D0068559

Time Out

Paris

timeout.com/paris

Time Out Guides Ltd
Universal House
251 Tottenham Court Road
London W1T 7AB
United Kingdom
Tel: +44 (0)20 7813 3000
Fax: +44 (0)20 7813 6001
Email: guides@timeout.com
www.timeout.com

Published by Time Out Guides Ltd, a wholly owned subsidiary
of Time Out Group Ltd. Time Out and the Time Out logo are
trademarks of Time Out Group Ltd.

© **Time Out Group Ltd 2014**
Previous editions 1989, 1990, 1992, 1995, 1997, 1998, 1999, 2000, 2001,
2002, 2003, 2004, 2005, 2006, 2007, 2008, 2009, 2010, 2011, 2012, 2013.

10 9 8 7 6 5 4 3 2 1

This edition first published in Great Britain in 2014 by Ebury Publishing.
A Random House Group Company
20 Vauxhall Bridge Road, London SW1V 2SA

Random House Australia Pty Ltd 20 Alfred Street, Milsons Point, Sydney,
New South Wales 2061, Australia

Random House New Zealand Ltd 18 Poland Road, Glenfield, Auckland 10,
New Zealand

Random House South Africa (Pty) Ltd Isle of Houghton, Corner Boundary
Road & Carse O'Gowrie, Houghton 2198, South Africa

Random House UK Limited Reg. No. 954009

Distributed in the US and Latin America by Publishers Group West
(1-510-809-3700)

For further distribution details, see www.timeout.com.

ISBN: 978-1-84670-324-9

A CIP catalogue record for this book is available from the British Library.

Printed and bound in China by Leo Paper Products Ltd.

The Random House Group Limited supports The Forest Stewardship Council®
(FSC®), the leading international forest-certification organisation. Our books
carrying the FSC label are printed on FSC®-certified paper. FSC is the only
forest-certification scheme supported by the leading environmental
organisations, including Greenpeace. Our paper procurement policy can be
found at www.randomhouse.co.uk/environment.

While every effort has been made by the author(s) and the publisher to ensure
that the information contained in this guide is accurate and up to date as at the
date of publication, they accept no responsibility or liability in contract, tort,
negligence, breach of statutory duty or otherwise for any inconvenience, loss,
damage, costs or expenses of any nature whatsoever incurred or suffered by
anyone as a result of any advice or information contained in this guide (except
to the extent that such liability may not be excluded or limited as a matter of
law). Before travelling, it is advisable to check all information locally, including
without limitation, information on transport, accommodation, shopping and
eating out. Anyone using this guide is entirely responsible for their own health,
well-being and belongings and care should always be exercised while travelling.

All rights reserved. No part of this publication may be reproduced, stored in
a retrieval system, or transmitted in any form or by any means, electronic,
mechanical, photocopying, recording or otherwise, without prior permission
from the copyright owners.

MIX
Paper from
responsible sources
FSC® C020056
www.fsc.org

Contents

59

115

54

342

110

Time Out Paris

Editorial
Editor Dominic Earle
Listings Editor Barbara Chossis
Proofreader Marion Moisy
Indexer Olivia Rye

Editorial Director Sarah Guy
Management Accountant Margaret Wright

Design
Senior Designer Kei Ishimaru
Designer Thomas Havell
Group Commercial Senior Designer Jason Tansley

Picture Desk
Picture Editor Jael Marschner
Deputy Picture Editor Ben Rowe
Freelance Picture Researchers Lizzy Owen, Olly Puglisi

Advertising
Managing Director of Advertising St John Betteridge
Advertising (Paris) Jinga Media Ltd
(www.jingamedia.com)

Marketing
Senior Publishing Brand Manager Luthfa Begum
Head of Circulation Dan Collins

Production
Production Controller Katie Mulhern-Bhudia

Time Out Group
Chairman & Founder Tony Elliott
Chief Executive Officer Tim Arthur
Publisher Alex Batho
Group IT Director Simon Chappell
Group Marketing Director Carolyn Sims

Contributors

Paris Today Alison Culliford. **Diary** Dominic Earle. **Explore** Anna Brooke, Alison Culliford, Dominic Earle, Natasha Edwards, Rich Woodruff. **Restaurants** Rosa Jackson, Ellen Hardy. **Cafés & Bars** Anna Brooke, Ellen Hardy. **Shops & Services** Alison Culliford; *Fashion* Katie Walker; *Galleries* Natasha Edwards. **Hotels** Alison Culliford, Dominic Earle, Katie Walker. **Children** Anna Brooke. **Film** Anna Brooke. **Gay & Lesbian** Robert Vallier. **Nightlife** Anna Brooke, Julien Sauvalle. **Performing Arts** Anna Brooke, Stephen Mudge, Estelle Ricoux. **Escapes & Excursions** Anna Brooke, Alison Culliford, Dominic Earle, Julien Sauvalle. **History** Simon Cropper. **Architecture** Natasha Edwards. **Essential Information** Barbara Chossis.

Maps JS Graphics Ltd (john@jsgraphics.co.uk), except pp396-397. New mapping on p113, pp162-163 and pp176-177 is supplied by © OpenStreetMap contributors (www.openstreetmap.org).

Cover photograph Arnaud Chicurel/Hemis/Corbis. With thanks to the Eiffel Tower/© SETE-illuminations Pierre Bideau and Louvre Pyramid/© arch.I.M.Pei, Musée du Louvre

Back cover photography Clockwise from top left: W Hotel; © Miss Ko; Lilyana Vynogradova/Shutterstock.com; Oliver Knight; Jean-Luc Pehau-Ricau (MOULIN ROUGE); Viacheslav Lopatin/Shutterstock.com

Photography Page 10 (left & middle), 16 (top), 129, 199 (left & right), 284 Heloise Bergman; 11 (right), 17 (middle), 42 (top), 43, 67, 110, 178, 209, 234, 260, 275, 283, 299, 341 (top), 350, 380 Olivia Rutherford; 12 (middle) Sophie Lloyd; 12 (bottom) Alamy; 13 (top), 169 www.foodsnobblog.wordpress.com; 13 (middle), 28 (top & middle), 29, 40, 46, 94, 139, 157 (top left & right), 161, 172, 182, 206, 213 (top & bottom), 227, 230 (left), 259, 262, 263, 271, 272, 279, 290, 338, 351 (top & bottom), 357, 358 Oliver Knight; 16 (bottom), 88 Florent Michel; 17 (top), 218 Marc Dantan; 18 REX/LCHAM/SIPA; 23, 143, 152 (top & bottom) Paris Tourist Office/Amélie Dupont; 24 (bottom), 269 (top and bottom) Beair/Press; 24 (top), 332 Christian Mueller/Shutterstock.com; 27 (bottom left & right), 86 (top & bottom) Virginie Garnier; 28 (bottom), 84, 191, 266 (top & bottom), 267, 285, 293, 303, 352 Karl Blackwell; 32 (top) ostill/Shutterstock.com; 32 (middle) Zdenek Krchak/Shutterstock.com; 32 (bottom) Migel/Shutterstock.com; 34 (top) Olga Besnard/Shutterstock.com; 34 (bottom) Patrick Wang/Shutterstock.com; 35 Stephane Deroussent; 36 (top) Raynard Lyudmyla/Shutterstock.com; 36 (bottom) W.Alix/SIPAPRESS/CRT; 37 (bottom) O.Jobard/SIPAPRESS/CRT IdF; 38 Yoann Morin/Shutterstock.com; 39 (top) R.Yaghobzadeh/SIPAPRESS/CRT IdF; 39 (bottom) Pavel L Photo and Video/Shutterstock.com; 54 (top) Benoist Linero; 54 (bottom) Klunderbie; 56, 76 Stanislas Liban; 57 Lilyana Vynogradova/Shutterstock.com; 58 Kiev.Victor/Shutterstock.com; 59, 116, 301 David Blondin/CRT PIdF; 63, 226, 300 (left & right) Hélène Giansily; 64 cesc_assawin/Shutterstock.com; 65 (top) Zoran Karapancev/Shutterstock.com; 65 (bottom) Theresasc75/Shutterstock.com; 91 Gousset Fabrice Paris; 95 Tung Cheung/Shutterstock.com; 97 (bottom left, top & bottom) Di Messina; 97 (top right) Pierre Antoine; 98 (top left & right) Edouard Sicot; 98 (bottom) Miss Kō; 101 Thomas Depin; 102 Oliver Dixon/Imagewise; 111 Viacheslav Lopatin/Shutterstock.com; 112 CTatiana/Shutterstock.com; 115 nito/Shutterstock.com; 118 Tutti Frutti/Shutterstock.com; 122 Manuelle Gautrand Architecture/Vincent Fillon; 123 vvoe/Shutterstock.com; 124 Dmitry Brizhatyuk/Shutterstock.com; 130 Anastasia Petrova/Shutterstock.com; 132 Jessica Orchard; 133, 151 Britta Jaschinski; 142 (bottom left) 242 Elena Dijour/Shutterstock.com; 158, 258, 287, 341 (bottom) Jean-Christophe Godet; 159 Walter Bibikow/Getty Images; 164 Julien Weber; 167 Marie Genel/Picturetank; 179 Luciano Mortula; 186 La Tour d'Argent/Press; 188 Jakob and Macfarlane; 189 (bottom) Ian River; 205 Elan Fleisher; 207 Paris Tourist Office/David Lefranc; 224 (top right) Marc Verhille/Mairie de Paris; 224 (bottom left & right) Sophie Robichon/Mairie de Paris; 228 Annabelle Schachmes; 229 Agence Moatti-Riviere; 230 (right) Alison Culliford; 235 dubassy/Shutterstock.com; 237 Charles Duprat; 238 Tupungato/Shutterstock.com; 240 Marie-Sophie Tekian; 247 AJOA-BTuA-SYNTHESE-Labtop; 249 Giuseppe Nocera/Shutterstock.com; 250 Thierry Valletoux; 252 Dmitry Brizhatyuk/Shutterstock.com; 253 Rex Features; 255, 256, 257 Alfred; 270 Emmanuel Trousse; 274 Stephane Monier; 280 Julieta Cervantes; 281 (top) Ateliers Jean Nouvel; 281 (bottom) Jean Nouvel - Arte Factory/Press; 286 Samantha Siegel; 286 Stephanie Berger; 288 Jérôme Delatour; 289 (top & bottom) P.Tourneboeuf/Tendance Floue; 292 (top left) Lesley Leslie-Spinks; 292 (bottom) vvoe/shutterstock.com; 294, 306 (top & bottom) Fondation Claude Monet, Giverny; 314 Getty Images/The Bridgeman Art Library; 319 Daily Mail/Rex Features; 320 UIG/Getty Images; 323 Serge De Sazo/Getty Images; 324 Christophe Simon/AFP/Getty Images; 330 photogolfer/shutterstock.com; 331 Bucchi Francesco/Shutterstock.com; 334, 336, 342, 347 Christophe Bielsa; 339 (top & bottom) feat/east; 345 Jacques Lebar; 353 Patrick Lazic; 355 DR; 359 (left & right) Cyrille Thomas; 381 Ming-Tang Evans

The following images were supplied by the featured establishments: pages 15, 22, 30, 33, 75, 109, 117, 190, 121, 215, 244, 248, 276, 337

The Editor would like to thank all contributors to the Time Out Paris website (www.timeout.fr) and previous editions of *Time Out Paris*, whose work forms the basis for parts of this book.

© **Copyright Time Out Group Ltd**
All rights reserved

About the Guide

GETTING AROUND

Each sightseeing chapter contains a street map of the area marked with the locations of sights and museums (❶), restaurants (❶), cafés and bars (❶), and shops (❶). There are also street maps of Paris at the back of the book, along with an overview map of the city and métro map. In addition, there is now a detachable fold-out street and métro map inside the back cover.

THE ESSENTIALS

For practical information, including visas, disabled access, emergency numbers, lost property, websites and local transport, see the Essential Information section. It begins on page 334.

THE LISTINGS

Addresses, phone numbers, websites, transport information, hours and prices are all included in our listings, as are selected other facilities. All were checked and correct at press time. However, business owners can alter their arrangements at any time, and fluctuating economic conditions can cause prices to change rapidly.

The very best venues in the city, the must-sees and must-dos in every category,

have been marked with a red star (★). In the sightseeing chapters, we've also marked venues with free admission with a FREE symbol.

THE LANGUAGE

Many Parisians speak a little English, but a few basic French phrases go a long way. You'll find a primer on page 379, along with some help with restaurants on page 380.

PHONE NUMBERS

The area code for Paris is 01. Even if you're calling from within Paris, you'll need to use the code. From outside France, dial your country's international access code (00 from the UK, 011 from the US) or a plus symbol, followed by the French country code (33), 1 for Paris (dropping the initial zero) and the eight-digit number. So, to reach the Louvre, dial +33.1.40.20.50.50. For more on phones, *see p377*.

FEEDBACK

We welcome feedback on this guide, both on the venues we've included and on any other locations that you'd like to see featured in future editions. Please email us at guides@timeout.com.

Paris Overview

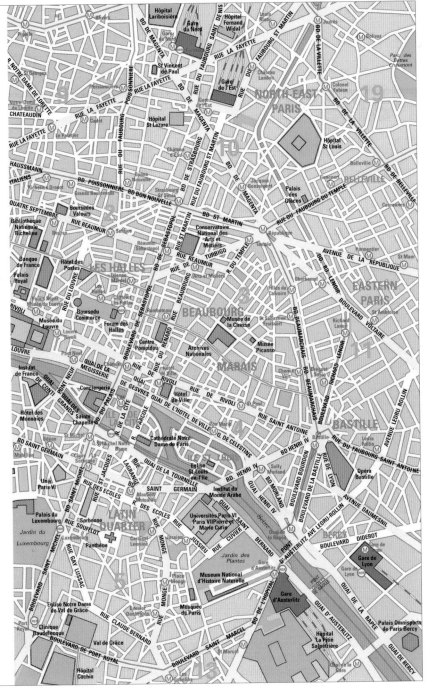

Paris's
Top 20

From concept stores to chanson venues, we count down the capital's finest.

1 Musée du Louvre
(page 64)

If any place demonstrates the central importance of culture in French life, this is it. The world's most popular museum (it welcomed just shy of ten million visitors during 2012) is a masterpiece inside and out, and the stunning new Islamic Arts department, beneath the Cour Visconti, means the Louvre is marching boldly onwards.

2 Musée d'Orsay
(page 225)

The groundbreaking revamp of the Musée d'Orsay hasn't changed the former railway station's exterior one iota – the wonder is all inside. On the museum's 25th anniversary, director Guy Cogeval finally achieved a long-held dream to obliterate white walls, 'the enemy of painting', and give the Impressionist movement the brush-up it so richly deserved. As an extra treat, the classical concerts held in the auditorium are consistently top-notch.

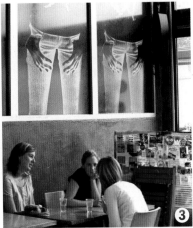

3 Point Ephémère
(page 267)

Housed in a former warehouse for art deco construction materials, Point Ephémère is a buzzing breeding ground for all things artistic and its location on Canal Saint-Martin makes it a summer hit. In 2004 it was an artist's squat, but today it organises everything from art exhibitions to pop, rock, electro and hip hop gigs, all within reach of youthful budgets. You can eat on the pretty terrace and the food is decent. You may jump every time a fire engine zooms out of the next-door fire station, but you'll soon settle back into the canalside vibe.

4 Eiffel Tower
(page 231)

Originally built for
the 1889 World Fair,
Gustave Eiffel's iconic
Iron Lady strikes a pose
like no other building
in Paris. The radical
cast-iron tower was
the tallest structure in
the world until it was
overtaken by New York's
Empire State Building in
the 1930s and views can
reach 65km on a clear
day. Oh, and they're building a glass
floor if you fancy looking down instead.

5 Musée de la Chasse et de la Nature
(page 131)

Whether tracking deer or snaffling
wild boar, the French adore *la chasse*,
and this grand Marais mansion makes
for a stunning trophy cabinet. It may
be a long way from the wild forests
of the Auvergne, but all manner of
stuffed treats await.

6 Canal Saint-Martin
(page 160)

Before it harboured stalwarts of Paris's
nightlife, Point Ephémère and Chez
Prune, the Canal Saint-Martin served
an entirely different purpose. Built
between 1805 and 1825, it brought
drinking water and merchandise to
the capital; then, from the late 19th
century onwards, it housed factories
and industrial warehouses. Nowadays,
many of the factories have become lofts
for Paris's bobo crowd, and dozens of
bars, restaurants and shops line the
quaysides. Its charming footbridges
and locks are ideal for a weekend stroll
– especially on Sundays when the roads
are reserved for walkers and cyclists.

7 La Pagode
(page 254)

We challenge you to find a more gorgeous picturehouse than the 19th-century Japanese-style Pagode on rue de Babylone. What started out in 1896 as an eccentric present for the wife of Bon Marché department store founder François-Emile Morin is now a supremely romantic cinema for art-house aesthetes: period touches include woven fabric on the walls, golden lights and dragon carvings over the grandiose doorways. On a warm day, have a cup of tea in the Pagode's bamboo-speckled Japanese garden.

8 Chateaubriand
(page 168)

The last few years have seen the meteoric rise of the neo-bistro scene, and Le Chateaubriand is the *coeur d'artichaut* of this new dining trend. So what are the magic ingredients? Flair, innovation and world-beating ingredients, all crafted together by chef-owner Inaki Aizpitarte in a get-what-you're-given *menu unique*.

9 Merci
(page 140)

At Merci – a concept store in the Haut Marais – you can pick up everything from furniture, clothes and jewellery to perfume, accessories and books. Nothing new there. What is different, though, is the fact that Merci's proceeds go to charity, so shopping here could make a real difference to people's lives. Ethics aside, the products on sale are generally gorgeous, as are the cakes in the café.

jack gomme
PARIS

BAGS AND ACCESSORIES · MADE IN FRANCE

16, Rue St-Claude//
1, Impasse St-Claude
75003 Paris
tel : (33)1 42 78 73 45
stclaude@jackgomme.com
www.jackgomme.com

Open Tuesday to Saturday - From 11 am to 2 pm - 2.30 pm to 7 pm

Family Twist

French bread baking class

Treasure hunt in the Louvre

Ride in a vintage car

Historic puzzle

Experiments

Looking for a treat for your family?

How about a truly memorable family holiday in Paris?
You choose from our selection of fun-filled activities and family-friendly
accommodation. We organise everything for you to make your life easier
and your break a unique experience with your family.

www.family-twist.com   -   +44 2 031 304 853   -   +33 9 83 84 40 54

10 Boulogne-Billancourt
(page 238)

Paris's suburbs often play second fiddle to the main attractions, but you'd be wrong to ignore Boulogne-Billancourt. There's the Bois de Boulogne for a start – Paris's western lung, filled with lakes and parkland. Then there are three museums worth an afternoon of your time. Head to the Musée Belmondo if you're into sculpture, the Musée des Années 30 for everything art deco, and the Musée Albert Kahn for wonderful sculpted gardens and collections of 19th-century photography.

11 Les Caves Augé
(page 102)

If you want a slice of history served with your wine head to Les Caves Augé. It has been open since 1850 and was the store where Proust used to go to stock up his cellar: the decor, awash with mouldings and panelling, has changed little since then. You can choose from thousands of bottles, the savvy *cavistes* can aid your selection, and there's an ever-increasing focus on 'natural' wines. If you fancy a *dégustation*, there's a tasting day one Saturday each month.

12 Cathédrale Notre-Dame de Paris
(page 51)

Quasimodo certainly had good taste: the views from Notre-Dame's towers are nothing short of stupendous, especially on a cloudy day when the skies spin a moody hue across the Seine. From the top, you also get the best view of the 850-year-old cathedral's famous gargoyles – cheeky little chimeras watching over the city below. They're actually not originals; architect Viollet-le-Duc added them in the mid 19th century when he restored the cathedral to its former glory.

13 Promenade Plantée
(page 156)

Fifty years ago Bastille had a train station with a viaduct that carried trains into the centre from Vincennes. The station is no more (the Opéra Bastille stands there now), but the viaduct is a firm fixture thanks to the Promenade Plantée – an elevated garden (like New York's High Line) that you can follow across Paris's 12th arrondissement.

14 Contemporary art
(pages 95, 96, 161, 209)

Paris may look stately on the outside, but on the inside it's a different story: cool contemporary art joints pepper the capital, from the Musée d'Art Moderne to the experimental Palais de Tokyo next door. Cross the river to Fondation Cartier to see highlights of Paris's art scene during the past 20 years, or if you're looking for art so contemporary you can watch it being made, try 104, where resident artists frequently open their workshops to the public.

101BEST
Looking for even more inspiration? Visit the Time Out Paris website (www.timeout.com/paris) for a full list of the 101 best things to do in the capital.

15 Centre Pompidou
(page 124)

As cutting-edge as ever, the extra-skeletal Centre Pompidou is home to modern art treasures by, among others, Braque, Dubuffet, Matisse and Ernst, plus rotating exhibitions that ensure that no two visits are ever the same. Arrive at 6pm and stay until closing time at 9pm, after which Georges, the Pompidou's trendy rooftop bar-restaurant, serves moreish cocktails in a futuristic setting with panoramic views over the city.

16 Les Catacombes
(page 216)

Descend, if you dare, into the entrails of the city. The Catacombs are without doubt the spookiest attraction Paris has to offer, with kilometres of tunnels lined with the bones of defunct Parisians. Created in the late 18th century to stop disease from spreading from overrun inner-city cemeteries, they now make for a chilling stroll.

17 Les Trois Baudets
(page 276)

While Britain was living it up with the Beatles, France was developing its text-led *chanson*. And in Paris, the launchpad for budding Brassens and Gainsbourgs (both of whom sang here) was Les Trois Baudets. It remains committed to *chanson* and is the place to hear France's finest modern talent.

18 Seine cruise
(page 368)

Yes, you'll get cheesy commentary, but seeing Paris in one majestic sweep from a boat is something everyone should do at least once. Many of the city's most gorgeous monuments cling to the banks of the Seine and the river's bridges are truly stunning.

19 Palais Garnier
(page 284)

The 'wedding cake', as the Garnier is nicknamed, wows a highbrow crowd with some of the world's best ballet and the occasional opera. The building is an ode to opulence, dripping in marble and gold leaf. It's also fascinating, with an underground lake that inspired Gaston Leroux to write *Phantom of the Opera* and beehives on the roof that produce the honey on sale in the boutique.

20 St-Germain-des-Prés
(page 190)

Whether you're tasting st-marcellin at Fromagerie Quatrehomme, sampling scents at L'Artisan Parfumeur or picking up a stuffed tiger at Deyrolle, shopping on the Left Bank is a sensual pleasure. Whereas we have window-shopping, the French have window-licking (*lèche-vitrine*), and a morning spent mooching around St-Germain-des-Prés will show you why.

Paris Today

All eyes on the mayoral prize.

TEXT: ALISON CULLIFORD

On a sunny day in June 2013, children skated through the mists of the new 'dry fountain' on place de la République, while lovers evoked the famous Brassens song, 'Les Amoureux des Bancs Publics', on modern *bancs publics* hewn from a single tree trunk. Among them moved a beaming Paris mayor, delighted to have fulfilled his promise to give this emblematic square back to the people. But it was also a chance for Socialist Bertrand Delanoë to showcase his intended successor in the March 2014 mayoral race, Anne Hidalgo, the daughter of a Spanish emigré whose grandparents fled to France during the Spanish Civil War. Hidalgo is in competition with UMP candidate Nathalie Kosciusko-Morizet, Nicolas Sarkozy's spokeswoman during his presidential re-election campaign, and the Paris political map shows an astonishing split down the middle, with the west voting right and the east left.

Bertrand Delanoë and Anne Hidalgo.

FONDATION CLAUDE MONET

GIVERNY

The Fondation Claude Monet is open every day from the
1st April to the 1st of November 9:30AM to 6:00PM
Latest time of entry: 5:30PM

Tel: +33 (0) 2 32 51 28 21 - Fax: +33 (0) 2 32 51 54 18
www.fondation-monet.com - contact@fondation-monet.com

Would the Paris that embraced its first openly gay mayor in 2011 stick with the Socialist model? Only one thing was for sure at the beginning of 2014: Marianne, the embodiment of France and a symbol of equality in a country that didn't give women the vote until 1944, smiled benignly down on two women hell-bent on being the city's standard bearer.

MAPPING OUT THE FUTURE

The new mayor's challenges will include a possible Olympics bid in 2015 after the French capital was pipped to the post by London for the 2012 event. She will also have to oversee several city planning projects that are already underway, including the modernisation of the Gare d'Austerlitz with hotels and shops, and a bouquet of new green spaces such as the 'People of the Grass' park that's part of the Seine City Park project. The city's town planning will have to go hand-in-hand with the Grand Paris scheme, a Sarkozy initiative to bring the suburbs into the city with the extension of several métro lines.

She will also have to deal with the less palatable question of crime in the capital. A slightly arch press release from the Paris tourist office says that crime is 'the price of fame' and blames a frenzy of videos that went viral on the internet for giving tourism a knock. But the malaise is probably less to do with the prevalence of pickpockets and child phone thieves than the blasé attitude of officials and Parisians when a crime is committed. The authorities seem to have taken note and deployed more cops on the beat, as well as installing a software system in police stations for giving statements in foreign languages. They claim pickpocketing in Trocadéro has dropped by almost a third as a result of the measures.

At the time of writing, Hidalgo was in the lead – less because of Socialist president François Hollande, whose popularity rating remained low, and more because of the legacy of Delanoë's two terms. As the first Socialist in the Mairie since the Commune of 1871, Delanoë knew how to spread the love, bringing in such crowd-pleasers as the Paris Plages summer beach by the Seine, the offbeat Nuit Blanche art extravaganza, the Vélib' bike scheme and Autolib' cars.

'Delanoë knew how to spread the love, bringing in such crowd-pleasers as Paris Plages, the offbeat Nuit Blanche and the Vélib' bike scheme.'

Whether presenting dustmen with prizes for completing night school courses or hosting a free Paul Auster event for the Shakespeare and Co literary festival, the Mayor laid on a party worthy of Marie-Antoinette, and everybody could eat the cake. After Chirac and Jean Tiberi's scandal-ridden tenures, it was a breath of fresh air.

Hidalgo, who is deputy mayor for town planning and architecture, has been associated with some of Delanoë's greatest successes – the Vélib' bikes and place de la République in particular. Her 'Paris that dares' manifesto, which launched on 8 December 2013, was certainly attractive with its promises of 60,000 homes, 20,000 trees, wild swimming in the Lac de Daumesnil and the Canal d'Ourcq, and sparkling water drinking fountains. One Socialist policy that will be unpopular with visitors, though, is the crackdown on holiday rentals through such sites as airbnb.com. It's a policy that's also employed in New York in an attempt to give back housing to residents and boost the hotel industry.

Nathalie Kosciusko-Morizet, or NKM as she's known, had yet to release a manifesto at the time of writing. She's been tasked by the UMP party with wooing the bobo (bourgeois-bohemian) vote. In November 2013, NKM's offensive saw her propping up the bar in an Algerian café in the 18th arrondissement in the company of the 'mayor of the night', Clément Léon R, a title voted on by the clientele of 42 bars and nightclubs as part of an ongoing campaign to reignite the capital's nightlife. The stage-managed appearance saw her texting her 'mates' to come and join her, and smoking several fags on the pavement. But her propositions to have the métro running

Candelaria.

24 hours a day at the weekends, and to organise parties in 'phantom stations', have been jeered at ever since a gaffe when she guessed the price of a métro ticket at €4 (it costs €1.70).

PARIS, BROOKLYN

The Chope du Château-Rouge bar, where NKM arranged her photocall, remains a fabulous example of the Paris melting pot, but the city is in the midst of an identity crisis. In short, it wants to be Brooklyn. For two or three years now, hipsters in beanie hats and retro glasses have been spotted wheeling their fixies around the 9th and 10th arrondissements, and an assortment of burger and bagel places have sprung up. The PNY (Paris New York) burger joint on rue du Faubourg St-Denis sports the motto 'Cheaper than a psychiatrist', and Hutch Hot-Dogs House opposite has plastic bottles of French's mustard crowding the window.

The quest for the perfect burger has become something of a Paris obsession – it's as if the city has discovered patties for the first time. In Chez Jeannette, a café popular with hipsters for its unreconstructed 1950s decor and moody servers, local writer and agitator Laurent Laurent (www.laurentlaurent.com) went misty-eyed as he described the burger in general as

'*une merveille*', before going on to give a potted personal history of burgers in France, from the seminal moment of his first 'McDo' in the 1970s near the Jardin du Luxembourg through the '*mauvaise periode*' when McDonald's closed and the French version, Quick, was 'not good'.

Having now Gallicised its menu with McBaguettes, McCamemberts, and that most aristocratic of pâtisseries, the *macaron*, the Golden Arches are once again marching apace in France, but it's the artisanal gourmet burger that has Parisians salivating. PNY's version features Le Ponclet beef and vintage Cheddar. The food truck trend has also arrived in the capital courtesy of Cantine California (www.cantinecalifornia.com) and Le Camion qui Fume (www.lecamion quifume.com), and there's even a gourmet fish and chip shop on rue des Vinaigriers (www.thesunkenchip.com). Our prediction is that Mexican will be next, with taste buds already attuned by the fresh tacos and enchiladas at Candelaria.

The emergence of London and New York as food capitals has also pushed Paris's more traditional restaurants to up their game, resulting in a spate of affordable bistros serving creative, often organic, fare. Beware, though, even if you manage to snaffle a table you'll probably find yourself sitting next to a group of American foodies complaining vociferously that the cheese is Shropshire blue (newly discovered, and appreciated, by Parisians) and not French.

In November 2013, author Thomas Chatterton Williams mourned in the pages of the *New York Times* the passing of old Pigalle, where hostess bars are rapidly being replaced by 'upscale cocktail lounges' – a demise that won't bring tears to the eye of any tourist who's been fleeced by the €500 glass of champagne trick. 'Today, the neighbourhood has been rechristened South Pigalle or, in a disheartening aping of New York, SoPi,' he complained. Ahem, rechristened by whom? An American ad man, apparently, who has succeeded in getting the British and US press to latch on to the moniker while Parisians have nonchalantly ignored it.

At Balades Sonores – a small record label, vinyl shop, clothing store and mini concert venue that is the very epitome of hipster – no one had even heard of 'SoPi'. Neither had Yannick, who runs the vintage clothing store Mamie located in a former girly bar. Brooklyn-based webzine www.bkmag.com's Kristin Iversen soon bit back with a scathing critique of Chatterton Williams's piece entitled: 'Hipsters ruined Paris,' says former Brooklyn hipster.

THE BIG SMOKE

Some Parisian habits die hard, but they do mutate. The electronic cigarette has taken off so successfully in the capital that there's an '*e-clope*' boutique on almost every street. Rather than being a slightly embarrassing admission that you're still hooked on nicotine, e-cigarettes have been embraced as a fashion accessory, worn nonchalantly on a chain around the neck and brandished at parties. If the trend doesn't burn itself out and the tobacconists' lobby doesn't succeed in its quest to get the e-cigarette shops closed down, non-smokers can look forward to finally reclaiming bar and restaurant terraces for themselves.

Another welcome arrival on the capital's streets is the minicab. Several companies have managed to cleverly circumvent Paris's protectionist laws by operating via phone apps, such as lecab.fr, chauffeur-privé.com, snapcar.com, allocab.com, uber.com and voituresjaunes.com. As well as allowing you to know the price and pay in advance, the drivers also show a courtesy rarely seen in the French capital.

Safe, polite, non-smoking, app-friendly and cosmopolitan – can this really be Paris? Don't worry, it takes more than a manifesto to erode the grit and romance of the city we know and love.

Place de la République.
See p18.

Itineraries

*Plot out your perfect trip
to the capital with our
step-by-step Paris planner.*

10AM

Day 1

9PM

10AM If 1960s Nouvelle Vague films are anything to go by, you'd be forgiven for thinking that most Paris couples spend all day in bed. But if you're in the City of Love for a weekend only, and are too eager for sightseeing to indulge in breakfast *en lit*, then you should kick things off with the city's best coffee at **La Caféothèque** (*p135*). This boutique café is located on a picture-postcard stretch of Seine,

an easy stroll from beautiful 17th-century **Place des Vosges** (*p131*). The Marais is abuzz with culture, shops, bars and, in its imposing *hôtels particuliers*, important cultural institutions: take your pick from the **Musée Carnavalet** (*p131*), the **Musée d'Art et d'Histoire du Judaïsme** (*p130*), the **Maison Européenne de la Photographie** (*p128*) or the newly expanded (and long delayed) **Musée Picasso**

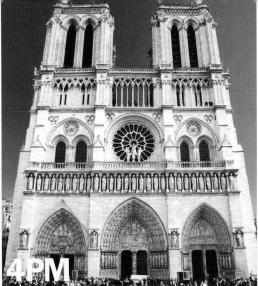

4PM

NOON

(*p129*). Shoppers will also find rich pickings in the streets leading off the main shopping thoroughfare of rue des Francs-Bourgeois.

NOON From the Marais, head across the Seine via the Pont de Sully to the **Institut du Monde Arabe** (*p184*), which holds a fine collection of Middle Eastern art and a rooftop café with fabulous views. (Other wonderful panoramas in Paris include the summit of the Parc des Buttes-Chaumont and the Sacré-Coeur, although the

latter is worth saving for dusk.) After a wander along the Left Bank to lunch in the back room at **La Palette** (*p196*), meander along the stone quays that border the Seine and leaf through tatty paperbacks at the riverside *bouquinistes*, before ducking into the recently revamped **Musée d'Orsay** (*p225*) for an Impressionist masterclass.

4PM From here, either hop on a boat tour or explore the islands. Snag an ice-cream from **Berthillon** (*p55*) on Ile St-Louis, before popping over to Ile de la Cité to visit **Notre-Dame** (*p51*).

9PM Evenings start with aperitifs. Join the crowd on the terrace seats at **Le Bar du Marché** (*p196*) and watch the Left Bank people-traffic pass by over a kir. Then head along the river to party at **Wanderlust** (*p270*). Post-club hunger pangs can be satiated 24/7 at **Au Pied de Cochon** (6 rue Coquillière, 1st, www.pieddecochon.com).

Clockwise from top left:
La Caféothèque;
Institut du Monde Arabe;
Notre-Dame;
Wanderlust.

The Sightseeing Cruise
Get the best of Paris in 1 hour

Special offer for Time Out Readers

€3 OFF
(Code VDP: 86)

Sightseeing cruise
Pleasure cruise
Snacking cruise
Snacking + cruise

The Parisian sightseeing cruise has to be at the top of your list of things to do when in the French Capital. Ideally located, it's charming boats enhance the pleasure of a guided cruise on the Seine.

The river banks offer you some of the most well-known monuments such as the Eiffel Tower, the Louvre, the Orsay Museum and Notre Dame Cathedral amongst others. Recorded multilingual commentary and a bar service on board.

Departures every day of the year from October to March from 11.15am to 21pm (every 45 min), from April to September from 10.30am to 22pm(every 30 min).

1 hour Sightseeing or "By Night" Cruises: Adult: 13€;
Children 4-11 y.o: 6€; free under 4 y.o

Exclusive: The Champagne Cruise
1 hr Sightseeing Cruise + 1 glass of Champagne for **19€**

*On this guide's presentation, valid for adult ticket for 2014. Terms and conditions apply. Not Cumulative offer.

At the foot of the Eiffel Tower
Port de Suffren - 75007 Paris
M° Bir Hakeim RER C Champs de Mars
+33 (0) 1 44 18 19 50
www.vedettesdeparis.com

vedettes de paris

Day 2

9AM

9AM If you'd like to see the marvels of the **Musée du Louvre** (*p64*), now's the time: early, before the crowds have descended (and preferably not on a weekend). Otherwise, cross the Pont des Arts and head south through the narrow Left Bank streets to the city's oldest church, **Eglise St-Germain-des-Prés** (*p192*), followed by a cup of coffee at **Le Rostand** (*p203*). Then stroll down to the **Jardin du Luxembourg** (*p199*), pull up two green chairs (using one as a footrest) and size up the park life. The adjacent **Musée National du Luxembourg** (*p199*) hosts world-class art exhibitions.

NOON From here, hop on the métro to Jacques Bonsergent. Amble along the tree-lined Canal St-Martin, crossing over its romantic bridges to explore little shops and waterside cafés, and maybe stopping at *cave à vins* **Le Verre Volé** (*p166*) for a plate of charcuterie and cheese washed down

with a couple of glasses of Touraine. On Sundays, traffic is outlawed from the Quai de Valmy and the bar-lined Quai de Jemmapes. There are plenty of boutiques in the area, alongside kitsch merchants **Antoine et Lili** (*p166*). For a swift *demi* near the water's edge, head to friendly **Chez Prune** (*p165*), before catching the métro to Alma Marceau.

5PM Modern art lovers should make a point of visiting the superb collection at the **Musée d'Art Moderne de la Ville de Paris** (*p95*); it's a neighbour to the **Palais de Tokyo** (*p96*), a dynamic

contemporary art space that has recently tripled in size. From here, you can walk to the Champs-Elysées and take a night-time hike up the **Arc de Triomphe** (*p91*) to see the lights of the avenue stretching into the city.

8PM Head back to the Palais de Tokyo and relax with an expertly shaken cocktail at the hip bar overlooking the Seine. Then head up to Les Halles for supper at the more accessible branch of Grégory Lemarchand's loft-style bistro, **Frenchie Bar à Vins** (*p87*), next to rue Montorgueil. Still got energy? Our Nightlife section awaits...

Top: **Musée du Louvre**. Bottom: **Frenchie Bar à Vins**.

8PM

Vintage Paris

Paris is dripping in everything your vintage heart could desire, from rare 1920s Chanel accessories and art deco lighting to '60s rock LPs and '80s kitten boots. And the good news is that many of the best vintage boutiques are condensed on the Right Bank between Palais-Royal and Faidherbe Chaligny.

Top: **Noir Kennedy**. Middle: **Didier Ludot**. Bottom: **Bistrot Paul Bert**.

To look the part, and for whizzing between the shops for maximum rifling time, hire a vintage-style Vespa from **Left Bank Scooters** (www.leftbankscooters.com). There are two models to choose from, each with a handy compartment for stashing your shopping.

Park your Vespa on the corner of rue Paul Bert and rue Faidherbe, 11th. Most vintage boutiques on this tour only open in the afternoon, so start with a retro lunch on rue Paul Bert. If you're looking for old-school Paris, **Bistrot Paul Bert** (p145) never fails to deliver, with its zinc bar, 1930s tiles and dishes such as suckling pig with potato gratin.

After lunch, leave your Vespa and walk down rue Faidherbe, pausing to admire **Les Années Scooter** (23 rue Faidherbe, 11th, www.lesanneesscooter.com), a den of mid 20th-century scooters, table lights, clocks, jukeboxes and street signs. Philippe, the owner, can tell you the story behind every piece on display. A few doors further on, **Restaur'Bronze** (41 rue Faidherbe, www. restaurbronze.com) is one of the last places in Paris to specialise in metal objects from the 1930s and '40s, including show-stopping art deco lights.

TWOWHEELS

All Left Bank Scooters rentals include a lock, two helmets, insurance, plus winter riding gloves and wet weather gear if needed. 50cc prices start from 70 euros per day.

You can't scoot around town with a 1932 crystal candelabra in tow, so head back to your Vespa. Drive back down rue Faidherbe and turn left down rue de Charonne. Park up opposite the Bistrot du Peintre café (where you'll be coming back for coffee in a while). Take a right down rue Keller, then turn left on to rue de la Roquette. **Adöm** (35 & 56 rue de la Roquette) is split into two small boutiques. Girls head to no.56 for 1970s and '80s jeans and '60s shift dresses, while boys drop into no.35 for 1950s baseball jackets, cowboy boots and a selection of sneakers.

Now retrace your steps to the art nouveau surroundings of **Le Bistro du Peintre** (116 av Ledru-Rollin, 11th, www.bistrotdupeintre. com), where you can peruse your purchases over a coffee. Sustenance over, the boutique-filled Haut Marais beckons. Return to your Vespa and head south down av Ledru-Rollin, then right on to rue du Faubourg-St-Antoine.

At place de la Bastille, take a right up bd Beaumarchais and park near St-Sébastien Froissart métro station.

During the last few years, this previously forgotten area has been transformed with numerous one-off boutiques – including the wonderful **Matières à Reflexion** (19 rue de Poitou, 3rd, www.matieresareflexion.com) – a place where old leather jackets and clothes are crafted into one-off bags and satchels fastened with aged brass hardware.

From here, hop back on the bike and whizz down rue du Pont-au-Choux, left on to rue de Turenne and then right on to rue St-Antoine. Park near St-Paul métro station. Walk up rue Pavée, then left on to rue du Roi de Sicile for two vintage hotspots. For punky London retro style, try **Noir Kennedy** (22 rue du Roi de Sicile, 4th, www.noirkennedyparis.com), which is chock full of leather coats, lumberjack shirts, ripped jeans and funky 1980s T-shirts. If '40s fashion is more your style, try **Mam'Zelle Swing** (35 rue du Roi de Sicile, 4th, www.mamzelle-swing.com).

Back on your Vespa, drive down rue de Rivoli, turn right up rue de l'Echelle and right down rue St-Honoré, then park wherever you can at Palais-Royal. From here, take a stroll under the arcades to Paris's ultimate temple of luxury vintage, **Didier Ludot** (see p71). You just have to catch a glimpse of the window displays to see there is something special about Ludot's pieces, many of which look like they could have been cast-offs from Audrey Hepburn or Marilyn Monroe.

Shopping over for the afternoon, head for a fittingly retro-style dinner at red- and white-checked **Astier** (44 rue Jean-Pierre Timbaud, 11th, www.restaurant-astier.com), where Cyril Boulet and Nicolas Frezel revive vintage French dishes with sophisticated flair.

PARIS FOR FREE

Not everything costs the earth in the capital.

FESTIVAL FEVER

From cinema under the stars in Parc de la Villette and jazz gigs in the Bois de Vincennes to Bastille Day fireworks and Nuit Blanche's all-night arts and culture extravaganza, several of Paris's finest festivals are free to attend.

CULTURE ON THE CHEAP

Time it right and you can visit many of Paris's museums without spending a single cent. On the first Sunday of each month, cultural giants such as the Louvre, Musée d'Orsay, Centre Pompidou, Musée de l'Orangerie and many more can be ticked off without reaching for your wallet.

HEAVEN SENT

Plenty of the capital's stunning churches are essential viewing, and free entry to most means you can admire everywhere from Notre-Dame's nave to St-Sulpice's Delacroix murals and the Sacré-Coeur's lavish interior without having to shell out a hefty entrance fee.

IN THE PICTURE

Timing your trip to coincide with a night of free *vernissages* (private views) gives a taste not only of the art on offer but also of the personalities who frequent the art scene, a real entrée into Paris life. The journal *L'Officiel Galeries & Musées*, which you can pick up in most galleries, has a diary of forthcoming *vernissages*.

PARK LIFE

Many of Paris's parks may be preened to within an inch of their life, but they're still free to all and sundry if you fancy stretching out in the sunshine. So get a picnic together and take your pick from the smart lawns of the Jardin des Tuileries, the rolling hills of the Parc des Buttes-Chaumont or the postmodern pathways of the Parc André Citroën.

Diary

*Plan your perfect weekend
with our year-round guide
to the French capital.*

Paris-Plages. *See p36.*

Paris is bursting with culture, and a spate
of new festivals has added to the already
crowded calendar. Eco-friendly music festival
We Love Green and culinary champion Fête de
la Gastronomie both started up in 2011, while
2012 saw the launch of Nuit Blanche-style
Paris Face Cachée. During summer, many of
the capital's parks turn into alfresco classical
concert venues and theatrical stages. Among
them is the lovely Parc Floral de Paris, which
holds weekend concerts throughout the warmer
months. Elsewhere, Solidays, Rock en Seine,
Festival des Inrockuptibles and the Techno Parade
all attract top rock acts. And if sports fans don't
manage to get tickets for the Six Nations, there's
always the finale of the Tour de France, which
celebrated its centennial edition in 2013 with a
win for, *sacré bleu*, an Englishman for the second
year running as Chris Froome inherited Bradley
Wiggins's yellow jersey.

Spring

Paris Face Cachée
*Various venues (01.43.48.08.02, www.parisface
cachee.fr).* **Tickets** varies. **Date** early Feb.
Quirky and educational, Paris Face Cachée is in the
same vein as autumn's Nuit Blanche, where the public is invited into unusual or industrial spaces for art
happenings. But this new festival is not exclusively
an art event. A huge variety of venues and activities
lift the lid on places you might never have known
existed, and give participants a chance to experience
Paris at work behind the scenes. *Photos p33.*

Six Nations
*Stade de France, 93210 St-Denis (www.rbs6nations.
com). RER B La Plaine Stade de France or RER D
Stade de France St-Denis.* **Admission** varies.
Date Feb-Mar.
Paris hosts two massive rugby weekends during the
spring. Log on to the website at least three months
in advance to be in with any chance of getting tickets
to a match. France managed to end up with the
wooden spoon in 2013.

Fashion Week
Various venues (www.modeaparis.com).
Date Mar, July, Oct & Jan.
Paris presents its haute couture and prêt-à-porter
collections at a variety of venues across the capital,
but to invited guests only. Visit the website for
accreditation details. *Photo p32.*

Le Printemps des Poètes
*Various venues (01.53.80.08.00, www.printemps
despoetes.com).* **Date** Mar.
The 16th edition of this long-running national poetry
festival featured 'Au Coeur des Arts' as its theme in
2014, and included a major celebration of the work
of French poet and painter Max Jacob on the 70th
anniversary of his death.

Printemps du Cinéma
Various venues (www.printempsducinema.com).
Date mid Mar.
Film tickets at a variety of cinemas all across
the city are cut to a bargain €3.50 for this hugely
popular three-day film bonanza.

IN THE KNOW ONLINE UPDATE

The comprehensive *Time Out Paris*
website (www.timeout.fr/paris) lists
everything that matters in the capital's
cultural calendar; get news of key events
via Facebook, Twitter and the weekly
newsletter. Always confirm details well
in advance – events can be cancelled
and dates may change with little notice.

PUBLIC HOLIDAYS

**Easter Monday
(Lundi de Pâques)**
6 April 2015

May Day (Fête du Travail)
1 May

VE Day (Victoire 1945)
8 May

**Ascension Day
(Jour de l'Ascension)**
29 May 2014, 14 May 2015

Whit Monday (Pentecôte)
9 June 2014, 25 May 2015

Bastille Day (Quatorze Juillet)
14 July

**Feast of the Assumption
(Fête de l'Assomption)**
15 Aug

All Saints' Day (Toussaint)
1 Nov

**Remembrance Day
(L'Armistice 1918)**
11 Nov

Christmas Day (Noël)
25 Dec

New Year's Day (Jour de l'An)
1 Jan

Bastille Day

★ **Marathon de Paris**
*Av des Champs-Elysées, 8th, to av Foch, 16th
(01.41.33.15.68, www.parismarathon.com).*
Date early Apr.
One of the world's most picturesque marathons, with
up to 40,000 runners heading off from the Champs-
Elysées along the Right Bank to the Bois de
Vincennes, and back along the Left Bank to the Bois
de Boulogne. Registration begins in the previous
September. If you're looking for something to aim at,
the 2013 men's winner was Kenyan Peter Some in
2hrs 5mins 38secs.

★ **Banlieues Bleues**
*Various venues in Seine-St-Denis (01.49.22.10.10,
www.banlieuesbleues.org).* **Admission** varies.
Date Apr.
A five-week festival of French and international jazz,
blues, R&B, soul, funk, flamenco and world music.
▶ *For more on music festivals in and around
Paris, see p265.*

Clockwise from top: **Paris Face Cachée** (*see p31*); **Marathon de Paris**; **Fashion Week** (*see p31*).

WWW.PARISFACECACHEE.FR

Le Chemin de la Croix

Square Willette, 18th. M° Abbesses or Anvers.
Date Good Friday.
A crowd of pilgrims follows the Archbishop of Paris from the bottom of Montmartre up to Sacré-Coeur as he performs the Stations of the Cross.

Foire du Trône

Pelouse de Reuilly, 12th (www.foiredutrone.com). M° Porte Dorée. **Admission** free; rides €2-€5.
Date Apr-May.
France's biggest funfair runs for nearly two months, with a mix of stomach-churning rides, bungee jumping and candyfloss aplenty. It's well worth investing in a pass (around €30) in advance. At the weekends the Mairie runs a free shuttle bus service from Bercy and Nation.

Fête du Travail

Date 1 May.
May Day is strictly observed. Key sights (the Eiffel Tower aside) close, and unions march in eastern Paris via Bastille. Sweet-smelling posies of lily of the valley (*muguet*) are sold on every street corner.

Foire de Paris

Paris-Expo, pl de la Porte de Versailles (01.49.09.60.00, www.foiredeparis.fr). M° Porte de Versailles. **Admission** €12; €7 reductions; free under-7s. **Date** early May.
This enormous lifestyle fair includes world crafts and foods, the latest health gizmos, plus everything you need to know about buying a swimming pool or doing up your home.

Le Printemps des Rues

Various venues (01.47.97.36.06, www.leprintemps-desrues.com). **Admission** free. **Date** mid May.
This annual two-day street-theatre festival takes place along the Canal St-Martin and has a distinctly experimental vibe.

★ La Nuit des Musées

All over France (www.nuitdesmusees.culture.fr).
Admission free. **Date** mid May.
During this pan-European one-night culture fest, museums open their doors late for special events and entertainment, including concerts, dance, lectures, unique access and special exhibitions.

Festival Jazz à Saint-Germain-des-Prés

Various venues, St-Germain-des-Prés (www.festivaljazzsaintgermainparis.com).
Date mid May-early June.
This two-week festival of jazz and blues celebrated its 13th anniversary in 2013 with everything from piano cruises on the Seine to gigs in the Eglise St-Germain-des-Prés. Many of the concerts are free.

Art Saint-Germain-des-Prés

Various venues (www.artsaintgermaindespres.com).
Admission free. **Date** end May.
Timing your trip to Paris to coincide with a night of *vernissages* (private views) gives a taste not only of the art on offer but also of the personalities who frequent the art scene. The big rendezvous of the year is Art St-Germain-des-Prés. Nicknamed the 'block

party', it sees more than 50 galleries get together to showcase their top artists. The galleries involved are mostly concentrated on rue de Seine, rue des Beaux-Arts, rue Visconti, rue Guénégaud and rue Mazarine.

French Tennis Open

Stade Roland-Garros, 2 av Gordon-Bennett, 16th (01.47.43.48.00, www.frenchopen.org). M° Porte d'Auteuil. **Admission** €21-€75. **Date** late May-early June.

Paris plays host to the second event in the Grand Slam calendar and the most prestigious clay court competition in the world. Rafael Nadal and Serena Williams took the spoils in 2013.

Summer

Quinzaine des Réalisateurs

Forum des Images, Porte St-Eustache, Forum des Halles, 1st (01.44.76.63.00, www.quinzaine-realisateurs.com). M° Les Halles. **Admission** €5.50. **Date** June.

The Cannes Directors' Fortnight sidebar comes to Paris; 2013 was the 45th anniversary of this festival of screenings and events.

Festival de St-Denis

Various venues in St-Denis (01.48.13.06.07, www.festival-saint-denis.com). M° St-Denis Basilique. **Admission** €17-€60. **Date** June.

The Gothic St-Denis basilica and other historic buildings in the neighbourhood host four weeks of top-quality classical concerts.

Fête du Vélo

Across Paris (www.feteduvelo.fr). **Date** Early June.

The Fête du Vélo is a celebration of urban riding with thousands of cyclists invited to meet up at various points in the suburbs and pedal to Paris en masse. The result is what the organisation calls *'la convergence'*, with a procession of two-wheelers meeting up for a huge picnic in the city centre. During the two-day festival visitors can also try in-line skating, as well as bicycles specially designed for children and people of reduced mobility.

Prix de Diane

Hippodrome de Chantilly, 16 av du Général-Leclerc, 90209 Chantilly (03.44.62.44.00, www.prix-de-diane.com). **Admission** €8; €4 reductions; free under-18s. **Date** mid June.

The French Derby draws the crème de la crème of high society to Chantilly, sporting silly hats and keen to have a flutter at this handsome racecourse next to the famous château and stables.

★ Fête de la Musique

All over France (01.40.03.94.70, www.fetedelamusique.culture.fr). **Admission** free. **Date** 21 June.

Free gigs, encompassing all genres, take place across the country and around the world as part of this festival on the summer solstice. In Paris, concerts take place in theatres, bars, on street corners, in parks and even on balconies.

★ Marche des Fiertés (Gay Pride)

Information: Centre Gai et Lesbien (01.43.57.21.47, www.centrelgbtparis.org). **Date** end June.

Outrageous floats and flamboyant costumes parade towards Bastille; then there's an official fête and various club and nightlife events.

Festival Chopin à Paris

Orangerie de Bagatelle, Parc de Bagatelle, Bois de Boulogne, 16th (01.45.00.22.19, www.frederic-chopin.com). M° Porte Maillot, then bus 244. **Admission** €17-€34 (plus €5.50 park entry). **Date** mid June-mid July.

Top: **French Open**. Bottom: **Quatorze Juillet**.

Organised by the Chopin Society, candlelit evening recitals of the composer's works are performed in the idyllic Parc de la Bagatelle.

★ Paris Jazz Festival

Parc Floral de Paris, Bois de Vincennes, 12th (www.parisjazzfestival.fr). M° Château de Vincennes. **Admission** *Park €5.50; €2.75 reductions; free under-7s.* **Date** *June-July.*
Two months of free jazz weekends take place in the Parc Floral. Highlights for 2013 included Hugh Masekela and Manu Katché.

Solidays

Longchamp Hippodrome (01.53.10.22.22, www.solidays.org). M° Porte Maillot. **Admission** *Day €39. Weekend €54.* **Date** *end June.*
A three-day music festival, for the benefit of AIDS charities. The 2013 event welcomed more than 170,000 festivalgoers and saw performances from the likes of Bloc Party and David Guetta.

Paris Cinéma

Various venues (01.55.25.55.25, www.paris cinema.org). **Admission** *varies.* **Date** *early July.*
Premieres, tributes and restored films make up the diverse programme at the city's excellent summer filmgoing initiative.

Le Quatorze Juillet (Bastille Day)

All over France. **Date** *14 July.*
France's national holiday commemorates the storming of the Bastille in 1789. The evening before the holiday, Parisians dance at place de la Bastille. At 10am on the 14th, crowds line up along the Champs-Elysées as the President reviews a full military parade. By night, the Champ de Mars fills for the fireworks display.

LOUD & PROUD

Fanfare provides the soundtrack for many a Paris celebration.

A cacophonous hybrid of Baltic brass band, New Orleans marching band and student rag day parade, *fanfare* is the true sound of the Paris streets. If you're in the capital for Fête de la Musique, Beaujolais Nouveau, a rugby match, political protest or just about any other mass gathering, you're sure to hear and see one. Though they take many strange forms today, Paris's *fanfares* – or *fanfares des beaux-arts* – have their roots in the carnivalesque antics of the city's architecture students. Every spring from 1892 to 1966, the students held a Bal des Quat'z'arts, a costumed procession through the streets followed by an orgiastic 'pagan' ball accompanied by *fanfares*, originally playing *bigotphones* (a kind of papier mâché kazoo), and later brass and woodwind instruments.

'A *fanfare* should be *faux, fort et pas en place* – false, loud and with no rhythm,' says Raphael Pluot, trombonist with the Chili Kipu's, whose costumes include Rod Stewart wigs, leopardskin Spandex and drag. 'The idea is that most people don't know how to play an instrument when they start out. We were formed at the end of the 1980s so we play a lot of Madonna, The Cure and anything else that makes us laugh.' Every four years or so there's a battle of the bands organised by the Grande Masse des Beaux-Arts alumni association (www.grandemasse.org). The next one is scheduled for 2015.

Paris's funkiest *fanfare* is the Tarace Boulba collective (www.taraceboulba.com), formed by two members of Les Négresses Vertes in 1993. With 1,000 members, it turns out in groups of anything from ten to 70, playing funk and Afrobeat in an atmosphere of crazed abandon.

★ Le Tour de France

*Av des Champs-Elysées, 8th (01.41.33.14.00,
www.letour.fr).* **Date** July.

The ultimate spectacle in cycling is reserved for
the end of July, when the world's biggest bike race
arrives in Paris. After three weeks of racing, the
battle for the leader's famed yellow jersey is all but
over, and the final stage usually climaxes in a mass
sprint with everyone finishing together. It's an
incredible spectacle as the riders propel themselves
at speeds of up to 65 km/h (40mph) around nine laps
of a four-mile finishing circuit that takes in the
Champs-Elysées and Tuileries area. Turn up early
for a front-row spot.

Etés de la Danse

*Théâtre du Châtelet, 1st (01.40.28.28.40,
www.lesetesdeladanse.com). M° Châtelet.*
Tickets €13-€100. **Date** July.

Every year, the sumptuous Théâtre du Châtelet
brings a major dance company from overseas to the
capital. Most theatres in Paris take a break over the
summer, so it's one of July's few opportunities to see
classical ballet. The 2013 edition saw the Vienna
National Ballet performing *Don Quixote*, and a special tribute to Rudolf Nureyev.

Paris, Quartier d'Eté

*Various venues (01.44.94.98.00, www.
quartierdete.com).* **Admission** free-€20.
Date mid July-mid Aug.

Global in outlook, ambitious in scope, citywide and
often free, the Quartier d'Eté festival offers a fantastic summer programme of dance, theatre, concerts
and circus. Previous years have seen open-air films,
gypsy music, ballet by Merce Cunningham, and
an opera composed specially for the occasion by
Youssou N'Dour.

★ Paris-Plages

Various venues (08.20.00.75.75, www.paris.fr).
Admission free. **Date** mid July-mid Aug.

If there's one event that sums up Paris in the summer, this is it. Back in 2002, Mayor Bertrand Delanoë
began the tradition of lining the banks of the Seine
with sand, deckchairs, food stalls and volleyball
nets, creating a series of city beaches for those stuck
in town during the long, hot months. Since 2007, the
project has extended along the length of the canal in
Bassin de la Villette, making an idyllic summer landscape of pétanque, boules, picnicking, sunbathing
and watersports. *Photo p30.*
► *A stretch of the Left Bank from the Musée
d'Orsay to just before the Eiffel Tower has
now become a permanent park, footpath and
cycle track. See p224.*

Le Cinéma en Plein Air

*Parc de la Villette, 19th (01.40.03.75.75,
www.villette.com). M° Porte de Pantin.*
Admission free. **Date** mid July-end Aug.

Clockwise
from top:
**Tour de
France**;
**Rock en
Seine**;
**Cinéma en
Plein Air.**

Outdoor movie going at its finest, with films
screened for free at sundown in Parc de la Villette,
the cutting-edge architectural, music and art hub
that's a big part of the recent buzz around north-east
Paris. Expect everything from *Ocean's Eleven* to
Kaurismäki gems, and an easygoing crowd of
happy, summery locals and tourists.

Festival Classique au Vert

*Parc Floral de Paris, Bois de Vincennes, 12th
(01.45.43.81.18, www.classiqueauvert.fr). M°
Château de Vincennes.* **Admission** *Park* €5.50;
€2.75 reductions; free under-7s. **Date** Aug-Sept.
Free classical music recitals in a park setting every
weekend throughout August and September.

Autumn

Jazz à la Villette
*Cité de la Musique & various venues
(01.44.84.44.84, www.jazzalavillette.com).*
Admission €6-€30. **Date** early Sept.
The first fortnight in September brings one of Paris's best jazz festivals with big-name stars such as Bryan Ferry and Jamie Cullum taking to the stage. There's also a series of Jazz for Kids concerts running alongside the main festival.

Festival Paris Ile-de-France
Various venues (01.58.71.01.01, www.festival-ile-de-france.com). **Tickets** varies. **Date** early Sept-mid Oct.
Each year, the Paris Ile-de-France Festival offers a brilliantly varied programme of music from classical to contemporary, traditional and folk to cutting-edge electronic, at venues ranging from central Paris to Vincennes via Fontainebleau.

We Love Green Festival
Parc de Bagatelle, Bois de Boulogne, 16th (www.welovegreen.fr). **Tickets** varies.
Date mid Sept.
This three-day eco festival, which had its first outing in 2011, is held in the verdant surroundings of the Parc de Bagatelle. It's a bucolic celebration of music and nature, and the audience is positively expected to dance barefoot in the grass, wear coronets of flowers and eat nothing but vegetables for three days. Past highlights have included Norah Jones and Django Django.

Techno Parade
www.technoparade.fr. **Date** mid Sept.
The Saturday parade (which finishes up at Bastille) is followed by several late, late club nights around the capital.

Journées du Patrimoine
All over France (www.journeesdupatrimoine.culture.fr). **Date** mid Sept.
Embassies, ministries, scientific establishments and corporate headquarters open their doors to the public, allowing for some fascinating glimpses of their interiors. The festive Soirée du Patrimoine takes place on the first Journée. Get *Le Monde* or *Le Parisien* for a full programme.

★ Festival d'Automne
Various venues. Information: 156 rue de Rivoli, 1st (01.53.45.17.00, www.festival-automne.com). **Admission** €7-€45. **Date** mid Sept-mid Jan.
This major annual arts festival focuses on bringing challenging contemporary theatre, dance and modern opera to Paris. It is also intent on bringing non-Western culture into the French consciousness. Apart from its exceptional length, the Festival

Fête de l'Assomption
Cathédrale Notre-Dame de Paris, pl du Parvis Notre-Dame, 4th (01.42.34.56.10, www.cathedraledeparis.com). Mº Cité/RER St-Michel Notre-Dame. **Admission** free.
Date 15 Aug.
A national holiday. Notre-Dame becomes a place of religious pilgrimage for Assumption Day.

★ Rock en Seine
Domaine National de St-Cloud (www.rockenseine.com). Mº Porte de St-Cloud.
Admission *Day* €45. *3 days* €99. **Date** end Aug.
The city's premier rock festival, Rock en Seine has been held in the Domaine National de Saint-Cloud every last weekend in August since 2003. Last year's line-up included Alt-J, Tame Impala, Laura Mvula, Nine Inch Nails and Black Rebel Motorcycle Club. For the best experience, buy a three-day pass and camp in the historic park grounds, which include Marie Antoinette's rose garden.

d'Automne also has enormous means at its disposal and an exceptionally high quality line-up. As well as name-checking theatre's big players (the likes of Maguy Marin, Robert Wilson, Trisha Brown and Christoph Marthaler) and venues (Théâtre de la Ville, Musée du Quai Branly, Centre Pompidou), the festival also lays great emphasis on less famous names such as director Gwenaël Morin or choreographer Latifa Laâbissi, and on less well-known venues (Scène Watteau, the Nouveau Théâtre de Montreuil), making it one of the most democratic arts festivals in Europe.

Fête de la Gastronomie
Various venues (www.fete-gastronomie.fr). **Admission** varies. **Date** late Sept.
This recently launched nation-wide festival is aimed at celebrating the wonders of French cuisine. The inaugural theme was 'terroir', with more than 3,000 events across the country: Michelin-starred chef Guy Martin set up market stalls in his cooking workshop L'Atelier Guy Martin, so that visitors could choose ingredients before being shown how to cook a gourmet dish with them. He also offered diners free kitchen tours around his temple of gastronomy, Le Grand Véfour, in Palais Royal.

Mondial de l'Automobile
Paris-Expo, pl de la Porte de Versailles (01.56.88.22.40, www.mondial-automobile.com). Mº Porte de Versailles. **Admission** €13; €7 reductions; free under-10s. **Date** early Oct.
Started in 1898, the biennial Paris Motor Show features cutting-edge design from all over the world. The next shows are due to pull into Paris-Expo in 2014 and 2016.

★ Nuit Blanche
Various venues (http://nuitblanche.paris.fr). **Admission** free. **Date** early Oct.
Nuit Blanche is a free dusk-to-dawn carnival of arts and culture inspired by St Petersburg's 'White Nights'. The premise is simple: an ever-changing roster of artistic directors takes over different portions of the city every year, commissioning hundreds of works that are all about finding new ways for citizens to interact with the urban space. From clouds of paper butterflies settling on neoclassical columns to church naves sprouting enormous bejewelled skulls, Nuit Blanche is a riotously popular way to engage with cutting-edge artistry.

Prix de l'Arc de Triomphe
Hippodrome de Longchamp, Bois de Boulogne, 16th (www.prixarcdetriomphe.com). Mº Porte d'Auteuil, then free shuttle bus. **Admission** €8; €4 reductions; free under-18s. **Date** early Oct.
France's richest flat race meeting attracts the elite of horse racing for a traditional autumn weekend of pomp and ceremony. The big race gallops off on Sunday afternoon.

Fête des Vendanges de Montmartre
Rue des Saules, 18th (www.fetedesvendanges demontmartre.com). Mº Lamarck Caulaincourt. **Date** early Oct.
This is perhaps the most quintessentially Gallic of the capital's annual festivals. The event takes place in Montmartre in the vicinity of the Clos Montmartre vineyard, which sits on the northern side of the Butte. Although the vines cover a mere 1,560sq m and produce an average of just 1,000 bottles a year, the modest harvest is the pretext for a long weekend of Bacchanalian street parties.

FIAC (Foire Internationale d'Art Contemporain)
Various venues (01.47.56.64.20, www.fiacparis.com). **Admission** €35; €20 reductions; free under-12s. **Date** mid Oct.
The Grand Palais is the main venue for this week-long international contemporary art fair featuring more than 180 galleries, along with a series of outdoor installations in the Jardins des Tuileries.

Clockwise from top: **Nouvel An Chinois**; **Noël**; **Nuit Blanche**.

Armistice Day

Arc de Triomphe, 8th.
M° Charles de Gaulle Etoile.
Date 11 Nov.
To commemorate French combatants who served in the World Wars, the President lays wreaths at the Tomb of the Unknown Soldier underneath the Arc de Triomphe. The *bleuet* (a cornflower) is worn.

Africolor

Various suburbs, including Montreuil, St-Denis & St-Ouen (01.47.97.69.99, www.africolor.com).
Admission €5-€15. **Date** late Nov-late Dec.
This month-long music and dance festival has been running for more than 20 years, featuring artists from all across Africa.

Fête du Beaujolais Nouveau

Various venues (www.beaujolaisgourmand.com).
Date late Nov.
The third Thursday in November sees cafés and wine bars buzzing in the capital as the young red *vin de primeur* Beaujolais nouveau is released on to the market. Just six to eight weeks old, the wine is intended for immediate consumption.

Noël (Christmas)

Date 24, 25 Dec.
Christmas is a family affair in France, with a dinner on Christmas Eve (*le Réveillon*), normally after mass. Usually the only bars and restaurants open are the ones in the city's main hotels.

★ New Year's Eve/New Year's Day

Date 31 Dec, 1 Jan.
Jubilant crowds swarm along the Champs-Elysées. Nightclubs and restaurants hold expensive New Year's Eve soirées, and on New Year's Day the Grande Parade de Paris brings floats, bands and dancers.

Fête des Rois (Epiphany)

Date 6 Jan.
Pâtisseries sell *galettes des rois*, cakes with a frangipane filling in which a *fève*, or tiny charm, is hidden.

Mass for Louis XVI

Chapelle Expiatoire, 29 rue Pasquier, 8th
(01.42.65.35.80). M° St-Augustin. **Date** Jan.
On the Sunday closest to 21 January – the anniversary of the beheading of Louis XVI in 1793 – rightwing crackpots mourn the end of the monarchy.

Nouvel An Chinois

Around av d'Ivry & av de Choisy, 13th.
M° Porte de Choisy or Porte d'Ivry. Also
av des Champs Elysées, 8th. **Date** Jan/Feb.
Lion and dragon dances, and lively martial arts demonstrations to celebrate the Chinese New Year.

Les Puces du Design

Bercy Village, 12th (01.53.40.78.77, www.puces dudesign.com). M° Jaurès. **Admission** free.
Date Oct & May.
Having moved to a new location in Bercy Village in 2011, this biannual weekend-long fair continues to specialise in modern and vintage furniture, and design classics.

Winter

★ Festival des Inrockuptibles

Various venues (01.42.44.16.16, www.lesinrocks. com). **Admission** varies. **Date** early Nov.
Famous indie cultural journal *Les Inrockuptibles* has changed a lot in its 25-year history, but the annual festival has always kept its spirit alive. *The* champion of independent rock music in France, the festival also welcomes folk, soul and electronica acts. The 2013 line-up included the likes of London Grammar, Laura Mvula, Foals and Suede.

Paris's Best

*There's something
for everyone with our
hand-picked highlights.*

Sightseeing

VIEWS

Arc de Triomphe p91
Gaze out across place
Charles-de-Gaulle and
its 12 arterial avenues.
Eiffel Tower p231
Brave the queues for a
glimpse of Paris in panorama.
**Institut du Monde
Arabe** p184
Fabulous vista from the roof
of this revamped treasure.
Sacré-Coeur p116
Hilltop views as heavenly
as the surroundings.
Tour Montparnasse p212
The capital laid bare from
56 floors up.

ART

Centre Pompidou p124
The largest collection of
modern art in Europe.
Musée du Louvre p64
Extravagant architecture
and extraordinary art.
Musée d'Orsay p225
Gleaming after a
groundbreaking revamp.
Musée Picasso p129
Bigger and brighter, Paris's
Picasso showcase is finally
back for 2014.
104 p161
Artistic creation in motion at
this community art space.
Palais de Tokyo p96
Tripled in size and still
pushing the boundaries.

HISTORY

Musée de Montmartre p115
This 17th-century manor
displays the history of the hill.
**Cité Nationale de l'Histoire
de l'Immigration** p156
Moving tribute to over 200
years of immigration history.
Musée de la Musique p164
Historic instruments
innovatively displayed.
Musée Edith Piaf p168
France's greatest singer.

OUTDOORS

Jardin des Plantes p185
Botanical bliss, including
a tree planted in 1636.
Bois de Vincennes p156
Space to roam in Paris's
biggest park.
**Parc des Buttes-
Chaumont** p168
Skip the Tuileries and head
for the 19th instead.
Parc de la Villette p164
Postmodern paradise: themed
gardens and fun activities.

CHURCHES

**Cathédrale Notre-Dame
de Paris** p51
Glorious Gothic grandeur
on the Ile de la Cité.
Eglise St-Séverin p175
The city's most charming
medieval church.
**Eglise St-Etienne-
du-Mont** p181
Resting place of Pascal,
Racine and Ste-Geneviève.

DEAD FAMOUS

Le Panthéon p182
Celebrity crypt, from Voltaire
to Marie Curie.
**Cimetière de
Montmartre** p115
Truffaut, Berlioz and Dalida
are all buried here.
**Cimetière de
Père-Lachaise** p142
Home to some of France's
most creative corpses.

CHILDREN

**Grande Galerie de
l'Evolution** p184
The natural world in all its
majestic modelled glory.
**Cité des Sciences et
de l'Industrie** p158
Science *can* be fun at this
superb museum.
Disneyland Paris p248
Mickey magic and scary
rides galore.
Musée des Egouts p245
Take your sewer rats on a trip
through Paris's tunnels.

WILDLIFE

**Parc Zoologique de
Paris** p247
The animals are back in style
after a handsome revamp.
Cinéaqua p246
Get up close and personal
with sharks and sturgeon.
Parc de Thoiry p246
Head out of town for this
suburban safari.

Eating & drinking

BISTROS

A la Biche au Bois p157
Prix fixe perfection at this
atmospheric eaterie.
Le Bistrot Paul Bert p145
Everything you imagine from
a classic bistro.
Le Chateaubriand p168
The leading light of Paris's
neo-bistro trend.
Frenchie p85
Grégory Marchand's
legendary loft-style eaterie.
Granterroirs p98
Terroir treats abound.
Pétrelle p120
Style and substance combine
in this quirky dining room.
Ribouldingue p178
Indulge your appetite for offal
at this classic bistro.

BLOWOUTS

Alain Ducasse au Plaza Athénée p98
Glamour guaranteed (if you can swallow the *haute* bill).
L'Arpège p226
Lofty cuisine at Alain Passard's Left Bank eatery.
Jules Verne p233
Elegant Eiffel Tower dining from Alain Ducasse.

GLOBAL

Pho 14 p187
This Vietnamese canteen is the place to come for *pho*.
Rose Bakery p120
Great British classics, from scones to sticky toffee pud.
Le Souk p150
Dream tagines at this lively Moroccan eatery.

BARS

Le Crocodile p183
Mix it up with more than 300 cocktails on the menu.
Candelaria p136
Tequila time at this hugely popular taqueria.
Rouge Passion p120
Well-picked wines from €4 and free *assiettes apéros*.
Le Verre Volé p166
Wondrous wine bar with dining to match.
Café Charbon p170
Hugely popular bar wrapped in belle époque surroundings.
Chez Jeannette p165
Retro chic abounds at this hip aperitif spot.
Chez Prune p165
Bobos and beer by the Canal Saint-Martin.
Les Furieux p153
Join the locals for a heady mix of absinthe and rock.
Le Fantôme p166
Cocktails and classic arcade games at this hip new venue.
La Bellevilloise p170
Brilliant multitasker with food, drink, art, gigs and clubbing.

FIVE SLEEPS
Hôtel le Bristol (p345)
Royal Monceau (p347)
Mama Shelter (p354)
Auberge Flora (p354)
St Christopher's Inn
Gare du Nord
(p364)

Shopping

CONCEPT

Colette p71
Must-have accessories from the original concept store.
L'Eclaireur p138
Sophisticated picks.
LE66 p104
Champs-Elysées cool.
Merci p140
Charity first at this most generous of general stores.

FOOD & DRINK

Arnaud Delmontel p121
Legendary baguettes.
Fromagerie Quatrehomme p228
Seriously tasty cheeses, from beaufort to brie.
Causses p121
Deli delights and expat treats.
Première Pression Provence p155
Single-producer olive oils from the Provençal groves.

Clockwise from far left: **Causses**; **Le Louxor**; **Candelaria**; **Colette**.

GIFTS & SOUVENIRS
Le Bon Marché p227
Chic shopping at Paris's oldest department store.
Diptyque p179
Divine scents, from Figuier to Violette.

BOOKS & MUSIC
Fargo p154
A cornucopia of good ol' country music.
Shakespeare & Co p179
An unmissable destination for bibliophiles the world over.
Album p178
Geek heaven at this king of the comic scene.

FASHION
Lanvin p103
Classic couture.
K Jacques p140
Making sandals sexy (Picasso was a fan).
Sonia Rykiel p198
The queen of Left Bank chic.

CHILDREN
DPAM p154
Classic kids' clothing with a touch of French flair.
Un Zèbre O Grenier p171
Charming toy shop where tradition rules.

MARKETS
Marché aux Puces de St-Ouen p118
Probably the biggest flea market in the world.
Marché aux Puces d'Aligre p155
Junk joy at this central Paris flea market.

Nightlife

CLUBS
Wanderlust p270
The 13th is Paris's new clubbing capital.
Batofar p270
Seineside swaying on the legendary lightship.
Rex p267
Paris's techno king.

MUSIC
Mécanique Ondulatoire p275
Rocking three-floor Bastille venue.
El Alamein p188
Climb aboard this moored boat for jazz and *chanson*.
New Morning p278
One of the city's finest jazz joints.

Arts

FESTIVALS
Paris Jazz Festival p35
Free summer jazz weekends in the lovely Parc Floral.
Cinéma en Plein Air p36
Deckchair delights at this free outdoor movie festival.
Festival d'Automne p37
Top-notch treats await at this annual arts extravaganza.

THEATRE
Comédie Française p289
Stage classics at the gilded mother of French theatres.
Théâtre de la Ville p292
Innovation rules at the 'City Theatre'.

FILM
Le Grand Rex p251
Biggest screen in town.
La Pagode p254
One of the loveliest cinemas in the world.
Le Louxor p254
1920s art deco revamped for the 21st century.

OPERA & BALLET
Palais Garnier p284
The jewel in the crown of Paris music-making.
Salle Pleyel p284
The leading symphonic hall handsomely restored.
Opéra Bastille p283
Hideous building, heavenly opera classics.

Explore

The Seine & Islands

Paris owes its very existence to the Seine, and dutifully acknowledges the importance of its river on the city's coat of arms. The Seine was the transport route that brought settlers here in the first place, many millennia ago. As the city grew, so did the river's cultural importance, until it became what it still is today – the symbolic boundary between intellectual Left Bank Paris and the mercantile activities of the Right Bank. In between the two sides, like a double bullseye, are the islands: the western Ile de la Cité, with its heavy payload of history, state machinery and religious grandeur; and the Ile St-Louis, once a mess of marshland and islets, and now one of the most exclusive residential districts in the city. In 2013, ambitious redesign plans for the traffic-choked *berges* saw a stretch of Left Bank road converted into a pedestrian promenade with play areas, cafés and bars. Forget the Côte d'Azur next August – and head for the Seine instead.

EXPLORE

Berthillon.

Don't Miss

1 Cathédrale Notre-Dame de Paris 850 years of Gothic glory (p51).

2 La Conciergerie Forbidding fortress with a fascinating past (p51).

3 Sainte-Chapelle Stunning stained-glass shrine (p54).

4 Berthillon Naughty but very nice (p55).

5 Le Sergent Recruteur Designer dinner (p55).

ALONG THE SEINE

The banks of the Seine have always been a place for romance, exhibitionism and breathing space in a city whose parks are all too regimented and close at dusk on the dot. Novelist Edmund White has written about the frisson of being lit up by a Bateau Mouche while cruising on the quays, and for either sex the rules of social behaviour were more akin to the louche South of France than Paris once you went down the steps to the river.

When Paris-Plage was introduced in 2002, the sunbathing and picnicking on the quayside became more of a family-friendly affair, harking back to the early years of the 20th century. In those days people didn't just sunbathe by the Seine, they swam in it too – swimming, rowing and water polo events all took place on the river during the 1900 Summer Olympics. The floating Piscine Josephine Baker, which launched in 2006, is the closest you'll get to swimming in the Seine at the moment, although the water has been significantly cleaned up of late and 33 species of fish now live in the river, against just three in 1970.

The bridges

From the honeyed arches of the oldest, the **Pont Neuf**, to the handsome, swooping lines of the newest, the **Passerelle Simone-de-Beauvoir**, the bridges spanning the Seine are among the best-known landmarks in the city, and enjoy some of its finest views.

There was already a bridge on the site of the **Petit Pont** in the first century BC, when the Parisii Celts ran their river trade and toll-bridge operations. The Romans put up a cross-island thoroughfare in the form of a reinforced bridge to the south of Ile de la Cité, and another one north of it (where the **Pont Notre-Dame** now stands), thus creating a straight route all the way from Orléans through to Belgium. Since then, the city's *ponts* have been bombed, bashed by buses and boats, weather-beaten and even trampled to destruction: in 1634, the Pont St-Louis collapsed under the weight of a religious procession. In the Middle Ages, the handful of bridges linking the islands to the riverbanks were lined with shops and houses, but the flimsy wooden constructions regularly caught fire or got washed away. The Petit Pont sank 11 times before councillors decided to ban building on top of bridges.

The Pont Neuf was inaugurated in 1607 and has been standing sturdy ever since. This was the first bridge to be built with no houses to obstruct the view of the river. It had a raised stretch of road at the edge to protect walkers from traffic and horse dung (the new-fangled 'pavement' soon caught on); the alcoves that now make pit stops for lovers were once filled with tooth-pullers, peddlers and *bouquinistes*.

The 19th century was boom time for bridge-building: 21 were built in all, including the city's first steel, iron and suspension bridges. The **Pont de la Concorde** used up what was left of the Bastille after the storming of 1789; the romantic **Pont des Arts** was the capital's first solely pedestrian crossing (built in 1803 and rebuilt in the 1980s). The most exuberant bridge is the **Pont Alexandre III**, with its bronze and glass, garlanding and gilded embellishments. More practical is the **Pont de l'Alma**, with its Zouave statue that has long been a flood monitor: when the statue's toes get wet, the state raises the flood alert and starts to close the quayside roads; when he's up to his ankles, it's no longer possible to navigate the river by boat.

The 20th century brought some spectacular additions. **Pont Charles-de-Gaulle**, for example, stretches resplendently like the

IN THE KNOW
THE SEINE DISTILLED

Length 776km
(France's second longest river)

Source Source-Seine
(30km north-west of Dijon)

Mouth Le Havre

Widest point in Paris 200m
(Pont de Grenelle)

Narrowest point in Paris 30m
(Quai de Montebello)

Speed Approx 2km/h

Bridges in Paris 37
(two rail, four pedestrian
and 31 road)

Oldest bridge Pont Neuf (1607)

Newest bridge Passerelle Simone
de Beauvoir (2006)

Most bridges built in a year 15 (in 1870)

Goods carried per year 21.3 million
tonnes

Most bodies found in a year 55 (in 2007)

Biggest flood 1910 (6.1m above average)

EXPLORE

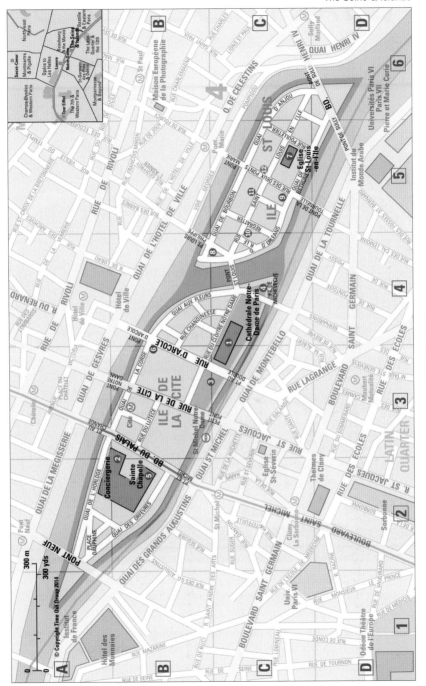

EXPLORE

BATOBUS
PARIS

RIVER-BOAT SHUTTLE SERVICE

1 PASS / 8 STOPS
to discover Paris by boat

CHAMPS-ELYSÉES   LOUVRE   HÔTEL DE VILLE

HOP ON, HOP OFF *as you please…*

TOUR EIFFEL   MUSÉE D'ORSAY   SAINT-GERMAIN-DES-PRÉS   NOTRE DAME   JARDIN DES PLANTES

Batobus shows you a different view of Paris…
Your ticket is a pass: you can get on and off the boat where you like,
when you like for 1 day , 2 days, 5 days or a year.

Information and booking:
0 825 05 01 01 (0.15€/min) www.batobus.com

a **sodexo** company

wing of a huge aeroplane, and iron **Viaduc d'Austerlitz** (1905) is striking yet elegant as it cradles métro line 5. The city's newest crossing (and its 37th in total), the Passerelle Simone-de-Beauvoir, links up the Bibliothèque Nationale to the Parc de Bercy.

ILE DE LA CITE

In the 1st & 4th arrondissements.

The Ile de la Cité is where Paris was born around 250 BC, when the Parisii, a tribe of Celtic Gauls, founded a settlement on this convenient bridging point of the Seine. Romans, Merovingians and Capetians followed, in what became a centre of political and religious power right into the Middle Ages: royal authority at one end, around the Capetian palace; the Church at the other, by Notre-Dame.

When Victor Hugo wrote *Notre-Dame de Paris* in 1831, the Ile de la Cité was still a bustling quarter of narrow medieval streets and tall houses: 'the head, heart and very marrow of Paris'. Baron Haussmann performed a marrow extraction when he supervised the expulsion of around 25,000 people from the island, razing tenements and some 20 churches, and leaving behind large, official buildings – the law courts, the **Conciergerie**, Hôtel-Dieu hospital, the police headquarters and the cathedral. The lines of the old streets are traced into the parvis in front of **Notre-Dame**.

Sainte-Chapelle, Pierre de Montreuil's masterpiece of stained glass and slender Gothic columns, stands among the nearby law courts. Enveloping the chapel, the Palais de Justice was built alongside the Conciergerie. Behind elaborate wrought-iron railings, most of the present buildings around the fine neoclassical entrance courtyard date from the 1780s reconstruction by Desmaisons and Antoine. After passing through security, you can visit the **Salle des Pas Perdus**, busy with plaintiffs and barristers, and sit in on cases in the civil and criminal courts. The Palais is still the centre of the French legal system.

Across boulevard du Palais, behind the Tribunal de Commerce, place Louis-Lépine is occupied by the Marché aux Fleurs. The Hôtel-Dieu, east of the market place, was founded in the seventh century. During the Middle Ages, your chances of survival here were, at best, slim. The hospital originally stood on the other side of the island facing the Latin Quarter, but after a series of fires in the 18th century it was rebuilt here in the 1860s.

Notre-Dame cathedral dominates the eastern half of the island. On the parvis in front of the cathedral is the bronze 'Kilomètre Zéro' marker, the point from which distances between Paris and the rest of France are measured. The **Crypte Archéologique** hidden under the parvis gives a sense of the island's multi-layered past, when it was a tangle of alleys, houses, churches and cabarets. Notre-Dame is still a place of worship, and holds its Assumption Day procession, Christmas Mass and Nativity scene on the parvis.

Walk through the garden by the cathedral to appreciate its flying buttresses. To the north-east, a medieval feel persists in the few streets untouched by Haussmann, such as rue Chanoinesse, rue de la Colombe and rue des Ursins, though the crenellated medieval remnant on the corner of rue des Ursins and rue des Chantres was redone in the 1950s for the Aga Khan. The capital's oldest love story unfolded in the 12th century at 9 quai aux Fleurs, where Héloïse lived with her uncle Canon Fulbert, who had her tutor and lover, the scholar Abélard, castrated. Héloïse was sent to a nunnery. Behind the cathedral, at the eastern end of the island, is the **Mémorial des Martyrs de la Déportation**, remembering people sent to Nazi concentration camps.

Sights & Museums

★ FREE Cathédrale Notre-Dame de Paris

Pl du Parvis-Notre-Dame, 4th (01.42.34.56.10, www.cathedraledeparis.com). M° Cité/RER St-Michel. **Open** 8am-6.45pm Mon-Fri; 8am-7.15pm Sat, Sun. *Towers* Apr-Sept 10am-6.30pm daily *(June-Aug* until 11pm Sat, Sun). Oct-Mar 10am-5.30pm daily. **Admission** free. *Towers* €8.50; €5.50 reductions; free under-18s, under-26s (EU citizens). PMP. **Map** p49 C4 **①**

Notre-Dame was constructed between 1163 and 1334, and the amount of time and money spent on it reflected the city's growing prestige. The west front remains a high point of Gothic art for the balanced proportions of its twin towers and rose window, and the three doorways with their rows of saints and sculpted tympanums: the *Last Judgement* (centre), *Life of the Virgin* (left) and *Life of St Anne* (right). Inside, take a moment to admire the long nave with its solid foliate capitals and high altar with a marble Pietà by Coustou. To truly appreciate the masonry, climb up the towers. The route runs up the north tower and down the south. Between the two you get a close-up view of the gallery of chimeras – the fantastic birds and hybrid beasts designed by Viollet-le-Duc along the balustrade. As of February 2013, Notre-Dame has eight new bells, forged as part of the cathedral's 850th anniversary year.

★ La Conciergerie

2 bd du Palais, 1st (01.53.40.60.80). M° Cité/ RER St-Michel Notre-Dame. **Open** 9.30am-6pm daily. **Admission** €8.50; €5.50 reductions; free

EXPLORE

EXPLORE

WALK REVOLUTIONARY ROAD

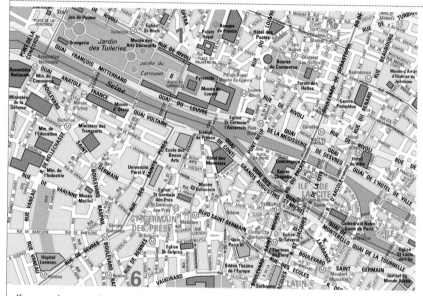

If you can keep your head while those around you are losing theirs, get on the blocks for our promenade through the goriest spots of regicidal fever. You'll need stout shoes and a fervent imagination. Start at place de la Concorde.

The key date here is 21 January 1793. Since 8am the gates of Paris have been locked, the shutters barred. A crowd of 20,000 has assembled in place Louis XV, renamed place de la Révolution. At 10am there is a drum roll, Louis XVI is strapped to a plank and pushed towards the guillotine. The device slices through his neck, the crowd roars and clamours to soak their hankies in the monarch's blood. But to see how the nation reached this bloodthirsty state, we have to step back in time.

Walk through the gates from Concorde into the Tuileries gardens. The palace that used to stand here was the scene of repeated revolutionary fracas. On 13 July 1789, the eve of Bastille Day, a crowd ransacked the royal *garde-meubles* for weapons. This was only a taster of what was to come, though. On the night of King Louis' arrest in 1792, 600 of his Swiss Guards were murdered, their genitals hacked off and fed to dogs.

Turn right on to rue de Rivoli and walk to the Palais-Royal. The Duc d'Orléans' pleasure palace was a revolutionary hotbed as nobles and plebs mingled among the coffee shops and sideshows.

Walk through the arch in the Louvre's north wing to place du Carrousel, where the guillotine briefly stood. Cross Pont des Arts and head down rue Bonaparte. On your left you'll see the Ecole des Beaux-Arts, where Alexandre Lenoir tried to save France's heritage from the mob – he threw himself on the grave of Richelieu and took a stab in the back for his pains.

Rue de l'Abbaye was the site of one of the revolution's worst atrocities, in September 1792, when 115 priests were trapped in the garden and butchered. The red brick Abbot's Palace is now the Institut Catholique. Take rue Garancière past St-Sulpice to the Palais du Luxembourg. Now the Senate, the palace was commandeered as a prison and housed, among others, activists Danton and Thomas Paine. Take rue Rotrou through place de l'Odéon, where influential pamphleteer Camille Desmoulins lived at no.2, and follow rue de l'Odéon, where Paine, having escaped the guillotine, lived at no.10. Cross boulevard St-Germain

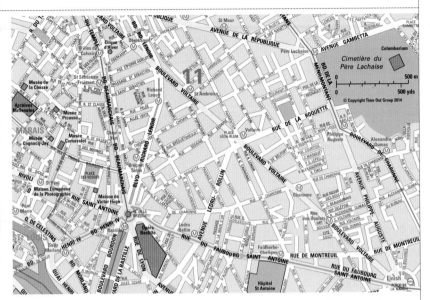

© Copyright Time Out Group 2014

EXPLORE

to Café Procope at 13 rue de l'Ancienne Comédie. A favourite slugging ground of Voltaire, Rousseau, Danton and Marat, it contains Voltaire's desk.

Head back across boulevard St-Germain and take rue de l'Ecole de Médecine, where the Cordeliers' Club met at no.15 in the former Couvent des Cordeliers. No.18 was the scene of pamphleteer Marat's infamous demise, when Charlotte Corday stabbed him in the bath with a kitchen knife.

Follow the road east and cut up rue St-Jacques and rue Dante until you meet rue Galande. By the time the Terror started, every available space was being used as a prison. At no.52, the Caveau des Oubliettes jazz club gets its name from a gory death sentence whereby prisoners were thrown into cells and 'forgotten'.

At Pont St-Michel, cross on to Ile de la Cité and call in at the Conciergerie. This 'vast antechamber of death' was one of the most appalling prisons of the revolution, where prisoners slept in their own excrement. Not so Marie-Antoinette, who had a room with a bed and wallpaper.

Cross the Seine again and you'll find yourself in front of the Hôtel de Ville. In October 1789, a mob of 3,000 fishwives

and others commandeered guns and cannon from here before marching to Versailles to lynch the King. They returned with the severed heads of two guards.

Take rue du Temple, the road of no return for Louis XVI, turn right into rue St-Croix-de-la-Bretonnerie and left into rue Vieille-du-Temple. Now take rue des Francs-Bourgeois on the right, which will bring you to the Musée Carnavalet with its fine collection of revolutionary history.

Follow rue de Sévigné south to the church of St-Paul-St-Louis on rue St-Antoine, from which the hearts of Louis XIII and XIV were seized and sold to a painter. Take boulevard Henri IV and notice the brown bricks in the road as you approach place de la Bastille. These mark the spot where the Bastille prison stood; similar marks can be seen on rue St-Antoine, where no.5 is the site of the main gate and the famous 'storming' on 14 July 1789. On place de la Bastille, in June 1794, the guillotine claimed 73 victims in three days.

Finally, walk east to place de la Nation (or hop on a bus). Nation, formerly place du Trône, was the guillotine's last stand before the murderous device moved back to Concorde to give Robespierre the chop.

EXPLORE

under-18s (accompanied by an adult), under-26s (EU citizens). *With Sainte-Chapelle* €12.50; €8.50 reductions. PMP. **Map** p49 B2 ②

The Conciergerie looks every inch the forbidding medieval fortress. However, much of the façade was added in the 1850s, long after Marie-Antoinette, Danton and Robespierre had been imprisoned here. The 13th-century Bonbec tower, built during the reign of St Louis, the 14th-century twin towers, César and Argent, and the Tour de l'Horloge all survive from the Capetian palace. The visit takes you through the Salle des Gardes, the medieval kitchens with their four huge chimneys, and the Salle des Gens d'Armes, a vaulted Gothic hall built between 1301 and 1315 for Philippe 'le Bel'. After the royals moved to the Louvre, the fortress became a prison under the watch of the Concierge. The wealthy had private cells with their own furniture, which they paid for; others crowded on beds of straw. A list of Revolutionary prisoners, including a hairdresser, shows that not all victims were nobles. In Marie-Antoinette's cell, the Chapelle des Girondins, are her crucifix, some portraits and a guillotine blade.

La Crypte Archéologique

Pl Jean-Paul II, 4th (01.55.42.50.10, www.crypte. paris.fr). M° Cité/RER St-Michel Notre-Dame. **Open** 10am-6pm Tue-Sun. **Admission** €5; €2.50-€3.50 reductions; free under-14s. PMP. **Map** p49 C3 ③

Hidden under the forecourt in front of the cathedral is a large void that contains bits and pieces of Roman quaysides, ramparts and hypocausts, medieval cellars, shops and pavements, the foundations of the Église Ste-Geneviève-des-Ardens (the church where Geneviève's remains were stored during the Norman invasions), an 18th-century foundling hospital and a 19th-century sewer, all excavated since the 1960s. It's not always easy to work out exactly which wall, column or staircase is which – but you do get a vivid sense of the layers of history piled one atop another during 16 centuries.

FREE Mémorial des Martyrs de la Déportation

Sq de l'Ile de France, 4th (01.46.33.87.56). M° Cité/RER St-Michel Notre-Dame. **Open** Oct-Mar 10am-5pm Tue-Sun. Apr-Sept 10am-7pm Tue-Sun. **Admission** free. **Map** p49 C4 ④

This sober tribute to the 200,000 Jews, Communists, homosexuals and *résistants* deported to concentration camps from France in World War II stands on the eastern tip of the island. A blind staircase descends to river level, where simple chambers are lined with tiny lights and the walls are inscribed with verse. A barred window looks out at the Seine.

Sainte-Chapelle

4 bd du Palais, 1st (01.53.40.60.80). M° Cité/RER St-Michel Notre-Dame. **Open** Mar-Oct 9.30am-6pm daily. Nov-Feb 9am-5pm daily. **Admission** €8.50;

Le Sergent Recruteur.

€5.50 reductions; free under-18s (with an adult), under-26s (EU citizens). *With Conciergerie* €12.50; €8.50 reductions. **Map** p49 B2 ⑤

Devout King Louis IX (St Louis, 1226-70) had a hobby of accumulating holy relics. In the 1240s, he bought what was advertised as the Crown of Thorns, and ordered Pierre de Montreuil to design a shrine. The result was Sainte-Chapelle. With 15m (49ft) windows, the upper level appears to consist almost entirely of stained glass. The windows depict hundreds of scenes from the Old and New Testaments.

Shops & Services

L'Occitane en Provence

1 rue d'Arcole, 4th (01.55.42.06.11, www. loccitane.com). M° Cité. **Open** 10.30am-7.30pm daily. **Map** p49 B3 ⑥ **Health & beauty**

The many branches of this popular Provençal chain offer natural beauty products in neat packaging.

ILE ST-LOUIS

In the 4th arrondissement.

For hundreds of years, the island was a swampy pasture belonging to Notre-Dame, known as Ile Notre-Dame and used as a retreat for fishermen, swimmers and courting couples. In the 14th century, Charles V built a fortified canal through the middle, thus creating the Ile aux Vaches ('Island of Cows'). Its real-estate potential wasn't realised until 1614, though, when speculator Christophe Marie persuaded Louis XIII to fill in the canal (present-day rue Poulletier) and plan streets, bridges and houses. The island was renamed in honour of the king's pious predecessor, and the venture proved a huge success, thanks to architect Louis Le Vau, who from the 1630s built fashionable residences along the quai d'Anjou, quai de Bourbon and quai de Béthune, as well as the **Eglise St-Louis-en-l'Ile**. By the 1660s the island was full; its smart reception rooms were set at the front of courtyards to give residents riverside views.

Rue St-Louis-en-l'Ile runs the length of the island. The grandiose **Hôtel Lambert** at no.2 was built by Le Vau in 1641 for Louis XIII's secretary. At no.51 – **Hôtel Chenizot** – look out for the bearded faun adorning the rocaille doorway, flanked by stern dragons. Across the street, the **Hôtel du Jeu de Paume** at no.54 was once a tennis court; at no.31, famous ice-cream maker **Berthillon** still draws a crowd. At 6 quai d'Orléans, the **Adam Mickiewicz library-museum** (01.55.42.83.88) is dedicated to the poet, journalist and campaigner for Polish freedom.

Sights & Museums

FREE Eglise St-Louis-en-l'Ile

19bis rue St-Louis-en-l'Ile, 4th (01.46.34.11.60, www.saintlouisenlile.catholique.fr). M° Pont Marie. **Open** 9.30am-1pm, 2-7.30pm Mon-Sat; 9am-1pm, 2-7pm Sun. **Admission** free. **Map** p49 C5 **7**
The island's church was built between 1664 and 1765. The Baroque interior boasts Corinthian columns and a sunburst over the altar.

Restaurants

Brasserie de l'Ile St-Louis

55 quai de Bourbon, 4th (01.43.54.02.59). M° Pont Marie. **Open** noon-11pm Mon, Tue, Thur-Sun. Closed Aug. **Main courses** €20. **Map** p49 C4 **8** **Brasserie**

IN THE KNOW CHEEP THRILLS

Every Sunday, the Ile de la Cité's flower market comes alive with a cacophony of squawking and chirping birds as the Marché aux Fleurs is joined by the Marché aux Oiseaux. Kids will love the line-up of parrots, chickens and canaries. Other animals such as ferrets and mice are on sale, too, plus ridiculously cute dwarf bunnies for some intense petting. It's a great way to spend time after braving the queues at nearby Notre-Dame.

Happily, this old-fashioned brasserie soldiers on while a stream of exotic juice bars on the Ile St-Louis come and go. The terrace has one of the best summer views in Paris and is invariably packed, though nothing here is gastronomically gripping: a well-dressed *frisée aux lardons* perhaps, or a more successful pan of warming tripes.

Isami

4 quai d'Orléans, 4th (01.40.46.06.97). M° Pont Marie. **Open** noon-2pm, 7-10pm Tue-Sat. **Main courses** €40. **Map** p49 C5 **9** **Japanese**
Isami is one of the best sushi restaurants in Paris. The small dining room is simply decorated with rows of Japanese earthenware stacked behind the bar, and in front of them the *itamae* (master sushi chef) works away in a frenzy. When the food arrives in a large terracotta vessel, it's hard to know where to begin. The salmon? The raw prawns? The tuna? The squid? Everything is bursting with subtle flavours and served as it should be, at room temperature.

Mon Vieil Ami

69 rue St-Louis-en-l'Ile, 4th (01.40.46.01.35, www.mon-vieil-ami.com). M° Pont Marie. **Open** noon-2.30pm, 7-10.30pm daily. **Main courses** €15-€25. **Prix fixe** €46. **Map** p49 C4 **10** **Bistro**
Antoine Westermann has created a true foodie destination here. Starters such as tartare of finely diced raw vegetables with sautéed baby squid on top impress with their deft seasoning. Typical of the mains is a cast-iron casserole of roast duck with caramelised turnips and couscous.

Le Sergent Recruteur

41 rue St-Louis-en-l'Ile, 4th (01.43.54.75.42, www.lesergentrecruteur.fr). M° Pont Marie or Sully-Morland. **Open** 12.30-2pm, 7.30-10pm Tue-Sat. **Prix fixe** *Lunch* €35, €75, €95. *Dinner* €145. **Map** p49 C5 **11** **Haute cuisine**
Avant-garde Spanish designer Jaime Hayon and chef Antonin Bonnet have turned this former pub into a handsome restaurant. The 'carte blanche' menus, where you're led by the whims of the chef, offer daring versions of classic French dishes: perhaps foie gras with rhubarb confit, wild duck with spelt, and mango and herb ice-cream. Service is adroit and professional.

Cafés & Bars

Berthillon

29-31 rue St-Louis en l'Ile, 4th (01.43.54.31.61, www.berthillon.fr). M° Pont Marie. **Open** 10am-8pm Wed-Sun. **No credit cards**. **Map** p49 C5 **12**
The flavours at this famous ice-cream parlour change throughout the season. In winter Berthillon serves delicious hot chocolate and – even naughtier – a chocolate *affogato* (a ball of vanilla ice-cream served in a white porcelain mug with hot chocolate poured over and topped with praline cream).

EXPLORE

Opéra to Les Halles

In centuries gone by, these two districts – bounded by the Grands Boulevards to the north and the river to the south – were the city's commercial and provisioning powerhouses, home to most of the newspapers, banks and major mercantile institutions. Nowadays, although there is still a strong financial slant thanks to the presence of the two stock exchanges and the Banque de France, the focus is firmly on shopping: mass-market stuff in and around Les Halles, shading into more exclusive brands the further one moves west, in particular on and just off rue St-Honoré. Les Halles itself was, famously, the city's wholesale food market until 1969, when the Second Empire iron-framed buildings that housed it were ripped out, and a thousand commentators gnashed their teeth in print. The soulless shopping centre that filled the gap in the 1970s has been one of the city's least liked features, and is itself being replaced by what promises to be a 21st-century glory of gardens, glass, and brighter, more open spaces.

EXPLORE

La Conserverie

Don't Miss

1 **Musée de l'Orangerie** Monet displayed in all his majesty (p65).

2 **Colette** The original concept store (p71).

3 **La Conserverie** Cool cocktails (p77).

4 **Musée du Louvre** A masterpiece – inside and out (p64).

5 **Frenchie** Essential eats if you get a table (p85).

TUILERIES & PALAIS-ROYAL

In the 1st & 8th arrondissements.

Once the monarchs had moved from the Ile de la Cité to spacious new quarters on the Right Bank, the Louvre and, later, the palaces of the **Tuileries** and **Palais-Royal** became the centres of royal power. **The Louvre** still exerts considerable influence today: first as a grandiose architectural ensemble; and, second, as a symbol of the capital's cultural pre-eminence. What had been simply a fortress along Philippe-Auguste's city wall in 1190 was transformed by Charles V into a royal residence with all the latest Gothic comforts; François I turned it into a sumptuous palace. For centuries, it was a work in progress: everyone wanted to make their mark – including the most monarchical of presidents, François Mitterrand, who added IM Pei's glass pyramid, doubled the exhibition space and added the Carrousel du Louvre shopping mall, auditorium and food halls.

The palace has always attracted crowds: first courtiers and ministers; then artists; and, since 1793, when it was first turned into a museum, art-lovers – though the last department of the Finance Ministry moved out as late as 1991. Around the Louvre, other subsidiary palaces grew up: Catherine de Médicis commissioned Philibert Delorme to begin work on one in the Tuileries; and Richelieu built the Palais Cardinal, which later became the Palais-Royal.

On place du Louvre, opposite Claude Perrault's grandiose eastern façade of the Louvre, is **Eglise St-Germain-l'Auxerrois**, once the French kings' parish church and home to the only original Flamboyant Gothic porch in Paris, built in 1435. Mirroring it to the left of the belfry is the 19th-century first arrondissement *mairie*, with its fanciful rose window and classical porch. Next door is the stylish **Le Fumoir** (*see p70*), with a Mona Lisa of its own: amaretto, orange juice and champagne.

Across rue de Rivoli from the Louvre, past the **Louvre des Antiquaires** antiques emporium (*see p73*), stands the understatedly elegant **Palais-Royal**, once Cardinal Richelieu's private mansion and now the Conseil d'Etat and ministry of culture. After a stroll in its quiet gardens, it's hard to believe that this was once the most debauched corner of Paris.

In the 1780s, the Palais was a boisterous centre of Paris life, where aristocrats and the financially challenged inhabitants of the *faubourgs* rubbed shoulders. The coffee houses in its arcades generated radical debate: here Camille Desmoulins called the city to arms on the eve of the storming of the Bastille; and after the Napoleonic Wars, Wellington and Field

Marshal von Blücher lost so much money in the gambling dens that Parisians claimed they had won back their entire dues for war reparations. Only haute cuisine restaurant **Le Grand Véfour** (*see p66*), founded as Café de Chartres in the 1780s, survives from this era, albeit with decoration dating from a little later.

The **Comédie Française** theatre ('La Maison de Molière'; *see p289*) stands on the south-west corner. The company, created by Louis XIV in 1680, moved here in 1799. Molière himself is honoured with a fountain on the corner of rue Molière and rue de Richelieu. Brass-fronted Café Nemours on place Colette – Colette used to buy cigars from old-fashioned **A la Civette** nearby (157 rue St-Honoré, 1st, 01.42.96.04.99) – is another thespian favourite. In front of it, the métro entrance by artist Jean-Michel Othoniel, all glass baubles and aluminium struts, is a kitsch take on Guimard's celebrated art nouveau métro entrances.

Today, the stately arcades of the Palais-Royal house an eclectic succession of antiques dealers, philatelists, specialists in tin soldiers and musical boxes – and fashion showcases. Here you'll find the European flagship of renowned New York designer **Marc Jacobs** (*see p73*), chic vintage clothes specialist **Didier Ludot** (*see p71*), and the elegant perfumery **Salons du Palais-Royal Shiseido** (*see p74*). Passing through the arcades to rue de Montpensier, the neo-rococo Théâtre du Palais-Royal and the centuries-old café **L'Entr'acte** (*see p69*), you'll find narrow, stepped passages that run between here and rue de Richelieu.

Palais-Royal. See p66.

EXPLORE

On the other side of the palace towards Les Halles is galerie Véro-Dodat. Built by rich *charcutiers* during the Restoration period, it features wonderfully preserved neoclassical wooden shopfronts.

At the western end of the Louvre, by rue de Rivoli, are the **Musée des Arts Décoratifs**, the **Musée de la Mode et du Textile** and the **Musée de la Publicité**. All of these are administered independently of the Musée du Louvre, but were refreshed as part of the Grand Louvre scheme. Across place du Carrousel from the Louvre pyramid, the **Arc du Carrousel**, a mini-Arc de Triomphe, was built in polychrome marble for Napoleon Bonaparte from 1806 to 1809. The chariot on the top was originally drawn by the antique horses from San Marco in Venice, snapped up by Napoleon but returned in 1815. From the arch, the extraordinary axis along the **Jardin des Tuileries**, the Champs-Elysées up to the Arc de Triomphe and on to the Grande Arche de la Défense is plain to see.

The Jardin des Tuileries stretched as far as the Tuileries palace, until that was destroyed in the 1871 Paris Commune. The garden was laid out in the 17th century by André Le Nôtre and remains a pleasure area, with a funfair in summer; it also serves as an open-air gallery for modern art sculptures. Overlooking focal **place de la Concorde** is the **Musée de l'Orangerie** and the **Jeu de Paume**, built as a court for real tennis and now a centre for photographic exhibitions.

The stretch of rue de Rivoli running beside the Louvre towards Concorde was laid out by Napoleon's architects Percier and Fontaine from 1802 to 1811, and is notable for its arcaded façades. It runs in a straight line between place de la Concorde and rue St-Antoine, in the Marais; at the western end it's filled with tacky souvenir shops – though old-fashioned hotels remain, and there are also gentlemen's outfitters, bookshop **WH Smith** (*see p74*) and tearoom **Angelina** (*see p68*). The area was inhabited by English aristocrats, writers and artists in the 1830s and '40s after the Napoleonic Wars, sleeping at **Le Meurice** (*see p338*) and dining in the fancy restaurants of the Palais-Royal.

Place des Pyramides, at the junction of rue de Rivoli and rue des Pyramides, contains a gleaming gilt equestrian statue of Joan of Arc. One of four statues of her in the city, it's fêted as a proud symbol of French nationalism every May Day by supporters of the Front National.

Ancient rue St-Honoré, running parallel to rue de Rivoli, is one of those streets that changes style as it goes along: smart shops line it near place Vendôme, small cafés and inexpensive bistros predominate towards Les Halles. The Baroque **Eglise St-Roch** is still pitted with bullet holes made by Napoleon's troops when they crushed a

Jardin des Tuileries. *See p63.*

royalist revolt in 1795. With its old houses, adjoining rue St-Roch still feels wonderfully authentic; a couple of shops are built into the side of the church. Further up stands **Chapelle Notre-Dame de l'Assomption** (1670-76), now used by the city's Polish community, its dome so disproportionately large that locals have dubbed it *sot dôme* ('stupid dome'; a pun on 'Sodom').

Concept store **Colette** (*see p71*) brought some glamour to a once-staid shopping area, drawing a swarm of similar stores along in its wake. All are ideally placed for the fashionistas and film stars who touch down at **Hôtel Costes** (*see p338*). Opposite Colette is rue du Marché-St-Honoré, which once led to the covered Marché St-Honoré, since replaced by offices, in a square lined with trendy restaurants; to the north, rue Danielle-Casanova boasts 18th-century houses.

Further west along rue St-Honoré lies the wonderful, eight-sided **place Vendôme** and a perspective stretching from rue de Rivoli up to Opéra. At the end of the Tuileries, place de la Concorde, originally laid out for the glorification of Louis XV, is a masterclass in the use of open space, and spectacular when lit up at night. The winged Marly horses (only reproductions, the originals are in the Louvre) frame the entrance to the Champs-Elysées.

Smart rue Royale has tearoom **Ladurée** (*see p100*) and famed restaurant **Maxim's** (3 rue Royale, 8th, 01.42.65.27.94), with a fabulous museum of art nouveau, **La Collection 1900**, attached. Rue Boissy d'Anglas proffers stylish shops and the trendy **Buddha Bar** (no.8, 8th, 01.53.05.90.00); and high-end designs at **Yves Saint Laurent** (*see p205*) and others set the plush tone.

EXPLORE

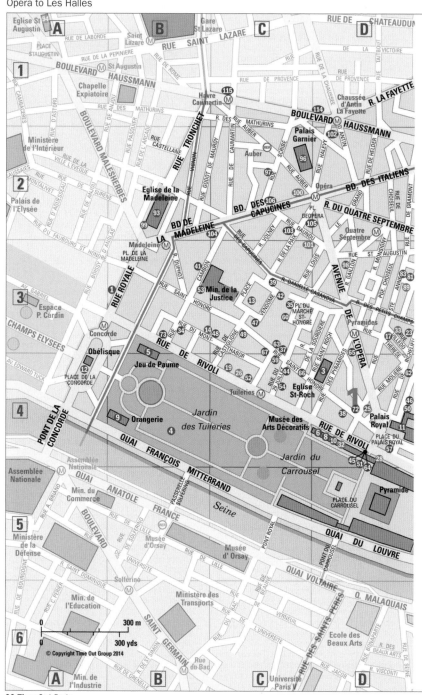

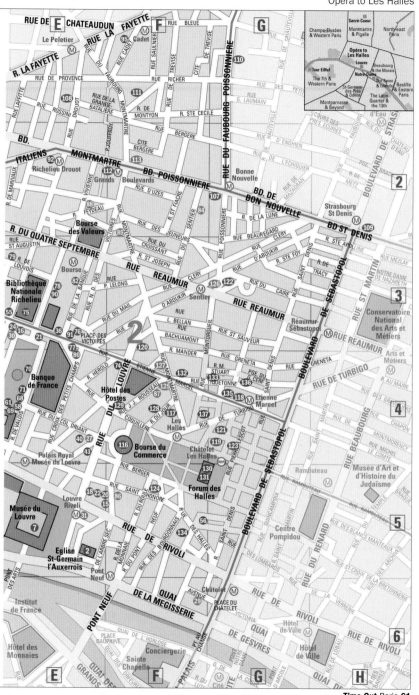

EXPLORE

My museum in Paris...

SIGHTSEEING CRUISE, LUNCH CRUISE, DINNER CRUISE

Information and booking : +33(0)1 76 64 14 45 - **www.bateauxparisiens.com**

Boarding at the foot of the Eiffel Tower

Bateaux Parisiens, a **sodexo** Company

Bateaux Parisiens

Le Paris d'un grand voyage

Musée des Arts Décoratifs.
See p64.

Sights & Museums

La Collection 1900

*Maxim's, 3 rue Royale, 8th (01.42.65.30.47,
www.maxims-musee-artnouveau.com). M°
Madeleine.* **Open** *Guided tours (reservations
essential)* 2pm Wed-Sun (English); 3.15pm, 4.30pm
(French). **Admission** €15. **No credit cards.**
Map p60 B3 ❶

Couturier Pierre Cardin has owned belle époque
restaurant Maxim's since 1981, and now he has
added a museum of art nouveau, which he has been
collecting since the age of 18. There are rooms and
rooms of exhibits, arranged so as to evoke a 19th-
century courtesan's boudoir. Read Zola's *Nana*
before your visit to grasp the full effect of the dreamy
lake maidens sculpted in glistening faience, pewter
vanity sets in the shape of reclining nudes, and beds
inlaid with opium flowers to promote sleep. Dinner
settings on display include Gustave Eiffel's own
chunky tureens, just crying out for turtle soup.

FREE Eglise St-Germain-l'Auxerrois

*2 pl du Louvre, 1st (01.42.60.13.96,
www.saintgermainauxerrois.cef.fr). M° Louvre
Rivoli or Pont Neuf.* **Open** 8am-7pm Mon-Sat;
9am-8pm Sun. **Admission** free. **Map** p61 E5 ❷

The architecture of this former royal church spans
several eras: the elaborate Flamboyant Gothic porch
is the most striking feature. The interior is home to
the 13th-century Lady Chapel and a canopied, carved
bench by Le Brun, which was made for the royal
family in 1682. The church achieved notoriety
on 24 August 1572, when its bell signalled the St
Bartholomew's Day massacre.

★ FREE Eglise St-Roch

*296 rue St-Honoré, 1st (01.42.44.13.20,
www.saintrochparis.cef.fr). M° Pyramides or
Tuileries.* **Open** 8.30am-7pm daily. **Admission**
free. **Map** p60 D4 ❸

Begun in the 1650s in what was then the heart of
Paris, this long church was designed chiefly by

Jacques Lemercier; work took so long, the church
was consecrated only in 1740. Famed parishioners
and patrons are remembered in funerary monuments: Le Nôtre, Mignard, Corneille and Diderot are
all here, as are busts by Coysevox and Coustou,
Falconet's statue *Christ on the Mount of Olives* and
Anguier's superb *Nativity.* Bullet marks from a 1795
shoot-out between royalists and conventionists still
pit the façade.

★ FREE Jardin des Tuileries

Rue de Rivoli, 1st. M° Concorde or Tuileries.
Open *Apr, May, Sept* 7am-9pm daily; *June-Aug*
7am-11pm daily; *Oct-Mar* 7.30am-7.30pm daily.
Admission free. **Map** p60 B4 ❹

Between the Louvre and place de la Concorde, the
gravelled alleyways of these gardens have been a chic
promenade ever since they opened to the public in the
16th century; and the popular mood persists with the
funfair that sets up along the rue de Rivoli side in summer. André Le Nôtre created the prototypical French
garden with terraces and central vista running down
the *Grand Axe* through circular and hexagonal ponds.
When the Tuileries palace was burned down during
the Paris Commune in 1871, the park was expanded.
As part of Mitterrand's Grand Louvre project, fragile
sculptures such as Coysevox's winged horses were
transferred to the Louvre and replaced by reproductions, and the Maillol sculptures were returned to the
Jardins du Carrousel; a handful of modern sculptures
has been added, including bronzes by Laurens, Moore,
Ernst and Giacometti, and Dubuffet's *Le Bel Costumé.*
Replanting has restored parts of Le Nôtre's design
and replaced damaged trees, and there's a gardeners'
bookshop by place de la Concorde. *Photo p59.*

Jeu de Paume

*1 pl de la Concorde, 8th (01.47.03.12.50,
www.jeudepaume.org). M° Concorde.* **Open**
11am-9pm Tue; 11am-7pm Wed-Sun (last entry
30mins before closing). **Admission** €8.50; €5.50
reductions; free under-26s 5-9pm last Tue of mth.
Map p60 B3 ❺

Musée du Louvre.

The Centre National de la Photographie moved into this site in 2005. The building, which once served as a tennis court, has been divided into two white, almost hangar-like galleries. It is not an intimate space, but it works well for showcase retrospectives. A video art and cinema suite in the basement shows new digital installation work, as well as feature-length films made by artists. There's also a sleek café and a decent bookshop.

★ Musée des Arts Décoratifs

107 rue de Rivoli, 1st (01.44.55.57.50, www.lesarts-decoratifs.fr). M° Palais Royal Musée du Louvre or Pyramides. **Open** 11am-6pm Tue, Wed, Fri-Sun; 11am-9pm Thur (late opening during exhibitions only). **Admission** (with Musée de la Mode & Musée de la Publicité) €9.50; €8 reductions; free under-18s, under-26s (EU citizens). PMP. **Map** p60 D4 ❻

Taken as a whole along with the Musée de la Mode et du Textile and Musée de la Publicité (for both, *see p65*), this is one of the world's major collections of design and the decorative arts. Located in the west wing of the Louvre since its opening a century ago, the venue reopened a few years ago after a decade-long, €35-million restoration of the building and of 6,000 of the 150,000 items donated mainly by private collectors. The major focus here is French furniture and tableware. From extravagant carpets to delicate crystal and porcelain, there is much to admire. Clever spotlighting and black settings show the exquisite treasures – including *châtelaines* made for medieval royalty and Maison Falize enamel work – to their best advantage. Other galleries are categorised by theme: glass, wallpaper, drawings and toys. There are cases devoted to Chinese head jewellery and the Japanese art of seduction with combs. Of most immediate attraction to the layperson are the reconstructed

period rooms, ten in all, showing how the other (French) half lived from the late 1400s to the early 20th century. *Photo p63.*

Musée du Louvre

Rue de Rivoli, 1st (01.40.20.50.50, recorded information 01.40.20.53.17, disabled access 01.40.20.59.90, www.louvre.fr). M° Palais Royal Musée du Louvre. **Open** 9am-6pm Mon, Thur, Sat, Sun; 9am-9.45pm Wed, Fri. **Admission** *Permanent collections* €12 (incl entry to the Musée Delacroix but not shows at the Salle Napoléon); free under-18s, under-26s (EU citizens), all under-26s 6-9.45pm Fri, all 1st Sun of mth. PMP. *Exhibitions* €13. *Combined ticket* €16. **Map** p61 E5 ❼

The world's largest museum is also its most visited, with a remarkable 9.7 million visitors in 2012. It is a city within the city, a vast, multi-level maze of galleries, passageways, staircases and escalators. It's famous for the artistic glories within, but the very fabric of the museum is a masterpiece in itself – or rather, a collection of masterpieces modified and added to from one century to another. And the additions and modifications continue into the present day, with the opening of a wonderful new two-storey Islamic Arts department beneath the Cour Visconti in late 2012 (*see p65*) and the franchising of the Louvre 'brand' via new outposts in Lens in northern France (www.louvrelens.fr) and Abu Dhabi.

Much like the building itself, the Louvre's collections were built up over the centuries. They encompass a rich visual history of the western world, from Ancient Egypt and Mesopotamia to the 19th century. Indeed, one of the most impressive things about the Louvre is the way it juxtaposes architecture and content. Look up from a case of Greek or Roman antiquities and you might

see an 18th-century painted ceiling, or two doves by Braque. In the Egyptian section you'll find Louis XIV's bedchamber, complete with gilded bed, while Renaissance art is housed in the Grande Galerie, where the Sun King performed the 'scrofula ceremony', blessing the sick. In between exhibits, the Louvre's long windows afford stunning views of the building's façades, gardens and lovely interior courtyards.

Some 35,000 works of art and artefacts are on show, split into eight departments and housed in three wings: Denon, Sully and Richelieu. Under the atrium of the glass pyramid, each wing has its own entrance, though you can pass from one to another. Treasures from the Egyptians, Etruscans, Greeks and Romans each have their own galleries in the Denon and Sully wings, as do Middle Eastern and Islamic art, now accommodated in a new space in the Cour Visconti. The first floor of Richelieu is taken up with European decorative arts from the Middle Ages up to the 19th century, including room after room of Napoleon III's lavish apartments.

The main draw, though, is the painting and sculpture. Two glass-roofed sculpture courts contain the famous Marly horses on the ground floor of

IN THE KNOW ISLAMIC ART

After a nine-year, €100 million makeover, the Louvre's stunning Département des Arts de l'Islam has opened its doors. Set in the Visconti wing, the two-storey, 3,000sq m gallery hosts 3,000 works, including gold treasures from Syria, ivories, miniatures, Ottoman ceramics and textiles, all displayed in chronological order.

Richelieu, with French sculpture below and Italian Renaissance pieces in the Denon wing. The Grande Galerie and Salle de la Joconde (home to the *Mona Lisa*), like a mini Uffizi, run the length of Denon's first floor with French Romantic painting alongside. Dutch and French painting occupies the second floor of Richelieu and Sully. Jean-Pierre Wilmotte's minimalist galleries in the Denon wing were designed as a taster for the Musée du Quai Branly, with art from Africa, the Americas and Oceania.

Musée de la Mode et du Textile

107 rue de Rivoli, 1st (01.44.55.57.50, www. lesartsdecoratifs.fr). M° Palais Royal Musée du Louvre or Pyramides. **Open** 11am-6pm Tue, Wed, Fri-Sun; 11am-9pm Thur (late opening during exhibitions only). **Admission** (with Musée des Arts Décoratifs & Musée de la Publicité) €9.50; €8 reductions; free under-18s, under-26s (EU citizens). PMP. **Map** p60 D4 ❽

This municipal fashion museum holds Elsa Schiaparelli's entire archive and hosts exciting themed exhibitions. Dramatic black-walled rooms make a fine background to the clothes, and video screens and a small cinema space show how the clothes move, as well as interviews with the creators.

★ Musée de l'Orangerie

Jardin des Tuileries, 1st (01.44.77.80.07, www.musee-orangerie.fr). M° Concorde. **Open** 9am-6pm Mon, Wed-Sun. **Admission** €10; €7.50 reductions & all after 5pm; free under-18s, under-26s (EU citizens), all 1st Sun of mth. PMP. **Map** p60 B4 ❾

This Monet showcase is a firm fixture on the tourist radar: expect long queues. The look is utilitarian and fuss-free, with the museum's eight tapestry-sized *Nymphéas* (water lilies) paintings housed in two plain oval rooms. They provide a simple backdrop for the astonishing, ethereal romanticism of Monet's works, painted late in his life. Depicting Monet's 'jardin d'eau' at his house in Giverny, the *tableaux* have an intense, dreamy quality – partly reflecting the artist's absorption in the private world of his garden. Downstairs, the Jean Walter and Paul Guillaume collection of Impressionism and the Ecole de Paris is a mixed bag of sweet-toothed Cézanne and Renoir portraits, along with works by Modigliani, Rousseau, Matisse, Picasso and Derain.

Musée de la Publicité

107 rue de Rivoli, 1st (01.44.55.57.50, www.les artsdecoratifs.fr). M° Palais Royal Musée du Louvre or Pyramides. **Open** 11am-6pm Tue, Wed, Fri-Sun; 11am-9pm Thur (late opening during exhibitions only). **Admission** (with Musée des Arts Décoratifs & Musée de la Mode) €9.50; €8 reductions; free under-18s, under-26s (EU citizens). PMP. **Map** p60 D4 ❿

The upstairs element of the trio of museums in the Louvre west wing, the advertising museum has a

EXPLORE

distressed interior by Jean Nouvel. Only a fraction of the vast collection of posters, promotional objects and packaging can be seen at any one time; vintage posters are accessed in the multimedia space.

★ FREE Palais-Royal

Pl du Palais-Royal, 1st. M° Palais Royal Musée du Louvre. **Open** *Gardens* Apr, May 7am-10.15pm daily; June-Aug 7am-11pm daily; Sept 7am-9.30pm daily; Oct-Mar 7am-8.30pm daily. **Admission** free. **Map** p60 D4 ⓫

Built for Cardinal Richelieu by Jacques Lemercier, this building was once known as the Palais Cardinal. Richelieu left it to Louis XIII, whose widow Anne d'Autriche preferred it to the chilly Louvre and rechristened it when she moved in with her son, the young Louis XIV. In the 1780s, the Duc d'Orléans, Louis XVI's fun-loving brother, enclosed the gardens in a three-storey peristyle and filled it with cafés, shops, theatres, sideshows and accommodation to raise money for rebuilding the burned-down opera. In stark contrast to Versailles, the Palais-Royal was a place where people of all classes could mingle, and its arcades became a trysting venue. Today, Daniel Buren's installation of black-and-white columns graces the main courtyard. *Photo p58.*

FREE Place de la Concorde

1st, 8th. M° Concorde. **Map** p60 A4 ⓬

This is the city's largest square, its grand east–west perspectives stretching from the Louvre to the Arc de Triomphe, and north–south from the Madeleine to the Assemblée Nationale across the Seine. Royal architect Gabriel designed it in the 1750s, along with the two colonnaded mansions astride rue Royale; the west one houses the chic Hôtel de Crillon (currently closed for renovations) and the Automobile Club de France, the other is the Naval Ministry. In 1792, the centre statue of Louis XV was replaced with the guillotine that would be used on Louis XVI, Marie-Antoinette and many more. The square was embellished in the 19th century with sturdy lamp-posts, the Luxor obelisk (from the Viceroy of Egypt), and ornate tiered fountains.

FREE Place Vendôme

1st. M° Opéra or Tuileries. **Map** p60 C3 ⓭

Elegant place Vendôme got its name from a *hôtel particulier* built by the Duc de Vendôme that stood on the site. Opened in 1699, the eight-sided square was conceived by Hardouin-Mansart to show off an equestrian statue of the Sun King, torn down in 1792 and replaced in 1806 by the Colonne de la Grande Armée. Modelled on Trajan's Column in Rome and featuring a spiral comic strip illustrating Napoleon's military exploits, it was cast from 1,250 Russian and Austrian cannon captured at the Battle of Austerlitz. During the 1871 Commune this symbol of 'brute force and false glory' was pulled down; the present column is a replica. Hardouin-Mansart designed only the façades, with their ground-floor arcade and

giant Corinthian pilasters; the buildings behind were put up by nobles and speculators. Today, the square houses sparkling jewellers, top fashion houses and the justice ministry. At no.12, you can visit the Grand Salon where Chopin died in 1849; its fabulous allegorical decoration dates from 1777 and has been restored as part of the new museum above the jewellers Chaumet (01.44.77.26.26).

Restaurants

★ L'Ardoise

28 rue du Mont-Thabor, 1st (01.42.96.28.18, www.lardoise-paris.com). M° Concorde or Tuileries. **Open** noon-3pm, 6.30-11pm Mon-Sat; 6.30-11pm Sun. **Main courses** €25. **Prix fixe** €36. **Map** p60 B3 ⓮ **Bistro**

This plain-looking bistro attracts a fair number of foreigners given its location near place Vendôme and early opening hours, but the food proves their judgement to be spot-on. Chef Pierre Jay doesn't skimp on quality ingredients in dishes such as shellfish papillote or chicken in parmesan cream sauce, making his €36 set menu a bargain. A lightly chilled Chinon is a perfect complement. Unusually for Paris, the restaurant is open on Sundays.

Chez La Vieille

37 rue de l'Arbre-Sec, 1st (01.42.60.15.78). M° Louvre Rivoli. **Open** 12.30-2pm, 7.30-10pm Mon-Fri; 7-10pm Sat. Closed Aug. **Prix fixe** €28, €38. **Map** p61 F5 ⓯ **Bistro**

The rustic ground floor of this bistro bursts with well-rounded regulars, whereas upstairs is plain and bright. A wondrous ad-lib selection of starters might include hot *chou farci* and home-made *terrine de foie gras*. Equally impressive is *foie de veau*, coated in a pungent reduction of shallots and vinegar and served with potato purée. Puddings follow the same cornucopian principle as the starters. Opening hours are limited and booking ahead is essential, but the lunchtime prix fixe is a bargain.

Le Grand Véfour

17 rue de Beaujolais, 1st (01.42.96.56.27, www.grand-vefour.com). M° Palais Royal Musée du Louvre. **Open** 12.30-2pm, 8-10pm Mon-Fri. Closed Aug. **Main courses** €85-€110. **Prix fixe** *Lunch* €98. *Dinner* €298. **Map** p61 E3 ⓰ **Haute cuisine**

Opened in 1784 (as the Café de Chartres), this is one of the oldest and most historic restaurants in the French capital. An à la carte meal begins with a fantasia suite of delicacies: tiny frogs' legs, for example, arranged within a circle of sage sauce; a first course of creamed Breton sea urchins served in their spiny shells with a quail's egg and topped with caviar. Fish dishes may be a touch overcooked, and the adventurous desserts are not always entirely successful, but you'll forgive all after a glass or two of vintage armagnac.

EXPLORE

Le Meurice.

& mid July-end Aug. **Main courses** €95-€185.
Prix fixe *Breakfast €40-€72. Lunch* €130, €380.
Dinner €380. **Map** p60 C4 ⑲ **Haute cuisine**
With the departure of Yannick Alléno in 2013, Alain
Ducasse has now taken over the reins at Le
Meurice's gorgeous dining room, launching a new
menu that eschews excess and focuses instead on a
simpler approach (to the food, not the prices). Head
chef Christophe Saintagne turns out delightfully
deconstructed dishes such as 'turbot, olives', 'mal-
lard, grapes' and 'spicy lamb, artichokes'.

Racines 2
39 rue de l'Arbre Sec, 1st (01.42.60.77.34).
Mᵒ Louvre Rivoli. **Open** noon-2.30pm, 7.45-
10.30pm Mon-Wed; noon-2.30pm, 7.45-11pm
Thur, Fri. **Main courses** €25-€33. **Map**
p61 F5 ⑳ **Bistro**
Racines' little brother is the rebellious one, with its
tattooed young chef and Scandinavian-influenced
decor from bad-boy designer Philippe Starck (we
particularly like the antler lamps). The feel is modern bistro with attitude: starters might include puff
pastry *feuilleté* with snails, cream of shallots and
fresh herbs or *vitello tonnato*, followed by pork belly
with crisp vegetables or beef with herby potato
purée and mesclun salad. Prices are on the steep
side, but the area's upmarket clientele are unlikely
to be too fazed by the bill.

★ Restaurant du Palais-Royal
110 galerie Valois, 1st (01.40.20.00.27,
www.restaurantdupalaisroyal.com). Mᵒ Bourse
or Palais Royal Musée du Louvre. **Open**
noon-2.30pm, 7-10pm daily (closed Mon,
Sun in winter). **Main courses** €34-€50.
Map p61 E3 ㉑ **Bistro**
There can be few more magical places to dine on a
summer evening than the terrace of the Restaurant
du Palais-Royal. Inside is memorable too: you sit in
a red dining room alongside the commissars of arts
and letters who work at the ministry of culture a
few doors down. Risotto is a speciality and the
Black, Black and Lobster is tremendous; rice simmered in rich squid ink is served al dente, topped
with tender but fleshy pink lobster, sun-dried
tomato and spring vegetables. Don't miss out on the
baba au rhum.

Spring
6 rue Bailleul, 1st (01.45.96.05.72, www.spring
paris.fr). Mᵒ Louvre Rivoli. **Open** 6.30-10.30pm
Tue-Sat. **Prix fixe** *Dinner* €84. **Map** p61 E5
㉒ **Bistro**
To join the privileged few who dine at Spring, you'll
have to book months in advance and arm yourself
with plenty of patience. You'll also need to leave any
cravings at the door and just let chef Daniel Rose do
his thing. Rose's unique menu changes daily, and
sometimes at the last minute, depending on the
availability of market produce. So in autumn, you

€ Higuma
32bis rue Ste-Anne, 1st (01.47.03.38.59,
www.higuma.fr). Mᵒ Pyramides. **Open** 11.30am-
10pm daily. **Main courses** €7-€9.50. **Prix fixe**
€10.50-€13.50. **Map** p60 D3 ⑰ **Japanese**
Higuma's no-nonsense food and service make it one
of the area's most popular destinations. On entering, customers are greeted by plumes of aromatic
steam emanating from the open kitchen-cum-
bar, where a small team of chefs ladle out giant
bowls of noodle soup piled with meat, vegetables
or seafood. You can slurp at the counter or sit at a
plastic-topped table.
Other location 163 rue St-Honoré, 1st
(01.58.62.49.22).

Kaï
18 rue du Louvre, 1st (01.40.15.01.99). Mᵒ
Louvre Rivoli. **Open** 12.30-2.15pm, 7.30-10.30pm
Tue-Sat. Closed 1wk Apr & 3wks Aug. **Main
courses** €27. **Prix fixe** *Lunch* €25-€42.
Dinner €69, €110. **Map** p61 E5 ⑱ **Japanese**
This restaurant has developed a following among
fashionable diners. The 'Kaï-style' sushi is a zesty
take on a classic: marinated and lightly grilled yel-
lowtail is pressed on to a roll of *shiso*-scented rice.
Not to be outdone, the grilled aubergine with miso,
seemingly simple, turns out to be a smoky, luscious
experience. A generous main of breaded pork lacks
the finesse and refinement of the starters, but is still
satisfying. Thoroughly French desserts come courtesy of celebrity pastry chef Pierre Hermé.

★ Le Meurice
Hôtel Meurice, 228 rue de Rivoli, 1st
(01.44.58.10.55, www.lemeurice.com). Mᵒ
Tuileries. **Open** 7-10.30am, 12.30-2pm, 7.30-10pm
Mon-Fri; 7-11am Sat, Sun. Closed 2wks Feb

EXPLORE

might sample wild mushrooms with a crab emulsion and a slow-cooked egg or duck with celeriac, quince and mustard leaves. Just watch out for the pricey wine list, which can quickly send the bill sky high.

★ Thaïm

46 rue de Richelieu, 1st (01.42.96.54.67).
Mº Bourse or Palais Royal Musée du Louvre.
Open noon-2.30pm, 7-11pm Mon-Fri; 7-11pm Sat. **Prix fixe** *Lunch* €16.50. *Dinner* €26.50.
Map p60 D3 ㉓ **Thai**

Steering well away from Thai clichés, Thaïm has an elegant decor of dark wood and plum fabrics, and a brief menu that changes often, keeping the regulars coming back. Particularly good value is the three-course lunch menu, which might bring crisp fried parcels filled with spiced vegetables, an aromatic green fish curry (there is a choice of fish, meat or poultry every day), and sweet coconut-pumpkin soup. There is an extensive choice of teas, including a delicious iced ginger-coconut version.

Verjus

52 rue de Richelieu, 1st (01.42.97.54.40,
www.hkmenus.com). Mº Pyramides. **Open** 6-11pm Mon; 12.30-2pm, 6-11pm Tue-Fri. **Prix fixe** *Lunch* €15. *Dinner* €60. **Map** p61 E3 ㉔ **Bistro**

Braden Perkins and Laura Adrian started out in Paris running a well-regarded supper club, 'Hidden Kitchen', so it's little surprise that Verjus – opened in 2012 after rave reviews paved the way for a full-blown restaurant – hasn't quite lost its word-of-mouth feel. You reach the small, stylish dining room through an unmarked iron gate. There's one eight-course tasting menu at dinner, updated monthly (plus an optional cheese board, and optional matched wines). At €60 a head without the extras, save it for a special occasion – but it will be special. On our visit, a Scandinavian-inspired plate of trout and potatoes brought a vivid citrus-cured curl of fish with slices of smoked potatoes and a salty scoop of bright orange roe, while thick slices of tender pink duck breast with their rich fat and golden skin nestled snugly on a bed of sharp winter sauerkraut.

Zen

8 rue de l'Echelle, 1st (01.42.61.93.99). Mº Louvre Rivoli. **Open** noon-2.30pm, 7-10.30pm Mon-Fri; noon-3pm, 7-10.30pm Sun. Closed Aug. **Prix fixe** *Lunch* €12-€20. *Dinner* €20-€65. **Map** p60 D4 ㉕ **Japanese**

There's no shortage of Japanese restaurants in this neighbourhood, but the recently opened Zen is refreshing in a couple of ways. First, there is no pale wood in sight; the colour scheme here is sharp white, green and yellow for a cheerful effect. Second, the menu has a lot to choose from – bowls of ramen, sushi and *chirashi*, hearty dishes such as chicken with egg on rice or *tonkatsu* – yet no detail is neglected. A perfect choice if you're spending a day at the Louvre – you can be in and out in 30 minutes.

Cafés & Bars

★ Angelina

226 rue de Rivoli, 1st (01.42.60.82.00, www.
angelina-paris.fr). Mº Tuileries. **Open** 7.30am-7pm Mon-Fri; 8.30am-7pm Sat, Sun. **Map** p60 C4 ㉖

Angelina is home to Paris's most lip-smackingly scrumptious desserts – all served in the faded grandeur of a belle époque salon just steps from the Louvre. The hot chocolate is pure decadence; try the speciality 'African', a velvety potion so thick that you need a spoon to consume it. Epicurean delights include the Mont Blanc dessert, a ball of meringue covered in whipped cream and sweet chestnut, and, for those with a waistline to watch, a sugar- and butter-free *brioche aux fruits rouges*. The place heaves at weekends, so be prepared to queue.

Le Café des Initiés

3 pl des Deux-Ecus, 1st (01.42.33.78.29,
www.lecafedesinities.com). Mº Louvre Rivoli or Les Halles. **Open** 7.30am-2am Mon-Fri; 9am-2am Sat, Sun. **Map** p61 E4 ㉗

Friendly staff and a central location have turned this designer hangout into a top spot for a trendy tipple, especially after work – cocktails are just €6.50 between 5pm and 8pm. The main room is lined with aerodynamic red banquettes, a long zinc bar provides character, and sleek, black, articulated lamps peer down from the ceiling. When hunger strikes, homely favourites such as shoulder of lamb baked in honey or tartare of salmon never fail to please.

Café Marly

93 rue de Rivoli, cour Napoléon, 1st
(01.49.26.06.60, www.beaumarly.com).
Mº Palais Royal Musée du Louvre. **Open** 8am-2am daily. **Map** p60 D4 ㉘

In the arcaded terrace overlooking the Louvre's glass pyramid, this classy, Napoleon III-style hangout (reached through the passage Richelieu, the entrance for advance Louvre ticket holders) is in an unrivalled location. One would expect nothing else from the ubiquitous Costes brothers – it's just a shame about the beer prices: it's €7 for a Heineken, so you might as well splash out €18 on a mojito. Most wines are under €15 a glass, and everything is impeccably served by razor-sharp staff. Brasserie fare and sandwiches are on offer too.

Le Dernier Bar Avant la Fin du Monde

19 av Victoria, 1st (01.53.00.98.95,
www.dernierbar.com). Mº Châtelet. **Open** 10am-midnight daily. **Map** p61 F6 ㉙

The cult of the geek in Paris received a well-oiled boost with the opening of this bar. Medieval and steampunk dominate the decor, with plenty of other bonkers sci-fi touches: as you walk in, a replica of the Millennium Falcon overlooks a timer counting down to the apocalypse predicted by the Mayans next to a window full of *Star Wars* memorabilia.

EXPLORE

Inside, the big, friendly bar is as much about alternative and popular culture as it is about drinking. A library, board games and science fiction books rub shoulders with the holy grail from *Indiana Jones and the Last Crusade* and other philtres, potions and skeletons. The prevailing atmosphere of heroic collaboration keeps prices low.

L'Entr'acte

47 rue de Montpensier, 1st (01.42.97.57.76).
Mº Pyramides or Palais Royal Musée du Louvre.

Open 10.30am-1.30am Mon-Sat; 1.30-8.30pm Sun.
Map p61 E3 ③

Take a little detour off avenue de l'Opéra, down an 18th-century staircase, and you'll find an unexpected congregation spread across the pavement: half are here for this little bar near the Comédie Française, half for the adjoining Sicilian pizzeria. There's food to be had at L'Entr'acte too – €10 plates of cheese and charcuterie, standard pastas and so on – but most come to enjoy an early-evening glass of house Bourgueil. The interior is tiny.

ART CART

Paris's museums offer quirky souvenirs aplenty.

107Rivoli.

EXPLORE

If you're still stuck for a unique Paris gift after a trip round the department stores and a trawl through the Marais, don't just leave it until duty free. Instead, step inside one of the city's museums. Paris's museums aren't just strong on world-class art. Many also have boutiques that sell gifts you can't find anywhere else in town, from limited-edition jewellery to quirky gadgets and beautiful coffee-table books.

One of the best is **107Rivoli**, in the Musée des Arts Décoratifs (107 rue de Rivoli, 1st, 01.42.60.64.94, www.lesarts decoratifs.fr), devoted to design books, jewellery (much of it inspired by the museum collections), fashion accessories, vintage toys, glassware and avant-garde furniture by up-and-coming designers.

For tech treats head to Paris's first digital arts centre, the Gaîté Lyrique. Its boutique, **Amusement** (3bis rue Papin, 3rd, 01.42.74.50.16, www.gaite-lyrique.net),

features gadgetry galore. Stock is linked to current exhibitions, so might include limited-edition skateboards, solar-activated robots or even fluffy balls of sushi to cuddle.

For something more traditional, the boutique at the **Musée Jacquemart André** (158 bd Haussmann, 8th, 01.45.62.11.59, www.musee-jacquemart-andre.com) sells delicate porcelain and 18th century-themed stationery, jewellery and candles. It's also handily situated near the museum café, so you can fill up on cake and coffee as you peruse your purchases.

Finally, another wonderful souvenir spot is the **Centre Pompidou**'s boutique (place Georges Pompidou, 4th, www.centre pompidou.fr), which sells all manner of art-inspired design gifts, from comedy mugs and watches to serious art books on everything from cubism to pop art. For a full list of Paris's museum shops, check out www.boutiquesdemusees.fr.

Le Fumoir

6 rue de l'Amiral-de-Coligny, 1st (01.42.92.00.24, www.lefumoir.com). Mº Louvre Rivoli. **Open** 11am-2am daily. **Map** p61 E5 ③①

There aren't many places around the Louvre that can compete with this elegant local institution: neo-colonial fans whirr lazily and oil paintings adorn the walls. A sleek crowd sips martinis or reads papers at the long mahogany bar (originally from a Chicago speakeasy), giving way to young professionals in the restaurant and pretty things in the library. It all feels a wee bit try-hard and resolutely well behaved, but the cocktails get tongues wagging soon enough, and food is consistently top notch.

Le Saut du Loup

107 rue de Rivoli, 1st (01.42.25.49.55, www.lesautduloup.com). Mº Palais Royal Musée du Louvre. **Open** noon-1am daily (until 7pm Sun in winter). **Map** p60 D4 ③②

Museums are usually daytime destinations, places of discovery that welcome their guests then politely expel them well before dusk. However the Saut du Loup, set inside the Musée des Arts Décoratifs, has made a concerted effort to reel in the Parigots after hours with a dapper restaurant, terrace views to die for over the Tuileries gardens, and a bar that'll knock you up a decent cocktail or two before bedtime. You can always tell a good joint from the quality of its mojitos, and Le Saut du Loup's version of the drink passes the test with flying colours: not too sweet and not too sour; you get an initial slap from the rum and lime, before the fresh mint and sugar settle things down. Perfect.

Télescope Café

5 rue Villedo, 1st (01.42.61.33.14, www.telescopecafe.com). Mº Pyramides. **Open** 8.30am-5pm Mon-Fri; 9.30am-6.30pm Sat. **No credit cards.** **Map** p60 D3 ③③

David Flynn is something of a coffee purist, and his newly opened Télescope Café has a stripped-down look to it; whitewashed walls, a pale blue wooden counter with a plate of cakes, Marzocco espresso machine and a strange water-heating device that he says is called an 'über-boiler'. Even the coffee menu looks pretty minimalist – no trendy flat whites here – but it turns out that Télescope also doubles as a coffee roaster, only keeping small stocks of beans to ensure freshness.

Shops & Services

★ Alice Cadolle

4 rue Cambon, 1st (01.42.60.94.22, www.cadolle.com). Mº Concorde or Madeleine. **Open** 10.30am-6.30pm Mon, Tue; 10am-7pm Wed-Sat. Closed Aug. **Map** p60 B3 ③④ **Fashion**

Five generations of lingerie-makers are behind this boutique, founded by Hermine Cadolle, who claimed to be the original inventor of the bra. Now

Colette.

her great-great-granddaughter, Poupie Cadolle, continues the tradition in a cosy space devoted to a luxury ready-to-wear line of bras, panties and corsets.
► *For a special treat, Cadolle Couture (255 rue St-Honoré, 1st, 01.42.60.94.94) will create indulgent bespoke lingerie (by appointment only).*

American Apparel

29 pl du Marché-St-Honoré, 1st (01.44.50.10.65, www.americanapparel.net). Mº Opéra, Pyramides or Tuileries. **Open** 11am-8pm Mon-Fri; 10am-8pm Sat; noon-7pm Sun. **Map** p60 C3 ③⑤ **Fashion**

Paris has acquired a taste for American Apparel's sweatshop-free, unisex cotton basics.
Other locations throughout the city.

Anne Sémonin

2 rue des Petits Champs, 2nd (01.42.60.94.66, www.annesemonin.com). Mº Bourse. **Open** 10am-7pm Tue-Sat. **Map** p61 E3 ③⑥ **Health & beauty**

Facials involve delicious concoctions of basil, lavender, lemongrass, ginger and plant essences. Also on offer are reflexology and a selection of massage styles, from Thai to ayurvedic. Body treatments cost from €70 to €210. Sémonin's renowned seaweed skincare products and essential oils are also on sale.

Appartement 217

217 rue St-Honoré, 1st (01.42.96.00.96, www.lappartement217.com). Mº Tuileries. **Open** 10am-7pm Tue-Sat. **Map** p60 C3 ③⑦ **Health & beauty**

A beautiful feng-shuied Haussmannian apartment is the setting for facials using organic beauty guru Dr Hauschka's products and ayurvedic or deep tissue massages. The water has been decalcified, electrical currents are insulated, and the silky-soft kimonos are made from organic wood pulp.

Astier de Villatte

173 rue St-Honoré, 1st (01.42.60.74.13, www.astierdevillatte.com). M° Palais Royal Musée du Louvre. **Open** 11am-7.30pm Mon-Sat. **Map** p60 D4 ❸ **Homewares**
Once home to Napoleon's silversmith, this ancient warren now houses ceramics inspired by 17th- and 18th-century designs, handmade by the Astier de Villatte siblings in their Bastille workshop.

Boucheron

26 pl Vendôme, 1st (01.42.61.58.16, www. boucheron.com). M° Opéra. **Open** 10.30am-7pm Mon-Sat. **Map** p60 C3 ❸ **Accessories**
Boucheron was the first *joaillier* to set up shop on place Vendôme. Owned by Gucci, the grand jeweller produces stunning pieces, using traditional motifs with new accents.
Other location 32 rue du Fbg-St-Honoré, 8th (01.44.51.95.20).

By Terry

21 & 36 passage Véro-Dodat, 1st (01.44.76.00.76, www.byterry.com). M° Palais Royal Musée du Louvre. **Open** 10am-7pm Mon-Sat. **Map** p61 E4 ❹ **Health & beauty**
Terry de Gunzburg, who earned her reputation at Yves Saint Laurent, offers made-to-measure 'haute couleur' make-up by skilled chemists and colourists combining high-tech treatments and handmade precision. There's prêt-à-porter too.
Other locations 30 rue de la Trémoille, 8th (01.44.43.04.04); 10 av Victor-Hugo, 16th (01.55.73.00.73).

★ Chanel

31 rue Cambon, 1st (01.44.50.72.50, www.chanel. com). M° Concorde or Madeleine. **Open** 10am-7pm Mon-Sat. **Map** p60 B3 ❹ **Fashion**
Fashion legend Chanel has managed to stay relevant, thanks to Karl Lagerfeld. Coco opened her first boutique in this street, at no.21, in 1910, and the tradition continues in this elegant interior. Lagerfeld has been designing for Chanel since 1983, and keeps on revamping the classics – the little black dress and the Chanel suit – with great success.
Other locations 42 av Montaigne, 8th (01.44.50.73.00); 25 rue Royale, 8th (01.44.51.92.93); 21 rue du Fbg-St-Honoré, 8th (01.53.05.98.95).

Chanel Joaillerie

18 pl Vendôme, 1st (01.40.98.55.55, www.chanel. com). M° Opéra. **Open** 11am-7pm Mon; 10.30am-7pm Tue-Sat. **Map** p60 C3 ❹ **Accessories**

Chanel launched its fine jewellery in the 1990s, reissuing the single collection – big on platinum and diamonds – that Coco herself designed some 60 years previously. The current line reinterprets the motifs – camellias, stars and comets – to create a collection of contemporary classics.

Christian Louboutin

19 rue Jean-Jacques-Rousseau, 1st (01.42.36.53.66, www.christianlouboutin.com). M° Palais Royal Musée du Louvre. **Open** 10.30am-7pm Mon-Sat. Closed 2wks Aug. **Map** p61 E4 ❹ **Accessories**
Every fashionista, WAG and shoe fiend worth her salt owns or hankers after a pair of Louboutin's trademark red-soled creations. Each design is displayed to maximum advantage in an individual frame.
Other locations 38 rue de Grenelle, 7th (01.42.22.33.07); 68 rue du Fbg-St-Honoré, 8th (01.42.68.37.65).

★ Colette

213 rue St-Honoré, 1st (01.55.35.33.90, www. colette.fr). M° Pyramides or Tuileries. **Open** 11am-7pm Mon-Sat. **Map** p60 C4 ❹ **Fashion**
The renowned one-stop concept and lifestyle store features a highly eclectic selection of must-have accessories, fashion, sneakers, books, media, shiny new gadgets, and hair and beauty brands, all in a swanky space. Expect to find Zippo lighters a few feet away from Smythson diaries, a few feet away from Ladurée macaroons, all one flight of stairs away from Alexander Wang and Valentino.

Delfonics

Carrousel du Louvre, 99 rue de Rivoli, 1st (01.47.03.14.24, www.delfonics.fr). M° Palais Royal Musée du Louvre. **Open** 10am-8pm daily. **Map** p60 D4 ❹ **Books & music**
Concentrating on minimalist designs using durable materials (linen, rayon, canvas, leather and resin), Delfonics is a haven for stationery addicts looking for Japanese and European notebooks, files, pens and much more. This flagship wood-lined store near the Louvre is the only one in Europe for the moment, offering nearly 55sq m of temptingly affordable things such as Post-it notes in cute designs, vinyl pencil cases and electronic letter-openers.

Didier Ludot

24 galerie de Montpensier, 1st (01.42.96.06.56, www.didierludot.fr). M° Palais Royal Musée du Louvre. **Open** 10.30am-7pm Mon-Sat. **Map** p60 D4 ❹ **Fashion**
Didier Ludot's temples to vintage haute couture appear in Printemps, Harrods and New York's Barneys. The prices may be on the steep side, but the pieces are stunning: Dior, Molyneux, Balenciaga, Pucci, Féraud and, of course, Chanel, from the 1920s onwards. Ludot also curates exhibitions, using the exclusive shop windows around the Palais-Royal as a gallery.

EXPLORE

> ▶ *Didier Ludot stocks his own line of vintage little black dresses, also available at La Petite Robe Noire (125 galerie de Valois, 1st, 01.40.15.01.04).*

Dior Joaillerie
8 pl Vendôme, 1st (01.42.96.30.84, www.dior. com). M° Opéra or Tuileries. **Open** 10.30am-7pm daily. **Map** p60 C3 ❼ **Accessories**
The unabashed bling of Victoire de Castellane's designs is responsible for the fad of semi-precious coloured stones and runaway success of the 'Mimi Oui', a ring with a tiny diamond on a slim chain. **Other location** 28 av Montaigne, 8th (01.47.23.52.39).

Eglé Bespoke
26 rue du Mont-Thabor, 1st (01.44.15.98.31, www.eglebespoke.com). M° Concorde. **Open** 11am-7.30pm Mon-Sat. **Map** p60 C3 ❽ **Fashion**
Two young entrepreneurs are reviving bespoke for a new generation in this tiny shop. Custom shirts start from about €120 and can be delivered in a week or so; they will also make or copy shirts for women and produce made-to-order jeans for both sexes. Laser-printed buttons are perfect for stamping your beloved's shirt with a saucy message.

★ Fifi Chachnil
231 rue St-Honoré, 1st (01.42.61.21.83, www.fifichachnil.com). M° Tuileries. **Open** 11am-7pm Mon-Sat. **Map** p60 C3 ❾ **Fashion**
Chachnil has a new approach to frou-frou underwear in the pin-up tradition. Her chic mixes – deep red silk bras with boudoir-pink bows, and pale turquoise girdles with orange trim – will have ladies and their male admirers purring in delight. The transparent black babydoll negligées with an Empire-line bust are classic saucy retro. **Other locations** 68 rue Jean-Jacques-Rousseau, 1st (01.42.21.19.93); 34 rue de Grenelle, 7th (01.42.22.08.23).

★ Gabrielle Geppert
31 & 34 galerie Montpensier, 1st (01.42.61.53.52, www.gabriellegeppert.com). M° Palais Royal Musée du Louvre. **Open** 10am-7.30pm Mon-Sat. **Map** p60 D4 ❺⓪ **Fashion**
Much fun can be had here rummaging in the back room or trying on the outrageous collection of '70s sunglasses (about €380 a pop, but they will get you into any party worth going to). No.31 is dedicated to luxury vintage with a selection of clothes and accessories by Hermès, Chanel and Dior, plus shoes by Chanel and Louboutin. At no.34, Geppert sells her own-brand jewellery and clothes.

La Galerie du Carrousel du Louvre
99 rue de Rivoli, 1st (01.43.16.47.10, www.carrouseldulouvre.com). M° Palais Royal Musée du Louvre. **Open** 10am-8pm daily. **Map** p60 D4 ❺❶ **Mall**

IN THE KNOW AND RELAX

Pioneer Swiss urban spa **After the Rain** (www.aftertherain.ch) makes a glorious retreat from the designer shopping stresses of nearby rue du Faubourg-St-Honoré. Signature massages include Honey Release and Aroma Stone Therapy, or enjoy a romantic massage *à deux* – complete with rose petal bath, strawberries and champagne.

This massive underground centre – open every day of the year – is home to more than 35 shops, mostly big-name chains vying for your attention and cash. Options include an Apple Store, Swatch Store and L'Occitane en Provence.

Galignani
224 rue de Rivoli, 1st (01.42.60.76.07, www.galignani.com). M° Palais Royal Musée du Louvre or Tuileries. **Open** 10am-7pm Mon-Sat. **Map** p60 C4 ❺❷ **Books & music**
Opened in 1802, this was the first English-language bookshop in mainland Europe. Today, it stocks fine art books, French and English literature, philosophical tomes and magazines.

Hervé Léger
24 rue Cambon, 1st (01.42.60.02.00, www.herve leger.com). M° Concorde. **Open** 10am-7pm Mon-Sat. **Map** p60 B3 ❺❸ **Fashion**
A couple of decades ago, Hervé Léger's silhouette-cinching bandage dresses were as evocative of the era as supermodels Linda, Christy, Naomi and Cindy. But somewhere in the mid-'90s women lost their love of Lycra, longing for the more conventional figure-flattering techniques of bias cut and tailoring. In the past few seasons, however, updated reinterpretations of Léger's style, by the likes of Christopher Kane and Marios Schwab, have been nothing short of a fashion phenomenon. Less modified versions, sold by the Léger label itself (now owned and designed by Max Azria of BCBG fame), have been less critically acclaimed, but celebrities just adore them.

★ Jay Ahr
2-4 rue du 29 Juillet, 1st (01.42.96.95.23, www.jayahr.com). M° Tuileries. **Open** 10am-7pm Mon-Fri; 11am-7pm Sat. **Map** p60 C4 ❺❹ **Fashion**
Former jewellery designer Jonathan Riss opened this shop as a fashion stylist in 2004, and soon struck gold with simple, figure-flaunting, 1960s-inspired dresses. Think plunging necklines and Bianca Jagger in her heyday, with Ali MacGraw and Anita Pallenberg in the mix. There are no price tags on the dresses, so you have to ask; they start at around €800 (€400 for skirts).

EXPLORE

Kitsuné
52 rue de Richelieu, 1st (01.42.60.34.28,
www.kitsune.fr). M° Palais Royal Musée du Louvre
or Pyramides. **Open** 11am-7.30pm Mon-Sat.
Map p61 E3 ⑤⑤ **Fashion**
The London/Paris style collective now has its own
boutique, which offers the entire catalogue of music
compilations, as well as branded clothing that takes
a back-to-basics approach using quality producers.
You'll find Scottish cashmere, Japanese jeans and
Italian shirts, together with items made in collaboration with Pierre Hardy, Scheisser underwear and
James Heeley.

Laguiole Galerie
1 pl Ste-Opportune, 1st (01.40.06.09.75, www.forge-
de-laguiole.com). M° Châtelet. **Open** 10.30am-1pm,
1.40-7pm Mon-Sat. **Map** p61 F5 ⑤⑧ **Homewares**
Philippe Starck designed this chic boutique, a showcase for France's classic knife, the Laguiole.

Louvre des Antiquaires
2 pl du Palais-Royal, 1st (01.42.97.27.27,
www.louvre-antiquaires.com). M° Palais Royal
Musée du Louvre. **Open** 11am-7pm Tue-Sun.
Closed Sun in July & Aug. **Map** p60 D4
⑤⑦ **Homewares**
This upmarket antiques centre houses 250 antiques
dealers: perfect for Louis XV furniture, tapestries,
porcelain, jewellery, model ships and tin soldiers.

★ Maison Fabre
128 galerie de Valois, 1st (01.42.60.75.88,
www.maisonfabre.com). M° Palais Royal Musée
du Louvre. **Open** 11am-7pm Mon-Sat. **Map**
p61 E4 ⑤⑧ **Accessories**
This Millau glovemaker, which was founded in
1924, has capitalised on its racy designs from the
sports-car eras of the 1920s and '60s. Classic gloves
made from the softest leather (€100) come in 20 wild
colours. Then there are the variations: crocodile,
python, coyote, fur-trimmed, fingerless. But the ultimate lust object is the patent leather 'Auto' glove
fastened with a massive button.
Other location 60 rue des Sts-Pères, 7th
(01.42.22.44.86).

Manoush
217 rue St Honoré, 1st (01.40.20.04.44, www.
manoush.com). M° Tuileries. **Open** 10.30am-
7.30pm Mon-Sat. **Map** p60 C4 ⑤⑨ **Fashion**
Manoush, which means 'gypsy' in French slang, has
proved more than a flash in the pan from the boho
craze of 2005 and now has five Paris boutiques tout-
ing designer Frédérique Trou-Roy's kooky vision.
Other locations throughout the city.

Marc by Marc Jacobs
19 pl du Marché-St-Honoré, 1st (01.40.20.11.30,
www.marcjacobs.com). M° Tuileries. **Open** 11am-
7pm Mon-Sat. **Map** p60 C3 ⑥⓪ **Fashion**
The new store for Jacobs' casual, punky line has
fashionistas clustering like bees round a honeypot,
not least for the fabulously inexpensive accessories
that make great gifts. A skateboard table and giant
pedalo in the form of a swan are the centrepieces of
the store, which stocks men's and women's prêt-
à-porter, shoes and special editions.

Marc Jacobs
34 galerie de Montpensier, 1st (01.55.35.02.60,
www.marcjacobs.com). M° Palais Royal Musée
du Louvre. **Open** 11am-7pm Mon-Sat. **Map**
p61 E4 ⑥① **Fashion**
By choosing the Palais-Royal for his first signature
boutique in Europe, Marc Jacobs brought new life
– and an influx of fashionistas – to these elegant
cloisters. Stocking womenswear, menswear, accessories and shoes, the boutique has become a place
of pilgrimage for the designer's legion of admirers,
who snap up his downtown New York style.

Martin Margiela
23 & 25bis rue de Montpensier, 1st (womenswear
01.40.15.07.55, menswear 01.40.15.06.44,
www.maisonmartinmargiela.com). M° Palais
Royal Musée du Louvre. **Open** 11am-7pm Mon-
Sat. **Map** p60 D4 ⑥② **Fashion**
The original Paris outlet for the JD Salinger of fashion is a pristine, white, unlabelled space. His collection for women (Line 1) has a blank label but is
recognisable by its external white stitching. You'll
also find Line 6 (women's basics) and Line 10
(menswear), plus a range of accessories and shoes.
Other location 13 rue de Grenelle, 7th
(01.45.49.06.68).

Miu Miu
219 rue St-Honoré, 1st (01.58.62.53.20, www.
miumiu.com). M° Tuileries. **Open** 10.30am-
7.30pm Mon-Sat. **Map** p60 C3 ⑥③ **Fashion**
Prada's younger sister has this rue St-Honoré store
as its main boutique, selling its quirky women's
fashions, shoes and bags.

Nature et Découvertes
Carrousel du Louvre, 99 rue de Rivoli, 1st
(01.47.03.47.43, www.natureetdecouvertes.com).
M° Palais Royal Musée du Louvre. **Open** 10am-
8pm daily. **Map** p60 D4 ⑥④ **Gifts & souvenirs**
This store stocks a great range of stuff for junior and
grown-up gadgeteers, from infrared parent detectors
to high-tech weather stations. Ten per cent of all the
group's profits go to support environmental causes.
Other locations throughout the city.

Nouvelles Frontières
13 av de l'Opéra, 1st (01.42.61.02.62, www.
nouvelles-frontieres.fr). M° Pyramides. **Open**
10am-7pm Mon-Sat. **Map** p60 D3 ⑥⑤ **Travel**
Travel agent with several branches in the capital.
Other locations throughout the city.

EXPLORE

EXPLORE

Olympia Le-Tan

Colette, 213 rue St-Honoré, 1st (01.55.35.33.90, www.colette.fr). Mᵒ Pyramides or Tuileries. **Open** 11am-7pm Mon-Sat. **Map** p60 C4 ⑥ **Accessories**
If you saw Olympia Le-Tan DJing at the Baron, you'd never think her passion was embroidery. But this über-cool night owl has indeed given up the decks to become one of the city's most sought-after accessory designers. Her limited-edition, 1950s-style purses and clutch bags, all hand-sewn and hand-embroidered, are inspired by Olympia's fetish authors (including Ernest Hemingway and Gustave Flaubert). In fact, at first glance, the bags look like little books; it's only when you examine the detail that you realise there's a clasp and embroidery. Olympia's collection (www.olympialetan.com) is available at Colette.

Paule Ka

223 rue St-Honoré, 1st (01.42.97.57.06, www. pauleka.com). Mᵒ Tuileries. **Open** 10.30am-7pm daily. **Map** p60 C3 ⑥ **Fashion**
Serge Cajfinger's '60s couture-influenced collections continue to gather a loyal following. With the opening of his rue St-Honoré boutique, he now has a foot in each of the city's fashion districts.
Other locations 20 rue Malher, 4th (01.40.29.96.03); 192 bd St-Germain, 6th (01.45.44.92.60); 45 rue François 1er, 8th (01.47.20.76.10).

★ Pierre Hardy

156 galerie de Valois, 1st (01.42.60.59.75, www.pierrehardy.com). Mᵒ Palais Royal Musée du Louvre. **Open** 11am-7pm Mon-Sat. **Map** p61 E4 ⑥ **Accessories**
This classy black-and-white shoebox is home to Hardy's range of superbly conceived footwear – with a price tag to match – for men and women.
Other location 9-11 pl du Palais Bourbon, 7th (01.45.55.00.67).

Rick Owens

130 galerie de Valois, 1st (01.40.20.42.52, www.owenscorp.com). Mᵒ Palais Royal Musée du Louvre. **Open** 10.30am-7pm Mon-Fri; 11am-7pm Sat. **Map** p61 E4 ⑥ **Fashion**
The Los Angeles designer and rock-star favourite brings his glamour-meets-grunge style to the Palais-Royal, with a selection of hoods, zips and asymmetrical wrappings for men and women. It's not the place for animal lovers – the upstairs has a dedicated mink section.

★ Salons du Palais-Royal Shiseido

Jardins du Palais-Royal, 142 galerie de Valois, 1st (01.49.27.09.09, www.sergelutens.com). Mᵒ Palais Royal Musée du Louvre. **Open** 10am-7pm Mon-Sat. **Map** p61 E4 ⑦ **Health & beauty**
Under the arcades of the Palais-Royal, Shiseido's perfumer Serge Lutens practises his aromatic arts. A former photographer at Paris *Vogue* and artistic director of make-up at Christian Dior, Lutens is a maestro of rare taste. Bottles of his concoctions – Tubéreuse Criminelle, Rahat Loukoum and Ambre Sultan – can be sampled by visitors. Look out for Fleurs d'Oranger, which the great man defines as the smell of happiness. Many of the perfumes are exclusive to the Salons; prices start at €69.
Other locations 2 pl Vendôme, 1st (01.42.60.68.61); 29 rue de Sèvres, 6th (01.42.22.46.60); 66 bd du Montparnasse, 15th (01.43.20.95.40).

Stella McCartney

114-121 galerie du Valois, Jardin du Palais-Royal, 1st (01.47.03.03.80, www.stellamccartney.com). Mᵒ Palais Royal Musée du Louvre. **Open** 10.30am-7pm Mon-Sat. **Map** p61 E4 ⑦ **Fashion**
McCartney is crazy about the 'clash of history, fashion and contemporary art' at the Palais-Royal, where she opened her sumptuous boutique. Thick carpets, maplewood and metal sculptures create a rarefied setting for women's prêt-à-porter, bags, shoes, sunglasses, lingerie, perfume and skincare.

Torréfacteur Verlet

256 rue St-Honoré, 1st (01.42.60.67.39, www.cafesverlet.com). Mᵒ Palais Royal Musée du Louvre. **Open** 9.30am-7pm Mon-Sat. Closed Aug. **Map** p60 D4 ⑦ **Food & drink**
Eric Duchossoy roasts rare coffee beans to perfection – sip a cup here or take some home to savour.

WH Smith

248 rue de Rivoli, 1st (01.44.77.88.99, www.whsmith.fr). Mᵒ Concorde. **Open** 9am-7pm Mon-Sat; 12.30-7pm Sun. **Map** p60 B3 ⑦ **Books & music**
With 70,000 English-language titles and extensive magazine shelves, this is a home from home for Brits craving a fix of their native periodicals; the first floor has books, DVDs and audiobooks.

Yohji Yamamoto

25 rue du Louvre, 1st (01.42.21.42.93, www.yohjiyamamoto.co.jp). Mᵒ Les Halles. **Open** 10.30am-7pm Mon-Sat. **Map** p61 F4 ⑦ **Fashion**
One of the few true pioneers working in fashion today, Yamamoto is a master of cut and finish, both strongly inspired by the kimono and traditional Tibetan costume. His dexterity with form makes for unique shapes and styles, largely in black. But when he does colour, it's a blast of brilliance.
Other location 4 rue Cambon, 1st (01.40.20.00.71).

THE BOURSE

In the 1st & 2nd arrondissements.

Far less frenzied than Wall Street, the city's traditional business district is squeezed between the elegant calm of the Palais-Royal and shopping hub the Grands Boulevards.

Liza. *See p76.*

Along rue du Quatre-Septembre, **La Bourse** (the stock exchange) is where financiers and stockbrokers beaver away in grandiose buildings. The Banque de France, France's national central bank, has occupied the 17th-century Hôtel de Toulouse since 1811, its long gallery still hung with Old Masters. Nearby, fashion and finance meet at stylish **place des Victoires**, designed by Hardouin-Mansart.

West of the square is shop-lined galerie Vivienne, the smartest of the covered passages in Paris, adjoining galerie Colbert. Also look out for temporary exhibitions at the **Bibliothèque Nationale de France – Richelieu**. You can linger at the luxury food and wine merchant **Legrand** (*see p77*), or head along passage des Petits-Pères to admire the 17th- to 18th-century **Eglise Notre-Dame-des-Victoires**, the remains of an Augustine convent with a cycle of paintings around the choir by Carle van Loo.

Rue de la Banque leads to the Bourse, behind a neoclassical colonnade. The area has a relaxed feel – it's dead at weekends – but lively pockets exist at such places as **Le Vaudeville** (29 rue Vivienne, 2nd, 01.40.20. 04.62, www.vaudeville paris.com) and **Gallopin** (40 rue Notre-Dame-des-Victoires, 2nd, 01.42.36.45.38, www.brasserie gallopin.com), busy brasseries frequented by stockbrokers and journalists. Rue des Colonnes is a quiet street lined with porticoes and acanthus motifs from the 1790s; its design nemesis, the 1970s concrete-and-glass HQ of Agence France-Presse, the nation's biggest news agency, stands on the other side of rue du Quatre-Septembre.

Sights & Museums

FREE Bibliothèque Nationale de France – Richelieu & Musée du Cabinet des Médailles
58 rue de Richelieu, 2nd (01.53.79.59.59, www.bnf.fr). M° Bourse. **Open** times vary. **Admission** varies. **Map** p61 E3 ⑦⑤

The history of the French National Library began in the 1660s, when Louis XIV moved manuscripts that couldn't be housed in the Louvre to this lavish Louis XIII townhouse. The library was first opened to the public in 1692, and by 1724 it had received so many new acquisitions that the adjoining Hôtel de Nevers had to be added. Some of the original painted decoration by Romanelli and Grimaldi can still be seen in Galeries Mansart and Mazarine. The highlights, however, are the two circular reading rooms: the Salle Ovale, which is full of researchers, note-takers and readers, and the magnificent Salle de Travail, a temple to learning, with its arrangement of nine domes supported on slender columns. On the first floor is the Musée du Cabinet des Médailles, a modest two-room collection of coins and medals, including Greek, Roman and medieval examples. There is also a miscellany of other items, including Merovingian king Dagobert's throne, Charlemagne's chess set and small artefacts from the Classical world and ancient Egypt. The whole site is undergoing major renovations until at least 2017 and some of the collection has had to be transferred to the BNF François Mitterrand (*see p188*).

FREE Place des Victoires
1st, 2nd. M° Bourse. **Map** p61 E3 ⑦⑥

This circular square, the first of its kind, was designed by Hardouin-Mansart in 1685 to show off a statue of Louis XIV that marked victories against Holland. The original statue was destroyed after the Revolution (although the massive slaves from its base are now in the Louvre), and replaced in 1822 with an equestrian statue by Bosio. Among the occupants of the grand buildings that encircle the 'square' are boutiques Kenzo and Victoire.

Restaurants

★ € Bistrot Victoires
6 rue de la Vrillière, 1st (01.42.61.43.78). M° Bourse. **Open** noon-3pm, 7-11pm daily. **Main courses** €11. **Map** p61 E3 ⑦⑦ **Bistro**

EXPLORE

Bistros with vintage decor serving no-nonsense food at generous prices are growing thin on the ground in Paris, so it's no surprise that this gem is packed to the gills with bargain-loving office workers and locals every day. The *steak-frites* are exemplary, featuring a slab of entrecôte topped with a smoking sprig of thyme, but *plats du jour* such as *blanquette de veau* (veal in cream sauce) are equally comforting. The wines by the glass can be rough, but the authentic buzz should make up for any flaws.

La Bourse ou la Vie

*12 rue Vivienne, 2nd (01.42.60.08.83). M°
Bourse.* **Open** noon-10pm Mon-Fri. Closed 1wk Aug & 1wk Dec. **Main courses** €16.90-€24.90.
Map p61 E3 ⑦ **Bistro**
After a career as an architect, the round-spectacled owner of La Bourse ou la Vie has a new mission in life: to revive the dying art of the perfect *steak-frites*. The only decision you'll need to make is which cut of beef to order with your chips, unless you pick the cod. Choose between ultra-tender *coeur de filet* or a huge, surprisingly tender *bavette*. Rich, creamy pepper sauce is the speciality here, but the real surprise is the chips, which gain a distinctly animal flavour from the suet in which they are cooked.

★ Chez Miki

*5 rue de Louvois, 2nd (01.42.96.04.88). M°
Bourse.* **Open** noon-2.30pm Mon; noon-10.30pm Tue-Sat; 7-10.30pm Sun. **Main courses** €15-€20.
Prix fixe €15. **Map** p61 E3 ⑦ **Japanese**
There are plenty of Japanese restaurants to choose from along nearby rue Ste-Anne, but none is as original – nor as friendly – as this tiny bistro run entirely by women, next to the square Louvois. The speciality here is bento boxes, which you compose yourself from a scribbled blackboard list (in Japanese and French). For €15 you can choose two small dishes – marinated sardines and fried chicken wings are especially popular – and a larger dish, such as grilled pork with ginger.

Les Fines Gueules

*43 rue Croix-des-Petits-Champs, 1st
(01.42.61.35.41, www.lesfinesgueules.fr).
M° Bourse or Sentier.* **Open** noon-2.30pm, 7.30-10.30pm Mon-Fri; noon-3pm, 7.30-11pm Sat, Sun.
Main courses €18-€26. **Map** p61 E4 ㉚ **Bistro**
At first glance, Les Fines Gueules might seem like an ordinary corner café, but a closer look at the menu reveals unusual attention to ingredients at this mini wine bar/bistro. Even if you've never heard of Hugo (Desnoyer, star butcher and supplier to some of the city's finest restaurants) or Jean-Luc (Poujauran, a celebrity Paris baker), you can taste the difference when the pedigree steak tartare arrives with a salad of baby leaves dressed in truffle oil. There are just a few seats around the bar, but upstairs is a buzzy dining room. A good selection of wines comes by the glass and the bottle.

Hokkaido

*14 rue Chabanais, 2nd (01.42.60.50.95).
M° Bourse.* **Open** 11.30am-10.30pm Mon, Tue, Thur-Sun. **Main courses** €7-€14.
Map p60 D3 ㉛ **Japanese**
A tiny canteen on rue Chabanais, Hokkaido is very basic but always promisingly full of regulars. Generous, well-priced dishes are offered to take away or eat *sur place* – a bowl of ramen noodles will set you back around €8, pork gyoza with white cabbage and ginger around €5.50 for seven.

★ Liza

*14 rue de la Banque, 2nd (01.55.35.00.66,
www.restaurant-liza.com). M° Bourse.* **Open** noon-2.15pm, 8-10.30pm Mon-Thur; noon-2.15pm, 8-11pm Fri; 8-11pm Sat; noon-3.30pm Sun. **Main courses** €25. **Prix fixe** *Lunch* €16, €21, €22.
Dinner €42, €49. **Map** p61 E3 ㉜ **Lebanese**
Liza Soughayar's restaurant showcases the style and superb food of contemporary Beirut. Lentil, fried onion and orange salad is delicious. Main courses, such as minced lamb with coriander-spiced spinach and rice, are light, flavoursome and well presented. Try one of the excellent Lebanese wines to accompany your meal, and finish with the halva ice-cream with carob molasses. *Photos p75.*

Michi

*58bis rue Sainte-Anne, 2nd (01.40.20.49.93).
M° Quatre-Septembre.* **Open** noon-2pm, 7-10pm Tue-Sat. **Prix fixe** *Lunch* €14, €18. *Dinner* €23.
Map p60 D3 ㉝ **Japanese**

La Conserverie.

Rue Sainte-Anne and its surroundings are full of Japanese treasures, tiny restaurants serving excellent ramen, gyoza, udon and soba – but not sushi. However, at no.58, 'sushi' is spelled out in big letters across a slightly decrepit-looking front window. Don't be put off – this is the real deal. Sit at the bar if you can and watch the chef preparing the dishes with disconcerting speed. At midday, the set sushi menus come with soup, salad, rice and dessert. Salmon, tuna, prawn, bream, eel and scallop sushi will all come out in a long procession, with flavours that put most of Paris's sushi dives to shame.

Cafés & Bars

★ La Conserverie

37bis rue du Sentier, 2nd (01.40.26.14.94, www.laconserveriebar.com). M° Bonne-Nouvelle. **Open** 7pm-midnight Mon, Tue; 7pm-2am Wed-Fri; 8pm-2am Sat. **Map** p61 F2 ❸
The gorgeous *nuit bleue* interior will win you over as soon as you step inside, and by the time you sit on the velvet sofas and taste the cocktails you'll want to make this your favourite hangout. The staff are incredibly friendly by Parisian standards. There's a quirky selection of nibbles in tin cans – sardines, anyone? – and regular music nights (live gipsy jazz bands on Mondays; electro on Thursdays and Fridays). Highly recommended.

Dédé la Frite

135 rue Montmartre, 2nd (01.40.41.99.90). M° Sentier or Bourse. **Open** 8am-2am Mon-Sat; 9am-2am Sun. **Map** p61 F2 ❸
Suits from the nearby Bourse flock here for after-work cocktails and beers, before giving in to the tempting aromas emanating from the kitchen: Dédé's frites at just €3 a tray are legendary and the rest of the food, reminiscent of an American diner (burgers, fries, ketchup on the bar), is an absolute bargain too. The place looks cool as well, with distressed walls, long bar and bright colours. After hours, when the alcohol flows and the munchies have been satisfied, the music is cranked up and the party really starts.

★ La Garde Robe

41 rue de l'Arbre-Sec, 1st (01.49.26.90.60). M° Louvre Rivoli. **Open** 12.30-2.30pm, 6.30-11pm Mon-Fri; 6.30-11pm Sat. **Map** p61 F5 ❸
This tiny wine bar, where bottles line the walls like books in a library, is perfect for an end-of-the-day snifter, preferably accompanied by one of the platters of delicious parma ham, cheese or oysters. Organic and bio-dynamic wines stand their ground next to vintages from around the world.

O Château

68 rue Jean-Jacques Rousseau, 1st (01.44.73.97.80, www.o-chateau.com). M° Les Halles. **Open** 4pm-midnight daily. **Map** p61 F4 ❸

The food is great and the vibe convivial, but a night here is all about the wine. There are no less than 500 by the bottle and 40 by the glass, including the chance to taste some very rare and expensive bottles in *soupçon*-sized quantities thanks to high-tech wine-saving devices. Tastings take place in the intimate tasting rooms at 12.15pm daily.

Le Truskel

12 rue Feydeau, 2nd (01.40.26.59.97, www. truskel.com). M° Bourse. **Open** 8pm-5am Tue-Sat. Closed mid July-mid Aug. **Map** p61 E2 ❸
The formula is quite simple at this pub-cum-club: an excellent selection of beers slakes your thirst, while an extensive repertoire of Britpop – sometimes live (ex-Pulp man and Paris resident Jarvis Cocker has been known to splice the night here, as have Pete Doherty and Franz Ferdinand) – assaults your ears. As a cheeky touch, a bar bell rings for no reason whatsoever, causing first-time visitors from the UK to down their drinks in one and dive for the bar.

Zenzoo

13 rue Chabanais, 2nd (01.42.96.27.28, www.zen-zoo.com). M° Quatre-Septembre. **Open** noon-7pm Mon-Sat. **Map** p60 D3 ❸
Between 2.30pm and 7pm, this tiny Taiwanese restaurant doubles as a 'tea bar', one of the few places in Paris that serves China's famous tapioca cocktails – sometimes known as 'bubble tea', they are served with an extra-wide straw to suck up the little tapioca balls at the bottom. The sensation may seem strange at first, but the tastes are great; among the flavours are mango, coconut and kumquat. Up the road at no.2, a spin-off boutique sells excellent oolong flower teas.

Shops & Services

Jean-Paul Gaultier

6 rue Vivienne, 2nd (01.42.86.05.05, www. jeanpaulgaultier.com). M° Bourse. **Open** 9am-7pm Mon-Sat. **Map** p61 E3 ❸ **Fashion**
Having celebrated his 30th year in the fashion business, Gaultier is still going strong. His boudoir boutique stocks men's and women's ready-to-wear and the reasonably priced JPG Jeans lines.
Other location 44 av George V, 8th (01.44.43.00.44).

Legrand Filles et Fils

1 rue de la Banque, 2nd (01.42.60.07.12, www. caves-legrand.com). M° Bourse. **Open** 11am-7pm Mon; 10am-7.30pm Tue-Fri; 10am-7pm Sat. Closed Mon in Aug. **Map** p61 E3 ❸ **Food & drink**
Fine wines and brandies, teas and *bonbons,* and a showroom for regular wine tastings.

Village Joué Club

3-5 bd des Italiens, 2nd (01.53.45.41.41). M° Richelieu Drouot. **Open** 10am-8pm Mon-Sat. **Map** p61 E2 ❸ **Children**

EXPLORE

Le Marrakech

Serving Moroccan specialties since 1948

The restaurant Marrakech welcomes
you with a family atmosphere to
help you discover the many flavors
of authentic Moroccan cuisine.
A stone's throw away from the
Arc de Triomphe.

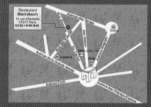

Restaurant Marrakech
12, rue d'Armaillé 75017 PARIS
+33 (0) 1 43 80 26 65   www.restaurant-marrakech.fr

the moose
canadian sports bar & grill

sundays
american style brunch
11:30am - 3:30pm

Monday - Friday
happy hour
4:00pm - 8:00pm

Open 11am - 2am daily

www.mooseparis.com
16 rue des quatre vents 75006 paris metro odeon tel 01 46 33 77 00

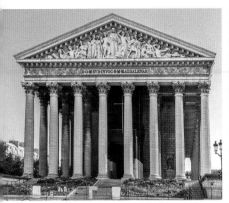

Eglise de la Madeleine.

Village Joué Club, the largest toy store in Paris, is spread out in and around passage des Princes. There's even a children's hairdresser and room for birthday parties.

OPERA & AROUND

In the 2nd, 8th & 9th arrondissements.

Charles Garnier's wedding-cake **Palais Garnier** is all gilt and grandeur, as an opera house should be. Garnier was also responsible for the ritzy **Café de la Paix** (*see p80*) and the **InterContinental Paris Le Grand** (*see p339*) overlooking place de l'Opéra. Behind, in the basement of what is now the Hôtel Scribe, the Lumière brothers held the world's first public cinema screening in 1895. The **Olympia** concert hall (*see p275*), the celebrated host of the Beatles, Piaf and anyone in *chanson*, was knocked down, but rose again nearby. Over the road at no.35, pioneering portrait photographer Nadar opened a studio in the 1860s, frequented by the likes of Dumas père, Offenbach and Doré. In 1874, it hosted the first Impressionists' exhibition. Pedestrianised rue Edouard VII, laid out in 1911, leads to the octagonal square of the same name with Landowski's equestrian statue of the English monarch. Through an arch, another square contains the belle époque **Théâtre de l'Athénée-Louis Jouvet**.

The **Eglise de la Madeleine**, a monument to Napoleon's army, stands guard at the end of the boulevard. At the head of rue Royale, its classical portico mirrors the Assemblée Nationale on the other side of place de la Concorde and over the river, and the interior is a riot of marble and altars. Well worth a browse is wonderfully extravagant delicatessen **Fauchon** (24-26 place de la Madeleine) and other luxury food shops; here, too, is haute cuisine restaurant **Senderens** (*see p80*).

Sights & Museums

FREE Eglise de la Madeleine

Pl de la Madeleine, 8th (01.44.51.69.00, www.eglise-lamadeleine.com). M° Concorde or Madeleine. **Open** 9.30am-7pm daily. **Admission** free. **Map** p60 B2 ❸

The building of a church on this site began in 1764, and in 1806 Napoleon sent instructions from Poland for Barthélémy Vignon to design a 'Temple of Glory' dedicated to his Grand Army. After the emperor's fall, construction slowed and the building, by now a church again, was finally consecrated in 1845. The exterior is ringed by huge, fluted Corinthian columns, with a double row at the front, and a frieze of the Last Judgement just above the portico. Inside are giant domes, an organ and side altars in a sea of multicoloured marble.

FREE Eglise St-Augustin

46 bd Malesherbes, 8th (01.45.22.23.12, www.saintaugustin.net). M° St-Augustin. **Open** 8.30am-7pm Mon-Fri; 9am-12.30pm, 2.30-7.30pm Sat; 8.30am-12.30pm, 4-8pm Sun. **Admission** free. **Map** p60 A1 ❹

St-Augustin, designed between 1860 and 1871 by Victor Baltard, architect of the defunct Les Halles pavilions, is not what it seems. The domed, neo-Renaissance stone exterior is merely a shell: inside is an iron vault structure; even the decorative angels are cast in metal. Impressive paintings by Adolphe William Bouguereau hang in the transept.

Musée de la Franc-Maçonnerie

16 rue Cadet, 9th (01.45.23.74.09, www.museefm.org). M° Cadet. **Open** 10am-12.30pm, 2-6pm Tue-Fri; 10am-1pm, 2-7pm Sat. **Admission** €6; €4 reductions; free under-18s. **No credit cards**. **Map** p61 F1 ❺

Tucked away at the back of the French Masonic Great Lodge, the Musée de la Franc-Maçonnerie first opened in 1973. It traces the history of French

EXPLORE

freemasonry, ranging from detailed information on stonemasons' guilds to prints of masons General Lafayette and the 1848 revolutionary leaders Blanc and Barbès. The museum reopened in 2010 after a hefty makeover.

Musée de l'Opéra

Palais Garnier, 1 pl de l'Opéra, 9th (01.53.79.37.47, www.bnf.fr). M° Opéra. **Open** 10am-5pm Mon-Sat. **Admission** €7; €5 reductions; free under-18s. **No credit cards**. **Map** p60 C2 ⓰

The Palais Garnier (*see also p284*) houses temporary exhibitions relating to current opera or ballet productions, along with a permanent collection of paintings, scores and bijou opera sets housed in delightful period cases.

FREE Musées des Parfumeries-Fragonard

9 rue Scribe, 9th (01.47.42.04.56, www. fragonard.com) & 39 bd des Capucines, 2nd (01.42.60.37.14, www.fragonard.com). M° Opéra. **Open** 9am-6pm Mon-Sat; 9am-5pm Sun (rue Scribe only). **Admission** free. **Map** p60 C2 ⓱

The rue Scribe museum showcases the collection of perfume house Fragonard: five rooms range from Ancient Egyptian ointment flasks to Meissen scent bottles; the boulevard des Capucines museum has bottles by Lalique and Schiaparelli.

Restaurants

Drouant

18 pl Gaillon, 2nd (01.42.65.15.16, www.drouant.com). M° Pyramides or Quatre Septembre. **Open** noon-2.30pm, 7-11.30pm daily. **Main courses** €19-€32. **Prix fixe** *Lunch* €44-€60. *Dinner* (10.30pm-midnight) €46-€58. **Map** p60 D3 ⓳ Brasserie

Star chef Antoine Westermann has whisked this landmark 1880 brasserie into the 21st century with bronze-coloured banquettes and butter-yellow fabrics. Westermann has dedicated this restaurant to the art of the hors d'oeuvre: they're served in themed sets of four ranging from global (Thai beef salad with brightly coloured vegetables, coriander, and a sweet and spicy sauce) to nostalgic (silky leeks in vinaigrette). The bite-sized surprises continue with the main course accompaniments.

Senderens

9 pl de la Madeleine, 8th (01.42.65.22.90, www.senderens.fr). M° Madeleine. **Open** noon-2.45pm, 7.30-11pm daily. Closed 1st 3wks Aug. **Main courses** €40-€51. **Prix fixe** €116, €160 (with wine). **Map** p60 B2 ⓳ Haute cuisine

Alain Senderens reinvented his art nouveau institution (formerly Lucas Carton) a few years ago with a *Star Trek* interior and a mind-boggling fusion menu. Now, you might find dishes such as roast duck foie gras with a warm salad of black figs and liquorice powder, or monkfish steak with Spanish mussels and green curry sauce. Each dish comes with a suggested wine, whisky, sherry or punch (to match a rumdoused *savarin* with slivers of ten-flavour pear), and although these are perfectly chosen, the mix of flavours and alcohols can prove overwhelming.

Cafés & Bars

★ Café de la Paix

12 bd des Capucines, 9th (01.40.07.36.36, www.cafedelapaix.fr). M° Opéra. **Open** 7am-midnight daily. **Map** p60 C2 ⓰⓿⓿

Lap up every detail – this is once-in-a-holiday stuff. Whether you're out on the historic terrace or looking up at the ornate stucco ceiling, you'll be sipping in the footsteps of the likes of Oscar Wilde, Josephine Baker, Emile Zola, and Bartholdi and the Franco-American Union (as they sketched out the Statue of Liberty). Let the immaculate staff bring you a kir or, for an afternoon treat, the vanilla millefeuille – possibly the best in Paris.

★ Harry's New York Bar

5 rue Daunou, 2nd (01.42.61.71.14, www.harrys-bar.fr). M° Opéra. **Open** noon-2am Mon-Thur, Sun; noon-3am Fri, Sat. **Map** p60 C3 ⓰⓿⓵

The city's most stylish American bar is an institution beloved of expats, visitors and hard-drinking Parisians (there are over 300 whiskies). The white-coated bartenders mix some of the most sophisticated cocktails in town, from the trademark bloody mary and white lady (both invented here, so they say) to the Pétrifiant, an aptly named elixir of half a dozen spirits splashed into a beer mug. They can also whip up personalised creations that will have you swooning in the downstairs piano bar, where Gershwin composed *An American in Paris*, and where jazz concerts are held most Thursday and Friday nights.

Shops & Services

Apple Store

12 rue Halévy, 9th (01.44.83.42.00, www.apple.com). M° Opéra. **Open** 9am-8pm Mon-Sat. **Map** p60 D2 ⓰⓿⓶ Electronics & photography

Apple's second Paris store opened a couple of years ago in a stunning belle époque former bank facing the Opéra Garnier. To fit in with such hallowed surroundings, Apple strayed from its standard store model, retaining the original carved wooden staircase, wrought-iron railings, marble columns and mosaic tile floor.

Other location 99 rue de Rivoli, 1st (01.43.16.78.00).

★ Cartier

13 rue de la Paix, 2nd (01.58.18.23.00, www.cartier.com). M° Opéra. **Open** 11am-7pm Mon-Sat. **Map** p60 C2 ⓰⓿⓷ Accessories

EXPLORE

This iconic French jeweller and watchmaker has impressive landmark headquarters. Downstairs, pearls, panthers and the Trinity ring jostle for attention among historic pieces commissioned by crowned heads; the upper salons house perfumer Mathilde Laurent's bespoke scents.
Other locations throughout the city.

★ Lavinia

3 bd de la Madeleine, 1st (01.42.97.20.20, www. lavinia.fr). M° Madeleine. **Open** 10am-8.30pm Mon-Sat. **Map** p60 C2 ⓘⓄⓋ **Food & drink**
Lavinia stocks a wonderfully broad selection of French vintages alongside many non-French wines; its glassed-in *cave* has everything from a 1945 Mouton-Rothschild at €22,000 to trendy and 'fragile' wines for under €10.

★ Repetto

22 rue de la Paix, 2nd (01.44.71.83.12, www.repetto.com). M° Opéra. **Open** 9.30am-7.30pm Mon-Sat. **Map** p60 D2 ⓘⓄⓈ **Accessories**
This ballet shoe-maker struck gold when it decided to reissue its dance shoes with pavement soles. The prowly *ballerines* and showbiz dance boots in black, metallic and spangly finishes are fun, stylish and exceptionally comfortable. They are sold alongside the full range of real balletwear; you can try out your *pointes* on a red carpet with a *barre* if you really want to show off.
Other locations 51 rue du Four, 6th (01.45.44.98.65); 51 rue des Francs Bourgeois, 4th (01.70.79.89.37); 36 rue de Passy, 16th (01.70.79.89.41).

Talents – Création Contemporaine

1bis rue Scribe, 9th (01.40.17.98.38, www. ateliersdart.com). M° Opéra. **Open** 11am-7pm Mon-Sat. **Map** p60 C2 ⓘⓄⓋ **Homewares**
This contemporary showroom for 70 creators affiliated to the craftworkers' federation Ateliers d'Art de France is a pure white space in which you'll find one-off designs in furniture, lighting, glass, ceramics and jewellery. If you want something made to measure they can put you in touch directly with the designers.
Other location 26 av Niel, 17th (01.44.40.22.80).

THE GRANDS BOULEVARDS

In the 2nd & 9th arrondissements.

Contrary to popular belief, the string of Grands Boulevards between Madeleine and République (des Italiens, Montmartre, Poissonnière, Bonne-Nouvelle, St-Denis, St-Martin) was not built by Baron Haussmann, but by Louis XIV in 1670, replacing the fortifications of King Philippe-Auguste's city wall. Their ramparts have left their traces in the strange changes of levels, with stairways climbing up to side streets at the eastern end. The boulevards burgeoned after the French Revolution, as residences, theatres and covered passages were put up on land taken from aristocrats and monasteries. To this day, they offer a glimpse of the city's divergent personalities – a stroll from Opéra to République runs from luxury shops via St-Denis prostitutes – and the phrase *théâtre des boulevards* is still used for lowbrow theatre. Between boulevard des Italiens and rue de Richelieu is place Boïeldieu and the **Opéra Comique** (*see p285*), where Bizet's *Carmen* had its première in 1875.

The 18th-century Hôtel d'Angny, now the town hall of the ninth arrondissement, was once home to the infamous *bals des victimes*, where every guest had to have a relative who had lost his or her head to the guillotine. The **Hôtel Drouot** auction house is ringed by antiques shops, coin- and stamp-dealers and wine bar Les Caves Drouot. There are several grand *hôtels particuliers* on rue de la Grange-Batelière, which leads on one side down the curious passage Verdeau, occupied by a range of antiques dealers, and on the other back to the boulevards via passage Jouffroy. With its grand, barrel-vaulted glass-and-iron roof, this is home to the delightful **Hôtel Chopin** (*see p343*), shop windows of doll's houses, antique walking sticks, art books and film posters, and the colourful entrance of the **Grévin** waxworks (*see p244*).

Over the boulevard, passage des Panoramas is the oldest remaining covered arcade in Paris. When it opened in 1800, panoramas – vast illuminated circular paintings – of Rome, Jerusalem, London and other cities drew large crowds. Today, the passage contains a selection of coin- and stamp-sellers, furniture-makers and old-fashioned printers. It leads into a tangle of other little passages and the stage door of the **Théâtre des Variétés** (7 bd Montmartre, 2nd, 01.42.33.09.92, www.theatre-des-varietes.fr), a pretty neoclassical theatre where Offenbach premièred *La Belle Hélène*.

Rue du Fbg-Montmartre is home to celebrated belle époque *bouillon* Chartier, which serves up hundreds of meals a day to the budget-minded. The street is also part of a significant Jewish quarter, less well known than the Marais, that grew up in the 19th century. There are several kosher bakers and restaurants, and France's largest synagogue at 44 rue de la Victoire, an opulent Second Empire affair completed in 1876. Cobbled Cité Bergère, constructed in 1825 with desirable residences, now houses budget hotels, though the pretty iron-and-glass *portes-cochères* remain. On rue Richer stands the art deco **Folies-Bergère** (no.32, 9th, 08.92.68.16.50, www.foliesbergere.com), nowadays used for cabaret revues. To the south of boulevard Bonne-Nouvelle lies the **Sentier** district, and to the north

EXPLORE

rue du Fbg-Poissonnière is a mixture of rag-trade outlets and *hôtels particuliers*.

Back on the boulevard is evidence of a move north of the Marais by trendsetting hubs, including **Rex** (*see p267*). East of here are Louis XIV's twin triumphal arches, the **Porte St-Denis** and **Porte St-Martin**, which were erected to commemorate his military victories.

Sights & Museums

★ Grand Rex

1 bd Poissonnière, 2nd (www.legrandrex.com). M° Bonne Nouvelle. **Tour** *Les Etoiles du Rex* every 5mins 10am-7pm Wed-Sun; daily during school hols. **Admission** €11; €9 reductions. **Map** p61 G2 ⑩

Opened in 1932, this huge art deco cinema (*see also p251*) was designed by Auguste Bluysen with fantasy Hispanic interiors by US designer John Eberson. Go behind the scenes in the crazy 50-minute Etoiles du Rex guided tour, which includes a presentation about the construction of the auditorium and a visit to the projection room, complete with nerve-jolting Sensurround effects.

Hôtel Drouot

9 rue Drouot, 9th (01.48.00.20.20, www.drouot.fr). M° Richelieu Drouot. **Open** 11am-6pm Mon-Sat. **Auctions** 2pm Mon-Sat. **Map** p61 E1 ⑩

A spiky aluminium-and-marble concoction is the unlikely location for France's second largest art market. Inside, escalators take you up to a number of small salerooms, where everything from medieval manuscripts and antique furniture to oriental arts, modern paintings, posters, jewellery and fine wines might be up for sale. Details of forthcoming auctions are published in the weekly *Gazette de l'Hôtel Drouot*, sold at various newsstands around the city. Not as daunting as it might seem, an afternoon at Drouot can be great fun, even if you don't fancy spending. On the day before the auction (and on the morning itself), drool over the objects for sale, then come back for the show (usually 2pm). Anyone can take part; and you don't have to sign up beforehand. Neither do you have to worry about sneezing or scratching your head – it's the role of Drouot's *commissaires des ventes* (auctioneers) to distinguish a real bid from nose twitching.

Other location Drouot-Montmartre, 64 rue Doudeauville, 18th (01.48.00.20.99).

FREE Porte St-Denis & Porte St-Martin

Rue St-Denis/bd St-Denis, 2nd; 33 bd St-Martin, 10th. M° Strasbourg St-Denis. **Map** p61 H2 ⑩

These twin triumphal gates were erected in 1672 and 1674 at important entry points to the city as part of Colbert's strategy to glorify Paris and celebrate Louis XIV's victories on the Rhine. They are modelled on the triumphal arches of ancient Rome. The Porte St-Denis is based on a perfect square with a single arch, bearing Latin inscriptions and decorated with military trophies and battle scenes. Porte St-Martin bears allegorical reliefs of Louis XIV's campaigns.

Restaurants

Big Fernand

55 rue du Faubourg Poissonnière, 9th (01.73.70.51.52, www.bigfernand.com). M° Cadet or Poissonnière. **Open** noon-2.30pm, 7.30-10.30pm Mon-Sat. **Main courses** €10-€20. **Map** p61 G1 ⑩ **Burgers**

This trendy takeaway burger joint has been dubbed '*l'atelier du hamburger*' – 'the hamburger workshop'. The concept is for customers to build their own burgers, selecting a combination of meat (beef, chicken, lamb or veal), cheese (goat's cheese, saint nectaire, tomme de savoie), grilled vegetables, spices and an array of sauces.

Les Fils à Maman

7 bis Rue Geoffroy-Marie, 9th (01.48.24.59.39, www.lesfilsamaman.com). M° Grands Boulevards. **Open** 11.30am-2.30pm, 7-11pm Mon-Fri; 7-11pm Sat. **Main courses** €12-€30. **Prix fixe** *Lunch* €11, €15, €19. **Map** p61 F1 ⑪ **Bistro**

In the up-and-coming neighbourhood near the Folies Bergère a band of five 'mothers' boys' has created a restaurant evoking their mums' home cooking. Even the mums themselves get into the kitchen on the first Tuesday of the month to turn out *blanquette de veau*, chicken cordon bleu with beaufort cheese and Nutella-flavoured puddings. Whether or not you think Babybel has a place in Gallic cuisine, it's a chance to relive the school French exchange or 1980s après-ski in the company of an ebullient crowd.

Racines

8 passage des Panoramas, 2nd (01.40.13.06.41). M° Bourse or Bonne Nouvelle. **Open** noon-2.30pm, 8-10.30pm Mon-Fri. **Main courses** €19-€32. **Map** p61 F2 ⑫ **Wine bar**

The 19th-century passage des Panoramas contains an eclectic collection of shops and restaurants – among them this wildly popular wine bar opened by the former owners of La Crèmerie in St-Germain-des-Prés. The menu is limited to superb-quality cheese and charcuterie plates, plus a couple of hot dishes, perhaps pork cheeks stewed in red wine or braised lamb, and a few comforting desserts. Many of the intense-tasting wines are biodynamic and, despite the rather hectic atmosphere, lingering over an extra glass or two is cheerfully tolerated.

Cafés & Bars

Le Brébant

32 bd Poissonnière, 9th (01.47.70.01.02, www.cafelebrebantparis.com). M° Grands Boulevards. **Open** 7.30am-6am daily. **Map** p61 F2 ⑬

Fontaine des Innocents.

The change that continues to sweep the Grands Boulevards is embodied in this prominent, round-the-clock bar-bistro. There's a permanently busy terrace beneath a colourful, stripy awning, and the cavernous, split-level interior has a cool neo-industrial feel. Prices are steep, so push the boat out and opt for an expertly made fruit daiquiri, or a Bonne Nouvelle of Bombay Sapphire gin and Pisang Ambon. There are rarer bottled beers too – Monaco, Picon and sundry brews from Brabant. A board advertises a decent range of proper eats: *burger-frites* (€20.50) and so on.

Shops & Services

Galeries Lafayette
40 bd Haussmann, 9th (01.42.82.34.56, fashion shows 01.42.82.30.25, fashion advice 01.42.82.35.50, www.galerieslafayette.com). M° Chaussée d'Antin/RER Auber. **Open** 9.30am-8pm Mon-Wed, Fri, Sat; 9.30am-9pm Thur. **Map** p60 D1 ⓮ **Department store**
The store has been undergoing a massive renovation programme of late, with the opening of Espace Luxe on the first floor, featuring luxury prêt-à-porter and accessories, and the unveiling of a vast new shoe department in the basement featuring some 150 brands. The men's fashion space on the third floor, Lafayette Homme, has natty designer corners and a 'Club' area with internet access. On the first floor, Lafayette Gourmet has exotic foods galore, plus a vast wine cellar including its own Bordeauxthèque.
▶ *Lafayette Maison, located over the road, has five floors of home furnishings and interior design products.*
Other location Centre Commercial Montparnasse, 22 rue du Départ, 14th (01.45.38.52.87).

★ Printemps
64 bd Haussmann, 9th (01.42.82.50.00, www.printemps.com). M° Havre Caumartin/RER Auber. **Open** 9.35am-8pm Mon-Wed, Fri, Sat; 9.35am-10pm Thur. **Map** p60 C1 ⓯ **Department store**
In the magnificently appointed Printemps you'll find everything you didn't even know you wanted and English-speaking assistants to help you find it. But fashion is where it really excels; an entire floor is devoted to shoes, and the beauty department stocks more than 200 brands. In all, there are six floors of men's and women's fashion. In Printemps de la Mode, French designers sit alongside all the big international designers. The Fashion Loft offers a younger take on current trends. Along with furnishings, Printemps de la Maison stocks everything from tableware to design classics.
▶ *For fast refuelling, Printemps has a tearoom, sushi bar and Café Be, an Alain Ducasse bakery. Or head up to Le Déli-cieux, on the ninth floor of Printemps Maison, for a drink on the terrace.*

LES HALLES & SENTIER

In the 1st & 2nd arrondissements.

For centuries, Les Halles was the city's wholesale food market. Covered markets were set up here in 1181 by King Philippe-Auguste; in the 1850s Baltard's spectacular cast-iron and glass pavilions were erected. In 1969, the market was relocated to the suburb of Rungis. Baltard's ten pavilions were knocked down (one was saved and now stands at Nogent-sur-Marne), leaving a giant hole. After a long political dispute, it was filled in the early 1980s by the miserable **Forum des Halles** underground mall and transport hub, and the unloved Jardin des Halles.

The Forum is currently undergoing a vast makeover, with a new canopy, revamped park and completion date of 2016. If you want to check out the progress of this *grand projet*, visit www.forumdeshalles.com.

East of the Forum, in the middle of place Joachim-du-Bellay, stands the Renaissance **Fontaine des Innocents**. The canopied fountain has swirling stone reliefs of water nymphs and titans by Jean Goujon (the ones you see today are replicas; the originals are in the Louvre). It was inaugurated for Henri II's arrival in Paris in 1549 on the traditional royal route along rue St-Denis. It was moved and reconstructed here when the nearby Cimetière des Innocents, the city's main burial ground, was demolished in 1786, after flesh-eating rats started gnawing into people's living rooms; the bones were transferred to the catacombs.

Pedestrianised rue des Lombards is a beacon of live jazz, with **Sunset/Sunside** (*see p279*), **Baiser Salé** (*see p278*) and **Au Duc des Lombards** (*see p278*). In 1610, King Henri IV

EXPLORE

EXPLORE

was assassinated by a Catholic fanatic named François Ravaillac on nearby rue de la Ferronnerie. Today, the street has become an extension of the Marais gay circuit.

The ancient, easternmost stretch of rue St-Honoré runs into the southern edge of Les Halles. The Fontaine du Trahoir stands at the corner with rue de l'Arbre-Sec. Opposite, the **Hôtel de Truden** (52 rue de l'Arbre-Sec) was built in 1717 for a rich wine merchant; in the courtyard on rue des Prouvaires, the market-traders' favourite **La Tour de Montlhéry** (*see p85*) serves up meaty fare through the night. Fashion chains line the commercial stretch of the rue de Rivoli south of Les Halles. Running towards the Seine, ancient little streets such as rue des Lavandiers-Ste-Opportune and rue Jean-Lantier show a different side of Les Halles. Between rue de Rivoli and the Pont Neuf is former department store La Samaritaine, which is due to reopen in 2015 as luxury hotel Le Cheval Blanc.

Looming over the northern edge of the Jardin des Halles is the massive **Eglise St-Eustache**, with Renaissance motifs inside and chunky flying buttresses outside. At the western end of the gardens is the circular, domed **Bourse de Commerce**. In front of it, an astrological column is all that remains from a grand palace belonging to Marie de Médicis that stood here.

The empire of French designer **Agnès b** (*see p87*) stretches along most of rue du Jour, with outlets such as **Kiliwatch** (*see p87*) clustered along rue Tiquetonne. On rue Etienne-Marcel, the restored **Tour Jean Sans Peur** is a weird Gothic relic of the fortified medieval townhouse of Jean Sans Peur, duke of Burgundy.

Busy, pedestrianised rue Montorgueil is lined with grocers, delicatessens and cafés. Some historic façades remain from when this was an area in which the well-heeled and the working class mingled: **Pâtisserie Stohrer** (no.51, 2nd, 01.42.33.38.20, www.stohrer.fr), founded in 1730 and credited with the invention of the sugary *puits d'amour*; and the golden snail sign in front of **L'Escargot Montorgueil** (no.38, 01.42.36.83.51), a restaurant established in 1832.

Stretching north, bordered by boulevard de Bonne-Nouvelle to the north and boulevard Sébastopol to the east, lies Sentier, the historic garment district, and cocky rue St-Denis, which has long relied on strumpets and strip joints. The grime is unremitting along its northern continuation, rue du Fbg-St-Denis.

Rue Réaumur is lined with striking art nouveau buildings. Between rue des Petits-Carreaux and rue St-Denis is the site of the medieval Cour des Miracles – a refuge where paupers would 'miraculously' regain use of their eyes or limbs. A disused aristocratic estate, it was a sanctuary for the underworld until it was cleared out in 1667.

Sentier's streets buzz with porters shouldering linen bundles, as sweatshops churn out copies of catwalk creations. Streets such as rue du Caire, rue d'Aboukir and rue du Nil reflect the craze that followed Napoleon's Egyptian campaign in 1798 and 1799.

Sights & Museums

FREE **Bourse de Commerce**

2 rue de Viarmes, 1st (01.55.65.55.65). M° Louvre Rivoli. **Open** *tour groups* 9am-6pm Mon-Fri. **Admission** free. **Map** p61 F4 ⑯

Housing the Paris chamber of commerce, this trade centre for coffee and sugar was built as a grain market in 1767. The circular building was then covered by a wooden dome, replaced by an avant-garde iron structure in 1809. In his 1831 novel *Notre-Dame de Paris*, Victor Hugo summed up the building thus: '*Le dôme de la Halle-au-Blé est une casquette de jockey anglais sur une grande échelle.*'

FREE **Eglise St-Eustache**

Rue du Jour, 1st (01.42.36.31.05, www.saint-eustache.org). M° Les Halles. **Open** 9.30am-7pm Mon-Fri; 10am-7pm Sat; 9am-7pm Sun. **Admission** free. **Map** p61 F4 ⑰

This barn-like church, built between 1532 and 1640, has a Gothic structure but Renaissance decoration in its façade and Corinthian capitals. Among the paintings in the side chapels are a *Descent from the Cross* by Luca Giordano.

★ **Tour Jean Sans Peur**

20 rue Etienne-Marcel, 2nd (01.40.26.20.28, www.tourjeansanspeur.com). M° Etienne Marcel.

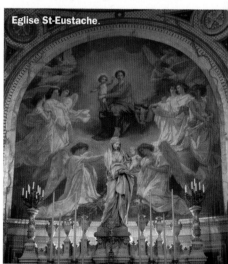

Eglise St-Eustache.

Open 1.30-6pm Wed-Sun. Tour 3pm Sat, Sun.
Admission €5; €3 reductions; free under-7s.
Tour €8. **No credit cards**. Map p61 G4 **⑱**
This Gothic turret (1409-11) is the remnant of the townhouse of Jean Sans Peur, duke of Burgundy. He was responsible for the assassination of his rival Louis d'Orléans, which sparked the Hundred Years' War and saw Burgundy become allied to the English crown. You can climb the tower.

Restaurants

L'Autobus Impérial
14 rue Mondétour, 1st (01.42.36.00.18, www.autobus-imperial.fr). M° Les Halles. **Open** 10am-2am Mon-Sat. **Main courses** €18. **Prix fixe** *Lunch* €13.50, €15.50. *Dinner* €24.50, €29.50. Map p61 G4 **⑲** Brasserie
Tucked away in a corner of Les Halles, L'Autobus Impérial is a hidden gem. The rather unattractive entrance does little justice to the superb art nouveau dining room, built in 1910 and boasting a listed glass ceiling. Food is traditional but inventive, and remains very reasonably priced. The bar has the longest zinc counter in Paris.

Blend
44 rue d'Argout, 2nd (01.40.26.84.57, www.blend-hamburger.com). M° Bourse or Sentier. **Open** noon-11pm daily. **Main courses** €10. **Prix fixe** *Lunch* €15 (Mon-Fri). Map p61 F3 **⑳** Burgers
Parisians have officially gone burger bonkers: after Camion qui Fume (www.lecamionquifume.com), Blend has opened its doors in the bobo quarters of Etienne Marcel. The secret is in the ingredients: made with hand-cut veal and beef mince, provided by star butcher Yves-Marie le Bourdonnec, burgers are succulent and flavoursome, and marry wonderfully with the fresh toppings (think bacon, bleu d'Auvergne cheese, spinach leaves, chorizo, mint and cheddar). The bread and fries (both potato and sweet potato) are also home-made.

Chez Vong
10 rue de la Grande-Truanderie, 1st (01.40.26.09.36, www.chez-vong.com). M° Etienne Marcel or Les Halles. **Open** noon-2pm, 7-11.30pm Mon-Sat. Closed 3wks Aug. **Main courses** €24-€58. **Prix fixe** *Lunch* €26. Map p61 G4 **㉑** Chinese
The staff at this cosy Chinese restaurant take pride in its excellent cooking. From the greeting at the door to the knowledgeable, trilingual service (Cantonese, Mandarin and French), each part of the experience is thoughtfully orchestrated. Any doubts about authenticity are extinguished with the arrival of the beautifully presented dishes. Expertly cooked spicy shrimp glistens in a smooth, characterful sauce of onions and ginger, and *ma po* tofu melts in the mouth, its spicy and peppery flavours melding with those of the fine pork mince.

★ Frenchie
5 rue du Nil, 2nd (01.40.39.96.19, www.frenchie-restaurant.com). M° Sentier. **Open** 7-11pm Mon-Fri. **Prix fixe** €48. Map p61 G3 **㉒** Bistro
Grégory Marchand honed his craft with Jamie Oliver in London before opening this loft-style bistro next to the market street rue Montorgueil. It has been a hit thanks to the bold flavours of dishes such as crab with cape gooseberry; braised lamb with roasted aubergine and spinach; and wild blackberries with lime and hazelnut. Book several days ahead for a table.

Le Pharamond
24 rue de la Grande Truanderie, 1st (01.40.28.45.18, www.pharamond.fr). M° Etienne Marcel. **Open** noon-2.30pm, 7-11pm daily. **Main courses** €15-€25. **Prix fixe** *Lunch* €14.90 (Tue-Fri), €29.50, €39.50. *Dinner* €29.50, €39.50. Map p61 G4 **㉓** Brasserie
There has been a restaurant on this site for well over a century and the interior is a joy to behold, with its carved wood panelling, elaborate tiling and stunning painted mirrors. The menu runs the gamut from *terrine de lapin* and *escargots* to *tripes à la mode de Caen* and *baba Normand au Calvados*. One thing's for sure – you won't be going home hungry.

★ La Tour de Montlhéry (Chez Denise)
5 rue des Prouvaires, 1st (01.42.36.21.82). M° Les Halles/RER Châtelet Les Halles. **Open** noon-3pm, 7.30pm-5am Mon-Fri. Closed mid July-mid Aug. **Main courses** €25. Map p61 F5 **㉔** Bistro
At the stroke of midnight, this place is packed, jovial and hungry. Savoury traditional dishes, washed down by litres of the house Brouilly, are the order of the day. Les Halles was the city's wholesale food market, and game, beef and offal still rule here. Diners devour towering rib steaks served with marrow and a heaped platter of chips, among the best in town. Brave souls can also try the *tripes au calvados* or grilled *andouillette*, or perhaps go for a stewed venison, served up with celery root and home-made jam.

Cafés & Bars

Le Cochon à l'Oreille
15 rue Montmartre, 1st (01.42.36.07.56). M° Les Halles. **Open** 7am-midnight. **No credit cards**. Map p61 F4 **㉕**
Some old bistros have the setting, others get the food. This place does a good job with both: the antique public telephone, the imposing zinc counter and the cosy wooden booths are charming reminders of Les Halles' heyday as the city's celebrated food market – note the tiles that depict scenes of the market in all its chaotic splendour. Food-wise, expect hearty dishes like stuffed pork on a bed of lentils and *confit de canard*, best accompanied by one of the 50 wines on the list. Enjoyed your meal? Write about it in the notebooks tucked away in little nooks.

EXPLORE

EXPLORE

GOOD GRAPES

Vintage treats at Frenchie's wine bar offshoot.

You'd be forgiven for suspecting that **Frenchie Bar à Vins** (*see p87*) was opened merely as a solution to the near impossible problem of getting a table – or even getting them to answer the phone – at the hugely successful Frenchie across the street. But it has quickly become a destination in its own right, drawing an agreeably eclectic mix of ages and nationalities to a part of Sentier otherwise deserted at night.

The look is similar to the sister restaurant – exposed stone walls and bare lightbulbs suspended from copper tubing – but here there are no reservations. You simply turn up (early or after 10pm is easiest) and grab one of the stools grouped around the high communal tables.

A similarly flexible approach applies to the food, with the choice of tucking into several courses or simply snacking on a starter or two. Plates are generally smaller and less complex than in the main restaurant, but the quality of dishes such as poached egg in frothy Jerusalem artichoke velouté, salsify with black mushrooms, and lamb shoulder with butternut squash helps you to understand why Frenchie has had such enormous acclaim since it opened.

Wines range in price from a simple €20 Loire to a Mouton Rothschild 1998 that'll set you back more than €1,000. 'Many are natural but not all, but we like to understand how the winemaker makes their wines,' says Canadian sommelier Laura Vidal, who chooses the wines with chef Gregory Marchand. 'The chef and I believe in having a very wide selection of wines and regions: a light red Beaujolais or a full-bodied Cahors to cater to different tastes and palates. His cuisine is often a twist on Italian and we serve a couple of pasta dishes, so we have a nice selection of Italian wines.' The list itself is curiously uninformative, simply arranged by colour and price, although on-the-spot sommelier Aurélien Massay can offer guidance.

★ Frenchie Bar à Vins

6 rue du Nil, 2nd (01.40.39.96.19, www.frenchie-restaurant.com). M° Sentier. **Open** 7-11pm Mon-Fri. **Map** p61 G3 ⓳
See p86 **Good Grapes**.

Le Tambour

41 rue Montmartre, 2nd (01.42.33.06.90). M° Sentier. **Open** 8.30am-5am daily. **Map** p61 F4 ⓲
Decked out with vintage public transport paraphernalia, slatted wooden banquettes and bus stop-sign bar stools, the Tambour has a split personality: there's the daytime Tambour, frequented by pretty much everybody; and then there's the nighttime Tambour, a well-loved nighthawks' bar where the chatty regulars give the 24-hour clock their best shot.

Shops & Services

Agnès b

2, 3, 4 & 6 rue du Jour, 1st (men 01.42.33.04.13, women 01.45.08.56.56, www.agnesb.com). M° Les Halles. **Open** Oct-Apr 10am-7pm Mon-Sat. *May-Sept* 10.30am-7.30pm Mon-Sat. **Map** p61 F4 ⓲ **Fashion**
Agnès b rarely wavers from her design vision: pure lines in fine quality cotton, merino wool and silk. Her mini-empire of men's, women's, children's, travel and sportswear shops is compact.
Other locations throughout the city.

★ E Dehillerin

18 rue Coquillière, 1st (01.42.36.53.13, www.e-dehillerin.fr). M° Les Halles. **Open** 9am-12.30pm, 2-6pm Mon; 9am-6pm Tue-Sat. **Map** p61 F4 ⓲ **Homewares**
This no-nonsense warehouse stocks just about every kitchen utensil ever invented.

Fnac Forum

Levels -1 to -3, Porte Lescot, Forum des Halles, 1st (08.25.02.00.20, ticket office 08.92.68.36.22, www.fnac.com). M° Les Halles. **Open** 10am-8pm Mon-Sat. **Map** p61 F5 ⓲ **Books & music**
Fnac is a supermarket of culture: books, DVDs, CDs, audio kit, computers and photographic equipment. Most branches stock everything; others specialise. All branches operate as a concert box office.
Other locations throughout the city.

Forum des Halles

Rue Pierre-Lescot & rue Rambuteau, 1st (01.44.76.96.56, www.forumdeshalles.com). M° Les Halles/RER Châtelet Les Halles. **Open** 10am-8pm Mon-Sat. **Map** p61 F5 ⓲ **Mall**
The Forum des Halles is Paris's least pleasant shopping mall, although a facelift due to be completed in 2016 should improve matters. Extending three levels underground, it incorporates métro stations, multiplex, gym, swimming pool and numerous restaurants. High-street retailers dominate.

Kiliwatch

64 rue Tiquetonne, 2nd (01.42.21.17.37, http://espacekiliwatch.fr). M° Etienne Marcel. **Open** 2-7pm Mon; 11am-7.30pm Mon-Sat. **Map** p61 F4 ⓲ **Fashion**
The trailblazer of the rue Etienne-Marcel revival is filled with hoodies, casual shirts and washed-out jeans. Brands such as Gas, Edwin and Pepe Jeans accompany pricey, good-condition second-hand garb.

Kokon To Zai

48 rue Tiquetonne, 2nd (01.42.36.92.41, www.kokontozai.co.uk). M° Etienne Marcel. **Open** 11.30am-7.30pm Mon-Sat. **Map** p61 G4 ⓲ **Fashion**
Always a spot-on spotter of the latest creations, this tiny style emporium is sister to the Kokon To Zai in London. The neon-lit club feel of the mirrored interior matches the dark glamour of the designs. Unique pieces straight off the catwalk share space with creations by Marjan Peijoski, Noki, Raf Simons, Ziad Ghanem and new Norwegian designers.

Monster Melodies

9 rue des Déchargeurs, 1st (01.40.28.09.39, www.monstermelodies.fr). M° Les Halles. **Open** noon-7pm Mon-Sat. **Map** p61 F5 ⓲ **Books & music**
The owners are very willing to help you hunt down your treasured tracks – and with more than 10,000 second-hand CDs of every variety, that's just as well.

Pull-In Underwear

8 rue Française, 2nd (01.42.36.91.06, www.pull-in.com). M° Etienne Marcel. **Open** 11am-1.30pm, 2.30-7.30pm Mon, Thur; 11am-7.30pm Tue, Wed, Fri-Sun. **Map** p61 G4 ⓲ **Accessories**
Hailing from south-west France, Pull-In is the official underwear supplier to the French rugby team. The ultra-trendy brand makes swimwear, but its boxers in wacko patterns have now supplanted Calvin Kleins as *the* visible waistband for Gallic hip hoppers.

Royal Cheese

22-24 rue Tiquetonne, 2nd (01.42.21.30.65, www.royalcheese.com). M° Etienne Marcel. **Open** 11am-8pm daily. **Map** p61 G4 ⓲ **Fashion**
Clubbers hit Royal Cheese to snaffle up hard-to-find imports: Stüssy, Cheap Monday and Lee for the boys; Insight, Sessun, Edwin and Lazy Oaf for the girls. Prices are hefty: Japanese jeans cost €200.
Other locations throughout the city.

Spa Nuxe

32 rue Montorgueil, 1st (01.42.36.65.65, www.nuxe.com). M° Les Halles. **Open** 10am-9pm Mon-Fri; 9.30am-7.30pm Sat. **Map** p61 F4 ⓲ **Health & beauty**
This luxurious day spa housed in stone vaults with wooden cabins and safari-style tents offers massages and skin treatments using Nuxe's gentle, plant-based products.

EXPLORE

Champs-Elysées & Western Paris

There seems to be an unwritten law in France that no mention of the capital's most famous thoroughfare can be made without calling it 'la plus belle avenue du monde'. In truth, it's not that beautiful and it heaves with cars, crowds and overpriced restaurants. The hordes aren't here for beauty, though. They're here for the shops, which the avenue, after years in the retail doldrums, now supplies in abundance thanks to an influx of megabrands. Fortunately, in the midst of all this consumerism are museums covering such topics as architecture, human evolution and life on the ocean waves, plus a greatly extended Palais de Tokyo that now lays claim to the title of Europe's largest contemporary art centre.

EXPLORE

Palais de Tokyo.

Don't Miss

1 Arc de Triomphe Head up for one of the best views in the city (p91).

2 Palais de Tokyo Tripled in size and still pushing the boundaries (p96).

3 Granterroirs Come for the *épicerie*, stay for the *table d'hôte* (p98).

4 Balenciaga Fabrics that the *haut monde* can't wait to slip into (p102).

5 Ladurée Indulge your senses in hot chocolate heaven (p100).

CHAMPS-ELYSEES

In the 8th, 16th & 17th arrondissements.

The Champs-Elysées is, and has long been, a symbolic gathering place. Sports victories, New Year's Eve, displays of military might on 14 July – all are celebrated here. Over the past decade, the avenue has undergone a renaissance, thanks initially to a facelift instigated by Jacques Chirac.

Chi-chi shops and chic hotels have set up in the 'golden triangle' (avenues George V, Montaigne and the Champs): **Louis Vuitton** (*see p104*), **Dior** (*see p102*) and **Balenciaga** (*see p102*), the **Marriott** (70 av des Champs-Elysées, 8th, 01.53.93.55.00) and **Pershing Hall** (*see p347*). The **Four Seasons George V** (*see p345*) has undergone a revamp, and fashionable restaurants draw affluent and screamingly fashionable diners. Crowds line up for the glitzy **Le Lido** cabaret (*see p271*), the now commercialised **Queen** nightclub (*see p267*) and numerous cinemas, or stroll down the avenue to floodlit place de la Concorde. The famous **Drugstore Publicis** (*see p103*) is where locals head to stock up on late-night wines and groceries.

This great spine of western Paris started life as an extension to the Tuileries, laid out by Le Nôtre in the 17th century. By the Revolution, the avenue had reached its full extent, but it

IN THE KNOW
CHAMPS-ELYSEES

Bismarck was so impressed with the Champs-Elysées when he arrived with the conquering Prussian army in 1871 that he had a replica, the Ku'damm, built in Berlin, and Hitler's troops made a point of marching down it in 1940, as did their Allied counterparts four years later.

was during the Second Empire that it became a focus for fashionable society, military parades and royal processions.

The lower, landscaped reach of the avenue hides two theatres and elegant restaurants **Laurent** (41 av Gabriel, 8th, 01.42.25.00.39, www.le-laurent.com) and **Ledoyen** (1 av Dutuit, 8th, 01.53.05.10.01, www.ledoyen.com), housed in fancy Napoleon III pavilions. At the Rond-Point des Champs-Elysées, no.7 (now the Artcurial gallery bookshop and auction house) and no.9 give visitors some idea of the magnificent mansions that once lined the avenue. From here on, it's platinum cards and lanky women aplenty, as avenue Montaigne rolls out a full deck of fashion houses.

Models and magnates nibble on the terrace at fashionable restaurant **L'Avenue** (no.41, 8th, 01.40.70.14.91, www.avenue-restaurant.com). You can admire the lavish **Hôtel Plaza Athénée** (*see p346*) and Auguste Perret's innovative 1911-13 **Théâtre des Champs-Elysées** concert hall (*see p285*), with an auditorium painted by Maurice Denis.

South of the avenue, the glass-domed **Grand Palais** and Petit Palais, both built for the 1900 Exposition Universelle and still used for major art exhibitions, create a magnificent vista across the Pont Alexandre III to Les Invalides. The rear wing of the Grand Palais, opening on to avenue Franklin-D-Roosevelt, contains the **Palais de la Découverte** science museum.

To the north lie more smart shops, antiques dealers and bastions of officialdom; on circular place Beauvau, wrought-iron gates herald the Ministry of the Interior. The 18th-century Palais de l'Elysée, the official presidential residence, is at 55-57 rue du Fbg-St-Honoré. Nearby, with gardens extending to avenue Gabriel, are the palatial **British Embassy** and ambassadorial residence, which was once the Hôtel Borghèse.

The western end of the Champs-Elysées is dominated by the **Arc de Triomphe** towering above place Charles-de-Gaulle, also known as L'Etoile. Built by Napoleon, the arch was modified to celebrate the Revolutionary armies. From the top, visitors can gaze over the

EXPLORE

Champs-Elysées.

square (commissioned later by Haussmann), with 12 avenues radiating out in all directions.

South of the arch, avenue Kléber leads to the monumental buildings and terraced gardens of the panoramic Trocadéro, now housing the aquarium and cinema, **Cinéaqua**. The vast 1930s **Palais de Chaillot** dominates the hill and houses four museums, plus the **Théâtre National de Chaillot** (*see p290*).

To the west of Chaillot, on avenue du Président-Wilson, are two major museums: the **Musée d'Art Moderne de la Ville de Paris** and the **Palais de Tokyo: Site de Création Contemporaine** are both inside the **Palais de Tokyo** building. Opposite is the newly revamped **Palais Galliera**, and up the hill at place d'Iéna are the Asian and oriental art collections of the **Musée National des Arts Asiatiques – Guimet**.

Towards the Champs-Elysées, the former townhouse of avant-garde patron Marie-Laure de Noailles has been given a cheeky revamp. It now houses the **Galerie-Musée Baccarat**.

Sights & Museums

★ Arc de Triomphe

Pl Charles-de-Gaulle (access via underpass), 8th (01.55.37.73.77). Mᵒ Charles de Gaulle Etoile. **Open** *Oct-Mar* 10am-10.30pm daily. *Apr-Sept* 10am-11pm daily. **Admission** €9.50; €6 reductions; free under-18s, under-26s (EU citizens). PMP. **Map** p92 C3 ❶

The Arc de Triomphe is the city's second most iconic monument after the Eiffel Tower – older, shorter, but far more symbolically important: indeed, the island on which it stands, in the centre of the vast traffic junction of l'Etoile, is the nearest thing to sacred ground in all of secular France, indelibly associated as it is with two of French history's greatest men – Napoleon and Charles de Gaulle. Despite such grand associations, until recently the interior of the Arc was far less impressive, having changed little since the 1930s. But now, after a revamp by architect Christophe Girault and artist Maurice Benayouna, there is an impressive museum with interactive screens allowing visitors to look at other famous arches throughout Europe and the world, as well as displays exploring the Arc's tumultuous 200-year history. But the main reason to head up here is the rooftop view, one of the finest in the city.

★ Chapelle Expiatoire

29 rue Pasquier, 8th (01.44.32.18.00). Mᵒ St-Augustin. **Open** 1-5pm Thur-Sat. **Admission** €5.50; €4 reductions; free under-18s, under-26s (EU citizens). PMP. **Map** p92 C6 ❷

The chapel was commissioned by Louis XVIII in memory of his executed predecessors, his brother Louis XVI and Marie-Antoinette. Their remains, along with those of 3,000 victims of the Revolution,

Pinacothèque. *See p96.*

including Camille Desmoulins, Danton, Malesherbes and Lavoisier, were found in 1814 on the spot where the altar stands. The bodies of Louis XVI and Marie-Antoinette were transferred the following year to the Basilique St-Denis; the pair are now represented by marble statues, kneeling at the feet of Religion. Every January, ardent (albeit unfulfilled) royalists gather here for a memorial service.

FREE Cimetière de Passy

2 rue du Commandant-Schloesing, 16th (01.53.70.40.80). Mᵒ Trocadéro. **Open** *16 Mar-5 Nov* 8am-5.30pm Mon-Fri; 8.30am-5.30pm Sat; 9am-5.30pm Sun. *6 Nov-15 Mar* 8am-6pm Mon-Fri; 8.30am-6pm Sat; 9am-6pm Sun. **Admission** free. **Map** p93 E2 ❸

Since 1874, this cemetery has been one of the most desirable Paris locations in which to be laid to rest. Here you'll find Debussy and Fauré, Manet and his sister-in-law Berthe Morisot, and writer Giraudoux, along with various generals and politicians.

★ Cinéaqua

2 av des Nations Unies, 16th (01.40.69.23.23, www.cineaqua.com). Mᵒ Trocadéro. **Open** 10am-7pm daily. **Admission** €19.90; €12.90-€15.90 reductions; free under-3s. **Map** p93 F2 ❹

This aquarium and three-screen cinema is a wonderful attraction and a key element in the renaissance of the once moribund Trocadéro. Children in particular love the shark tunnel and the petting pool (*bassin de caresses*) where you can stroke friendly

EXPLORE

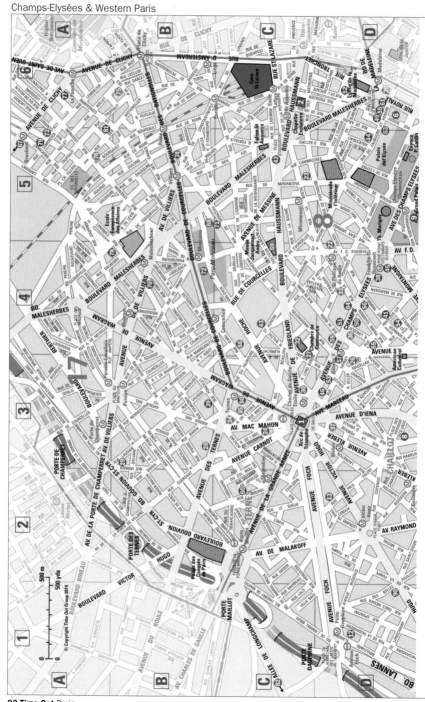

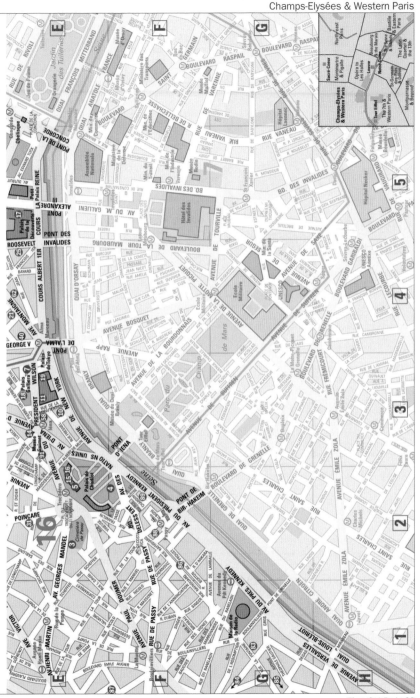

Galerie-Museé Baccarat.

Fondation Pierre Bergé Yves Saint Laurent

*3 rue Léonce-Reynaud, 16th (01.44.31.64.31,
www.fondation-pb-ysl.net). M° Alma Marceau.*
Open 11am-6pm Tue-Sun (only during
exhibitions). Closed Aug. **Admission** €7;
€5 reductions; free under-10s. Map p93 E3 **7**
When the late Yves Saint Laurent bowed out of
designing in 2002, he reopened his fashion house as
this foundation, exhibiting Picasso and Warhol
paintings with the dresses they closely inspired.
Every sketch and every *toile* has been carefully catalogued, and many of Saint Laurent's friends and
clients presented the designer with the dresses he
created for them. The foundation stages two or
three exhibitions every year.

★ Galerie-Musée Baccarat

*11 pl des Etats-Unis, 16th (01.40.22.11.00,
www.baccarat.fr). M° Boissière or Iéna.* **Open**
10am-6pm Mon, Wed-Sat. **Admission** €5; €3.50
reductions; free under-18s. Map p92 D3 **8**
Philippe Starck has created a neo-rococo wonderland
in the former mansion of the Vicomtesse de Noailles.
From the red-carpet entrance with a chandelier in a
fish tank to the Alchemy room, decorated by Gérard
Garouste, there's a play of light and movement that
makes Baccarat's work sing. See items by designers
Georges Chevalier and Ettore Sottsass, services
made for princes and maharajahs, and monumental
items made for the great exhibitions of the 1800s.
▶ *If you want to eat at the opulent Le Cristal Room
restaurant (01.40.22.11.10), be sure to book.*

Galeries Nationales du Grand Palais

*3 av du Général-Eisenhower, 8th (01.44.13.17.17,
www.grandpalais.fr). M° Champs-Elysées
Clemenceau.* **Open** times vary. **Admission**
prices vary. Map p92 D5 **9**
Built for the 1900 Exposition Universelle, the Grand
Palais was the work of three different architects,
each of whom designed a façade. During World War
II it accommodated Nazi tanks. In 1994, the magnificent glass-roofed central hall was closed when bits
of metal started falling off. After major restoration,
the Palais reopened in 2005. The space hosts blockbuster exhibitions, including a major Braque retrospective in 2014.

Mona Bismarck American Center for Art & Culture

*34 av de New-York, 16th (01.47.23.38.88, www.
monabismarck.org). M° Alma Marceau.* **Open**
11am-6pm Wed-Sun. Closed Aug. **Admission**
€7; €5 reductions; free under-12s. Map p93 E3 **10**
The Mona Bismarck Foundation supports this Paris
cultural centre set in Countess Bismarck's former
townhouse across the Seine from the Eiffel Tower.
The Foundation puts on an eclectic programme,
including a 2014 exhibition celebrating the work of
comic book artist Alex Ross.

sturgeon. Also interesting (though less theatrical) is
the section on the River Seine, showing the sorts of
fish that still survive in Paris's river despite the pollution. Many people baulk at the admission fee, but
you can easily spend a long afternoon here, watching
cartoons in the cinemas and observing the sealife.
On Wednesdays and weekends, there are special
children's shows too.

★ Cité de l'Architecture et du Patrimoine

*Palais de Chaillot, 1 pl du Trocadéro, 16th
(01.58.51.52.00, www.citechaillot.fr). M°
Trocadéro.* **Open** 11am-7pm Mon, Wed,
Fri-Sun; 11am-9pm Thur. **Admission** €8;
€6 reductions; free under-18s, under-26s
(EU citizens). Map p93 E2 **5**
This architecture and heritage museum impresses
principally by its scale. The expansive ground floor
is filled with life-size mock-ups of cathedral façades
and heritage buildings, and interactive screens
place the models in context. Upstairs, darkened
rooms house full-scale copies of medieval and
Renaissance murals and stained-glass windows.
The highlight of the modern architecture section
is the walk-in replica of an apartment from Le
Corbusier's Cité Radieuse in Marseille. Temporary
exhibitions are housed in the large basement area.

FREE Fondation d'Enterprise Paul Ricard

*12 rue Boissy d'Anglas, 8th (01.53.30.88.00, www.
fondation-entreprise-ricard.com). M° Concorde.*
Open 11am-7pm Tue-Sat. **Admission** free.
Map p92 D6 **6**
The Pastis firm promotes modern art with the Prix
Paul Ricard – young French artists are shortlisted
by an independent curator for an annual prize.
▶ *The Prix Paul Ricard coincides with FIAC
(see p38) each autumn.*

EXPLORE

FREE Musée d'Art Moderne de la Ville de Paris

11 av du Président-Wilson, 16th (01.53.67.40.00, www.mam.paris.fr). M° Alma Marceau or Iéna. **Open** *10am-6pm Tue-Sun.* **Admission** *free. Temporary exhibitions €5-€11; €2.50-€5.50 reductions; free under-13s.* **No credit cards.** **Map** p93 E3 ⑪

This monumental 1930s building, housing the city's modern art collection, features painting, sculpture, installation, photography and video. The museum is particularly strong on the Cubists, Fauves, Delaunays, Rouault and Ecole de Paris artists Soutine and van Dongen.

Musée de la Contrefaçon

16 rue de la Faisanderie, 16th (01.56.26.14.03, www.unifab.com). M° Porte Dauphine. **Open** *2-5.30pm Tue-Sun.* **Admission** *€4; €3 reductions; free under-12s.* **No credit cards.** **Map** p92 D1 ⑫

This museum was set up by the French anti-counterfeiting association with the aim of deterring forgers – but playing spot-the-fake with such brands as Reebok, Lacoste and Vuitton is fun for visitors.

Musée Dapper

35bis rue Paul-Valéry, 16th (01.45.00.91.75, www.dapper.com.fr). M° Victor Hugo. **Open** *11am-7pm Mon, Wed, Fri-Sun.* **Admission** *€6; €4 reductions; free under-26s, all last Wed of mth.* **Map** p92 D2 ⑬

Named after the 17th-century Dutch humanist Olfert Dapper, the Fondation Dapper began as an organisation dedicated to preserving sub-Saharan art. Reopened in 2000, the venue created by Alain Moatti houses a performance space, bookshop and café.

★ Musée National des Arts Asiatiques – Guimet

6 pl d'Iéna, 16th (01.56.52.53.00, www.guimet.fr). M° Iéna. **Open** *10am-6pm Mon, Wed-Sun.* **Admission** *€7.50; €5.50 reductions; free under-18s, under-26s (EU citizens).* PMP. **Map** p93 E3 ⑭

Founded by the industrialist Emile Guimet in 1889 to house his collection of Chinese and Japanese religious art, and later incorporating oriental collections from the Louvre, the museum has 45,000 objects from neolithic times onwards. Lower galleries focus on India and South-east Asia, centred on stunning Hindu and Buddhist Khmer sculpture from Cambodia. Don't miss the Giant's Way, part of the entrance to a temple complex at Angkor Wat. Upstairs, Chinese antiquities include mysterious jade discs. Afghan glassware and Moghul jewellery also feature.

Musée National de la Marine

Palais de Chaillot, 16th (01.53.65.69.69, www.musee-marine.fr). M° Trocadéro. **Open** *11am-6pm Mon, Wed-Fri; 11am-7pm Sat, Sun.* **Admission** *Main collection & temporary exhibitions €10; €2-€8 reductions. Main collection €7; €5 reductions; free under-18s, under-26s (EU citizens).* PMP. **Map** p93 E2 ⑮

Four centuries of French naval history are outlined in detailed models of battleships and Vernet's series of paintings of French ports (1754-65). There's also an imperial barge, built when Napoleon's delusions of grandeur were reaching their zenith in 1810.

FREE Palais de Chaillot

Pl du Trocadéro, 16th. M° Trocadéro. **Admission** *free.* **Map** p93 E2 ⑯

Palais de Chaillot.

EXPLORE

Palais de Tokyo.

This immense pseudo-classical building was constructed by Azéma, Boileau and Carlu for the 1937 international exhibition, with giant sculptures of Apollo by Henri Bouchard, and inscriptions by Paul Valéry. The Palais houses the Musée National de la Marine and the Musée de l'Homme (closed for renovation until 2015). In the east wing are the Théâtre National de Chaillot (*see p290*) and the Cité de l'Architecture et du Patrimoine (*see p94*).

★ Palais de la Découverte

Av Franklin-D.-Roosevelt, 8th (01.56.43.20.21, www.palais-decouverte.fr). M° Champs-Elysées Clemenceau or Franklin D. Roosevelt. **Open** 9.30am-6pm Tue-Sat; 10am-7pm Sun (last entry 30mins before closing). **Admission** €8; €6 reductions; free under-6s. *Planetarium* €3 supplement. **Map** p93 E5 ⑰
This science museum houses designs dating from Leonardo da Vinci's time to the present. Models, real apparatus and audio-visual material bring displays to life, and permanent exhibits cover astrophysics, astronomy, biology, chemistry, physics and earth sciences. The Planète Terre section highlights meteorology, and one room is dedicated to the sun.

Palais Galliera – Musée de la Mode

10 av Pierre 1er de Serbie, 16th (01.56.52.86.00, www.palaisgalliera.paris.fr). M° Alma Marceau or Iéna. **Open** 10am-6pm Tue, Wed, Fri-Sun; 10am-9pm Thur. **Admission** varies. **Map** p93 E3 ⑱
See p97 **Fashion Show**.

Palais de Tokyo: Site de Création Contemporaine

13 av du Président-Wilson, 16th (01.81.97.35.88, www.palaisdetokyo.com). M° Alma Marceau or Iéna. **Open** noon-midnight Mon, Wed-Sun. **Admission** €10; €8 reductions; free under-18s. **Map** p93 E3 ⑲

Paris's most happening major art space since it opened in 2002, the Palais de Tokyo has now virtually tripled in size to become the largest contemporary art centre in Europe. The organisation is known for its highly international approach, and for blurring boundaries between art, music, science and politics – as well as for its artist-designed Tokyo Eat restaurant and Black Block shop. Architects Lacaton & Vassal, who transformed the 1937 building in 2002, employing a deliberately raw, distressed style (as much for budget reasons as aesthetics), have now tackled the vast remaining spaces, many of them unused for over 30 years.

Pinacothèque

28 place de la Madeleine, 8th (01.42.68.02.01, www.pinacotheque.com). M° Madeleine. **Open** 10.30am-6.30pm Mon, Tue, Thur, Sat, Sun; 10.30am-9pm Wed, Fri. **Admission** *Main collection & temporary exhibitions* €18-€22; €15-€18 reductions. *Main collection* €8; €6 reductions; free under-12s. **Map** p92 D6 ⑳
At place de la Madeleine, every square metre of real estate is so sought after that you'd never think there'd be room for a large museum. So imagine Paris's surprise when Credit Agricole turned its office block into the Pinacothèque – an art museum dedicated to expression through the ages, displaying a steadily rotating series of exhibitions focusing on everything from archaeological finds to modern art. Roy Lichtenstein, Goya and Jackson Pollock have all had retrospectives. *Photo p91.*

Restaurants

Alain Ducasse au Plaza Athénée

Hôtel Plaza Athénée, 25 av Montaigne, 8th (01.53.67.65.00, www.alain-ducasse.com). M° Alma Marceau. **Open** 7.45-10.15pm Mon-Wed; 12.45-2.15pm, 7.45-10.15pm Thur, Fri. Closed late

FASHION SHOW

The Palais Galliera has reopened with a stunning display.

Since the reopening of the **Palais Galliera** (*see p96*), it's been hard to decide whether to be more impressed by the building or the clothes on show inside. This extraordinary mock-Renaissance folly, as only the 19th century knew how to do them, has been brought back to its full glory of Pompeian red walls, black woodwork, mosaic floors and vaulted ceilings painted with grotesqueries and arabesques. The fanciful villa was built in 1879-94 by architect Paul-René-Léon Genain for Marie Brignole-Sale, Italian aristocrat and widow of the Duc de Galliera, a wealthy banker. Surrounded by pleasure gardens, it was originally intended to house Brignole-Sale's art collection (ultimately left to the town of Genoa). The house then became the property of the Ville de Paris and has played host to exhibitions, salons, auctions and, since 1977, the municipal fashion museum. It has also regained its name of 'Palais' rather than 'Musée' – an appropriately theatrical showcase for some theatrical clothes.

As before, the Galliera is dedicated solely to temporary exhibitions – due to the fragility of the fabrics, clothes can only

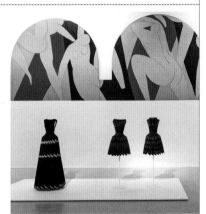

be exhibited for four months at a time under strictly controlled lighting – but the shows manage to provide a decent glimpse of the Palais' incredibly rich collection, which stretches from late 17th-century period costume, via the birth of haute couture, to the creators of today.

After reopening in September 2013 with an exhibition dedicated to the sculptural figure-hugging dresses of Azzedine Alaïa, forthcoming treats include 'Glossy Paper', fashion photography from Condé Nast magazines (28 Feb-25 May 2014); and the glamorous belle époque wardrobe of the Countess Greffulhe (Dec 2014-Feb 2015).

Flamboyant new director Olivier Sainsard, a fashion historian and former curator of the Musée de la Mode in Marseille, has undoubtedly introduced a new dynamism to the Galliera. As well as the internal exhibitions, he's organising adventurous collaborations with other institutions and crossover events with contemporary art and theatre.

Part of the Alaïa show took place inside the Musée d'Art Moderne de la Ville de Paris across the street. And 'Eternity Dress', at the Ecole Nationale Supérieure des Beaux-Arts as part of the 2013 Festival d'Automne, saw Sainsard performing the entire process of making a single dress in a show with British actress Tilda Swinton. A follow-up is already planned in the Palais Galliera itself.

EXPLORE

July-late Aug & 1wk Dec. **Main courses** €80-€135. **Prix fixe** €260-€380. **Map** p93 E4
㉑ Haute cuisine
The sheer glamour factor would be enough to recommend this restaurant, Alain Ducasse's most lofty Paris undertaking. The dining room ceiling drips with 10,000 crystals. An *amuse-bouche* of a single langoustine in a lemon cream with a touch of Iranian caviar starts the meal off beautifully, but other dishes can be inconsistent: a part-raw/part-cooked salad of autumn fruit and veg in a red, Chinese-style sweet-and-sour dressing, or Breton lobster in an overwhelming sauce of apple, quince and spiced wine. Cheese is predictably delicious, as is the *rum baba comme à Monte-Carlo*. The restaurant will be closed until June 2014 while the hotel is undergoing renovations.

Le Bistrot Napolitain

18 av Franklin D. Roosevelt, 8th (01.45.62.08.37). M° St-Philippe-du-Roule. **Open** noon-2.30pm, 7-10.30pm Mon-Fri. Closed late July-early Sept & 24 Dec-3 Jan. **Main courses** €18-€25. **Map** p92 D4 **㉒ Italian**
This chic Italian bistro is as far from a tourist joint as it is possible to be. At lunchtimes, it is full of suave Italianate businessmen. Generosity defines the food – not just big plates, but lashings of the ingredients that others skimp on, such as the slices of tangy parmesan piled high over rocket on the tender beef carpaccio. The pizzas are very good: the Enzo comes with milky, almost raw *mozzarella di bufala* and tasty tomatoes. For pasta you can choose between dried and fresh, with variations such as fresh saffron tagliatelle.

★ Granterroirs

30 rue de Miromesnil, 8th (01.47.42.18.18, www.granterroirs.com). M° Miromesnil. **Open** 9am-5.30pm Mon-Fri. Closed 2wks Aug. **Main courses** €16-€25. **Map** p92 C5 **㉓ Bistro**
This *épicerie* with a difference is the perfect remedy for anyone for whom the word *'terroir'* conjures up visions of grease-soaked peasant food. Here, the walls heave with more than 600 enticing specialities from southern France, including Périgord foie gras, charcuterie from Aubrac and a fine selection of wines. All make excellent gift ideas – but why not sample some of the goodies by enjoying the midday *table d'hôte* feast? Come in early to ensure that you can choose from the five *plats du jour* on offer (such as marinated salmon with dill on a bed of warm potatoes).

Miss Kō.

€ Le Hide

10 rue du Général-Lanrezac, 17th (01.45.74.15.81, www.lehide.fr). M° Charles de Gaulle Etoile. **Open** noon-2pm, 7-10pm Mon-Fri; 7-10pm Sat. **Main courses** €14-€18. **Prix fixe** *Lunch* €19.80, €27. *Dinner* €25, €32.50. **Map** p92 C3 ❷ **Bistro**

This snug bistro is packed with a happy crowd of bistro-lovers who appreciate Japanese-born chef Hide Kobayashi's superb cooking and good-value prices. Expect such dishes as duck foie gras terrine with pear-and-thyme compôte to start, followed by tender *faux-filet* steak in a light foie gras sauce or skate wing with a lemon-accented *beurre noisette*. Desserts are excellent: perfect tarte tatin comes with crème fraîche from Normandy. Good, affordable wines explain the merriment, with glasses starting at €3.80.

Lasserre

17 av Franklin-Roosevelt, 8th (01.43.59.02.13, www.restaurant-lasserre.com). M° Franklin D Roosevelt. **Open** 7-10pm Tue, Wed, Sat; noon-2pm, 7-10pm Thur, Fri. **Main courses** €80-€120. **Prix fixe** *Lunch* €90, €120, €220. *Dinner* €220. **Map** p93 E4 ❷ **Haute cuisine**

Lasserre's rich history is definitely a part of the dining experience: Audrey Hepburn, André Malraux and Salvador Dali were regulars. But its illustrious past is nothing next to the food: chef Christophe Moret (ex-Plaza Athénée) and his pastry chef Claire Heitzler (ex-Ritz) create lip-smacking delicacies to die for. The upstairs dining room, accessed by a bellboy-operated lift, is a sumptuous affair in taupe and white, with solid silver table decorations and a retractable roof that opens just enough for you to see the stars at night.

Miss Kô

49 av George V, 8th (01.53.67.84.60, www.miss-ko.com). M° George V. **Open** noon-2am daily. **Main courses** €17-€29. **Map** p92 D3 ❷ **Chinese**

Philippe Starck's latest venture is set up to look like a narrow Chinatown street, bustling and colourful at night with open kitchens at the end where chefs work away beneath an array of suspended woks and neon lights. There are a dozen dishes, of which the star is beef tataki at €29 – a sort of carpaccio with teriyaki sauce, shiitake mushrooms and purée perfumed with ginger. The 'black salmon & Kô' burger at €19.50 is equally alluring, the bread coloured black with squid ink and garnished with avocado, mizuna, gravlax and tempura-fried green beans. For lighter meals, the creative sushi (gyoza with foie gras, perhaps) go perfectly with a cocktail or bubble tea. The bar and terrace are suitably hip.

Pierre Gagnaire

6 rue Balzac, 8th (01.58.36.12.50, www.pierre-gagnaire.com). M° Charles de Gaulle Etoile or George V. **Open** noon-1.30pm, 7.30-9.30pm Mon-Fri. Closed Aug. **Prix fixe** *Lunch* €115, €290. *Dinner* €290. **Map** p92 C4 ❷ **Haute cuisine**

At Pierre Gagnaire the prix fixe starts at a staggering €115, which seems to be the price of culinary experimentation these days. This cheaper lunch menu is far from the full-blown experience of the *carte*: the former is presented in three courses, whereas the latter involves four or five plates for each course. Even the *amuse-bouches* fill the table: an egg 'raviole', ricotta with apple, fish in a cauliflower jelly, and glazed monkfish. The best thing about the lunch menu is that it includes four very indulgent desserts: clementine, raspberry and vanilla, chocolate, and passion fruit.

Rech

62 av des Ternes, 17th (01.45.72.29.47, www.restaurant-rech.fr). M° Ternes. **Open** noon-2pm, 7.30-10pm Tue-Sat. Closed Aug & 1wk Dec. **Main courses** €34-€65. **Prix fixe** *Lunch* €39, €72. *Dinner* €54, €72. **Map** p92 B3 ❷ **Bistro**

Alain Ducasse's personal touches are everywhere in this art deco seafood restaurant, from the Japanese fish prints on the walls of the upstairs dining room to the blown-glass candleholders on the main-floor tables. The kitchen turns out the kind of precise, Mediterranean-inspired cooking you would expect from Ducasse: glistening sardine fillets marinated with preserved lemon, silky lobster ravioli, and octopus carpaccio painted with pesto. As the fish dishes are light, you can justify indulging in a perfectly aged camembert and the XL éclair, an event in itself.

★ Restaurant L'Entredgeu

83 rue Laugier, 17th (01.40.54.97.24). M° Porte de Champerret. **Open** noon-2pm, 7.30-11pm Tue-Sat. Closed 1wk Apr, 1st 3wks Aug & 1wk Dec. **Prix fixe** *Lunch* €25, €35. *Dinner* €35. **Map** p92 B3 ❷ **Bistro**

Reading the menu here will make you seriously doubt your capacity for pudding. But have no fear. The heartiness of the dishes belies refined, perfectly gauged cooking, served in civilised portions. The table turnover is fast, but this is not a place to linger smoochily in any case – you'll be too busy marvelling at the sharp *gribiche* sauce cutting through the milky crisp-battered oysters, the depth and aroma of the saffron-infused fish soup, the perfect layered execution of the caramelised pork belly, and the delicate desserts. The wine list is creative and assured.

★ Stella Maris

4 rue Arsène-Houssaye, 8th (01.42.89.16.22, www.stellamaris-paris.com). M° Charles de Gaulle Etoile. **Open** 12.30-2.30pm, 7.30-10pm Mon-Fri; 7.30-10pm Sat. Closed 2wks Aug. **Main courses** €41-€75. **Prix fixe** *Lunch* €52. *Dinner* €75, €130. **Map** p92 C3 ❸ **Haute cuisine**

Tateru Yoshino has divided his life between Paris and Tokyo for many years. Trained by Robuchon and Troisgros, he turns out food that is resolutely

EXPLORE

French. The service is at times faltering, but charmingly so, and the space is beautiful. You might float your way through foie gras with carrots, truffles and pistachio oil, pan-fried sea bass with saffron risotto, and a perfectly lopsided Grand Marnier soufflé. The exquisite, powdery blandness of the tasting menu going-home present, *cake aux marrons glacés*, brings it all softly, dreamily, back next morning at breakfast. Expensive but wonderful.

La Table Lauriston

129 rue de Lauriston, 16th (01.47.27.00.07, www.restaurantlatablelauriston.com). M°
Trocadéro. **Open** noon-2.30pm, 7-10.30pm Mon-Fri; 7-10.30pm Sat. Closed Aug & 1wk Dec.
Main courses €21-€44. **Prix fixe** *Lunch* €26.
Map p93 E2 ㉛ **Bistro**
Serge Barbey's dining room has a refreshingly feminine touch. The emphasis here is firmly on good-quality ingredients, skilfully prepared to show off their freshness. In spring, stalks of asparagus from the Landes are expertly trimmed to avoid any trace of stringiness and delightfully served with the simplest *vinaigrette d'herbes*. More extravagant is the *foie gras cuit au torchon*, in which the duck liver is wrapped in a cloth and poached in a bouillon. Skip the crème brûlée, which you could have anywhere, and order a dessert with attitude instead: the giant *baba au rhum*.

Taillevent

15 rue Lamennais, 8th (01.44.95.15.01, www.taillevent.com). M° George V. **Open** 12.15-1.30pm, 7.15-9.30pm Mon-Fri. Closed Aug.
Main courses €54-€240. **Prix fixe** *Lunch* €88, €104, €218, €320. *Dinner* €218, €320.
Map p92 C4 ㉜ **Haute cuisine**
Prices here are not quite as shocking as in some restaurants at this level; for instance, there's an €88 lunch menu. *Rémoulade de coquilles St-Jacques* is a technical feat, with slices of raw, marinated scallop wrapped in a tube shape around a finely diced apple filling, encircled by a mayonnaise-like *rémoulade* sauce. An earthier and lip-smacking dish is the signature *épeautre* – an ancient wheat – which is cooked 'like a risotto' with bone marrow, black truffle, whipped cream and parmesan, and topped with sautéed frogs' legs. *Ravioli au chocolat araguani* is a surprising and wonderful dessert. Men must wear a jacket.

Cafés & Bars

Charlie Birdy

124 rue La Boétie, 8th (01.42.25.18.06, www.charliebirdy.com). M° Franklin D. Roosevelt.
Open noon-5am daily. **Map** p92 D4 ㉝
Take a New York loft and meld it with a colonial English gentleman's club and you're looking at Charlie Birdy – a large 'pub' with a live music programme of jazz, soul and funk that's worth listening

to. If you're in a hurry, stay away – the service can be irritatingly slow. But if you take your time choosing from the 50-strong cocktail menu, sink into a comfy chesterfield and let the evening wash over you, it'll be worth it. Between 4pm and 8pm Monday to Friday, cocktails are half-price.

Le Dada

12 av des Ternes, 17th (01.43.80.60.12).
M° Ternes. **Open** 6am-2am Mon-Sat; 7am-8pm Sun. **Map** p92 C3 ㉞
Perhaps the hippest café in this stuffy part of town, Le Dada is best known for its well-placed, sunny terrace. Inside, the wood-block carved tables and red walls provide a warm atmosphere for a crowd that tends towards the well-heeled, well-spoken and, well, loaded. That said, the atmosphere is friendly; if terracing is your thing, you could happily spend a summer's day here – just remember to bring along your Prada shades.

Flute l'Etoile

19 rue de l'Etoile, 17th (01.45.72.10.14, www.flutebar.com). M° Ternes. **Open** 5pm-2am Tue-Sat. **Map** p92 C3 ㉟
With a menu of some 23 different champagnes and designer decor (slick wooden panelling, blue walls and red velvet), Paris's first champagne lounge may be minuscule, but it certainly looks the part. Indeed the only indication that it's not French (it's American) is the sneaky appearance of a Californian sparkler on the champagne list. For drinkers wishing to sample different vintages without buying a whole glass (from €9), the small tasting glasses (from €5) are a thoughtful touch. And for anyone bored by plain old bubbly, cocktails such as champagne sangria and Rossini-Tini (champagne, raspberry juice, liqueur and Grey Goose vodka) are sophisticated alternatives.

★ Ladurée

75 av des Champs-Elysées, 8th (01.40.75.08.75, www.laduree.fr). M° George V or Franklin D. Roosevelt. **Open** 7.30am-11pm Mon-Fri; 8.30am-midnight Sat; 8.30am-10pm Sun. **Map** p92 D4 ㊱
Decadence permeates this elegant tearoom, from the 19th century-style interior and service to the labyrinthine corridors that lead to the toilets. While you bask in the warm glow of bygone wealth, indulge in tea, pastries (the pistachio pain au chocolat is heavenly) and, above all, the hot chocolate. It's a rich, bitter, velvety tar that will leave you in the requisite stupor for any lazy afternoon.
▶ *The original branch at 16 rue Royale (8th, 01.42.60.21.79) is famed for its macaroons.*
Other location 21 rue Bonaparte, 6th (01.44.07.64.87).

Sir Winston

5 rue de Presbourg, 16th (01.40.67.17.37).
M° Charles de Gaulle Etoile. **Open** 9am-2am Mon-Sat; noon-2am Sun. **Map** p92 D3 ㊲

WELL HUNG

The Fondation Louis Vuitton is taking shape in the Bois de Boulogne.

EXPLORE

Like a butterfly emerging from its chrysalis, a daring glass structure has been slowly unfolding on the edge of the Bois de Boulogne. The **Fondation Louis Vuitton** (www.fondationlouisvuitton.fr), designed by star architect Frank Gehry, is described by LVMH chairman Bernard Arnault as 'an emblematic building of the 21st century', an ambitious statement project that proclaims the arrival of Louis Vuitton – previously active as a sponsor of exhibitions and heritage restoration – as an art-world force. The Foundation will open in autumn 2014, four years later than planned.

Gehry has described his inspiration behind the design: 'Within the Bois de Boulogne and the Jardin d'Acclimatation, the idea of a glass pavilion was the only way forward. It seemed inappropriate to me to create a solid object. I wanted to express a notion of transparency.'

This is not, of course, the first building by Frank Gehry in the capital. Well before the Guggenheim Bilbao put him on the European art map, he designed what was originally the American Center (now the Cinémathèque Française) in 1994, giving the city a taste of his deconstructionist style. But the Fondation involves a new level of scale and complexity.

In a combination of extravagance and apparent weightlessness, a series of glass sails hover over the white concrete 'icebergs' of the galleries beneath. The building is intended to change with the light at different times of day and be integrated with the surrounding nature, right down to tree-lined terraces beneath the glass. The seemingly fluid glass sails are composed of thousands of panels of curved glass, developed with the help of a 3D modelling programme adapted from the same aerospace technology used by Dassault Aviation. All very high-tech, but it's also intended to have a low environmental impact, using the sails to create shade and reduce energy consumption.

The appointment of Suzanne Pagé, highly respected long-time director of the Musée d'Art Moderne de la Ville de Paris, has given the project credibility within the Paris art world. As to what will actually be on show, that remains a mystery. The Foundation is keeping details of its first exhibition firmly under wraps and, at the time of writing, refused even to confirm any of the artists. However, we can probably expect to see some of the artists who have created handbags for Louis Vuitton, such as Takashi Murakami and Richard Prince, along with Danish artist Olafur Eliasson, who designed the pitch-black lift leading to the rooftop gallery at Louis Vuitton's Champs-Elysées flagship. Then there are artists who Arnault is said to have purchased during the past 20 years – a panoply of big names including Jean-Michel Basquiat, Pierre Huyghe, Jeff Koons, Gilbert & George, Andreas Gursky and Chinese artist Zang Huan.

A bit of an anomaly, this. Grand and imperial, with a bit of Baroque thrown in for good measure, and located within sight of high-end glitz, Sir Winston does a nice line in jazz and gospel brunches on a Sunday. Colonial knick-knacks, chesterfields and chandeliers make up the decor, with Winnie himself framed behind a sturdy bar counter. A battalion of whiskies stands guard beside him, and the wine list is equally *recherché*.

Shops & Services

Abercrombie & Fitch
23 av des Champs-Elysées, 8th (08.05.11.15.59, www.abercrombie.com). M° Franklin D Roosevelt. **Open** 10am-8pm Mon-Sat; 11am-7pm Sun. **Map** p92 D4 ❸ **Fashion**
The US brand's store has been causing a stir on the Champs since it opened in 2011, with banging tunes and topless male models in the doorway. Like its sister stores in London and New York, the box-hedged garden, dimmed lighting and scent of aftershave make the place feel more like a club than a shop.

★ Alléosse
13 rue Poncelet, 17th (01.46.22.50.45, www.fromage-alleosse.com). M° Ternes. **Open** 9am-1pm, 4-7pm Tue-Thur; 9am-1pm, 3.30-7pm Fri, Sat; 9am-1pm Sun. **Map** p92 B3 ❸ **Food & drink**
People cross town for these cheeses – wonderful farmhouse camemberts, delicate st-marcellins, a choice of *chèvres* and several rarities.

★ Balenciaga
10 av George V, 8th (01.47.20.21.11, www.balenciaga.com). M° Alma Marceau. **Open** 10am-7pm Mon-Sat. **Map** p93 E4 ❹ **Fashion**
With Alexander Wang now at the helm, the Spanish fashion house is ahead of Japanese and Belgian designers in the hip stakes. Floating fabrics contrast with dramatic cuts, producing a sophisticated urban style. Bags and shoes are also available.

Balmain
44 rue François 1er, 8th (01.47.20.57.58, www.balmain.com). M° George V. **Open** 10.30am-7pm Mon-Sat. **Map** p92 D4 ❹ **Fashion**
A large portrait of the late Pierre Balmain surveys the scene at his eponymous shop. What would he have made of the clothes around him? Long gone are the afternoon dresses with perfectly positioned waists, full skirts and trapezoidal necklines. While the clothes are still astonishingly expensive and exquisitely finished, the racks are these days lined with studded jackets and animal print drainpipes.

Les Caves Augé
116 bd Haussmann, 8th (01.45.22.16.97, www.cavesauge.com). M° St-Augustin. **Open** 10am-7.30pm Mon-Sat. Closed Mon in Aug. **Map** p92 C5 ❹ **Food & drink**

Marks & Spencer. *See p104.*

Les Caves Augé is the oldest wine shop in Paris – Marcel Proust was a regular customer – and offers a serious and professional service.

Les Caves Taillevent
228 rue du Fbg-St-Honoré, 8th (01.45.61.14.09, www.taillevent.com). M° Charles de Gaulle Etoile or Ternes. **Open** 10am-7.30pm Mon-Sat. Closed 1st 3wks Aug. **Map** p92 C4 ❹ **Food & drink**
Choose from a vast range of wines at this boutique arm of the smart Taillevent restaurant. Sommeliers are on hand to help you choose and there are bottles for every budget.

Comme des Garçons
54 rue du Fbg-St-Honoré, 8th (01.53.30.27.27, www.comme-des-garcons.com). M° Concorde. **Open** 11am-7pm Mon-Sat. **Map** p92 D5 ❹ **Fashion**
Rei Kawakubo's design ideas and revolutionary mix of materials have heavily influenced fashions of the past two decades, and are showcased in this fibreglass store.
▶ *Comme des Garçons Parfums (23 pl du Marché-St-Honoré, 1st, 01.47.03.15.03) provides a futuristic setting for the brand's fragrances.*

Dior
26-30 av Montaigne, 8th (01.40.73.73.73, www.dior.com). M° Franklin D. Roosevelt. **Open** 10am-7pm Mon-Sat. **Map** p92 D4 ❹ **Fashion**

EXPLORE

The Dior universe is here on avenue Montaigne, from the main prêt-à-porter store and jewellery, menswear and eyewear to Baby Dior.
Other locations throughout the city.

Drugstore Publicis
133 av des Champs-Elysées, 8th (01.44.43.79.00, www.publicisdrugstore.com). Mº Charles de Gaulle Etoile. **Open** 8am-2am Mon-Fri; 10am-2am Sat, Sun. **Map** p92 D3 ⑯ **Department store**
A 1960s legend, Drugstore Publicis was clad with neon swirls following a renovation a few years ago; a glass-and-steel café stretches out on to the pavement. On the ground floor there's a newsagent, pharmacy, bookshop and upmarket deli full of quality olive oils and elegant biscuits. The basement is a macho take on Colette, keeping selected design items and lifestyle magazines, and replacing high fashion with fine wines and a cigar cellar.

Erès
2 rue Tronchet, 8th (01.47.42.28.82, www.eres.fr). Mº Madeleine. **Open** 10am-7pm Mon-Sat. **Map** p92 D6 ⑰ **Fashion**
Erès's beautifully cut swimwear has embraced a sexy '60s look complete with buttons on the low-cut briefs. To make life easier, the top and bottom can be purchased in different sizes or you can buy one piece of a bikini.
Other locations throughout the city.

Fauchon
26 & 30 pl de la Madeleine, 8th (01.70.39.38.00, www.fauchon.com). Mº Madeleine. **Open** *No.26* 8am-8.30pm Mon-Sat. *No.30* 9am-8pm Mon-Sat. **Map** p92 D6 ⑱ **Food & drink**
The city's most famous food shop is worth a visit, particularly for the beautifully packaged gift items and the stunning pastries and cakes – or, as Fauchon likes to call them, *'le snacking chic'*.

Givenchy
28 rue du Fbg-St-Honoré, 8th (01.42.68.31.00, www.givenchy.com). Mº Madeleine. **Open** 10.30am-7pm Mon-Sat. **Map** p92 D6 ⑲ **Fashion**
A few years ago, Givenchy opened this handsome flagship store for men's and women's prêt-à-porter and accessories. It incorporates surreal rooms within rooms – cut-out boxes lined with white, black or mahogany panelling – providing an art gallery setting for Givenchy's cutting-edge, sculptural and monochrome designs.

Glup's
84 av des Champs-Elysées, 8th (01.42.89.84.11, www.glups.fr). Mº George V. **Open** 11am-11.45pm Mon, Fri; 10am-11.45pm Tue-Thur, Sat, Sun. **Map** p92 D4 ⑳ **Food & drink**
With 33 stores throughout France and one in Switzerland, Glup's is the brash younger sibling to the charming, wood-panelled village *confiserie.*

Among the 250 kinds of candy sold in help-yourself dispensers are fizzy Smurfs, sugar-speckled Eiffel Towers, kilos of jelly beans, giant spider gummies, chocolate marshmallows and Magnificat milk caramels wrapped in gold paper.

Guerlain
68 av des Champs-Elysées, 8th (01.45.62.52.57, www.guerlain.com). Mº Franklin D. Roosevelt. **Open** 10.30am-8pm Mon-Sat; noon-7pm Sun. **Map** p92 D4 ㉑ **Health & beauty**
The golden oldie of luxury beauty products and scents is looking as ravishing as ever. Head to the first floor to get the full measure of the history behind the house that created the mythic Samsara, Mitsouko and L'Heure Bleue.
Other locations 2 pl Vendôme, 1st (01.42.60.68.61); 29 rue de Sèvres, 6th (01.42.22.46.60); 66 bd du Montparnasse, 15th (01.43.20.95.40).

★ Hédiard
21 pl de la Madeleine, 8th (01.43.12.88.88, www.hediard.fr). Mº Madeleine. **Open** 9am-8pm Mon-Sat. **Map** p92 D6 ㉒ **Food & drink**
Hédiard's charming shop dates back to 1880, when it introduced exotic foods to Paris, specialising in rare teas and coffees, spices, jams and candied fruits.
Other locations throughout the city.

Hugo Boss
115 av des Champs-Elysées, 8th (01.53.57.35.40, www.hugoboss.com). Mº George V. **Open** 10.30am-8pm Mon-Sat; 11am-6.30pm Sun. **Map** p92 D4 ㉓ **Fashion**
Hugo Boss's flagship store is all straight lines and steely greys – rather like the signature Boss suits worn by the sales assistants. Big screens flash images of Hugo Boss catwalk shows – inspiration for your shopping as you browse the minimalist rows of the brand's smart designer garb. Boss has other outlets dotted around town, but this is its biggest store.

★ Jabugo Ibérico & Co
11 rue Clément-Marot, 8th (01.47.20.03.13). Mº Franklin D. Roosevelt. **Open** 10am-9pm Mon-Sat. **Map** p92 D4 ㉔ **Food & drink**
Spanish hams here have the Bellota-Bellota label, meaning that the pigs have been allowed to feast on acorns. Manager Philippe Poulachon compares his cured hams to the delicacy of truffles.
▶ *Restaurant Bellota-Bellota (18 rue Jean-Nicot, 7th, 01.53.59.96.96) also sells hams at its adjoining épicerie.*

Lanvin
22 rue du Fbg St-Honoré, 8th (01.44.71.31.73, www.lanvin.com). Mº Concorde or Madeleine. **Open** 10.30am-7pm daily. **Map** p92 D6 ㉕ **Fashion**
The couture house that began in the 1920s with Jeanne Lanvin has been reinvented by the talented and indefatigable Albert Elbaz. In October 2007, he

EXPLORE

unveiled this, the revamped showroom that set new aesthetic standards for luxury fashion retailing, incorporating original furniture from the Lanvin archive that has been restored. All this would be nothing, of course, if the clothes were not exquisite.

LE66

66 av des Champs-Elysées, 8th (01.53.53.33.80, www.le66.fr). M° George V. **Open** 11am-8pm Mon-Fri; 11am-8.30pm Sat; 1-8pm Sun. **Map** p92 D4 ⑤⑤ **Fashion**

This fashion concept store is youthful and accessible, with an ever-changing selection of hip brands. Assistants, who are also the buyers and designers, make for a motivated team. The shop takes the form of three transparent modules.

★ Louis Vuitton

101 av des Champs-Elysées, 8th (01.53.57.52.00, www.louisvuitton.fr). M° George V. **Open** 10am-8pm Mon-Sat; 11am-7pm Sun. **Map** p92 D3 ⑤⑦ **Fashion**

The 'Promenade' flagship sets the tone for Vuitton's global image, from the 'bag bar', bookstore and jewellery department to the women's and men's ready-to-wear. Contemporary art, videos by Tim White Sobieski and a pitch-black elevator by Olafur Eliasson complete the picture. Accessed by lift, the Espace Vuitton hosts temporary art exhibits – but the star of the show is the view over Paris. **Other locations** 6 pl St-Germain-des-Prés, 6th (01.45.49.62.32); 22 av Montaigne, 8th (01.45.62.47.00).

Marché Président-Wilson

Av Président-Wilson, 16th. M° Alma-Marceau or Iéna. **Open** 7am-2.30pm Wed; 7am-3pm Sat. **Map** p92 E3 ⑤⑧ **Market**

A classy market attracting the city's top chefs, who snap up ancient vegetable varieties.

Marks & Spencer

100 av des Champs-Elysées & 1 rue de Berri, 8th (01.56.69.19.20, www.marksandspencer.fr). M° George V. **Open** 10am-10pm daily. **Map** p92 D4 ⑤⑨ **Department store**

Marks opened its new Paris store in late 2011. While most French people love nothing more than criticising British food, give them an M&S chicken tikka sarnie and the superlatives flow like wine from a barrel. They're also secret admirers of British fashion, and M&S offers cuts, colours and fabrics not readily available in France. *Photo p102.*

Nauti Store

18bis rue Brunel, 17th (01.44.09.04.48, www. nautistore.fr). M° Argentine. **Open** 10am-7pm Mon-Sat. **Map** p92 C2 ⑥⓪ **Accessories**

This shop stocks a vast range of sailing clothes and shoes from labels such as Helly Hansen, Musto, Aigle and Sebago.

Paul Smith

3 rue du Fbg-St-Honoré, 8th (01.42.68.27.10, www.paulsmith.co.uk). M° Concorde. **Open** 10.30am-7pm Mon-Sat. **Map** p92 D6 ⑥① **Fashion**

A 'so British' atmosphere is cultivated with '40s wallpaper, antiques, old books and bric-a-brac, much of it for sale along with the colourful shirts and knitwear in which Smith excels. Collections for men, women and children, along with eyewear and accessories, are all gathered in this elegant apartment. **Other locations** 70 rue de Grenelle, 6th (01.42.22.66.67); 22 bd Raspail, 7th (01.53.63.08.74).

Prada

10 av Montaigne, 8th (01.53.23.99.40, www.prada.com). M° Alma Marceau. **Open** 10am-7pm Mon-Sat. **Map** p92 E4 ⑥② **Fashion**

Miuccia Prada's elegant stores pull in fashionistas of all ages. Handbags of choice are complemented by the coveted ready-to-wear range. **Other locations** 5 rue de Grenelle, 6th (01.45.48.53.14); 6 rue du Fbg-St-Honoré, 8th (01.58.18.63.30).

Roger Vivier

29 rue du Fbg-St-Honoré, 8th (01.53.43.00.85, www.rogervivier.com). M° Madeleine. **Open** 11am-7pm Mon-Sat. **Map** p92 D6 ⑥③ **Accessories**

The fashion editors' shoeman of choice, Vivier is credited with inventing the stiletto.

Sephora

70 av des Champs-Elysées, 8th (01.53.93.22.50, www.sephora.fr). M° Franklin D. Roosevelt. **Open** 10am-8.30pm daily. **Map** p92 D4 ⑥④ **Health & beauty**

Founded in 1969, the Sephora chain has more than 750 shops around the globe. The Champs-Elysées flagship houses 12,000 brands of scent and slap. **Other locations** throughout the city.

Sony Style

39 av George V, 8th (09.69.39.39.39, www. boutiquegeorge5.fr). M° George V. **Open** 11am-7pm Mon-Sat. **Map** p92 D4 ⑥⑤ **Electronics & photography**

Sony's concept store brings high-tech gadgets and zen decor together in an *hôtel particulier*. Phones, cameras, computers and PlayStations are all here.

MONCEAU & BATIGNOLLES

In the 8th & 17th arrondissements.

Parc Monceau, with its wonderful neo-antique follies and large lily pond, lies at the far end of avenue Hoche (the main entrance is on boulevard de Courcelles, the circular pavilion by Ledoux). Three museums capture the extravagance of the area when it was newly fashionable in the 19th century: the

EXPLORE

Alexander Nevsky Cathedral.

Musée Jacquemart-André, with its Old Masters, the **Musée Nissim de Camondo** (superb 18th-century decorative arts), and the **Musée Cernuschi** (Chinese art). There are some nice exotic touches too, such as the red lacquer **Galerie Ching Tsai Too** (48 rue de Courcelles, 8th), built in 1926 for a dealer in oriental art near the wrought-iron gates of Parc Monceau, and the onion domes of the Russian Orthodox **Alexander Nevsky Cathedral** on rue Daru. Built in the mid 19th century, when a stay in Paris was essential to the education of every Russian aristocrat, it is still very much at the heart of an émigré little Russia.

The Quartier des Batignolles to the north-east towards place de Clichy is more working class, housing the rue de Lévis market, tenements lining the deep railway canyon and square des Batignolles park, with the pretty **Eglise Ste-Marie-de-Batignolles**. It's fast becoming trendy, with a good restaurant scene.

Sights & Museums

★ FREE Alexander Nevsky Cathedral
12 rue Daru, 8th (01.42.27.37.34, www.cathedrale-orthodoxe.com). M° Courcelles. **Open** times vary. **Admission** free. Map p92 C4 ⑥⑤
All onion domes, icons and incense, this Russian Orthodox church was completed in 1861 in the neo-Byzantine Novgorod style of the 1600s by the tsar's architect Kouzmin, who was also responsible for the Fine Arts Academy in St Petersburg.

FREE Cimetière des Batignolles
8 rue St-Just, 17th (01.53.06.38.68). M° Porte de Clichy. **Open** *16 Mar-6 Nov* 8am-5.45pm Mon-Fri; 8.30am-5.45pm Sat; 9am-5.45pm Sun & public hols. *7 Nov-15 Mar* 8am-5.15pm Mon-Fri; 8.30am-5.15pm Sat; 9am-5.15pm Sun & public hols. **Admission** free. Map p92 A5 ⑥⑦

Squeezed inside the Périphérique are the graves of poet Paul Verlaine, Surrealist André Breton, and Léon Bakst, costume designer of the Ballets Russes.

★ FREE Musée Cernuschi
7 av Vélasquez, 8th (01.53.96.21.50, www.cernuschi.paris.fr). M° Monceau or Villiers. **Open** 10am-6pm Tue-Sun. **Admission** free. *Temporary exhibitions* €7; €3.50-€5 reductions; free under-14s. Map p92 B5 ⑥⑧
Since the banker Henri Cernuschi built a *hôtel particulier* by the Parc Monceau for the treasures he found in the Far East in 1871, this collection of Chinese art has grown steadily. The fabulous displays range from legions of Han and Wei dynasty funeral statues to refined Tang celadon wares.

★ Musée Jacquemart-André
158 bd Haussmann, 8th (01.45.62.11.59, www.musee-jacquemart-andre.com). M° Miromesnil or St-Philippe-du-Roule. **Open** 10am-6pm daily (late opening Mon & Sat until 8.30pm during exhibitions). **Admission** €11; €9.50 reductions; free under-7s. Map p92 C4 ⑥⑨
Long terrace steps and a pair of handsome stone lions usher visitors into this grand 19th-century mansion, home to a collection of *objets d'art* and fine paintings. The collection was assembled by Edouard André and his artist wife Nélie Jacquemart, using money inherited from his rich banking family. The mansion was built to order to house their art hoard, which includes Rembrandts, Tiepolo frescoes and various paintings by Italian masters Uccello, Mantegna and Carpaccio.
▶ *The adjacent tearoom (open 11.45am-5.30pm daily) is a favourite with the smart lunch set.*

★ Musée National Jean-Jacques Henner
43 av de Villiers, 17th (01.47.63.42.73, www.musee-henner.fr). M° Malesherbes. **Open** 11am-6pm Mon, Wed-Sun (11am-9pm 1st Thur

Parc Monceau.

of mth). **Admission** €5; €3 reductions; free under-18s, under-26s (EU citizens), all 1st Sun of mth. **Map** p92 B4 🕖

The Musée National Jean-Jacques Henner traces the life of one of France's most respected artists, from his humble beginnings in Alsace in 1829 to his rise as one of the most sought-after painters in Paris. On the first floor, Alsatian landscapes and family portraits are a reminder of the artist's lifelong attachment to his native region. What brought Henner most acclaim (and criticism), however, was his trademark nymph paintings. The museum will be closed until 1 April 2015 for renovations.

Musée Nissim de Camondo

63 rue de Monceau, 8th (01.53.89.06.50, www. lesartsdecoratifs.fr). M° Monceau or Villiers. **Open** 10am-5.30pm Wed-Sun. **Admission** €7.50; €5.50 reductions; free under-18s, under-26s (EU citizens). PMP. **Map** p92 C5 🕗

Put together by Count Moïse de Camondo, this collection is named after his son Nissim, who was killed in World War I. Moïse replaced the family's two houses near Parc Monceau with this palatial residence and lived here in a style in keeping with his love of the 18th century. Grand first-floor reception rooms are filled with furniture by craftsmen of the Louis XV and XVI eras, Sèvres and Meissen porcelain, Savonnerie carpets and Aubusson tapestries.

FREE Parc Monceau

Bd de Courcelles, av Hoche, rue Monceau, 8th. M° Monceau. **Open** *Nov-Mar* 7am-8pm daily. *Apr-Oct* 7am-10pm daily. **Admission** free. **Map** p92 B4 🕘

Surrounded by grand *hôtels particuliers* and elegant Haussmannian apartments, Monceau is a favourite with well-dressed children and their nannies. It was laid out in the 18th century for the Duc de Chartres in the English style, with a lake, lawns and a variety of follies: an Egyptian pyramid, a Corinthian colonnade, a Venetian bridge and sarcophagi.

Restaurants

Atao

86 rue Lemercier, 17th (01.46.27.81.12). M° La Fourche. **Open** noon-2pm, 7-10pm Tue-Sun. **Main courses** €30. **Map** p92 A5 🕖 **Seafood**

Atao looks like a dream of a fisherman's cabin – marine blue on the outside, then wood, white and colourful touches inside, with an old mariner's portrait, an anchor and a black-and-white flag. At night, soft candlelight enhances the atmosphere even further. This pretty place is owned by the daughter of an oyster farmer from Morbihan, who serves up platters of fine oysters – flat native *plates* and huge Japanese *creuses* (alive and cooked). Main dishes – fish stew, dorado with basil, scallop carpaccio – are pricey but worth every cent.

Bar à Sushi Izimi

55 bd des Batignolles, 8th (01.45.22.43.55, www.lebarasushi.com). M° Villiers. **Open** noon-2.30pm, 7.30-10pm Tue-Sat. **Main courses** €4.50-€28. **Prix fixe** *Lunch* €12.50-€17.50. *Dinner* €23-€90. **Map** p92 B5 🕖 **Sushi**

Blink and you'll miss it, but this tiny sushi bar punches far above its size. It quickly made a name for itself when it opened in 2011, educating Paris diners about the delights of fatty tuna, eel and wagyu beef. The eel arrives still smoking, perfectly grilled, swiped with a delicious sweet sauce then arranged in a *chirachi* bowl with fish, omelette and prawns on a warm bed of rice and sesame. The wagyu beef, with its remarkable texture and nutty flavour, is served as *tataki* (a sort of half-cooked carpaccio) or sushi. Have it with one of the sakes – a fruity Tatenokawa, a flavourful Muroka, an intense Kenbishi, or a taster of all three.

Cafés & Bars

Les Caves Populaires
22 rue des Dames, 17th (01.53.04.08.32).
M° Place de Clichy. **Open** 8am-2am Mon-Sat;
11am-2am Sun. **Map** p92 B6 ⑦
An old soak props up the bar with his *petit rouge*,
while others play chess and groups of bobos (bourgeois bohemians) revel in the cheap prices – from
€2.40 for a glass of quaffable wine, €2.70 for a beer
and €5.50 for a cheese platter. It's a charming place
and vaguely reminiscent of a wooden chalet, hence
its second name, Les Caves du Châlet.

L'Endroit
67 pl du Dr-Félix-Lobligeois, 17th (01.42.29.50.00).
M° La Fourche or Rome. **Open** 11am-2am Mon,
Tue; 11am-3am Thur; 11am-4am Fri, Sat; 11am-
midnight Sun. **Map** p92 A5 ⑦
L'Endroit is one of the best spots in old Batignolles
village, with views over neoclassical Ste-Marie-des-
Batignolles church, a cool thirtysomething crowd,
decent wines, cocktails a go-go and excellent food
that won't break the bank.

Shops & Services

French Touche
1 rue Jacquemont, 17th (01.42.63.31.36,
www.frenchtouche.com). M° La Fourche.
Open 1-8pm Tue-Fri; 11am-8pm Sat. **Map**
p92 A6 ⑦ **Accessories**
Bags adorn the walls, trinkets sit atop small wooden
shelves, and lamps are dotted around the room –
French Touche is a shop where one could happily
rummage for hours on end. Nestled in the heart of
the 17th for the past decade, this 'gallery of touching
objects' was one of the first concept stores in the capital. Dreamed up by the lovely Valérie, it's teeming
with original creations, from retro knitted cat badges
to Beatles patches and micro-notebook keychains.
At the back is a fascinating selection of clothing,
boots and crockery unearthed from antiques stores.

Fromagerie Dubois et Fils
80 rue de Tocqueville, 17th (01.42.27.11.38). M°
Malesherbes or Villiers. **Open** 8am-1pm, 4-8pm
Tue-Thur; 8am-8pm Fri, Sat; 9am-1pm Sun. Closed
1st 3wks Aug. **Map** p92 A4 ⑦ **Food & drink**
Superchef darling Dubois stocks 80 types of goat's
cheese, plus prized, aged st-félicien.

Marché Batignolles
Rue Lemercier, 17th. M° Brochant. **Open**
8.30am-1pm, 3.30-8pm Tue-Fri; 8.30am-8pm
Sat; 8.30am-2pm Sun. **Map** p92 A5 ⑦ **Market**
Batignolles is more down to earth than the better-
known Raspail organic market, with a quirky selection of stallholders, many of whom produce what
they sell. Prices are higher here than at ordinary
markets, but the goods are worth it.

Thomas Cook
45 av de Wagram, 17th (01.55.37.72.72,
www.thomascook.fr). M° Opéra. **Open** 10am-
7pm Mon-Fri; 10am-1pm, 2-6.30pm Sat. **Map**
p92 C3 ⑨ **Travel**
Travel agent with more than 30 branches in and
around Paris.
Other locations throughout the city.

Le Vin en Tête
30 rue des Batignolles, 17th (01.44.69.04.57,
www.levinentete.fr). M° Place de Clichy or Rome.
Open 10am-2pm, 4-9pm Mon-Thur; 10am-
9pm Fri, Sat; 10.30am-1.30pm, 4.30-8pm Sun.
Map p92 A5 ⑨ **Food & drink**
Le Vin en Tête has been supplying wine enthusiasts
for more than a decade now. Not content with stocking more than 1,200 wines and spirits, it also seeks
to explain the science behind wine-making to as
many people as possible. If you're interested in learning the subtle differences between natural and bio-
dynamic wine (80% of the wines here are produced
biodynamically), you can sign up for one of the
numerous courses or go to the weekly tastings.

PASSY & AUTEUIL

In the 16th arrondissement.

West of l'Etoile, the extensive 16th
arrondissement is the epitome of bourgeois
respectability, with grandiose apartments and
exclusive residences lining the private roads.
It's also home to some seminal examples of
modernist architecture, plus several of the city's
most important museums. When Balzac lived
at no.47 rue Raynouard in the 1840s, Passy was
a country village (it was absorbed into the city
in 1860) where the rich came to take cures at its
mineral springs – a history alluded to by rue
des Eaux. The novelist's former abode, **Maison
de Balzac**, is open to the public. The **Musée
du Vin** is of interest if only for its setting in
the cellars of the wine-producing Abbaye de
Minimes, destroyed in the Revolution. Rue de
Passy, formerly the village high street, and
parallel rue de l'Assomption, are the focus of
local life, with fashion shops and *traiteurs*, the
department store **Franck et Fils** (80 rue de
Passy, 16th, 01.44.14.38.00, www.francketfils.fr)
and a covered market.

West of the former high-society pleasure
gardens of the Jardin du Ranelagh you'll find
the **Musée Marmottan**, with its superb
collection of Monet's late water-lily canvases,
other Impressionists and Empire furniture.

Next to the Pont de Grenelle stands the circular
Maison de Radio France, the giant home of
state broadcasting, which is currently undergoing
a massive six-year renovation. From here, in
more upmarket Auteuil, you can head up rue

EXPLORE

La Fontaine, the best place to find art nouveau architecture by Hector Guimard, of *métro* entrance fame. He also designed the less ambitious nos.19 and 21. At no.96 pay homage to Marcel Proust, who was born here.

Nearby, the **Fondation Le Corbusier** occupies two of the architect's avant-garde houses in square du Dr-Blanche. A little further up rue du Dr-Blanche sculptor Henri Bouchard himself commissioned the studio and house that is now the dusty Atelier-Musée Henri Bouchard. Much of the rest of Auteuil is private territory, with exclusive streets of residences off rue Chardon-Lagache; the studio of 19th-century sculptor Jean-Baptiste Carpeaux remains, looking rather lost, at no.39 boulevard Exelmans. The top storey was added later by Guimard.

West of the 16th, across the Périphérique, sprawls the parkland of **Bois de Boulogne**. At porte d'Auteuil is the romantic **Jardin des Serres d'Auteuil** and sports venues the **Parc des Princes**, home of football club Paris St-Germain, and **Roland Garros**, host of the French Tennis Open. Another attraction is slated to open in 2014: the much-delayed **Fondation Louis Vuitton** (*see p101*).

Sights & Museums

★ FREE Bois de Boulogne
16th. Mᵒ Les Sablons or Porte Dauphine.
Admission free. **Map** p92 C1 ③②
Covering 865 hectares, the Bois was once the Forêt de Rouvray hunting grounds. It was landscaped in the 1860s, when artificial grottoes and waterfalls were created around the Lac Inférieur. The Jardin de Bagatelle is famous for its roses, daffodils and water lilies, and contains an orangery that rings to the sound of Chopin in summer. The Jardin d'Acclimatation (*see p249*) is a children's amusement park. The Bois also boasts two racecourses (Longchamp and Auteuil), sports clubs and stables, and restaurants, including the smart Le Pré Catelan (01.44.14.41.00, www.precatelanparis.com).

Castel Béranger
14 rue La Fontaine, 16th. Mᵒ Jasmin.
Map p93 G1 ③③
Guimard's masterpiece of 1895-98 epitomises art nouveau in Paris. From outside you can see his love of brick, wrought iron and asymmetry, and his renunciation of harsh angles not found in nature. The faces on the balconies are thought to be self-portraits, inspired by Japanese figures, to ward off evil spirits.

Fondation Le Corbusier
Maison La Roche, 10 square du Dr-Blanche, 16th (01.42.88.75.72, www.fondationlecorbusier.fr). Mᵒ Jasmin. **Open** 1.30-6pm Mon; 10am-6pm Tue-Sat. Closed Aug. **Admission** €5; €3 reductions; free under-14s. **No credit cards. Map** p93 G1 ③④

Designed by Le Corbusier in 1923 for a Swiss art collector, this house shows the architect's ideas in practice, with its stilts, strip windows, roof terraces and balconies, built-in furniture and an unsuspected use of colour inside: sludge green, blue and pinky beige. A sculptural cylindrical staircase and split volumes create a variety of geometrical vistas; inside, Le Corbusier's own neo-Cubist paintings and furniture sit alongside pieces by Perriand. The adjoining Maison Jeanneret houses the foundation's extensive library.

FREE Le Jardin des Serres d'Auteuil
3 av de la Porte d'Auteuil, 16th. Mᵒ Porte d'Auteuil. **Open** *Winter* 10am-5pm daily. *Summer* 10am-6pm daily. **Admission** free. **Map** p93 G1 ③⑤
These romantic glasshouses were opened in 1895 to cultivate plants for Paris parks and public spaces. Today, there are seasonal displays of orchids and begonias. Look out for the tropical pavilion, which is home to palms, birds and Japanese ornamental carp.

FREE Maison de Balzac
47 rue Raynouard, 16th (01.55.74.41.80). Mᵒ Passy. **Open** 10am-6pm Tue-Sun. **Admission** free. *Exhibitions* €4; €2-€3 reductions; free under-13s. **Map** p93 F2 ③⑥
Honoré de Balzac rented this apartment in 1840 to escape his creditors. Mementos include first editions and letters, plus portraits of friends and the novelist's mistress Mme Hanska. Along with a 'family tree' of his characters that extends across several walls, you can see Balzac's desk and the monogrammed coffee pot that fuelled all-night work on *La Comédie Humaine*.

★ Musée Marmottan – Claude Monet
2 rue Louis-Boilly, 16th (01.44.96.50.33, www.marmottan.com). Mᵒ La Muette. **Open** 10am-6pm Tue, Wed, Fri-Sun; 10am-8pm Thur. **Admission** €10; €5 reductions; free under-7s. **Map** p93 F1 ③⑦
Originally a museum of the Empire period left to the state by collector Paul Marmottan, this old hunting pavilion has become a famed holder of Impressionist art thanks to two bequests: the first by the daughter of the doctor of Manet, Monet, Pissarro, Sisley and Renoir; the second by Monet's son Michel. Its Monet collection, the largest in the world, numbers 165 works, plus sketchbooks, palette and photos. A special circular room was created for the breathtaking late water-lily canvases; upstairs are works by Renoir, Manet, Gauguin, Caillebotte and Berthe Morisot, 15th-century primitives, a Sèvres clock and a collection of First Empire furniture.

Musée du Vin
5 square Charles Dickens, Rue des Eaux, 16th (01.45.25.63.26, www.museeduvinparis.com). Mᵒ Passy. **Open** 10am-6pm Tue-Sun. **Admission**

EXPLORE

La Pâtisserie des Rêves.

(with guidebook and glass of wine) €11.90; €9.90 reductions; free under-14s, diners in the restaurant. **Map** p93 F2 ⊛

Here the Confrères Bacchiques defend French wines from imports and advertising laws. In the cellars of an old wine-producing monastery are displays on the history of viticulture, with waxwork peasants, old tools, bottles and corkscrews. Visits finish with a wine tasting and, a paid extra, a meal. The museum is a reminder that, for centuries, Passy was a wine-growing area. Louis XIII used to stop off for a drink here after hunting in the Bois de Boulogne.

Restaurants

Astrance
4 rue Beethoven, 16th (01.40.50.84.40, www.astrancerestaurant.com). M° Passy. **Open** 12.15-1.30pm, 8.15-9pm Tue-Fri. Closed 2wks Dec, 1wk May & late July-early Aug. **Prix fixe** *Lunch* €70, €150, €230. *Dinner* €230. **Map** p93 F2 ⊛
Haute cuisine
When Pascal Barbot opened Astrance, he was praised for creating a new style of Paris restaurant – refined, yet casual and affordable. A few years later, this small, slate-grey dining room feels just like an haute cuisine restaurant. Most customers, having reserved at least a month ahead, give free rein to the chef with the 'Menu Astrance'. Barbot has an original touch, combining foie gras with slices of white mushrooms and a lemon condiment, or sweet lobster with candied grapefruit peel, a grapefruit and rosemary sorbet, and raw baby spinach. Wines are reasonably priced.

Shops & Services

La Maison du Chocolat
120 av Victor-Hugo, 16th (01.40.67.77.83, www. lamaisonduchocolat.com). M° Victor Hugo. **Open** 10am-7.30pm Mon-Sat; 10am-1pm Sun. Closed Sun in July & Aug. **Map** p92 D1 ⑳ **Food & drink**
Robert Linxe opened his first Paris shop in 1977, and has been inventing new chocolates ever since, using Asian spices, fresh fruits and herbal infusions. **Other locations** throughout the city.

La Pâtisserie des Rêves
11 rue de Longchamp, 16th (01.47.04.00.24, www.lapatisseriedesreves.com). M° Victor Hugo. **Open** *Shop* 10am-7pm Tue-Fri; 9am-7pm Sat, Sun. *Salon de thé* noon-6.30pm Fri; 9am-6.30pm Sat, Sun. **Map** p92 E3 ㉑ **Food & drink**
Looking for your dream pâtisserie? Look no further than cake-maker extraordinaire Philippe Conticini's contemporary boutique and tearoom in the 16th. The Saint-Honoré (a circular puff-pastry delight filled with whipped cream and caramelised sugar) is rectangular so that you can cut it into slices, and the famous Paris-Brest (a praline cream éclair) comes with a runny praline centre.

EXPLORE

Montmartre & Pigalle

Alas, long gone are the days when Montmartre was a tranquil village packed with windmills and vineyards, although two *moulins* and a small patch of vines do still survive. Today, perched high on the 'Butte' (Paris's highest hill), the area is tightly packed with houses spiralling round the mound below the sugary-white dome of the Sacré-Coeur. Despite the thronging tourists (chiefly around place du Tertre), it remains the most unabashedly romantic district in Paris – a place in which to climb quiet stairways, peer down narrow alleys on to ivy-clad houses, and watch the world go by in atmospheric cafés. At the foot of Montmartre, Pigalle has long had a reputation as Paris's centre for sleaze. But while peep shows do still tout for business, a younger, hipper and more wholesome crew also line the pavements nowadays, queuing to get into cool gigs and clubs.

Causses

Don't Miss

1 **Sacré-Coeur** All of Paris spread out before you (p116).

2 **Causses** Top treats at this delish deli (p121).

3 **Cimetière de Montmartre** Resting place of Truffaut, Nijinsky and others (p115).

4 **Marché de St-Ouen** Flea market fantasy (p118).

5 **Musée de Montmartre** History of the hill (p115).

MONTMARTRE

In the 18th arrondissement.

For centuries, Montmartre was a tranquil village. When Haussmann sliced through the capital during the mid 19th century, working-class families started to move out, and migrants poured into an industrialising Paris from across France. The population of Montmartre swelled. The *butte* was absorbed into the city of Paris in 1860, but remained proudly independent. Its key role in the Commune in 1871, fending off government troops, is marked by a plaque on rue du Chevalier-de-la-Barre.

Artists started to move into the area from the 1880s. Renoir found plenty of subject matter in the cafés and *guinguettes*, while Toulouse-Lautrec patronised the local bars and immortalised its cabarets in his famous posters. Later, it was frequented by Picasso and artists of the Ecole de Paris.

You can start a wander from Abbesses métro station, one of only two in Paris (along with Porte Dauphine) to retain its original art nouveau metal-and-glass awning designed by Hector Guimard. Across place des Abbesses is art nouveau **St-Jean-de-Montmartre** church, a pioneering reinforced concrete structure with turquoise mosaics around the door. Along rue des Abbesses and adjoining rue Lepic, which winds its way up the hill, are food shops, boutiques, wine merchants and cafés, including the ever-popular **Le Sancerre** (*see p118*).

**IN THE KNOW
RUE DES ABBESSES**

Rue des Abbesses got its title because it once led to the Women's Abbey of Montmartre, which was nicknamed the 'army's whorehouse on the hill' following the seduction of the abbess in 1590 by the besieging Henri de Navarre.

In the other direction from Abbesses, at 11 rue Yvonne-Le-Tac, is the Chapelle du Martyr. According to legend, St Denis picked up his head here after his execution during the third century. Rue Orsel, with a cluster of retro design, ethnic and second-hand clothes shops, leads to place Charles-Dullin, where a few cafés overlook the respected Théâtre de l'Atelier (1 pl Charles-Dullin, 18th, 01.46.06.49.24, www.theatre-atelier.com).

Up the hill, the cafés of rue des Trois-Frères are popular spots for evening drinks. The street leads into sloping place Emile-Goudeau, whose staircases, wrought-iron streetlights and old houses are particularly evocative of days gone by. The Bâteau Lavoir, a piano factory that stood at no.13, witnessed the birth of Cubism. Divided in the 1890s into a warren of studios for impoverished artists of the day, it was here that Picasso painted *Les Demoiselles d'Avignon* in 1906 and 1907, when he, Braque and Juan Gris were all residents. The building burned down in 1970, but has since been reconstructed.

On rue Lepic, which winds up the hill from rue des Abbesses, are the village's two remaining windmills: the **Moulin Radet**, which was moved here in the 17th century from its hillock in rue des Moulins near the Palais-Royal; and the **Moulin de la Galette**, site of the celebrated dancehall depicted by Renoir (now in the Musée d'Orsay) and today a smart restaurant (www.lemoulindelagalette.fr). Vincent van Gogh and his beloved brother Theo lived at no.54 from 1886 to 1888.

On tourist-swamped **place du Tertre** (*photo p115*) at the top of the hill, painters flog lurid views of Paris or offer to draw your portrait; nearby **Espace Dalí** (11 rue Poulbot, 18th, 01.42.64.40.10, www.daliparis.com) has rather more illustrious art. Round here, so legend has it, the bistro concept was born in the early 1800s, when Russian soldiers shouted '*Bistro!*' ('Quickly!') to be served. Just off the square is **St-Pierre-de-Montmartre**, the oldest church in the district, its columns bent with age. Founded by Louis VI in 1133, it's an example of early Gothic, in contrast to its extravagant mock Romano-Byzantine neighbour, the Sacré-Coeur.

For all its kitsch and swarms of tourists, **Sacré-Coeur** is well worth the visit for its 19th-century excess. Rather than the main steps, take the staircase down rue Maurice-Utrillo to pause on a café terrace on the small square at the top of rue Muller, or wander down through the adjoining park to the Halle St-Pierre. The old covered market is now used for shows of naïve art, but the surrounding square and streets, known as the **Marché St-Pierre**, are packed with fabric shops.

On the north side of place du Tertre in rue Cortot is the quiet 17th-century manor that houses the **Musée de Montmartre**, dedicated

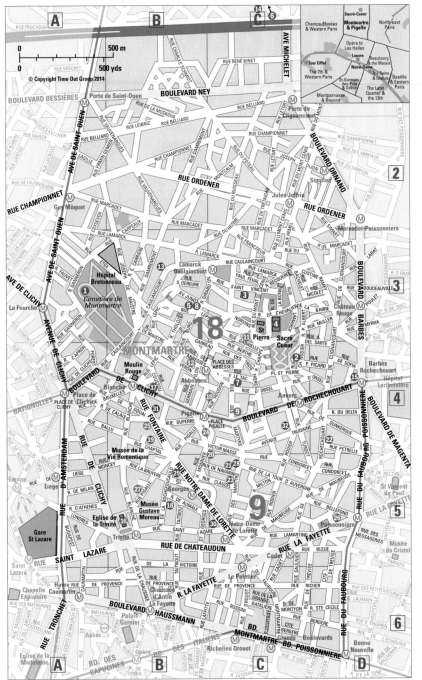

Inspiration wherever you are

REVIEWS
TICKETS
BOOKINGS

TimeOut

Our FREE apps do it all

Download them today at
timeout.com/apps

Place du Tertre. *See p112.*

to the neighbourhood and its famous former inhabitants. Dufy, Renoir and Utrillo all used to have studios in the entrance pavilion. Nearby in rue des Saules is the Montmartre vineyard, planted by local artist Poulbot in 1933 in commemoration of the vines that once covered the area. The grape harvest here every autumn is a local highlight, celebrated with great pomp. Further down the hill, among rustic, shuttered houses, is the cabaret **Au Lapin Agile** (*see p272*). This old artists' meeting point got its name from André Gill, who painted the inn sign of a rabbit (the 'lapin à Gill').

A series of squares leads to rue Caulaincourt, crossing the **Cimetière de Montmartre** (enter on avenue Rachel, reached by stairs from rue Caulaincourt or place de Clichy). A stone's throw south of here is the pocket-sized *chanson* venue **Les Trois Baudets** (*see p276*), which saw the Paris debuts of Brel, Brassens, Vian, Gainsbourg, Gréco and others. Winding down the back of the hill, avenue Junot is lined with exclusive residences, such as the avant-garde house built by Adolf Loos for poet Tristan Tzara at no.15, exemplifying his Modernist maxim: 'Ornament is crime.'

La Goutte d'Or is primarily an African and Arab neighbourhood, and can seem like a slice of the Middle East or a state under perpetual siege owing to the frequent police raids. Down rue Doudeauville, you'll find lively ethnic music shops; rue Polonceau contains African grocers and Senegalese restaurants. Mayor Delanoë has tried to attract young designers to the area by designating rue des Gardes 'rue de la mode', and square Léon is the focus for La Goutte d'Or en Fête in June, which brings together local musicians. Some of them, such as Africando and the Orchestre National de Barbès, have become well known across the capital. A market sets up under the métro tracks along boulevard de la Chapelle on Monday, Wednesday and Saturday mornings, with stalls selling exotic vegetables and rolls of African fabrics.

Further north, at porte de Clignancourt, is the city's largest flea market, the **Marché aux Puces de St-Ouen** (*see p118*), which teems with 3,000 traders and up to 180,000 bargain-hunters each weekend.

Sights & Museums

★ FREE Cimetière de Montmartre

20 av Rachel, access by staircase from rue Caulaincourt, 18th (01.53.42.36.30). Mº Blanche or Place de Clichy. **Open** *6 Nov-15 Mar* 8am-5.30pm Mon-Fri; 8.30am-5.30pm Sat; 9am-5.30pm Sun & public hols. *16 Mar-5 Nov* 8am-6pm Mon-Fri; 8.30am-6pm Sat; 9am-6pm Sun & public hols. **Admission** free. **Map** p113 A3 ❶

Truffaut, Nijinsky, Berlioz, Degas, Offenbach and German poet Heine are all buried here. So, too, are La Goulue, the first great cancan star and model for Toulouse-Lautrec, celebrated local beauty Mme Récamier, and the consumptive heroine Alphonsine Plessis, inspiration for Dumas's *La Dame aux Camélias* and Verdi's *La Traviata*, who died at the tender age of 23. Flowers are still left on the grave of pop diva and gay icon Dalida (*see p116*).

▶ *For a review of celebrity-filled Père-Lachaise cemetery, see p145.*

Musée d'Art Halle St-Pierre

2 rue Ronsard, 18th (01.42.58.72.89, www.halle saintpierre.org). Mº Anvers. **Open** *Jan-July, Sept-Dec* 10am-6pm Mon-Fri; 10am-7pm Sat; 11am-6pm Sun; *Aug* noon-6pm Mon-Fri. **Admission** prices vary. **Map** p113 C4 ❷

The former covered market in the shadow of Sacré-Coeur specialises in *art brut, art outsider* and *art singulier* from its own and other collections.

Musée de Montmartre

12 rue Cortot, 18th (01.49.25.89.37, www.museedemontmartre.fr). Mº Anvers or Lamarck-Caulaincourt. **Open** 10am-6pm daily. **Admission** €9; €5-€7 reductions; free under-10s. **Map** p113 C3 ❸

EXPLORE

EXPLORE

At the back of a garden, this 17th-century manor displays the history of the hill, with rooms devoted to composer Gustave Charpentier and a tribute to the Lapin Agile cabaret, with original Toulouse-Lautrec posters. There are paintings by Suzanne Valadon, who had a studio above the entrance pavilion, as did Renoir, Raoul Dufy and Valadon's son Maurice Utrillo. Valadon's studio is undergoing restoration and will open to the public in late 2014. The museum's three gardens have recently been renovated and make a delightful place for a stroll away from the tourist bustle of Montmartre.

▶ *In October 2014, the museum will reopen the Hôtel Demarne, doubling the exhibition space.*

★ `FREE` Sacré-Coeur

35 rue du Chevalier-de-la-Barre, 18th (01.53.41.89.00, www.sacre-coeur-montmartre.com). M° Abbesses or Anvers. **Open** *Basilica* 6am-11pm daily. *Crypt & dome* Winter 10am-5.45pm daily. Summer 9am-6.45pm daily. **Admission** free. *Crypt & dome* €8. **Map** p113 C3 ❹
Work on this enormous mock Romano-Byzantine edifice began in 1877. It was commissioned after the nation's defeat by Prussia in 1870, voted for by the Assemblée Nationale and built from public subscription. Finally completed in 1914, it was consecrated in 1919 – by which time a jumble of architects had succeeded Paul Abadie, winner of the original competition. The interior boasts lavish mosaics, including 'Christ in Majesty' in the apse – one of the world's largest. It sits atop Paris's highest point, and the views are as heavenly as the surroundings.

Restaurants

Le Coq Rico

98 rue Lepic, 18th (01.42.59.82.89, www.lecoqrico.com). M° Abbesses, Blanche or Lamarck-Caulincourt. **Open** noon-2.30pm, 7.30-11pm daily. **Main courses** €21-€38. **Map** p113 B3 ❺ Bistro
Coq Rico is a classy *'bistrotisserie'*, a place where comfort food standards are transformed into gourmet treats – boiled egg comes with crunchy soldiers and

Sacré-Coeur.

truffle-infused butter, and the *planchette de béatilles* features nibble-sized pieces of chicken heart, gizzards and sticky chicken wings, all perfectly seasoned. There's a list of poultry suppliers on the menu, a transparency that appeals to health-conscious locals – even if prices are high (€95 for a whole chicken serving two to four). Wine choice is excellent.

Ma Cocotte

106 rue des Rosiers, 93400 St-Ouen (01.49.51.70.00, www.macocotte-lespuces.com). **Open** noon-3pm, 7-11pm Mon-Fri; 8am-11pm Sat, Sun. **Main courses** €17-€33. **Map** p113 C1 ❻ Bistro
See p117 **Designer Diner.**

Le Miroir

94 rue des Martyrs, 18th (01.46.06.50.73). M° Abbesses. **Open** noon-2pm, 7.30-10.30pm Tue-Sat. **Main courses** €20. **Prix fixe** *Lunch* €19, €26, €33, €42. *Dinner* €26, €33, €42. **Map** p113 C4 ❼ Bistro
This friendly modern bistro is a welcome addition to the neighbourhood. Big mirrors, red banquettes and a glass ceiling at the back give it character, while the very professional food and service reflect the owners' haute cuisine training. Expect such dishes as a salad of whelks with white beans, crisp-skinned duck and chanterelle mushrooms, and a *petit pot de crème vanille* with little chocolate cakes.

Le Moulin de la Galette

83 rue Lepic, 18th (01.46.06.84.77, www.lemoulindelagalette.eu). M° Notre-Dame-de-Lorette. **Open** noon-11pm daily. **Main courses** €25. **Prix fixe** *Lunch* €23, €29. *Dinner* €59. **Map** p113 B3 ❽ Bistro
The Butte Montmartre was once dotted with windmills, and this survivor houses a chic restaurant with a few tables in the cobbled courtyard. It's hard to

---

**IN THE KNOW
DALIDA'S MONTMARTRE**

During her 30-year career, Egyptian-born icon Dalida recorded more than 1,000 songs, scoring 45 gold records and two platinum albums, before committing suicide in the late 1980s. Much of the Dalida myth is rooted in Montmartre: she lived in the 'Castle of Sleeping Beauty', a four-storey house on rue d'Orchampt; place Dalida is graced by a bronze bust of the idol; and her grave in the Montmartre cemetery is a place of pilgrimage.

imagine a lovelier setting in Montmartre, but the kitchen makes an effort nonetheless, coming up with dishes such as foie gras with melting beetroot cooked in lemon balm and juniper, and suckling pig alongside potato purée.

Cafés & Bars

La Fourmi
74 rue des Martyrs, 18th (01.42.64.70.35). M° Pigalle. **Open** 8am-2am Mon-Thur; 8am-4am Fri, Sat; 10am-2am Sun. **Map** p113 C4 **❾**
La Fourmi is an old bistro that has been converted for today's tastes, with picture windows lighting the spacious, roughshod interior, cool staff (and customers) and excellent music. The classic zinc bar is crowned by industrial lights, which helps you to see what you're reading as you rifle through the piles of flyers deciding where to go on to next.

Le Kremlin
6 rue André Antoine, 18th (no phone). M° Abbesses or Pigalle. **Open** 6pm-2am daily. **Map** p113 C4 **❿**
This new Russian outpost has been heaving from the word go – it's difficult to navigate a path to the bar to order one of the fantastic imported vodkas or original cocktails. Try the Red Star (mezcal, fresh beetroot and Carpano) or the Red Army (Gin Carpano, green chartreuse and orange bitters). Once you've finally got hold of your drink, pass an eye over the sumptuous communist red decor, punctuated with propaganda posters and Soviet-style furniture.

DESIGNER DINER
Starck is serving in the Puces de St-Ouen.

It's official: Philippe Starck has finally got over 'baroque modern' with not a single Perspex Louis XVI chair in sight at his 250-seat restaurant, **Ma Cocotte** (*see p116*), in the vast Marché aux Puces de St-Ouen flea market.

Housed in a handsome red-brick loft building at the entrance to the gorgeous Serpette antiques market, it has rather more in common with Terence Conran's taste for steel open kitchens and tiles, although perhaps that's no accident. Surfing on the current retro vogue for 1960s and '70s furniture, Habitat has opened up a 'vintage space' (77-81 rue des Rosiers, St-Ouen, www.habitat.fr/vintage) just down the road for owners of old Habitat classics to re-sell their vintage pieces.

On a wet Sunday afternoon, Ma Cocotte bustled with families and young couples queuing for a seat at the high communal tables or regular Formica ones. On the menu, conviviality is the order of the day, with litre pitchers of Starck (champagne, passionfruit, cucumber, ginger and mint); sharing plates of radish, foie gras or caviar; and mains such as rôtisserie farm chicken for four (€80) or côte de boeuf for two or three (€89), prepared by head chef Yannick Papin and a vast army of kitchen staff all decked out in Chairman Mao-style blue cap and overalls.

After years in the doldrums, the Puces is starting to show signs of life again, and the weekend crowds are sure to fancy a post-browse brunch at Ma Cocotte.

EXPLORE

Au Rendez-vous des Amis

*23 rue Gabrielle, 18th (01.46.06.01.60). M°
Abbesses.* **Open** 10am-2am daily. **Map** p113 C3 ⑪
Considering its proximity to the honeypot that is
the Sacré-Coeur, Au Rendez-vous des Amis is still
remarkably cheap, especially during happy hour
(6-9pm), making it popular with locals and foreign
students, and the odd tourist. There are some cosy
nooks round the back with plenty of upholstered
spots to choose from.

Le Sancerre

*35 rue des Abbesses, 18th (01.42.58.08.20).
M° Abbesses.* **Open** 7am-2am daily. **Map**
p113 B4 ⑫
It's official: Le Sancerre, a rock bar that attracted
everyone from alcohol-fuelled transvestites to
tourists and local bobos, has cleaned up its act. Gone
forever are the cheap beer and trashy music. Instead
you'll find a buzzing 1930s-style café with traditional
fare and bourgeois punters who fight for a spot on
the terrace. If you're in the area, pop by for a glass
of chardonnay and the special triple burgers.

Shops & Services

Arnaud Larher

*53 rue Caulaincourt, 18th (01.42.57.68.08, www.
arnaud-larher.com). M° Lamarck Caulaincourt.*
Open 10am-7.30pm Tue-Sat; 10am-1pm Sun.
Map p113 B3 ⑬ **Food & drink**
Look out for the strawberry-and-lychee flavoured
bonheur and the chocolate-and-thyme *récif* from this
master *pâtissier*.

★ Marché aux Puces de St-Ouen

*Av de la Porte de Clignancourt, 18th. M° Porte
de Clignancourt.* **Open** 11am-5pm Mon; 9am-
6pm Sat, Sun. **Map** p113 C1 ⑭ **Market**

With 3,000 traders and up to 180,000 visitors each
weekend, this is thought to be the biggest flea market
in the world. The fleas left long ago, and since 1885
what started as a rag-and-bone shantytown outside
the city limits has been organised into a series of
enclosed villages. It's now also home to Philippe
Starck's restaurant, Ma Cocotte (*see p116*).

Tati

*4 bd de Rochechouart, 18th (01.55.29.52.20,
www.tati.fr). M° Barbès Rochechouart.* **Open**
10am-7pm Mon-Fri; 9.30am-7pm Sat. **Map**
p113 D4 ⑮ **Department store**
Expect to find anything from T-shirts to wedding
dresses, as well as bargain children's clothes and
household goods at this discount heaven.
Other locations throughout the city.

PIGALLE & LA NOUVELLE ATHENES

In the 9th & 18th arrondissements

In the 1890s, Toulouse-Lautrec's posters of Jane
Avril at the Divan Japonais, Chat Noir and
Moulin Rouge, and of *chanson* star Aristide
Bruant, were landmarks of art and advertising
and immortalised Pigalle's cabarets. It's still
a happening area: Le Divan Japonais is now
Le Divan du Monde (*see p265*), a club and
music venue; a hip young crowd packs into
La Fourmi (*see p117*) opposite; and up the
hill, there's a cluster of *atelier*-boutiques where
designers have set up their sewing machines.

Along the boulevard, behind its bright red
windmill, the **Moulin Rouge** (*see p271*), once
the image of naughty 1890s Paris, is now a
cheesy tourist draw. Its befeathered dancers still
cavort across the stage, but are no substitute for

Moulin Rouge.

La Goulue and Joseph Pujol – *le pétomane* who could pass wind melodically. In stark contrast is the **Cité Véron** next door, a cobbled alley with a small theatre and cottagey buildings.

Just south of Pigalle and east of rue Blanche lies this often overlooked quarter, dubbed New Athens when it was colonised by a wave of artists, writers and composers in the early 19th century. Long-forgotten actresses and *demi-mondaines* had mansions built here; some are set in tiny rue de la Tour-des-Dames.

Just off rue Taitbout is square d'Orléans, a remarkable housing estate that was built in 1829 by English architect Edward Cresy. These flats and studios attracted the glitterati of the day, including George Sand and her lover Chopin. In the house built for Dutch painter Ary Scheffer in nearby rue Chaptal, the **Musée de la Vie Romantique** displays Sand's mementos.

The **Musée National Gustave Moreau** is reason alone to visit, featuring the artist's apartment and magnificent studio (the museum is undergoing renovations, with a full reopening in winter 2014). Fragments of bohemia can still be gleaned in the area, although Café La Roche, where Moreau met Degas for drinks and rows, has been downsized to **Café Matisse** (57 rue Notre-Dame-de-Lorette, 9th, 01.53.16.44.58). Degas painted most of his memorable ballet scenes in rue Frochot, and Renoir hired his first proper studio at 35 rue St-Georges. A few streets away in Cité Pigalle, a collection of studios, is van Gogh's last Paris house (no.5), from where he moved out to Auvers-sur-Oise. There is a plaque here, but nothing marks the building in rue Pigalle where Toulouse-Lautrec slowly drank himself to an early grave.

The area around the neoclassical **Eglise Notre-Dame-de-Lorette** was built up in Louis-Philippe's reign and was famous for its courtesans or *lorettes*, elegant ladies named after their haunt of rue Notre-Dame-de-Lorette. In 1848, Gauguin was born at no.56; from 1844 to 1857, Delacroix had a studio at no.58.

The lower stretch of rue des Martyrs is packed with tempting food shops, and a little further up the hill you should look out for the prosperous residences of the Cité Malesherbes and avenue Trudaine. Circular place St-Georges was home to the true Empress of Napoleon III's Paris: the Russian-born Madame Païva. La Païva shot herself after a passionate affair with the millionaire cousin of Chancellor Bismarck.

Sights & Museums

FREE Eglise de la Trinité
Pl Estienne-d'Orves, 9th (01.48.74.12.77, www.latriniteparis.com). M° Trinité. **Open** 7.15am-8pm Mon-Fri; 11am-8pm Sat; 8.30am-8.30pm Sun. **Admission** free. **Map** p113 B5 ⑯

Noted for its tiered bell tower, this neo-Renaissance church was constructed between 1861 and 1867. Composer Olivier Messiaen (1908-92) was organist at the church for over 30 years.

Musée de l'Erotisme
72 bd de Clichy, 18th (01.42.58.28.73, www.musee-erotisme.com). M° Blanche. **Open** 10am-2am daily. **Admission** €10; €8 reductions. **Map** p113 B4 ⑰

Seven floors of erotic art and artefacts amassed by collectors Alain Plumey and Joseph Khalif. The first three run from first-century Peruvian phallic pottery through Etruscan fertility symbols to Yoni sculptures from Nepal; the fourth gives a history of Paris brothels; and the refurbished top floors host exhibitions of modern erotic art.

★ Musée National Gustave Moreau
14 rue de La Rochefoucauld, 9th (01.48.74.38.50, www.musee-moreau.fr). M° Trinité. **Open** 10am-12.45pm, 2-5.15pm Mon, Wed, Thur; 10am-5.15pm Fri-Sun. **Admission** €5; €3 reductions; free under-18s, under-26s (EU citizens), all 1st Sun of mth. PMP. **Map** p113 B5 ⑱

This wonderful museum combines the small private apartment of Symbolist painter Gustave Moreau (1825-98) with the vast gallery he built to display his work – set out as a museum by the painter himself, and opened in 1903. Downstairs shows his obsessive collector's nature with family portraits, Grand Tour souvenirs and a boudoir devoted to the object of his unrequited love, Alexandrine Durem. Upstairs is Moreau's fantasy realm, which plunders Greek mythology and biblical scenes for canvases filled with writhing maidens, trance-like visages, mystical beasts and strange plants.

FREE Musée de la Vie Romantique
Hôtel Scheffer-Renan, 16 rue Chaptal, 9th (01.55.31.95.67, www.vie-romantique.paris.fr). M° Blanche or St-Georges. **Open** 10am-6pm Tue-Sun. *Tearoom* Apr-mid Oct 10am-5.30pm Tue-Sun. **Admission** free. *Exhibitions* prices vary. **Map** p113 B4 ⑲

When Dutch artist Ary Scheffer lived in this small villa, the area teemed with composers, writers and artists. Aurore Dupin, Baronne Dudevant (George Sand) was a guest at Scheffer's soirées, along with great names such as Chopin and Liszt. The museum is devoted to Sand, although the watercolours, lockets, jewels and plastercast of her right arm that she left behind reveal little of her ideas or affairs.

Restaurants

Buvette Gastrothèque
28 rue Henry Monnier, 9th (01.44.63.41.71, www.ilovebuvette.com). M° Pigalle or Saint-Georges. **Open** 10am-midnight Tue-Sun. **Main courses** €10. **Map** p113 C5 ⑳ **Bistro**

EXPLORE

EXPLORE

Jody Williams, a purebred New Yorker, has brought a bit of Greenwich Village to Pigalle. There's nothing ostentatious about the interior, all rough brick walls and wooden tables that sit well around the huge marble bar. The menu is a selection of small plates and fresh sandwiches, with an interesting wine list arranged by region. Sandwiches contain things like freshly made ratatouille or *brandade de morue* (cod and potato pie), or there are more substantial dishes such as *coq au vin en cocotte*.

La Maison Mère

4 rue de Navarin, 9th (01.42.81.11.00, www. lamaisonmere.fr). M° Pigalle or Saint-Georges. **Open** noon-2.30pm, 7.30-11pm Mon-Thur; noon-2.30pm, 7.30-11.30pm Fri; noon-4pm, 7.30-11.30pm Sat; noon-4pm Sun. **Main courses** €15-€24. **Prix fixe** *Lunch* €15 Mon-Fri. **Map** p113 C5 ㉑ **Bistro**

Forget any ideas of a traditional French kitchen: this place is more Mom than Mère. Embrace, instead, the New York-style decor, with white tiles, vintage furniture, enamelled mirrors, lamps disguised as bowler hats and a sign declaring: 'In food we trust'. The menu is much what you'd expect given the setting, with a few dashing bourgeois touches. Leek vinaigrette, eggs 'mimosa', bone marrow sandwiches, grilled cockerel and chocolate mousse all appear alongside crab cake, Brooklyn platters, Long Island platters and so on. The five burgers will delight enthusiasts, be it a breaded cod burger or the Black Label with its thick-cut Black Angus steak. Friendly service, decent wine and top cheesecake all go a long way towards sweetening the bill.

★ € Pétrelle

34 rue Pétrelle, 9th (01.42.82.11.02, www. petrelle.fr). M° Anvers. **Open** 8-10pm Tue-Sat. Closed 1st wk May, 4wks July/Aug & 1wk Dec. **Main courses** €25-€40. **Prix fixe** €40. **Map** p113 D4 ㉒ **Bistro**

Jean-Luc André is as inspired a decorator as he is a cook, and the quirky charm of his dining room has made it popular with fashion designers and film stars. But behind the style there's some serious substance. André seeks out the best ingredients from local producers, and the quality shines through. The no-choice menu is very good value for money (marinated sardines with tomato relish, rosemary-scented rabbit with roasted vegetables, deep-purple poached figs) – or you can splash out with luxurious à la carte dishes such as tournedos Rossini.

€ Rose Bakery

46 rue des Martyrs, 9th (01.42.82.12.80). M° Notre-Dame-de-Lorette. **Open** 9am-6pm Tue-Sun. **Main courses** €8.50-€17. **Map** p113 C5 ㉓ **British**

This English-themed café stands out for the quality of its ingredients – organic or from small producers – as well as the too-good-to-be-true puddings: carrot

cake, sticky toffee pudding and, in winter, chocolate-chestnut tart. The DIY salad plate is crunchily satisfying, but the thin-crusted *pizzettes*, soups and risottos are equally good choices. Don't expect much beyond scones in the morning except at weekends, when brunch is served to a packed-out house. **Other location** 30 rue Debelleyme, 3rd (01.49.96.54.01).

Cafés & Bars

Dirty Dick

10 rue Frochot, 9th (no phone). M° Pigalle. **Open** 7pm-2am daily. **Map** p113 B4 ㉔

SoPi (South Pigalle) welcomes another hip new venue to this once down-at-heel area. A former hostess bar (they've kept the name, evidently), the only phallic elements now are the Polynesian totems scattered throughout the bar, which has a kitsch, exotic 'tiki' vibe and lots of free-flowing rum. The flower-shirted barmen cater to the crowds with a list of 20 or so cocktails served in giant shells or miniature volcanoes (€7-€14). Enjoy a Cannibal's Dilemma or the famous Zombie. Dirty Dick is slightly bonkers and super fun – SoPi can celebrate.

Le Mansart

1 rue Mansart, 9th (01.56.92.05.99). M° Blanche or Pigalle. **Open** 9am-2am daily. **Map** p113 B4 ㉕

With its large terrace occupied by a small army of young mustachioed men wearing lumberjack shirts, Le Mansart wears its hipster credentials proudly – not surprising given its location in trendy SoPi. Inside it's packed with people elbowing each other to get to the bar, and music so loud it's hard to make yourself heard. It's not particularly cheap, but it does have table football, rare in Parisian bars.

Le Poussette Café

6 rue Pierre Sémard, 9th (01.78.10.49.00, www. lepoussettecafe.com). M° Poissonnière or Cadet. **Open** 10.30am-6.30pm Tue-Sat. **Map** p113 D5 ㉖

Fed up with the impracticalities of pushing her pram (*poussette*) into the local café, mother of two Laurence Constant designed her own parent- and child-friendly establishment. This upmarket *salon de thé* caters for the harassed parent (herbal teas, smoothies, quiches and salads) and demanding baby (purées, solids and cuddly toys).

★ Rouge Passion

14 rue Jean-Baptiste Pigalle, 9th (01.42.85.07.62, www.rouge-passion.fr). M° St Georges or Pigalle. **Open** noon-3pm Mon; noon-3pm, 7pm-midnight Tue-Fri; 7pm-midnight Sat. Closed 3wks Aug. **Map** p113 B5 ㉗

Two bright upstarts (Anne and Sébastien) determined to make their mark on Paris's bar scene are behind this venture – and they're going about it the right way. Offering a long list of wines (from just €4), free *assiettes apéros* (peanuts, olives, tapenades

La Fausse Boutique.

on toast) and decor that is perfect vintage chic, the formula is spot on. A small but mouthwatering selection of hot dishes, salads, cheese and *saucisson* platters (set lunch menus €19 or €24, mains from €15) help to soak up the wine. Look out for the tasting classes, given by a guest sommelier.

Shops & Services

★ Arnaud Delmontel
39 rue des Martyrs, 9th (01.48.78.29.33, www.arnaud-delmontel.com). M° St-Georges. **Open** 7am-8.30pm Mon, Wed-Sun. **Map** p113 C5 ㉘ **Food & drink**
With its crisp crust and chewy crumb shot through with irregular holes, Delmontel's Renaissance bread is one of the finest in Paris.
Other locations 25 rue de Levis, 17th (01.42.27.15.45); 57 rue Damrémont, 18th (01.42.64.59.63); 43 rue Douai, 9th (01.49.70.68.22).

★ Causses
55 rue Notre-Dame de la Lorette, 9th (01.53.16.10.10, www.causses.org). M° Pigalle or St-Georges. **Open** 10am-9pm Mon-Sat. **Map** p113 B5 ㉙ **Food & drink**
Causses, SoPi's (South Pigalle) new *alimentation générale extraordinaire*, offers a winning formula of quality seasonal produce (fruit 'n' veg, hams and cheeses), gourmet preserves and take-away breads, sandwiches and salads, plus a fill-your-own-bottle area next to the orange squeezing machine. You'll also find an array of interesting seasonings, including smoked salt and *sel fou* (salt mixed with oriental spices and pink peppercorns). For expats in need of a taste of home, Tyrrell's crisps, Covent Garden soups, HP sauce and English biscuits abound.

Détaille 1905
10 rue St-Lazare, 9th (01.48.78.68.50, www.detaille. com). M° Notre-Dame-de-Lorette. **Open** 11am-1pm, 2-7pm Tue-Sat. **Map** p113 C5 ㉚ **Health & beauty**
Step back in time at this gorgeous perfume shop, opened, as the name suggests, in 1905 by war artist Edouard Détaille. There are six fragrances available (three for men and three for women), all conjured up from century-old recipes.

La Fausse Boutique
32 rue Pierre Fontaine, 9th (09.52.43.25.71, www.lafausseboutique.com). M° Blanche or Pigalle. **Open** 2-8pm Mon; 11am-8pm Tue-Sat. **Map** p113 B4 ㉛ **Gifts & souvenirs**
As its name suggests, the False Boutique is an unusual spot – half-office, half-retail store. Unlike most shops labelled as 'concept stores', it doesn't sell designer clothing or luxury goods in the usual meaning of the terms, but instead focuses on so-called surrealist products. As such, you might find offbeat tourist guides such as *Paris à Gratter* (modelled on a scratchcard, where you scratch to reveal monuments) and satirical board games such as Méditations Foireuses (half-assed meditations), produced by a collective of designers who work in the offices at the back of the showroom. This is a great place to find original and unique gifts.

Marché Anvers
Pl d'Anvers, 9th. M° Anvers. **Open** 3-8.30pm Fri. **Map** p113 C4 ㉜ **Market**
An afternoon market that adds to the village atmosphere of a peaceful *quartier* down the hill from Montmartre. Among its highlights are regional vegetables, hams from the Auvergne, lovingly aged cheeses and award-winning honey.

EXPLORE

Beaubourg & the Marais

EXPLORE

For the last two decades the Marais has been one of the hippest parts of the city, packed to the hilt with modish hotels, vintage boutiques, restaurants and bars – in no small part due to its popularity with the gay crowd (this is the only part of Paris where the blokes tend to get winked at more than the ladies). But it's also prime territory for art-lovers. A vast concentration of galleries and museums, more often than not set in aristocratic 18th-century mansions spared by Haussmann, make it a charming place in which to get lost for a few hours. And as an extra bonus in 2014, the Musée Picasso is finally reopening its doors with triple the exhibition space after a five-year renovation fraught with controversy. The Marais' neighbour to the west is Beaubourg, the focal point of which is the iconic Centre Pompidou, with the city's all-important Hôtel de Ville a stone's throw to the south.

Gaîté Lyrique.

Don't Miss

1 Centre Pompidou A modern must-see – inside and out (p124).

2 Gaîté Lyrique Digital design download (p128).

3 Musée de la Chasse et de la Nature Hunting in all its stuffed glory (p131).

4 Merci Concept store with class (p140).

5 K Jacques Making sandals sexy (p140).

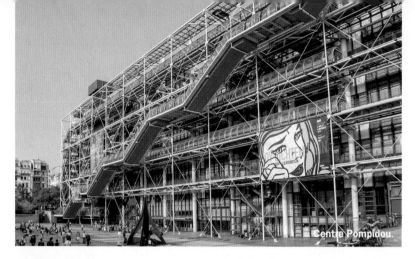
Centre Pompidou.

BEAUBOURG & HOTEL DE VILLE

In the 3rd & 4th arrondissements.

Modern architecture in Paris took off with the **Centre Pompidou**, a benchmark of inside-out high tech designed by Richard Rogers and Renzo Piano that's as much an attraction as the **Musée National d'Art Moderne** within. The piazza outside attracts all manner of street performers and artists; the reconstructed **Atelier Brancusi**, left by the sculptor to the state, was moved here from the 15th arrondissement.

On the other side of the piazza, rue Quincampoix houses galleries, bars and cobbled passage Molière. Beside the Centre Pompidou is place Igor-Stravinsky and the Fontaine Stravinsky – full of spraying kinetic fountains, and a colourful snake by the late artists Niki de Saint Phalle and Jean Tinguely – as well as the red-brick **IRCAM** music institute (*see p283*), also designed by Renzo Piano.

South of here stands the spiky Gothic **Tour St-Jacques**. Towards the river, on the site of the Grand Châtelet (a fortress put up in the 12th century to defend Pont au Change), place du Châtelet's Egyptian-themed fountain is framed by twin theatres designed by Davioud as part of Haussmann's urban improvements in the 1860s. They're now two of the city's main arts venues: the **Théâtre de la Ville** (*see p292*) and the **Théâtre du Châtelet** (*see p290*).

Beyond Châtelet, the **Hôtel de Ville** (city hall) has been the symbol of municipal power since 1260. The equestrian statue out front is of 14th-century merchant leader and rebel Etienne Marcel. Revolutionaries made the Hôtel de Ville their base in the 1871 Commune, but it was set on fire by the Communards themselves and wrecked during savage fighting. It was rebuilt according to the original model, on a larger scale, in fanciful neo-Renaissance style, with knights in armour along the roof and statues of French luminaries dotted all over the walls. The square outside was formerly called place de Grève, after the nearby riverside wharf where goods were unloaded for market. During the 16th-century Wars of Religion, Protestant heretics were burned in the square, and the guillotine stood here during the Terror, when Danton, Marat and Robespierre made the Hôtel de Ville their own seat of government. Today, the square hosts an ice rink every December, and screenings of major sports events. Across the road stands the BHV (Bazar de l'Hôtel de Ville) department store, newly restyled and retitled **BHV Marais** (*see p127*).

Sights & Museums

FREE Atelier Brancusi

Piazza Beaubourg, 4th (01.44.78.12.33, www.centrepompidou.fr). M° Hôtel de Ville or Rambuteau. **Open** 2-6pm Mon, Wed-Sun. **Admission** free. **Map** p125 B3 ❶
When Constantin Brancusi died in 1957, he left his studio and its contents to the state, and it was later moved and rebuilt by the Centre Pompidou. His fragile works in wood and plaster, the endless columns and streamlined bird forms show how Brancusi revolutionised sculpture.

★ Centre Pompidou (Musée National d'Art Moderne)

Rue St-Martin, 4th (01.44.78.12.33, www.centre pompidou.fr). M° Hôtel de Ville or Rambuteau. **Open** 11am-10pm (last entry 8pm) Mon, Wed-Sun (until 11pm some exhibitions). **Admission** *Museum & exhibitions* €11-€13; €9-€10 reductions; free under-18s, under-26s (EU citizens), all 1st Sun of mth (museum only). PMP. **Map** p125 B3 ❷
The primary colours, exposed pipes and air ducts make this one of the best-known sights in Paris. The

EXPLORE

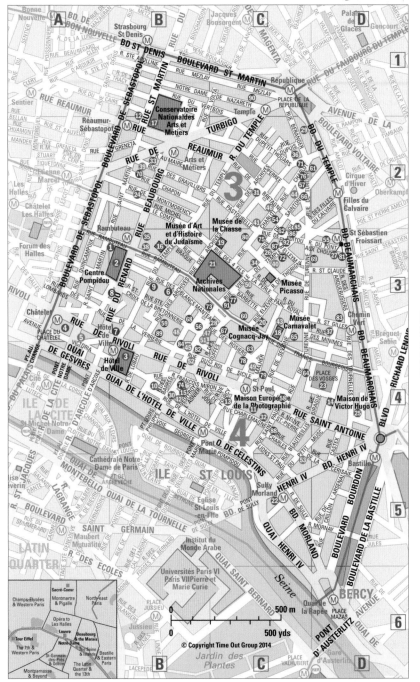

EXPLORE

EXPLORE

then-unknown Italo-British architectural duo of Renzo Piano and Richard Rogers won the competition with their 'inside-out' boilerhouse approach, which put air-conditioning, pipes, lifts and the escalators on the outside, leaving an adaptable space within. The multidisciplinary concept of modern art museum (the most important in Europe), library, exhibition and performance spaces, and repertory cinema was also revolutionary. When the centre opened in 1977, its success exceeded all expectations. After a two-year revamp, the centre reopened in 2000 with an enlarged museum, renewed performance spaces, vista-rich Georges restaurant and a mission to get back to the stimulating interdisciplinary mix of old. Entrance to the forum is free (as is the library, which has a separate entrance), but you now have to pay to go up the escalators (€3).

The Centre Pompidou (or 'Beaubourg') holds the largest collection of modern art in Europe, rivalled only in its breadth and quality by MoMA in New York. Sample the contents of its vaults (50,000 works of art by 5,000 artists) on the website, as only a fraction – about 600 works – can be seen for real at any one time. There is a partial rehang each year. For the main collection, buy tickets on the ground floor and take the escalators to level four for post-1960s art. Level five spans 1905 to 1960. There are four temporary exhibition spaces on each of these two levels (included in the ticket). Main temporary exhibitions take place on the ground floor, in gallery two on level six, in the south gallery, level one and in Espace 315, which is devoted to artists aged under 40.

On level five, the historic section takes a chronological sweep through the history of modern art, via Primitivism, Fauvism, Cubism, Dadaism and Surrealism up to American Color-Field painting and Abstract Expressionism. Masterful ensembles let you see the span of Matisse's career on canvas and in bronze, the variety of Picasso's invention, and the development of cubic orphism by Sonia and Robert Delaunay. Others on the hits list include Braque, Duchamp, Mondrian, Malevich, Kandinsky, Dalí, Giacometti, Ernst, Miró, Calder, Magritte, Rothko and Pollock. Don't miss the reconstruction of a wall of André Breton's studio, combining the tribal art, folk art, flea-market finds and drawings by fellow artists that the Surrealist artist and theorist had amassed. The photography collection also has an impressive roll call, including Brassaï, Kertész, Man Ray, Cartier-Bresson and Doisneau.

Level four houses post-'60s art. Its thematic rooms concentrate on the career of one artist or focus on movements such as Anti-form or *arte povera*. Recent acquisitions line the central corridor, and at the far end you can find architecture and design. Video art and installations by the likes of Mathieu Mercier and Dominique Gonzalez-Foerster are in a room devoted to *nouvelle création*.

▶ *An 80-minute TGV ride from Paris, the Centre Pompidou Metz (see p305) opened in 2010.*

FREE Hôtel de Ville

29 rue de Rivoli, 4th (01.42.76.40.40, www.paris.fr). M° Hôtel de Ville. **Open** 10am-7pm Mon-Sat. **Map** p125 B4 ❸
Rebuilt by Ballu after the Commune, the palatial, multi-purpose Hôtel de Ville is the very heart of the city administration, and a place in which to entertain visiting dignitaries. Free exhibitions are held in the Salon d'Accueil (open 10am-6pm Mon-Fri). The rest of the building, which is accessible by weekly guided tours (you need to book in advance), has parquet floors, marble statues, crystal chandeliers and painted ceilings.

Tour St-Jacques

Square de La-Tour-St-Jacques, 4th. M° Châtelet. **Map** p125 A3 ❹
Loved by the Surrealists, this solitary Flamboyant Gothic belltower with its leering gargoyles is all that remains of St-Jacques-La-Boucherie church, which was built for the powerful Butchers' Guild in 1508-22. The statue of Blaise Pascal at the base commemorates his experiments on atmospheric pressure, carried out in the 17th century. A weather station now crowns the 52m (171ft) tower.
▶ *After being closed to the public for the best part of 500 years, the tower now opens for a couple of months during the summer, with access to the roof – and stunning views – via a 300-step spiral staircase. Tours (€3-€6) last 45 minutes and run daily from 10am to 5pm (reservations on site).*

Cafés & Bars

Café Livres

10 rue St-Martin, 4th (01.42.72.18.13). M° Châtelet or Hôtel de Ville. **Open** 8am-midnight Mon-Fri; 9am-midnight Sat; 10am-7pm Sun. **Map** p125 A3 ❺
This charming café with a terrace in the shade of the Tour Saint-Jacques has lines and lines of books surrounding patrons inside. Since this is as central as can be, a cappuccino will set you back €6, but the atmosphere is pleasantly relaxing after a shopping marathon on rue de Rivoli. Food is served non-stop from noon to 11pm.

Shops & Services

Les Bains du Marais

31-33 rue des Blancs-Manteaux, 4th (01.44.61.02.02, www.lesbainsdumarais.com). M° St-Paul. **Open** *Men* 10am-11pm Thur; 10am-8pm Fri. *Women* 10am-11pm Tue; 10am-7pm Wed. *Mixed (swimwear required)* 7-11pm Wed; 10am-8pm Sat; 10am-11pm Sun. **Map** p125 B3 ❻ **Health & beauty**
This hammam and spa mixes the modern and traditional (lounging beds and mint tea). Facials, waxing and essential oil massages (€70) are also available. The hammam and standard massage are €35 each.

Tour St-Jacques.

carved doorways and early street signs carved into the stone. The Marais, or 'marsh', started life as a piece of swampy ground inhabited by a few monasteries, sheep and market gardens. This was one of the last parts of central Paris to be built up. In the 16th century, the elegant Hôtel Carnavalet and Hôtel Lamoignon sparked the area's phenomenal rise as an aristocratic residential district; Henri IV began building **place des Vosges** in 1605. Nobles and royal officials followed, building smart townhouses where literary ladies such as Mme de Sévigné held court. The area fell from fashion a century later; many of the narrow streets remained unchanged as mansions were transformed into workshops, studios, schools and tenements.

Rue des Francs-Bourgeois, crammed with impressive mansions and original boutiques, runs like a backbone right through the Marais, becoming more aristocratic as it leaves the food shops of rue Rambuteau behind. Two of the most refined early 18th-century residences are **Hôtel d'Albret** (no.31), a venue for jazz concerts during the Paris, Quartier d'Eté festival (*see p36*), and the palatial **Hôtel de Soubise** (no.60), the national archives. Begun in 1704 for the Prince and Princesse de Soubise, it has interiors by Boucher and Lemoine and currently hosts the **Musée de l'Histoire de France**, along with the neighbouring Hôtel de Rohan. There's also a surprising series of rose gardens.

Facing the Archives Nationales, the **Crédit Municipal** (no.55) acts as a sort of municipal pawnshop: people exchange goods for cash, and items never reclaimed are sold at auction. On the corner of rue Pavée is the Renaissance Hôtel Lamoignon. Built in 1585, it now contains the **Bibliothèque Historique de la Ville de Paris** (no.24, 01.44.59.29.40). Further up, the **Musée Carnavalet** runs across the Hôtel Carnavalet and Hôtel le Peletier de St-Fargeau.

At its eastern end, rue des Francs-Bourgeois leads into the beautiful brick-and-stone place des Vosges. At one corner is the **Maison de Victor Hugo**, where the writer lived from 1833 to 1848. An archway in the south-west corner leads to the **Hôtel de Sully**, which houses the Centre des Monuments Nationaux headquarters. Designed in 1624, the building belonged to the Duc de Sully.

Several other important museums are also found in sumptuous *hôtels*. The Hôtel Salé on rue de Thorigny, built in 1656, was nicknamed ('salty') after its owner, Fontenay, who collected the salt tax. Home to the **Musée National Picasso**, it is currently under restoration until spring 2014 (*see p129* **Growing Pains**). Nearby, the pretty Hôtel Donon, built in 1598, contains the **Musée Cognacq-Jay** and has remarkable 18th-century panelled interiors, and the Hôtel Guénégaud contains the **Musée de la Chasse et de la Nature**.

BHV Marais

52-64 rue de Rivoli, 4th (01.42.74.90.00, www.bhv.fr). M° Hôtel de Ville. **Open** 9.30am-8pm Mon, Tue, Thur-Sat; 9.30am-9pm Wed. **Map** p125 B3 ❼ **Department store**
Homeware heaven at this department store. The upper floors have a good range of men's outdoor wear, bedlinen, toys, books and household appliances.

★ FR66

25 rue du Renard, 4th (01.44.54.35.36, www.fr66. com). M° Hôtel de Ville. **Open** 10am-7pm Mon-Sat. Closed Aug. **Map** p125 B3 ❽ **Gallery**
Somewhere between a gallery and a shop, this two-level space accommodates artists and designers who produce exciting and original products for the home.

I Love My Blender

36 rue du Temple, 3rd (01.42.77.50.32, www.ilovemyblender.fr). M° Hôtel de Ville. **Open** 10am-7pm Tue-Sat; 10am-5pm Sun. **Map** p125 B3 ❾ **Books & music**
Christophe Persouyre left a career in advertising to share his passion for literature: all the books he stocks were originally penned in English and here you can find mother-tongue and translated versions.

THE MARAIS

In the 3rd & 4th arrondissements.

The narrow streets of the Marais contain aristocratic *hôtels particuliers*, art galleries, boutiques and stylish cafés, with beautiful

EXPLORE

EXPLORE

IN THE KNOW
HERE LAY HENRY

In 1559, Henri II was fatally wounded
jousting on today's rue St-Antoine,
marked by Pilon's marble *La Vierge de
Douleur* in the Eglise St-Paul-St-Louis.

The Marais has also long been a focus for the
Jewish community. Today, Jewish businesses
are clustered along rue des Rosiers, rue des
Ecouffes and rue Pavée, where there's a
synagogue designed by Guimard. Originally
made up mainly of Ashkenazi Jews, who fled
the pogroms in eastern Europe at the end of the
19th century (many were later deported during
World War II), the community expanded in
the 1950s and '60s with a wave of Sephardic
Jewish immigration after French withdrawal
from North Africa.

The lower ends of rue des Archives and rue
Vieille-du-Temple are the centre of café life and
the hub of the gay scene. Bars such as the **Open
Café** (*see p257*) draw gay crowds in the early
evening. In their midst, the 15th-century **Cloître
des Billettes** at 22-26 rue des Archives is the
only surviving Gothic cloister in Paris.

Workaday rue du Temple is full of surprises.
Near rue de Rivoli, **Le Noveau Latina** (*see
p254*) specialises in Latin American films and
holds tango balls in the room above. At no.41,
an archway leads into the former Aigle d'Or
coaching inn, now the **Café de la Gare** *café-
théâtre* (*see p272*). Further north, at no.71, the
grandiose Hôtel de St-Aignan, built in 1650,
contains the **Musée d'Art et d'Histoire du
Judaïsme**. The top end of rue du Temple and
adjoining streets, such as rue des Gravilliers,
are packed with costume jewellery, handbag
and rag-trade wholesalers in what is the city's
oldest Chinatown.

The north-west corner of the Marais hinges
on the **Musée des Arts et Métiers**, a science
museum with early flying machines displayed
in the 12th-century chapel of the former priory
of St-Martin-des-Champs, and the adjoining
Conservatoire des Arts et Métiers. Across rue
St-Martin on square Emile-Chautemps, the belle
époque **Gaîté Lyrique** theatre reopened in
2011 as a centre for contemporary music and
the 'digital arts'.

Despite the Marais' rise to fashion, the less
gentrified streets around the northern stretch
of rue Vieille-du-Temple towards place de la
République are awash with designers on the rise
and old craft workshops. Rue Charlot, housing
an occasional contemporary art gallery at the
passage de Retz at no.9, is typical of the trend.
At the top, the **Marché des Enfants-Rouges**

(once an orphanage whose inhabitants were
attired in red uniforms) is one of the city's
oldest markets, founded in 1615.

Sights & Museums

FREE Eglise St-Gervais-St-Protais

*Pl St-Gervais, 4th (01.48.87.32.02). M° Hôtel
de Ville.* **Open** times vary. **Admission** free.
Map p125 B4 ⑩
Gothic at the rear and classical at the front, this
church also has an impressive Flamboyant Gothic
interior, most of which dates from the 16th century.
The nave gives an impression of enormous height,
with tall columns that soar up to the vault. There are
plenty of fine funerary monuments.

FREE Eglise St-Paul-St-Louis

*99 rue St-Antoine, 4th (01.42.72.30.32,
www.saintpaulsaintlouis.com). M° St-Paul.*
Open 8am-8pm Mon-Fri; 8am-7.30pm Sat;
9am-8pm Sun. **Admission** free. **Map** p125 C4 ⑪
This domed Baroque Counter-Reformation church
is modelled, like all Jesuit churches, on the Chiesa
del Gesù in Rome. Completed in 1641, it features a
single nave, side chapels and a three-storey façade
featuring statues of Saints Louis, Anne and
Catherine – all replacements. The provider of con-
fessors to the kings of France, the Eglise St-Paul-St-
Louis was richly endowed until Revolutionary
iconoclasts pinched its treasures, including the
hearts of Louis XIII and XIV. Afterwards, in 1802,
it was converted back into a church, and today it
houses Delacroix's *Christ in the Garden of Olives*.

★ Gaîté Lyrique

*3bis rue Papin, 3rd (01.53.01.51.51, www.gaite-
lyrique.net). M° Réaumur Sébastopol.* **Open** *Box
office* 2-8pm Tue-Sat; 2-6pm Sun. **Map** p125 B2 ⑫
After a huge revamp, the belle époque Gaîté Lyrique
theatre, built in 1862, has been turned into Paris's
first digital cultural centre; a seven-floor, multidisciplinary concert hall-cum-gallery that thrusts
visitors deep into the realms of digital art, music,
graphics, film, fashion, design and video games.
After being an haut-lieu of operetta and Russian ballet, it was pillaged by the Nazis, only to become a
circus school in the 1970s and a mini-theme park in
the 1980s. But this time its multi-million euro interior, which combines the original belle époque foyer
with starkly modern spaces by architect Manuelle
Gautrand, is set to become a permanent fixture on
the cultural scene. There are no fewer than three electronic music concerts each week and around 120 live
multimedia performances a year.

Maison Européenne de la Photographie

*5-7 rue de Fourcy, 4th (01.44.78.75.00, www.
mep-fr.org). M° St-Paul.* **Open** 11am-8pm Wed-
Sun. **Admission** €8; €4.50 reductions; free
under-8s, all 5-8pm Wed. **Map** p125 C4 ⑬

Probably the capital's best photography exhibition space, hosting major retrospectives alongside work by emerging photographers. The building, an airy mansion with a modern extension, contains a huge permanent collection.

FREE Maison de Victor Hugo

Hôtel de Rohan-Guéménée, 6 pl des Vosges, 4th (01.42.72.10.16, www.musee-hugo.paris.fr). Mº Bastille or St-Paul. **Open** 10am-6pm Tue-Sun. **Admission** free. *Exhibitions* prices vary. **Map** p125 D4 ⓴

Victor Hugo lived here from 1833 to 1848, and today the house is a museum devoted to his life and work. On display are his first editions, nearly 500 drawings and, more bizarrely, Hugo's home-made furniture.

★ FREE Le Mémorial de la Shoah

17 rue Geoffroy-l'Asnier, 4th (01.42.77.44.72, www.memorialdelashoah.org). Mº Pont Marie or St-Paul. **Open** 10am-6pm Mon-Wed, Fri, Sun; 10am-10pm Thur. *Research centre* 10am-5.30pm Mon-Wed, Fri, Sun; 10am-7.30pm Thur. **Admission** free. **Map** p125 B4 ⓰

GROWING PAINS

The Musée Picasso finally reopens after a lengthy revamp.

After being closed for five years, the **Musée Picasso** (www.musee-picasso.fr) is finally reopening in 2014, tripled in size and with more works on show, yet keeping the domestic scale that has always made the museum so attractive and which, says head curator Anne Baldessari, is essential to appreciating Picasso's work.

For the first time, visitors will be able to roam the whole of the magnificent Hôtel Salé, built in 1659 for Pierre Aubert de Fontenay, collector of the *gabelle* or salt tax. Like many Marais mansions, the Hôtel Salé has had a chequered history, serving as an embassy and technical school before becoming a museum.

Architect Jean-François Bodin, working in collaboration with Monuments Historiques head architect Stéphane Thouin, was keen to respect not only the original 17th-century *hôtel particulier* but also the modern style of the prize-winning 1985 conversion by Roland Simounet, who intended 'to give it the atmosphere of a grand residence'.

The newly enlarged museum will still be centred on the grand Baroque stairway, but has now also colonised the two upper storeys previously occupied by offices and archives. A new entrance lobby and ticket desk have been created in the former stable wing lining the Cour d'Honneur, with technical services and educational facilities moved into old garages in the garden.

While the old display seemed remarkably comprehensive, spanning the artist's prolific career from early Spanish paintings and his Blue period to bawdy late artist-and-model works, it was always short of space; only a fraction of the museum's vast holding of some 5,000 works has ever been on show. The new display will

present around 550 works (rather than 450 in the past) in a less convoluted route, along with a series of temporary exhibitions deemed essential for getting locals to make return visits alongside the tourists.

The revamp has had its difficulties, finishing more than a year late, with a budget said to have more than doubled from the original estimate of €25 million amid tales of union discontent. But with the rehung display opening in spring 2014 and the first temporary exhibitions scheduled for 2015, the revamped space should hopefully be worth the wait.

EXPLORE

Airport-style security checks mean queues, but don't let that put you off: the Mémorial du Martyr Juif Inconnu is an impressively presented and moving memorial to the Holocaust. Enter via the Wall of Names, where limestone slabs are engraved with the first and last names of each of the 76,000 Jews deported from France from 1942 to 1944 with, as an inscription reminds the visitor, the say-so of the Vichy government. The basement-level permanent exhibition documents the plight of French and European Jews through photographs, texts, films and individual stories: 'The French,' reads one label (captioning is also given in English), 'were not particularly interested in the fate of French Jews at this point.'

▶ *The Shoah Memorial organises free guided tours in English on the second Sunday of the month. Tours start at 3pm and no reservation is needed.*

★ Musée d'Art et d'Histoire du Judaïsme

Hôtel de St-Aignan, 71 rue du Temple, 3rd (01.53.01.86.60, www.mahj.org). M° Rambuteau. **Open** 11am-6pm Mon-Fri; 10am-6pm Sun. Closed Jewish hols. **Admission** €6.80; €4.50 reductions; free under-26s. **Map** p125 B3 ⑯

It's fitting that a museum of Judaism should be lodged in one of the grandest mansions of the Marais, for centuries the epicentre of local Jewish life. It sprang from the collection of a private association formed in 1948 to safeguard Jewish heritage after the Holocaust. Pick up a free audio-guide in English to help you navigate through displays illustrating ceremonies, rites and learning, and showing how styles were adapted across the globe through examples of Jewish decorative arts. Photographic portraits of modern French Jews, each of whom tells his or her own story on the audio soundtrack, bring a contemporary edge. There are documents and paintings relating to the emancipation of French Jewry after

the Revolution and the infamous Dreyfus case, from Zola's *J'Accuse!* to anti-Semitic cartoons. Paintings by the early 20th-century avant-garde include works by El Lissitsky and Chagall. The Holocaust is marked by Boris Taslitzky's stark sketches from Buchenwald and Christian Boltanski's courtyard memorial to the Jews who lived in the building in 1939, 13 of whom died in the camps.

Musée des Arts et Métiers

60 rue Réaumur, 3rd (01.53.01.82.00, www. arts-et-metiers.net). M° Arts et Métiers. **Open** 10am-6pm Tue, Wed, Fri-Sun; 10am-9.30pm Thur. **Admission** €6.50; €4.50 reductions; free under-26s (EU citizens), all 6-9.30pm Thur & 1st Sun of mth. PMP. **Map** p125 B2 ⑰

The 'arts and trades' museum is, in fact, Europe's oldest science museum, founded in 1794 by the constitutional bishop Henri Grégoire, initially as a way to educate France's manufacturing industry in useful scientific techniques. Housed in the former Benedictine priory of St-Martin-des-Champs, it became a museum proper in 1819; it's a fascinating, attractively laid out and vast collection of treasures. Here are beautiful astrolabes, celestial spheres, barometers, clocks, weighing devices, some of Pascal's calculating devices, amazing scale models of buildings and machines that must have demanded at least as much engineering skill as the originals, the Lumière brothers' cinematograph, an enormous 1938 TV set, and still larger exhibits such as Cugnot's 1770 'Fardier' (the first ever powered vehicle) and Clément Ader's bat-like, steam-powered Avion 3. The visit concludes in the chapel, which now contains old cars, a scale model of the Statue of Liberty, the monoplane in which Blériot crossed the Channel in 1909, and a Foucault pendulum.

▶ *Try to time your visit to coincide with one of the spellbinding demonstrations of the museum's old music boxes in the Théâtre des Automates.*

▶ **Place des Vosges**.

★ **FREE** Musée Carnavalet

*23 rue de Sévigné, 3rd (01.44.59.58.58, www.
carnavalet.paris.fr). Mᵒ St-Paul.* **Open** 10am-6pm
Tue-Sun. **Admission** free. *Exhibitions* prices
vary. **Map** p125 C3 ⑱

Here, 140 chronological rooms depict the history of
Paris, from pre-Roman Gaul to the 20th century. Built
in 1548 and transformed by Mansart in 1660, this fine
house became a museum in 1866, when Haussmann
persuaded the city to preserve its beautiful interiors.
Original 16th-century rooms house Renaissance collections, with portraits by Clouet and furniture and
pictures relating to the Wars of Religion. The first
floor covers the period up to 1789, with furniture and
paintings displayed in restored period interiors;
neighbouring Hôtel Le Peletier de St-Fargeau covers
the period from 1789 onwards. Displays relating to
1789 detail that year's convoluted politics and
bloodshed, with prints and memorabilia, including a
chunk of the Bastille. There are items belonging to
Napoleon, a cradle given by the city to Napoleon III,
and a reconstruction of Proust's cork-lined bedroom.

★ Musée de la Chasse et de la Nature

*Hôtel Guénégaud, 62 rue des Archives, 3rd
(01.53.01.92.40, www.chassenature.org). Mᵒ
Rambuteau.* **Open** 11am-6pm Tue, Thur-Sun;
11am-9.30pm Wed. **Admission** €6; €4.50
reductions; free under-18s, all 1st Sun of mth.
Map p125 C3 ⑲

A two-year overhaul turned the three-floor hunting
museum from a musty old-timer into something
really rather special. The history of hunting and
man's larger relationship with the natural world are
examined in such things as a quirky series of
wooden cabinets devoted to the owl, wolf, boar and
stag, each equipped with a bleached skull, small
drawers you can open to reveal droppings and foot-
print casts, and a binocular eyepiece you can peer
into for footage of the animal in the wild. A cleverly
simple mirrored box contains a stuffed hen that is
replicated into infinity on every side; and a stuffed
fox is set curled up on a Louis XVI chair as though
it were a domestic pet. Thought-provoking stuff.

FREE Musée Cognacq-Jay

*Hôtel Donon, 8 rue Elzévir, 3rd (01.40.27.07.21,
www.cognacq-jay.paris.fr). Mᵒ St-Paul.* **Open** 10am-
6pm Tue-Sun. **Admission** free. **Map** p125 C3 ⑳

This cosy museum houses a collection put together
in the early 1900s by La Samaritaine founder Ernest
Cognacq and his wife Marie-Louise Jay. They stuck
mainly to 18th-century French works, focusing on
rococo artists such as Watteau, Fragonard, Boucher,
Greuze and pastellist Quentin de la Tour, though
some English artists (Reynolds, Romney, Lawrence)
and Dutch and Flemish names (an early Rembrandt,
Ruysdael, Rubens), plus Canalettos and Guardis,
have managed to slip in. Pictures are displayed in
panelled rooms with furniture, porcelain, tapestries
and sculpture of the same period.

Musée de l'Histoire de France (Musée des Archives Nationales)

*Hôtel de Soubise, 60 rue des Francs-Bourgeois, 3rd
(01.40.27.60.96, www.archivesnationales.culture.
gouv.fr/chan/chan/musee). Mᵒ Hôtel de Ville or
Rambuteau.* **Open** 10am-5.30pm Mon, Wed-Fri;
2-5.30pm Sat, Sun. **Admission** €4-€6; €2-€4
reductions; free under-26s. **Map** p125 C3 ㉑

Documents and artefacts covering everything from
the founding of the Sorbonne to an ordinance about
umbrellas are displayed in the recently renovated
Hôtel de Soubise. Its rococo interiors feature paintings by François Boucher and Carle van Loo.

FREE Pavillon de l'Arsenal

*21 bd Morland, 4th (01.42.76.33.97, www.pavillon-
arsenal.com). Mᵒ Sully Morland.* **Open** 10.30am-
6.30pm Tue-Sat; 11am-7pm Sun. **Admission** free.
Map p125 C5 ㉒

The setting is a fantastic 1880s gallery with an iron
frame and glass roof; the subject is the built history
of Paris. Exhibits were previously limited to a few
storyboards, maps and photos, and three city models
set into the floor (done far more impressively at the
Musée d'Orsay), but a brand new permanent exhibition, Paris, a City in the Making, boasts a 37sq m
Google Earth model of the city with four touch-
screens to explore the different *quartiers* in delicious
digital detail.

FREE Place des Vosges

4th. Mᵒ St-Paul. **Map** p125 D4 ㉓

Paris's first planned square was commissioned in
1605 by Henri IV and inaugurated by his son Louis
XIII in 1612. With harmonious red-brick and stone
arcaded façades and steeply pitched slate roofs, it
differs from the later pomp of the Bourbons. It was
called place Royale prior to the Napoleonic Wars,
when the Vosges was the first region to pay its war
taxes. Mme de Sévigné, salon hostess and letter-
writer, was born at no.1bis in 1626. At that time the
garden hosted duels and trysts; now it attracts children from the nearby nursery school.

Restaurants

★ L'Ambassade d'Auvergne

*22 rue du Grenier-St-Lazare, 3rd (01.42.72.31.22,
www.ambassade-auvergne.com). Mᵒ Arts et
Métiers.* **Open** noon-2pm, 7.30-10pm daily.
Main courses €18. **Prix fixe** *Lunch* €22.
Dinner €32. **Map** p125 B2 ㉔ **Bistro**

This rustic-style *auberge* is a fitting embassy for the
hearty fare of central France. An order of cured ham
comes as two hefty, plate-filling slices, and the salad
bowl is chock-full of green lentils cooked in goose
fat, studded with bacon and shallots. The *rôti
d'agneau* arrives as a pot of melting chunks of lamb
in a rich, meaty sauce with a helping of tender white
beans. Dishes arrive with the flagship *aligot*, the
creamy, elastic mash-and-cheese concoction.

EXPLORE

Chez Omar.

EXPLORE

Bofinger

*5-7 rue de la Bastille, 4th (01.42.72.87.82,
www.bofingerparis.com). M° Bastille.* **Open**
noon-3pm, 6.30pm-midnight Mon-Sat; noon-
3pm, 6.30-11.30pm Sun. **Main courses**
€21.50-€46. **Prix fixe** €29.50, €36.50, €59.
Map p125 D4 **㉕ Brasserie**

Bofinger draws big crowds for its authentic art nouveau setting and brasserie atmosphere. Downstairs
is the prettiest place in which to eat, but the upstairs
room is air-conditioned. An à la carte selection might
start with plump, garlicky escargots or a well-made
langoustine terrine, followed by an intensely seasoned salmon tartare, a generous (if unremarkable)
cod steak, or calf's liver accompanied by cooked
melon. Alternatively, you could have the foolproof
brasserie meal of oysters and fillet steak, washed
down with the fine Gigondas.

€ Breizh Café

*109 rue Vieille-du-Temple, 3rd (01.42.72.13.77,
www.breizhcafe.com). M° Filles du Calvaire.*
Open 11.30am-11pm Wed-Sat; 11.30am-10pm
Sun. Closed 3wks Aug. **Main courses** €7-€15.
Map p125 C3 **㉘ Crêperie**

With its modern interior of pale wood and its choice
of 15 artisanal ciders, this outpost of a restaurant in
Cancale, Brittany, is a world away from the average
crêperie. For the complete faux-seaside experience,
you might start with a plate of creuse oysters from
Cancale before indulging in an inventive buckwheat
galette such as the Cancalaise, made with potato,
smoked herring from Brittany and herring roe.
The choice of fillings is fairly limited, but the ingredients are of high quality – including the use of
Valrhona chocolate with 70% cocoa solids in the
dessert crêpes.

★ € Cantine Merci

*111 bd Beaumarchais, 3rd (01.42.77.78.92).
M° St-Sébastien Froissart.* **Open** noon-3.30pm
Mon-Sat (until 6pm for tea). **Main courses**
€8-€19. **Map** p125 D3 **㉗ Café**

Fairtrade concept store Merci is all about feeling
virtuous even as you indulge, and its basement
canteen is a perfect example. Fresh and colourful
salads, soup and risotto of the day, an organic
salmon plate, and the *assiette merci* (perhaps chicken
kefta with two salads) make up the brief, Rose
Bakery-esque menu, complete with invigorating
teas and juices. Rustic desserts add just the right
handmade touch.

★ € Chez Hanna

*54 rue des Rosiers, 4th (01.42.74.74.99). M°
St-Paul.* **Open** noon-midnight Tue-Sun. **Main
courses** €12-€16. **Map** p125 C3 **㉘ Jewish**

By noon on a Sunday, there is a queue outside almost
every falafel shop along rue des Rosiers. The long-
established L'As du Fallafel, a little further up the
street, still reigns supreme, whereas Chez Hanna

remains something of a locals' secret, quietly serving
up falafel and shawarma sandwiches to rival any in
the world. A pitta sandwich bursting with crunchy
chickpea-and-herb balls, tahini sauce and vegetables
costs just €5.50 if you order from the takeaway window, €9.50 if you sit at one of the tables in the buzzy
dining room. Either way, you really can't lose.

Chez Jenny

*39 bd du Temple, 3rd (01.44.54.39.00, www.
chez-jenny.com). M° République.* **Open** noon-
midnight Mon-Thur, Sun; noon-1am Fri, Sat.
Main courses €19-€30. **Prix fixe** €19.80,
€25.90. **Map** p125 C2 **㉙ Brasserie**

Chez Jenny is a legendary Alsatian brasserie. As
well as the famous *choucroute* (sauerkraut) and traditional oyster bar, the menu features specialities
such as *flammekueche*, caramelised pork shank,
strudel and kouglof. Sitting down to eat at Chez
Jenny is like taking a train from Gare de L'Est to the
Alsatian foothills. Just be aware that outside of the
well-chosen set menus (which don't include any of
the local specialities), the bill can mount up alarm-
ingly – for example, allow €20-€30 for sauerkraut.
A real regret is that there aren't any speciality
Alsatian beers on the menu.

Chez Julien

*1 rue du Pont Louis-Philippe, 4th
(01.42.78.31.64). M° Pont Marie.* **Open** noon-
2.30pm, 7.30-10.30pm Mon-Fri; 12.30-3pm, 7.30-
11pm Sat, Sun. **Main courses** €23-€36. **Prix
fixe** *Lunch* €22, €65, €85, €115. *Dinner* €65,
€85, €115. **Map** p125 B4 **㉚ Bistro**

Thierry Costes discreetly took over this vintage
bistro overlooking the Seine in 2007. The zebra ban-
quette near the loo upstairs is most reminiscent of
the Costes style, but the 1920s dining room is also
unmistakably chic with plum walls, a big chandelier
and red banquettes, and the terrace outside stretches
across the pedestrian street. The food is predictable

– crab salad, steak with shoestring fries – and pricey, but it's hard not to enjoy this slice of Paris life.

★ € Chez Omar

47 rue de Bretagne, 3rd (01.42.72.36.26).
M° Arts et Métiers or Temple. **Open** noon-2.30pm, 7-11.30pm Mon-Sat; 7-11.30pm Sun.
Main courses €12-€26. **No credit cards.**
Map p125 C2 ③① **North African**
The once-fashionable Omar doesn't take any reservations, and the queue can often stretch the length of the zinc bar and through the door. Everyone is waiting for the same thing: couscous. Prices range from €11 (vegetarian) to €26 (*royale*); there are no tagines or other traditional Maghreb mains, only a handful of French classics (duck, fish, steak). Overstretched waiters slip through the crowds with mounds of semolina, vats of vegetable-laden broth and steel platters heaving with meat, including the stellar *merguez*. Even on packed nights, there's an offer of seconds – gratis – to encourage you to stay.

Cru

7 rue Charlemagne, 4th (01.40.27.81.84,
www.restaurantcru.fr). M° St-Paul. **Open** 12.30-2.30pm, 7-11pm Tue-Sat; 12.30-3pm Sun. **Main courses** €9-€25. **Prix fixe** *Lunch* €19 (Mon-Fri).
Brunch (Sun) €24. **Map** p125 C4 ③② **Bistro**
Opening a raw-food restaurant is a gamble, so the owners of Cru cheat here and there, offering root vegetable 'chips' and a few *plancha* dishes. Still, the extensive menu has plenty for the crudivore, such as some unusual carpaccios (the veal with preserved lemon is particularly good) and intriguing 'red' and 'green' plates, variations on the tomato and cucumber. The food is perfectly good, but the real reason to come here is the gorgeous courtyard terrace.

★ Derrière

69 rue des Gravilliers, 3rd (01.44.61.91.95,
www.derriere-resto.com). M° Arts et Métiers.

Open noon-2.30pm, 8-11.30pm Mon-Sat; noon-4pm, 8-11.30pm Sun. **Main courses** €15-€35.
Prix fixe *Lunch* €25. **Map** p125 B2 ③③ **Bistro**
Mourad Mazouz, the man behind Momo and Sketch in London, has hit on another winning formula with this apartment-restaurant in the same street as his North African restaurant 404 and bar Andy Wahloo. The cluttered-chic look mixes contemporary fixtures and antique furniture, such as the beat-up armchairs in the smoking room hidden behind a wardrobe door upstairs. It attracts a young, hip crowd that appreciates the high-calorie comfort food: roast chicken with buttery mashed potatoes, macaroni gratin with taramasalata, and chocolate mousse.

Glou

101 rue Vieille du Temple, 3rd (01.42.74.44.32,
www.glou-resto.com). M° St-Sébastien Froissart.
Open 12.30-2.30pm, 8-11pm Mon-Fri; noon-5pm, 8-11.30pm Sat; noon-3pm, 8-10.30pm Sun. **Main courses** €17-€24. **Prix fixe** *Lunch* €16, €21.
Map p125 C3 ③④ **Bistro**
For a restaurant founded by a man the *New York Times* dubbed the 'wizard of offal', it's initially disappointing that Glou keeps its tongue (and heart, testicles and other offcuts) in cheek and off the menu. Instead this charming bistro plays things straight and pan-continental with Spanish meat boards, subtle pasta dishes and bold French desserts. Smoked duck stuffed with foie gras might be followed by a seasonal cep ravioli. To finish, a crispy chocolate and praline tartlet with a glass of 'Sugar Baby Love', a dessert wine. Glou is a 'food with friends' affair, with friendly staff and a communal table that reverberates with the laughter of Marais hipsters.

Le Hangar

12 impasse Berthaud, 3rd (01.42.74.55.44).
M° Rambuteau. **Open** noon-2.30pm, 7.30-11pm Tue-Sat. Closed Aug. **Main courses** €18-€28.
No credit cards. Map p125 B3 ③⑤ **Bistro**

EXPLORE

Andy Wahloo. *See p134.*

La Caféotheque.

It's worth making the effort to find this bistro by the Centre Pompidou, with its terrace tucked away in a hidden alley and excellent cooking. A bowl of tapenade and toast is supplied to keep you going while choosing from the comprehensive *carte*. It yields, for starters, tasty and grease-free *rillettes de lapereau* (rabbit) alongside perfectly balanced pumpkin and chestnut soup. Main courses include pan-fried foie gras on a smooth potato purée.

★ L'Îlot

*4 rue de la Corderie, 3rd (06.95.12.86.61). M°
Filles du Calvaire, République or Temple.* **Open**
7-10pm Tue; noon-3pm, 7-10pm Wed-Sat. **Main
courses** €10. **Prix fixe** *Lunch* €12.50. *Dinner*
€50 (for 2). **Map** p125 C2 ❸ **Seafood**
At l'Îlot, you don't have to pay Paris prices for the best catch of the day. The venue is tiny but beautiful, with big slate menus, earthenware pots and white parquet, a bay window, a few photos on the walls and a terrace for nice days – it all has a solid charm. Perch yourself on a stool and order a glass of white wine, then browse the menu: €5 for a serving of tuna or salmon rillettes, €4.50 to €9.50 for grey or pink Madagascan prawns, €6.50 for whelks and €8 for a half crab (€14 for the whole). There are also beautiful oysters, while the fish is smoked or marinated. The value of the set menu is unbeatable, at €12.50 for a starter, main and glass of wine. A delight.

Le Petit Marché

*9 rue de Béarn, 3rd (01.42.72.06.67). M°
Chemin Vert.* **Open** 8am-2am daily. *Food
served* noon-4pm, 7.30pm-midnight daily.
Main courses €19. **Prix fixe** *Lunch* €14.50.
Map p125 D3 ❸ **Bistro**
Petit Marché's menu is short and modern with Asian touches. Raw tuna is flash-fried in sesame seeds and served with a Thai sauce, making for a refreshing

starter; crispy-coated deep-fried king prawns have a similar lightness. The main vegetarian risotto is rich in basil, coriander, cream and al dente green beans. Pan-fried scallops with lime are precision-cooked and accompanied by a good purée and more beans. There's a short wine list.

Le Potager du Marais

*24 rue Rambuteau, 4th (01.57.40.98.57,
www.lepotagerdumarais.fr). M° Rambuteau.*
Open noon-3pm, 7-10.30pm Wed-Sun. **Main
courses** €16-€19. **Map** p125 B3 ❸ **Vegetarian**
This organic vegetarian restaurant is proof that you can fit an entire restaurant into a shoebox. But what the Potager lacks in space, it makes up for on the plate with luscious dishes brimming with pulses, tofu, crunchy vegetables and beans. The mushroom terrine, served with gherkins and salad, is a real winner, as are mains such as sweet pumpkin *hachis parmentier* (veggie shepherd's pie). If you require gluten-free, the Potager gets brownie points for its multiple choice of dishes – a real rarity in Paris.

Cafés & Bars

★ Andy Wahloo

*69 rue des Gravilliers, 3rd (01.42.71.20.38).
M° Arts et Métiers.* **Open** 7pm-2am Tue-Sat.
Map p125 B2 ❸
Andy Wahloo, created by the people behind its neighbour 404 and London's Momo and Sketch, is Arabic for 'I have nothing'. Bijou? This place brings new meaning to the word. The formidably fashionable crowd fights for coveted 'seats' on upturned paint cans; from head to toe, it's a beautifully designed venue, crammed with Moroccan artefacts and a spice rack of colours. It's quiet early on, with a surge around 9pm, and the atmosphere heats up as the night goes on. *Photo p133.*

EXPLORE

L'Apparemment Café

18 rue des Coutures St-Gervais, 3rd (01.48.87.12.22). M° St-Sébastien Froissart. **Open** noon-2am Mon-Sat; 12.30pm-midnight Sun. **Map** p125 C3 ⓴

The 'Apparently' feels more like a communal living room than a café. The low lighting, cosy nooks and board games (Trivial Pursuit and Taboo, both in French) make for an excellent place to while away an afternoon. Staff even organise the occasional fortune-telling evening. The location is perfect for shoppers too, being just off the rue Vieille-du-Temple. Lunches consist of simple DIY platters of meats, cheeses and salads, but at €15 for the basic version they're a bit rudimentary for the price. Eating is obligatory during busy periods.

Le Baromètre

17 rue Charlot, 3rd (01.48.87.04.54). M° Arts et Métiers. **Open** 9am-midnight Mon-Sat. Closed 3wks Aug. **Map** p125 C2 ⓴

This unpretentious wine bar is popular with artisan types. Lunchtimes are heaving, so unless you're after the sit-down *menu du jour* (€13-€14) served at the back, you're better off coming along for a lazy afternoon. Order a plate of cheese or the house speciality, bacon and andouillette gratin, and choose from a 20-strong list of wines by the glass, most under €3.50.

La Caféotheque

52 rue de l'Hotel de Ville, 4th (01.53.01.83.84, www.lacafeotheque.com). M° St-Paul. **Open** 9.30am-7.30pm daily. **Map** p125 B4 ⓴

The Caféotheque is where the coffee revolution in Paris kicked off seven years ago. The café is next door to artist's residence La Cité Internationale des Arts, which ensures a cosmopolitan clientele, while its picture-postcard location on the banks of the Seine means tourists are always dropping by as well.

Café Suédois

11 rue Payenne, 3rd (01.44.78.80.11). M° Chemin Vert or St-Paul. **Open** noon-6pm Tue-Sun. **No credit cards**. **Map** p125 C3 ⓴

The Café Suédois is an integral part of the Swedish Cultural Institute in the Hôtel de Marle, a magnificent mansion in the Marais built between the 15th and 18th centuries. You can while away a sunny afternoon with a good book in its peaceful paved courtyard, or retreat to the pretty café if it's cold and wet. Every morning before opening, a passionate team of Swedish pastry chefs prepare fresh bread, elderflower cordial and a range of seasonal delicacies. The lunch menu consists of a selection of sandwiches, including succulent marinated salmon, as well as carrot cake, cinnamon rolls, cranberry tart and a daily soup special in winter.

★ Candelaria

52 rue de Saintonge, 3rd (01.42.74.41.28, www.candelariaparis.com). M° Filles du Calvaire or

République. **Open** 12.30-11pm Mon-Wed, Sun; noon-midnight Thur-Sat. **Map** p125 C2 ⓴ *See p136* **Perfect Mix**.

Comme à Lisbonne

37 rue du Roi de Sicile, 4th (07.61.23.42.30, www.commealisbonne.com). M° Hôtel de Ville. **Open** 11am-7pm Tue-Sun. **Map** p125 B4 ⓴

Opened in 2011 by the cheerful Portuguese barista Victor Silveira, this hole-in-the-wall bar in a chic corner of the Marais may be impossibly small, but it has become a runaway success with its irresistible freshly-baked *pasteis de nata* accompanied by traditional Portuguese coffee. The *pasteis*, succulent custard tarts, are baked according to Victor's mother's secret recipe. Although there are no seats and just a small bar at which to sip your coffee and nibble a *pasteis*, there is a deli section with a host of traditional Portuguese goodies.

L'Estaminet

39 rue de Bretagne, 3rd (01.42.72.28.12, www.lestaminetdesenfantsrouges.com). M° Temple. **Open** 9am-8pm Tue-Sat; 9am-3pm Sun. **Map** p125 C2 ⓴

L'Estaminet is tucked away in the Marché des Enfants-Rouges, a charming neighbourhood market and one of the city's oldest. The café has a warm interior, with a grandfather clock in the corner and guests eating €13 *plats du jour* off Limoges porcelain. Wines from €3.50 a glass.

★ L'Etoile Manquante

34 rue Vieille-du-Temple, 4th (01.42.72.48.34, www.cafeine.com). M° Hôtel de Ville or St-Paul. **Open** 9am-2am daily. **Map** p125 B3 ⓴

L'Etoile Manquante is the hippest of Xavier Denamur's merry Marais bars. Cocktails are punchy, traditional tipples just as good, and the salads and snacks reasonably priced and tasty – but it's the design and buzz that are the main draws. The decor is trendy but comfortable, embellished with interesting art. As in all Denamur's places, no visit is complete without a trip to the toilets: here, an electric train shuttles between cubicles, starlight beams down from the ceiling, and a hidden camera films you washing your hands. Just watch the small screen on the wall behind you.

Lizard Lounge

18 rue du Bourg-Tibourg, 4th (01.42.72.81.34, www.cheapblonde.com). M° Hôtel de Ville. **Open** noon-2am daily. **Map** p125 B3 ⓴

An anglophone favourite located deep in the heart of the Marais, this loud and lively (hetero) pick-up joint provides lager in pints (€6), plus cocktails (€7) and a viewing platform for beer-goggled oglers. Bare brick and polished woodwork are offset by the occasional lizard and a housey soundtrack. Bargain boozing (cocktails €5) kicks off at 5pm; from 8pm to 10pm, there's another happy hour in the

EXPLORE

sweaty cellar bar (complete with minuscule dance-floor); on Mondays, it lasts all day. A popular weekend brunch of bacon, sausages and eggs benedict caters to the homesick.

Le Loir dans la Théière

3 rue des Rosiers, 4th (01.42.72.90.61). M° St-Paul. **Open** 9am-7.30pm daily. **Map** p125 C4 ⓯
Le Loir is named after the unfortunate dormouse that gets dunked in the pot at the Mad Hatter's tea party in *Alice in Wonderland*. Its squishy sofas are the perfect complement to its comfort food: it specialises in baked goods, and the famed lemon meringue and chocolate fondant are divine. At weekends, it's packed out with tourists in search of brunch; long queues of people looking enviously at your plate, plus occasionally patchy service, can mar the experience. Be prepared to queue.

La Perle

78 rue Vieille-du-Temple, 3rd (01.42.72.69.93). M° Chemin Vert or St-Paul. **Open** 6.30am-2am Mon-Fri; 8am-2am Sat, Sun. **Map** p125 C3 ⓾
The Pearl achieves a rare balance between all-day and late-night venue, and has a good hetero/homo mix. In the morning, it draws early risers; lunchtime is for a business crowd; the afternoon reels in retired locals, and in the evening, screenwriters rub elbows with young dandies, keeping one eye on the mirror and an ear on the electro-rock. The menu runs the gamut from omelettes to *salade marine*. Expect a DJ later on.

Le Petit Fer à Cheval

30 rue Vieille-du-Temple, 4th (01.42.72.47.47, www.cafeine.com). M° St-Paul. **Open** 9am-2am daily. **Map** p125 B3 ⓾

PERFECT MIX

A new breed of bar is shaking up the capital's cocktail scene.

EXPLORE

Having lagged behind London and New York for years in the cocktail stakes, Paris is now being flooded with a host of cool new mixology bars. The trend was started by the Experimental Cocktail Club a few years ago, and the new wave includes Sherry Butt, Candelaria and L'Entrée des Artistes, all three run by ex-Experimental bartenders. Each one has its speciality – **Candelaria** (*see p135*) is a taqueria specialising in tequila cocktails; the **Sherry Butt** (www.sherrybuttparis.com) favours a whisky base, as its name subtly suggests; and **L'Entrée des Artistes** (8 Rue de Crussol, 11th) is embracing the aged cocktails trend started by molecular mixology pioneer Tony Conigliaro. What they all have in common is that they are small, tucked away and packed with a new breed of imbiber who approaches cocktails as if they were fine wines.

The icing on the cake is the fact that Conigliaro himself, star of the London cocktail scene, has now opened a bar in Paris, **Le Coq** (www.barlecoq.com), near place de la République.

Conigliaro is excited about the host of French drinks gathering dust on the shelves of forgotten bars, and discovering artisanal cognacs and armagnacs to make specifically French cocktails.

Moving on from the speakeasy style of Experimental, Le Coq is themed around 1970s glamour – think Françoise Hardy, the Gainsbourgs and Marianne Faithful.

Romée de Gorianoff, one of Experimental's founders, is delighted to see the group's young talent take flight on their own. 'In France we've been like a sponge,' he says. 'We take from everywhere because we've been very behind. But things have changed. Now the barman is respected, like a chef. People are ready to take risks.'

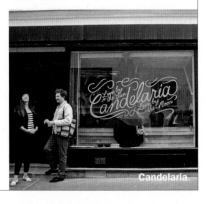

Candelaria.

Even a miniature Shetland pony would be pushed to squeeze his hoof into this *fer à cheval* (horseshoe) – the adorable little café, which has been in business for more than 100 years, has one of France's smallest bars. Tucked in behind the glassy façade is a friendly dining room lined with reclaimed métro benches; if you want scenery, the tables out front overlook the bustle of rue Vieille-du-Temple. As with its sister bar L'Etoile Manquante (*see p135*), the loos are worth the detour – they look as if they've been pummelled out of a defunct Dalek, with metal panels and strange knobs everywhere.

Stolly's

16 rue Cloche-Perce, 4th (01.42.76.06.76, www.cheapblonde.com). M° Hôtel de Ville or St-Paul. **Open** 4pm-2am daily. **Map** p125 B4 ②

This seen-it-all drinking den has been serving a mainly anglophone crowd for nights immemorial. The staff make the place what it is, and a summer terrace eases libation, as do the long happy hours; but don't expect anyone at Stolly's to faff about with food. There's football on TV and a plastic shark to compensate.

Le Temps des Cérises

31 rue de la Cerisaie, 4th (01.42.72.08.63). M° Bastille. **Open** 8.30am-2am daily. **Map** p125 C5 ③

Not to be confused with several other cafés of the same name, this one-room *bistro à vins* has changed very little over the years. Faded net curtains, Duralex tumblers behind the zinc bar and prices that begin at €3.50 for a *vin* or €2.50 for a beer are all reminiscent of a bygone age. The blackboard wine list is limited but the selection is always well chosen, and food is old-fashioned and hearty (think beef stew and *blanquette de veau*). The general banter is football-centred, so get ready to rumble with the natives about the goings-on at PSG.

Shops & Services

AB33

33 rue Charlot, 3rd (01.42.71.02.82). M° Filles du Calvaire. **Open** 10.30am-7.30pm Tue-Sat; 11am-7pm Sun. **Map** p125 C2 ④ **Fashion**

Delicate in summer, cosy in winter, the pretty, unstructured clothes in AB33 may not make the wish list of any sultry, groomed Parisienne, but would be perfect for her up-from-the-country Bardot-esque cousin. Owner Agathe Buchotte sells Forte, Forte, Kristina Ti and Philip Lim.

Anikalena Skärström

16 rue du Pont aux Choux, 3rd (09.83.82.32.85, www.anikalena.com). M° St-Sébastien Froissart. **Open** 10am-7pm Mon-Fri; noon-7pm Sat. Closed 2wks Aug. **Map** p125 D3 ⑤ **Fashion**

Clean lines and streamlining are the guiding aesthetic for Anikalena Skärström's collections of sporty, sexy day and evening dresses and separates, with the occasional wow piece like the grass-green suede coat a few seasons ago.

Anne et Valentin

4 rue Ste-Croix-de-la-Bretonnerie, 4th (01.40.29.93.01, www.anneetvalentin.com). M° Hôtel de Ville or St-Paul. **Open** noon-8pm Mon; 11am-8pm Tue-Sat. Closed 1wk Aug. **Map** p125 B3 ⑤ **Accessories**

This modish eyewear firm occupies a three-floor boutique. A&V design chic unisex frames: light titanium models have names like Tarzan and Truman; coloured acetate frames have inventive details.

April 77

49 rue de Saintonge, 3rd (01.40.29.07.30, www.april77.fr). M° Filles du Calvaire. **Open** 2-7.30pm Mon; 11am-7.30pm Tue-Sat. **Map** p125 C2 ⑤ **Fashion**

The cult skinny jeans brand has acquired its own boutique, designed by Steven Thomas, to show off a collection inspired by the mid-'80s music scene. **Other location** 7-9 rue Charonne, 11th (01.43.38.39.74).

Au Nom de la Rose

87 rue St-Antoine, 4th (01.42.71.34.24, www.aunomdelarose.fr). M° St-Paul. **Open** Sept-July 10am-9pm Mon-Sat; 9am-2pm, 3-6pm Sun. *Aug* 10am-9pm Mon-Sat. **Map** p125 C4 ⑤ **Gifts & souvenirs**

Specialising in roses, Au Nom can supply a bouquet, as well as rose-based beauty products and candles. **Other locations** throughout the city.

Azzedine Alaïa

7 rue de Moussy, 4th (01.42.72.30.69, www.alaia.fr). M° Hôtel de Ville. **Open** 10am-7pm Mon-Sat. **Map** p125 B3 ⑤ **Fashion**

Ringing the doorbell gains you entry to the factory-style showroom in the same building as Alaïa's headquarters and apartment, where the Tunisian creator continues to astound with his originality. Stunning haute couture creations are in the back room, and sexy shoes are scattered among the rails.

ba&sh

22 rue des Francs-Bourgeois, 3rd (01.42.78.55.10, www.ba-sh.com). M° Jacques Bonsergent. **Open** 11am-7.30pm Mon-Sat; noon-7pm Sun. **Map** p125 C3 ⑥ **Fashion**

At this fresh, Paris-based label, you'll find dresses, skirts and blouses with ethnic touches on one side and drapey jersey on the other. **Other locations** throughout the city.

Byzance Home

129 rue de Turenne, 3rd (01.42.77.89.42). M° Filles du Calvaire. **Open** 11am-1pm, 2-7pm Tue-Sat. **Map** p125 D2 ⑥ **Homewares**

EXPLORE

EXPLORE

In a cool loft space, interior designer Soraya Belhadia displays her *coups de coeur* for the home. Italian designers are in the majority, with Zanotta pouffes, Lana leather chaise longues from Palomba and one-off marquetry chests by Camobio.

★ Christophe Lemaire
28 rue de Poitou, 3rd (01.44.78.00.09, www.christophelemaire.com). M° St-Sébastien Froissart. **Open** 1-7pm Mon; noon-7.30pm Tue-Fri; 11am-7.30pm Sat. **Map** p125 C3 ❷ **Fashion**
Creative director for Lacoste for seven years, Lemaire opened his own boutique in an old pharmacy. It's decorated like a fantasy apartment: the salon, in '70s gold and glitz, stocks his own-label menswear and womenswear in high-tech Japanese textiles, and leads into a soundproofed music room with a wall of old speakers where you can buy collectable Lacoste and Lemaire's own fave CDs. Next door the seductive 'Japanese salon' holds the jeans range. You can also buy the vintage lighting on display here.

COS
4 rue des Rosiers, 4th (01.44.54.37.70, www. cosstores.com). M° St-Paul. **Open** 10am-7.30pm Mon-Sat. **Map** p125 C4 ❸ **Fashion**
H&M's upmarket brand Collection of Style (COS) now has a Paris outpost, designed by William Russell, in rue des Rosiers, causing some consternation among those who'd rather have kept this a chain-free zone.

Dammann Frères
15 pl des Vosges, 4th (01.44.54.04.88, www.dammann.fr). M° St-Paul. **Open** 11am-7pm Mon-Fri; 10am-8pm Sat, Sun. **Map** p125 C4 ❹ **Food & drink**
Dammann Frères, fine tea importers since 1825, have finally opened their own boutique, a wonderful den of a place with a beamed roof and mahogany shelves displaying hundreds of their exquisite black boxes. The *orgue à thés* allows you to sniff the aromas of 160 blends. A small tin of loose tea or 24 tea bags costs around €10-€12 and they also sell traditional oriental iron teapots. Everything is attractively gift-wrapped.

★ L'Eclaireur
40 rue de Sévigné, 4th (01.48.87.10.22, www. leclaireur.com). M° St-Paul. **Open** 11am-7pm Mon-Sat; 2-7pm Sun. **Map** p125 C3 ❺ **Fashion**
Housed in a dandified warehouse, L'Eclaireur stocks designs by the likes of Comme des Garçons, Martin Margiela, Dries van Noten, Carpe Diem and Junya Watanabe. Among its exclusive finds, check out smocks by Finnish designer Jasmin Santanen. At the secretive rue Hérold branch you have to ring the doorbell to enter. A space in rue Boissy d'Anglas, near Concorde, sells chic fashions for men and women.

▶ *Men are catered for separately at L'Eclaireur Homme (12 rue Malher, 4th, 01.44.54.22.11).* **Other locations** 10 rue Hérold, 1st (01.40.41.09.89); 26 av des Champs-Elysées, 8th (01.45.62.12.32); 10 rue Boissy d'Anglas, 8th (01.53.43.03.70); 39 av Hoche, 8th (01.56.68.10.47).

★ Finger in the Nose
60 rue Saintonge, 3rd (01.42.71.43.40, www.fingerinthenose.com). M° St-Sébastien Froissart. **Open** 11am-7pm Tue-Sat. **Map** p125 C2 ❻ **Children**
As the name suggests, there is nothing twee about the kidswear from this Norwegian designer. In this Marais boutique blackboard walls with chalk slogans and drawings set off tough rebel urban wear for six- to 16-year-olds. **Other location** 11 rue de l'Echaudé, 6th (09.83.01.76.75).

Finkelsztajn
27 rue des Rosiers, 4th (01.42.72.78.91, www. laboutiquejaune.com). M° St-Paul. **Open** 11am-7pm Mon; 10am-7pm Wed, Thur; 10am-7.30pm Fri-Sun. Closed 15 July-15 Aug. **Map** p125 C3 ❼ **Food & drink**
This motherly, yellow-fronted shop, in business since 1946, stocks dense Jewish cakes filled with poppy seeds, apples or cream cheese.

Free 'P' Star
8 rue Ste-Croix-de-la-Bretonnerie, 4th (01.42.76.03.72, www.freepstar.com). M° St-Paul. **Open** 11am-9pm Mon-Sat; noon-9pm Sun. **Map** p125 B3 ❽ **Fashion**
Late-night shopping is fun at this Aladdin's cave of retro glitz, ex-army wear and glad rags that has provided fancy dress for many a Paris party. **Other locations** 61 rue de la Verrerie, 4th (01.42.78.00.76); 20 rue de Rivoli, 4th (01.42.77.63.43).

★ Galerie Emmanuel Perrotin
76 rue de Turenne & 10 impasse St-Claude, 3rd (01.42.16.79.79, www.galerieperrotin.com). M° St-Sébastien Froissart. **Open** 11am-7pm Tue-Sat. **Map** p125 D3 ❾ **Gallery**
Perrotin is one of the sharpest figures in town: not content with owning a gallery in Miami and a glossy magazine, he has recently jumped on the design

---

IN THE KNOW KEEPING FIT

Espace Vit'Halles (48 rue Rambuteau, 3rd, 01.42.77.21.71, www.vithalles.fr) is a Marais health club with Technogym fitness machines, a sauna and some of the best classes in the city, particularly for step and spinning.

Galerie Emmanuel Perrotin.

Galerie Yvon Lambert
108 rue Vieille-du-Temple, 3rd (01.42.71.09.33, www.yvon-lambert.com). M° Filles du Calvaire or St-Sébastien Froissart. **Open** 10am-7pm Tue-Sat. **Map** p125 C3 ⓱ **Gallery**
Lambert celebrated 35 years in the business in 2011, and remains a powerhouse of the French scene, with plenty of big-name stuff, a New York offshoot and a personal collection granted museum status in Avignon. The gallery includes a dedicated area for video installations, and the main space shows leading international names – American bigwigs Andres Serrano, Sol LeWitt, Nan Goldin and Jenny Holzer, plus next-generation artists Douglas Gordon and Jonathan Monk. The street-front art bookshop has a basement gallery for younger talents.

★ Iro
53 rue Vieille-du-Temple, 4th (01.42.77.25.09, www.iro.fr). M° St-Paul. **Open** 10.30am-7.30pm Mon-Sat; noon-7pm Sun. **Map** p125 B3 ⓱ **Fashion**
Fashion editors have tipped designers Laurent and Arik Bitton for stardom with what they call 'basic deluxe': skinny knits, skinny jeans, babydoll dresses and the 'perfecto' mini leather jacket. With a background in music, the brothers know how to hit just the right note for a French silhouette.
Other locations throughout the city.

Izraël
30 rue François-Miron, 4th (01.42.72.66.23). M° Hôtel de Ville. **Open** 11am-1pm, 2-7pm Tue-Fri; 11am-7pm Sat. Closed Aug. **Map** p125 B4 ⓱ **Food & drink**
A Marais fixture, this narrow shop stocks spices and other delights from Mexico, Turkey and India.

Jacenko
38 rue de Poitou, 3rd (01.42.71.80.38). M° St-Sébastien Froissart. **Open** 12.30-8pm Tue-Sat. **Map** p125 C3 ⓱ **Fashion**
The owner of this tasteful little boutique has a faultless eye for shirts, jackets, woollens and accessories that are dandy but not downright gay. McQ, Viktor & Rolf, Givenchy and John Smedley all appear.

Jacques Génin
133 rue de Turenne, 3rd (01.45.77.29.01). M° Filles du Calvaire. **Open** 11am-7pm Mon-Fri; 11am-8pm Sat. **Map** p125 C2 ⓱ **Food & drink**
Jacques Génin was voted the 'best *chocolatier* in the world' by critic Mort Rosenblum, but his creations could previously be tasted only in top restaurants. But now his impressive Marais boutique allows you to taste *sur place* or take a bag home. The signature éclairs and tarts glisten in glass cases, and the millefeuilles are made to order for perfect freshness. The chocolate ganaches include Menthe Amante, a two-phase taste sensation. One part of the space is given over to a tearoom, and a spiral staircase leads to the *ateliers*.

EMMANUEL
ne - 10 impasse Saint
6 79 79 www.gale
1h-19h / tuesday-sa

bandwagon with shows by Robert Stadler and Eric Benqué. As well as the quirky Japanese set of Takashi Murakami, Mariko Mori et al, and big French names such as Sophie Calle, Xavier Veilhan, Tatiana Trouvé and Bernard Frize, he also features radical Austrian collective Gelatin.

Galerie Fatiha Selam
58 rue Chapon, 3rd (09.83.33.65.69, www.fatiha selam.com). M° Arts et Métiers. **Open** 11am-7pm Tue-Sat. **Map** p125 B2 ⓱ **Gallery**
This new addition to a burgeoning gallery street opened in late 2012 with an exhibition of US artist Stephen Schultz's dreamlike canvases. Fatiha Selam brings a fresh eye to the NoMa art scene and promises to explore figurative and abstract contemporary artists both known and emerging.

Galerie Simone
77 rue Charlot, 4th (www.galerie-simone.com). M° Filles du Calvaire or Temple. **Open** noon-7.30pm daily. **Map** p125 C2 ⓱ **Gallery**
Simone Gaubatz sources and cultivates talented young designers from around the world, displaying their most eye-catching creations on mannequins in this gallery-style space.

EXPLORE

Jimmy Fairly

64 rue Vieille du Temple, 4th (01.79.72.60.20,
www.jimmyfairly.com). M° St-Paul. **Open** 11am-
7pm daily. **Map** p125 C3 🐓 **Accessories**
Probably the city's largest supplier of eyewear to
bearded hipsters, Jimmy Fairly launched as a website
before opening a store in 2012. There are around 30
retro-style designs: pick up a Monroe, Hamilton or
Watson for just €95, lenses included (if you don't need
a prescription or to have them fitted with anti-reflec-
tive glass). What's more, the 'Buy one give one' model
means that for every pair of glasses sold, Jimmy
Fairly gives a brand new pair to someone in need.

★ K Jacques

16 rue Pavée, 4th (01.40.27.03.57, www.
kjacques.fr). M° St-Paul. **Open** 10am-7.15pm Mon-
Sat; 1-7.15pm Sun. **Map** p125 C4 🐓 **Accessories**
Set up in Saint-Tropez in 1933 by Jacques Keklikian
and his wife, the K Jacques workshop started life
stitching together basic leather sandals for visitors
to the Med resort. The Homère (or Homer) was, and
still is, the signature piece – Picasso loved them.

Margo Milin

4 rue Malher, 4th (06.61.77.14.76, www.margo
milin.com). M° St-Paul. **Open** noon-7.30pm
Tue-Sat; 2-6.30pm Sun. **No credit cards.**
Map p125 C4 🐓 **Fashion**
St Martin's graduate Marguerite Milin studied theatrical design and produces kimono-influenced wraparound jumpers and party dresses that play with a
contrast of textures and pattern versus plain.

Martin Grant

10 rue Charlot, 3rd (01.42.71.39.49, www.
martingrantparis.com). M° Temple. **Open**
10am-1pm, 2-6pm Mon-Fri. Closed 3wks Aug.
Map p125 C3 🐓 **Fashion**
This high-end shop is tucked away in a second-floor
Marais apartment. If you're a stickler for steady cuts,
pure textiles and unfussy designs, Australian
Martin Grant's interpretation of couture is for you.

★ Merci

111 bd Beaumarchais, 3rd (01.42.77.00.33, www.
merci-merci.com). M° St-Sébastien Froissart. **Open**
10am-7pm Mon-Sat. **Map** p125 D3 🐓 **Homewares**
Merci is housed in a 19th-century fabric factory.
Inside, three loft-like floors heave with furniture, jewellery, stationery, fashion, household products, childrenswear and a haberdashery. That's not all. In a
move that takes the trend for retailer responsibility
to a new level, this most generous of general stores
gives all its profits to charity.

Nodus

22 rue Vieille-du-Temple, 4th (01.42.77.07.96,
www.nodus.fr). M° Hôtel de Ville or St-Paul.
Open 10.45am-2pm, 3-7.30pm Mon-Sat; 1-7.30pm
Sun. **Map** p125 B4 🐓 **Fashion**

Under the wooden beams of this men's shirt specialist are neat rows of striped, checked and plain dress
shirts, silk ties and silver-plated crystal cufflinks.
Other locations throughout the city.

Polka Galerie

Cour de Venise, 12 rue Saint-Gilles, 3rd
(01.76.21.41.30, www.polkagalerie.com). M°
Bréguet-Sabin or Chemin Vert. **Open** 11am-
7.30pm Tue-Sat. **Map** p125 D3 🐓 **Gallery**
'Every photo has a tale to tell': such is the leitmotif
at Polka Galerie, where Adélie de Ipanema and
Edouard Genestar have devoted their art space to
photojournalism. Works on display are signed by
photographers such as Ethan Levitas, Marc Riboud,
Reza and Daido Morayima. While you're there, pick
up a copy of *Polka Magazine*, a fortnightly spread
brimming with picture-rich articles, many of which
tie in with the exhibitions in the gallery.

Pozzetto

39 rue du Roi de Sicile, 4th (01.42.77.08.64,
www.pozzetto.biz). M° Hôtel de Ville or St-Paul.
Open noon-11pm Mon-Thur, Sun; noon-12.15am
Fri, Sat. **Map** p125 B4 🐓 **Food & drink**
Pozzetto might not be the most famous *gelateria* in
Paris, but it's one of the best, serving classic Italian
flavours such as *gianduia torinese* (a Turin speciality
of chocolate and hazelnuts), *fior di latte* (made from
milk, cream and sugar) and *pistacchio* (a creamy
Sicilian pistachio blend). Fruit-lovers are in for a treat,
too, with peach, berry, pear and orange sorbets all
made from real fruit. Order your scoop through the
little window overlooking rue du Roi Sicile.

★ Les Prairies de Paris

23 rue Debelleyme, 3rd (01.48.04.91.16, www.
lesprairiesdeparis.com). M° St-Sébastien Froissart.
Open 11.30am-2pm, 3-7.30pm Tue-Sat; 2-7pm
Sun. **Map** p125 C2 🐓 **Fashion**
The ground floor of Laeticia Ivanez's boutique is
given over to art shows, gigs and happenings.
Downstairs the 1960s theme continues, with a
cocoon-like setting in which to commune with the
disco-glam separates and cute children's collection.
Other location 6 rue du Pré aux Clercs, 7th
(01.40.20.44.12).

Shine

15 rue de Poitou, 3rd (01.48.05.80.10). M° Filles
du Calvaire. **Open** 11am-7.30pm Mon-Sat; 1-7pm
Sun. **Map** p125 C3 🐓 **Fashion**
See By Chloe, Marc by Marc Jacobs and Acne Jeans,
plus Repetto shoes and Véronique Branquino, are
among the goodies in this glossy showcase.

Surface 2 Air

108 rue Vieille-du-Temple, 3rd (01.44.61.76.27,
www.surface2airparis.com). M° St-Sébastien
Froissart. **Open** 11.30am-7.30pm Mon-Sat;
1.30-7.30pm Sun. **Map** p125 C3 🐓 **Fashion**

This non-concept concept store also acts as an art gallery. The cult clothing selection takes in Alice McCall's sassy frocks, Fifth Avenue Shoe Repair jeans and printed dresses by Wood Wood. For men, labels include Marios, Wendy & Jim and F-Troupe.

Le Village St-Paul

Rue St-Paul, rue Charlemagne & quai des Célestins, 4th (www.levillagesaintpaul.com). M° St-Paul. **Open** 11am-7pm Mon, Thur-Sun. **Map** p125 C4 ❸ **Homewares**

This colony of antiques sellers is a source of retro furniture, kitchenware and wine gadgets.

Vintage Bar

16 rue de la Verrerie, 4th (09.82.24.56.95). M° Hôtel de Ville or St-Paul. **Open** noon-8pm daily. **Map** p125 B3 ❸ **Fashion**

Vintage Bar is pretty luxurious, in an area where clothes can usually be found at bargain prices. Once inside, though, it's hard to imagine that the clothes have three-figure labels; it couldn't feel further from a high-end hangout. Trinkets clutter up the floor, and fur coats hanging from the ceiling casually brush your face as you walk by. The boutique also acts as a *dépôt-vente* – if you have designer threads lying about you want to get rid of, they'll sell them on, with a percentage of the price returning to you.

WAIT

9 rue Notre-Dame de Nazareth, 3rd (09.82.52. 84.34, www.wait-paris.com). M° République. **Open** 11am-7pm Mon-Sat. **Map** p125 C1 ❸ **Accessories**
See below **Bachelor Bliss**.

Zadig & Voltaire

42 rue des Francs-Bourgeois, 3rd (01.44.54.00.60, www.zadig-et-voltaire.com). M° Hôtel de Ville or St-Paul. **Open** 10.30am-7.30pm Mon-Sat; noon-7.30pm Sun. **Map** p125 C3 ❸ **Fashion**

Z&V's relaxed, urban collection is a winner. Popular separates include cotton tops, shirts and faded jeans; its winter range of cashmere jumpers is superb.
▶ *The more upmarket Zadig & Voltaire De Luxe is at 18 rue François 1er, 8th (01.40.70.97.89).* **Other locations** throughout the city.

Zef

15 rue Debelleyme, 3rd (01.42.76.09.65, www.zef.eu). M° St-Sébastien Froissart. **Open** 10.30am-7pm Mon-Sat; 2-7pm Sun. **Map** p125 C3 ❸ **Children**

Zef's trendy children's separates have a classic Italian look with adorable details such as elbow patches on the jackets.
Other locations throughout the city.

BACHELOR BLISS

All the modern man needs at WAIT.

Imagine a man's ultimate fantasy living room and you have **WAIT** (*see above*), a shop filled with everything from retro video game consoles, surfboards, skateboards and shades to a reconditioned racing bike, vintage furniture, cool shirts, T-shirts and baseball caps. Plus the crucial accessory for the modern man – scented candles.

'It's not just a concept shop, but it's our office, showroom and ideas lab,' says Antoine Mocquard, one half of the duo behind the store. He and Julien Tual, both from Brittany, met in Rennes and started designing ultra-light glasses and sunglasses made from wood five years ago. Having outgrown their premises in the St-Paul area, the pair moved to this up-and-coming district and decided to fill the space with 'everything we like', which ranges

from Thomas Bexon Australian surfboards to Fabrice Houdry art. Brands sourced from all over the world include Australian fashion label TCSS, La Paz checked shirts, Moupia baseball caps, Good Guys vegan shoes and delightful Papier Tigre notebooks.

The bike is on *depôt-vente* from La Bicyclette, which repairs and customises vintage racers. Antoine and Julien have also designed a trio of white steel tables, and in 2013 launched their own fashion brand. Also called WAIT, it offers a unique take on traditional Breton togs, such as a densely knitted navy jumper with three different-coloured wooden buttons on the shoulder. 'It's 90 per cent Breton and ten per cent Parisian,' says Antoine. A little like these guys, who have brought a touch of Atlantic surf to the city.

Bastille & Eastern Paris

EXPLORE

Place de la Bastille has remained a symbol of popular revolt ever since the storming of the grim fortress-prison that kicked off the Revolution in 1789. The square is still a gathering point for demonstrations and Bastille Day festivities, but the only remnants of the prison are found in the métro station underneath. In fact, with its opera house, lively market along boulevard Richard-Lenoir, and bobo bars and restaurants, Bastille is positively hip these days – especially at night when rue Amelot, rue de la Roquette and rue de Charonne serve party-crazed Parisians enough drinks to sink the canal boats in the nearby Port de l'Arsenal. The Bercy district has seen its star rise, too, thanks to the Cinémathèque Française, and the shops and cafés at Bercy Village.

Bois de Vincennes

Don't Miss

1 Cimetière du Père-Lachaise Home to some of France's most creative corpses (p145).

2 A la Biche au Bois Great food, great wine, great vibe (p157).

3 Bois de Vincennes Paris's biggest park is buzzing with activity (p156).

4 Cité Nationale de l'Histoire de l'Immigration Immigration laid bare at this moving museum (p157).

5 Isabel Marant Designer Paris chic to a T (p155).

Cimetière du Père-Lachaise

BASTILLE & FURTHER EAST

In the 11th, 12th & 20th arrondissements.

The area around place de la Bastille was transformed in the 1980s with the arrival of the **Opéra Bastille** (*see p283*), along with a slew of fashionable cafés, restaurants and bars. The present-day square occupies the site of the long-vanished prison ramparts, and is dominated by the Opéra's curved façade. Opened in 1989 on the bicentenary of Bastille Day, the venue remains controversial, criticised for its poor acoustics and design. South of the square is the Port de l'Arsenal marina, where the Canal St-Martin meets the Seine. The canal continues underground north of the square, running beneath boulevard Richard-Lenoir.

Rue du Fbg-St-Antoine has been the heart of the furniture-makers' district for centuries. Showrooms still line the street, though they've been joined by clothes shops and bars. Cobbled rue de Lappe typifies the shift, as the last remaining furniture workshops hold out against theme bars overrun at weekends by suburban youths. Pockets of bohemian resistance remain

IN THE KNOW EAU DE PARIS

The French capital is littered with more than 800 water fountains; from simple taps on the sides of *sanisettes* (Paris's self-cleaning public loos) to arty-looking modern street units. And now Eau de Paris has gone one step further by installing three chilled sparkling water fountains in the capital, including La Pétillante in the Jardin de Reuilly in the 12th.

on rue de Charonne, however, with the **Pause Café** (*see p153*) and its busy terrace, bistro **Chez Paul** (no.13, 11th, 01.47.00.34.57, www.chezpaul.com) and dealers in colourful 1960s furniture. Rue des Taillandiers and rue Keller are a focus for record stores, streetwear shops and fashion designers.

Narrow street frontages hide cobbled alleys, lined with craftsmen's workshops or quirky bistros dating from the 18th century. Note the cours de l'Ours, du Cheval Blanc, du Bel Air (and hidden garden) and de la Maison Brûlée, the passage du Chantier on rue du Fbg-St-Antoine, the rustic-looking passage de l'Etoile d'Or and the passage de l'Homme, with wooden shopfronts on rue de Charonne. This area was originally located outside the city walls on the lands of the Convent of St-Antoine (parts of which survive as the Hôpital St-Antoine). In the Middle Ages, skilled furniture-makers not belonging to the city's restrictive guilds earned the neighbourhood a reputation for free thinking that was cemented a few hundred years later during the Revolution.

Further down rue du Fbg-St-Antoine is place d'Aligre, home to a rowdy, cheap produce market, a more sedate covered food hall and the only flea market within the city walls. The road ends in the major intersection of place de la Nation, another grand square. It was originally called place du Trône, after a throne that was positioned here when Louis XIV and his bride Marie-Thérèse entered the city in 1660. After the Revolution, between 13 June and 28 July 1794, thousands were guillotined on the site, their bodies carted to the nearby Cimetière de Picpus. The square still has two of Ledoux's toll houses and tall Doric columns from the 1787 Mur des Fermiers-Généraux. In the centre stands Jules Dalou's sculpture *Le Triomphe*

EXPLORE

de la République, erected for the centenary of the Revolution in 1889. East of place de la Nation, broad cours de Vincennes has a market on Wednesday and Saturday mornings.

North of place de la Bastille, boulevard Beaumarchais divides Bastille from the Marais. East of place Voltaire, on rue de la Roquette, which heads east towards the Ménilmontant area and **Père-Lachaise** cemetery, a small park and playground marks the site of the prison of La Roquette, where a plaque remembers the 4,000 Resistance members imprisoned here in World War II.

East of Père-Lachaise on rue de Bagnolet, **La Flèche d'Or** (*see p274*), a converted station on the defunct Petite Ceinture railway line, is a landmark music venue. Beyond, the medieval Eglise St-Germain-de-Charonne (currently closed for renovations) is at the heart of what is left of the village of Charonne. Set at the top of steps next to its presbytery, below a hill once covered with vines, it is one of only two churches in Paris still to have its own graveyard. Below here, centred on the old high street of rue St-Blaise, is a prettified backwater of quiet tearooms and bistros, where old shops have been taken over by art classes.

Towards porte de Bagnolet, where rue de Bagnolet and rue des Balkans meet on the edge of a small park, the **Pavillon de l'Hermitage** is a small aristocratic relic built in the 1720s for Françoise-Marie de Bourbon, the daughter of Louis XIV, when it was in the grounds of the Château de Bagnolet. A little further south at porte de Montreuil, cross the Périphérique for the Puces de Montreuil market (7am-7pm Mon, Sat, Sun).

Sights & Museums

★ FREE Cimetière du Père-Lachaise

*Bd de Ménilmontant, 20th (01.55.25.82.10). M°
Père-Lachaise.* **Open** *6 Nov-15 Mar* 8am-5.30pm
Mon-Fri; 8.30am-5.30pm Sat; 9am-5.30pm Sun.
16 Mar-5 Nov 8am-6pm Mon-Fri; 8.30am-6pm Sat;
9am-6pm Sun. **Admission** free. **Map** p146 B6 ❶
See p148 **Walk**.

La Maison Rouge – Fondation Antoine de Galbert

*10 bd de la Bastille, 12th (01.40.01.08.81,
www.lamaisonrouge.org). M° Quai de la Rapée.*
Open 11am-7pm Wed, Fri-Sun; 11am-9pm Thur.
Admission €8; €5.50 reductions; free under-13s.
Map p147 E2 ❷
Created by art collector Antoine de Galbert and set in a former printworks, the Red House is an independently run space focusing on contemporary works. Solo shows alternate with themed exhibitions featuring pieces from international collections. The bright on-site café is run by the Rose Bakery team.

Restaurants

Le 6 Paul Bert

*6 rue Paul Bert, 11th (01.43.79.14.32).
M° Charonne or Faidherbe Chaligny.* **Open**
7.30-11pm Mon; noon-2.30pm, 7.30-11pm
Tue-Fri. **Main courses** €10-€18. **Prix
fixe** *Lunch* €18, €19. *Dinner* €38, €44.
Map p146 D4 ❸ Bistro
Bertrand Auboyneau (Bistrot Paul Bert, Ecailler du Bistrot) opened Le 6 Paul Bert at the end of 2012. Charming, efficient staff welcome you into the light-filled room dominated by an enormous zinc bar, surrounded by Formica tables and studded with lamps made from forks and bottles of wine. The menu revisits bistro jazz standards (tartare, herring, seasonal vegetables), but they're adapted according to the produce available in the market and the whims of the chef. You might enjoy roasted scallops with parsley and lemon, or a little quail with beetroot purée and a bouquet of pickled carrots. In the best bistro tradition, a short but well-chosen wine list offers bottles from all over France.

★ Le Bistrot Paul Bert

*18 rue Paul-Bert, 11th (01.43.72.24.01).
M° Charonne or Faidherbe Chaligny.* **Open**
noon-2pm, 7.30-11pm Tue-Sat. Closed Aug.
Main courses €14-€27. **Prix fixe** *Lunch* €19.
Dinner €38. **Map** p146 D4 ❹ Bistro
This heart-warming bistro gets it right almost down to the last crumb. A starter salad of *ris de veau* illustrates the point, with lightly browned veal sweetbreads perched on a bed of green beans and baby carrots with a sauce of sherry vinegar. A roast shoulder of suckling pig and a thick steak with a raft of golden, thick-cut *frites* look inviting indeed. Desserts are superb too, including what may well be the best *île flottante* in Paris.

La Crêperie Bretonne Fleurie de l'Epouse du Marin

*67 rue de Charonne, 11th (01.43.55.62.29).
M° Charonne, Ledru-Rollin or Voltaire.* **Open**
noon-2.30pm, 7-11pm Mon-Sat; 7-11pm Sun.
Main courses €6.40-€10.40. **Prix fixe** *Lunch*
€9. **No credit cards. Map** p146 D3 ❺ Crêperie
The spectacularly named 'flower-filled Breton crêperie run by a sailor's wife' feels like the haunt of old sea-dogs, all wood, old posters, antiques and postcards from all over the world. The menu offers a wide choice of crêpes and galettes – the origin of the ingredients is carefully marked, as if to reassure those traumatised by the indigestible crêpes sold along rue Oberkampf. Prices range between €2.70 for a buckwheat pancake with butter to €10.40 for a version with goat's cheese, bacon and eggs. The picture is completed with a good bottle of cider at €9 and a fantastic classic sweet crêpe, the 'Gwenn ha Du' with own-made chocolate sauce and a scoop of vanilla ice-cream (€6.40).

EXPLORE

EXPLORE

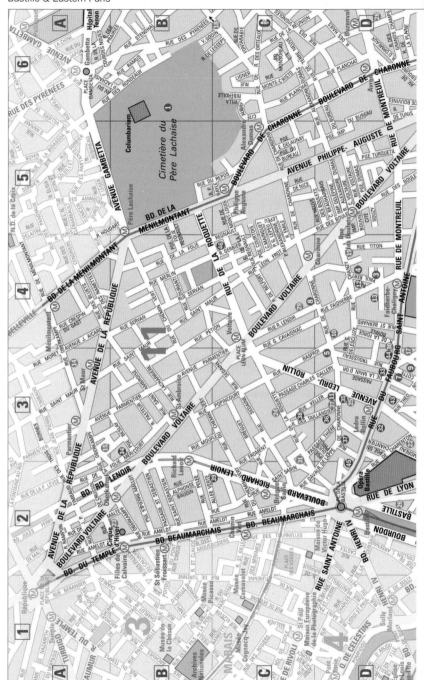

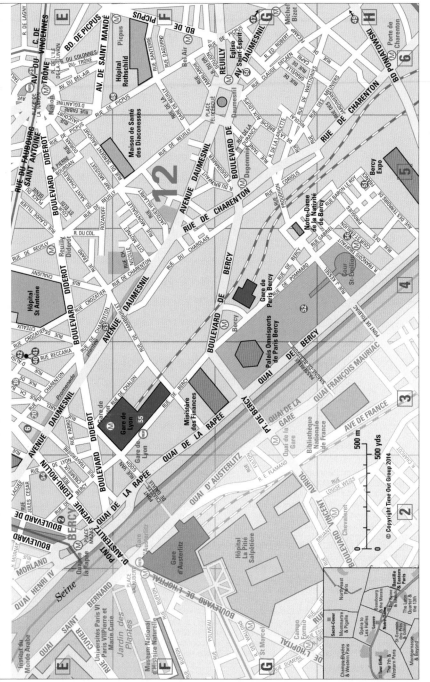

EXPLORE

WALK DEAD FAMOUS

Take a stroll round Père-Lachaise.

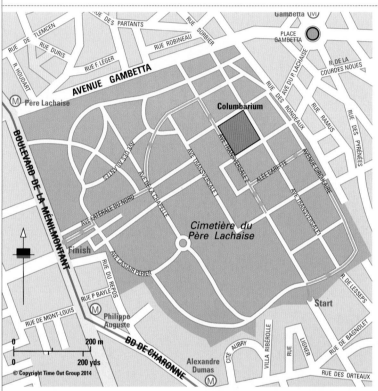

EXPLORE

The Cimetière du Père-Lachaise (*see p145*), Paris's largest cemetery, is probably still best known to foreign visitors as the final resting place of lead singer **James Douglas Morrison**, lead singer of the Doors. But ask a local what this 48-hectare site in the 20th arrondissement means to them, and they're more likely to mention the Mur des Fédérés or **Molière** than the Lizard King. On this walk, therefore, you'll pay tribute to the heroes and victims of French political history, and visit the tombs of some of France's greatest writers.

Rather than entering Père-Lachaise by the main entrance on boulevard Ménilmontant, start at the much more discreet gate set into the southern wall of the cemetery on rue de la Réunion, just off rue de Bagnolet.

You join avenue Circulaire, which hugs the cemetery wall. Turn right and then follow the path round until you reach the **Mur des Fédérés** in the south-east corner.

It was here, during the last week of May 1871, that the few remaining partisans of the **Paris Commune** (known as *fédérés* or communards) were lined up against a wall and summarily executed by troops loyal to the National Assembly at Versailles. A memorial procession to the wall, the Montée au Mur des Fédérés, takes place every year in May.

Across the path, in plot or '*division*' No.97, stand a number of memorials to the victims of Nazism and Fascism. Next to an urn containing ashes from the crematorium at the Flossenburg concentration camp is a striking ziggurat commemorating people who were 'tortured, gassed, shot or hanged'. And just behind this loom two enormous manacled hands hewn from stone, a deeply unsettling monument to the women who died at Ravensbrück. A little further along avenue Circulaire, on the same side, is the tomb of people who perished in 1962 at the hands of the police at Charonne métro station, after a demonstration in favour of Algerian independence.

Follow avenue Circulaire along the northern wall until you reach the Jardin du Souvenir. Turn left up avenue Carette, keeping an eye out on your right for the monumental sarcophagus housing the remains of **Oscar Wilde**, who died in Paris in 1900 aged just 46.

When you reach avenue Transversale no.2, turn left and walk down the hill until you reach a bronze effigy of **Victor Noir**, a journalist who was shot by a cousin of Napoleon III in 1870. You'll notice that the effigy depicts Noir with a distinct enlargement in the region of the groin, and also that the area in question appears to have been rubbed down rather energetically: many *parisiennes* have believed that a little *frottage* with Victor would make them fertile.

Now retrace your steps in the direction of the crematorium and columbarium. On your left hand side, in division 86, is the rough-hewn headstone of **Guillaume Appolinaire**. Across the path, **Marcel Proust** lies in an austere tomb with various other family members.

Continue along avenue Transversale No.2, until you reach avenue des Thuryas. Turn left and walk down the hill into gently curving chemin Casimir Delavigne. About halfway down on the right is a bronze bust of **Honoré de Balzac**. The bust is accompanied by a bronze book and quill, upon which, on a recent visit, an admirer had left an apple with a heart carved in it.

Walk straight on, down chemin Mont-Louis. Through the trees you'll catch a few tantalising glimpses of the Paris skyline as you head towards avenue Principale, and beyond that the main gate of the cemetery, and the din and traffic of boulevard Ménilmontant.

€ L'Encrier

55 rue Traversière, 12th (01.44.68.08.16). *M° Gare de Lyon or Ledru-Rollin.* **Open** noon-2.30pm, 7.30-11pm Mon-Sat. Closed Aug. **Main courses** €10.50-€25. **Prix fixe** *Lunch* €13.50-€25.50. *Dinner* €17, €20.40, €25.50. **Map** p147 E3 **6** Bistro

Through the door and past the velvet curtain, you find yourself face to face with the kitchen – and a crowd of locals, many of whom seem to know the charming boss personally. Start with fried rabbit kidneys on a bed of salad dressed with raspberry vinegar, perhaps, an original and wholly successful combination, and follow with goose *magret* with honey – served with crunchy, thinly sliced sautéed potatoes. To end, share a chocolate cake, or try the popular profiteroles. The Chinon is a classy red.

La Gazzetta

29 rue de Cotte, 12th (01.43.47.47.05, www. lagazzetta.fr). M° Ledru-Rollin. **Open** noon-3pm, 8-10.30pm Tue-Sat. Closed Aug. **Main courses** €25. **Prix fixe** *Lunch* €19. *Dinner* €45, €55, €65. **Map** p146 D3 **7** Bistro

Opened by the team behind Le Fumoir, La Gazzetta has a similarly moody feel, with dim lighting, a long zinc bar and retro decor. Chef Petter Nilssen is Swedish, but he made his name in the south of France, and his food shows a strong Scandinavian influence in dishes such as bonito in a sweet-salty marinade with caraway, borage leaves, radish and pomelo, or new potatoes from the Ile de Noirmoutier off the Atlantic coast with seaweed butter and dill. The €45 menu is a pretty good bet, with five courses.

La Pulpería

1 rue Richard Lenoir, 11th (01.40.09.03.70). M° Charonne or Voltaire. **Open** 8-11pm Mon, Sat; noon-2.30pm, 8-11pm Tue-Fri. **Main courses** €23-€30. **Prix fixe** *Lunch* €18, €22. **Map** p146 C4 **8** South American

The Meat at La Pulpería comes with a capital M, served in a noisy, welcoming little dining room and whipped up in the white-tiled kitchen by talented Argentinian chef Fernando Di Tomaso and his South American team. The menu changes daily, but dishes might include a pretty cod ceviche surrounded with fine slices of sweet potato, avocado purée and a splash of lemon juice, or a bloody, magnificent *churrasco* cut of beef served with rissole potatoes and garlicky chimichurri sauce. Prices might seem a bit high (starters €8 to €14, mains €23 to €30, desserts around €9), but for the quality of the products and cooking, it's really very reasonable.

Restaurant Boucherie les Provinces

20 rue d'Aligre, 12th (01.43.43.91.64). M° Faidherbe-Chaligny or Ledru-Rollin. **Open** noon-2pm Tue, Wed; noon-2pm, 7-10.30pm Thur, Fri; noon-3pm Sat, Sun. **Main courses** €13.50-€24. **Map** p146 D3 **9** Bistro

EXPLORE

IN THE KNOW KITCHEN CRAFT

Miss Lunch (Claude Cabri) is famed for her secret lunch parties, Lunch in the Loft, but she was giving cooking classes way before she opened her home as a *table d'hôte*. Nowadays these lessons take place at Première Pression Provence (*see p155*), an olive oil shop just a stone's throw from the Marché d'Aligre (one of the city's best food markets). Sign up for the morning demonstrations (10.30am-2pm) or opt for a culinary evening (7-9.30pm).

The Marché d'Aligre is already one of Paris's favourite foodie markets, and now there's a new reason to visit. Young artisan butcher Christophe Dru began to make a name for himself hosting events in his shop during the annual Le Fooding festival. The success of these tastings gave him the idea to transform his butcher's shop into a no-reservations restaurant as well, and the place has been packed out since the day it opened. As you walk in, all the meat is displayed on the left as usual, with Aligre locals lining up to do their shopping, while the rest of the space is a jumble of tables and counters, heaving with hungry meat-eaters tucking into a giant entrecôte, sweet lamb chops or juicy pork ribs. Prices are very reasonable, basically the same 'per kilo' rate as at the meat counter plus €9 for the cooking. There's a small but excellent wine list.

Septime

80 rue de Charonne, 11th (01.43.67.38.29, www. septime-charonne.fr). M° Charonne, Faidherbe-Chaligny or Ledru-Rollin. **Open** 7.30-10pm Mon; 12.15-2pm, 7.30-10pm Tue-Sat. **Prix fixe** *Lunch* €28, €55. *Dinner* €58. **Map** p146 D4 ⑩ Bistro
The Faubourg Saint-Antoine area has been making waves on the food scene for quite a while, so it's no surprise to find Bertrand Grébaut's latest restaurant venture here. Grébaut is a former pupil at Penninghen design school and the decor reflects his background: huge mirrors, industrial installations, antique flooring and furniture, reinforced concrete and bare wood. The cooking is direct, pure and serious: raw horse mackerel with yoghurt and red cabbage was superb; Iberico ham and pumpkin was tender and delicious. Dessert was a lovely mixture of apples, fromage blanc, honey and thyme. It's all topped off with charming service.

★ Le Souk

1 rue Keller, 11th (01.49.29.05.08). M° Bastille or Ledru-Rollin. **Open** 7.30-11.30pm Tue-Fri; 11.30am-2.30pm, 7.30pm-midnight Sat; 11.30am-2.30pm, 7.30-11.30pm Sun. **Main courses** €13-€16. **Prix fixe** €16.50, €22.50. **Map** p146 D3 ⑪ North African

Potted olive trees mark the entrance to this lively den of Moroccan cuisine. Start with savoury *b'stilla*, a pastry stuffed with duck, raisins and nuts, flavoured with orange-blossom water and sprinkled with cinnamon and powdered sugar. Don't fill up, though, as the first-rate tagines and couscous are enormous. The *tagine canette* (duckling stewed with honey, onions, apricots, figs and cinnamon, then showered with toasted almonds) is terrific. For dessert, try the excellent millefeuille with fresh figs, while sweet mint tea is poured in a long stream by a *djellaba*-clad waiter.

Unico

15 rue Paul-Bert, 11th (01.43.67.68.08, www.resto-unico.com). M° Faidherbe-Chaligny. **Open** 8-11pm Mon; noon-3pm, 8-11pm Tue-Sat. **Main courses** €27-€39. **Prix fixe** *Lunch* €17. **Map** p146 D4 ⑫ South American
Architect Marcelo Joulia and photographer Enrique Zanoni were wise enough to retain the vintage 1970s decor of this former butcher's shop when they opened their temple to Argentinian beef. Orange tiles and matching light fixtures provide the backdrop for the fashionable, black-dressed crowd that comes here for thick slabs of meat grilled over charcoal and served with a selection of sauces. If you find yourself hesitating, opt for the *lomo* (fillet) with *chimichurri*, a mild salsa – and don't forget to wash it down with Argentinian wine, a rarity in Paris.

★ Au Vieux Chêne

7 rue du Dahomey, 11th (01.43.71.67.69, www.vieuxchene.fr). M° Faidherbe-Chaligny. **Open** noon-2pm, 8-10.30pm Mon-Fri. Closed 1wk July & 2wks Aug. **Main courses** €20-€25. **Prix fixe** *Lunch* €15, €19. *Dinner* €28, €33. **Map** p146 D4 ⑬ Bistro
Although everyone loves the zinc-capped bar by the entrance, and the tiled floor, what makes this bistro so special is its desire to please. A starter of langoustines encased in fine crunchy angel hair and garnished with slices of fresh mango is delicious and refreshing, and chilled tomato soup is garnished with mint, a ball of tomato sorbet and a drizzle of olive oil. Stéphane Chevassus is a gifted game cook, too, as proved by the tender roast pigeon sautéed with Chinese cabbage.

Cafés & Bars

Le 114

114 rue Oberkampf, 11th (www.le-114.fr). M° Ménilmontant or Parmentier. **Open** 8pm-4.30am Tue-Sat. **Map** p146 A3 ⑭
Opened in partnership with Puma Social and in association with the new magazine *Plugged*, Le 114 proudly parades its motto on its front window: 'C'est comme chez toi, mais en mieux' (It's just like home, but better). Squishy armchairs and huge sofas back up this assertion, even if the atmosphere isn't quite

as warm as the sign might suggest. However, the bar's creators hit on a great concept when they decided to invite groups to play for free on the small stage. The schedule displays decent taste in rock and pop, and the door policy is run according to time-honoured principles: first come, first served.

★ Ave Maria
1 rue Jacquard, 11th (01.47.00.61.73).
Mº Parmentier. **Open** 7pm-2am daily.
Map p146 A3 🅯
Unlike some places that eschew good food for alcohol and a funky interior, colourful Ave Maria scores highly for all three. The kitsch interior is decked out in a canopy of chinoiserie parasols and a vast collection of Hindu gods. Music, a combination of reggae, funk, soul and dub, is cool but unobtrusive. Strangers sharing wooden benches devour exotic dishes from the Brazilian-inspired menu, which combines meat, spices, lentils, rice and fruit. Cocktails are equally quirky – try the Aguas Borobora (with mango, rose, vodka and champagne).

Ave Maria.

Le Baron Rouge
1 rue Théophile-Roussel, 12th (01.43.43.14.32).
Mº Ledru-Rollin. **Open** 10am-2pm, 5-10pm Tue-Fri; 10am-10pm Sat; 10am-4pm Sun.
Map p147 E3 🅯
It sells wine, certainly – great barrels of the stuff are piled high and sold by the glass at very reasonable prices. But the Red Baron is not just a wine bar; it's more like a local chat room, where regulars congregate to yak over their *vin*, or perhaps one of the few draught beers, and maybe a snack of sausages or oysters. Despite its lack of seating (there are only four tables), it's a popular pre-dinner spot, so arrive early and don't expect too much elbow room.

Café Aouba
30 rue d'Aligre, 12th (01.43.43.22.24). Mº Ledru-Rollin. **Open** 8am-1.30pm, 4-7pm Tue-Fri; 8am-7pm Sat; 8am-2.30pm Sun. **No credit cards**.
Map p146 D3 🅯
To really feel the authentic pulse of the Marché d'Aligre and taste some great coffee, nothing compares to stopping off at Café Aouba, tucked away behind teeming fruit and vegetable stalls. Opened in 1938 by a Portuguese butcher, this is the ultimate market bar, tiny and packed with boisterous stallholders, shoppers and curious tourists. Aouba has had a new lease of life since it was bought two years ago by Emmie Bolatoglu, a dynamic young Turkish woman who has always lived in the neighbourhood. Don't expect any designer deco here, just a basic red Formica counter with elbow room for half-a-dozen customers, and a shining Faema espresso machine.

Le Café Noir
15 rue St-Blaise, 20th (01.40.09.75.80). Mº Alexandre Dumas or Porte de Bagnolet. **Open** noon-2pm, 7.30-11pm Mon-Fri; 7.30-10.30pm Sat.
Map p146 C6 🅯
In the St-Blaise district (the former village of Charonne annexed to Paris in 1860), with views on to the village church, this gorgeous high-ceilinged café, decorated with old cafetières, draws in artists, workers and an upbeat crowd of local trendies. At mealtimes expect inventive French cuisine, with the likes of magret of duck with cardamom and vanilla, and pineapple and mango trifle.

Café Titon
34 rue Titon, 11th (09.53.17.94.10, www.cafe titon.com). Mº Faidherbe-Chaligny or Rue des Boulets. **Open** 8am-2am Mon-Sat; 9am-8pm Sun.
Map p146 D4 🅯
The funky Titon is Paris's only Franco-German café – and certainly the only place in town to flog *currywurst* (German sausage in curry sauce) and chips for a bargain €5.90. It even transforms into a giant *biergarten* during Oktoberfest. Its Parisian side doesn't get forgotten, though, with *croques*, *tartines*, an unbeatable lunch menu (€11.60 for a main and a *café*) and scrumptious cocktails.

EXPLORE

REVAMPING REPUBLIQUE

Paris's most symbolic square has been given a brush-up.

Nowhere is more symbolic for Parisians than place de la République. Originally an avenue of trees created for Louis XIV, then a pleasure garden just before the Revolution, it was laid out in its current grandiose dimensions by Baron Haussmann in 1865. It became place de la République following the Paris Commune, when it acquired its statue of Marianne to celebrate the centenary of the Revolution in 1889. The tradition of protesters climbing on to the statue began almost immediately, and the square remains a key gathering point for the *manifestations* (marches) that are an intrinsic part of city life.

This key right to protest was one of the central considerations when the Mairie decided to revamp the square in 2011 – the space had to remain symbolically open and even the fountains now disappear into the ground during mass gatherings (though this removes the chance of dancing through them dressed only in a *tricolore*). Doubling the pedestrian area and making it into a huge plaza that runs right up to the military barracks on the north side provides Paris with its largest public square. The architects, TVK, describe it as a 'supersurface' that can be adapted to multiple uses, from a venue for large cultural events to a simple place to cool off in the summer among the raised terraces and fountains.

The existing plane trees have been retained and 18 new honey locust trees planted. The 19th-century lampposts have been moved to the back of the square, where they cast a moody green-blue light into the trees, and there's column lighting to make the area safer and more attractive at night. While the disruption has given Parisians another thing to complain about, the work will once again make place de la République worthy of its illustrious name.

Le Calbar

*82 rue de Charenton, 12th (01.84.06.18.90,
www.lecalbarcocktail.com). M° Ledru-Rollin.*
Open 3pm-1.30am Mon-Fri; 5pm-1.30am Sat.
Map p147 E3 ㉚

The look of this former wine bar recalls a New York
loft, with bare bricks, street art, wooden furniture –
and waiters decked out in underwear, aprons, braces
and bow ties. You have to climb a caged stairway to
find the lounge furnished with comfortable chesterfields and post-industrial coffee tables, and hip hop
and electro playing in the background. Cocktails feature premium spirits such as Monkey 47 (a German
liqueur with 47 ingredients), Nikka Japanese whisky
or even Tanqueray Ten (gin made from fresh fruit).
There's no happy hour, but instead a monthly *apéro*
where underwear as outerwear is a prerequisite for
both sexes (free dressing room available) to get hold
of the special cocktail, the Dagobear.

★ Chez Prosper

7 av du Trône, 11th (01.43.73.08.51). M° Nation.
Open 8am-1am daily. **Map** p147 E6 ㉛

Chez Prosper welcomes punters all day long with
that simplest of gestures: a smile. Yes, even when
squeezing past people queuing for a spot on the sun
terrace, the waiters are positively beaming. The din-
ing/drinks area – tiled floor, large mirrors, wooden
furniture – is run with military precision, and orders
arrive promptly. The *steak-frites* and *croques* (served
on Poilane bread) are hearty, and the naughty
Nutella tiramisu is worth crossing town for.

China

*50 rue de Charenton, 12th (01.43.46.08.09,
www.lechina.eu). M° Bastille or Ledru Rollin.*
Open 10am-2am Mon-Thur, Sun; 10am-4am
Fri, Sat. Closed Aug. **Map** p146 D3 ㉜

This sexy take on a 1930s Shanghai gentleman's club,
with red walls, leather chesterfields and the longest
bar in Paris, serves some of the finest cocktails in town
(including its signature singapore sling). The
Cantonese cuisine is pricey, so skip dinner and head
upstairs to the cigar bar (if you're romantically
inclined) or downstairs to the cellar for weekly jazz,
pop and world music concerts (website has details).

L'Entrée des Artistes

*8 rue de Crussol, 11th (09.50.99.67.11). M° Filles
du Calvaire or Oberkampf.* **Open** 7pm-2am Mon-
Sat. **Map** p146 B2 ㉝

Having mixed drinks at Murano and the
Experimental Cocktail Club, two friends decided to
open Entrée des Artistes. The relaxed venue offers
sophisticated cocktails and a more straightforward
wine list, plus smart snacks such as foie gras, Italian
cheeses and a classy *plat du jour*. Warm and intimate, the small space has an old-world feel cluttered
with beautiful vintage objects, from soda siphons to
an old metal cash register. Dandified city slickers
and Marais hipsters have quickly appropriated the

handful of tables, and the place is packed out from
cocktail hour onwards, fuelled by a mix of hip hop,
jazz, funk, disco and soul.

★ Les Furieux

*74 rue de la Roquette, 11th (01.47.00.78.44,
www.lesfurieux.fr). M° Bastille or Voltaire.*
Open 4pm-2am Tue-Thur; 4pm-5am Fri, Sat.
Map p146 C3 ㉞

Just when it looked as if 'lounge attitude' would con-
taminate every bar on rue de la Roquette, Les Furieux
fought back with a healthy dose of rock and metal,
padded red walls, faux-leather banquettes, black
paint, and rotating photography exhibitions. Locals
flock here for the happy hour (6pm to 8pm), when
cocktails with rockin' names like Grunge, Scud, and,
er, Boris are half price. Diehards can pay tribute to
Paris's hedonistic heyday with 12 different absinthes.

Le Motel

*8 passage Josset, 11th (01.58.30.84.68, www.
lemotel.fr). M° Ledru-Rollin.* **Open** 6pm-1.45am
Tue-Sun. **Map** p146 D3 ㉟

Le Motel has a simple formula: cheap drinks and
excellent music. During happy hour (6pm to 9pm) a
pint of *blonde* costs €3.50 and cocktails €5. With DJs
almost every night, the music ranges from cutting-
edge indie to contemporary neo-folk and rock classics, with the odd Motown hit thrown in for good
measure. Friendly twentysomethings cluster around
faux Louis XVI armchairs or try their luck in the
Sunday pop quiz.

L'Opa

*9 rue Biscornet, 12th (01.46.28.12.90, www.opa-
paris.com). M° Bastille.* **Open** 8pm-2am Wed, Thur;
8pm-6am Fri, Sat. **Map** p146 D2 ㊱

Late opening and Eric Perier's diverse range of
nightly entertainment – DJs (weekends), videos, live
acts and the odd open mic event – are the attractions
here, along with free admission and fairly reasonable drinks prices. A couple of comfortable sofas
take the edge off the loft-like, institutional interior,
with a modest stage in one corner and an upstairs
chill-out space and separate bar.

Pause Café

*41 rue de Charonne, 11th (01.48.06.80.33). M°
Ledru-Rollin.* **Open** 8am-2am Mon-Sat; 9am-8pm
Sun. **Map** p146 D3 ㊲

Featured in Cedric Klapisch's 1996 film *Chacun
Cherche son Chat*, which was shot on location in the
neighbourhood, the Pause Café has managed to pro-
long its moment of glory thanks to its large terrace
on the corner of rues Charonne and Keller. Inside,
the modern salons benefit from a smattering of primary colours with ornately plastered ceilings and
plenty of light. The food – traditional French café
fare with an Asian twist – is not bad, but you might
be waiting for a while; best to order a well-mixed
cocktail to pass the time.

EXPLORE

EXPLORE

Les Pères Populaires

46 rue de Buzenval, 20th (01.43.48.49.22,
www.myspace.com/perespopulaires). M° Buzenval.
Open 8am-2am Mon-Fri; 10am-2am Sat, Sun.
Map p146 D6 ㉘
Could this funky number be the cheapest bar in
Paris? Wine is a mere €2.20 a glass, beer is €2.80
(€5.30 for a pint) and flavoured rums cost €4. To get
an idea of the look of the place, think 1970s canteen-
cum-retro classroom and you'll come close. During
the day, the freelance media crowd and a handful of
musicians squat the tables for free Wi-Fi; at night DJs
spin electro sounds and a party atmosphere reigns.

Le P'tit Bar

7 rue Richard Lenoir, 11th (no phone). M°
Charonne. **Open** 5pm-2am daily. **No credit**
cards. Map p146 C4 ㉙
You couldn't invent this place if you tried: local
soaks, immigrant South Americans, twentysome-
thing students, Brits and retired war veterans all
pop in for a taste of the most surreal experience in
town, courtesy of the elderly Madame Polo, her
fluffy cat and her canaries. A word of warning,
though: don't drink out of the glasses – Madame
Polo isn't too keen on cleaning. We recommend you
opt instead for a €3 bottle of beer.

Le Red House

1bis rue de la Forge Royale, 12th (01.43.67.06.43).
M° Bastille, Faidherbe-Chaligny or Ledru-Rollin.
Open 5pm-2am daily. **Map** p146 D4 ㉚
Le Red House, dominated by a majestic bull's skull
hanging over the bar, has the air of a Texan saloon
in the middle of Bastille, and the crowd is colourful,
young, lively and loud. DJs spin rock, punk, funk
and electro, and the place never seems to be empty
– luckily it's huge, with two connected rooms with
exposed beams, each equipped with its own bar. Try
a Wild West Side (tequila, chilli, cucumber and lime)
or Red House Flambeau (bourbon, apricot brandy,
spicy syrup, lemon and ginger). Also look out for the
menu of off-the-wall seasonal cocktails.

Tape Bar

21 rue de la Roquette, 11th (01.43.38.69.28).
M° Bastille or Bréguet-Sabin. **Open** 6pm-2am
daily. **Map** p146 C3 ㉛
To get away from the overloaded rue de Lappe,
frequented by students and tourists, follow rue de la
Roquette to a little bar that's close by but a world
away. Tape Bar recalls New York's underground
dive scene with its mix-tape and street-art feel, and
is owned by friendly, dynamic young people who
leave graffiti artists to express themselves on the
walls and the DJs to mix mostly hip hop and funk
sets, with some dubstep, drum'n'bass and rock as
well. The ambience is relaxed, the drinks are affordable, the hipster crowd is young, and it all stays
humming until late. During happy hour, cocktails
and hot dogs are €4, a real bargain.

Shops & Services

★ Caravane Chambre 19

19 rue St-Nicolas, 12th (01.53.02.96.96,
www.caravane.fr). M° Ledru-Rollin. **Open**
11am-7pm Tue-Sat. Closed 2wks Aug.
Map p146 D3 ㊷ **Homewares**
This offshoot of Françoise Dorget's original Marais
shop has goodies such as exquisite hand-sewn quilts
from west Bengal, crisp cotton and organdie tunics,
Berber scarves, lounging sofas and daybeds.
Other locations 6 rue Pavée, 4th (01.44.61.04.20);
22 rue St-Nicolas, 12th (01.53.17.18.55).

★ DPAM

120-122 rue du Fbg-St-Antoine, 12th (01.43.44.
67.46, www.dpam.com). M° Ledru-Rollin. **Open**
10am-7pm Mon-Sat. **Map** p146 D3 ㉝ **Children**
Bright, cleverly designed and well made basics for
children aged three months to 14 years, at refreshingly low prices. The Bébé branch, with fashionable
accessories and clothing for kids up to two years, is
a good source of gifts.
Other locations throughout the city.

Fargo

42 rue de la Folie-Méricourt, 11th
(01.48.05.49.52, www.fargostore.com). M°
Parmentier or St-Ambroise. **Open** 11am-7.30pm
Mon-Sat. **Map** p146 B3 ㉞ **Books & music**
With its handsome wooden façade and neon lights,
Fargo wouldn't look out of place in San Francisco.
It's got a Far West feel inside, too, with collections
that cover country music in all its forms (rock, pop,
folk and new wave). The shop has only been around
since 2010, but it's got good connections: regular free
showcases draw the crowds (Moriarty and Steve
Smyth have both played here).

Les Fleurs

6 passage Josset, 11th (01.43.55.12.94,
www.boutiquelesfleurs.com). M° Ledru-Rollin.
Open noon-7.30pm Mon-Sat. **Map** p146 D3 ㉟
Accessories
There are two reasons to walk down passage Josset:
it's quaint and off the beaten track; and it's home to
Les Fleurs, a girly boutique extraordinaire that drips
with funky jewellery, bags, rococo mirrors and all
sorts of gizmos and gadgets for little and grown-up
girls alike. Owner Lucie Deniset has hand-picked
designers such as Nat&Nin, Adeline Affre and
Titlee to create a range of desirables quite unlike any
other in Paris.

Galerie Patrick Seguin

5 rue des Taillandiers, 11th (01.47.00.32.35,
www.patrickseguin.com). M° Bastille or Ledru-
Rollin. **Open** 10am-7pm Mon-Sat. **Map**
p146 D3 ㊱ **Homewares**
Seguin specialises in French design from the 1950s:
items by Jean Prouvé and Charlotte Perriand are on

IN THE KNOW BARGAIN HUNT

Less famous than its older brother in St-Ouen, Montreuil's flea market (Sat, Sun, Mon) on av du Professeur André Lemierre in the 20th is where real folk rifle for antiques nowadays; mostly because it's off the beaten tourist track so you can still hunt uncork the occasional treasure. You'll find everything from vintage clothes to old cutlery, 1940s light fittings, furniture and antique glassware.

display in this handsome showroom designed by Jean Nouvel. Seguin has also collaborated on some ground-breaking exhibitions around the world.

★ Isabel Marant

16 rue de Charonne, 11th (01.49.29.71.55, www.isabelmarant.tm.fr). M° Ledru-Rollin. **Open** 11am-7pm Mon; 10.30am-7.30pm Tue-Sat. **Map** p146 D3 ❻ **Fashion**
Isabel Marant's style is easily recognisable in her ethno-beach brocades, blanket-like coats and decorated sweaters. It's a firm favourite among Paris's young trendies.
Other locations 47 rue Saintonge, 3rd (01.42.78.19.24); 1 rue Jacob, 6th (01.43.26.04.12); 151 av Victor Hugo, 16th (01.47.04.99.95).

Loulou Addict

25 rue Keller, 11th (01.49.29.00.61, www.loulou addict.com). M° Bastille, Ledru-Rollin or Voltaire. **Open** 11.30am-2pm, 3-7pm Tue-Fri; 11am-7pm Sat. **Map** p146 C3 ❽ **Accessories**
Retro motifs, English flourishes, Japanese ornaments and bright colours abound in this boutique, which specialises in home decor and accessories for children (especially girls) and their mothers. This is the place to invest in a mini 2CV in lacquered wood by Vilac or a crocheted doll by Anne-Claire Petit. For *madame*, perhaps a 1970s maroon purse with orange flowers by Blafre or an arty cushion by La Cerise.

★ Marché Bastille

Bd Richard-Lenoir, 11th. M° Richard-Lenoir. **Open** 7am-2.30pm Thur; 7am-3pm Sun. **Map** p146 C2 ❾ **Market**
One of the biggest markets in Paris. A favourite of political campaigners, it's also a great source of local cheeses, farmers' chicken and excellent fish.

Marché Beauvau

Pl d'Aligre, 12th. M° Ledru-Rollin. **Open** 9am-1pm, 4-7.30pm Tue-Fri; 9am-1pm, 3.30-7.30pm Sat; 9am-1.30pm Sun. **Map** p147 E3 ❿ **Market**
This market remains proudly working class. Stallholders do their best to out-shout each other, and price-conscious shoppers don't compromise on quality.

Marché aux Puces d'Aligre

Pl d'Aligre, rue d'Aligre, 12th. M° Ledru-Rollin. **Open** 7am-2pm Tue-Sun. **Map** p147 E3 ⓬ **Market**
The only flea market in central Paris, Aligre stays true to its junk tradition with a handful of *brocanteurs* peddling books, phone cards, kitchenware and oddities at what seem to be optimistic prices.

Moisan

5 pl d'Aligre, 12th (09.50.27.67.04, www.painmoisan.fr). M° Ledru-Rollin. **Open** 6.30am-8.30pm Tue-Sat; 6.30am-2pm Sun. **Map** p147 E3 ⓬ **Food & drink**
Moisan's organic bread, *viennoiseries* and rustic tarts are outstanding. At this branch, situated by the market, there's always a healthy queue.
Other locations throughout the city.

Première Pression Provence

3 rue Antoine Vollon, 12th (01.53.33.03.59, www.premiere-pression-provence.com). M° Ledru Rollin. **Open** 10.30am-3.30pm Wed, Sat; 10.30am-3.30pm, 7-9.30pm Thur, Fri. **Map** p146 D3 ⓭ **Food & drink**
PPP is L'Occitan creator Olivier Baussan's project, where you're encouraged to taste spoonfuls of single-producer olive oil to educate your palate about the nuances of *vert*, *mûr* and *noir*. Two dozen small producers send oils direct from their Provençal olive groves to the boutiques, where they're sold in aluminium cans with colour-coded labels.
Other locations 35 rue Charlot, 3rd (01.57.40.69.58); 9 rue des Martyrs, 9th (01.48.78.86.51); 37 rue du Roi de Sicile, 4th (01.49.96.55.40).

★ A La Providence (Quincaillerie Leclercq)

151 rue du Fbg-St-Antoine, 11th (01.43.43.06.41). M° Ledru-Rollin. **Open** 10am-1pm, 2.30-6pm Tue-Sat. **Map** p146 D3 ⓮ **Homewares**
Step into the past at this museum-piece *quincaillerie* in which 170-year-old wooden cabinets are filled with knobs, locks and other brass accoutrements for dolling up or restoring old furniture and doors.

Silvera

41 rue du Fbg-St-Antoine, 11th (01.43.43.06.75, www.silvera.fr). M° Bastille or Ledru-Rollin. **Open** 10am-7pm Mon-Sat. Closed 2wks Aug. **Map** p146 D2 ⓯ **Homewares**
The former Le Bihan was taken over by Silvera in 2005 and is now a three-floor showcase for modern design. Look out for furniture and lighting from Perriand, Pesce, Pillet, Morrison, Arad and others.
Other locations throughout the city.

Souffle Continu

22 rue Gerbier, 11th (01.40.24.17.21, www.souffle continu.com). M° Philippe Auguste. **Open** noon-8pm Mon-Sat. **Map** p146 C4 ⓰ **Books & music**

EXPLORE

Souffle Continu is one of the musical stars of the neighbourhood thanks to its owners, Bernard and Théo, a pair passionate about vinyl. From jazz improv to harsh noise, from indie rock to black metal, the stands groan with rare treasures.

BERCY & DAUMESNIL

In the 12th arrondissement.

The **Viaduc des Arts** is a former railway viaduct along avenue Daumesnil; its row of glass-fronted arches enclose craft boutiques and workshops. Above sprout the blooms and bamboo of the **Promenade Plantée**. In 1969, the steam engines on avenue Daumesnil's viaduct whistled their last and the train line between Bastille and Vincennes closed forever. While the Bastille station was replaced by today's opera house, the old lines became a 5km-long trail (the Promenade Plantée), made up of elevated gardens, the Jardin de Reuilly and tree-lined cycling paths.

Eglise du Saint-Esprit is a copy of Istanbul's Hagia Sofia; the nearby **Cimetière de Picpus** contains the graves of many of the victims of the Terror, as well as American War of Independence hero General La Fayette.

Just before the Périphérique, the **Palais de la Porte Dorée** was built in 1931 for the Exposition Coloniale. Originally the Musée des Colonies, then the Musée des Arts d'Afrique et d'Océanie, it's home to the **Cité Nationale de l'Histoire de l'Immigration**.

As recently as the 1980s, wine was unloaded from barges at Bercy, but this stretch of the Seine is now home to the vast Ministère de l'Economie et du Budget. To the east is the Bercy Expo centre. In between lie the modern **Parc de Bercy** and the former American Center, built in the 1990s by Frank Gehry. It now houses the Cinémathèque Française. At the eastern edge of the park is **Bercy Village**, where warehouses have been sympathetically restored and opened as shops and cafés.

EXPLORE

Sights & Museums

★ FREE Bois de Vincennes

12th. M° Château de Vincennes or Porte Dorée. **Map** p147 G6 ㊼

This is Paris's biggest park, created when the former royal hunting forest was landscaped by Alphand. There are boating lakes, a Buddhist temple, a racecourse, restaurants, a baseball field and a farm. The park also contains the Cartoucherie theatre complex (*see p289*). The Parc Floral is a cross between a botanical garden and an amusement park, including crazy golf and an adventure playground. Next to the park stands the Château de Vincennes, where England's Henry V died in 1422 (*see p238*).

Cimetière de Picpus

35 rue de Picpus, 12th (01.43.44.18.54). M° Daumesnil, Nation or Picpus. **Open** *15 Apr-14 Oct* 2-6pm Tue-Sun. *15 Oct-14 Apr* 2-4pm Tue-Sun. **Admission** €3. **No credit cards. Map** p147 F6 ㊽

This cemetery in a working convent is the resting place for the thousands of victims of the Revolution's aftermath, guillotined at place du Trône (now place de la Nation) between 13 June and 28 July 1794. At the end of a walled garden is a graveyard of aristocratic French families. In one corner is the tomb of General La Fayette, who fought in the American War of Independence and was married to the aristocratic Marie Adrienne Françoise de Noailles. In the chapel, two tablets list the names and occupations of the executed: 'domestic servant' and 'farmer' figure alongside 'lawyer' and 'prince and priest'.

★ Cité Nationale de l'Histoire de l'Immigration

293 av Daumesnil, 12th (01.53.59.58.60, www.histoire-immigration.fr). M° Porte Dorée. **Open** 10am-5.30pm Tue-Fri; 10am-7pm Sat, Sun. **Admission** €4.50-€6; free under-26s. *Aquarium* €5-€7; €3.50-€5 reductions. PMP. **No credit cards. Map** p147 H6 ㊾

Set in the stunning, colonial-themed Palais de la Porte Dorée, the collections trace over 200 years of immigration history. There are thought-provoking images (film and photography), everyday objects (suitcases, accordions, sewing machines and so on) and artworks that symbolise the struggles immigrants had to face when integrating into French society. Don't miss the permanent Repères (bearings) exhibition that looks at why many immigrants chose France, the problems they faced upon arrival, and the way sport, work, language, religion and culture can ease integration. One of the most moving areas is the Galerie des Dons – memorabilia donated by individuals whose families came from foreign countries. There's also an aquarium in the basement.

FREE Eglise du Saint-Esprit

186 av Daumesnil, 12th (01.44.75.77.50, www.st-esprit.org). M° Daumesnil. **Open** 9.30am-noon, 3-7pm Mon-Fri; 9.30am-noon, 4-6pm Sat; from 9am Sun. **Admission** free. **Map** p147 G6 ㊿

Behind a red-brick exterior cladding, this unusual 1920s concrete church follows a square plan around a central dome, lit by a scalloped ring of windows. Architect Paul Tournon was directly inspired by the Hagia Sofia cathedral in Istanbul, though the inside is decorated with frescoes rather than mosaics.

Musée des Arts Forains

53 av des Terroirs-de-France, 12th (01.43.40.16.22, www.pavillons-de-bercy.com). M° Cour St-Emilion. **Open** groups only, min 15 people, by appointment. **Admission** €14; €5 reductions. **No credit cards. Map** p147 H5 (51)

Musée des Arts Forains.

Housed in a collection of Eiffel-era wine warehouses is a fantastical collection of 19th- and early 20th-century fairground attractions. The venue is hired out for functions on most evenings, and staff may well be setting the tables when you visit. Of the three halls, the most wonderful is the Salon de la Musique, where a musical sculpture by Jacques Rémus chimes and flashes in time with the 1934 Mortier organ and a modern-day digital grand piano playing *Murder on the Orient Express*. In the Salon de Venise you are twirled round on a gondola carousel; in the Salon des Arts Forains you can play a ball-throwing game that sets off a race of moustached waiters. The venue is open only to groups of 15 or more, but individuals can visit on the occasional guided tours. Call ahead.

FREE Parc de Bercy
Rue de Bercy, 12th. M° Bercy or Cour St-Emilion. **Open** *Winter* 8am-5.30pm Mon-Fri; 9am-5.30pm Sat, Sun. *Summer* 8am-9pm Mon-Fri; 9am-9pm Sat, Sun. **Map** p147 G4 ⓷②

Created in the 1990s, the Bercy park features a large lawn, a grid with square rose, herb and vegetable plots, an orchard, and gardens laid out to represent the four seasons.

FREE Le Viaduc des Arts
15-121 av Daumesnil, 12th (www.viaducdesarts.fr). M° Gare de Lyon or Ledru-Rollin. **Map** p147 E4 ⓷③

Glass-fronted workshops in the arches beneath the Promenade Plantée provide showrooms for furniture and fashion designers, picture-frame gilders, tapestry restorers, porcelain decorators, and chandelier, violin and flute makers.

Restaurants

★ € A la Biche au Bois
45 av Ledru-Rollin, 12th (01.43.43.34.38). M° Gare de Lyon. **Open** 7-11pm Mon; 12.30-2pm, 7-11pm Tue-Fri. Closed 4wks July-Aug

& Christmas wk. **Main courses** €17. **Prix fixe** €29.80. **Map** p147 E2 ⓷④ Bistro

However crowded it gets here, it doesn't matter because everyone always seems so happy with the food and the convivial atmosphere. It's impossible not to be enthusiastic about the more than generous portions offered with the prix fixe menu. Mains might include wild duck in blackcurrant sauce, partridge with cabbage or wild venison stew. If you can still do dessert, go for one of the home-made tarts laden with seasonal fruits. The wine list has a reputation as one of the best-value selections in town.

Le Train Bleu
Gare de Lyon, pl Louis-Armand, 12th (01.43.43.09.06, www.le-train-bleu.com). M° Gare de Lyon. **Open** 11.30am-2.45pm, 7-10.45pm daily. **Main courses** €40. **Prix fixe** *Lunch* €60, €75. *Dinner* €60, €75, €102. **Map** p147 F3 ⓷⑤ Brasserie

This listed dining room – with vintage frescoes and big oak benches – exudes a pleasant air of expectation. Don't expect cutting-edge cooking, but rather fine renderings of French classics. Lobster served on walnut oil-dressed salad leaves is a beautifully prepared starter, as is pistachio-studded *saucisson de Lyon* with a warm salad of small *ratte* potatoes.

Shops & Services

Bercy Village 2
Cour St Emilion, 12th (08.25.16.60.75, www.bercy village.com). M° Cour St-Emilion. **Open** 11am-9pm daily. **Map** p147 H4 ⓷⑥ Mall

This retail and leisure development housed in old wine warehouses is a relaxed place in which to shop. Squarely aimed at tourists and out-of-towners, the shops include Agnès b, Nature et Découvertes, Pacific Adventure, L'Occitane, Oliviers & Co and Sephora. There are also several cafés and restaurants, a park and a multiplex cinema.

EXPLORE

North-east Paris

EXPLORE

The Canal St-Martin's iron footbridges and tree-shaded quays formed the backdrop for some of *Amélie*'s most atmospheric scenes, and nowadays this 19th-century waterway draws a hipster crowd to its shabby-chic bars and bistros. Heading north along the Canal, the must-visit den of multidisciplinary artistic creation is Point Ephemère. From here the Canal widens into the Bassin de la Villette and Canal de l'Ourcq, famed for its twin MK2 cinemas, retro-futurist 1970s tower blocks and watersports during Paris-Plages. Once you've crossed the quirky 1885 hydraulic lift bridge, Pont de Crimée, you're in Parc de la Villette territory. Futuristic and cutting-edge, this is where you can visit major science and music museums, picnic on the lawns, and take in concerts at major venues such as the Cité de la Musique, Cabaret Sauvage, Trabendo and Zénith (and Jean Nouvel's Philharmonie come 2015).

Cité des Sciences et de l'Industrie.

Don't Miss

1 Cité des Sciences et de l'Industrie Edutainment galore at this science museum (p161).

2 104 Accessible art (p161).

3 Parc des Buttes-Chaumont Great park, glorious views (p168).

4 Le Chateaubriand Neo-bistro brilliance (p168).

5 Chez Prune Lounge by the canal with bobos and beer (p165).

EXPLORE

PORTE ST-DENIS TO LA VILLETTE

In the 10th & 19th arrondissements.

North of Porte St-Denis and Porte St-Martin, two of the oldest thoroughfares leading out of the city, rue du Fbg-St-Denis and rue du Fbg-St-Martin, traverse an area that was transformed in the 19th century by the railways, when it became the site of the Gare du Nord and Gare de l'Est. The grubby rue du Fbg-St-Denis is almost souk-like with its food shops, narrow passages and sinister courtyards. Garishly lit passage Brady is a surprising piece of India in Paris, full of restaurants, hairdressers and costume shops, whereas the art deco passage du Prado is more a continuation of the Sentier rag trade. Rue du Fbg-St-Martin follows the trace of the Roman road out of the city, and is home to clothes wholesalers, atmospheric courtyards and the ornate Mairie for the tenth.

Rue de Paradis is known for its porcelain and glass outlets, and rue d'Hauteville shows traces of the area's grander days (notably the **Petit Hôtel Bourrienne**, at no.58). Opposite, Cité Paradis is an alley of early industrial buildings. At the top of the street are the twin towers and terraced gardens of the **Eglise St-Vincent-de-Paul**. On boulevard Magenta, **Marché St-Quentin**, built in the 1860s, is one of the city's last remaining cast-iron, covered market halls.

Boulevard de Strasbourg was cut through in the 19th century to create a vista up to the Gare de l'Est. At no.2, a neo-Renaissance creation houses the last fan-maker in Paris and the **Musée de l'Eventail**. Towards the station, Eglise St-Laurent (69 bd de Magenta, 119 rue du Fbg-St-Martin, 10th) is one of the city's oldest churches, an eclectic composition with a 12th-century tower, Gothic nave, Baroque lady chapel, 19th-century façade and 1930s stained glass. Between the Gare de l'Est and **Canal St-Martin** are the restored **Couvent des Récollets** and Square Villemin park.

Canal St-Martin, built between 1805 and 1825, begins at the Seine at Pont Morland, disappears underground at Bastille, hides under boulevard

Richard-Lenoir, then emerges after crossing rue du Fbg-du-Temple, east of place de la République. Rue du Fbg-du-Temple itself is scruffy and cosmopolitan, lined with cheap grocers and discount stores, hidden courtyards and stalwarts of Paris nightlife: **Le Gibus**, bar-restaurant **Favela Chic** and vintage dancehall **La Java** (for all, *see p265*).

The first stretch of the canal, lined with shady trees and crossed by iron footbridges and locks, has the most appeal. The quays are traffic-free on Sundays. Many canalside warehouses have been snapped up by artists and designers or turned into loft apartments.

East of here, the Hôpital St-Louis was commissioned in 1607 by Henri IV to house plague victims, and was built as a series of isolated pavilions in the same brick-and-stone style as place des Vosges, far enough from the town to prevent risk of infection. Behind the hospital, the rue de la Grange-aux-Belles housed the Montfaucon gibbet, put up in 1233, where victims were hanged and left to the elements. East of the hospital, the lovely cobbled rue Ste-Marthe and place Ste-Marthe have a provincial air, busy at night with multi-ethnic eateries.

North, on place du Colonel-Fabien, is the head-quarters of the **Parti Communiste Français**, a modernist masterpiece built between 1968 and 1971 by Oscar Niemeyer with Paul Chemetov and Jean Deroche. The canal disappears briefly again under place de Stalingrad, a locale best avoided after dark. The square was landscaped in 1989 to showcase the Rotonde de la Villette, one of Ledoux's grandiose 1780s toll houses that once marked the boundary of Paris; it now displays exhibitions and archaeological finds.

Here the canal widens into the Bassin de la Villette, and the new developments along the quai de Loire and further quai de la Marne, as well as some of the worst 1960s and '70s housing in the blocks that stretch along rue de Flandres. At 104 rue d'Aubervilliers, the old municipal undertaker's today houses art space **104**.

At the eastern end of the basin is an unusual 1885 hydraulic lifting bridge, Pont de Crimée. Thursday and Sunday mornings add vitality with a market at place de Joinville. East of here, the Canal de l'Ourcq (created in 1813 to provide drinking water, as well as for freight haulage) divides: Canal St-Denis runs north towards the Seine, and Canal de l'Ourcq continues east through La Villette and the suburbs. Long the city's main abattoir district (still reflected in the Grande Halle de la Villette and in some of the old meaty brasseries along boulevard de la Villette), the area has been revitalised since the late 1980s by the postmodern **Parc de la Villette** complex, with the **Cité des Sciences et de l'Industrie** science museum and the **Cité de la Musique** concert hall.

IN THE KNOW CANAL CRUISE

For a cruise with a difference, take a trip along the city's second waterway, the pretty tree-lined Canal St-Martin, with **Canauxrama** (www.canauxrama.com). The cruise takes in four double locks and two swing bridges, and even heads underground, where the tunnel walls are enlivened by a light show.

104.

Sights & Museums

★ FREE 104
5 rue Curial, 19th (01.53.35.50.00, www.104.fr).
M° Riquet. **Open** noon-7pm Tue-Fri; 11am-
7pm Sat, Sun. **Admission** free. *Exhibitions*
prices vary. **Map** p162 C4 ➊
104, described as a 'space for artistic creation',
occupies a vast 19th-century building on the rue
d'Aubervilliers that used to house Paris's municipal
undertakers. The site was saved from developers by
Roger Madec, the mayor of the 19th, who made its
renovation the centrepiece of a massive project of cultural and urban renewal. There aren't any constraints
on the kind of work the resident artists do – 104 is
open to 'all the arts' – but they're expected to show
finished pieces in one of four annual 'festivals'. And
they're also required to get involved in projects with
the public, the fruits of which are shown in a space
next door. The community vibe continues via the
onsite café, bookshop and kids' play area.

★ La Cité des Sciences
et de l'Industrie
La Villette, 30 av Corentin-Cariou, 19th (01.40.
05.70.00, www.cite-sciences.fr). M° Porte de la
Villette. **Open** 10am-6pm Tue-Sat; 10am-7pm Sun.
Admission €8; €6 reductions; free under-6s.
PMP. **Map** p162 B5 ➋
This ultra-modern science museum pulls in several
million visitors a year. Explora, the permanent show,
occupies the upper two floors, whisking visitors
through 30,000sq m (320,000sq ft) of space, life, matter and communication: scale models of satellites
including the Ariane space shuttle, planes and robots,
plus the chance to experience weightlessness, make
for an exciting journey. In the Espace Images, try the
delayed camera and other optical illusions, draw 3D
images on a computer or lend your voice to the *Mona
Lisa*. The hothouse garden investigates developments in agriculture and biotechnology.
▶ *The brilliant Cité des Enfants, which spreads*
across several themed zones and is aimed at
under-12s, runs loads of workshops for younger
children. See the website for details.

FREE Couvent des Récollets
148 rue du Fbg-St-Martin, 10th. M° Gare de l'Est.
Admission free. **Map** p163 E2 ➌
Founded as a monastery in the 17th century when
still outside the city walls, this barracks, spinning
factory and hospice was a military hospital from
1860 to 1968. Left empty, the convent was squatted
by artists, Les Anges des Récollets, in the early
1990s. The buildings were renovated and reopened
in 2004. One half, the Maison de l'Architecture
(www.maisonarchitecture-idf.org), hosts a garden
café and architectural debates. The other is the
Centre International d'Accueil et d'Echanges des
Récollets: studios and duplexes for foreign 'creators'
– artists and researchers (from painters to neuro-
biologists) – invited to stay for extended periods.

★ FREE Eglise St-Vincent-de-Paul
5 rue de Belzunce, 10th (01.48.78.47.47,
www.paroissesvp.fr). M° Gare du Nord. **Open**
2-7.30pm Mon; 8am-noon, 2-7pm Tue-Fri; 8am-noon,
2-7.30pm Sat; 9.30am-noon, 4.30-7.30pm Sun.
Admission free. **Map** p163 E1 ➍
Set at the top of terraced gardens, this church was
begun in 1824 by Jean-Baptiste Lepère and completed in 1844 by his son-in-law, Jacques Hittorff,
who also designed the Gare du Nord (*see below*) and
Cirque d'Hiver (*see p248*). The twin towers, pedi-
mented Greek temple portico and sculptures of the
four evangelists along the parapet are in high classical mode. The interior has a splendid double-storey
arcade of columns, murals by Jean-Hippolyte
Flandrin and church furniture by François Rude.

Gare du Nord
Rue de Dunkerque, 10th. M° Gare du Nord.
Map p162 D2 ➎
The grandest of the great 19th-century train stations
(and Eurostar terminal since 1994) was designed by
Jacques Hittorff between 1861 and 1864. A conventional stone façade, with Ionic capitals and statues
representing towns served by the station, hides a
vast iron-and-glass vault. The Gare du Nord is the
busiest station in Europe, with more than 550,000
passengers passing through every day.

Musée de l'Eventail
2 bd de Strasbourg, 10th (01.42.08.90.20,
www.annehoguet.fr). M° Strasbourg St-Denis.
Open 2-6pm Mon-Wed. *Children's activities*
Wed afternoons. Closed Aug. **Admission** €6;
€3-€4 reductions; free under-8s. **No credit
cards.** **Map** p163 F2 ➏

EXPLORE

EXPLORE

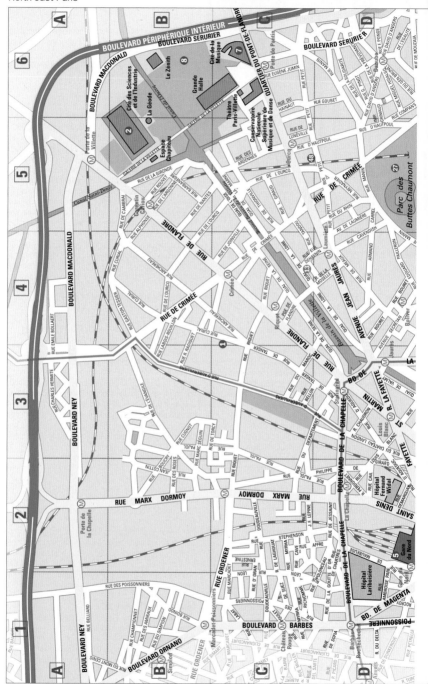

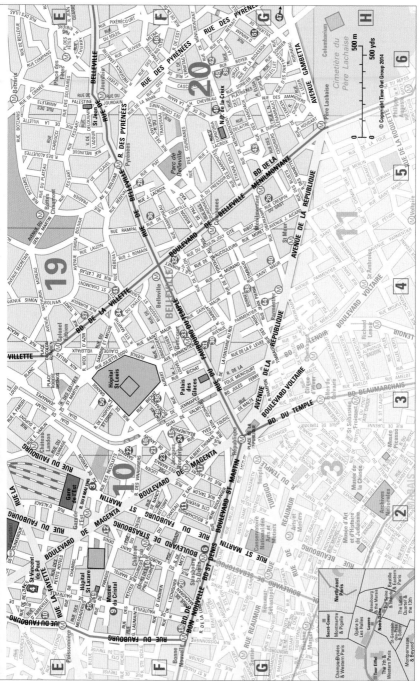

EXPLORE

Anne Hoguet keeps the tradition of her ancestors alive in this arcane museum, which has been a fan-maker's *atelier* since 1805. One room houses the tools of the trade; beside it is Hoguet's studio, where she works on fans for fashion and the stage. The former *salle d'exposition*, lined in blue silk, is where the collection of almost 1,000 historic fans is shown.

Musée de la Musique
Cité de la Musique, 221 av Jean-Jaurès, 19th (01.44.84.44.84, www.cite-musique.fr). M° Porte de Pantin. **Open** *noon-6pm Tue-Sat; 10am-6pm Sun.* **Admission** *€7; €5.60 reductions; free under-26s. PMP.* **Map** p162 C6 **7**
Alongside the concert hall, this innovative music museum houses a gleamingly restored collection of instruments from the old Conservatoire, interactive computers and scale models of opera houses and concert halls. Visitors are supplied with an audio-guide in a choice of languages, and the musical commentary is a joy, playing the appropriate instrument as you approach each exhibit. Alongside the trumpeting brass, curly woodwind instruments and precious strings (highlights include a Stradivarius violin and Django Reinhardt's guitar) are more unusual items, such as the Indonesian gamelan orchestra, whose sounds influenced the work of Debussy and Ravel. Concerts in the amphitheatre use instruments from the collection.

★ FREE Parc de la Villette
Av Corentin-Cariou, 19th (01.40.03.75.75, www. villette.com). M° Porte de la Villette. Av Jean-Jaurès, 19th. M° Porte de Pantin. **Map** p162 B6 **8**
Dotted with red pavilions, or *folies*, the park was designed by Bernard Tschumi and is a postmodern feast. The *folies* serve as glorious giant climbing frames, as well as a first-aid post, burger bar, chil-

dren's art centre and gig venue. As well as the lawns, which are used for an open-air film festival in summer, there are ten themed gardens bearing evocative names, such as the Garden of Mirrors, of Mists, of Acrobatics and of Childhood Frights. South of the canal are the Zénith concert venue (*see p276*), and the Grande Halle de la Villette – now used for trade fairs, exhibitions and September's jazz festival (*see p37*). It is flanked by the Conservatoire de la Musique and the Cité de la Musique, with rehearsal rooms, concert halls and the Musée de la Musique, but come 2015 the whole will be overshadowed by Jean Nouvel's 2,400-seat Philharmonie. When the dramatic symphony hall finally opens, two years late and hugely over budget, visitors will be able to climb up its sloping metal-clad roof, while concert listings will be projected on to a 52-metre aluminium slab visible from the neighbouring ring road.

Petit Hôtel Bourrienne
58 rue d'Hauteville, 10th (01.47.70.51.14). M° Bonne Nouvelle or Poissonnière. **Open** *Guided visits 1-15 July, Sept noon-6pm daily. Rest of year by appointment Sat.* **Admission** *€7.* **No credit cards.** **Map** p163 F1 **9**
A rare example of the Consulaire style, this small *hôtel particulier* was built between 1789 and 1798. It was occupied by Fortunée Hamelin, born (like her friend the Empress Josephine) on the French Caribbean island of Martinique, and notorious for parading topless down the Champs-Elysées. A bedroom boudoir painted with tropical birds was her only decoration before the site was taken over by Louis Fauvelet de Bourrienne, Napoleon's private secretary. He had it decorated according to the latest fashion, making sure to keep his political options open (the dining room ceiling is painted with motifs favourable to monarchy and empire).

Le Fantôme. *See p166.*

Restaurants

Abri
*92 rue du Fbg-Poissonnière, 10th
(01.83.97.00.00). Mº Poissonnière.* **Open**
noon-3pm Mon; 12.30-3pm, 8-10pm Tue-Sat.
Prix fixe *Lunch* €25 (Tue-Fri). *Dinner* €40.
Map p163 E1 ➓ **Bistro**
A pocket-sized restaurant next to the Poissonière
métro, Abri ('shelter') serves everything from multi-
layered sandwiches (Mondays and Saturdays) to
sophisticated French cuisine enhanced with Far
Eastern touches: marinated mackerel, for example,
with almost transparent sliced vegetables, or a winter squash soup with pumpkin seeds and coffee.
The tasting menus are a big draw (four dishes at
lunch, six at dinner). You'll need to be patient and
reserve far in advance to secure a table in the
postage stamp-sized room, where the open kitchen
takes up half the floor space, but it's definitely
worth the effort. Service is charming.

Au Comptoir de Brice
*33 rue du Château-d'Eau, 10th (07.87.36.77.38,
www.aucomptoirdebrice.com). Mº Château d'Eau.*
Open noon-6pm Tue-Sat; 11am-1.45pm Sun.
Main courses €15-€25. **Prix fixe** *Brunch*
€29 (Sun). **Map** p163 F2 ➓ **Burgers**
This popular joint is run by TV chef Brice Morvent.
Serving gourmet cheeseburgers at the weekend
made with sesame-, pistachio- and peanut-sprinkled
buns, comté cheese, candied onions and generous
helpings of mustard, the friendly green and white
space is a popular Saturday go-to.

★ La Fidélité
*12 rue de la Fidélité, 10th (01.47.70.19.34,
www.lafidelite.com). Mº Gare de L'Est.* **Open**
8pm-2am Mon-Sat. **Main courses** €17-€26.
Prix fixe *Dinner* €45, €55 (groups of 15 or
more). **Map** p163 E2 ➓ **Brasserie**
There was a huge buzz when La Clique took this
place over. The neighbourhood is arguably one of
the least attractive in the capital, but La Fidélité has
become an A-list magnet with its stylish interior
and expensive drinks list. Food can be rather hit-
and-miss, but the *joue de boeuf* is a safe bet. On
Thursdays and Fridays, the basement morphs into
Cave de la Fidélité, a jukebox bar.

Cafés & Bars

Bar Ourcq
*68 quai de la Loire, 19th (01.42.40.12.26,
http://barourcq.free.fr). Mº Laumière.* **Open**
Summer 3pm-midnight Wed, Thur; 3pm-2am Fri,
Sat; 3-10pm Sun. *Winter* 3pm-2am Sat; 3-10pm
Sun. **No credit cards. Map** p162 C4 ➓
This was one of the first hip joints to hit the Canal
de l'Ourcq, with an embankment broad enough to
accommodate *pétanque* games (ask at the bar) and

a cluster of deckchairs. It's a completely different
scene from the crowded bustle along Canal St-Martin
– more discerning and less self-satisfied. The cabin-
like interior is cosy, and drinks are listed in a hit
parade of prices, starting with €2.50 for a *demi* or
glass of red. Pastas at €9, exhibitions and a regular
DJ spot keep the cool clientele sated. Closed on rainy
weekdays in summer.

★ Chez Jeannette
*47 rue du Fbg-St-Denis, 10th (01.47.70.30.89,
www.chezjeannette.com). Mº Strasbourg St-Denis
or Château d'Eau.* **Open** 9am-1.45am daily.
Map p163 F2 ➓
When she sold her café a few years ago, Jeannette
handed over to the young team from Chez Justine
because they promised not to change a thing. The
monstrous 1940s dust-coated lights, leaky loos,
tobacco-stained wallpaper depicting the Moulin
Rouge and PVC-covered banquettes have finally
been cleaned up, and the café has become one of
Paris's hippest spots for an aperitif. There's a *plat
du jour* at lunch and plates of cheese and charcuterie
at night; at 8pm, the fluorescent lights go off and
candlelight takes over, to a cheer.

Chez Prune
*36 rue Beaurepaire, 10th (01.42.41.30.47).
Mº Jacques Bonsergent.* **Open** 8am-2am
Mon-Sat; 10am-2am Sun. **Map** p163 F3 ➓
Chez Prune is still one of the best places in which to
spend an evening on the Canal St-Martin. The local
bobo HQ, this traditional café, with high ceilings and
low lighting, sticks to a simple formula: groups of
friends crowd around the cosily ordered banquettes,
picking at moderately priced cheese or meat platters.
Mostly, though, they come for a few leisurely drinks
or an *apéro* before heading off to one of the late-night
venues in the area.

Le Cinquante
*50 rue de Lancry, 10th (01.42.02.36.83).
Mº Jacques Bonsergent.* **Open** 5.30pm-2am
daily. Closed Aug. **Map** p163 F3 ➓
The bare brick, Formica and framed '50s ads of this
funky venue attract an inner circle of regulars. These
days, it's established enough to produce its own
T-shirts and customised bar stools. Reasonable prices
– half-litre pitchers of sauvignon, Brouilly and Chablis
in the €10 range – attract a mixed bag of tastes and
generations. The two rooms behind the main bar are
set aside for dining (affordable classics) and music
(generally acoustic). Sunday is open-mic night.

Le Coq
*12 rue du Château d'Eau, 10th (01.42.40.85.68,
www.barlecoq.com). Mº Jacques Bonsergent.*
Open 6pm-2am Tue-Sat. **Map** p163 F2 ➓
Here's a cocktail bar that gives its cutting-edge
neighbours a run for their money. Tony Conigliaro,
joint owner with Thierry Daniel and Eric Fossard,

EXPLORE

knows what he's doing: he also opened 69 Colebrook Row and Zetter Townhouse in London. There are 12 mixes on the menu, at €11 a throw. The black walls host exhibitions of work by 1970s-influenced artists, with a soundtrack ranging from Serge Gainsbourg to Grace Jones via Fela Kuti. The shelves behind the bar, stocked with vintage bottles of chartreuse, vermouth, cognac and other rare liquors, enhance the speakeasy vibe.

Delaville Café

34 bd de Bonne-Nouvelle, 10th (01.48.24.48.09, www.delavillecafe.com). M° Bonne Nouvelle. **Open** 8.30am-2am daily. **Map** p163 F1 ⑱
The Delaville Café is an unmissable stop on the Grands Boulevards, possessed as it is of a vast sunny terrace open from springtime onwards. The vibe is a little precious, but the decor of the huge venue is a delight, a lively mixture of ancient gilt rococo and post-industrial baroque (it used to be a *maison close*). The high glass ceiling between the bar and the terrace is stunning, full of light even in winter, and the back room surprises with all the decadence of an upmarket London club: think red leather banquettes, stuffed animals and plasma screens. DJs mix unobtrusive electro lounge sets at weekends.

★ Le Fantôme

36 rue de Paradis, 10th (09.66.87.11.20, www.lefanto.me). M° Poissonnière or Château d'Eau. **Open** 11am-2am Mon-Fri; 6pm-2am Sat. **Map** p163 E1 ⑲
Only the black lacquered tiles give away the location of Le Fantôme, the new venue from the crew behind Le Baron. The enormous space is a fantasy venue for fans of retrogaming: as well as a huge bar, Formica chairs and faux leather banquettes, the Fantôme offers a fistful of arcade games, a Pacman table (often reserved) and table football. Drinks-wise, the resident mixologist is an inspired Californian called David West who refuses to churn out mojitos, but has instead produced a list of five inventive cocktails to go with the menu of hefty pizzas (we liked one with porcini, pancetta, ceps, buffalo mozzarella and artichoke hearts) or salads. *Photo p164.*

L'Inconnu

17-19 rue de Mazagran, 10th (01.45.23.95.37, www.inconnu-bar.com). M° Bonne Nouvelle or Strasbourg St-Denis. **Open** 6pm-2am Tue-Sat. **Map** p163 F1 ⑳
This new bar is in Strasbourg St-Denis, an area that's becoming an increasingly attractive nightlife alternative to Pigalle, Oberkampf and Bastille. The friendly welcome, comfy sofas, soft lighting and cheap Paris beer (Gallia) encourage chat, while the DJ sets on Thursdays, Fridays and Saturdays often feature big names such as Teki Latex, Supa Never Smiles or Acid Washed. The downstairs dancefloor keeps going until 2am and is a good place to meet the local crowd of hipsters, artists and musicians.

Le Verre Volé

67 rue de Lancry, 10th (01.48.03.17.34, www. leverrevole.fr). M° Jacques Bonsergent. **Open** 9.30am-1am daily (4pm-1am 2wks mid Aug). **Map** p163 F3 ㉑
See p167 **All in Good Taste**.
▶ *For lunch on the hoof, head for the Verre Volé's deli offshoot (54 rue de la Folie-Méricourt, 11th), which serves up gourmet sandwiches such as calf's head pâté, gribiche sauce and watercress.*

Shops & Services

Antoine et Lili

95 quai de Valmy, 10th (01.40.37.41.55, www.antoineetlili.com). M° Jacques Bonsergent. **Open** 11am-7pm Mon, Sun; 11am-8pm Tue-Sat. **Map** p163 F3 ㉒ **Fashion**
Antoine et Lili's fuchsia-pink, custard-yellow and apple-green shopfronts are a new raver's dream. The bobo designer's clothes, often in wraparound styles, adapt to all sizes and shapes. The Canal St-Martin 'village' comprises womenswear, a kitsch home decoration boutique and childrenswear.
Other locations throughout the city.

★ Culture(s)

46 rue de Lancry, 10th (09.81.74.58.71). M° Jacques Bonsergent. **Open** 10.30am-7.30pm Tue-Sat. **Map** p163 F2 ㉓ **Gifts & souvenirs**
In a loft-style studio, this unusual florist combines exotic flowers, trees and garden-themed items, such as floral printed rain hats. Truly original.

★ Du Pain et des Idées

34 rue Yves Toudic, 10th (01.42.40.44.52, www.dupainetdesidees.com). M° Jacques Bonsergent. **Open** 6.45am-8pm Mon-Fri. **Map** p163 F3 ㉔ **Food & drink**
Christophe Vasseur is a former winner of the Gault-Millau prize for Best Bakery. Among his specialities are Le Pagnol aux Pommes, bread studded with apple (skin on), raisins and orange flower water.

Jamin Puech

61 rue de Hauteville, 10th (01.40.22.08.32, www.jamin-puech.com). M° Poissonnière. **Open** 10am-7pm Mon, Wed, Fri; 11am-7pm Tue, Sat. **Map** p163 E1 ㉕ **Accessories**
The complete collection of Benoît Jamin and Isabelle Puech's dazzling handbags is displayed in a bohemian setting complete with antler-horn chairs.
Other locations throughout the city.

BELLEVILLE & MENILMONTANT

In the 11th, 19th & 20th arrondissements.

When the city boundaries were expanded in 1860, Ménilmontant and Belleville, once villages that provided Paris with fruit, wine and weekend escapes, were absorbed. They were built up with housing for migrants, first from rural France and later from former colonies in North Africa and South-east Asia. The area encompasses one of the city's most beautiful parks, the **Buttes-Chaumont**.

On boulevard de Belleville, Chinese and Vietnamese shops rub shoulders with Muslim and kosher groceries, and couscous and falafel eateries; a street market takes place here on Tuesday and Friday mornings. North of here, along avenue Simon-Bolivar, is the Parc des Buttes-Chaumont. This is the most desirable part of north-east Paris, with Haussmannian apartments overlooking the park: to the east, near place de Rhin-et-Danube, is a small area of tiny, hilly streets lined with small houses and gardens, known by locals as Quartier Mouzaïa.

Up on the slopes of the Hauts de Belleville, there are views over the city from rue Piat and rue des Envierges, which lead to the modern but charming **Parc de Belleville** with its Maison des Vents devoted to birds and kites. Below the park, rue Ramponneau mixes new housing and relics of old Belleville. At no.23 an old smithy has been turned into La Forge, an artists' squat.

'Mesnil-Montant' used to be a few houses on a hill with vines and fruit trees – then came the bistros, bordellos and workers' housing. It became part of Paris in 1860 along with Belleville, and has a similar history. These days it's a thriving centre of alternative Paris, as artists and young professionals have moved in. Although side streets still have male-only North African cafés, rue Oberkampf is home to some of the city's most humming bars.

The area mixes 1960s and '70s housing projects with older dwellings, some gentrified, some derelict. Just below rue des Pyrénées, which cuts through the 20th, you can rummage around the rustic Cité Leroy or Villa l'Ermitage, cobbled cul-de-sacs of little houses and gardens,

ALL IN GOOD TASTE

Eat, drink and be merry at cult cave à manger pioneer Le Verre Volé.

EXPLORE

To first-timers, **Le Verre Volé** (*see p166*) seems like a basic wine shop with a few rickety tables, but reserve a spot one night and you'll understand why *New York Times* food writer Alec Lobrano calls it his favourite wine bar in the city. Located by the Canal St-Martin, the tiny bistro has become a neighbourhood staple over the past few years, which means reservations are strongly urged for lunch or dinner, with two services in the evening. Two other Paris locations, as well as a recently opened Tokyo outpost, sell wine and sandwiches, but only the Canal address is fit for proper dining with reliable dishes in an unpretentious atmosphere, despite the area's bobo tendencies.

Locals pop in for a bottle of the natural or unfiltered wines hand-selected from producers across France, a far cry from most wine *caves*. The knowledgeable staff will help you pick out something in your price range, be it for a posh dinner party

or just to share along the adjacent canal with some bread and cheese. Fruity red? Chilled white? The Verre Volé has it all. With less expensive bottles hovering around €10, there's no need to break the budget, though you certainly could.

While the wine is the centrepiece, the dining is anything but below par. Rich *boudin noir* with buttery mash and small charcuterie plates are always on the menu, but the daily specials are where it's really at. Monkfish *beignets* with sea urchin mayonnaise or horse steak tartare to start, perhaps, followed by veal saltimbocca with polenta and anchovy sauce.

You can pair your meal with the wine of your choice from the well-stocked shelves on either side of the cosy dining room, but it's best to trust the staff's suggestions. Affordable bottles and a reasonable €7 corkage fee leaves you with an entirely manageable tab for innovative, fun, yet homey cuisine in a hip neighbourhood.

EXPLORE

IN THE KNOW PINK PIZZA

Pink Flamingo (67 rue Bichat, 10th, www.pinkflamingopizza.com) is one of the least traditional pizza joints in Paris, but the quirky toppings (think eight cheeses or aubergine and houmous) never fail to hit the spot. If you fancy eating canalside on warmer evenings, they'll hand you a helium balloon when you order, and the delivery boy will come and find your picnic spot on the Canal St-Martin. How's that for service?

and old craft workshops. Rue de l'Ermitage has a curious neo-Gothic house at no.19 – and a bird's-eye view from the junction with rue de Ménilmontant, right down the hill to the Centre Pompidou. On rue Boyer, **La Maroquinerie** (*see p171*) puts on an eclectic mix of literary events, political debate and live music, and at 88 rue de Ménilmontant, graffiti-covered art squat **La Miroiterie** opens house for art shows and the *magasin gratuit*, a free swap shop.

Sights & Museums

FREE Musée Edith Piaf

5 rue Crespin-du-Gast, 11th (01.43.55.52.72). M° Ménilmontant. **Open** *By appointment only* 1-6pm Mon-Wed; 10am-noon Thur. **Admission** free (donations welcome). **Map** p163 G5 ㉖
Set in an apartment where Piaf lived at the age of 18, when she sang on the streets of Ménilmontant, this tiny museum consists of two red-painted rooms crammed with letters, pictures, framed discs and objects belonging to the singer. The museum's real treasures are two letters, one a chatty number written on her 28th birthday, and another more passionate pen to actor Robert Dalban. She died at the age of 47 and is buried in Père-Lachaise (*see p145*).

★ FREE Parc des Buttes-Chaumont

Rue Botzaris, rue Manin, rue de Crimée, 19th. M° Buttes Chaumont. **Open** *Oct-Apr* 7am-8pm daily. *May-Sept* 7am-10pm daily. **Map** p162 D5 ㉗
When the city's boundaries were expanded in 1860, Belleville was absorbed and the Buttes-Chaumont was created on the site of a former gypsum and limestone quarry. The park, with its meandering paths, waterfalls, temples and vertical cliffs, was designed by Adolphe Alphand, and was opened as part of the celebrations for the Universal Exhibition in 1867. After lounging with the locals, head for the park's Rosa Bonheur *guinguette* (www.rosabonheur.fr). Open till midnight, it makes the perfect place to sip an *apéro* and take in the stunning views of the city below. Also worth a look is the Pavillon du Lac (www.pavillondulac.fr), one of five pavilions opened

in 1868. Restored in 2010 after lying abandoned for ten years, it has been transformed into a high-class restaurant with chef Fabien Borgel in the kitchen. The park is undergoing major renovations until 2015, but will remain open throughout.

Restaurants

★ Le Baratin

3 rue Jouye-Rouve, 20th (01.43.49.39.70). M° Pyrénées. **Open** noon-2pm, 7.30-11pm Tue-Fri; 7.30-11pm Sat. **Main courses** €18-€30. **Prix fixe** *Lunch* €19. **Map** p163 F5 ㉘ Bistro
Star pastry chef Pierre Hermé visits this cheerful little bistro and wine bar high up in Belleville at least every two weeks to fill up on Raquel Carena's homely cooking with the occasional exotic twist. Typical of her style, which draws on her native Argentina, are tuna carpaccio with cherries, roast Basque lamb with new potatoes and spinach, and hazelnut pudding. If the food weren't so fantastic, it would still be worth coming for the mostly organic wines.

€ Le Cambodge

10 av Richerand, 10th (01.44.84.37.70, www.lecambodge.fr). M° Goncourt or République. **Open** noon-2.30pm, 7-11pm Mon-Thur; noon-2.30pm, 7-11.30pm Fri, Sat. Closed 1 Aug-8 Sept, 24 Dec-1 Jan. **Main courses** €13. **Map** p163 F3 ㉙ Cambodian
The system at Le Cambodge is simple: you write your order on a piece of paper, including any preferences such as 'no coriander', 'no peanuts' or 'extra rice', and after a short wait the dishes appear. Two favourites are the *bobun spécial*, a hot and cold mix of sautéed beef, noodles, salad, bean sprouts and imperial rolls, and *banhoy*, a selection of the same ingredients to be wrapped in lettuce and mint leaves and dipped in a sauce.

★ Le Chateaubriand

129 av Parmentier, 11th (01.43.57.45.95, www.lechateaubriand.net). M° Goncourt. **Open** 7.30-11pm Tue-Sat. Closed 2wks Dec. **Prix fixe** *Dinner* €60. **Map** p163 G4 ㉚ Bistro
Self-taught Basque chef Iñaki Aizpitarte runs this stylish bistro. Dishes have been deconstructed down to their very essence and put back together again. You'll understand if you try starters like chunky steak tartare with a quail's egg, or asparagus with tahini foam and little splinters of sesame-seed brittle. The cooking's not always so cerebral – Aizpitarte's Spanish goat's cheese with stewed apple jam is brilliant. Be sure to book ahead.

Le Dauphin

131 av Parmentier, 11th (01.55.28.78.88, www.restaurantledauphin.net). M° Goncourt. **Open** noon-1.30pm, 7-11pm Tue-Fri; 7-11pm Sat. **Prix fixe** *Lunch* €23-€27. **Tapas** €8-€18 (dinner only). **Map** p163 F3 ㉛ Wine bar

Le Chateaubriand.

Iñaki Aizpitarte's Le Dauphin, a Rem Koolhaus-designed tapas-style place, offers sub-€15 dishes such as *magret séché, tempura de gambas* and *tarte au citron meringuée*. As at Le Chateaubriand, sourcing is all-important – bread comes from award-winning Du Pain et des Idées.

★ € Dong Huong
14 rue Louis-Bonnet, 11th (01.43.57.42.81).
M° Belleville. **Open** noon-11pm Mon, Wed-Sun.
Closed 3wks summer. **Main courses** €7.50.
Map p163 F4 ❷ Vietnamese
The excellent food at this Vietnamese noodle joint attracts a buzzy crowd. The delicious *bành cuôn*, steamed Vietnamese ravioli stuffed with minced meat, mushrooms, bean sprouts, spring onions and deep-fried onion, are served piping hot. *Com ga lui*, chicken kebabs with lemongrass, though not as delicate, come with tasty rice. *Bò bùn chà giò* (noodles with beef and small *nem* topped with onion strips, spring onion and crushed peanuts) makes a meal in itself. For dessert, the mandarin, lychee and mango sorbets are tasty and authentic.

Le Floréal
73 rue du Fbg-du-Temple, 10th (01.40.18.46.79).
M° Goncourt. **Open** 8am-1.30am Mon-Sat; 9.30am-1.30am Sun. **Main courses** €12-€35. **Prix fixe** *Lunch* €16, €18. **Map** p163 F4 ❸ Diner
The proprietors of Chez Jeannette and Chez Justine chose this prime site opposite Le Chateaubriand and Le Dauphin for their latest venture, Le Floréal – an American-style diner serving hamburgers and cupcakes (and favourite of actor Mathieu Amalric).

Le Galopin
34 rue Ste-Marthe, 10th (01.42.06.05.03, www. le-galopin.com). M° Belleville or Colonel Fabien.
Open 7.30-10.30pm Tue-Fri; 7.30-11pm Sat.
Prix fixe *Dinner* €48. **Map** p163 F4 ❷ Bistro
Award-winning chef Romain Tischenko serves up a creative, daily-changing menu at this little restau-

rant on pretty place Sainte-Marthe. The avant-garde Tischenko's USP is taking unfashionable vegetables and turning them into fusion cuisine 2.0 – think parsnips, artichokes, pumpkins and celery combined with cocoa, scallops and caramel. Staff are young, attentive and full of good advice on the wines, all of which are produced by independent winemakers. Make sure you reserve in advance.

€ La Madonnina
10 rue Marie-et-Louise, 10th (01.42.01.25.26).
M° Goncourt or Jacques Bonsergent. **Open** 12.15-2.30pm, 7.30-11pm Mon-Thur; 12.15-2.30pm, 7.30-11.30pm Fri; 7.30-11.30pm Sat. Closed 2wks Aug.
Main courses €13-€18. **Prix fixe** *Lunch* €13.
Map p163 F3 ❸ Italian
La Madonnina flirts with kitsch so skilfully that it ends up coming off as cool. With its candles, mustard yellow walls and red-checked tablecloths, it's the perfect place for a romantic night out. La Madonnina describes itself as a *trattoria napoletana*, but most of the dishes are pan-southern Italian. The short menu changes monthly; don't miss the homemade pastas, such as artichoke and ricotta ravioli. The *cassata*, an extremely sweet Sicilian version of cheesecake, is authentic and unusual to see on menus outside Italy.

Le Rouleau de Printemps
42 rue de Tourtille, 20th (01.46.36.98.95).
M° Belleville or Pyrénées. **Open** 11.30am-3.30pm, 7.30-11pm Mon, Tue, Thur-Sun. **Main courses** €7-€14. **Map** p163 F5 ❸ Vietnamese
The secret's been out about Rouleau de Printemps for some time, but it never disappoints. You can't reserve a place in the two postcard-sized rooms, so arrive early to get a space on the shared tables. A coriander-scented *bo bun*, some plump crunchy egg rolls, a vegetarian spring roll and some steamed prawn ravioli washed down with jasmine tea or Tsingtao beer won't cost you much more than €20, so go easy on the sometimes chaotic service.

EXPLORE

Cafés & Bars

Le 9b

*68 bd de la Villette, 19th (01.40.18.08.10,
www.le9b.com). M° Colonel Fabien.* **Open**
8am-2am Mon-Sat. **Map** p163 E4 ③

Does the name remind you of anything? It's our old
favourite, Le 9 Billards. This bar – which preceded
Les Disquaires on rue Jean-Pierre Timbaud – has
been reborn on boulevard de la Villette. It's already
full to bursting each night with a grand blend of electro, hip hop, funk and rock on the crammed dancefloor, and cocktails and couscous on the menu.

L'Alimentation Générale

*64 rue Jean-Pierre-Timbaud, 11th (01.43.55.42.50,
www.alimentation-generale.net). M° Parmentier.*
Open 7pm-2am Wed, Sun; 7pm-4am Thur-Sat.
Map p163 G4 ③

The 'Grocery Store' is a big old space filled with junk.
Cupboards of kitsch china and lampshades made
from kitchen sponges are an inspired touch. The beer
is well chosen – Flag, Sagres, Picon and Orval by the
bottle – and the unusual house cocktail involves basil
and figs. DJs rock the joint: expect a €5-€10 cover
price for big names or live bands.

La Bellevilloise

*19 rue Boyer, 20th (01.46.36.07.07, www.la
bellevilloise.com). M° Gambetta.* **Open** 7pm-1am
Wed, Thur; 7pm-2am Fri; times vary Sat, Sun.
Map p163 G6 ③

The Bellevilloise is the latest incarnation of a building
that once housed the capital's very first workers' co-
operative. Now it competently multitasks as a bar,
restaurant, club and exhibition space, hosting regular
film and music festivals on the top level (where there's
a fake lawn with deckchairs and a massage area).
Enjoy brunch in the Halle aux Oliviers or decent
views of the *quartier* from the charming terrace;
downstairs the club-cum-concert venue has launched
some of Paris's most exciting new bands, and on '80s
nights you can hardly move for the fortysomethings
living it up like they were teens again. There's also
live jazz music with the Sunday brunch.

Café Charbon

*109 rue Oberkampf, 11th (01.43.57.55.13).
M° Parmentier or Ménilmontant.* **Open** 9am-
2am Mon-Wed, Sun; 9am-4am Thur-Sat.
Map p163 G4 ④

The bar contained within this beautifully restored
belle époque building sparked the Oberkampf
nightlife boom. Its booths, mirrors and adventurous
music policy put trendy locals at ease, capturing the
essence of café culture spanning each end of the 20th
century. After more than 15 years, the formula still
works – and is copied by nearby bars. Avoid coming
on weekend evenings, as the bar is always rammed
and the waiters overwhelmed. The terrace is a particularly good bet in summer.

Café Chéri(e)

*44 bd de la Villette, 19th (01.42.02.02.05,
http://cafecherie.blogspot.com). M° Belleville.*
Open noon-2am daily. **Map** p163 F4 ④

This splendid DJ bar is also an all-day café – but it
doesn't compromise any of the cool that keeps it well
ahead of the pack after dark. Music comes from all
over, and runs from electro, rock, funk, hip hop,
indie, dance and jazz to golden oldies and ghetto-
inspired grooves. The interior sparkles with wit and
invention – note the marvellous mural alluding to
the personal sacrifices made for a life of coupledom.
There's a front terrace if you need a smoke or con-
versational respite from the BPM.

▶ *There's music from Thursdays to Saturdays
after 9pm; see p262.*

Le Café des Sports

*94 rue de Ménilmontant, 20th (01.46.36.48.18,
www.lecafedessports.org). M° Gambetta.* **Open**
10am-2am daily. Closed Aug. **Map** p163 G6 ④

Le Café des Sports' eclectic music programme
ranges from electro (Saturdays), to pop or *chanson*
(Tuesdays and Thursdays) to world dub. Beer and
wine are fabulously cheap (just €2 from 6pm to 8pm)
and there's sometimes free couscous or tapas with
your drink on a Monday evening. Unlike its sprawling neighbours, Le Café des Sports has just one room
to call home. DJs play in the space at the back.

La Cale Sèche

*18 rue des Panoyaux, 20th (no phone).
M° Ménilmontant.* **Open** 11am-2am Tue-Sat;
3pm-2am Sun. **Map** p163 G5 ④

This little bar is easy to miss, thanks to its unpretentious façade. But once inside, you'll find a long
bar with a surprise at the back – a pretty, leafy terrace flanked by public tennis courts. It's a mellow
place to sit and read, admire the flowers and watch
the locals playing tennis while you drink your coffee.
Inside, the decor is a jumble of storm lamps, old
shoes suspended from the ceiling and posters for
punk, rock and French *chanson* artists (who also
make up the soundtrack). The well-chosen range of
beers includes Maes, Chimay, Chouffe and Cuvée des
Trolls. An excellent neighbourhood address.

La Gouttière

*96 av Parmentier, 11th (01.43.55.46.42).
M° Parmentier.* **Open** 5pm-2am Mon-Sat.
Map p163 G4 ④

Far enough (five minutes) from rue Oberkampf to
feel off the beaten track, the Gutter is not out-and-
out libertine, but you're on the right lines. Certainly,
a come-what-may approach to music, drinking and
eye contact abounds in the crowded venue. Decor
consists of a few LP covers and the kind of colour
scheme often put to good use in adventure playgrounds. Reasonably priced lunches (food is a mix
of French and North African), the occasional live
band, chess and card games complete the picture.

EXPLORE

IN THE KNOW TABLE SERVICE

The **Gossima Ping Pong Bar** (www. gossima.fr) is the first of its kind in the city; the owners, a pair of former world champions, have filled the cavernous premises in Ménilmontant (formerly a garage) with eight tables, leaving enough elbow room to avoid accidental bat-induced beatings. The equipment is in top condition (for now), but you pay accordingly: €7.50/pint, €6 per half hour of play (€5 before 6pm).

La Maroquinerie

23 rue Boyer, 20th (01.40.33.35.05, www. lamaroquinerie.fr). M° Gambetta. **Open** 6pm-2am daily. Closed Aug. **Map** p163 G6 ㊺

La Maroquinerie's former life as a leather factory is little in evidence these days. It's now a bright café and bar in competition with La Bellevilloise (*see p170*), with a coveted downstairs music venue that hosts the odd literary debate and a wealth of cool acts. The food is excellent – you can eat your way through the menu for around €25 – and wine sourced from across France starts at €3 a glass. The interior, with exposed brick, is cosy, and in summer chirpy locals invade the shaded terrace.

Les Trois Arts

21 rue des Rigoles, 20th (01.43.49.36.27, http://les3arts.free.fr). M° Jourdain. **Open** 5pm-2am Tue-Sat; 11am-11pm Sun. **Map** p163 F6 ㊻

This Breton tavern offers a mix of live arts and lessons on the art of living. You can hear folk, jazz, klezmer or classical concerts, or take part in French, Irish, Mediterranean and Eastern European storytelling evenings. Occasionally, you'll happen upon plays, improv and comedy. All that goes on in the basement, but the bar upstairs also lays on activities. You can borrow board games to pore over in the library, and they'll even lend you works of art on show as part of the *De l'art chez toi* (Art at Your Place) initiative. Every Friday, food offerings include *kig ha farz*, a traditional Breton dish from Léon in Finistère. Enjoy with a barley ale, glass of cider or *chouchen*, a honey-based Breton aperitif.

Shops & Services

GoldyMama

14 rue du Surmelin, 20th (01.40.30.08.00, www.goldymama.com). M° Pelleport. **Open** 11am-7.30pm Tue-Sat. **Map** p163 G6 ㊼ **Fashion**

Finding well-presented vintage clothes that have been washed, ironed and don't smell like dirty underpants is possible – GoldyMama is the proof. This small boutique in the heights of the 20th has retro treasures aplenty and makes an original spot for gift

hunting. The walls are lined with 1950s skirts, '40s suits, empire dresses, wacky '70s tops and multi-era accessories. Once you've tried on half the shop, free your inner child at GoldyMama's 'Bar à Bonbons' filled with boiled sweets, caramels and all sorts of other naughty treats.

★ Hammam Medina Center

43-45 rue Petit, 19th (01.42.02.31.05, www.hammam-medina.com). M° Ourcq. **Open** *Women* 11am-10pm Mon-Fri; 9am-7pm Sun. *Mixed (swimwear required)* 10am-9pm Sat. **Map** p162 D5 ㊽ **Health & beauty**

This hammam is hard to beat – spotless mosaic-tiled surroundings, flowered sarongs and a relaxing pool. The exotic 'Forfait floral' option (€125) will have you enveloped in rose petals and massaged with *huile d'Argan* from Morocco, and the more simple hammam and *gommage* followed by mint tea and pastries is €44. Plan to spend a few hours here.

Le Monte-en-l'air

71 rue de Ménilmontant, 20th (01.40.33.04.54). M° Ménilmontant. **Open** 1-8pm Mon-Fri; 10am-8pm Sat. **Map** p163 G6 ㊾ **Books & music**

Guillaume Dumora's glorious shop is a literary hybrid, a triple-purpose space with a 'curiosity shop' for atypical and disturbing novels, a 'gallery' where different paintings and photos are hung every three weeks, and the main '*librairie*', where you'll find everything from graphic novels to classic literature and modern poetry. Hang around long enough and you might even catch some live music or meet an author on a book signing.

Viveka Bergström

23 rue de la Grange aux Belles, 10th (01.40.03.04.92, www.viveka-bergstrom.com). M° Colonel Fabien. **Open** noon-7pm Tue-Sat. **Map** p163 E3 ㊿ **Accessories**

The daughter of Saab's aeroplane designer in the 1950s, Viveka Bergström makes slinky tassel necklaces, oversized beaten gold rings and brooches, and conversation starters like the angel-wing bracelet and a necklace featuring a map of Paris.

Un Zèbre O Grenier

16 rue Villiers de l'Isle Adam, 20th (09.52.62.88.70, www.unzebreaugrenier.fr). M° Gambetta. **Open** 10.30am-1.30pm, 3-7pm Tue-Fri; 10.30am-7pm Sat. **Map** p163 G6 ㊿ **Children**

This charming children's toy shop is hidden away near Gambetta. Catering for 0-8s, it has thought of everything – you can find things for tots to wear, play with, read and rest on. Another little plus is that the shop welcomes pre-loved toys through its ingenious system of reselling used items. So you'll find beautiful second-hand books for sale from €3 next to Petit Prince Music boxes for €26. What you won't find are the latest electronic gadgets – it's all about soft toys, wooden games and puzzles.

EXPLORE

The Latin Quarter & the 13th

EXPLORE

The Latin Quarter holds considerable mystique for foreign visitors, thanks to the historical presence of Hemingway, Orwell and Miller, and to it being the seedbed of the 1968 revolt. Granted, many of the narrow, crooked streets (the Latin Quarter was a part of Paris largely untouched by Haussmann) are charming, and there are some real architectural glories, especially ecclesiastical ones; but the crowds can make the experience dispiriting. To the east of the Latin Quarter, the part of the 13th known as the ZAC Rive Gauche, anchored by the four towers of the Bibliothèque Nationale, is one of the city's fastest rising quarters, and the Cité de la Mode, which finally opened its doors in 2012, is swiftly transforming the area into an essential Left Bank hangout.

Institut du Monde Arabe.

Don't Miss

1 Diptyque Finest candles money can buy (p179).

2 Institut du Monde Arabe One of the city's most innovative museums (p184).

3 Ribouldingue Offally good food (p178).

4 Docks en Seine Left Bank party HQ (p189).

5 Shakespeare & Co Literary legend (p179).

ST-SEVERIN & ST-JULIEN-LE-PAUVRE

In the 5th arrondissement.

Boulevard St-Michel used to be synonymous with student rebellion; now it's a ribbon of fast-food joints and clothing shops, though Gibert Joseph continues to furnish books and stationery to students. East of here, the semi-pedestrianised patch by the Seine has retained much of its medieval street plan. Rue de la Huchette and rue de la Harpe are now best known for their kebabs and pizzas, though there are 18th-century wrought-iron balconies and carved masks in the latter street. At the tiny **Théâtre de la Huchette** (*see p293*), Ionesco's absurdist drama *La Cantatrice Chauve* (*The Bald Soprano*) has been playing continuously since 1957. Also of interest are rue du Chat-qui-Pêche, supposedly the city's narrowest street, and rue de la Parcheminerie, named after the parchment sellers and copyists who once lived here. Among the tourist shops stands the city's most charming medieval church, the **Eglise St-Séverin**, with leering gargoyles, spiky gabled side chapels and an exuberantly vaulted Flamboyant Gothic interior.

Across ancient rue St-Jacques is the **Eglise St-Julien-le-Pauvre**, built as a resting place for 12th-century pilgrims. Nearby rue Galande has old houses and the Trois Mailletz cabaret (5th, 01.43.54.42.94, www.lestroismailletz.fr). The medieval cellars of the **Caveau des Oubliettes** jazz club (*see p279*) were used as a prison after the French Revolution (*oubliette* is the French word for a pit into which prisoners were thrown, then forgotten). At no.42 is arts cinema **Studio Galande** (*see p254*). Nearby, in place Viviani, stands what is perhaps the city's oldest tree, a false acacia that was planted in 1602; it's now half-swamped by ivy and propped up by concrete buttresses.

The little streets between here and the eastern stretch of boulevard St-Germain are among the city's oldest: streets such as rue de Bièvre, which follows the course of the Bièvre river that flowed into the Seine in the Middle Ages; rue du Maître-Albert; and rue des Grands-Degrès, with traces of old shop signs painted on its buildings' façades. Remnants of the Collège des Bernardins, built for the Cistercian order, can be seen in rue de Poissy, where the 13th- to 14th-century Gothic monks' refectory has been restored after service as firemen's barracks. Nearby are the **Eglise St-Nicolas du Chardonnet** (23 rue Bernardins, 5th, 01.44.27.07.90), associated with the schismatic Society of St Pius X and one of a small number of churches where you can hear the Tridentine Mass in Paris, and the art deco

Maison de la Mutualité (24 rue St-Victor, 5th, 01.83.92.24.00, www.maisondelamutualite. com), home to everything from trade unions meetings to rock concerts.

Place Maubert, now a breezy morning marketplace (Tue, Thur, Sat), witnessed the hanging of Protestants during the 16th-century Wars of Religion. Just behind the square, the modern police station is home to an array of grisly criminal evidence in the **Musée de la Préfecture de Police**.

On the corner of boulevard St-Germain and boulevard St-Michel stand the striking ruins of the late second-century **Thermes de Cluny**, the Romans' main baths complex; the adjoining Gothic Hôtel de Cluny provides a suitable setting for the **Musée National du Moyen Age**, the national collection of medieval art. Adjoining boulevard St-Germain, its garden has been replanted with species portrayed in medieval tapestries, paintings and treatises.

Sights & Museums

FREE Eglise St-Julien-le-Pauvre
Rue St-Julien-le-Pauvre, 5th (01.43.54.52.16, www.sjlpmelkites.fr). M° Cluny La Sorbonne. **Open** 9.30am-1pm, 3-6.30pm daily. **Admission** free. **Map** p176 B2 ❶

Eglise St-Séverin.

IN THE KNOW NIGHT HIKE

The thought of going for a hike in the dark may not be to everyone's liking, but insomniac ramblers turn up in their hundreds for the **Marche de la Bièvre** (http://marche.bievre.org) in May, which follows the route of Paris's underground river, the Bièvre, out towards its source beyond Versailles. Setting off en masse at midnight from Notre-Dame, hikers are guided through the Latin Quarter and the 13th, before heading out of the city's sprawling suburbs and following painted arrows through forests and farmland. Those who don't want to go the whole distance can choose from shorter courses, beginning around dawn.

A former sanctuary for pilgrims en route to Compostela, this much-mauled church dates from the late 12th century, on the cusp of Romanesque and Gothic, and has capitals richly decorated with vines, acanthus leaves and winged harpies. Once part of a priory, it became the university church when colleges migrated to the Left Bank. Since 1889, it has been used by the Greek Orthodox Church.

★ FREE Eglise St-Séverin

3 rue des Prêtres-St-Séverin, 5th (01.42.34.93.50, www.saint-severin.com). M° Cluny La Sorbonne or St-Michel. **Open** 11am-7.30pm Mon-Sat; 9am-8.30pm Sun. **Admission** free. **Map** p176 B2 ❷
Built on the site of the chapel of the hermit Séverin, itself set on a much earlier Merovingian burial ground, this lovely Flamboyant Gothic edifice was long the parish church of the Left Bank. It was rebuilt on various occasions to repair damage after ransacking by Normans and to meet the needs of the growing population. The church dates from the 15th century, though the doorway, carved with foliage, was added in 1837 from the demolished Eglise St-Pierre-aux-Boeufs on Ile de la Cité. The double ambulatory is famed for its forest of 'palm tree' vaulting, which meets at the end in a unique spiral column that inspired a series of paintings by Robert Delaunay. The bell tower, a survivor from one of the earlier churches on the site, has the oldest bell in Paris (1412). Around the nave are stained-glass windows dating from the 14th and 15th centuries, and the choir apse has stained glass designed by Jean René Bazaine in the 1960s. Next door, around the former cemetery, is the only remaining charnel house in Paris.

★ Musée National du Moyen Age – Thermes de Cluny

6 pl Paul-Painlevé, 5th (01.53.73.78.00, www. musee-moyenage.fr). M° Cluny La Sorbonne. **Open** 9.15am-5.45pm Mon, Wed-Sun. **Admission**

€8; €6 reductions; free under-18s, under-26s (EU citizens), all 1st Sun of mth. PMP. **Map** p176 B1 ❸
The national museum of medieval art is best known for the beautiful, allegorical *Lady and the Unicorn* tapestry cycle, which is gleaming after a two-year restoration project, but it also has important collections of medieval sculpture and enamels. The building itself, commonly known as Cluny, also a rare example of 15th-century secular Gothic architecture, with its foliate Gothic doorways, hexagonal staircase jutting out of the façade and vaulted chapel. It was built from 1485 to 1498 – on top of a Gallo-Roman baths complex. The baths, built in characteristic Roman bands of stone and brick masonry, are the finest Roman remains in Paris. The vaulted *frigidarium* (cold bath), *tepidarium* (warm bath), *caldarium* (hot bath) and part of the hypocaust heating system are all still visible. A themed garden fronts the whole complex. Recent acquisitions include the illuminated manuscript *L'Ascension du Christ* from the Abbey of Cluny, dating back to the 12th century, and the 16th-century triptych *Assomption de la Vierge*.

FREE Musée de la Préfecture de Police

4 rue de la Montagne-Ste-Geneviève, 5th (01.44.41.52.50, www.prefecturedepolice. interieur.gouv.fr). M° Maubert Mutualité. **Open** 9am-5.30pm Mon-Fri; 10.30am-5.30pm Sat. **Admission** free. **Map** p176 C2 ❹
The police museum is housed in a working *commissariat*, which makes for a slightly intimidating entry procedure. You need to walk boldly past the police officer on guard outside and up the steps to the lobby, where you have to ask at the reception booth to be let in – queuing, if necessary, with locals there on other, but usually police-related, errands. The museum is on the second floor; start from the *Accueil* and work your way clockwise. None of the displays is labelled in English (though there is a bilingual booklet), and a handful are not labelled at all; but if you have basic French and any sort of interest in criminology, this extensive collection is well worth seeing. It starts in the early 17th century and runs to the Occupation, via the founding of the Préfecture de Police by Napoleon in 1800. Exhibits include a prison register open at the entry for Ravaillac, assassin of Henri IV; a section on the Anarchist bombings of the 1890s; the automatic pistol used to assassinate President Doumer in 1932; a blood-chilling collection of murder weapons – hammers, ice picks and knives; sections on serial killers Landru and Petiot; and less dangerous items, such as a gadget used to snag banknotes from the apron pockets of market sellers.

Restaurants

Atelier Maître Albert

1 rue Maître-Albert, 5th (01.56.81.30.01, www. ateliermaitrealbert.com). M° Maubert Mutualité or St-Michel. **Open** noon-2.30pm, 6.30-11pm Mon-Wed; noon-2.30pm, 6.30pm-1am Thur, Fri;

EXPLORE

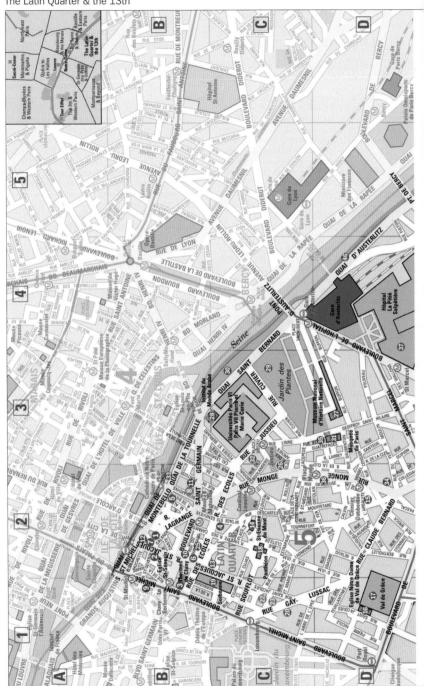

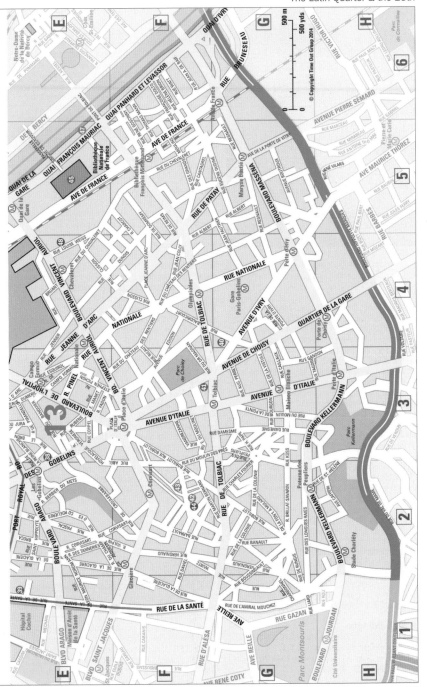

EXPLORE

Diptyque.

6.30pm-1am Sat; 6.30-11.30pm Sun. **Main courses** €21.50-€33. **Prix fixe** *Lunch* €26, €31. *Dinner* €36. **Map** p176 B2 **5** **Bistro**
This Guy Savoy outpost in the fifth arrondissement has slick decor designed by Jean-Michel Wilmotte. The indigo-painted, grey marble-floored dining room with open kitchen and rôtisseries on view is attractive, but it does mean that the place can get very noisy. The short menu lets you have a Savoy classic or two to start with, including oysters in seawater *gelée*, perhaps, or more inventive dishes such as the ballotine of chicken, foie gras and celeriac in a chicken-liver sauce. Next up could be tuna served with tiny iron casseroles of dauphinois potatoes, accompanied by cauliflower in béchamel sauce.

Le Pré Verre
8 rue Thénard, 5th (01.43.54.59.47, www.lepreverre.com). M° Maubert Mutualité. **Open** noon-2pm, 7.30-10.30pm Tue-Sat. Closed 22 Dec-6 Jan. **Main courses** €19.50. **Prix fixe** *Lunch* €13.90, €30.50. *Dinner* €30.50. **Map** p176 B2 **6** **Bistro**
Philippe Delacourcelle knows how to handle spices like few other French chefs. He also trained with the late Bernard Loiseau, and learned the art of French pastry at Fauchon. Salt cod with cassia bark and smoked potato purée is a classic: what the fish lacks in size it makes up for in rich, cinnamon-like flavour and crunchy texture, and smooth potato cooked in a smoker makes a startling accompaniment. Spices have a way of making desserts seem esoteric, but the roast figs with olives are an exception to the rule.

★ Ribouldingue
10 rue St-Julien-le-Pauvre, 5th (01.46.33.98.80, www.restaurant-ribouldingue.com). M° St-Michel. **Open** noon-2pm, 7-11pm Tue-Sat. **Prix fixe** €28, €34. **Map** p176 B2 **7** **Bistro**

This bistro facing St-Julien-le-Pauvre church is the creation of Nadège Varigny, who spent ten years working with Yves Camdeborde before opening a restaurant inspired by the food of her childhood in Grenoble. It's usually full of people, including critics and chefs, who love simple, honest bistro fare, such as *daube de boeuf* or seared tuna on a bed of melting aubergine. And if you have an appetite for offal, go for the gently sautéed brains with new potatoes, or the veal kidneys with a perfectly prepared potato gratin. For dessert, try the fresh ewe's cheese with bitter honey.

Cafés & Bars

Da Zavola
24 rue des Bernadins, 5th (01.46.34.66.97, www.dazavola.com). M° Maubert-Mutualité. **Open** 10.30am-10pm Tue-Sat. **Map** p176 B2 **8**
Da Zavola is a contemporary café of the sort the Italians term a *gastronomia*, where you can taste gourmet treats from across Italy and get an outstanding espresso. The bar is open all day serving everything from prosciutto crudo and mozzarella to grilled aubergines and toasted foccacia, pasta at lunch and dinner, and *aperitivi* in the early evening. And for the perfect treat after *cannoli*, a traditional Sicilian dessert, order a *marocchino*, a lethal glass of syrupy liquid chocolate topped off with an espresso and a drop of frothy milk.

Shops & Services

Abbey Bookshop
29 rue de la Parcheminerie, 5th (01.46.33.16.24). M° St-Michel. **Open** 10am-7pm Mon-Sat. **Map** p176 B1 **9** **Books & music**
The tiny Abbey Bookshop is the domain of Canadian renaissance man Brian Spence, who organises weekend hikes as well as dressing up in doublet and hose for a spot of 17th-century dancing. The tiny, narrow shop stocks old and new works, a specialised Canadian section, and highbrow subjects down the rickety staircase. Several thousand more books are tucked away in storage, and he can normally order titles for collection within two days.

Album
67 bd Saint-Germain, 5th (01.53.10.00.60, www.album.fr). M° Cluny La Sorbonne. **Open** 10am-8pm Mon-Sat; noon-7pm Sun. **Map** p176 B2 **10** **Books & music**
Proud denizens of boulevard Saint-Germain for more than 20 years, the three 'Album' shops reign supreme over the Paris comic scene. Under the watchful eye of the owners who dispense both advice and anecdotes, this is a comic-lover's paradise, with titles for children and adults (Marvel, DC comics, TPB Vertigo), and whole shelves dedicated to merchandising. From classic posters signed by Hugo Pratt to umbrellas and Star Wars-branded

USB sticks, there's something here to make every geek and figurine collector happy. Imported limited-edition mangas and book signings are the specialities of this address, open seven days a week.
Other locations 84 bd St-Germain, 5th (01.43.25.25.68, French and Belgian comics); 8 rue Dante, 5th (01.43.25.85.19, action figures).

★ Diptyque

34 bd St-Germain, 5th (01.43.26.77.44, www.diptyqueparis.com). M° Maubert Mutualité.
Open 10am-7pm Mon-Sat. **Map** p176 B2 ⓫
Gifts & souvenirs
Diptyque's divinely scented candles are the quintessential gift from Paris. They come in 48 different varieties, from wild fennel to pomander. Prices are not cheap, but with 50 to 60 hours' burn time, they're worth every euro.

★ Shakespeare & Company

37 rue de la Bûcherie, 5th (01.43.25.40.93, www.shakespeareandcompany.com). M° St-Michel.
Open 10am-11pm Mon-Fri; 11am-11pm Sat, Sun.
Map p176 B2 ⓬ **Books & music**
Unequivocally the best bookshop in Paris, the historic and ramshackle Shakespeare & Company is always packed with expat and tourist book-lovers. There is a large second-hand section, antiquarian books next door, and just about anything you could ask for new.

THE SORBONNE, MONTAGNE STE-GENEVIÈVE & MOUFFETARD

In the 5th arrondissement.

An influx of well-heeled residents in the 1980s put paid to the days of horn-rims, pipes and turtlenecks: accommodation here is now well beyond the reach of most students. The intellectual tradition persists, however, in the concentration of academic institutions around Montagne Ste-Geneviève, and students throng the specialist bookstores and art cinemas on rue Champollion and rue des Ecoles.

The district's long-running association with learning began in about 1100, when a number of renowned scholars, including Pierre Abélard, began to live and teach on the Montagne, independent of the established cathedral school of Notre-Dame. This loose association of scholars came to be referred to as a 'university'. The Paris schools attracted students from all over Europe, and the 'colleges' – in reality student residences dotted round the area (some still survive) – multiplied, until the University of Paris was given official recognition with a charter from Pope Innocent III in 1215.

By the 16th century, the university – named the **Sorbonne** after the most famous of its colleges – had been co-opted by the Catholic Church. A century later, Cardinal Richelieu rebuilt it. Following the Revolution, when it was forced to close, Napoleon revived the Sorbonne as the cornerstone of his new, centralised education system. The university participated enthusiastically in the uprisings of the 19th century; it was also a seedbed of the 1968 revolt, when it was occupied by protesting students. Also on rue des Ecoles, the independent **Collège de France** was founded in 1530 by a group of humanists led by Guillaume Budé under the patronage of François I. The neighbouring **Brasserie Balzar** (no.49, 5th, 01.43.54.13.67) has been fuelling amateur philosophy for years.

From here, climb rue St-Jacques to rue Soufflot for the most impressive introduction to place du Panthéon. Otherwise, follow rue des

EXPLORE

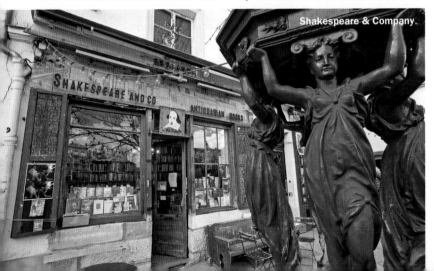
Shakespeare & Company.

La Sorbonne. *See p183.*

Carmes – with its Baroque chapel, now used by the Syrian Church – and continue on rue Valette past the brick and stone entrance of the **Collège Ste-Barbe**, where Ignatius Loyola, Montgolfier and Eiffel studied. Alternatively, follow the serpentine rue de la Montagne-Ste-Geneviève; at the junction of rue Descartes, cafés and eccentric wine bistros overlook the sculpted 19th-century entrance to what was once the elite Ecole Polytechnique (since moved to the suburbs) and is now the research ministry. There's a small park here, and popular bistro **L'Ecurie** (2 rue Laplace, 5th, 01.46.33.68.49) – an old stable burrowed into medieval cellars.

Louis XV commissioned the huge, domed **Panthéon** to honour Geneviève, the city's patron saint, but it was converted during the Revolution into a secular temple for France's *grands hommes*. The surrounding place du Panthéon, also conceived by Panthéon architect Jacques-Germain Soufflot, is one of the city's great set pieces: looking on to it are the elegant fifth arrondissement town hall and, opposite, the law faculty. On the north side, the Ste-Geneviève university library, built by Labrouste with an iron-framed reading room, contains medieval manuscripts. On the other side you'll find the historic **Hôtel des Grands Hommes** (no.17, 5th, 01.46.34.19.60, www.hotelesgrands hommes.com), where Surrealist mandarin André Breton invented 'automatic writing' in the 1920s.

Pascal, Racine and the remains of Sainte Geneviève are all interred within **Eglise St-Etienne-du-Mont**, on the north-east corner of the square. Just behind it, within the illustrious and elitist Lycée Henri IV, is the Gothic-Romanesque **Tour de Clovis**, part of the former Abbaye Ste-Geneviève. Take a look through the entrance (open during termtime) and you'll also catch glimpses of the cloister and other monastic structures.

Further from place du Panthéon, along rue Clovis, is a chunk of Philippe-Auguste's 12th-century city wall. The exiled monarch James II once resided at 65 rue du Cardinal-Lemoine, in the severe buildings of the former Collège des Ecossais (now a school), founded in 1372 to house Scottish students; the king's brain was preserved here until carried off and lost during the French Revolution. Other well known ex-residents include Ernest Hemingway, who lived at 79 rue du Cardinal-Lemoine (note the plaque) and 39 rue Descartes in the 1920s, and James Joyce; the latter completed *Ulysses* while staying at 71 rue du Cardinal-Lemoine. Rimbaud lived in rue Descartes, and Descartes himself lived on nearby rue Rollin.

This area is still a mix of tourist picturesque and gentle village, where some of the buildings hide surprising courtyards and gardens. Pretty place de la Contrescarpe has been a famous rendezvous since the 1530s, when writers as renowned as Rabelais, Ronsard and Du Bellay frequented the Cabaret de la Pomme de Pin at no.1; it still has some lively cafés. When George Orwell stayed at 6 rue du Pot-de-Fer in 1928 and 1929 (he described his time here and his work as a dishwasher in *Down and Out in Paris and London*), it was a place of astounding poverty; today, the street is lined with bargain bars and restaurants, and the restored houses along rue Tournefort bear little relation to the garrets of Balzac's *Le Père Goriot*.

Rue Mouffetard, originally the road to Rome and one of the oldest streets in the city, winds south as a suite of cheap bistros, Greek and Lebanese tavernas and knick-knack shops thronged with tourists; the vibe described by Hemingway – 'that wonderful narrow crowded market street, beloved of bohemians' – has faded. The street market (Tue-Sat, Sun morn) on the lower half seethes at weekends, when it spills on to the square and around the cafés in front of the **Eglise St-Médard**. There's another busy market, more frequented by locals, at place Monge (Wed, Fri, Sun morning).

Back to the west of the Panthéon, head south beyond rue Soufflot and you'll notice that rue St-Jacques becomes prettier. Here you'll find several ancient buildings, including the *hôtel* at no.151, good food shops and vintage bistro **Perraudin** (no.157, 5th, 01.46.33.15.75, www.restaurant-perraudin.com). Rue d'Ulm contains the elite **Ecole Normale Supérieure** (no.45, 5th, 01.44.32.30.00, www.ens.fr), occupied in protest by the unemployed in January 1998; in an echo of 1968, students also joined in.

Turn off up hilly rue des Fossés-St-Jacques to discover place de l'Estrapade; in the 17th century the *estrapade* was a tall wooden tower from which deserters were dropped repeatedly until they died. Nearby, in rue des Irlandais, the Centre Culturel Irlandais hosts concerts, exhibitions, films, plays and spoken-word events promoting Irish culture. Back to the west of rue St-Jacques, rue Soufflot and broad rue Gay-Lussac (a hotspot of the May 1968 revolt), with their Haussmannian apartment buildings, lead to boulevard St-Michel and the Jardin du Luxembourg.

Further south along rue St-Jacques, in the potters' quarter of Roman Lutetia, is the most ornate of the city's Baroque churches, the **Eglise du Val-de-Grâce**. Round the corner, at 6 rue du Val-de-Grâce, is the former home of Alfons Maria Mucha, the influential Moravian art nouveau artist, who was best known for his posters of Sarah Bernhardt.

Sights & Museums

FREE Collège de France
11 pl Marcelin-Berthelot, 5th (01.44.27.12.11, 01.44.27.11.47, www.college-de-france.fr). M° Cluny La Sorbonne or Maubert Mutualité/ RER Luxembourg. **Open** 9am-5pm Mon-Fri. **Admission** free. **Map** p176 C2 **⑬**
Founded in 1530 with the patronage of François I, the college is a place of learning and a research institute. The present building dates from the 16th and 17th centuries; there's also a later annexe. All lectures are free and open to the public; some have been given by such eminent figures as anthropologist Claude Lévi-Strauss, philosopher Maurice Merleau-Ponty and mathematician Jacques Tits.

★ FREE Eglise St-Etienne-du-Mont
Pl Ste-Geneviève, 5th (01.43.54.11.79, www.saintetiennedumont.fr). M° Cardinal Lemoine/ RER Luxembourg. **Open** 8.45am-7.45pm Tue-Fri; 8.45am-noon, 2-7.45pm Sat; 8.45am-12.15pm, 2-7.45pm Sun (*July, Aug* 10am-noon, 4-7.45pm Tue-Sun). **Admission** free. **Map** p176 C2 **⑭**

Geneviève, patron saint of Paris, is credited with having miraculously saved the city from the ravages of Attila the Hun in 451, and her shrine has been a site of pilgrimage ever since. The present church was built in an amalgam of Gothic and Renaissance styles between 1492 and 1626, and once adjoined the abbey church of Ste-Geneviève. The façade mixes Gothic rose windows with rusticated roman columns and reliefs of classically draped figures. The interior is wonderfully tall and light, with soaring columns and a classical balustrade. The stunning Renaissance rood screen, with its double spiral staircase and ornate stone strapwork, is the only surviving one in Paris, and was possibly designed by Philibert Delorme. The decorative canopied wooden pulpit by Germaine Pillon dates from 1651, and is adorned with figures of the Graces and supported by a muscular Samson sitting on the defeated lion. Sainte Geneviève's elaborate neo-Gothic brass-and-glass shrine (shielding the ancient tombstone) is located to the right of the choir, surrounded by an assortment of reliquaries and dozens of marble plaques bearing messages of thanks. At the back of the church (and reached through the sacristy), the catechism chapel constructed by Baltard in the 1860s contains a cycle of paintings relating the saint's life story.

FREE Eglise St-Médard
141 rue Mouffetard, 5th (01.44.08.87.00, www.saintmedard.org). M° Censier Daubenton. **Open** 8am-12.30pm, 2.30-7.30pm Tue-Sat; 8.30am-12.30pm, 4-8.30pm Sun. **Admission** free. **Map** p176 D2 **⑮**
The original chapel here was a dependency of the Abbaye Ste-Geneviève. The rebuilding towards the end of the 15th century created a somewhat larger, late Gothic structure best known for its elaborate vaulted ambulatory.

FREE Eglise du Val-de-Grâce
Pl Alphonse-Laveran, 5th (www.valdegrace.org). RER Luxembourg or Port-Royal. **Open** 2-6pm Mon-Sat; 9am-noon, 2-6pm Sun. **Admission** free. **Map** p176 D1 **⑯**
Anne of Austria, the wife of Louis XIII, vowed to erect 'a magnificent temple' if God blessed her with a son. She got two. The resulting church and surrounding Benedictine monastery – these days a military hospital and the Musée du Service de Santé des Armées (*see below*) – were built by François Mansart and Jacques Lemercier. This is the most luxuriously Baroque of the city's 17th-century domed churches, its ornate altar decorated with twisted barley-sugar columns. The swirling colours of the dome frescoes painted by Pierre Mignard in 1669 (which Molière himself once eulogised) are designed to give a foretaste of heaven. In contrast, the surrounding monastery offers the perfect example of François Mansart's classical restraint. Phone in advance if you're after a guided visit.

EXPLORE

MOVIE MAGIC
Pathé is opening up its archives.

As if film buffs weren't already spoilt for choice in Paris, they'll have another reason to get excited come 2014. The **Fondation Jérôme Seydoux-Pathé** (www.fondation-jeromeseydoux-pathe.com) is opening a showcase centre for its collection of film memorabilia and artefacts, including a space for temporary exhibitions.

Established in 1896, the Société Pathé Frères was one of the founders of cinema, building its reputation on savvy technical innovations and the famed pre-film Pathé newsreels. Today, the company remains one of Europe's leading distributors, producers and cinema exhibitors, and the foundation's mission is to promote the history of cinema via the Pathé story. Its collection is made up of the company's archives for everything except film reels, and includes movie posters, journals, props, cameras, and all sorts of projectionists' paraphernalia.

To house such a prestigious collection, Pathé commissioned Renzo Piano, architect of the Centre Pompidou, to design a new building on the site of a former cinema near Place d'Italie. The only stipulation was that the building's old façade had to be conserved, as it was embellished with an elaborate sculpture by iconic artist Auguste Rodin. Piano's solution was to take visitors through the old entrance, across a short corridor, and into a brand new oval complex that will house the foundation's offices and collection. This five-storey building will be glass-fronted, with tinted panes used on certain floors to protect the archives. On the ground floor, a temporary exhibition space, including a small cinema, will host exhibitions based on the Pathé collection. Visitors will be treated to original posters, props and stills from landmark movies such as Marcel Carné's post-war classic *Les Enfants du Paradis*, as well as more recent crowd-pleasers such as box-office smash *Bienvenue chez les Ch'tis*.

The centre will also exhibit Pathé studio cameras and film projectors through the ages, while the top floor will feature a research library, accessible to the public by appointment only. Outside, visitors will be able to admire the building's audacious architecture from a small garden.

Musée du Service de Santé des Armées
Val de Grâce, pl Alphonse-Laveran, 5th (01.40.51.51.92). RER Luxembourg or Port Royal. **Open** noon-6pm Tue, Wed, Sat, Sun. Closed Aug. **Admission** €5; €2.50 reductions; free under-6s. **No credit cards. Map** p176 D1 **⑰**
Housed in the royal convent designed by Mansart, this museum traces the history of military medicine via replicas of field hospitals and ambulance trains, as well as displays of antique medical instruments. The section on World War I demonstrates how much the conflict propelled medical progress.

★ Le Panthéon
Pl du Panthéon, 5th (01.44.32.18.00). M° Cardinal Lemoine/RER Luxembourg. **Open** 10am-6pm (until 6.30pm summer) daily. **Admission** €7.50; €4.50 reductions; free under-18s, under-26s (EU citizens). PMP. **Map** p176 C2 **⑱**

Soufflot's neoclassical megastructure was the architectural *grand projet* of its day, commissioned by a grateful Louis XV to thank Sainte Geneviève for his recovery from illness. But by the time it was ready in 1790, a lot had changed; during the Revolution, the Panthéon was rededicated as a 'temple of reason' and the resting place of the nation's great men. The austere barrel-vaulted crypt now houses such illustrious figures as Voltaire, Rousseau, Hugo and Zola. New heroes are installed but rarely: Pierre and Marie Curie's remains were transferred here in 1995; Alexandre Dumas in 2002. Inside are Greek columns and domes, along with 19th-century murals of Geneviève's life by Symbolist painter Puvis de Chavannes, a formative influence on Picasso during the latter's blue period.

Mount the steep spiral stairs to the colonnade encircling the dome for superb views. A replica of Foucault's Pendulum hangs here; the original proved that the earth does indeed spin on its axis, via a universal joint that lets the direction of the pendulum's swing rotate as the earth revolves.

La Sorbonne

17 rue de la Sorbonne, 5th (01.40.46.22.11, www.sorbonne.fr). M° Cluny La Sorbonne. **Open** 9am-5pm Mon-Fri. *Tours* by appointment. Closed July & Aug. **Map** p176 C1 **⑱**

Founded in 1253, the University of the Sorbonne was at the centre of the Latin Quarter's intellectual activity from the Middle Ages until 1968, when it was occupied by students and stormed by the riot police. The authorities then split the University of Paris into safer outposts, but the Sorbonne still houses the Faculté des Lettres. Rebuilt by Richelieu and reorganised by Napoleon, the present buildings date from the late 1800s, and have a labyrinth of classrooms and lecture theatres, as well as an observatory tower. The elegant dome of the 17th-century chapel dominates place de la Sorbonne; Cardinal Richelieu is buried inside. It's open to the public only for exhibitions or concerts. *Photo p180.*

Restaurants

Les Papilles

30 rue Gay-Lussac, 5th (01.43.25.20.79, www.lespapillesparis.fr). M° Luxembourg. **Open** noon-2pm, 7-10.30pm Tue-Sat. **Main courses** €20. **Prix fixe** €35. **Map** p176 C1 **⑳** **Bistro**

This quaint little bistro, which doubles as a wine shop and *épicerie*, is a safe bet in an otherwise touristy neighbourhood. Waiters rattle off the menu, then invite you to choose your bottle of wine from the wall. Wine aficionados will have a field day; wine amateurs, ask for help. A €7 corkage fee is applied to each bottle. On the plate, expect seasonal tastes such as carrot soup poured over crispy bacon and sour cream, cod with capers in a sizzling hot copper dish, and salted caramel and poached pear panna cotta. It gets crowded and the noise level picks up later on, but it's all part of the fun.

Cafés & Bars

Ciel

3 rue Monge, 5th (01.43.29.40.78, www.patisserie-ciel.com). M° Maubert-Mutualité. **Open** 10.30am-11pm Tue-Thur; 10.30am-1am Fri, Sat; 10.30am-5pm Sun. **Map** p176 B2 **㉑**

Macaroons, cupcakes and choux buns have all had their food fashion moments in Paris, and now it's the turn of the angel cake – light, fluffy American treats, here adapted by a Japanese kitchen. There are six flavours on offer at Ciel, a *salon de thé* entirely devoted to angel cake: from the classic (rose, chocolate and vanilla-caramel) to the more unusual (lemon *yuzu* or green tea *matcha*). In the evenings, the *salon de thé* becomes a trendy bar, where fans of Japanese whisky can indulge while snacking on savoury dishes such as parmesan bake or pata negra.

★ Le Crocodile

6 rue Royer-Collard, 5th (01.43.54.32.37). RER Luxembourg. **Open** 6pm-2am Mon-Sat. **No credit cards. Map** p176 C1 **㉒**

Ignore the apparently boarded-up windows at Le Crocodile; if you're here late, then it's open. Friendly young regulars line the sides of this small, narrow bar and try to decide what to drink – not easy, given the length of the cocktail list: at last count there were 317 varieties. The generous €6-per-cocktail happy hour (6-11pm Monday to Thursday) will allow you to start with a champagne *accroche-coeur*, followed up with a Goldschläger (served with gold leaf) before moving on to the rest of the list.

Le Pantalon

7 rue Royer-Collard, 5th (no phone). RER Luxembourg. **Open** 5.30pm-1.45am daily. **No credit cards. Map** p176 C1 **㉓**

A local café that seems familiar yet is utterly surreal. It has the standard fixtures, including the old soaks at the bar – but the regulars and staff are enough to tip the balance firmly into eccentricity. Friendly and funny French grown-ups and foreign students chat in a variety of languages; drinks are cheap enough to make you tipsy without the worry of a cash hangover.

Le Requin Chagrin

10 rue Mouffetard, 5th (01.44.07.23.24). M° Place Monge. **Open** 4pm-2am Mon-Thur, Sun; 4pm-4am Fri, Sat. **Map** p176 C2 **㉔**

The 'depressed shark' hasn't lost its bite. Students and beer guzzlers of all ages still cram in for the ten *bières* on tap and extended happy hour (4-9.30pm), when the cheapest pints are a steal at just €4. You'll find the usual Left Bank suspects: groups of friends, blokes trying to get laid and *intellos* from the nearby universities playing chess and quoits.

Shops & Services

Crocodisc

40-42 rue des Ecoles, 5th (01.43.54.47.95, www.crocodisc.com). M° Maubert Mutualité. **Open** 11am-7pm Tue-Sat. Closed last wk July & 1st 2wks Aug. **Map** p176 B2 **㉕** **Books & music**

The excellent albeit expensive range includes rock, funk, African, country and classical, in the form of new and second-hand vinyl and CDs. For jazz and blues, try sister shop Crocojazz.

Other locations Crocojazz, 64 rue de la Montagne-Ste-Geneviève, 5th (01.46.34.78.38).

AROUND THE JARDIN DES PLANTES

In the 5th arrondissement.

The quiet, easternmost part of the fifth arrondissement is home to yet more academic institutions, the Paris mosque and another

EXPLORE

Roman relic. Old-fashioned bistros on rue des Fossés-St-Bernard contrast with the forbidding 1960s architecture of the massive university campus of Paris VI and VII, the science faculty (known as Jussieu) built on what had been the site of the important Abbaye St-Victor. Between the Seine and Jussieu is the newly revamped, glass-faced **Institut du Monde Arabe**, which has a programme of concerts and exhibitions and a restaurant with a great view. The **Jardin Tino Rossi**, by the river, contains the slightly dilapidated **Musée de la Sculpture en Plein Air**; in summer this is a spot for dancing and picnicking.

Hidden among the hotels of rue Monge is the entrance to the **Arènes de Lutèce**, a Roman amphitheatre. The remains of a circular arena and its tiers of stone seating were discovered in 1869. Excavation started in 1883, thanks to lobbying by Victor Hugo. Nearby rise the white minaret and green pantiled roof of the **Mosquée de Paris**, built in 1922. Its beautiful Moorish tearoom is a student haunt.

The mosque looks over the **Jardin des Plantes** botanical garden. Opened in 1626 as a garden for medicinal plants, it features an 18th-century maze and a winter garden bristling with rare species. It also houses the Muséum National d'Histoire Naturelle, with its brilliantly renovated **Grande Galerie de l'Evolution**, and a zoo, La Ménagerie, an unlikely by-product of the Revolution, when royal and noble collections of wild animals were impounded. Street names and the lovely animal-themed fountain on the corner of rue Cuvier pay homage to the many naturalists and other scientists who worked here. A short way away, at 11-13bis rue Geoffroy-St-Hilaire, the words 'Chevaux', 'Poneys' and 'Anes' are still visible on the façade of the old horse market.

Sights & Museums

FREE Arènes de Lutèce

Rue Monge, rue de Navarre or rue des Arènes, 5th. M° Cardinal Lemoine or Place Monge. **Open** *Summer* 9am-9.30pm daily. *Winter* 8am-5.30pm daily. **Admission** free. **Map** p176 C2 ②
This Roman arena, where wild beasts and gladiators once fought, could seat 10,000 people. It was still visible during the reign of Philippe-Auguste in the 12th century, then disappeared under rubble. The site was only rediscovered in 1869 and now incorporates a romantically planted garden. These days, it attracts an assortment of skateboarders, footballers and boules players.

★ Grande Galerie de l'Evolution

36 rue Geoffroy-St-Hilaire, 2 rue Bouffon or pl Valhubert, 5th (01.40.79.56.01, www.mnhn.fr). M° Gare d'Austerlitz or Jussieu. **Open** *Grande*

Galerie 10am-6pm Mon, Wed-Sun. *Galerie de Paléontologie et d'Anatomie Comparée* 10am-5pm Mon, Wed-Fri; 10am-6pm Sat, Sun. **Admission** *Grande Galerie* €7; €5 reductions. *Galerie de Paléontologie et d'Anatomie Comparée* €7; €5 reductions; free under-26s. **No credit cards**.
Map p176 D3 ②
One of the city's most child-friendly attractions (*see also p246*), this is guaranteed to bowl adults over too. Located within the Jardin des Plantes (*see p185*), this beauty of a 19th-century iron-framed, glass-roofed structure has been modernised with lifts, galleries and false floors, and filled with life-size models of tentacle-waving squids, open-mawed sharks, tigers hanging off elephants and monkeys swarming down from the ceiling. The centrepiece is a procession of African wildlife across the first floor that resembles the procession into Noah's Ark. Glass-sided lifts take you up through suspended birds to the second floor, which deals with man's impact on nature (crocodile into handbag). The third floor focuses on endangered and extinct species. The separate Galerie de Paléontologie et d'Anatomie Comparée contains more than a million skeletons, as well as a world-class fossil collection.

Institut du Monde Arabe

1 rue des Fossés-St-Bernard, 5th (01.40.51.38.38, www.imarabe.org). M° Jussieu. **Open** *Museum* 10am-6pm Tue-Thur; 10am-9.30pm Fri; 10am-7pm Sat, Sun. *Library* 1-8pm Tue-Sat (July, Aug 1-6pm). *Tours* 3pm Tue-Fri; 3pm & 4.30pm Sat, Sun. **Admission** *Museum* €8; €4-€6 reductions; free under-18s, under-26s (EU citizens). PMP. *Library* free. *Exhibitions* varies. **Map** p176 C3 ②
One of Paris's most innovative museums reopened to the public in 2012 after a three-year revamp. The beautiful museum of the Institut du Monde Arabe, dedicated to the development of Islamic art and the history and culture of the Arab world, has been transformed, and reopened in time to mark its 25th anniversary. Collections from the 22 Arab countries that co-founded the museum can now be enjoyed once again, in an exciting and dynamic new interior. Some 600 items are on display, from places as diverse as Damascus, Aleppo, Latakia, Amman, Kairouan and Manama, as well as the Musée du Louvre, the Musée du Quai Branly and the Bibliothèque Nationale de France. And where before the collection was limited to art, the new museum has widened its scope (as well as its physical space), showcasing the Arab world in thematic ways, covering its ethno-linguistic, historical, cultural, anthropological and geographical diversity. What's more, there's a lively programme of events (exhibitions, film screenings, music and dance) and an excellent Middle East bookshop on the ground floor, and the views from the roof terrace (to which access is free) are fabulous.
▶ *Jean Nouvel's other landmark Paris buildings include the Musée du Quai Branly and the Fondation Cartier.*

EXPLORE

Jardin des Plantes

★ FREE Jardin des Plantes

36 rue Geoffroy-St-Hilaire, 2 rue Buffon, pl Valhubert or 57 rue Cuvier, 5th (01.40.79.56.01, www.jardindesplantes.net). M° Gare d'Austerlitz or Place Monge. **Open** *Main garden* Winter 8am-5.30pm daily. Summer 7.30am-8pm daily. *Alpine garden* Apr-Oct 8am-4.40pm Mon-Fri; 1.30-6pm Sat; 1.30-6.30pm Sun. Closed Nov-Mar. *Ménagerie* 9am-6pm Mon-Sat; 9am-6.30pm Sun. **Admission** *Alpine Garden* free Mon-Fri; €2 Sat, Sun. *Jardin des Plantes* free. *Ménagerie* €11; €9 reductions; free under-4s. **Map** p176 C3 ㉙

The Paris botanical garden – which contains more than 10,000 species and includes tropical greenhouses and rose, winter and Alpine gardens – is an enchanting place. Begun by Louis XIII's doctor as the royal medicinal plant garden in 1626, it opened to the public in 1640. The formal garden, which runs between two dead-straight avenues of trees parallel to rue Buffon, is like something out of *Alice in Wonderland*. There's also the Ménagerie (a small zoo) and the terrific Grande Galerie de l'Evolution (*see p184*). Ancient trees on view include a false acacia planted in 1636 and a cedar from 1734.

FREE Jardin Tino Rossi (Musée de la Sculpture en Plein Air)

Quai St-Bernard, 5th. M° Gare d'Austerlitz. **Admission** free. **Map** p176 C3 ㉚

This open-air sculpture museum by the Seine fights a constant battle against graffiti. Still, it's a pleasant place for a stroll. Most of the works are second-rate, aside from Etienne Martin's bronze *Demeure I* and the Carrara marble *Fenêtre* by Cuban artist Careras. ▶ *From May to September, the gardens turn into an open-air dance studio.*

La Mosquée de Paris

2 pl du Puits-de-l'Ermite, 5th (01.45.35.97.33, 01.43.31.18.14, www.mosquee-de-paris.net). M° Monge. **Open** *Tours* 9am-noon, 2-6pm Mon-Thur, Sat, Sun (closed Muslim hols). *Tearoom* 10am-11.30pm daily. *Restaurant* noon-2.30pm, 7.30-10.30pm daily. *Baths* (women) 10am-9pm Mon,

Wed, Sat; 2-9pm Fri; (men) 2-9pm Tue, Sun. **Admission** €3; €2 reductions; free under-7s. *Tearoom* free. *Baths* €15-€35. **Map** p176 D3 ㉛

Some distance removed from the Arabic-speaking inner-city enclaves of Barbès and Belleville, this vast Hispano-Moorish construct is nevertheless the spiritual heart of France's Algerian-dominated Muslim population. Built from 1922 to 1926 with elements inspired by the Alhambra and the Bou Inania Medersa in Fès, the Paris mosque is dominated by a stunning green-and-white tiled square minaret. In plan and function it divides into three sections: religious (grand patio, prayer room and minaret, all for worshippers and not curious tourists); scholarly (Islamic school and library); and, via rue Geoffroy-St-Hilaire, commercial (café and domed hammam). La Mosquée café is delightful – a modest courtyard with blue-and-white mosaic-topped tables shaded beneath green foliage and scented with the sweet smell of sheesha smoke (€6).

Restaurants

Le Buisson Ardent

25 rue Jussieu, 5th (01.43.54.93.02, www. lebuissonardent.fr). M° Jussieu. **Open** noon-2pm, 7.30-10pm Mon-Sat; noon-2.30pm Sun. Closed 2wks Aug. **Main courses** €26. **Prix fixe** *Lunch* €24, €27. *Dinner* €40. **Map** p176 C3 ㉜ **Bistro**

This bistro's square front dining room with its red banquettes and painted glass panels dating from 1923 has a quintessentially Paris charm, especially when compared to the surrounding kebab shops. There is plenty for adventurous eaters on the menu, such as pan-fried squid with chorizo and quinoa or white bean and pig's ear salad with pan-fried foie gras, but it also does conventional dishes (chestnut velouté with spice bread croûtons) very well. This is one of the area's best finds for the price.

La Tour d'Argent

15 quai de la Tournelle, 5th (01.43.54.23.31, www.latourdargent.com). M° Pont Marie or Cardinal Lemoine. **Open** noon-2pm, 7.30-10pm

EXPLORE

Tue-Sat. Closed Aug. **Main courses** €70-€140.
Prix fixe *Lunch* €75. *Dinner* €180, €200.
Map p176 B2 ❸ **Haute cuisine**
This Paris institution is regaining its lustre following the death of aged owner Claude Terrail in 2006.
In the kitchen, Breton-born Stéphane Haissant has brought a welcome creative touch to the menu, bringing in such creative dishes as a giant langoustine dabbed with kumquat purée and surrounded by lightly scented coffee foam. But he also shows restraint, as in duck (the house speciality) with cherry sauce and a broad-bean flan. Following in his father's footsteps, Terrail's soft-spoken son André now does the rounds.

La Tour d'Argent. *See p185.*

Shops & Services

Le Boulanger de Monge

123 rue Monge, 5th (01.43.37.54.20,
www.leboulangerdemonge.com). M° Censier
Daubenton. **Open** 7am-8.30pm Tue-Sun.
Map p176 D2 ❸ **Food & drink**
Dominique Saibron uses spices to give inimitable flavour to his organic sourdough *boule*. Every day about 2,000 bread-lovers visit his boutique, which also produces one of the city's best baguettes.
Other locations 53 rue Montorgueil, 2nd
(01.42.33.31.05); 48 rue de la Clef, 5th (01.47.07.28.19).

★ Hammam de la Grande Mosquée

39 rue Geoffrey St-Hilaire, 5th (01.43.31.38.20,
www.la-mosquee.com). M° Censier Daubenton.
Open 10am-9pm Mon, Wed-Sun. **Map**
p176 D3 ❸ **Health & beauty**
The authentic, women-only hammam experience in this beautiful 1920s mosque has become popular with locals, so avoid the weekends when the volume of traffic makes it less relaxing. Follow a steam session with a *gommage* (exfoliation with a rough mitt), then a massage. The hammam is €18, *gommage* €10 and massage €10 for 10mins. Swimwear is compulsory. Towel and gown hire is also available.

★ Marché Monge

Pl Monge, 5th. M° Place Monge. **Open** 7am-
2.30pm Wed, Fri; 7am-3pm Sun. **Map** p176 D2
❸ **Market**
This pretty, compact market is set on a leafy square.
It has a high proportion of producers and is much less touristy than nearby rue Mouffetard.

LES GOBELINS & LA SALPÊTRIÈRE

In the 13th arrondissement.

Its defining features might be 1960s tower blocks, but the 13th arrondissement is also historic, especially in the area bordering the fifth. The **Manufacture Nationale des Gobelins**, home to the state weaving companies, continues a tradition founded in the 15th century, when tanneries, dyers and weaving workshops lined the Bièvre river.
This putrid waterway became notorious, and the slums that grew up around it were depicted in Victor Hugo's *Les Misérables*.
The area was tidied up in the 1930s, when a small park, square René-Le-Gall, was laid out on the allotments used by tapestry workers.
The river was built over, but local enthusiasts have since opened up a small stretch in the park. Nearby, through a gateway at 17 rue des Gobelins, you can spot the turret and first floor of a medieval house. The so-called Château de la Reine Blanche on rue Gustave-Geffroy is named after Queen Blanche of Provence, who had a château here; it was probably rebuilt in the 1520s for the Gobelin family.
In the northern corner of the 13th, next to Gare d'Austerlitz, sprawls the huge Hôpital de la Pitié-Salpêtrière founded in 1656, with its striking **Chapelle St-Louis**.

FREE Chapelle St-Louis-de-la-Salpêtrière

47 bd de l'Hôpital, 13th (01.42.16.04.24). M° Gare
d'Austerlitz. **Open** 8.30am-6pm Mon-Fri, Sun;
11am-6pm Sat. **Admission** free. **Map** p176 D4 ❸
This austerely beautiful chapel, designed by Libéral Bruand and completed in 1677, features an octagonal dome in the centre and eight naves in which the sick were separated from the insane, the destitute from the debauched. Around the chapel sprawls the vast Hôpital de la Pitié-Salpêtrière, founded on the site of a gunpowder factory (hence the name, derived from saltpetre) by Louis XIV to house rounded-up vagrant women. It became a centre for research into insanity in the 1790s, when renowned doctor Philippe Pinel began to treat some of the inmates as sick rather than criminal; Jean-Martin Charcot later pioneered neuropsychology here, famously receiving a visit from Freud. Salpêtrière is today one of the city's

EXPLORE

main teaching hospitals, but the chapel is also used for contemporary art installations, notably during the Festival d'Automne (*see p37*), when its striking architecture provides a backdrop for artists such as Bill Viola, Anish Kapoor and Nan Goldin.

Manufacture Nationale des Gobelins

42 av des Gobelins, 13th (01.44.08.53.59). M° Les Gobelins. **Open** 11am-6pm Tue-Sun. **Admission** €6; €4 reductions; free last Sun of mth. *Tours* call for details. **No credit cards. Map** p177 E3 ⑱
The royal tapestry factory was founded by Colbert when he set up the Manufacture Royale des Meubles de la Couronne in 1662; it's named after Jean Gobelin, a dyer who owned the site. It reached the summit of its renown during the *ancien régime*, when Gobelins tapestries were produced for royal residences under artists such as Le Brun. Tapestries are still made here and visitors can watch weavers at work. Tours (in French; €7.50-€10) through the 1912 factory take in the 18th-century chapel and the Beauvais workshops.

CHINATOWN & THE BUTTE-AUX-CAILLES

In the 13th arrondissement.

South of rue de Tolbiac, the shop signs turn Chinese or Vietnamese. The city's main Chinatown runs along avenue d'Ivry, avenue de Choisy and into the 1960s tower blocks between. Whereas much of the public housing in and around Paris is pretty bleak, here a distinctly eastern vibe reigns, with restaurants, Vietnamese *pho* noodle bars and Chinese pâtisseries, hairdressers and purveyors of exotic groceries; not to mention the expansive **Tang Frères** supermarket (48 av d'Ivry, 13th, 01.45.70.80.00). There's even a Buddhist temple hidden in a car park beneath the tallest tower (av d'Ivry, opposite rue Frères d'Astier-de-la-Vigerie, 13th). Lion and dragon dances, and martial arts demonstrations, take place on the streets at **Chinese New Year** (*see p39*).

In contrast to Chinatown, the villagey Butte-aux-Cailles, occupying the wedge between boulevard Auguste-Blanqui and rue Bobillot, is a neighbourhood of old houses, winding streets, funky bars and restaurants. This area, which was home in the 19th century to many small factories, was one of the first to fight during the 1848 Revolution and the Paris Commune.

The Butte has preserved its rebellious character, with residents standing up to commercial developers. This predominantly *soixante-huitard* resistance is concentrated in the cobbled rue de la Butte-aux-Cailles and rue des Cinq-Diamants. Here you'll find inexpensive bistros such as **Le Temps des Cerises** (18 rue Butte-aux-Cailles, 13th, 01.45.89.69.48), run as a co-operative, and **Chez Gladines**

(30 rue des Cinq-Diamants, 13th, 01.45.80.70.10). The cottages built in 1912 in a mock-Alsatian style around a central green at 10 rue Daviel were among the earliest public-housing schemes in Paris. Just across rue Bobillot, the **Piscine Butte-aux-Cailles** (*see p248*) is a charming Arts and Crafts-style swimming pool.

Further south, you can explore passage Vandrezanne, the little houses and gardens of square des Peupliers, rue des Peupliers and rue Dieulafoy, and the flower-named streets of the Cité Florale. By the Périphérique, the **Stade Charléty** (17 av Pierre-de-Coubertin, 13th) is a superb piece of stadium architecture.

Restaurants

L'Auberge du 15

15 rue de la Santé, 13th (01.47.07.07.45, www.laubergedu15.com). M° Les Gobelins. **Open** noon-2.30pm, 7.30-11pm Tue-Thur; noon-2.30pm, 7-11pm Fri, Sat. **Main courses** €31-€49. **Prix fixe** *Lunch* €30. *Dinner* €68. **Map** p177 E1 ⑲ **Brasserie**
L'Auberge du 15 cultivates the air of a country brasserie, with Moroccan tiles lining the open kitchen and a hunting motif on the curtains. No more than ten tables fill the long room, waited on by hip young things. The seasonal menu echoes a farmhouse kitchen – soup from a tureen, cake sliced on its stand. You might get a silky *potage* of chestnuts and ceps poured over a scoop of crème fraîche. Then a hearty dish of tender veal with sweet vegetables and a cream and white wine sauce: pure indulgence.

€ Le Bambou

70 rue Baudricourt, 13th (01.45.70.91.75). M° Olympiades or Tolbiac. **Open** 11.30am-3.30pm, 6.30-10.30pm Tue-Sun. **Main courses** €7-€14.50. **Map** p177 G4 ⑳ **Vietnamese**
The Vietnamese fare here is a notch above what is normally served in Paris. Seating is elbow to elbow and, should you come on your own, the waiter will draw a line down the middle of the paper tablecloth and seat a stranger on the other side. That stranger might offer pointers on how to eat certain dishes, such as the no.42: grilled marinated pork to be wrapped in lettuce with beansprouts and herbs and eaten by hand, dipped into the accompanying sauce.

€ Pho 14

129 av de Choisy, 13th (01.45.83.61.15). M° Olympiades or Tolbiac. **Open** 9am-11pm daily. **Main courses** €7.60-€8.50. **No credit cards. Map** p177 F3 ⑳ **Vietnamese**
Vietnamese canteen Pho 14 is the place to come for delicious *pho* soups, filled with noodles, meatballs, beef or chicken, all served with fresh mint and basil. Other highlights include crispy pork spring rolls and dumplings. There's takeaway, too, if you don't want to wait for a table (there's usually a queue).

EXPLORE

Docks en Seine.

Cafés & Bars

Le Merle Moqueur
11 rue de la Butte aux Cailles, 13th (no phone).
Mº Place d'Italie. **Open** 5pm-2am daily.
No credit cards. Map p177 F2 ⓸
Amid semi-faded pseudo-tropical decor and '80s
music, the Teasing Blackbird – a Butte-aux-Cailles
institution – tantalises students and nostalgists with
its splendid selection of rums (over 20) and a long
list of cocktails. The atmosphere gets pretty raucous
after 10pm – make sure you get in early to grab one
of the three tables.

Sputnik
14 rue de la Butte aux Cailles, 13th (01.45.65.19.82,
www.sputnik.fr). Mº Place d'Italie. **Open** 2pm-2am
Mon-Sat (from 5pm in winter); 4pm-midnight Sun.
Map p177 F2 ⓸
A hip young crowd gathers in this rock-oriented
bar, which doubles as a sports bar during important
fixtures, and trebles as an internet café at other
times. Ever-changing art exhibitions add interest to
the walls, and live music once a month draws an
indie crowd. Fancy falling in love? Try the €8 love
potion cocktail Philtre d'Amour, which is made
from a fruity concoction of gin, Malibu, pineapple
and strawberries.

IN THE KNOW
BOARDING PARTY

El Alamein (http://elalamein.free.fr), a
charming purple *péniche* moored next to
the Bibliothèque Nationale de France, is a
breath of fresh air. On the terrace, a café
springs up in summer amid the plants. But
this boat also has a lot going on inside,
with an eclectic programme that ranges
from jazz to French *chanson* via rock and
theatrical performance.

Shops & Services

Les Abeilles
21 rue de la Butte-aux-Cailles, 13th (01.45.81.43.48,
www.lesabeilles.biz). Mº Corvisart or Place d'Italie.
Open 11am-7pm Tue-Sat. **Map** p177 F2 ⓸
Gifts & souvenirs
This tiny boutique sells everything from candles to
honey vinegar, honey mustard and speciality 'Miel
de Paris', gathered by owner Jean-Jacques from his
hives in Parc Kellerman. There's also a wonderful
selection of honey pots and soaps.

FURTHER EAST

The arrival in the 1990s of the **Bibliothèque
Nationale de France** breathed new life into
the desolate area, now known as the **ZAC Rive
Gauche**, between Gare d'Austerlitz and the
Périphérique. The ambitious, long-term ZAC
project includes a new university quarter, new
housing projects and a tramway linking to the
suburbs. The pedestrian **Passerelle Simone-
de-Beauvoir** spans the Seine between the BNF
and the Cinémathèque Française; the floating
Piscine Josephine-Baker (*see p248*) is now
a focus for the Paris-Plages entertainments; and
the much-delayed **Cité de la Mode et du
Design** (**Docks en Seine**), originally due to
open in 2009, is finally up and running.

Sights & Museums

Bibliothèque Nationale de France
François Mitterrand
10 quai François-Mauriac, 13th (01.53.79.59.59,
www.bnf.fr). Mº Bibliothèque François Mitterrand.
Open 2-7pm Mon; 9am-7pm Tue-Sat; 1-7pm Sun.
Admission *1 day* €3.50. *1 year* €38; €20
reductions. **Map** p177 E5 ⓸
Opened in 1996, the new national library was the last
and costliest of Mitterrand's *grands projets*. Its architect, Dominique Perrault, was criticised for his dated

EXPLORE

design, which hides readers underground and stores the books in four L-shaped glass towers. He also forgot to specify blinds to protect books from sunlight; they had to be added later. The library houses over ten million volumes and can accommodate 3,000 readers. Much of the library is open to the public: books, newspapers and periodicals are accessible to anyone over 18, and you can browse through photographic, film and sound archives.

Docks en Seine
28-36 quai d'Austerlitz, 13th (www.paris-docks-en-seine.fr). M° Chevaleret or Gare d'Austerlitz. **Map** p176 D4 ⑥
The apple-green caterpillar of Docks en Seine finally, belatedly opened its doors in 2012, transforming an industrial wasteland into a futuristic vision of culture and entertainment. A grassy terrace runs down to the water, there's a spanking new restaurant on the roof (the Moon Roof) and a bar/club (Wanderlust, by the team behind Silencio) on the first floor, and there are open-air screenings and exhibitions at the Cité de la Mode et du Design. The resurrection was completed with the opening of another club, Nüba, in late 2012.

Cafés & Bars

★ Petit Bain
7 port de la Gare, 13th (01.80.48.49.81, www.petit bain.org). M° Bibliothèque François Mitterrand or Quai de la Gare. **Open** 6.30pm-2am Wed-Sat; noon-5.30pm Sun (later in summer). **Map** p177 E5 ⑰
See below **Making Waves.**

Shops & Services

Air de Paris
32 rue Louise-Weiss, 13th (01.44.23.02.77, www.airdeparis.com). M° Chevaleret. **Open** 11am-7pm Tue-Sat. **Map** p177 E4 ⑱ **Gallery**
This gallery shows experimental, neo-conceptual and chaotic material. A hip stable of artists includes Liam Gillick, Carsten Höller and Sarah Morris.

MAKING WAVES
Join Paris's party flotilla for a night of Seine-side fun in the 13th.

The idea of an urban beach went down so well when it was first floated back in 2002 that now Paris-Plages is a victim of its own success: on sweltering summer days, the suncream-slathered crowds descend *en masse* to the banks of the Seine. But it still remains one of the best things to do in Paris during the summer, and has spawned a whole host of bars to soak up the post-beach party crowds. One of the best spots for Seine-side partying is the 13th, in the shadow of the Bibliothèque Nationale de France François Mitterrand, where a veritable flotilla of boat bars are moored up for drinks and dancing. Batofar was the original floating pleasure palace, but **Petit Bain** (*see above*) has been giving it a run for its money since it first lowered the gangplank in 2010.

Designed by the Encore Heureux collective, Petit Bain looks like a fluorescent green barge with a cubist wooden tree house plonked on top, and harbours an excellent line-up of concerts and art exhibitions, plus a coveted terrace that doubles as a bar, restaurant and octopus's garden, with all manner of aquatic plants housed in white bathtubs repurposed as planters. Below deck, the intimate stage hosts regular gigs with everything from minimalist Norwegian pop and indie folk to rock and jazz making the eclectic playlist.

EXPLORE

St-Germain-des-Prés & Odéon

St-Germain may be more Louis Vuitton than Boris Vian these days, but there are still enough small galleries and bookshops to ensure that it retains a whiff of its bohemian past. In the middle third of the 20th century, the area was prime arts and *intello* territory: the haunt of Picasso, Giacometti, Camus, Prévert and, *bien sûr*, Jean-Paul Sartre and Simone de Beauvoir; the hotspot of the Paris jazz boom after World War II; and the heart of the Paris book trade. This is where the cliché of café terrace intellectualising was coined, but nowadays most of the local patrons of the Flore and the Deux Magots are in the fashion business, and couturiers have largely replaced publishers. Never mind: it's a smart and attractive part of the city to wander around in, and also has some very good restaurants.

Hermès

Don't Miss

1 **La Palette** Sip in style at this gem (p196).

2 **Hermès** Stunning shop, spiffing scarves (p197).

3 **Jardin du Luxembourg** The quintessential Paris park (p199).

4 **Musée Zadkine** Modern art in a magical Left Bank setting (p200).

5 **Lapérouse** Blow the budget in style (p195).

Eglise St-Germain-des-Prés.

BOULEVARD ST-GERMAIN TO THE SEINE

In the 6th arrondissement.

Hit by shortages of coal during World War II, Sartre shunned his cold apartment on rue Bonaparte. 'The principal interest of the Café de Flore,' he noted at the time, 'was that it had a stove, a nearby métro and no Germans.' Although you can spend more on a few coffees here than on a week's heating these days, the **Café de Flore** remains an arty favourite, and hosts *café-philo* evenings in English. Its rival, **Les Deux Magots**, facing historic **Eglise St-Germain-des-Prés**, is frequented largely by tourists. Nearby is the celebrity favourite **Brasserie Lipp** (151 bd St-Germain, 6th, 01.45.48.53.91); art nouveau fans tend to prefer **Brasserie Vagenende** (142 bd St-Germain, 6th, 01.43.26.68.18, www.vagenende. com). Swish bookshop **La Hune** provides sustenance of a more intellectual kind.

St-Germain-des-Prés grew up around the medieval abbey, the oldest church in Paris. There are traces of its cloister and part of the abbot's palace behind the church on rue de l'Abbaye. Constructed in 1586 in red brick with stone facing, the palace prefigured the architecture of place des Vosges. Charming place de Furstemberg (once the palace stables) is home to the house and studio where the elderly Delacroix lived when painting the murals in St-Sulpice; it now houses the **Musée National Delacroix**. Wagner, Ingres and Colette lived on nearby rue Jacob; its elegant 17th-century *hôtels particuliers* now contain specialist book, design and antiques shops and a few pleasant hotels.

Further east, rue de Buci hosts a street market and upmarket food shops, and is home to legendary local **Bar du Marché** (no.16, 6th, 01.43.26.55.15). **Hôtel La Louisiane** (60 rue de Seine, 6th, 01.44.32.17.17, www.hotel-lalouisiane.com) has hosted jazz stars Chet Baker and Miles Davis, and Existentialist lovers Sartre and de Beauvoir. Rue de Seine, rue des Beaux-Arts and rue Bonaparte (Manet was born in the latter, at no.5, in 1832) are still packed with art galleries. It was in rue des Beaux-Arts, at the Hôtel d'Alsace, that Oscar Wilde complained about the wallpaper and then checked out for good. Now fashionably renovated, it houses the hip **L'Hôtel** (*see p358*). **La Palette** is a great pit stop with an enviable terrace; rue Mazarine, with shops selling lighting, vintage toys and jewellery, is also home to Terence Conran's bright, buzzing and wonderfully stylish **L'Alcazar** brasserie (no.62, 6th, 01.53.10.19.99, www.alcazar.fr). Set in the confines of a 17th-century real tennis court, and once a notorious transvestite bar, the space has been transformed with a glass roof, cool lighting and a changing series of photographic exhibits.

On quai de Conti stands the neoclassical Hôtel des Monnaies, built for Louis XV by architect Jacques-Denis Antoine; formerly the mint (1777-1973), it's now the **Musée de la Monnaie** (www.monnaiedeparis.fr) and traces the history of French coinage. Next door stands the domed **Institut de France**, cleaned to within an inch of its classical life. Opposite, the iron Pont des Arts footbridge leads directly to the Louvre. Further along, the city's main fine arts school, the **Ecole Nationale Supérieure des Beaux-Arts**, occupies an old monastery.

Sights & Museums

Ecole Nationale Supérieure des Beaux-Arts (Ensb-a)

14 rue Bonaparte, 6th (01.47.03.50.00, www. ensba.fr). M° St-Germain-des-Prés. **Open** 1-7pm Tue-Sun. **Admission** €4; €2 reductions. *Exhibitions* prices vary. **Map** p193 C2 ❶
The city's most prestigious fine arts school resides in what remains of the 17th-century Couvent des Petits-Augustins, the 18th-century Hôtel de Chimay, some 19th-century additions and some chunks of assorted French châteaux that were moved here after the Revolution (when the buildings briefly served as a museum of French monuments, before becoming the art school in 1816).

★ FREE Eglise St-Germain-des-Prés

3 pl St-Germain-des-Prés, 6th (01.55.42.81.10, www.eglise-sgp.org). M° St-Germain-des-Prés. **Open** 8am-7.45pm Mon-Sat; 9am-8pm Sun. **Admission** free. **Map** p193 C3 ❷

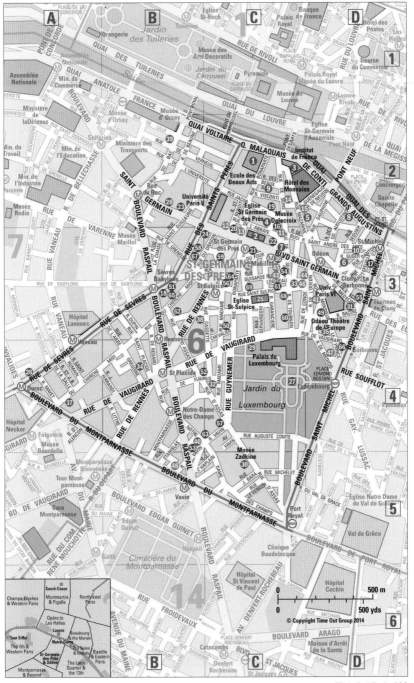

EXPLORE

Since 1832 this renowned establishment has kept up its impeccable reputation by cooking traditional French Cuisine.
In 1989, the building was officially listed as a historical monument.

Open every day except Sundays and Mondays.
24 Rue Grande Truanderie 75001 Paris, France
T. 01 40 28 45 18
le.pharamond@orange.fr

Le Pharamond
Depuis 1832

GRAND BOUILLON PARISIEN
depuis 1906

PARIS CHARM

BOUILLON
Racine

3 rue Racine, 6th. M° Odéon.
Tel: 01.44.32.15.60
Email.bouillon.racine@wanadoo.fr
www.bouillonracine.com

Difficult to surpass the beauty of this restaurant built in 1906 and listed as a Historic Building. The Chef will treat you to delicious French classics.

This is the oldest church in Paris. On the advice of Germain (later Bishop of Paris), Childebert, son of Clovis, had a basilica and monastery built here around 543. It was first dedicated to St Vincent, and came to be known as St-Germain-le-Doré ('the gilded') because of its copper roof, then later as St-Germain-des-Prés ('of the fields'). During the Revolution the abbey was burned and a saltpetre refinery installed; the spire was added in a clumsy 19th-century restoration. Still, most of the present structure is 12th century, and ornate carved capitals and the tower remain from the 11th. Tombs include those of Jean-Casimir, the deposed King of Poland who became Abbot of St-Germain in 1669, and of Scots nobleman William Douglas. Under the window in the second chapel is the funeral stone of philosopher-mathematician Descartes.

Institut de France

23 quai de Conti, 6th (01.44.41.44.41, www. institut-de-france.fr). M° Louvre Rivoli or Pont Neuf. **Open** *Guided tours only* (call 01.44.41.43.32 for times). **Admission** prices vary. **No credit cards. Map** p193 C2 ❸

This elegant domed building with sweeping curved wings was designed as a school by Louis Le Vau and opened in 1684. The five academies of the Institut (Académie Française, Académie des Inscriptions et Belles-Lettres, Académie des Beaux-Arts, Académie des Sciences, Académie des Sciences Morales et Politiques) moved here in 1805. Inside is Mazarin's ornate tomb, and the Bibliothèque Mazarine (open to over-18s with ID and two photos; €15/year). The Académie Française was founded by Cardinal Richelieu in 1635 with the aim of preserving the purity of the French language from corrupting outside influences (such as English). *Photo p196.*

Musée National Delacroix

6 rue de Furstenberg, 6th (01.44.41.86.50, www.musee-delacroix.fr). M° St-Germain-des-Prés. **Open** 9.30am-5pm Mon, Wed-Sun. **Admission** €5; free under-18s, under-26s (EU citizens), all 1st Sun of mth. PMP. **Map** p193 C2 ❹

Eugène Delacroix moved to this apartment and studio in 1857 in order to be near the Eglise St-Sulpice, where he was painting murals. This collection includes small oil paintings, free pastel studies of skies, sketches and lithographs, as well as his palette.

Restaurants

Le 21

21 rue Mazarine, 6th (01.46.33.76.90). M° Odéon. **Open** 12.30-2pm, 8-11pm Tue-Sat. **Main courses** €25-€56. **Map** p193 D2 ❺ **Bistro**

This clubby restaurant in St-Germain-des-Prés is a big hit with a *beau monde* crowd of antiques dealers, book editors and politicians. Chef Paul Minchelli's original minimalist style has evolved towards more homely preparations, as seen in a delicious sauté of flaked cod, potatoes, onions and green peppers, or squid in a squid ink sauce with black rice. To keep the waistline-watching regulars happy, a few of his old classics, including grilled red mullet, are still offered. Don't miss the chocolate fondant cake for dessert, and don't be shy about asking for help with the pricey wine list.

★ L'Epigramme

9 rue de l'Eperon, 6th (01.44.41.00.09). M° Odéon. **Open** noon-2.30pm, 7-10.30pm Tue-Sat. **Prix fixe** *Lunch* €24, €28. *Dinner* €38. **Map** p193 D3 ❻ **Bistro**

L'Epigramme is a pleasantly bourgeois dining room with terracotta floor tiles, wood beams, a glassed-in kitchen and comfortable chairs. Like the decor, the food doesn't aim to innovate but instead sticks to tried and true classics with the occasional twist. Marinated mackerel in a mustardy dressing on toasted country bread gets things off to a promising start, but the chef's skill really comes through in the main courses, such as perfectly seared lamb with glazed root vegetables and intense jus. Be sure to book well in advance.

Germain

25-27 rue de Buci, 6th (01.43.26.02.93). M° Mabillon or Odéon. **Open** 9am-2am daily. **Main courses** €20-€25. **Map** p193 C3 ❼ **Brasserie**

Quaint rue de Buci has been shaken up by the extravagance of Germain, a versatile brasserie halfway between *Alice in Wonderland* and London's Sketch. The heated terrace is great for people watching, and the main ground-floor room, which features the lower part of a vast yellow statue piercing through the ceiling above, is perfect for a quick lunch. There's also a cosy salon for cocktails, a more conservative dining room at the back, and a private room on the first floor with a snooker table and the top half of the yellow statue. The food is almost childishly classic, but always with a twist (ham and butter macaroni with truffle) and not as expensive as you might expect.

Lapérouse

51 quai des Grands-Augustins, 6th (01.43.26.68.04, www.laperouse.com). M° St-Michel. **Open** noon-2.30pm, 7.30-11pm Mon-Fri; 7.30-11pm Sat. **Main courses** €35. **Prix fixe** *Lunch* €40, €55. *Dinner* €115, €168. **Map** p193 D2 ❽ **Brasserie**

One of the most romantic spots in Paris, Lapérouse was formerly a clandestine rendezvous for French politicians and their mistresses; the tiny private dining rooms upstairs used to lock from the inside. Chef Christophe Guibert does a wonderful take on classic French cooking: chateaubriand is glazed with port in a hazelnut crust; tender saddle of rabbit is cooked in a clay crust, flavoured with lavender and rosemary and served with ravioli of onions. The only potential snag is the cost of a meal here.

EXPLORE

Institut de France. *See p195.*

★ Le Restaurant
*L'Hôtel, 13 rue des Beaux-Arts, 6th
(01.44.41.99.01, www.l-hotel.com). M° St-
Germain-des-Prés.* **Open** 7-10.30am, 12.30-2pm,
7.30-10pm Tue-Sat. **Main courses** €50. **Prix
fixe** *Breakfast* €18. *Lunch* €45, €55. *Degustation*
€110, €135. **Map** p193 C2 ❾ **Haute cuisine**
L'Hôtel's restaurant is a wonderfully atmospheric
spot for lunch or dinner, with a charming terrace
during the summer months. You can choose from a
short seasonal menu with such dishes as pan-fried
tuna, John Dory or suckling pig. But for the same
price you can also enjoy the marvellous four-course
menu dégustation or, even better, the *menu surprise*.
Highlights of the autumn menu were the wild Breton
crab stuffed with fennel, avocado and *huile d'Argan*,
and a main course of pigeon on a bed of beetroot.

Shu
*8 rue Suger, 6th (01.46.34.25.88, www.
restaurant-shu.com). M° St-Michel or Odéon.*
Open 6.30-11.30pm Mon-Sat. **Prix fixe** €38,
€48, €63. **Map** p193 D3 ❿ **Japanese**
Shu specialises in *kushi-agué* – a sort of Japanese
kebab, with different ingredients breaded and fired
on sticks. But where it really excels is in the starters,
often more refined than at the purest *kaïseki* bar.
Despite the price, opt for the more expensive menu,
which represents better value for money: €58 for an
amuse-bouche, a delicious assortment of incredibly
fresh sashimi, three seasonal dishes, nine *kushi-
agué* and a choice of *ochazuké* (rice with green tea
and condiments) or *inaniwa* (fine udon noodles)
served cold with their own cooking liquor. There
are some very good sakes on the wine list and the
service is impeccable.

Cafés & Bars

★ Le Bar du Marché
*75 rue de Seine, 6th (01.43.26.55.15). M°
Mabillon or Odéon.* **Open** 8am-2am daily.
Map p193 C3 ⓫

The market in question is the Cours des Halles, the
bar a convivial corner café opening on to the pleasing bustle of St-Germain-des-Prés. Simple dishes like
a ham omelette or a plate of herrings are in the €7
range, and Brouilly or muscadet is €4-€5 a glass –
all proffered by waiters dressed in matching dungarees. It couldn't be anywhere else in the world.

Café de Flore
*172 bd St-Germain, 6th (01.45.48.55.26,
www.cafedeflore.fr). M° St-Germain-des-Prés.*
Open 7am-2am daily. **Map** p193 C2 ⓬
Bourgeois locals crowd the terrace tables at lunch, eating club sandwiches with knives and forks as anxious
waiters frown at couples with pushchairs or single
diners occupying tables for four. This historic café,
former HQ of the Lost Generation intelligentsia,
attracts tourists and, yes, celebrities from time to time.
But a *café crème* is €4.60, and the omelettes and
croque-monsieurs are best eschewed in favour of the
better dishes on the menu (€15-€25). There are play
readings on Mondays and philosophy debates on the
first Wednesday of the month, at 8pm, in English.

Les Deux Magots
*6 pl St-Germain-des-Prés, 6th (01.45.48.55.25,
www.lesdeuxmagots.com). M° St-Germain-des-
Prés.* **Open** 7.30am-1am daily. **Map** p193 C3 ⓭
If you stand outside Les Deux Magots, you have to
be prepared to photograph tourists wanting proof of
their encounter with French philosophy. The former
haunt of Sartre and de Beauvoir now attracts a less
pensive crowd that can be all too *m'as-tu vu*, particularly at weekends. The hot chocolate is still good,
though, and served in generous portions. Visit on a
weekday afternoon when the editors return, manuscripts in hand, to the inside tables, leaving enough
elbow room for some serious discussion.

★ La Palette
43 rue de Seine, 6th (01.43.26.68.15). M° Odéon.
Open 7am-2am Mon-Sat; 10am-2pm Sun.
Map p193 C2 ⓮

EXPLORE

La Palette is the café-bar of choice for the very *beaux* Beaux-Arts students who study at the venerable institution around the corner, and young couples who steal kisses in the wonderfully preserved art deco back room decorated with illustrations. It ain't cheap – a glass of Chablis sets you back around €7, a demi €5 – but you're paying for the prime location once frequented by such luminaries as Jim Morrison, Picasso and Ernest Hemingway.

Prescription Cocktail Club

23 rue Mazarine, 6th (01.46.34.67.73, www.prescriptioncocktailclub.com). Mº Odéon. **Open** 7pm-2am Mon-Thur; 7pm-4am Fri, Sat; 8pm-2am Sun. **Map** p193 C2 ⑮
This stylish 1930s-style speakeasy has a retro Prohibition feel but remains severely Left Bank, with crowds of well-dressed people sipping cocktails by candlelight. It's always busy and almost impossible to navigate at weekends.

Shops & Services

Arty Dandy

1 rue de Furstemberg, 6th (01.43.54.00.36, www.artydandy.com). Mº Mabillon. **Open** 10.30am-7pm Mon-Fri; 10.30am-7.30pm Sat. **Map** p193 C2 ⑯ **Gifts & souvenirs**
'Dandyism is the last spark of heroism amid decadence,' said Baudelaire. Taking this as its motto, Arty Dandy is a concept shop that embraces the surreal, the tongue-in-cheek and the poetic – an R.MUTT sticker to create your own Duchampian loo, and the 'Karl who?' bag (which KL himself has carried) are instant pleasers. More sublime offerings include Jaime Hayon's 'Lover' figurines and Sebastien Le Gal watercolours.

Démocratie

14 bd St-Michel, 6th (01.56.24.05.55). Mº St-Michel. **Open** 11am-7.30pm Mon-Sat; 2-7pm Sun. **Map** p193 D3 ⑰ **Accessories**
This multi-brand boutique has injected a hint of underground culture into the tourist district of Saint-Michel. Sisters Kimo and Diana took over the former music and bookshop Silly Melody, which had been run by Kimo and her father. They have since breathed new life and a new philosophy into the place, modernising it in the style of a London or Berlin concept store. On the ground floor, you'll find a selection of designer objects and accessories, books and magazines with a retro touch. Fashion for women and men is on the first floor, with a good selection of streetwear and brands such as Vans, Dunderdone and Be Street, but also ethnic print bags by Pendelton and trendy shoes by Jeffrey Campbell.

Hermès

17 rue de Sèvres, 6th (01.42.22.80.83, www. hermes.com). Mº Sèvres Babylone. **Open** 10.30am-7pm Mon-Sat. **Map** p193 B3 ⑱ **Fashion**

If you thought that Hermès was about horsey scarves and little else, a visit to the rue de Sèvres shop should dispel the equestrian rumours forever. Designed by Denis Montel, the concept store is set in the Hôtel Lutetia's former indoor pool. The renovations have produced one of the best-looking retail spaces on the Left Bank. While the trademark scarves and ties are all present, the three-floor store also focuses on homewares, from wallpaper and carpets to sumptuous reproductions of 1930s-era furniture by renowned designer Jean-Michel Frank.

Huilerie Artisanale Leblanc

12 rue Jacob, 6th (01.44.07.36.58, www. huile-leblanc.com). Mº St-Germain-des-Prés. **Open** 11am-1.30pm, 2.30-7pm Tue-Sat. **Map** p193 C2 ⑲ **Food & drink**
The Leblanc family from Burgundy started making walnut oil before branching out to press pure oils from hazelnuts, almonds, pine nuts, grilled peanuts and olives. There are vinegars and mustards too.

★ La Hune

170 bd St-Germain, 6th (01.45.48.35.85). Mº St-Germain-des-Prés. **Open** 10am-11.45pm Mon-Sat; 11am-7.45pm Sun. **Map** p193 C3 ⑳ **Books & music**
This Left Bank institution boasts a global selection of art and design books, and a magnificent collection of French literature and theory.

Joseph

147 bd St-Germain, 6th (01.55.42.77.55, www. joseph.co.uk). Mº St-Germain-des-Prés. **Open** 10am-7pm Mon-Sat. **Map** p193 C3 ㉑ **Fashion**
Taking a cue from its London store, Joseph's multi-brand shop stocks pieces by the likes of Balmain and Lanvin, as well as accessories by Bijoux de Sophie and handbags by Jérôme Dreyfuss.
Other locations throughout the city.

Lefranc.ferrant

22 rue de l'Echaudé, 6th (01.40.21.03.29, www. lefranc-ferrant.fr). Mº St-Germain-des-Prés. **Open** 11am-7pm Tue-Sat. **Map** p193 C3 ㉒ **Fashion**
The opening of this boutique was eagerly awaited by keen followers of the talented Paris duo Béatrice Ferrant and Mario Lefranc. Their trademark is a surreal approach to tailoring, as in a strapless yellow evening gown made like a pair of men's trousers – complete with flies. Prices are in the €1,000 range.

Patrick Roger

108 bd St-Germain, 6th (01.43.29.38.42, www. patrickroger.com). Mº Odéon. **Open** 10.30am-7.30pm daily. **Map** p193 B2 ㉓ **Food & drink**
Roger is shaking up the art of chocolate-making. Whereas other *chocolatiers* aim for gloss, Roger may create a brushed effect on hens so realistic you almost expect them to lay (chocolate) eggs.
Other locations throughout the city.

EXPLORE

★ Sonia Rykiel

175 bd St-Germain, 6th (01.49.54.60.60, www.soniarykiel.com). M° St-Germain-des-Prés or Sèvres Babylone. **Open** 10.30am-7pm Mon-Sat. **Map** p193 C3 ❷ **Fashion**
The queen of St-Germain celebrated the 40th birthday of her flagship store with a glamorous black and smoked glass refit perfect for narcissists: tons of mirrors reflect the gorgeous flowing gowns. Menswear is just across the street, and two newer boutiques stock the younger, more affordable Sonia by Sonia Rykiel range (61 rue des Sts-Pères, 6th, 01.49.54.61.00) and kids' togs (4 rue de Grenelle, 6th, 01.49.54.61.10).
▶ *For something on the wild side, the main shop also stocks a range of designer sex toys.*
Other locations throughout the city.

ST-SULPICE & THE LUXEMBOURG

In the 6th arrondissement.

Crammed with historic buildings and inviting shops, the quarter south of boulevard St-Germain between Odéon and Luxembourg epitomises civilised Paris. Just off the boulevard lies the covered market of St-Germain, now the site of a shopping arcade, auditorium, food hall and underground swimming pool. There are bars and bistros along rue Guisarde, nicknamed rue de la Soif ('thirst street') thanks to its carousers; it contains the late-night **Birdland** bar (no.8, 6th, 01.43.26.97.59) and a couple of notable bistros, including **Mâchon d'Henri** (no.8, 6th, 01.43.29.08.70). Rue Princesse and rue des Canettes are a mix of budget restaurants and nocturnal haunts.

Pass the fashion boutiques, pâtisseries and antiquarian book and print shops and you come to **Eglise St-Sulpice**, a surprising 18th-century exercise in classical form with two unmatching turrets and a colonnaded façade. The square in front was designed in the 19th century by Visconti; it contains his lion-flanked Fontaine des Quatre Points Cardinaux (a pun on cardinal points and the statues of Bishops Bossuet, Fénelon, Massilon and Flechier, none of whom was actually a cardinal).

Among shops of religious artefacts, the chic boutiques on place and rue St-Sulpice include **Yves Saint Laurent**, **Vanessa Bruno** and milliner **Marie Mercié**. Prime shopping continues further west: clothes on rue Bonaparte and rue du Four, and accessory and fashion shops on rue du Dragon, rue de Grenelle and rue du Cherche-Midi. If you spot a lengthy queue in the latter, it's most likely for bread at **Poilâne**. Across the street, at the junction of rue de Sèvres and rue du Cherche-Midi, César's bronze *Centaur* is the sculptor's tribute to Picasso.

IN THE KNOW BOUQUINISTES

The green, open-air boxes along the Seine *quais* are one of the city's institutions. Most sell second-hand books – rummage through boxes packed with ancient paperbacks for something existential to peruse over a *chocolat chaud* at La Palette.

The early 17th-century chapel of St-Joseph-des-Carmes – once a Carmelite convent, now hidden within the **Institut Catholique** (21 rue d'Assas, 6th, 01.44.39.52.00, www.icp.fr) – was the scene of the murder of 115 priests during the Terror in 1792. To the east lies wide rue de Tournon, lined by such grand 18th-century residences as the elegant Hôtel de Brancas (no.6), with figures of Justice and Prudence over the door. This street opens up to the **Palais du Luxembourg**, which now serves as the Senate, and the adjoining **Jardin du Luxembourg**.

Towards boulevard St-Germain is the neoclassical **Odéon, Théâtre de l'Europe** (*see p292*), built in 1779. A house in the square in front was home to Revolutionary hero Camille Desmoulins, who incited the mob to attack the Bastille in 1789. It's now occupied by **La Méditerranée** (2 pl de l'Odéon, 6th, 01.43.26.02.30, www.la-mediterranee.com); the restaurant's menus and plates were designed by Jean Cocteau. Joyce's *Ulysses* was published in 1922 by Sylvia Beach at the celebrated **Shakespeare & Company** (*see p179*).

Further along the street, at 12 rue de l'Ecole-de-Médecine, is the neoclassical Université René Descartes (Paris V) medical school, and the Musée d'Histoire de la Médecine. The Club des Cordeliers, set up by Danton in 1790, devised revolutionary plots across the street at the **Couvent des Cordeliers** (no.15); the 14th-century refectory, all that remains of the monastery founded by St Louis, houses modern art exhibitions. Marat, one of the club's leading lights, was stabbed to death in the bathtub at his home in the same street; David depicted the moment after the crime in his iconic painting, the *Death of Marat*. This was the surgeons' district: observe the building at no.5, once the barbers' and surgeons' guild. Climb rue André-Dubois to rue Monsieur-le-Prince to budget restaurant **Polidor** (no.41, 6th, 01.43.26.95.34, www.polidor.com), open since 1845.

Sights & Museums

🆓 Eglise St-Sulpice

Pl St-Sulpice, 6th (01.42.34.59.98, www.paroisse-saint-sulpice-paris.org). M° St-Sulpice. **Open** 7.30am-7.30pm daily. **Admission** free. **Map** p193 C3 ❷

It took 120 years and six architects to finish St-Sulpice. The grandiose façade, with its two-tier colonnade, was designed by Jean-Baptiste Servandoni. He died in 1766 before the second tower was finished, leaving one tower a good five metres shorter than the other. The trio of murals by Delacroix in the first chapel – *Jacob's Fight with the Angel, Heliodorus Chased from the Temple* and *St Michael Killing the Dragon* – create a sombre atmosphere.

Fondation Dubuffet

137 rue de Sèvres, 6th (01.47.34.12.63, www.dubuffetfondation.com). M° Duroc. **Open** 2-6pm Mon-Fri. Closed Aug. **Admission** €6; €4 reductions; free under-10s. **No credit cards.** **Map** p193 A4 🔢

You walk up a winding garden path to get to this museum, founded by Jean Dubuffet, wine merchant and master of *art brut*. There's a changing display of Dubuffet's lively drawings, paintings and sculptures, as well as models of the architectural sculptures from the *Hourloupe* cycle.

▶ *The foundation also looks after the Closerie Falbala, the 3D masterpiece of the Hourloupe cycle, housed at Périgny-sur-Yerres, east of Paris.*

★ FREE Jardin & Palais du Luxembourg

Pl André Honnorat, pl Edmond-Rostand or rue de Vaugirard, 6th (01.44.54.19.49, www.senat.fr/ visite). M° Odéon/RER Luxembourg. **Open** *Jardin* summer 7.30am-dusk daily; winter 8am-dusk daily. **Map** p193 C4 🔢

The palace itself was built in the 1620s for Marie de Médicis, widow of Henri IV, by Salomon de Brosse. Its Italianate style was intended to remind her of the Pitti Palace in her native Florence. The palace now houses the French parliament's upper house, the Sénat (open only by guided visits). The mansion next door (Le Petit Luxembourg) is the residence of the Sénat's president. The gardens, though, are the real draw: part formal (terraces and gravel paths), part 'English garden' (lawns and mature trees). The garden is crowded with sculptures: a looming Cyclops (on the 1624 Fontaine de Médicis), queens of France, a miniature Statue of Liberty, wild animals, busts of Flaubert and Baudelaire, and a monument to Delacroix. The Musée du Luxembourg (*see below*) hosts prestigious exhibitions. Most interesting, though, are the people: a mixture of *flâneurs* and *dragueurs*, chess players and martial-arts practitioners, as well as children on ponies, in sandpits, on roundabouts and playing with boats on the pond.

★ Musée des Lettres et Manuscrits

222 bd St-Germain, 7th (01.42.22.48.48, www.museedeslettres.fr). M° Rue du Bac. **Open** 10am-7pm Tue, Wed, Fri-Sun; 10am-9.30pm Thur. **Admission** €7; €5 reductions; free under-12s. **Map** p193 B2 🔢

More than 2,000 documents and letters give an insight into the lives of the great and the good, from Magritte to Mozart. Einstein arrives at the theory of relativity on notes scattered in authentic disorder, Baudelaire complains about his money problems in a letter to his mother, and HMS *Northumberland*'s logbook records the day Napoleon boarded the ship to be exiled to St Helena.

Musée du Luxembourg

19 rue de Vaugirard, 6th (01.40.13.62.00, www. museeduluxembourg.fr). M° Cluny La Sorbonne or Odéon/RER Luxembourg. **Open** 10am-10pm Mon, Fri; 10am-7.30pm Tue-Thur, Sat, Sun. **Admission** Prices vary. **Map** p193 C4 🔢

Jardin du Luxembourg.

EXPLORE

When it opened in 1750, this small museum was the first public gallery in France. After closing for more than a year, the museum reopened in early 2011 with a Cranach exhibition, followed by a major Chagall retrospective in 2013. Book ahead to avoid queues.

★ FREE Musée Zadkine

100bis rue d'Assas, 6th (01.55.42.77.20, www. zadkine.paris.fr). M° Notre-Dame-des-Champs/ RER Port-Royal. **Open** 10am-6pm Tue-Sun. **Admission** free. *Exhibitions* €4; €2-€3 reductions; free under-13s. **Map** p193 C5 ㉚

This is one of the most intimate museums in Paris, a peaceful hideaway where you can also get a good dose of modern art. The former studio of Russian-born cubist sculptor Ossip Zadkine was converted into a museum in 1932, and has always had a particular charm, conserving the spirit of the place where the sculptor and his wife, painter Valentine Prax, lived for more than 40 years. There's barely a wink to Valentine, just a solitary canvas hung at the head of a staircase: Zadkine is the master of this place, dominated by his angular portraits and women's bodies carved out of tree trunks in African-inspired elliptical forms. Don't miss the garden planted with stylised bronze statues (including the famous *Monument à la Ville Détruite de Rotterdam*). The museum reopened in late 2012 after undergoing an extensive revamp.

Restaurants

★ Bouillon Racine

3 rue Racine, 6th (01.44.32.15.60, www.bouillon-racine.com). M° Odéon. **Open** noon-11pm daily. **Main courses** €17-€23. **Prix fixe** *Lunch* €15.50, €30.90, €41.90. *Dinner* €30.90, €41.90. **Map** p193 D3 ㉛ **Brasserie**

Originally opened as a *bouillon* (soup kitchen) in the early 20th century to feed hungry city workers, this beautifully renovated two-storey brasserie lives on as an art nouveau gem. Food is suitably traditional, with classic dishes such as foie gras, *escargots de Bourgogne* and *confit de canard* dominating the reasonably priced menu. Dishes are served non-stop from noon to 11pm, and you can even drop in for waffles and hot chocolate in the afternoon.

Bread & Roses

7 rue de Fleurus, 6th (01.42.22.06.06, www.breadandroses.fr). M° St-Placide. **Open** 8am-8pm Mon-Sat. **Main courses** €18. **Map** p193 C4 ㉜ **Bakery/café**

Come for a morning croissant and you might find yourself staying on for lunch, so tempting are the wares at this Anglo-influenced *boulangerie/épicerie/* café. Giant wedges of cheesecake sit alongside French pastries, and huge savoury puff-pastry tarts are perched on the counter. Attention to detail shows even in the authentically pale taramasalata, which is matched with buckwheat-and-seaweed bread.

Prices reflect the quality of the often organic ingredients, but that doesn't seem to deter any of the moneyed locals, who order towering birthday cakes here for their snappily dressed offspring.

Le Comptoir

Hôtel Le Relais Saint-Germain, 9 carrefour de l'Odéon, 6th (01.43.29.12.05). M° Odéon. **Open** noon-6pm, 8.30-11pm (last orders 9pm) Mon-Fri; noon-11pm Sat, Sun (no booking on weekends). **Main courses** €15. **Prix fixe** *Dinner* (Mon-Fri) €60. **Map** p193 C3 ㉝ **Brasserie**

Yves Camdeborde runs the bijou Hôtel Le Relais Saint-Germain (*see p361*), whose art deco dining room, Le Comptoir, serves brasserie fare from noon to 6pm and on weekend nights, and a five-course prix fixe feast on weekday evenings. The single dinner sitting lets the chef take real pleasure in his work. On the daily menu, you might find dishes like rolled saddle of lamb with vegetable-stuffed 'Basque ravioli'. The catch? The prix fixe dinner is booked up as much as six months in advance.

Ecole Ferrandi

28 rue de l'Abbé Grégoire, 6th (01.49.54.17.31, www.ferrandi-paris.fr). M° Saint-Placide. **Open** *Lunch* 12.30pm Wed-Fri. *Dinner* 7.30pm Mon, Tue. Closed school hols. **Prix fixe** *Lunch* €30. *Dinner* €45. **Map** p193 B4 ㉞ **Cookery school**

Ferrandi is one of the most important cookery schools in France, with over 1,300 students learning how to be bakers, barstaff, waiters and chefs. Of course they have to practise their skills on the general public, so the Ecole has set up two restaurants that are favourites with foodies-in-the-know (the waiting list can stretch for months). Le Premier is a showcase for students learning a basic cooking apprenticeship. Restaurant 28, though, is reserved for high-level students. The standard is hugely impressive and the bill comes to €30 for a five-course lunch.

La Ferrandaise

8 rue de Vaugirard, 6th (01.43.26.36.36, www. laferrandaise.com). M° Odéon/RER Luxembourg. **Open** 7-10.30pm Mon, Sat; noon-2.30pm, 7-10.30pm Tue-Fri. **Prix fixe** *Lunch* €16, €31, €35. *Dinner* €31, €35, €48. **Map** p193 D3 ㉟ **Bistro**

This bistro has quickly established a following for its solid, classic food with a twist. A platter of excellent ham, sausage and terrine arrives as you study the blackboard menu, and the bread is crisp-crusted, thickly sliced sourdough. Two specialities are the potato stuffed with escargots in a camembert sauce, and a wonderfully flavoured, slightly rosé slice of veal. Desserts might include intense chocolate with rum-soaked bananas. Wines start at €20.

Huîtrerie Régis

3 rue de Montfaucon, 6th (01.44.41.10.07, www. huitrerieregis.com). M° Mabillon. **Open** noon-2.30pm, 6.30-10.30pm Tue-Sun. Closed mid July-

EXPLORE

mid Sept. **Main courses** €32. **Prix fixe** €18.50-
€59. **Map** p193 C3 ㊱ **Oyster bar**
Paris oyster fans are often obliged to use one of the
city's big brasseries to get their fix of shellfish, but
what if you just want to eat a reasonably priced platter of oysters? Enter Régis and his cosy 14-seat oyster bar. The tiny room feels pristine and the tables
are properly laid. Here you can enjoy the freshest
oysters from Marennes for around €25 a dozen. The
bread and butter is fresh and wines are well chosen.
Hungry souls can supplement their feast with a slice
of home-made apple tart or the cheese of the day.

Joséphine Chez Dumonet
*117 rue du Cherche-Midi, 6th (01.45.48.52.40).
M° Duroc.* **Open** 12.30-2pm, 7.30-10.30pm Mon-
Fri. **Main courses** €30-€35. **Map** p193 A4
㊲ **Bistro**
This bastion of classic bistro cooking, where the use
of luxury ingredients brings a splash of glamour, is
guaranteed to please the faithful, well-heeled clientele. The good news is that several dishes are available as half portions, opening up the possibility of
exploring some classy numbers without your credit
card melting. A half portion of salad of lamb's
lettuce, warm potatoes and truffle shavings is a sexy
dish, with the perfume of black truffles gloriously
present. Tournedos Rossini, with fresh truffles and
a slice of foie gras on the tender fillet, comes with
sautéed potatoes, rich in goose fat and a touch of
garlic. Puddings make for a sumptuous finish.

Pizza Chic
*13 rue de Mézières, 6th (01.45.48.30.38,
www.pizzachic.fr). M° Rennes, Sèvres-Babylone
or St-Sulpice.* **Open** 12.30-2.30pm, 7.30-11pm
Mon-Thur; 12.30-2.30pm, 7.30-11.30pm Fri, Sat;
12.30-3.30pm, 7.30-10pm Sun. **Main courses**
€14-€19. **Map** p193 B3 ㊳ Pizza
An address that could only exist on the Left Bank,
where 'chic' is a religion in itself. But this contemporary, polished pizzeria isn't the least bit ostentatious
and the pizzas are among the best in Paris. White
(with no tomato base) or red, the pizzas are beautiful
as well as delicious: tuck into the luxurious spiciness
of the carciofi (artichoke cream, raw artichokes,
rocket, 24-month aged parmesan) or the simplicity
of the aurora (tomato, mozzarella, fresh basil). You'll
leave delighted at having found a Parisian version
of Italian chic for around €20 – an invigorating treat.

La Taverna degli Amici
*16 rue du Bac, 6th (01.42.60.37.74). M°
Assemblée Nationale or Solférino.* **Open** noon-3pm,
7.30-11pm Mon-Sat. **Main courses** €20-€22.
Prix fixe *Lunch* €18.50. **Map** p193 B2 ㊴ Italian
La Taverna degli Amici is the ideal spot for a quick
business lunch or a big, rumbustious dinner with
friends. Spread across two floors, the yellow-walled
rooms are well lit and airy. Run by the exceptionally
friendly Notaro family, who own, manage and cook,

the restaurant is constantly bustling. Don't miss the
mixed bruschette, which includes three vegetable
toppings, such as grilled courgettes marinated in
olive oil, lemon and parsley. Pastas feature fresh,
tasty toppings, such as their most popular dish,
penne with *caccioricotta* (made with ewe's milk) and
rocket. Most of the regulars finish things off with
home-made tiramisu.

Le Timbre
*3 rue Ste-Beuve, 6th (01.45.49.10.40,
www.restaurantletimbre.com). M° Vavin.*
Open noon-1.30pm, 7-10.30pm Tue-Sat.
Closed Aug & 1wk Dec. **Main courses** €17.
Prix fixe *Lunch* €22, €26. *Dinner* €32 (Sat).
Map p193 B4 ㊵ Bistro
Chris Wright's restaurant, open kitchen included,
might be the size of the average student garret, but
this Mancunian aims high. Typical of his cooking is
a plate of fresh green asparagus elegantly cut in half
lengthwise and served with dabs of anise-spiked
sauce and balsamic vinegar, and a little crumbled
parmesan. Main courses are also pure in presentation and flavour – a thick slab of pork, pan-fried but
not the least bit dry, comes with petals of red onion
that retain a light crunch.

Cafés & Bars

★ Le Bar Dix
*10 rue de l'Odéon, 6th (01.43.26.66.83, www.
lebar10.com). M° Odéon.* **Open** 6pm-2am daily.
No credit cards. Map p193 D3 ㊶
Generations of students have glugged back jugs of
the celebrated home-made sangría (€3 a glass during
happy hour) while squeezed into the cramped upper
bar, tattily authentic with its Jacques Brel record
sleeves, Yves Montand handbills and pre-war light
fittings. Spelunkers and hopeless romantics negotiate the hazardous stone staircase to drink in the
cellar bar, with its candlelight and century-old advertising murals. Can someone please come and slap a
preservation order on the place?

★ Chez Georges
*11 rue des Canettes, 6th (01.43.26.79.15).
M° Mabillon.* **Open** noon-2am Tue-Sat.
Closed Aug. **Map** p193 C3 ㊷
One of a dying breed of *cave-bars*, Chez Georges
is beloved of students, professionals and local
eccentrics. Regulars pop in during the day to sip wine
over a game of chess, and at night the *cave* fills up
with people dancing to *chanson*, pop and even the
odd bar mitzvah tune. The heat is mascara-melting
and it's not for the claustrophobic.

La Compagnie des Vins Surnaturels
*7 rue Lobineau, 6th (09.54.90.20.20,
www.compagniedesvinssurnaturels.com).
M° Mabillon or Odéon.* **Open** 6pm-2am daily.
Map p193 C3 ㊸

EXPLORE

CYCLE LEFT BANK LUNCH

Pedal your way to a perfect picnic.

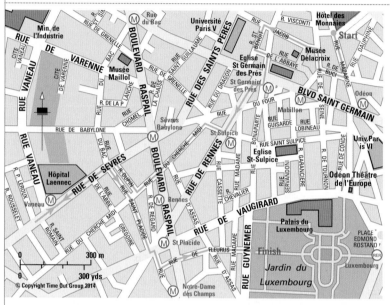

© Copyright Time Out Group 2014

Aside from art and books, the sixth arrondissement (and its neighbour the seventh) is also a great place to shop for food, since it has some of the finest artisanal bakeries and *traiteurs* in Paris.

And thanks to Velib (www.velib.paris.fr), it's easy to get around the *quartier* in order to stock up. What's more, the standard-issue bike is equipped with a basket that should carry all you'll need for a sumptuous picnic. This itinerary will probably take you the best part of two hours. Don't bother searching for a station each time you need to stop; just use the chain provided to lock your bike.

Detach your bike from the *borne* at 1 rue Jacques-Callot, 6th (M° Mabillon) and cycle down rue Mazarine as far as the carrefour de Buci. Turn left into rue de Buci and carry on until the junction with rue de Seine. The stretch of rue de Seine between here and boulevard St-Germain is lined with butchers and greengrocers. Ignore the smell of roasting chickens (you'll be getting cooked meat elsewhere), and just buy salad leaves and fruit. Then head back down rue de

Seine towards the river. Halfway down, turn left into rue Jacob. Cross rue Bonaparte and take the next left into rue St-Benoît. Pause to look in the window of **Librairie St-Benoît-des-Prés** (2 rue St-Benoît, 6th, 01.40.20.43.42), which specialises in rare books, manuscripts and letters.

Continue down rue St-Benoît as far as place St-Germain-des-Prés, where you'll find three venerable institutions: **Café de Flore** (*see p196*), **Les Deux Magots** (*see p196*) and **La Hune** bookshop (*see p197*). The Flore and the Deux Magots buzz more with tourists than writers these days, though the former is still a favoured haunt of *enfant terrible* Bernard-Henri Lévy. If you spot a man with a mane of black hair and a white shirt open to the navel poring over a notebook, it's probably BHL. Next door, La Hune is a kind of holy shrine for that nearly extinct species, the Left Bank Intellectual.

But it's not books we're after, it's bread; so cross boulevard St-Germain and follow rue Gozlin round into rue de Rennes. This is a busy main road lined with chain stores. There's not a great deal to distract as you

EXPLORE

bowl south for half a kilometre or so, until you reach rue du Vieux-Colombier on the right. You'll have to do battle with buses and taxis in this narrow cut-through, which leads to the far more charming rue du Cherche-Midi. On the left-hand side of the street, wedged among the boutiques, jewellers and galleries, stands **Poilâne** (*see p205*), the renowned family bakers. You can expect to have to queue here for the famous Poilâne loaf – but it's worth it: dark, firm and distinctively flavoured. The tarts and the biscuits are wonderful too.

Having loaded the bread into your basket, carry on down rue du Cherche-Midi. Go straight across boulevard Raspail, then take the first right into rue Dupin. You'll eventually reach rue de Sevres. Lock your bike against the railings here and cross the road on foot to La Grande Epicerie, the food hall in Paris's oldest department store, **Le Bon Marché** (*see p227*). Make your way to the *traiteurs* in the centre of the hall and choose from a staggering array of cooked meats. While you're here, you can pick up dressing for the salad and a bottle of wine (and a corkscrew if needed).

It just remains to buy some cheese, and for this you'll need to cycle a little further south down rue de Sèvres. You'll pass the wonderful art deco entrance to the Vaneau metro station on the right, with its green iron lattices and globe lanterns. A little further along on the same side of the street, on the corner of rue Pierre-Leroux, stands **Fromagerie Quatrehomme** (*see p228*). Run by Marie Quatrehomme, this place is famous across Paris for its comté fruité, beaufort and oozy st-marcellin.

Your basket will be near to overflowing. It's time to head for a picnic spot in the Jardin du Luxembourg. Turn round and cycle back up rue de Sèvres, then turn right into rue St-Placide. Shortly after you pass the St-Placide métro station, turn left into rue de Fleurus. The **Jardin du Luxembourg** (*see p199*) is ahead of you, on the far side of rue Guynemer. There's a Vélib station at 26 rue Guynemer. The grass in the park isn't for sitting on. So find a bench in the shade and tuck in.

Forget cheap plonk – both drinks and food here are nothing but the best. The wine list has more than 3,000 bottles listed, and to go with the booze there are some first-class treats such as *burrata, prosciutto al tartufo*, truffles and fine cheeses. The menu performs leaps and bounds from €6 to €40 a glass, and from €20 to €4,000 a bottle. But even if you don't have four months' rent to spare, the lower end of the selection is worth a look.

Les Editeurs

4 carrefour de l'Odéon, 6th (01.43.26.67.76, www.lesediteurs.fr). M° Odéon. **Open** 8am-2am daily. **Map** p193 C3 **❹**
It's no surprise to see row upon row of books in the bright, modern interior of Les Editeurs. A café with literary leanings, it sits on the lovely carrefour de l'Odéon. Bask in the glory of literary greats as portraits of authors and their editors look down on you. The weekend brunch is good value at €26.

★ J'Go

Rue Clément, 6th (01.43.26.19.02, www.lejgo.com). M° Mabillon or Odéon. **Open** 11am-midnight daily. **Map** p193 C3 **❺**
J'Go (pronounced gigot) is all about lamb – well, meat of various kinds, actually: a buzzing Toulouse-style wine bar in the Marché St-Germain by day, it becomes a *rôtisserie* at meal times, serving its speciality spit-roasted lamb from Quercy, black pigs from Bigorre, and whole roasted chickens. If you'd rather stick to wine and tapas, sidle up to one of the great wooden barrels, choose your poison and share a plate of charcuterie or foie gras *tartines* (€15).

Moose

16 rue des Quatre Vents, 6th (01.46.33.77.00, www.mooseparis.com). M° Odeon. **Open** 11am-2am daily. **Map** p193 C3 **❻**
This Canadian sports bar serves a vast selection of beers and even some organic Australian wines. A friendly atmosphere and delicious burgers make the Moose a great place to kick off the evening.

Le Rostand

6 pl Edmond-Rostand, 6th (01.43.54.61.58). RER Luxembourg. **Open** 8am-midnight daily. **Map** p193 D4 **❼**
Le Rostand has a truly wonderful view of the Jardin du Luxembourg from its classy interior, decked out with oriental paintings, a long mahogany bar and wall-length mirrors. It's a terribly well-behaved place. Whiskies and cocktails are pricey, as is the brasserie menu, but the snack menu serves delicious omelettes and *croques* for around €8 (salad €4 extra). Perfect for a civilised drink after a stroll round the gardens.

Le Select

99 bd du Montparnasse, 6th (01.45.48.38.24). M° Vavin. **Open** 7am-2am Mon-Thur, Sun; 7am-4am Fri, Sat. **Map** p193 B5 **❽**

EXPLORE

For a decade between the wars, the junction of boulevards Raspail and du Montparnasse was where Man Ray, Cocteau and Lost Generation Americans hung out in the vast, glass-fronted cafés. Eight decades on, Le Select is the best of what have inevitably become tourist haunts. Sure, its pricey menu is big on historical detail and short on authenticity, but it manages to hold on to its heyday with dignity.

Shops & Services

Adrenaline

30 rue Racine, 6th (01.44.27.09.05, www. adrenaline-vintage.com). M° Odéon. **Open** 11am-7pm Mon-Sat. **Map** p193 D3 ⑭ **Accessories**
This *dépot-vente* specialises in vintage luggage and handbags. Iconic Vuitton suitcases and Kelly and Birkin bags command enormous prices, but there are some slightly more affordable pieces and a small collection of '60s couture.

APC

38 rue Madame, 6th (01.42.22.12.77, www.apc.fr). M° St-Placide. **Open** 11am-7.30pm Mon-Sat; 12.30-6.30pm Sun. **Map** p193 C3 ⑳ **Fashion**
The look here is simple but stylish: think perfectly cut basics in muted tones. Hip without trying too hard, its jeans are a big hit with denim aficionados – the skinny version nearly caused a stampede when it first came out.
Other locations throughout the city.

Chantelivre

13 rue de Sèvres, 6th (01.45.48.87.90, www.chantelivre.com). M° St-Sulpice or Sèvres-Babylone. **Open** 1-7.30pm Mon; 10.30am-7.30pm Tue-Sat. **Map** p193 B3 ⑤ **Children**
Chantelivre was the first – and remains the best – children's bookshop in Paris, housing a vast catalogue of children's literature (75% of the 50,000 titles on the market). It also boasts activities for children (talks, concerts, special guests, book signings) all year round, and occasionally for adults too – such as a recent visit from author Jacques Lamalle.

Christian Constant

37 rue d'Assas, 6th (01.53.63.15.15). M° Rennes or St-Placide. **Open** 9.30am-8.30pm Mon-Fri; 9am-8pm Sat, Sun. **Map** p193 B4 ⑫ **Food & drink**
A master chocolate-maker and *traiteur*, Constant scours the globe for new ideas. His *ganaches* are subtly flavoured with verbena, jasmine or cardamom.

Fnac Junior

19 rue Vavin, 6th (08.92.35.06.66, www.eveil etjeux.com). M° Vavin. **Open** 10am-7.30pm Mon-Sat. **Map** p193 B4 ⑬ **Children**
Fnac Junior stocks a wide range of books, toys, DVDs, CDs and CD-Roms for under-12s. Storytelling and other activities take place for over-twos.
Other locations throughout the city.

Gérard Mulot

76 rue de Seine, 6th (01.43.26.85.77, www.gerard-mulot.com). M° Odéon. **Open** 6.45am-8pm Mon, Tue, Thur-Sun. Closed Easter & Aug. **Map** p193 C3 ⑭ **Food & drink**
Gérard Mulot rustles up stunning pastries. Try the *mabillon*: caramel mousse with apricot marmalade.
Other locations 6 rue du Pas de la Mule, 3rd (01.42.78.52.17); 93 rue de la Glacière, 13th (01.45.81.39.09).

Gibert Joseph

26 bd St-Michel, 6th (01.44.41.88.88, www.gibertjoseph.com). M° St-Michel. **Open** 10am-8pm Mon-Sat. **Map** p193 D3 ⑮ **Books & music**
Formed back in 1929, this string of bookshops is normally packed out with students.
▶ *Further up bd St-Michel (nos.30, 32 & 34) are branches specialising in stationery, CDs, DVDs and art materials.*

★ Hervé Chapelier

1bis rue du Vieux-Colombier, 6th (01.44.07.06.50, www.hervechapelier.fr). M° St-Germain-des-Prés. **Open** 10.15am-7pm Mon-Sat. **Map** p193 C3 ⑯ **Accessories**
Bag yourself a classic, chic, bicoloured tote at Hervé Chapelier. Sizes and prices range from a small handbag at €30 to a canvas travel bag at €500.
Other location 390 rue Saint-Honoré, 1st (01.42.96.38.04).

★ Jean-Paul Hévin

3 rue Vavin, 6th (01.43.54.09.85, www.jphevin. com). M° Vavin. **Open** 10am-7pm Tue-Sat. Closed Aug. **Map** p193 C4 ⑰ **Food & drink**
Hévin specialises in the beguiling combination of chocolate with potent cheese fillings, which loyal customers serve with wine as an aperitif.
Other locations 231 rue St-Honoré, 1st (01.55.35.35.96); 23bis av de La Motte-Picquet, 7th (01.45.51.77.48).

KarryO'

62 rue des Sts-Pères, 6th (01.45.48.94.67, www.karryo.com). M° St-Germain-des-Prés. **Open** 11am-7pm Tue-Sat. **Map** p193 B3 ⑱ **Accessories**
Paris socialites come here to source their vintage jewellery, as well as modern gems by owner Karine Berrebi. Her adjacent gallery, Unique, features one-of-a-kind finds, from jewels and decorative objects to Hermès bags and the occasional Schiaparelli fur.

Kenzo

60-62 rue de Rennes, 6th (01.45.44.27.88, www.kenzo.com). M° St-Sulpice. **Open** 10.30am-7.30pm Mon-Sat. **Map** p193 C3 ⑲ **Fashion**
This flagship store has three floors of men's and women's fashion, and is crowned with the Bulle Kenzo spa and Starck-designed Kong restaurant.
Other locations throughout the city.

EXPLORE

Poilâne

10am-7.30pm Thur, Fri; 10am-8pm Sat. Closed Sun in Aug. **Map** p193 C3 ❻ **Food & drink**
Pastry superstar Pierre Hermé attracts connoisseurs from St-Germain and further afield with his wonderful seasonal collections.
Other locations throughout the city.

★ Poilâne
8 rue du Cherche-Midi, 6th (01.45.48.42.59, www.poilane.com). M° Sèvres Babylone or St-Sulpice. **Open** 7.15am-8.15pm Mon-Sat. **Map** p193 B3 ❻ **Food & drink**
Apollonia Poilâne runs the family shop, where locals queue for fresh country *miches*, flaky-crusted apple tarts and buttery shortbread biscuits.
▶ *Poilâne has now opened a shop in the Marais (38 rue Debelleyme, 3rd, 01.44.61.83.39).*
Other locations 49 bd de Grenelle, 15th (01.45.79.11.49).

Princesse Tam-Tam
52 bd St-Michel, 6th (01.40.51.72.99, www.princessetamtam.com). M° Cluny La Sorbonne. **Open** 1.30-7pm Mon; 10.30am-7.30pm Tue-Sat (closed 3-4pm Wed, Thur). **Map** p193 D4 ❻ **Fashion**
This inexpensive underwear and swimwear brand has traffic-stopping promotions. Bright colours and sexily transparent and sporty gear rule.
Other locations throughout the city.

Sabbia Rosa
73 rue des Sts-Pères, 6th (01.45.48.88.37). M° St-Germain-des-Prés. **Open** 10am-7pm Mon-Sat. **Map** p193 B3 ❻ **Fashion**
Let Moana Moatti tempt you with feather-trimmed satin mules, or satin, silk and chiffon negligées in fine shades of tangerine, lemon, mocha or pistachio. All sizes are medium, others are made *sur mesure*; prices are just the right side of stratospheric.

Vanessa Bruno
25 rue St-Sulpice, 6th (01.43.54.41.04, www.vanessabruno.com). M° Odéon. **Open** 10.30am-7.30pm Mon-Sat. **Map** p193 C3 ❻ **Fashion**
Mercerised cotton tanks, flattering trousers and feminine tops have a Zen-like quality that stems from Bruno's stay in Japan, and they manage to flatter every figure type. She also makes great bags.
Other locations 12 rue de Castiglione, 1st (01.42.61.44.60); 100 rue Vieille-du-Temple, 3rd (01.42.77.19.41).

Yves Saint Laurent
6 pl St-Sulpice, 6th (01.43.29.43.00, www.ysl.com). M° St-Sulpice. **Open** 11am-7pm Mon; 10.30am-7pm Tue-Sat. **Map** p193 C3 ❻ **Fashion**
The memory of the founding designer, who died in 2008, lives on in this elegant boutique, which was splendidly refitted in red in the same year.
Other locations throughout the city.

★ Marie-Hélène de Taillac
8 rue de Tournon, 6th (01.44.27.07.07, www.mariehelenedetaillac.com). M° Mabillon. **Open** 11am-7pm Mon-Sat. **Map** p193 C3 ❻ **Accessories**
Marie-Hélène de Taillac is a fine jeweller. But unlike her colleagues across the Seine, her diamonds and emeralds in simple, unpretentious settings work well with jeans and don't make her customers look like ancestral portraits.

★ Marie Mercié
23 rue St-Sulpice, 6th (01.43.26.45.83, www.mariemercie.com). M° Odéon. **Open** 11am-7pm Mon-Sat. **Map** p193 C3 ❻ **Accessories**
Mercié's creations make you wish you lived in an era when hats were de rigueur. Step out in one shaped like curved fingers (complete with shocking-pink nail varnish and pink diamond ring).

Peggy Huyn Kinh
9-11 rue Coëtlogon, 6th (01.42.84.83.84, www.phk.fr). M° St-Sulpice. **Open** 11am-7pm Tue-Sat. **Map** p193 B3 ❻ **Accessories**
Once creative director at Cartier, Peggy Huyn Kinh now makes bags of boar skin and python, as well as silver jewellery.

Petit Bateau
26 rue Vavin, 6th (01.55.42.02.53, www.petitbateau.com). M° Vavin. **Open** 10am-7.30pm Mon-Sat. **Map** p193 C4 ❻ **Fashion**
Widely renowned for its comfortable, well-made cotton T-shirts, vests and other separates, Petit Bateau carries an equally coveted teen range.
Other locations throughout the city.

★ Pierre Hermé
72 rue Bonaparte, 6th (01.43.54.47.77, www.pierreherme.com). M° St-Germain-des-Prés or St-Sulpice. **Open** 10am-7pm Mon-Wed, Sun;

EXPLORE

Montparnasse & Beyond

Montparnasse's heyday was short, but for a few years between the two world wars it was the emblematic 'gay Paree' district of after-dark merriment and fruitful artistic exchange. A great number of its most prominent figures were expats (including its finest chronicler, the Hungarian photographer Brassaï), and the late-night bars and artists' studios formed a bubble of cordial international relations that was irreparably popped in 1939. The local atmosphere soured further with the completion in the early 1970s of the much-loathed Tour Montparnasse, a monolith that cast an ominous spell on the whole quarter. The dismay with which its construction was greeted prompted a change in building regulations in the city. Granted, this is rich territory for art museums, but with the exception of the Fondation Cartier, they're all about past glories.

Cimetière du Montparnasse.

Don't Miss

1 **Les Catacombes**
Bones galore in the 'empire of death' (p216).

2 **Fondation Cartier**
A work of art, inside and out (p209).

3 **Tour Montparnasse**
Views to savour (p212).

4 **Severo** Carnivore's paradise (p215).

5 **Cimetière du Montparnasse** From Sartre to Seberg (p209).

Fontaine de l'Observatoire.

MONTPARNASSE

In the 14th & 15th arrondissements.

Artists Picasso, Léger and Soutine fled to
'Mount Parnassus' in the early 1900s to escape
the rising rents of Montmartre. They were soon
joined by Chagall, Zadkine and other refugees
from the Russian Revolution, along with
Americans such as Man Ray, Henry Miller,
Ezra Pound and Gertrude Stein. Between the
wars the neighbourhood was the epitome of
modernity: studios with large windows were
built by avant-garde architects; artists, writers
and intellectuals drank and debated in the
quarter's showy bars; and naughty pastimes –
including the then risqué tango – flourished.

Sadly, the Montparnasse of today has lost
much of its former soul, dominated as it is by
the lofty **Tour Montparnasse** – the first
skyscraper to be built in central Paris. At its
foot are a shopping centre, the **Mix Club**
(www.mixclub.fr), and in winter an open-air ice
rink. There are fabulous panoramic views from
the newly renovated terrace on the 56th floor,
reaching up to 40km (25 miles) on a clear day.

Gare Montparnasse was rebuilt in the 1970s,
a grey affair above which can be found the
surprisingly oasis-like Jardin Atlantique, the
Mémorial du Maréchal Leclerc and the
Musée Jean Moulin. Rue du Montparnasse,
appropriately for a street near the station
that sends trains to Brittany, is dotted with

IN THE KNOW BACK TRACK

The old Gare Montparnasse witnessed two
events of historical significance. In 1898,
a runaway train burst through its façade;
and on 25 August 1944, the German
forces surrendered Paris here.

crêperies. Nearby, strip joints have replaced
most of the theatres on ever-saucy rue de la
Gaîté, but boulevard Edgar-Quinet has pleasant
cafés and a street market (Wed, Sat), plus the
entrance to the **Cimetière du Montparnasse**.
Boulevard du Montparnasse still buzzes at
night, thanks to its many cinemas and dining
spots: giant art deco brasserie **La Coupole** (*see
p214*); **Le Dôme** (no.108, 14th, 01.43.35.25.81),
now a top fish restaurant; and restaurant
La Rotonde (no.105, 6th, 01.43.26.48.26,
www.rotondemontparnasse.com). All were
popularised by the literati between the wars,
and now use this heritage to their advantage.
Nearby, on boulevard Raspail, stands Rodin's
statue of Balzac, whose rugged appearance
caused such a scandal that it was put in
place only after the sculptor's death.

For a whiff of Montparnasse's artistic history,
wander down rue de la Grande-Chaumière.
Bourdelle and Friesz taught at the venerable
Académie de la Grande-Chaumière (no.14,
01.43.26.13.72, www.grande-chaumiere.fr),
frequented by Calder, Giacometti and Pompon
among others (it still offers drawing lessons);
Modigliani died at no.8 in 1920, ruined by
tuberculosis, drugs and alcohol. Rue Vavin and
rue Bréa, leading to the Jardin du Luxembourg,
have become an enclave of children's shops.
Look out for no.6, the 1912 white-tiled
apartment building where art nouveau
architect Henri Sauvage lived.

Further east on boulevard du Montparnasse,
literary café **La Closerie des Lilas** (no.171,
01.40.51.34.50, www.closeriedeslilas.fr) was a
pre-war favourite with everyone from Lenin
and Trotsky to Picasso and Hemingway; brass
plaques on the tables indicate where each
historic figure used to sit. Next to it is the lovely
19th-century **Fontaine de l'Observatoire**,
featuring bronze turtles and thrashing sea
horses by Frémiet, and figures of the four
continents by Carpeaux.

From here, the Jardins de l'Observatoire form part of the green axis between the Palais du Luxembourg and the royal observatory, the **Observatoire de Paris**. A curiosity next door is the Maison des Fontainiers, built over an expansive (now dry-ish) underground reservoir that was originally commissioned by Marie de Médicis to supply water to fountains around the city.

A relatively recent addition to boulevard Raspail is the glass and steel **Fondation Cartier pour l'Art Contemporain**. Designed by architect Jean Nouvel, it houses the jewellers' head offices and an exhibition space dedicated to contemporary art and photography.

West of the train station, the redevelopment of Montparnasse is also evident in the circular place de Catalogne, a piece of 1980s postmodern neoclassicism by Mitterrand's favourite architect, Ricardo Bofill, and the housing estates of rue Vercingétorix.

There are still some traces of the old, arty Montparnasse for those willing to look for it: in impasse Lebouis, an avant-garde studio building houses the **Fondation Henri Cartier-Bresson**; at 21 avenue du Maine, an ivy-clad alleyway of old studios contains the artist-run exhibition space Immanence, as well as the **Musée du Montparnasse**, housed in the former academy and canteen of Russian painter Marie Vassilieff; on rue Antoine-Bourdelle, the **Musée Bourdelle** includes another old cluster of studios, where sculptor Antoine Bourdelle, Symbolist painter Eugène Carrière and, briefly, Marc Chagall all worked. Towards Les Invalides, on rue Mayet, craft and restoration workshops are still tucked away in the old courtyards.

Sights & Museums

FREE Cimetière du Montparnasse

*3 bd Edgar-Quinet, 14th (01.44.10.86.50). M°
Edgar Quinet or Raspail.* **Open** *16 Mar-5 Nov*
8am-6pm Mon-Fri; 8.30am-6pm Sat; 9am-6pm Sun.
6 Nov-15 Mar 8am-5.30pm Mon-Fri; 8.30am-
5.30pm Sat; 9am-5.30pm Sun. **Admission** free.
Map p211 F5 ❶

Formed by commandeering three farms (you can still see the ruins of a windmill by rue Froidevaux), the Montparnasse boneyard has plenty of literary clout: Beckett, Baudelaire, Sartre, de Beauvoir and Maupassant all rest here. There are also artists, including Brancusi, Frédéric Bartholdi (sculptor of the Statue of Liberty) and Man Ray. The celebrity roll-call continues with Serge Gainsbourg, André Citroën and actress Jean Seberg.

★ Fondation Cartier pour l'Art Contemporain

*261 bd Raspail, 14th (01.42.18.56.50, www.
fondation.cartier.fr). M° Denfert-Rochereau or
Raspail.* **Open** 11am-10pm Tue; 11am-8pm Wed-
Sun. **Admission** €9.50; €6.50 reductions; free
under-10s. **Map** p211 G5 ❷

Jean Nouvel's glass and steel building, an exhibition centre with Cartier's offices above, is as much a work of art as the installations inside. Shows by artists and photographers often have wide-ranging themes, such as 'Birds' or 'Desert'. Ron Mueck's sculptures took centre stage in 2013. Live events around the shows are called Soirées Nomades and feature concerts, screenings, lectures and performances.

★ Fondation Henri Cartier-Bresson

*2 impasse Lebouis, 14th (01.56.80.27.00,
www.henricartierbresson.org). M° Gaîté.* **Open**
1-6.30pm Tue, Thur, Fri, Sun; 1-8.30pm Wed; 11am-
6.45pm Sat. Closed Aug & between exhibitions.
Admission €6; €4 reductions; free 6.30-8.30pm
Wed. **No credit cards. Map** p211 F5 ❸

This two-floor gallery is dedicated to the work of acclaimed photographer Henri Cartier-Bresson. It consists of a tall, narrow *atelier* in a 1913 building, with a minutely catalogued archive, open to researchers, and a lounge on the fourth floor screening films. In the spirit of Cartier-Bresson, who assisted on three Jean Renoir films and drew and painted all his life, the Fondation opens its doors to other disciplines with three annual shows.

FREE Mémorial du Maréchal Leclerc de Hauteclocque et de la Libération de Paris & Musée Jean Moulin

*Jardin Atlantique, 23 allée de la 2e DB (above
Gare Montparnasse), 15th (01.40.64.39.44,
www.ml-leclerc-moulin.paris.fr). M° Montparnasse
Bienvenüe.* **Open** 10am-6pm Tue-Sun. **Admission**
free. *Exhibitions* €4; €2-€3 reductions; free
under-13s. **Map** p211 E5 ❹

EXPLORE

Fondation Cartier pour l'Art Contemporain.

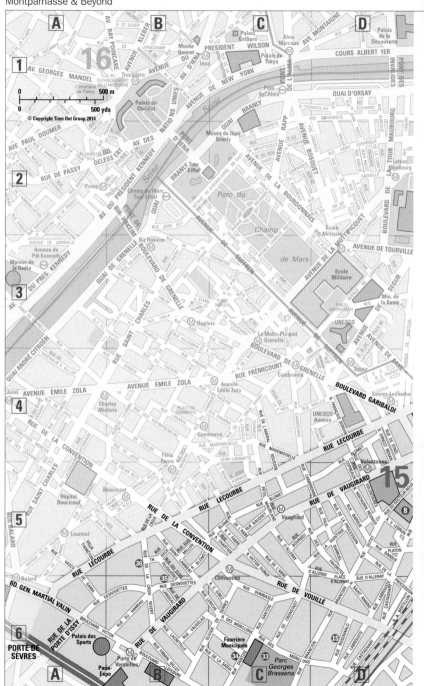

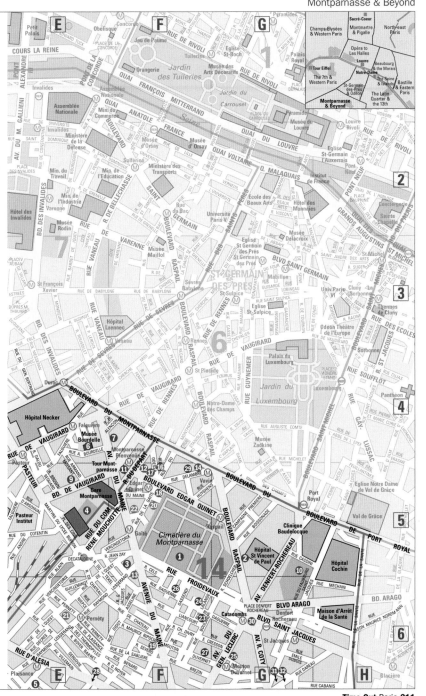

EXPLORE

EXPLORE

IN THE KNOW
HANGING GARDENS

The **Jardin Atlantique**, an oasis of green set high above Gare Montparnasse, has been offering Parisians a welcome breath of fresh air since 1994. The garden can be accessed by lift via rue du Commandant Mouchotte and boulevard de Vaugirard.

This double museum retraces World War II and the Resistance through the Free French commander Maréchal Leclerc and left-wing hero Jean Moulin. Documentary material and film archives complement an impressive 270° slide show, complete with sound effects, which tells the story of the Liberation of Paris.

FREE Musée-Atelier Adzak

*3 rue Jonquoy, 14th (01.45.43.06.98). M°
Plaisance.* **Open** usually 3-7pm Sat, Sun (call in advance). **Admission** free. **Map** p211 E6 ❺
The eccentric house, studio and garden built by the late Roy Adzak, a British-born painter and sculptor who died in 1987, harbour traces of the conceptual artist's plaster body columns and dehydrations. Now a registered British-run charity, it gives mostly foreign artists a chance to exhibit in Paris.

FREE Musée Bourdelle

*16-18 rue Antoine-Bourdelle, 15th (01.49.54.
73.73, www.bourdelle.paris.fr). M° Falguière
or Montparnasse Bienvenüe.* **Open** 10am-6pm
Tue-Sun. **Admission** free. *Exhibitions* €5; €2.50-
€3.50 reductions; free under-14s. **Map** p211 E4 ❻
The sculptor Antoine Bourdelle (1861-1929), who was a pupil of Rodin, produced a number of monumental works including the modernist relief friezes at the Théâtre des Champs-Elysées, which were inspired by Isadora Duncan and Nijinsky. The museum includes the artist's apartment and studios, which were also used by Eugène Carrière, Dalou and Chagall. A 1950s extension tracks the evolution of Bourdelle's equestrian monument to General Alvear in Buenos Aires, and his masterful *Hercules the Archer.* A modern wing by Christian de Portzamparc houses bronzes, including various studies of Beethoven in different guises.

Musée du Montparnasse

*21 av du Maine, 15th (01.42.22.91.96, www.
museedumontparnasse.net). M° Montparnasse
Bienvenüe.* **Open** 12.30-7pm Tue-Sun. **Admission**
€6; €5 reductions; free under-12s. **No credit
cards. Map** p211 F4 ❼
Set in one of the last surviving alleys of studios, this was home to Marie Vassilieff, whose academy and cheap canteen – 'la Cantine des Artistes' – welcomed poor artists, including famous names such as Picasso, Cocteau, Matisse, Braque and Modigliani.

Trotsky and Lenin were also guests. The museum's shows focus on present-day artists and the area's creative past.

Musée Pasteur

*Institut Pasteur, 25 rue du Dr-Roux, 15th
(01.45.68.82.83, www.pasteur.fr). M° Pasteur.*
Open 2-5.30pm Mon-Fri. Closed Aug.
Admission €7; €3 reductions. **Map** p210 D5 ❽
The flat where the famous chemist and his wife lived at the end of his life (1888-95) has not been touched; you can see their furniture and possessions, photos and instruments. An extravagant mausoleum on the ground floor houses Pasteur's tomb, decorated with mosaics depicting his scientific achievements.

Musée de la Poste

*34 bd de Vaugirard, 15th (01.42.79.24.24, www.
ladressemuseedelaposte.com). M° Montparnasse
Bienvenüe.* **Open** 10am-6pm Mon-Sat. **Admission**
€5; €3.50 reductions; free under-26s. PMP.
Temporary exhibitions €6.50; €5 reductions; free
under-13s. **No credit cards. Map** p211 E5 ❾
From among the uniforms, pistols, carriages, official decrees and fumigation tongs emerge snippets of history: during the 1871 Siege of Paris, hot-air balloons and carrier pigeons were used to get post out of the city, and *boules de Moulins,* balls crammed with hundreds of letters, were floated down the Seine in return, mostly never to arrive. The second section covers French and international philately.

FREE Observatoire de Paris

*61 av de l'Observatoire, 14th (01.40.51.23.97,
www.obspm.fr). Entry for visitors at 77 av
Denfert-Rochereau, 14th. M° St-Jacques/RER
Port-Royal.* **Tours** Email visite.paris@obspm.fr
or write to Observatoire de Paris, 61 av de
l'Observatoire, 75014 Paris. **Map** p211 G5 ❿
The Paris observatory was founded by Louis XIV's finance minister, Colbert, in 1667; it was designed by Claude Perrault (who also worked on the Louvre), with labs and an observation tower. The French meridian line drawn by François Arago in 1806 (which was used here before the Greenwich meridian was adopted as an international standard) runs north–south through the centre of the building. The dome on the observation tower was added in the 1840s.
▶ *You'll need to apply for an appointment at the
Observatoire by email, but it's also worth checking
the website for openings linked to astronomical
events – or visit on the Journées du Patrimoine
(see p37).*

★ Tour Montparnasse

*33 av du Maine, 15th (01.45.38.52.56,
www.tourmontparnasse56.com). M° Montparnasse
Bienvenüe.* **Open** *Oct-Mar* 9.30am-10.30pm
Mon-Thur, Sun; 9.30am-11pm Fri, Sat. *Apr-Sept*
9.30am-11.30pm daily. **Admission** €13; €6-
€9.50 reductions; free under-7s. **Map** p211 F5 ⓫

GLORIOUS GALETTES

Head to Montparnasse for pancake heaven.

If you picture the crêpe as the soggy letdown of French cuisine, then a trip down rue Montparnasse and rue Odessa on a weekend night could change your mind. According to the organisation Paris Breton there are some 300,000 Bretons living in Paris, and Montparnasse, close to the railway station that brought them here, is their *quartier*, with queues down the street for the 15 or so crêperies.

In its finest manifestation, the buckwheat pancake, or *galette de sarrasin*, is a crisp, melt-in-the-mouth envelope for an imaginative selection of fillings that go far beyond the egg and ham staple. At the **Crêperie du Manoir Breton** (18 rue Odessa, 14th, 01.43.35.40.73), the Périgord is filled with *magret de canard*, creamed prunes and caramelised pear; the Landaise is smartly presented with a round of foie gras and caramelised pear on top; and the Roquefort is laden with the Ardèchois blue cheese, crème fraîche and walnuts. At the **Crêperie du Pont-Aven** (54 rue du Montparnasse, 14th, 01.43.22.23.74),

with its attractive red interior dating back to 1920, the Gwazenn comes with scallops, mushrooms and cream; and the Pont-Aven is filled with salmon, leeks and cream; there are even several eel variations if you're feeling adventurous.

But the star crêperie of the area, and the one with the longest queues, is the prettily decorated **Josselin** (*see p214*), where the speciality is the Couple – two layers of galette with the filling in the middle. The savoury galette is followed by the dessert *crêpe de froment*, which comes in three varieties: classic (honey and lemon or wonderful caramel beurre salé); flambéed with calvados; and a fantasy creation oozing with chocolate, banana, ice-cream and whipped cream.

Wash it all down with bowls of cider, of which the brut is far better than the sweet. You'll be surprised how full you feel at the end and the bill should come to no more than €20 a head, a buckwheat bargain by Paris standards.

EXPLORE

Josselin.

EXPLORE

Built in 1974 on the site of the old station, this 209m (686ft) steel-and-glass monolith is actually shorter than the Eiffel Tower, but better placed for fabulous views of the city – including, of course, the Eiffel Tower itself. A lift whisks you up in 38 seconds to the 56th floor, where you'll find a display of aerial scenes of Paris, an upgraded café-lounge, a souvenir shop – and lots and lots of sky. On a clear day you can see up to 40km (25 miles). Another lift takes you all the way up to the roof. Classical concerts are held on the terrace.

Restaurants

★ La Cerisaie
70 bd Edgar Quinet, 14th (01.43.20.98.98, www.restaurantlacerisaie.com). M° Edgar Quinet or Montparnasse. **Open** noon-2pm, 7-10.30pm Mon-Fri. Closed mid July-mid Aug & 1wk Dec. **Main courses** €16-€21. **Map** p211 F5 ⑫ **Bistro**
Nothing about La Cerisaie's unprepossessing red façade hints at the talent that lurks inside. Chef Cyril Lalanne proves his ability to select and prepare the finest produce. On the daily changing blackboard menu you might find *bourride de maquereau*, a thrifty take on the garlicky southern French fish stew, or *cochon noir de Bigorre*, an ancient breed of pig that puts ordinary pork to shame. *Baba à l'armagnac*, a variation on the usual rum cake, comes with stunningly good chantilly.

Cobéa
11 rue Raymond Losserand, 14th (01.43.20.21.39, www.cobea.fr). M° Gaîté or Pernety. **Open** 12.15-1.45pm (last orders 1.15pm), 7.15-9.45pm (last orders 9.15pm) Tue-Sat. **Prix fixe** *Lunch* €44. *Dinner* €70, €85, €105. **Map** p211 F5 ⑬ **Haute cuisine**
Cobéa is a slick new restaurant launched by friends Jerome Cobou and Philippe Bellissent, who won a Michelin star when he was head chef at L'Hôtel. The ethos here is gastronomy without the snobbery. Set in a renovated 1920s house with big windows overlooking a green space, it feels wonderfully peaceful and cosy, while touches such as silverware and Bernardaud porcelain add a luxury feel. The set menus are a treasure chest of reworked classics, plus a daily-changing 'chef's surprise'. Each dish is accompanied by a well-sourced wine recommendation from Jerome.

La Coupole
102 bd du Montparnasse, 14th (01.43.20.14.20, www.flobrasseries.com/coupoleparis). M° Vavin. **Open** 8.30am-11pm Mon, Sun; 8.30am-midnight Tue-Sat. **Main courses** €21.50-€46. **Prix fixe** €29.50 (Mon-Fri, Sun dinner), €36.50, €59. **Map** p211 F5 ⑭ **Brasserie**
La Coupole still glows with some of the old glamour. The people-watching potential remains superb, inside and out, and the long ranks of linen-covered tables, professional waiters, 32 art deco columns painted by different artists of the epoch, mosaic floor and sheer scale of the operation still make coming here an event. The set menu offers unremarkable steaks, foie gras, fish and game stews, but the real treat is the shellfish. Take your pick from the *claires*, *spéciales* and *belons*, or go for a platter brimming with crabs, oysters, prawns, periwinkles and clams.

Le Grand Pan
20 rue Rosenwald, 15th (01.42.50.02.50). M° Convention. **Open** noon-2pm, 7.30-11pm Mon-Fri. **Main courses** €14-€20. **Prix fixe** *Lunch* €29. **Map** p210 D6 ⑮ **Bistro**
Young chef Benoît Gauthier trained with Christian Etchebest, and he's come up with a clever formula that surfs the current Paris preference for great produce simply cooked. At dinner, a complimentary starter of soup is served – maybe courgette or white bean – and then you choose from the selection of grilled meats and lobster. Everything comes with a delicious mountain of home-made chips and green salad. Desserts run to homely choices like strawberry crumble or rice pudding with caramel sauce.

€ Josselin
67 rue du Montparnasse, 14th (01.43.20.93.50). M° Edgar Quinet. **Open** 11am-3pm, 5.30-11.30pm Tue-Sat. Closed 1wk Jan & Aug. **Main courses** €10. **No credit cards. Map** p211 F5 ⑯ **Crêperie**
See p213 **Glorious Galettes**.

L'Opportun
64 bd Edgar Quinet, 14th (01.43.20.26.89). M° Edgar Quinet. **Open** noon-3pm, 7-11.30pm Mon-Sat. **Main courses** €20. **Prix fixe** *Lunch* €25. *Dinner* €25, €40. **Map** p211 F5 ⑰ **Bistro**
Owner-chef Serge Alzérat is passionate about Beaujolais, dubbing his convivial cream and yellow restaurant a centre of 'beaujolaistherapy' and a place for 'the prevention of thirst'. He's also an advocate for good, honest Lyonnais food. Thus his menu is littered with the likes of *sabodet* (thick pork sausage) with a purée of split peas, duck skin salad, *tête de veau* (a favourite of ex-president Chirac) and meat – lots of it. *Fromage* fans should try the st-marcellin by master cheesemaker Hervé Mons.

Le Plomb du Cantal
3 rue de la Gaîté, 14th (01.43.35.16.92). M° Gaîté. **Open** noon-midnight daily. **Main courses** €18. **Map** p211 F5 ⑱ **Bistro**
This homage to the Auvergne may suffer from its 1980s decor, but with food like this, who cares? *Aligot* (potato puréed with fresh tomme cheese) and *truffade* (potatoes sautéed with tomme) are scraped out of copper pots on to plates at the table, the shoestring fries arrive by the saucepan-load, and the omelettes are made with three eggs, 300g of potatoes, and, if you're really hungry, a supplement of tomme. Wines are excellent and the service is friendly.

★ Severo
8 rue des Plantes, 14th (01.45.40.40.91).
M° Alésia, Mouton-Duvernet or Pernety.
Open noon-2pm, 7.30-10pm Mon-Fri. **Main courses** €15-€40. **Map** p211 F6 ⑲ **Bistro**
Severo is all about well-bred meat selected by former butcher William Bernet and partner Hugo Desnoyer. On the menu, all sorts of piggy things to begin with, then mostly beef, from a modest *steak haché* with chips or green beans to a bloody entrecôte. The meat also deserves to be tried raw in a steak tartare – here, the naturally fatty meat is minimally seasoned: no egg, no spice, just an edge of capers and shallots. The chips – often neglected elsewhere – also stand out, set to one side in their own bowl. Among the nursery-style desserts, go for the crème caramel or a lovely plum tart.

Cafés & Bars

Le Café Tournesol
9 rue de la Gaîté, 14th (01.43.27.65.72). M° Gaîté.
Open 8am-2am daily. **Map** p211 F5 ⑳
The Tournesol is young, vibrant and the best of the cafés on rue de la Gaîté. There's outdoor seating in the shadow of the Tour Montparnasse, and an exposed brick interior with a soul, funk and electro soundtrack. A croque-monsieur will set you back €7, a cheeseburger €13, and a demi of Amstel €4.

L'Entrepôt
7-9 rue Francis de Pressensé, 14th (01.45.40.07.50, www.lentrepot.fr). M° Pernéty. **Open** 9am-2am daily. **Map** p211 E6 ㉑
L'Entrepôt, housed in a former warehouse, is a wonderful multitasker and has enough to keep you keen all week. There's a café where literary readings are held, a restaurant with a terrace (a godsend in the summer), and a bar on the ground floor with live music most Thursdays, Fridays, Saturdays and Mondays – mainly jazz, rap and *chanson*. There's also an arthouse cinema and exhibition space upstairs.

Storie. *See p216.*

KriZa Bar
9 rue Vandamme, 14th (01.43.21.57.58, www.krizabar.com). M° Edgar Quinet or Gaîté. **Open** noon-2pm, 6.30pm-2am Tue-Fri; 6.30pm-2am Sat. **Map** p211 F5 ㉒
KriZa has been a neighbourhood favourite for years. Aperitifs based around Suze gentian bitters or port (€4), decent draught beers and lethal cocktails make up a drinks list that's broad and well priced for the area. The food is classic tapas: manchego, tortilla, olives or foie gras. With big, cosy sofas inside and an interior patio for sunny days, it's a reliable bet.

Shops & Services

Bogato
7 rue Liancourt, 14th (01.40.47.03.51, www.chez bogato.fr). M° Denfert-Rochereau. **Open** 10am-7pm Tue-Sat. **Map** p211 F6 ㉓ **Food & drink**
If Hansel and Gretel had a cake shop in Paris it might look like Bogato (a name that sounds like '*beau gateau*'). Everything here is about temptation, from the quaint wooden furniture to pastry chef Anaïs Olmer's brightly coloured cupcakes, towering under glass bells on the counter like sugary art installations. Eat in or take out; and if you like what you've scoffed, sign up for a baking class.

La Cave des Papilles
35 rue Daguerre, 14th (01.43.20.05.74, www.lacavedespapilles.com). M° Denfert-Rochereau. **Open** 3.30-8.30pm Mon; 10am-1.30pm, 3.30-8.30pm Tue-Fri; 10am-8.30pm Sat; 10am-1.30pm Sun. **Map** p211 F6 ㉔ **Food & drink**
You can't miss the lemon-yellow frontage of La Cave des Papilles. The owner is a lover of 'natural' wine and 80% of the 1,200 wines on offer are produced organically. La Cave des Papilles itself has a hand in certain vintages, producing bottles under the Cave des Papilles brand. It's not outrageously priced either: with a choice of 60 to 80 bottles between €3 and €10, even budget quaffers will leave happy.

Jacadi
19bis av du Général Leclerc, 14th (01.43.21.46.03, www.jacadi.fr). M° Mouton-Duvernet. **Open** 10am-7pm Mon-Sat. **Map** p211 G6 ㉕ **Children**
Jacadi's well-made clothes for babies and children – pleated skirts, smocked dresses, dungarees and Fair Isle knits – are a hit with well-to-do parents.
Other locations throughout the city.

Madame de
65 rue Daguerre, 14th (01.77. 10.59.46, www.madamede.net). M° Denfert-Rochereau. **Open** 11am-7.30pm Tue-Sat. **Map** p211 F6 ㉖ **Fashion**
This delightful second-hand shop only stocks pieces 'that are like new' – even better, the prices wouldn't look out of place in the sales: a suede Vanessa Bruno bag for €154, APC jeans for €55, a checked Zara dress for €33. For retro decor fans, Madame de also

EXPLORE

Les Catacombes

stocks homeware treasures – an art deco carafe with smoked glass goblets, a vintage sewing machine, a Kodak Senior no.1 projector.

La Maison des Bonbons

14 rue Mouton-Duvernet, 14th (01.45.41.25.55). Mº Mouton-Duvernet. **Open** 11am-7pm Tue-Sat. **Map** p211 F6 ㉗ **Food & drink**
Those with a sweet tooth or a taste for cutesy bibelots will be in heaven here – start with the rows and rows of sugary treats ranged in glass jars, from liquorice to salted butter caramels. Then check out the miniature peacocks, rabbit-shaped lamps, classic games and pretty lunchboxes.

Marché aux Puces de Vanves

Av Georges-Lafenestre & av Marc-Sangnier, 14th. Mº Porte de Vanves. **Open** 7am-2pm Sat, Sun. **Map** p211 E6 ㉘ **Market**
Vanves is the smallest of the Paris flea markets, and the atmosphere is infinitely more tranquil than at Clingancourt. It's a favourite with serious collectors, so arrive early for the best pick of decent vintage clothes, dolls, costume jewellery and silverware.

Storie

20 rue Delambre, 14th (01.83.56.01.98, www.storie blog.com). Mº Vavin. **Open** 3-8pm Mon; 11am-2pm, 3-8pm Tue-Sat. **Map** p211 F5 ㉙ **Homewares**
Storie is a tiny, open space a few steps from the Tour Montparnasse. It's stocked with lightbulb-shaped vases, patterned cushions, pewter picture frames: everything needed to add a touch of luxury to a home. At the back of the shop you'll also find a fine selection of jewellery. *Photo p215.*

DENFERT-ROCHEREAU & MONTSOURIS

In the 14th & 15th arrondissements.

In the run-up to the 1789 Revolution, the bones of six million Parisians were taken from the handful of overcrowded city cemeteries and wheelbarrowed to the **Catacombes**, a vast network of tunnels that stretches under much of Paris. The sections under the 13th and 14th arrondissements are open to the public; the gloomy Denfert-Rochereau entrance is next to one of the toll gates of the Mur des Fermiers-Généraux, built by Ledoux in the 1780s.
The bronze *Lion de Belfort* dominates place Denfert-Rochereau, a favourite starting point for countless political demonstrations. The regal beast was sculpted by Bartholdi, of Statue of Liberty fame, and is a scaled-down replica of one in Belfort that commemorates the brave defence by Colonel Denfert-Rochereau of the town in 1870. Nearby, the southern half of rue Daguerre is a pedestrianised market street brimming with cafés and food stores.

One of the biggest draws of the area is the **Parc Montsouris**, with lovely lakes, dramatic cascades and an unusual history. Surrounding the western edge of the park are a number of modest, quiet streets – including rue du Parc Montsouris and rue Georges-Braque – that used to be lined during the 1920s and '30s with charming villas and artists' studios by avant-garde architects Le Corbusier and André Lurçat. On the southern edge of the park sprawls the **Cité Universitaire** complex.

Sights & Museums

★ Les Catacombes

1 av du Colonel-Henri-Rol-Tanguy, 14th (01.43.22.47.63, www.catacombes-de-paris.fr). Mº/RER Denfert Rochereau. **Open** 10am-5pm Tue-Sun (last entry 4pm). **Admission** €8; €4-€6 reductions; free under-14s. **Map** p211 G6 ㉚
This is the official entrance to the 3,000km (1,864-mile) tunnel network that runs under much of the city. With public burial pits overflowing in the late 18th century, the bones of six million people were transferred to the *catacombes*. The bones of Marat, Robespierre and their cronies are packed in with wall upon wall of their fellow citizens. A damp, cramped tunnel takes you through a series of galleries before you reach the ossuary, the entrance to which is announced by a sign engraved in the stone: 'Stop! This is the empire of death.'

FREE Cité Universitaire

17 bd Jourdan, 14th (01.44.16.64.00, www.ciup.fr). RER Cité Universitaire. **Map** p211 G6 ㉛
The Cité Universitaire is an odd mix. Created between the wars and inspired by Oxbridge colleges, its 37 halls of residence across landscaped gardens were designed in a variety of supposedly authentic national styles. Some are by architects of the appropriate nationality (Dutchman Willem Dudok, for instance, designed the De Stijl-style Collège Néerlandais); others, such as the Khmer sculptures and bird-beak roof of the Asie du Sud-Est building, are merely pastiches. You can visit the sculptural white Pavillon Suisse (01.44.16.10.16, www.fondationsuisse.fr), which has a Le Corbusier mural on the ground floor. The spacious landscaped gardens are open to the public.

EXPLORE

FREE Parc Montsouris

Bd Jourdan, 14th. RER Cité Universitaire. **Open** 8am-dusk Mon-Fri; 9am-dusk Sat, Sun. **Map** p211 G6 32

The most colourful of the capital's parks, Montsouris was laid out for Baron Haussmann by Jean-Charles Adolphe Alphand. It includes a series of gently sloping lawns, an artificial lake and cascades. On the opening day in 1878, the lake inexplicably emptied, and the engineer responsible committed suicide.

FURTHER WEST

In the 15th arrondissement.

The expansive 15th arrondissement has little to offer tourists, though as a largely residential district it has plenty of good restaurants and street markets, and some good small shops. It's worth making a detour to visit **La Ruche** ('beehive'), designed by Eiffel as a wine pavilion for the 1900 Exposition Universelle and moved here to serve as artists' studios. Nearby is **Parc Georges Brassens**, opened in 1983, and at the porte de Versailles the sprawling Paris-Expo exhibition centre was created in 1923.

Sights & Museums

FREE Parc Georges Brassens

Rue des Morillons, 15th. M° Porte de Vanves or Porte de Versailles. **Open** 8am-dusk Mon-Fri; 9am-dusk Sat, Sun. **Map** p210 C6 33

Built on the site of the old Abattoirs de Vaugirard, Parc Georges Brassens prefigured the industrial regeneration of Parc André Citroën and La Villette. The gateways, crowned by bronze bulls, have been kept, as have a series of iron meat-market pavilions, which house a second-hand book market at weekends. The Jardin des Senteurs is planted with aromatic species, and a small vineyard yields 200 bottles of Clos des Morillons every year. The park is named in honour of the famed French singer.

La Ruche

Passage de Dantzig, 15th (www.la-ruche.fr). M° Convention or Porte de Versailles. **Map** p210 C6 34

Have a peep through the fence to see the iron-framed former wine pavilion built by Gustave Eiffel for the 1900 Exposition Universelle, and later rebuilt by philanthropic sculptor Alfred Boucher to be let as studios for struggling artists. Chagall, Soutine, Brancusi, Modigliani, Lipchitz and Archipenko all spent periods here, and the 140 studios are still sought after by today's artists and designers.

Restaurants

Afaria

15 rue Desnouettes, 15th (01.48.42.95.90). M° Convention. **Open** noon-2pm, 7-11pm Tue-Sat. **Main courses** €16-€24. **Prix fixe** *Lunch* €22 (Mon-Fri), €26, €45. *Dinner* €45. **Map** p210 B6 35 **Bistro**

Basque-born chef Julien Duboué may have handed over the reins at Afaria to his talented young deputy, Ludivine Merlin, but the southern French-inspired menu remains intact. Several dishes are for sharing, in particular a caveman-sized duck *magret* with balsamic fig vinegar, served on a terracotta roof tile with potato gratin perched on a bed of twigs. Other creations show a willingness to borrow ingredients from around the world.

Jadis

208 rue de la Croix-Nivert, 15th (01.45.57.73.20, www.bistrot-jadis.com). M° Convention or Porte de Versailles. **Open** 12.15-2pm, 7.15-11pm Mon-Fri. **Main courses** €25. **Prix fixe** *Lunch* €26, €38. *Dinner* €38, €57. **Map** p210 B5 36 **Bistro**

The 15th has more than its fair share of great bistros, and Jadis confirms the trend. In this grey-painted dining room, young chef Guillaume Delage serves a gently updated take on classic French cuisine. The pared-down presentation of such dishes as snails in puff pastry with oyster mushrooms and romaine lettuce lets each element speak for itself.

Parc Montsouris.

The 7th & Western Paris

The seventh arrondissement has long played host to the heavy machinery of state and diplomacy: this is the home of France's parliament, several ministries and a gaggle of foreign embassies, as well as the headquarters of UNESCO. Thankfully, though, three of its greatest attractions – an A-shaped assembly of 19th-century iron lattice, a gallery in an old Beaux Arts train station and the river itself – have decided to embrace the future with thoroughly modern makeovers. The Eiffel Tower is installing a dramatic glass floor for 2014, the Musée d'Orsay has been nicknamed the 'Nouvel Orsay' after a stunning renovation, and the riverbanks are blissfully car-free after Bertrand Delanoë came good on his plans to pedestrianise parts of the Seineside expressway.

Deyrolle.

Don't Miss

1 **Eiffel Tower** Reach for the skies and check out the new glass floor (p231).

2 **Musée d'Orsay** The Nouvel Orsay has had a dynamic revamp (p225).

3 **Le Bon Marché** Push open the door to retail heaven (p227).

4 **Deyrolle** Pick up a bison to take home at this temple of taxidermy (p227).

5 **Musée National Rodin** Greatest hits, from *The Thinker* to *The Gates of Hell* (p225).

THE FAUBOURG ST-GERMAIN

In the 7th arrondissement.

In the early 18th century, when the Marais went out of fashion, aristocrats built palatial new residences on the Faubourg St-Germain, the district developing around the site of the former city wall. It is still a well-bred part of the city, government ministries and foreign embassies colouring the area with flags and diplomatic plates. Many fine *hôtels particuliers* survive; glimpse their elegant entrance courtyards on rue de Grenelle, rue St-Dominique, rue de l'Université and rue de Varenne.

Just west of St-Germain, the 'Carré Rive Gauche' – the quadrangle enclosed by quai Voltaire, rue des Sts-Pères, rue du Bac and rue de l'Université – is filled with antiques shops. On rue des Sts-Pères, *chocolatier* **Debauve & Gallais** (no.30, 7th, 01.45.48.54.67) has been making chocolates since 1800. Rue du Pré-aux-Clercs, named after a field where students used to duel, is now a favourite with fashion insiders. There are still students to be found on rue St-Guillaume, home of the prestigious **Fondation Nationale des Sciences-Politiques** (no.27), more commonly known as 'Sciences-Po'.

Rue de Montalembert is home to two of the Left Bank's most fashionable hotels: the **Hôtel Montalembert** (*see p363*) and the Hôtel Pont Royal, a gastronomic magnet ever since the addition of the trendy **Atelier de Joël Robuchon** (www.joel-robuchon.com). By the river, a Beaux-Arts train station – the towns once served still listed on the façade – houses

the unmissable art collections of the **Musée d'Orsay**; outside on the esplanade are 19th-century bronze animal sculptures.

Next door is the lovely 1780s Hôtel de Salm, once the Swedish embassy and now home to the **Musée National de la Légion d'Honneur et des Ordres de Chevalerie** (2 rue de la Légion d'Honneur, 7th, 01.40.62.84.25, www. musee-legiondhonneur.fr), devoted to France's honours system since Louis XI. The Legion of Honour was established by Napoleon in 1802. Across the street, a modern footbridge, the Passerelle Solférino, crosses the Seine to the Tuileries. The fancy Hôtel Bouchardon today houses the **Musée Maillol**. Right beside its curved entrance, the Fontaine des Quatre Saisons by Edmé Bouchardon features statues of the seasons surrounding allegorical figures of Paris above the rivers Seine and Marne.

You'll have to wait for the open-house **Journées du Patrimoine** (*see p37*) to see the decorative interiors and private gardens of other *hôtels*, such as the **Hôtel de Villeroy** (Ministry of Agriculture; 78 rue de Varenne, 7th), **Hôtel Boisgelin** (Italian Embassy; 51 rue de Varenne, 7th), **Hôtel d'Avaray** (Dutch ambassador's residence; 85 rue de Grenelle, 7th), **Hôtel d'Estrées** (Russian ambassador's residence; 79 rue de Grenelle, 7th) or **Hôtel de Monaco** (Polish Embassy; 57 rue St-Dominique, 7th). Among the most beautiful is the **Hôtel Matignon** (57 rue de Varenne, 7th), residence of the prime minister. It contains the biggest private garden in Paris. The Cité Varenne at no.51 is a lane of exclusive houses complete with private gardens.

Assemblée Nationale.

Rue du Bac is home to the city's oldest and most elegant department store, **Le Bon Marché** ('the good bargain'), and to an unlikely pilgrimage spot, the **Chapelle de la Médaille Miraculeuse**. On nearby rue de Babylone, budget bistro **Au Babylone** (no.13, 7th, 01.45.48.72.13) has been serving up cheap lunches for decades, but the Théâtre de Babylone, where Beckett's *Waiting for Godot* was premiered in 1953, is long gone.

At the foot of boulevard St-Germain, facing place de la Concorde across the Seine, is the **Assemblée Nationale**, the lower house of the French parliament. Behind, elegant place du Palais-Bourbon leads into rue de Bourgogne, a rare commercial thoroughfare amid the official buildings, with some delectable pâtisseries and designer-furniture showrooms.

Beside the Assemblée is the Foreign Ministry, often referred to by its address, 'quai d'Orsay'. Beyond it, a long, grassy esplanade leads up to golden-domed **Les Invalides**. The vast military hospital complex, with its Eglise du Dôme and St-Louis-des-Invalides churches, all built by Louis XIV, epitomises the official grandeur of the Sun King as expression of royal and military power. It now houses the **Musée de l'Armée**, as well as Napoleon's tomb inside the Eglise du Dôme. Stand with your back to the dome to survey the cherubim-laden Pont Alexandre III and the Grand and Petit Palais over the river, all put up for the 1900 Exposition Universelle.

Just beside Les Invalides is the **Musée National Rodin**, occupying the charming 18th-century Hôtel Biron and its romantic gardens. Many of Rodin's great sculptures, including the *Thinker*, the *Burghers of Calais* and the swarming *Gates of Hell*, are displayed in the building and around the gardens – as are those of his mistress, Camille Claudel.

Sights & Museums

★ FREE Assemblée Nationale

33 quai d'Orsay, 7th (www.assemblee-nationale.fr). M° Assemblée Nationale. **Map** p223 F1 ❶
Like the Sénat, the Assemblée Nationale (also known as the Palais Bourbon) is a royal building adapted for republicanism. It was built between 1722 and 1728 for the Duchesse de Bourbon, daughter of Louis XIV and Madame de Montespan, who also put up the neighbouring Hôtel de Lassay for her lover, the Marquis de Lassay. The *palais* was modelled on the Grand Trianon at Versailles, with a colonnaded *cour d'honneur* opening on to rue de l'Université and gardens running down to the Seine. The Prince de Condé extended the palace, linked the two *hôtels* and laid out place du Palais-Bourbon. The Greek temple-style façade facing Pont de la Concorde (the rear of the building) was added in 1806.

Flanking this riverside façade are statues of four great statesmen: L'Hôpital, Sully, Colbert and Aguesseau. The Napoleonic frieze on the pediment was replaced by a monarchist one after the restoration: between 1838 and 1841, Cortot sculpted the figures of France, Power and Justice. After the Revolution, the palace became the meeting place for the Conseil des Cinq-Cents. It was the forerunner of the parliament's lower house, which set up here for good in 1827. Visits are by arrangement through a serving *député* (if you're French) – or during the Journées du Patrimoine (*see p37*).

★ FREE Chapelle de la Médaille Miraculeuse

Couvent des Soeurs de St-Vincent-de-Paul, 140 rue du Bac, 7th (www.chapellenotredame delamedaillemiraculeuse.com). M° Sèvres Babylone. **Open** 7.45am-1pm, 2.30-7pm Mon, Wed-Sun; 7.45am-7pm Tue. **Admission** free. **Map** p223 G3 ❷
In 1830, saintly Catherine Labouré was said to have seen a vision of the Virgin, who told her to cast a medal that copied her appearance – standing on a globe with rays of light appearing from her outstretched hands. This kitsch chapel – murals, mosaics, statues and the embalmed bodies of Catherine and her mother superior – attracts two million pilgrims every year.

FREE Espace Fondation EDF

6 rue Récamier, 7th (http://fondation.edf.com). M° Sèvres Babylone. **Open** noon-7pm Tue-Sun. **Admission** free. **Map** p223 G3 ❸
This former electricity substation was constructed in 1910 under the guidance of architect Paul Friesé, known for his industrial-style buildings around Paris. Reconverted by EDF, the building has been used for exhibitions since 1990. Themes often deal with the environment or sustainable development.

★ Les Invalides & Musée de l'Armée

Esplanade des Invalides, 7th (08.10.11.33.99, www.invalides.org). M° La Tour Maubourg or Les Invalides. **Open** *Apr-Oct* 10am-6pm Mon, Wed-Sun (Dôme until 7pm July, Aug); 10am-9pm Tue. *Nov-Mar* 10am-5pm daily. **Admission** *Courtyard* free. *Musée de l'Armée & Eglise du Dôme* €9.50; €7.50 reductions; free under-18s, under-26s (EU citizens). PMP. **Map** p223 F2 ❹
Topped by its gilded dome, the Hôtel des Invalides was (and in part still is) a hospital. Commissioned by Louis XIV for wounded soldiers, it once housed as many as 6,000 invalids. Designed by Libéral Bruand (the foundations were laid in 1671) and completed by Jules Hardouin-Mansart, it's a magnificent monument to Louis XIV and Napoleon. Behind lines of cannon and bullet-shaped yews, the main (northern) façade has a relief of Louis XIV (Ludovicus Magnus) and the Sun King's sunburst. Wander through the main courtyard and you'll see

EXPLORE

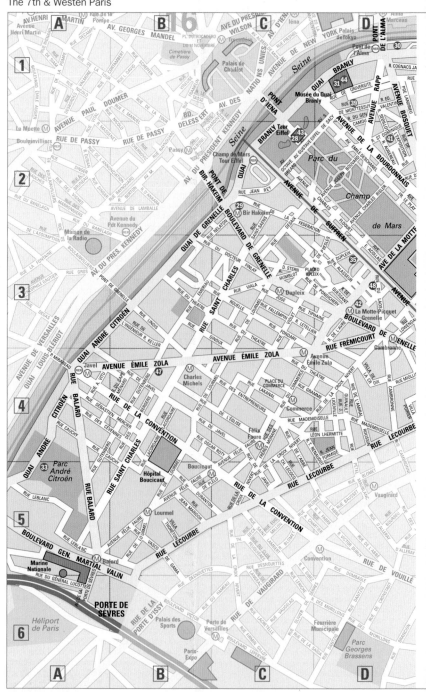

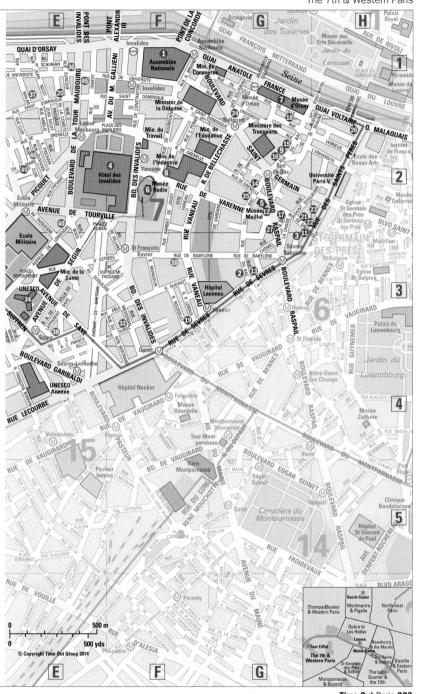

SEVENTH HEAVEN

Dip your toes in the revamped Berges de Seine.

Parisians have always loved their city's quays: over the centuries they've built iconic monuments along them, stretched bridges between them and written songs about them (check out Lucienne Delyle's 1939 rendition of 'Sur les Quais du Vieux Paris'). But in the 1960s, certain stretches were turned into roads that distanced locals and visitors from the banks and some of the best views in town.

Now the city council has given the quayside between Quai Anatole France and Quai Branly in the 7th back to the people by converting the roads into year-round, car-free promenades known as Les Berges (www.lesberges.fr), with floating gardens, a dramatic *emmarchement* (an apparently airborne flight of stairs connecting the upper and lower quays), activities for families, outdoor stages, restaurants, bars and cycle routes.

Outdoors is the name of the game for families with activities including 100m sprinting lanes, hopscotch zones, teepees, climbing walls, summer terraces filled with board games and renovated cargo crates called 'Zzz' that double as private chill-out cabins (available for hire). During spring and summer, a stream of free open-air concerts are performed on a stage called the Mikado (by Pont de Solferino), and throughout the year you can enrol for free yoga, tai chi, fitness and zumba classes organised for hundreds of people at a time.

A mix of seasonal and permanent eateries pepper the banks, too, including food truck Mozza & Co (www.mozzaandco.it) selling some of the finest mozzarella-based dishes in town. Rosa Bonheur sur Seine, a spin-off

of Rosa Bonheur (www.rosabonheur.fr), is set to be a summer fixture, along with neighbouring Le Flow (www.flow-paris.com), a café with a coveted summer 'beach' terrace overlooking the river. And if it's a river dance you're after, one all-year-rounder to look out for is über-trendy Le Faust. Iranian businessman Addy Bakhtiar's latest project beneath Pont Alexandre III gives the Showcase nightclub on the other side of the bridge a run for its money, with chic surroundings and champagne aplenty.

If that's not enough to whet your appetite, Les Berges are near a seventh heaven of another kind: top chef Jean-François Piège's stunning new pastry shop, Gâteaux Thoumieux (*see p228*). Opened in November 2013, it's a den of delectable naughties. Tuck into the likes of *kouign amann* (a buttery, sugary Breton cake) and indulgent chocolate éclairs, before heading back to the sprinting lanes to work it all off.

grandiose arcades and a statue of Napoleon glaring down from the end; the dormer windows around the courtyards are sculpted to resemble suits of armour.

The complex contains two churches – or, rather, a sort of double church: the Eglise St-Louis was for the soldiers, the Eglise du Dôme for the king. An opening behind the altar connects the two. The long, barrel-vaulted nave of the church of St-Louis is hung with flags captured from enemy troops. Since 1840 the Baroque Eglise du Dôme has been dedicated to the worship of Napoleon, whose body was brought here from St Helena. On the ground floor, under a dome painted by de la Fosse, Jouvenet and Coypel, are chapels featuring monuments to Vauban, Foch and Joseph Napoleon (Napoleon's older brother and King of Naples, Sicily and Spain). Napoleon II (King of Rome) is buried in the crypt opposite his father the emperor. Two dramatic black figures holding up the entrance to the crypt, the red porphyry tomb, the ring of giant figures, and the friezes and texts eulogising the emperor's heroic deeds give the measure of the cult of Napoleon, cherished in France for ruling large swaths of Europe and for creating an administrative and educational system that endures to this day.

The Invalides complex also houses the enormous Musée de l'Armée, in effect several museums in one. Even if militaria are not your thing, the building is splendid, and there's some fine portraiture, such as Ingres' *Emperor Napoleon on his Throne*. The Antique Armour wing is packed full of armour and weapons that look as good as new, from the 16th-century suit made for François I to cabinets full of swords, maces, crossbows and muskets and arquebuses. The Plans-Reliefs section is a collection of gorgeous 18th- and 19th-century scale models of French cities, used for military strategy; also here is a 17th-century model of Mont St-Michel, made by a monk from playing cards.

The World War I rooms bring the conflict into focus with uniforms, paintings, a scale model of a trench and, most sobering of all, white plastercasts of the hideously mutilated faces of two soldiers. The World War II wing covers the Resistance, the Battle of Britain and the war in the Pacific (there's a replica of Little Boy, the bomb dropped on Hiroshima), alternating artefacts with film footage. Also included in the entry price is the Historial Charles de Gaulle (closed Mon), an interactive multimedia space dedicated to the work of the founding President of the Fifth Republic.

Musée Maillol
59-61 rue de Grenelle, 7th (01.42.22.59.58, www.museemaillol.com). M° Rue du Bac. **Open** 10.30am-7pm (last admission 6.15pm) Mon-Thur, Sat, Sun; 10.30am-9.30pm (last admission 8.45pm) Fri. **Admission** €11; €9 reductions; free under-11s. **Map** p223 G2 ❺
Dina Vierny was 15 when she met Aristide Maillol and became his principal model for the next decade, idealised in such sculptures as *Spring*, *Air* and

Christian Liaigre
42 rue du Bac, 7th (01.53.63.33.66, www. christian-liaigre.fr). M° Rue du Bac. **Open** 10am-7pm Mon-Sat. Closed 3wks Aug. **Map** p223 G2 ❿ Homewares
This French interior decorator fitted out Marc Jacobs' boutiques. His showroom displays his elegant lighting and furniture designs.
Other locations 61 rue de Varenne, 7th (01.47.53.78.76); 33 rue de Verneuil, 7th (01.40.15.55.92).

Deyrolle
46 rue du Bac, 7th (01.42.22.30.07, www. deyrolle.com). M° Rue du Bac. **Open** 10am-1pm, 2-7pm Mon; 10am-7pm Tue-Sat. **Map** p223 G2 ⓰ Gifts & souvenirs
Opened in 1831 by Jean-Baptiste Deyrolle, a taxidermist and avid traveller, this shop has always been a curiosity, with its bizarre menagerie of lions, giraffes, polar bears, butterflies and bugs. After a fire swept through the shop in 2008, Parisians came together to save the place. It remains a great place to escape the city, buy a tiger for the living room or crank up your kids' imagination.

Editions de Parfums Frédéric Malle
37 rue de Grenelle, 7th (01.42.22.76.40, www.editionsdeparfums.com). M° Rue du Bac or St-Sulpice. **Open** noon-7pm Mon; 11am-7pm Tue-Sat. **Map** p223 G2 ⓱ Health & beauty

Le Bon Marché.

EXPLORE

Gâteaux Thoumieux.

Choose from a range of eight perfumes by Frédéric Malle, former consultant to Hermès and Lacroix. Carnal Flower is seduction in a bottle.
Other locations 21 rue du Mont-Thabor, 1st (01.42.22.16.89); 140 av Victor-Hugo, 16th (01.45.05.39.02).

Epicerie Générale
43 rue de Verneuil, 7th (01.42.60.51.78, www.epiceriegenerale.fr). M° Solférino or Rue du Bac. **Open** 11am-7.30pm Mon-Fri; 10.30am-7.30pm Sat. **Map** p223 G1 ⑱ **Food & drink**
Maud, Claude and Lucio opened Epicerie Générale in 2011. Here, gourmands can pick up cheese, charcuterie, fruit and vegetables, along with products such as Miel Béton ('concrete honey'), made on the roofs of Saint-Denis. L'Epicerie Générale is also developing its own range of branded products, such as La Strix, the first organic French vodka.

★ Fromagerie Quatrehomme
62 rue de Sèvres, 7th (01.47.34.33.45). M° Duroc or Vaneau. **Open** 9am-7.45pm Tue-Sat. **Map** p223 F3 ⑲ **Food & drink**
Marie Quatrehomme runs this *fromagerie*. Justly famous for her beaufort and st-marcellin, she also sells such specialities as goat's cheese with pesto.
Other location 9 rue du Poteau, 18th (01.46.06.26.03).

Gâteaux Thoumieux
58 rue St-Dominique, 7th (www.thoumieux.fr). M° Latour Maubourg. **Open** 9am-7pm Mon, Wed-Sat; 8.30am-2pm Sun. **Map** p223 E1 ⑳
Food & drink
See p224 **Seventh Heaven.**

Iris
28 rue de Grenelle, 7th (01.42.22.89.81, www.iris shoes.com). M° Rue du Bac or St-Sulpice. **Open** 10.30am-7pm Mon-Sat. **Map** p223 G2 ㉑ **Fashion**
This white boutique stocks shoes by the likes of Marc Jacobs, John Galliano and Viktor & Rolf.

Moss
22 rue de Grenelle, 7th (01.42.22.01.43). M° Rue du Bac or St-Sulpice. **Open** 11am-7pm Mon; 10.30am-7pm Tue-Sat. **Map** p223 G2 ㉒
Accessories
The three sisters who run this boutique pride themselves on sourcing cutting-edge shoes that can be hard to find elsewhere, such as creations by former Céline stylist Avril Gau and signature designs by Laurence Dacade, Duccio del Duca and Hartian Bourdin. You'll also find scarves by Octavio Pizzaro and jewellery by Karry O', the fourth sister.

★ Paul & Joe
64 rue des Sts-Pères, 7th (01.42.22.47.01, www.paulandjoe.com). M° Rue du Bac or St-Germain-des-Prés. **Open** 10am-7pm Mon-Sat. **Map** p223 H2 ㉓ **Fashion**
Fashionistas adore Sophie Albou's retro-styled creations, dressing leggy young things in a range of winter shorts, colourful minidresses and voluminous trousers, and their intellectual paramours in slouchy woollens, tailored jackets and chunky boots.
Other locations throughout the city.

Richart
258 bd St-Germain, 7th (01.45.55.66.00, www. richart.com). M° Solférino. **Open** 10am-7pm Mon-Sat. **Map** p223 G1 ㉔ **Food & drink**
Each of Richart's stunning chocolate *ganaches* has an intricate design, packages look like jewel boxes, and every purchase comes with a tract on how best to savour the stuff.

Ryst Dupeyron
79 rue du Bac, 7th (01.45.48.80.93, www. vintageandco.com). M° Rue du Bac. **Open** 12.30-7.30pm Mon; 10.30am-7.30pm Tue-Sat. Closed 2wks Aug. **Map** p223 G2 ㉕
Food & drink
The Dupeyrons have been selling armagnac for four generations. Treasures include 200 fine Bordeaux wines and an extensive range of vintage port.

★ Sennelier
3 quai Voltaire, 7th (01.42.60.72.15, www.
magasinsennelier.fr). M° St-Germain-des-Prés.
Open 2-6.30pm Mon; 10am-12.45pm, 2-6.30pm
Tue-Sat. **Map** p223 H2 **⊕ Gifts & souvenirs**
Old-fashioned colour merchant Sennelier sells oil
paints, watercolours and pastels, rare pigments,
primed canvases, varnishes and paper.
Other location 4bis rue de la Grande-Chaumière,
6th (01.46.33.72.39).

Sentou Galerie
26 bd Raspail, 7th (01.45.49.00.05, www.sentou.fr).
M° Rue du Bac. **Open** 10am-7pm Tue-Sat.
Map p223 G2 **⊕ Homewares**

A trend-setting shop for colourful tableware and
furniture: painted Chinese flasks, vases and so on.
Other location 29 rue François-Miron, 4th
(01.42.78.50.60).

WEST & SOUTH OF LES INVALIDES
In the 7th & 15th arrondissements.

South-west of the Invalides is the enormous
Ecole Militaire (av de La Motte-Picquet, 7th),
the military academy built by Louis XV to
educate the children of penniless officers;
it would later train Napoleon. The severe

WALKING IN THE AIR
The Iron Lady is getting a glass floor.

No building better symbolises Paris than
the **Eiffel Tower** (*see p231*). Maupassant
claimed he left Paris because of it, William
Morris visited daily to avoid having to see it
from afar – and it was originally meant to be
a temporary structure. The cast-iron tower
was built for the 1889 World Fair and the
centenary of the 1789 Revolution by
engineer Gustave Eiffel, who made use of
new technology that was already popular in
iron-framed buildings. Construction took
more than two years and used some 18,000
pieces of metal and 2,500,000 rivets. And
not much has changed since – until now.

In an attempt to brighten up the rather
dingy first floor and make it as much of an
attraction as the summit itself, the Eiffel
Tower is undergoing its third facelift since
opening 125 years ago – and what a facelift:
the €25m revamp is radical, to say the
least, with the central void being filled in with
a solid glass floor surrounded by inclined
safety barriers, so visitors will be able to
peer over and eyeball the queues of tourists
57m below. The 18-month project features
other future-proofing ideas too, including
environmentally friendly lighting and power,
new teaching areas and the introduction of
full disabled access to the first floor. Having
welcomed more than 200 million people, the
Dame de Fer is finally shedding a few rivets
in favour of a more 21st-century style.

EXPLORE

neoclassical building, designed by Jacques Ange Gabriel, is still used by the army and closed to the public.

From the north-western side of the Ecole Militaire begins the vast Champ de Mars, a market garden converted into a military drilling ground in the 18th century. It has long been home to the most celebrated Paris monument of all, the **Eiffel Tower**. At the south-eastern end of the Champ de Mars stands the Mur pour la Paix ('wall for peace'), erected in 2000 to articulate hopes for global peace. South-east of the Ecole are the Y-shaped **UNESCO** building,

built in 1958, and the modernist Ministry of Labour. Fashionable apartments line broad avenue Bosquet and avenue Suffren, though there's much architectural eclecticism in the area: look at the pseudo-Gothic and pseudo-Renaissance houses on avenue de Villars; Lavirotte's fabulous art nouveau doorway at 27 avenue Rapp; and the striking **Notre Dame de l'Arche de l'Alliance** church (81 rue d'Alleray, 15th, 01.56.56.62.56, www.ndarche. org), completed in 1998. For signs of life, visit the Saxe-Breteuil street market. The upper reaches of rue Cler contain classy food shops.

BLIND AMBITION

Explore the history of braille at the Musée Valentin Haüy.

The tiny **Musée Valentin Haüy** (*see p231*) is devoted to the history of braille, a story intimately connected with the French Enlightenment just before the Revolution. Valentin Haüy, whose statue you will see as you pass the gates of the Institut National des Jeunes Aveugles, was an 18th-century linguist and philanthropist. He established France's first school for the blind, and it was here that Louis Braille became a star pupil some 34 years later.

The one-room museum is hidden at the end of the nondescript corridors of the Valentin Haüy Association, which offers educational services to the blind. The door opens on to glass-fronted cases of exhibits with, in the centre, a huge braille globe. You can explore on your own with the aid of French, English or braille texts, or allow the curator, Noêle Roy, to show you round. She will give a tour in English if preferred.

The first exhibit is a shocking print, depicting the fairground freak show that inspired Valentin Haüy to devote his life to educating not only the blind, but also the

backward public who came to laugh at the likes of this blind orchestra forced to perform in dunce's hats. He wanted to prove that blind people had as great a capacity for learning and feeling as anyone else.

Next begins the tactile tour, with a chance to touch books printed by Haüy in embossed letters. After the Revolution, philanthopist Charles Barbier tried to develop a universal writing system using raised dots, but it was difficult to read. Braille, the son of a harness-maker, arrived at the school as a ten-year-old in 1819, having been blind since the age of four after he accidentally stabbed himself in the eye with a stitching awl. He spent his years at the school developing his six-dot fingertip system. He was only 16 when he completed it, and he went on to teach, write a treatise on arithmetic, and play the organ in two Paris churches. He died from tuberculosis at the age of 43. If it hadn't been for his childhood accident, this genius may never have had access to the education that led to his gift to humanity and his admission to the Pantheon.

Downstream from the Eiffel Tower is the **Musée du Quai Branly**, which opened in 2006. A short way further on, the high-tech **Maison de la Culture du Japon** stands near Pont Bir-Hakeim on quai Branly. Beyond, the 15th-arrondissement Fronts de Seine riverfront, with its tower-block developments, had some of the worst architecture of the 1970s inflicted upon it. The adjacent Beaugrenelle shopping centre has always been rather dingy, but the mall reopened in late 2013 with a spectacularly modern redesign and 120 shops to browse. Further west, things look up: the sophisticated former headquarters of the Canal+ TV channel (2 rue des Cévennes, 15th), designed by architect Richard Meier, is surrounded by fine modern housing; and the pleasant **Parc André Citroën**, created in the 1990s on the site of the former Citroën car works, runs down to the Seine.

Sights & Museums

★ Eiffel Tower

Champ de Mars, 7th (08.92.70.12.39, www.toureiffel.fr). Mº Bir-Hakeim/RER Champ de Mars Tour Eiffel. **Open** *By lift* Mid June-Aug 9am-12.45am daily (last ascent 11pm). Sept-mid June 9.30am-11.45pm daily (last ascent 10.30pm). *By stairs* (1st & 2nd levels) Mid June-Aug 9am-12.45am (last ascent midnight). Sept-mid June 9.30am-6.30pm (last ascent 6pm). **Admission** *By stairs* €5; €3-€3.50 reductions; free under-4s. *By lift* (1st & 2nd level) €8.50; €4-€7 reductions; (3rd level) €14.50; €10-€13 reductions; free under-4s. **Map** p222 C2 ㉘
See p229 **Walking in the Air**.

FREE Maison de la Culture du Japon

101bis quai Branly, 15th (01.44.37.95.01, www.mcjp.asso.fr). Mº Bir-Hakeim/RER Champ de Mars Tour Eiffel. **Open** noon-7pm Tue, Wed, Fri, Sat; noon-8pm Thur. Closed Aug. **Admission** free. **Map** p222 C2 ㉙
Constructed in 1996 by the architectural partnership of Kenneth Armstrong and Masayuki Yamanaka, this glass-fronted Japanese cultural centre screens films and puts on exhibitions and plays. It also contains a library, an authentic Japanese tea pavilion on the roof and a well-stocked bookshop and gift shop.

Musée des Egouts

Entrance opposite 93 quai d'Orsay, by Pont de l'Alma, 7th (01.53.68.27.81). Mº Alma Marceau/RER Pont de l'Alma. **Open** 11am-4pm Mon-Wed, Sat, Sun (until 5pm May-Sept). Closed 2wks Jan. **Admission** €4.30; €3.50 reductions; free under-6s. **No credit cards. Map** p222 D1 ㉚
For centuries, the main source of drinking water in Paris was the Seine, which was also the main sewer. Construction of an underground sewerage system began at the time of Napoleon. Today, the Egouts

de Paris constitutes a smelly museum; each sewer in the 2,100km (1,305-mile) system is marked with a replica of the street sign above.

★ Musée du Quai Branly

37 quai Branly, 7th (01.56.61.70.00, www.quaibranly.fr). RER Pont de l'Alma. **Open** 11am-7pm Tue, Wed, Sun; 11am-9pm Thur-Sat. **Admission** €8.50; €6 reductions; free under-18s, under-26s (EU citizens), all 1st Sun of mth. *Temporary exhibitions* €7; €5 reductions; free under-18s, all 1st Sun of mth. **Map** p222 D1 ㉛
Surrounded by trees on the banks of the Seine, this museum, housed in an extraordinary building by Jean Nouvel, is a vast showcase for non-European cultures. Dedicated to the ethnic art of Africa, Oceania, Asia and the Americas, it joins together the collections of the Musée des Arts d'Afrique et d'Océanie and the Laboratoire d'Ethnologie du Musée de l'Homme, as well as contemporary indigenous art. Treasures include a tenth-century anthropomorphic Dogon statue from Mali, a 19th-century Hawaiian chief's helmet, a Vietnamese bronze funeral drum, Gabonese masks, Aztec statues, Peruvian feather tunics and rare frescoes from Ethiopia.

FREE Musée Valentin Haüy

5 rue Duroc, 7th (01.44.49.27.27, www.avh.asso.fr). Mº Duroc. **Open** 2.30-5pm Tue, Wed (closed July-mid Sept). **Admission** free. **Map** p223 F3 ㉜
See p230 **Blind Ambition**.

FREE Parc André Citroën

Rue Balard, rue St-Charles or quai Citroën, 15th. Mº Balard or Javel. **Open** 8am-dusk Mon-Fri; 9am-dusk Sat, Sun, public hols. **Map** p222 A5 ㉝
This park is a fun, postmodern version of a French formal garden. It comprises glasshouses, computerised fountains, waterfalls, a wilderness and themed gardens, and is currently being extended. A tethered Eutelsat helium balloon takes visitors up for panoramic views. If the weather looks unreliable, call 01.44.26.20.00 to check the programme.

FREE UNESCO

7 pl de Fontenoy, 7th (01.45.68.10.00, tours (book in advance) 01.45.68.03.59, www.unesco.org). Mº Ecole Militaire. **Open** *Tours* call for details. **Admission** free. **Map** p223 E3 ㉞
The Y-shaped UNESCO headquarters, built in 1958, is home to a swarm of international diplomats. It's worth visiting for the sculptures and paintings – by Picasso, Arp, Giacometti, Moore, Calder and Miró – and for the Japanese garden. Tours need to be reserved three months in advance.

FREE Village Suisse

78 av de Suffren or 54 av de La Motte-Picquet, 15th (www.villagesuisse.com). Mº La Motte Picquet Grenelle. **Open** 10.30am-7pm Mon, Thur-Sun. **Map** p222 D3 ㉟

EXPLORE

The mountains and waterfalls created for the Swiss Village at the 1900 Exposition Universelle are long gone, but the village lives on. The street level has been colonised by some 150 boutiques offering various high-quality, pricey antiques and collectibles.

Restaurants

Le 144 Petrossian

144 rue de l'Université, 7th (01.44.11.32.32, www.petrossian.fr). M° La Tour Maubourg. **Open** 12.15-2.30pm, 7.30-10.30pm Tue-Sat. **Main courses** €35. **Prix fixe** *Lunch* €35, €90. *Dinner* €35, €90, €250. **Map** p223 E1 ❸❺ **Russian**
At this famed caviar house you'll find Russian specialities such as blinis, salmon and caviar (at €44 an ounce) from the Petrossian boutique downstairs, plus preparations and spices from all over the world. You might start with a divine risotto made with carnaroli rice, codfish caviar and parmesan. In similar Med-meets-Russia vein are such main courses as roast sea bream with a lemon-vodka sauce.

★ L'Ami Jean

27 rue Malar, 7th (01.47.05.86.89, www.amijean.eu). M° Ecole Militaire. **Open** noon-2pm, 7-10pm Tue-Sat. Closed Aug. **Main courses** *Dinner* €40. **Prix fixe** *Lunch* €35, €42, €55, €80. *Dinner* €75. **Map** p223 E1 ❸❼ **Bistro**
This long-running Basque address is an ongoing hit thanks to chef Stéphane Jégo. Excellent bread from baker Jean-Luc Poujauran is a perfect nibble when slathered with a tangy, herby *fromage blanc* – as is a starter of sautéed baby squid on a bed of ratatouille. Tender veal shank comes de-boned with a lovely side of baby onions and broad beans with tiny cubes of ham, and house-salted cod is soaked, sautéed and doused with an elegant vinaigrette. There's a great wine list, and some lovely Brana *eau de vie* should you decide to linger.

€ Le Bistro

17 rue Pérignon, 15th (01.45.66.84.03). M° Ségur. **Open** 8am-7pm Mon-Fri; Sat by reservation only. **Main courses** €12-€15. **Prix fixe** €17. **Map** p223 E3 ❸❽ **Bistro**
At first glance there is nothing to distinguish this corner bistro from hundreds of other cafés in Paris. In the front room, with its wood-panelled ceiling, are a plastic-topped bar and a few bare tables with black banquettes, and in the back is a larger room with red-and-white checked tablecloths. Then you see the plates going by, each one – from the goat's cheese salad to the *pavé de rumsteak* – loaded with golden fried potato rounds or hand-cut chips. This is the kind of neighbourhood bistro you had almost given up hope of finding in Paris.

★ Au Bon Accueil

14 rue de Monttessuy, 7th (01.47.05.46.11, www.aubonaccueilparis.com). M° Alma Marceau. **Open** noon-2.30pm, 7-10.30pm Mon-Fri. Closed 3wks Aug. **Main courses** €29-€46. **Prix fixe** €32-€50. **Map** p222 D1 ❸❾ **Bistro**
Jacques Lacipière runs Au Bon Accueil, and Keita Kitamura turns out the beautiful food. Perhaps most impressive is his elegant use of little-known fish, such as grey mullet and meagre (*maigre*), rather than the usual endangered species. The €32 lunch menu might highlight such posh ingredients as *suprême de poulet noir du Cros de la Géline*, free-range chicken raised on a farm run by two former cabaret singers. But the biggest surprise comes with desserts, worthy of the finest pastry shops. In summer, book a table on the pavement terrace with its view of the Eiffel Tower.

D'Chez Eux

2 av de Lowendal, 7th (01.47.05.52.55, www.chezeux.com). M° Ecole Militaire. **Open** noon-2pm, 7-11pm daily. Closed Aug. **Main courses** €29-€60. **Prix fixe** *Lunch* €29, €34 Mon-Fri; €44 Sat, Sun. **Map** p223 E2 ❹❶ **Bistro**
Arm yourself with serious stamina for a meal at this jovial south-western *auberge*, which looks touristy with its red-and-white checked tablecloths but attracts *bons vivants* from the neighbourhood. First come the help-yourself lyonnais-style 'salads' (cooked beetroot, lentils, celeriac rémoulade, ratatouille, etc), before hearty main dishes such as cassoulet or calf's liver with sherry vinegar. The heaving dessert cart will ensure that you waddle out overfed but happy.

Les Cocottes

135 rue St-Dominique, 7th (01.45.55.15.05, www.maisonconstant.com). M° Ecole Militaire/ RER Pont de l'Alma. **Open** noon-4pm, 6.30-11pm daily. **Main courses** €14-€29. **Map** p222 D2 ❹❶ **Bistro**
Christian Constant has found the perfect recipe for pleasing Parisians at his new bistro: a flexible menu of salads, soups, *verrines* (light dishes served in jars) and *cocottes* (served in cast-iron pots), all at bargain prices – for this neighbourhood. Service is swift and the food satisfying, though the *vraie salade César Ritz*, which contains hard-boiled egg, shouldn't be confused with US-style Caesar salad. Soups such as an iced pea velouté are spot-on, and *cocottes* range from sea bream with ratatouille to potatoes stuffed with pig's trotter.

IN THE KNOW UP MARKET

Saxe-Breteuil market (av de Saxe, 7th; Thur, Sat) has an unrivalled setting facing the Eiffel Tower, as well as the city's smartest produce. Look for farmer's goat's cheese, rare apple varieties, Armenian specialities, oysters and a handful of dedicated small producers.

L'Epicerie du Père Claude

La Gauloise
59 av de la Motte-Picquet, 15th (01.47.34.11.64).
M° La Motte-Picquet Grenelle. **Open** noon-2.30pm,
7-11pm daily. **Main courses** €22-€33. **Prix fixe**
€24.50, €29.50. **Map** p222 D3 ⓵ **Bistro**
This restaurant is chic, calm and welcoming, long
regulated by the etiquette of the Parisian bourgeoisie
(Mitterand was a longstanding customer). It's done
out in immaculate taste (long dark wood bar, plaster
mouldings, red velvet banquettes), with an eye to
discretion (well-spaced tables throughout multiple
rooms). The cooking has kept up with the times, but
never goes too far: soft-boiled eggs, a legendary *pot-
au-feu*, Aubrac beef, sole meunière, corn-fed poultry
with ceps, soufflés and profiteroles.

★ Jules Verne
*Pilier Sud, Eiffel Tower, 7th (01.45.55.61.44,
www.lejulesverne-paris.com). M° Bir Hakeim or
RER Tour Eiffel.* **Open** 12.15-1.30pm, 7-9.30pm
daily. **Main courses** €74-€92. **Prix fixe** *Lunch*
€90 Mon-Fri; €165, €175, €210 Sat, Sun. *Dinner*
€210, €310. **Map** p223 C2 ⓵ **Haute cuisine**
You have to have courage to take on the Eiffel
Tower, but Alain Ducasse has done just that. He has
transformed the cuisine and brought in designer
Patrick Jouin. Meanwhile, Ducasse protégé Pascal
Féraud updates French classics, combining all the
grand ingredients you'd expect with light, modern
textures. Try dishes like lamb with artichokes or turbot with champagne zabaglione. Book ahead.

Les Ombres
*27 quai Branly, 7th (01.47.53.68.00, www.les
ombres-restaurant.com). M° Alma-Marceau.* **Open**
noon-2.30pm, 7-11pm daily. **Main courses** €30-
€50. **Prix fixe** *Lunch* €32, €42. *Dinner* €68, €95.
Map p222 D1 ⓵ **Bistro**
The view of the Eiffel Tower at night would be reason enough to come to this glass-and-iron restaurant
on the top floor of the Musée du Quai Branly, but the
food also demands that you sit up and take notice.
In keeping with its location, the menu is themed by
continent, providing the chance to sample everything from tabouleh to NY strip steak.

Il Vino
*13 bd de La Tour-Maubourg, 7th (01.44.11.72.00,
www.ilvinobyenricobernardo.com). M° La Tour-
Maubourg.* **Open** 12.30-2pm, 7pm-midnight
Mon-Fri; 7pm-midnight Sat. **Main courses**
€12. **Prix fixe** *Lunch* €35. *Dinner* €75, €95.
Map p222 E1 ⓵ **Italian**
Enrico Bernardo, youngest winner of the World's
Best Sommelier award, runs this restaurant where
food plays second fiddle to wine. You are presented
with nothing more than a wine list. Each of 15 wines
by the glass is matched with a surprise dish, or the
chef can build a meal around a bottle of your choice.

Cafés & Bars

Le Café du Marché
*38 rue Cler, 7th (01.47.05.51.27). M° Ecole
Militaire.* **Open** 7am-midnight Mon-Sat;
7am-8pm Sun. **Map** p223 E2 ⓵
This well-loved address is frequented by trendy
locals, shoppers hunting down a particular type of
cheese and tourists who've managed to make it this
far from the Eiffel Tower. Le Café du Marché really
is a hub of activity. Its *pichets* of decent house plonk
always go down a treat.

Shops & Services

Les Délices d'Orient
*52 av Emile-Zola, 15th (01.45.79.10.00).
M° Charles Michels.* **Open** 8.30am-9pm
Tue-Sun. **Map** p222 B4 ⓵ **Food & drink**
Shelves here groan beneath the weight of stuffed
aubergines, halva, falafel and all manner of Middle
Eastern delicacies.
Other location 14 rue des Quatre-Frères-Peignot,
15th (01.45.77.82.93).

L'Epicerie du Père Claude
*4 rue du Général de Castelnau, 15th
(01.47.34.04.04, www.epicerieduperecclaude.com).
M° La Motte-Picquet Grenelle.* **Open** 10am-11pm
daily. **Map** p222 D3 ⓵ **Food & drink**
Père Claude's three businesses are just a few steps
from each other: the historic restaurant run by Père
Claude himself since 1988, a deli opened in 2009, and
a bar opened in 2012. The deli is top quality, its
shelves loaded with carefully sourced ingredients
(rock salt, fine spices), gourmet conserves, sauces
and home-made products: brie with truffles, terrines,
sausages, merguez, plus tarts, pâtés and foie gras.

Marie-Anne Cantin
*12 rue du Champ-de-Mars, 7th (01.45.50.43.94,
www.cantin.fr). M° Ecole Militaire.* **Open** 2-7.30pm
Mon; 8.30am-7.30pm Tue-Sat; 8.30am-1pm Sun.
Map p223 E2 ⓵ **Food & drink**
Cantin, a defender of unpasteurised cheese and supplier to many posh Paris restaurants, offers aged
chèvres and amazing morbier, mont d'or and comté.

EXPLORE

Beyond the Périphérique

Ten years ago, visitors might not have looked much further than a quick dash round the Louvre and a twilight cruise on the Seine to tick the boxes for their perfect Paris weekend. But now the capital's pleasures are spreading well beyond the cramped confines of the Grands Boulevards, even crossing the Périphérique and into the formerly forbidden lands of the banlieue. From art complexes to anatomy museums, Paris no longer stops at the 20th arrondissement, with big-hitters Thadaeus Ropac and Larry Gagosian both opening landmark galleries in the suburbs in late 2012. Big chunks of the Périphérique itself, long a symbolic frontier between 'inside' and 'outside', are set to be boxed over by gardens and other vote-winning urban amenities during the next decade, with a particular focus on beefed-up transport links across the greater Paris region, from the eastern extension of the tram network to the reopening of the Voguéo river shuttle between Suresnes and the Musée d'Orsay.

Musée de l'Air et de l'Espace.

Don't Miss

1 La Défense Soaring skyscrapers and stunning views (p236).

2 Basilique St-Denis Gothic grandeur (p236).

3 Musée de l'Air et de l'Espace Classic cockpit action (p236).

4 Stade de France Grand stands (p238).

5 MAC/VAL Modern art, 1950s to now (p238).

LA DEFENSE

The skyscrapers and walkways of La Défense – named after a stand against the Prussians in 1870 – create a whole new world. The area has been a showcase for French business since the mid 1950s, when the CNIT hall was built to host trade shows, but it was the arrival of the **Grande Arche** that gave the district its most dramatic monument. On the central esplanade are fountains and sculptures by Miró and Serra.

Grande Arche de La Défense

92044 Paris La Défense (01.49.07.27.27, www.grandearche.com). M° La Défense. **Open** *Apr-Aug* 10am-8pm daily. *Oct-Mar* 10am-7pm daily. **Admission** €10 (€5 Tue); €8.50 reductions; free under-6s.

Completed in 1989, the Grande Arche was designed by Danish architect Johan Otto von Spreckelsen. Though it lines up neatly on the Grand Axe – from the Louvre, up the Champs-Elysées to the Arc de Triomphe – the building itself is skewed. A vertigo-inducing glass lift soars up through canvas 'clouds' to the roof, for a fantastic view over Paris.

▶ *Also here is the Musée de l'Informatique (08.20.21.03.10, www.museeinformatique.fr), which traces the story of computing.*

ST-DENIS & THE NORTH

North of Paris, the *département* of Seine St-Denis (and part of adjoining Val d'Oise) best fulfils the negative stereotype of the *banlieue*. It's a victim of its 19th-century industrial boom and the 20th-century housing shortage, when colossal estates went up in La Corneuve, Aulnay-sous-Bois and Sarcelles. It includes some of the poorest *communes* in all of France. Yet the *département* boasts a buzzing theatre scene, with the **MC93** in Bobigny (*see p293*), the **Théâtre Gérard-Philipe** (*see p293*) in St-Denis, and the Théâtre de la Commune in Aubervilliers. Amid the sprawl stands one of the treasures of Gothic architecture: the **Basilique St-Denis**, final resting place for the majority of France's former monarchs.

Le Bourget, home to the city's first airport and still used for private jets and an air fair, contains the **Musée de l'Air et de l'Espace** in its original passenger terminals and hangars. In late 2012, the area also became home to a bold new Gagosian gallery (*see p237*) designed by Jean Nouvel. North-east of Paris, Pantin arrived on the cultural scene with the opening in 2004 of the **Centre National de la Danse** (*see p286*) in a cleverly revamped office block, and 2012 saw the opening of Thaddaeus Ropac's new art gallery space (*see p237*). North-west of St-Denis, Ecouen, noted for its Renaissance château, now the **Musée National de la Renaissance**, allows for a glimpse of a more rural past.

★ **Basilique St-Denis**

1 rue de la Légion-d'Honneur, 93200 St-Denis (01.48.09.83.54). M° St-Denis Basilique/tram 1. **Open** *Apr-Sept* 10am-6.15pm Mon-Sat; noon-6.15pm Sun. *Oct-Mar* 10am-5pm Mon-Sat; noon-5.15pm Sun. *Tours* 10.30am, 3pm Mon-Sat; 12.15pm, 3pm Sun. **Admission** €7.50; €4.50 reductions; free under-18s, under-26s (EU citizens). PMP.

Legend has it that when St Denis was beheaded, he picked up his noggin and walked with it to Vicus Catulliacus (now St-Denis) to be buried. The first church, parts of which can be seen in the crypt, was built over his tomb in around 475. The present edifice was begun in the 1130s by Abbot Suger. It is considered to be the first example of Gothic architecture, uniting the elements of pointed arches, ogival vaulting and flying buttresses. In the 13th century, master mason Pierre de Montreuil erected the spire and rebuilt the choir nave and transept. St-Denis was the burial place for all but three French monarchs between 996 and the end of the *ancien régime*, so the ambulatory is a museum of French funerary sculpture. It includes a fanciful Gothic tomb for Dagobert, the austere effigy of Charles V, and the Renaissance tomb of Louis XII and his wife Anne de Bretagne. In 1792, these tombs were desecrated, and the royal remains thrown into a pit.

★ FREE **Musée de l'Air et de l'Espace**

Aéroport de Paris-Le Bourget, 93352 Le Bourget Cedex (01.49.92.70.00, www.mae.org). M° Gare du Nord, then bus 350/RER Le Bourget, then bus 152. **Open** *Apr-Sept* 10am-6pm Tue-Sun. *Oct-Mar* 10am-5pm Tue-Sun. **Admission** free. *With 1-3 animations* €8-€16; €6-€12 under-26s; free under-4s. PMP.

Set in the former passenger terminal at Le Bourget airport, the collection begins with the pioneers, including the command cabin of a Zeppelin airship. On the runway are Mirage fighters, a US Thunderchief, a Boeing 747 and Ariane launchers 1 and 5. Hangars house the prototype Concorde 001 and a Dakota. Entry to the main collection is free, but there's a charge for each *animation* (Forfait Avions, Planète Pilote, Planétarium, Simulateurs, Cockpits Secrets).

Musée National de la Renaissance

Château d'Ecouen, 95440 Ecouen (01.34.38.38.50, www.musee-renaissance.fr). Train Gare du Nord to Ecouen-Ezanville then bus 269 or walk. **Open** *16 Apr-Sept* 9.30am-12.45pm, 2-5.45pm Mon, Wed-Sun. *Oct-14 Apr* 9.30am-12.45pm, 2-5.15pm Mon, Wed-Sun. **Admission** €5; €3.50 reductions; free under-26s, all 1st Sun of mth.

The Renaissance château completed in 1555 for Royal Constable Anne de Montmorency and wife Margaret de Savoie is the setting for a collection of 16th-century decorative arts (some sections are open only at certain times so it's a good idea to phone ahead). Best are the painted chimney pieces, decorated with biblical and mythological scenes.

PERIPHERAL VISION

Larry Gagosian and Thaddaeus Ropac are hanging in the suburbs.

First it was the 13th arrondissement, and now the Paris art world cognoscenti are having to get out their maps again and head off to the badlands beyond the Périphérique. Much as New York headed down to Chelsea in the early noughties, a handful of art dealers have headed out to the *banlieue* to open galleries with the sort of space that they could have only dreamed about in the Marais.

Larry Gagosian has complemented his elegant premises off avenue Matignon with the two-level **Gagosian Le Bourget** (800 avenue de l'Europe, 93350 Le Bourget, 01.48.16.16.47, www.gagosian.com), housed in a 1950s concrete hangar at Le Bourget airport (handy for jet-set collectors, less so if you're travelling by RER). Converted by Jean Nouvel, the massive white space can accommodate installations even many museums can't fit in, opening with Anselm Kiefer's spectacular *Morgenthau Plan*, a sculpture of a golden wheat field enclosed within a five-metre high iron cage.

After 30 years in Paris and Salzburg, Thaddaeus Ropac's new **Galerie Pantin** (69 avenue du General Leclerc, 93500 Pantin, 01.55.89.01.10, www.ropac.net) occupies a red-brick factory complex converted by architects Buttazzoni & Associés. The opening exhibition also featured paintings by Kiefer, displayed in four long, light-filled galleries, plus a re-creation of Joseph Beuys' last exhibition, complete with pony, in a separate glass-

fronted building. Pantin 'will give artists the opportunity to realise their vision without the restrictions of space,' says Ropac, who intends to mix shows by established and young artists, in-house and guest curators, as well as potential collaborations with the nearby Cité de la Musique at La Villette and the Centre National de la Danse in Pantin. The second show, 'Disaster – from Andy Warhol to Banks Violette', included works by Gilbert & George, Erwin Wurm, Mark Quinn and Liza Lou.

Even further out of town is Italian-owned Galleria Continua's **Le Moulin** (46 rue de la Ferté Gaucher, 77169 Boissy-le-Châtel, 01.64.20.39.50, www.galleriacontinua. com) in Boissy-le-Châtel, 65km east of Paris. The converted papermill has been left in an appealing semi-derelict state, housing a display of works by the likes of Daniel Buren, Michelangelo Pistoletto and Kader Attia, some of whom created pieces especially for the building; there are also temporary shows that are put on in an adjacent warehouse.

The gallery has recently acquired a second, even larger mill across the river, and embarked on an ambitious project with the local mayor and the Ville Rayée architects' collective. The idea is to create a complex that features art studios, an auditorium, galleries and a restaurant. Accessed by a riverside footpath and boat shuttle, it is intended as 'an exceptional gallery off the beaten track in the Parisian countryside'. Time to get the map out again.

EXPLORE

Gagosian Le Bourget.

Stade de France

For listings, see p246.

The 80,000-capacity Stade de France is the national stadium. It was built for the 1998 football World Cup and staged the final, when France beat Brazil 3-0 to claim the title for the first time. As well as hosting top football matches, it hosts home legs for rugby's Six Nations, athletics meetings and major league concerts. For details of stadium tours, *see p246.*

VINCENNES & THE EAST

The more upmarket residential districts in the east surround the **Bois de Vincennes**, such as Vincennes, with its royal château, St-Mandé and Charenton-le-Pont. **Joinville-le-Pont** and **Champigny-sur-Marne** draw weekenders for the riverside *guinguette* dancehalls.

Château de Vincennes.

Château de Vincennes

Av de Paris, 94300 Vincennes (01.48.08.31.20, www.chateau-vincennes.fr). M° Château de Vincennes. **Open** *Mid May-mid Sept* 10am-6pm daily. *Mid Sept-mid May* 10am-5pm daily. **Admission** €8.50; €5.50 reductions; free under-18s, under-26s (EU citizens).

An imposing curtain wall punctuated by towers encloses this 52m-high fortress, which is the tallest medieval fortified structure in Europe. Originally the site of a hunting lodge built for Louis VII in the 12th century, the square keep was begun by Philippe VI and completed in the 14th century by Charles V, who added the curtain wall. English king Henry V died here in 1422, and Louis XIII used the château for hunting expeditions.

★ MAC/VAL

Pl de la Libération, 94404 Vitry-sur-Seine (01.43.91.64.20, www.macval.fr). M° Porte de Choisy then bus 183/RER Gare de Vitry-sur-Seine then bus 180. **Open** 10am-6pm Tue-Fri; noon-7pm Sat, Sun. **Admission** €5; €2.50 reductions; free under-26s, students, all 1st Sun of mth.

This contemporary art museum's collection offers a stunning snapshot of French art from 1950 to the present, with installations by Gilles Barbier, Jesús Rafael Soto and Christian Boltanski.

Musée Fragonard

7 av du Général de Gaulle, 94704 Maisons-Alfort (01.43.96.71.72, http://musee.vet-alfort.fr). M° Ecole Vétérinaire de Maisons-Alfort. **Open** 2-6pm Wed-Sun. Closed Aug. **Admission** €7; free under-26s. **No credit cards**.

In 18th-century French medical schools, study aids were produced in one of two ways. They were either sculpted in coloured wax or made from the real things – organs, limbs, tangled vascular systems – dried or preserved in formaldehyde. Veterinary surgeon Honoré Fragonard was a master of the second method, and many of his most striking works are now on display here. Most grandiose of all, *Cavalier de l'apocalypse* is a flayed man on the back of a flayed galloping horse, inspired by a painting by Dürer.

BOULOGNE & THE WEST

The capital's most desirable suburbs lie to the west. La Défense, Neuilly-sur-Seine, Boulogne-Billancourt, Levallois-Perret and, over the river, Issy-les-Moulineaux have become accepted business addresses for Parisians.

Boulogne-Billancourt is the main town and a lively centre in its own right. In 1320, the Gothic Eglise Notre-Dame was begun in tribute to a miraculous statue of the Virgin that washed up at Boulogne-sur-Mer. By the 18th century, Boulogne was known for its wines and laundries, then, early in the 20th century, for its artist residents (Landowski, Lipchitz, Chagall, Gris), whereas Billancourt was known for car manufacturing, aviation and its film studios.

In the 1920s and '30s, Boulogne-Billancourt was proud of its modernity: Tony Garnier built the elegant new town hall on avenue André-Morizet; a new post office, apartments and schools all went up in the modern style; and private houses were built by the leading avant-garde architects of the day – Le Corbusier, Mallet-Stevens, Perret, Lurçat, Pingusson and Fischer. The **Musée des Années 30** focuses on artists and architects who lived or worked in the town at the time. The glass-fronted apartment block by Le Corbusier – including the flat where he lived from 1933 to 1965 – can be visited each Saturday at 24 rue Nungesser et Coli (reserve on 01.42.88.75.72, www.fondationlecorbusier.asso.fr).

In the 19th century, riverside towns such as **Chatou**, **Asnières** and **Argenteuil** became places of entertainment – for promenades, *guinguettes* and rowing on the Seine – as depicted in many Impressionist paintings.

EXPLORE

At Rueil-Malmaison, the romantic **Château de Malmaison** was loved by Napoleon and Josephine. Josephine had a second château, **La Petite Malmaison** (229bis av Napoléon-Bonaparte), built nearby. The empress is buried in the Eglise St-Pierre St-Paul in the old centre, as is her daughter Hortense de Beauharnais, Queen of Holland and mother of Napoleon III.

Suresnes, across the Seine from the Bois de Boulogne, has been a wine-producing village since Roman times, and still celebrates the Fête des Vendanges every autumn. The 162m (532ft) Mont Valérien was a place of pilgrimage. In 1841, a huge fortress was built here to defend Paris. It was occupied by the German army in World War II; French *résistants* were brought here at night to be shot. The fortress still belongs to the French army, and is the centre of its eaves-dropping network. On the surrounding hill is the **American Cemetery** (190 bd de Washington), which contains the graves of American soldiers from World Wars I and II.

St-Germain-en-Laye is a smart suburb with a historic centre and a château. Henri II lived here with his wife Catherine de Médicis and his mistress Diane de Poitiers; it was here also that Mary Queen of Scots grew up, Louis XIV was born and the deposed James II lived for 12 years. Napoléon III turned the château into the **Musée d'Archéologie Nationale**.

Château de Malmaison

Av du Château, 92500 Rueil-Malmaison (01.41.29.05.55, www.chateau-malmaison.fr). RER La Défense then bus 258. **Open** times vary. **Admission** €6.50; €5 reductions; free under-18s, under-26s (EU citizens), all 1st Sun of mth. PMP.
Napoleon and Josephine's love nest, bought by Josephine in 1799, was the emperor's favourite retreat during the Consulate (1800-03). After their divorce, Napoleon gave the château to his ex, who died here in 1814. The couple redesigned the entrance as a military tent; you can see Napoleon's office, the billiard room and Josephine's tented bedroom.

★ [FREE] Mémorial de la France Combattante

Rue du Professeur-Léon-Bernard, 92150 Suresnes (01.47.28.46.35, www.mont-valerien.fr). Train to Suresnes-Mont-Valérien/RER La Défense then bus 160, 360 or tram 2. **Open** tour times vary (see website for details). **Admission** free.
Sixteen bronze sculptures by 16 artists represent France's struggle for liberation. Behind an eternal flame, the crypt contains tombs of 16 heroes from 16 French battles in World War II. The memorial was built on the site where Resistance members were brought from prisons in Paris. A staircase from within the crypt leads visitors inside the curtain wall, then up to the chapel where prisoners were locked before execution, and down to the Clairière des Fusillés, the clearing where they were shot. The chapel walls were covered in the prisoners' last graffiti; it also contains five of the wooden firing posts. More than 1,000 men were shot here (women were deported). A monument lists the names of victims.

Musée Albert Kahn

10-14 rue du Port, 92100 Boulogne-Billancourt (01.55.19.28.00, www.albert-kahn.hauts-de-seine.net). M° Boulogne – Pont de Saint-Cloud. **Open** 11am-6pm Tue-Sun (until 7pm May-Sept). **Admission** €4; €2.50 reductions; free under-12s & all 1st Sun of mth.
The spectacular ten-acre *jardin* alone makes a visit here worthwhile: each section is modelled on a garden from around the world. Albert Kahn was an early 20th-century banker and philanthropist who financed several 'discovery' missions across the world. His main legacy is 'Les Archives de la Planète' on show here – a fascinating collection of film and snapshots brought back from missions in over 60 countries.

Musée des Années 30

Espace Landowski, 28 av André-Morizet, 92100 Boulogne-Billancourt (01.55.18.53.00, www. annees30.com). M° Marcel Sembat. **Open** 11am-6pm Tue-Sun. Closed 2wks Aug. **Admission** (incl Musée-Jardin Paul Landowski) €6; €4 reductions; free under-16s.
The Musée des Années 30 highlights just how much second-rate art was produced in the 1930s, though there are decent modernist sculptures by the Martel brothers, graphic designs, and Juan Gris still lifes and drawings. The star exhibits are the designs by avant-garde architects Auguste Perret, Le Corbusier and Louis-Raymond Fischer.

Musée d'Archéologie Nationale

Château St-Germain, pl Charles-de-Gaulle, 78105 St-Germain-en-Laye (01.39.10.13.00, www.musee-archeologienationale.fr). RER St-Germain-en-Laye. **Open** 10am-5pm Mon, Wed-Sun. **Admission** €7; €5.50 reductions; free under-18s, all 1st Sun of mth.
This awe-inspiring museum traces France's rich archaeological heritage. The redesigned Neolithic galleries feature statue-menhirs, female figures and an ornate tombstone from Cys-la-Commune.

Musée Belmondo

14 rue de L'Abreuvoir, 92100 Boulogne-Billancourt (01.55.18.54.40). M° Boulogne Jean Jaurès. **Open** 2-6pm Tue-Fri; 11am-6pm Sat, Sun. **Admission** €6; €4 reductions; free under-16s & all 1st Sun of mth.
Jean-Paul Belmondo's father, Paul, was one of France's most important 20th-century sculptors. The space is an interior designer's dream – the mix of stark white, black and timber materials lends a different mood to each section, and several of the rooms harbour alcoves in which Belmondo's sculptures sit enticingly.

EXPLORE

Arts & Entertainment

Children

For all its commotion and traffic-clogged boulevards, the capital is actually a very child-friendly place to visit. Most Parisians have to raise their children in gardenless apartments, so the city powers ensure that there is plenty of provision for youngsters to expend their energy outside the home: every *arrondissement* has spaces with playgrounds (including a brand new adventure playground at Les Halles), and in big parks such as the Jardin du Luxembourg and Buttes-Chaumont, pony rides, sandpits, swings, puppet shows and boating ponds spice up the childhood of many a young Parisian. And now a section of the Left Bank has been pedestrianised and transformed into Les Berges (www.lesberges.paris.fr), kids can sample everything from climbing walls and running tracks to tepees and hopscotch along the banks of the Seine.

WHAT'S ON WHEN

Paris's museums and other attractions cater to children as well as adults, and also offer blissful opportunities to offload your kids on to someone else with children's workshops, held on Saturdays and Wednesdays during the school year, and daily during school holidays. If your children don't speak French, you can usually request an English speaker in advance. To find out what's coming up, contact the individual museums or check out www.paris.fr. Listings magazines *Pariscope*, *L'Officiel des Spectacles*, *Figaroscope* (with Wednesday's *Le Figaro*) and Télérama's *Sortir* all have kids' sections; and the free bi-monthly magazine *Paris-Mômes* is distributed with daily newspaper *Libération* in the city's toy shops and public libraries.

Sightseeing with children can be made easier with planning. Queues at prime spots such as the **Eiffel Tower** (*see p230*), **Louvre** (*see p64*) and the towers at **Notre-Dame** (*see p51*) are less disheartening in the morning.

GETTING AROUND

One word of advice: walk whenever possible. The métro is difficult to negotiate with babies and toddlers. Two of you might just manage a pushchair, but lone travellers won't and passers-by are notoriously selfish about helping out. If your babe is small enough for a baby carrier, it will save you a lot of hassle when navigating the tight turnstiles and never-ending staircases. Also try to travel between 10.30am and 5pm to avoid the rush-hour crowds. The driverless line 14 (St-Lazare to Olympiades) is a big hit with kids, who can sit at the front and peer down the tunnel as the train advances; the mostly overground lines six (Nation to Charles de Gaulle Étoile) and two (Nation to Porte Dauphine) offer attractive city views; a number of RER stations have lifts, although they are frequently broken.

Buses, on the other hand, are easier thanks to priority seats near the front for passengers with young children; many, such as nos.24, 63 and 95 (www.ratp.fr), pass numerous sights. Three-to 11-year-olds qualify for a half-price *carnet* (a book of ten tickets) for all transport, including the Montmartrobus minibus and Montmartre funicular. Taxi drivers will usually take a family of four (charging €1 to carry a pushchair and a little extra for the fourth person). If you're stuck, try **G7 taxis** (36.07, www.taxisg7.fr), which has an English-speaking booking line.

For older kids, the addition of extra cycle paths across the centre (especially along the Seine, up the Canal St-Martin and along the Canal de l'Ourcq) makes a spin *en famille* an enjoyable way to get around the city while seeing the sights. Short distances are easily covered using the city's **Vélib** self-service scheme (www.velib.fr; *see p368*), and a new book, *Paris à Vélib* (also available in English), maps out seven scenic cycle routes around the city.

For day-long fun try **Paris à Vélo c'est Sympa** (22 rue Alphonse Baudin, 11th, 01.48.87.60.01, www.parisvelosympa.com). For a day out in beautiful surroundings, the Bois de Vincennes in the east and the Bois de Boulogne in the west provide woodlands, picnic areas, boating lakes and lawns.

EATING OUT

Affordable **Chartier** (7 rue du Fbg-Montmartre, 9th, 01.47.70.86.29, www.restaurant-chartier.com) is always a fun place to take the kids, with its belle époque dining room and waiters clad in black and white. Picky eaters can't help but love the timeless *steak-frites* at mini-chain **Relais d'Entrecote** (www.relaisentrecote.fr) where the only option is, well, steak and chips covered in the restaurant's secret sauce. Get there early to avoid a lengthy queue, but relax knowing there'll be no menu to translate. **Tokyo Eat** at the Palais de Tokyo (13 av du Président-Wilson, 16th, 01.47.20.00.29, www.palaisdetokyo.com) is good too, with wacky decor and round, family-sized tables. Everything at **Bogato** (7 rue Liancourt, 14th, 01.40.47.03.51, www.chezbogato.fr, *photos p244*) is designed around temptation. Kids will be in sweet heaven as they sample smooth Nutella tarts, cherry cheesecakes, chocolate-coated marshmallows and Cheshire Cat shortbreads with an edible rice paper smile.

BABIES & TODDLERS

Always pack a portable changing mat. A facility worth remembering is the WC chalet in the Jardin du Luxembourg, where €0.60 gives you access to loos with a padded changing table; the **Galeries Lafayette** and **Printemps** (for both, *see p83*) department stores have clean, well-equipped nappy-changing facilities, as does the **Poussette Café** (*see p120*). Breastfeeding in public is more common than ever, but still often frowned upon, so take a scarf for places where modesty is essential, or choose a quiet corner.

A city break with tots in tow doesn't have to mean missing out on the city's galleries and museums. Almost all of the main attractions have child-friendly activities or green spaces nearby – always handy as a reward for good behaviour. There's a carefully tended garden

THE TASTIEST SPOTS FOR A PICNIC

Parc des Buttes-Chaumont. *See p249*.
Jardin du Luxembourg. *See p249*.
Parc de la Villette. *See p249*.
Bois de Boulogne. *See p108*.
Bois de Vincennes. *See p156*.

by Notre-Dame, and the dignified **Musée Rodin** (*see p225*) has outdoor distractions such as a sandpit to dig in, a sculpture-filled garden to explore (free entry to parents with a pushchair) and a tempting ice-cream stand. And if the heady heights of the Eiffel Tower prove too daunting, more down-to-earth amusements can be found at the adjacent Champ de Mars, with its play areas and seasonal donkey rides; or there are old-style merry-go-rounds by the river.

BABYSITTING

Many hotels can organise babysitting (ask when you reserve). The **American Church in Paris** (65 quai d'Orsay, 7th, 01.40.62.05.00, www.acparis.org) has a noticeboard displaying ads from English-speaking babysitters and au pairs; **Baby Sitting Services** (01.46.21.33.16, www.babysittingservices.com) can organise babysitting at short notice.

MUSEUMS & SIGHTSEEING

Most museums offer children's workshops (in French) on Wednesday afternoons, at weekends and in the holidays. At the **Louvre** (*see p64*) the programme for kids varies from learning about facial expressions in paintings to Egyptian sculpture. Next door, the **Musée des Arts Décoratifs** (*see p64*) offers hands-on art workshops for ages four to 14 and special tours (tailored to different age groups). The **Palais de Tokyo** (*see p96*) has inventive 'Tok Tok' story-reading for three- to five-year-olds, workshops for five- to seven-year-olds and family visits (4.30pm Sun), often led by notable contemporary artists. The **Musée Rodin** (*see p225*) runs children's clay workshops.

★ Centre Pompidou – Galerie des Enfants
Rue St-Martin, 4th (01.44.78.12.33, www.centrepompidou.fr/enfants). M° Hôtel de Ville or Rambuteau/RER Châtelet Les Halles. **Open** *Museum* 11am-9pm Mon, Wed-Sun. *Workshops* most Wed, Sat & Sun afternoons & school holidays. **Admission** *Museum* €11-€13; €9-€10 reductions; free under-18s, under-26s (EU citizens). *Workshops* €10 (1 child & 1 adult). **Map** p402 K5.

Bogato. See p243.

In this ground-floor gallery, wonderfully thought-out exhibitions introduce children to interesting aspects of modern art, design and architecture. Kids are kept enthralled with interactive elements and the opportunity to touch. There are also hands-on workshops for three- to 12-year-olds, family workshops and a 13/16 studio for teens. Audio guides for six- to 12-year-olds can also be hired for €4. If you just fancy a gawp over the rooftops from the sixth floor, it's €4 (free under-26s). Outside, look for the colourful Stravinsky fountain on the south side.

Cité de l'Architecture
Palais de Chaillot, 1 pl du Trocadéro, 16th (01.58.51.52.00, www.citechaillot.fr). Mº Trocadéro. **Open** 11am-7pm Mon, Wed, Fri-Sun; 11am-9pm Thur. **Admission** €8; €6 reductions; free under-18s, under-26s (EU citizens). **Map** p400 B5.
More than 850 life-size copies of France's architectural treasures (including portions of great cathedrals such as Chartres) make for a fascinating visit for children of all ages. To help them understand the exhibits, colourful interactive games are dotted around the permanent displays, so they can try their hand at architecture and learn the concepts of Romanesque and Gothic as they create fantastical animal heads, design stained-glass windows or build a Romanesque arch. On Wednesday and Saturday afternoons, three- to seven-year-olds can have a go at doing some building themselves with wooden blocks. Entry is €8 and you don't need to reserve (just turn up about 30 minutes beforehand).

Etoiles du Rex
1 bd Poissonnière, 2nd (08.25.05.44.05, www.legrandrex.com). Mº Bonne Nouvelle. **Open** 10am-7pm Wed-Sun (tours leave every 5mins); daily during school holidays. **Admission** €11; €9 under-12s. **Map** p402 J4.

The slick but cheesy 50-minute backstage tour of the glorious art deco Grand Rex cinema is a treat for any kids with acting aspirations. Be prepared to ham your heart out when, propelled by automatic doors, lifts and mystery voices, you visit the projection room, climb behind the giant screen and are thrust into a whirlwind of sound dubbing, special effects and an audition for *King Kong*.

Grévin
10 bd Montmartre, 9th (01.47.70.85.05, www.grevin.com). Mº Grands Boulevards. **Open** 10am-6.30pm (last admission 5.30pm) Mon-Fri; 10am-7pm (last admission 6pm) Sat, Sun. **Admission** €23.50-€30; €13.50-€20.50 reductions; free under-6s. **Map** p402 H4.
This wonderfully kitsch version of Madame Tussauds is a hit with kids, who can have their photo taken alongside waxworks of showbiz stars and personalities such as Zinédine Zidane, Brigitte Bardot, the Queen and Barack Obama, plus new arrivals such as Lady Gaga, Penélope Cruz and Scrat from *Ice Age*. Landmark historical moments, such as Neil Armstrong walking on the moon, are re-enacted in the 'snapshots of the 20th century' area; a small gallery at the top of a spiral staircase near the end shows how waxworks are made; and an impressive hall of mirrors (designed by France's fetish illusionist Arturo Brachetti and with music by Manu Katche) plunges you into scenes such as an Aztec temple.
▶ *On Saturday and Sunday afternoons during termtime there are special children's guided tours (French only) for seven- to 12-year-olds (€20.50).*

Musée des Arts et Métiers
60 rue Réaumur, 3rd (01.53.01.82.00, www. arts-et-metiers.net). Mº Arts et Métiers. **Open** 10am-6pm Tue, Wed, Fri-Sun; 10am-9.30pm

Thur. **Admission** €6.50; €4.50 reductions; free under-18s, under-26s (EU citizens), all 1st Sun of mth & after 6pm Thur. *Audio guides* €5. **Map** p402 K5.

Abbot Grégoire founded the fascinating 'arts and trades' museum in the late 18th century as 'a store for useful, new inventions'. Today, it thrills budding scientists, mechanics, astronomers, pilots or kids simply curious about the world around them with highlights that include Foucault's original pendulum, used by physician Léon Foucault in 1851 to make the rotation of the earth visible to the human eye; Clément Ader's steam-powered Avion III, officially the world's first working plane (1897); and Henry Ford's Model T car.

Musée des Egouts

Entrance opposite 93 quai d'Orsay, by Pont de l'Alma, 7th (01.53.68.27.81). M° Alma-Marceau/ RER Pont de l'Alma. **Open** *May-Sept* 11am-5pm Mon-Wed, Sat, Sun. *Oct-Apr* 11am-4pm Mon-Wed, Sat, Sun. **Admission** €4.30; €3.50 reductions; free under-6s. **Map** p400 D5.

The sewer museum retraces the pungent history of all 2,100km (1,305 miles) of Paris's underworld through a genuinely fascinating series of films, exhibits and a trip through the tunnels. Go early, before all of Paris's homes and restaurants are functioning at full capacity, to avoid the worst of the odours. During bad weather, visiting times may change or the museum may close as sudden surges in water can make the sewers dangerous.

Musée Gourmand du Chocolat

28 bd de Bonne Nouvelle, 10th (01.42.29.68.60, www.museeduchocolat.fr). M° Bonne Nouvelle. **Open** 10am-6pm daily. **Admission** €9; €6-€8 reductions; free under-6s. **Map** p402 J4.

The chocolate museum – need we say any more? Choco-Story traces the history of every child's passion. The first part explores its Mayan and Aztec origins, before moving on to its introduction to Europe. The third part delves into chocolate today, including a demonstration of how it's made, a mere hurdle before getting to every kid's favourite part – the gift shop. Finish the visit off with a tasty hot chocolate (€3).

IN THE KNOW MASTER CHEF

Elsa and Emmanuelle Condet run **Atelier Cake** (www.cakeletraiteur.fr), a bread-baking workshop for ages six and up. The 90-minute class is held in a purpose-built studio and kitchen, where kids learn about different kinds of grains and flours, before getting up to their elbows in pastry dust. Children leave with a recipe and the loaf of bread they've baked.

Musée de la Magie

11 rue St-Paul, 4th (01.42.72.13.26, www.museedelamagie.com). M° St-Paul or Sully-Morland. **Open** 2-7pm Wed, Sat, Sun (open extra hours & days during school holidays, check website for details). **Admission** €9; €7 reductions. **No credit cards. Map** p409 L7.

Small kids love the distorting mirrors and putting their hands in the lion's mouth at this museum of magic and curiosities, which is housed in vaulted cellars. A short magic show is included in the visit – it's in French, but rabbits out of hats translate well into any language. There's a great automated museum too (extra charge), where 100 mechanical toys move into action before your kids' eyes.

Musée de la Musique

Parc de la Villette, 221 av Jean-Jaurès, 19th (01.44.84.44.84, www.cite-musique.fr). M° Porte de Pantin. **Open** noon-6pm Tue-Sat; 10am-6pm Sun. **Admission** €7; free under-26s. **Map** p403 inset.

This innovative music museum houses a gleamingly restored collection of instruments from the old Conservatoire, interactive computers and scale models of opera houses and concert halls. Visitors are supplied with an audio guide in a choice of languages, and the musical commentary is a joy, playing the appropriate instrument as you approach each exhibit. There are also regular free interactive workshops and concerts for children over seven.

★ Musée National de la Marine

Palais de Chaillot, 17 pl du Trocadéro, 16th (01.53.65.69.69, www.musee-marine.fr). M° Trocadéro. **Open** 11am-6pm Mon, Wed-Fri; 11am-7pm Sat, Sun. **Admission** €7-€10; €5 reductions; free under-18s, under-26s (EU citizens). **Map** p400 B5.

Sail your family back in time through 400 years of French naval history. Highlights include the *Océan*, a 19th-century sailing vessel equipped with an impressive 120 cannon; a gilded barge built for Napoleon; and some extravagant, larger-than-life figureheads, from serene-faced angels to leaping sea-horses. There are also dozens of model boats, dating from the 18th to the 20th century, and several old-fashioned divers' suits. Guided tours for children run during the school holidays.

Musée de la Poupée

Impasse Berthaud, 3rd (01.42.72.73.11, www.museedelapoupeeparis.com). M° Rambuteau. **Open** 1-6pm Tue-Sun. **Admission** €8; €4-€6 reductions; free under-3s. **No credit cards. Map** p406 L7.

This small, private museum and doll hospital enchants little girls with its collection of some 500 dolls (mostly of French origin) and their accompanying accessories and pets, which are arranged in thematic tableaux. A few teddies and quacking

ARTS & ENTERTAINMENT

ducks are thrown in for young boys, and storytelling sessions and workshops (along the lines of making doll's clothes or miniature food for dolls' houses) are held on Wednesday afternoons (in French, reserve in advance; €10-€14). There's even a *clinique pour poupées* if your doll is falling apart at the seams.

★ Muséum National d'Histoire Naturelle

36 rue Geoffroy-St-Hilaire, 2 rue Bouffon, 57 rue Cuvier, 5th (01.40.79.30.00, www.mnhn.fr). Mº Gare d'Austerlitz or Jussieu. **Open** 10am-6pm Mon, Wed-Sun. **Admission** *Grande Galerie de l'Evolution* €7; €5 reductions; free under-4s. *Galeries de Paléontologie et d'Anatomie Comparée* €7; €5 reductions; free under-26s. *Galerie des Enfants* €9; €7 reductions; free under-4s. *Combined 2-day ticket for all sites* €25; €20 reductions. **Map** p406 K9.

At the Natural History Museum's impressive Grande Galerie de l'Evolution, stuffed creatures parade majestically through their various habitats. Animals of all kinds teach children about the diversity of nature and, in the endangered and vanished section (where a dodo takes pride of place), about the importance of protecting them. Also in the Jardin des Plantes complex are the small Ménagerie zoo (*see right*); the bony remains of fish, birds, monkeys, dinosaurs and humans in the Galerie de Paléontologie et d'Anatomie Comparée; and the excellent Galerie des Enfants. This 600sq m space is specially designed to help children increase their awareness of the planet's future through three different environments – the city (Paris), the river (La Bassée), and the tropical forest (Kayapo native land in Brazil). Finally, scaling things up to planetary level, they can get to grips with a brief history of life and major ecological issues such as global warming, before finding out what action they can take now and in the future.

★ Stade de France

Guided visits via entrance Porte G, Stade de France, Seine St-Denis (01.55.93.00.00, tours 08.92.70.09.00, www.stadefrance.com). Mº St-Denis Porte de Paris/RER Stade de France St-Denis. **Tours** *French* every 2hrs 11am-5pm daily (every hr except lunchtime Apr-Aug). *English* 10.30am, 2.30pm daily. **Admission** €15; €10-€12 reductions; free under-5s.

Football- and rugby-crazy kids will absolutely love the behind-the-scenes tours of France's handsome national sports stadium. After a quick scan of the newly renovated museum (featuring photos, football shirts and electric guitars from the rock stars who also play here), the tour begins by sitting in the stands and ends with a runout through the tunnel to the sound of applause. On the way, you can visit the changing and shower rooms and learn about the on-site hospital and prison cells. On match or concert days, tours are not available.

AQUARIUMS & ZOOS

Cinéaqua

2 av des Nations Unies, 16th (01.40.69.23.23, www.cineaqua.com). Mº Trocadéro. **Open** 10am-7pm daily. **Admission** €20.50; €13-€16 reductions; free under-3s. **Map** p400 B5.

Paris's first 'ocean entertainment centre' is a hybrid aquarium-cinema complex containing more than 500 species of fish, invertebrates, sharks and coral, along with several film screens. There are kids' clubs, with face-painting and games, from 2pm to 5pm daily, plus a touch pool offering the chance to stroke carp and sturgeon. The section on the Seine is fascinating.

Ménagerie du Jardin des Plantes

57 rue Cuvier, 5th (01.40.79.37.94, www.mnhn.fr). Mº Gare d'Austerlitz, Jussieu or Place Monge. **Open** 9am-5pm daily. **Admission** €11; €9 reductions; free under-4s. **Map** p406 K8.

Heads rolled during the Terror, leaving many an aristocratic collection of exotic animals without a home. This *ménagerie* became the solution in 1794. Nowadays, its inhabitants include vultures, monkeys, orang-utans, ostriches, flamingos, a century-old turtle plus another one rescued from the sewers, a lovely red panda and lots of satisfyingly scary spiders and snakes. There's a petting zoo with farm animals for small kids, and older ones can zoom in on microscopic species in the Microzoo.

Palais de la Porte Dorée Aquarium Tropical

293 av Daumesnil, 12th (01.53.59.58.60, www.palais-portedoree.fr). Mº Porte Dorée. **Open** 10am-5.30pm Tue-Fri; 10am-7pm Sat, Sun. **Admission** €5; €3.50 reductions; free under-4s. **No credit cards.**

The basement of this art deco palace, built for the Colonial Exhibition in 1931, contains the small but much-loved city aquarium. Four alligators were introduced recently when the last of the aquarium's original crocodiles, brought from Senegal in 1948, died; other watery residents include cuttlefish, sharks and luminous deep-water species.

▶ *Palais de la Porte Dorée is also home to the Cité Nationale de l'Histoire de l'Immigration (see p157).*

Parc de Thoiry

78770 Thoiry-en-Yvelines (01.34.87.53.76, www.thoiry.net). 45km (28 miles) west of Paris; by car A13, A12, then N12 towards Dreux until Thoiry. **Open** times vary, see website for details. **Admission** *Safari park, park & château* €28.50; €12.50-€26 reductions; free under-3s.

As well as a beautiful château, the Parc de Thoiry houses one of Europe's first animal reserves. Follow the long safari park trail, accessible only by car, and see zebras rub their noses over your windscreen and bears amble down tracks. In the adjoining zoo, rarities include Siberian lynx and Tonkean macaques.

ARTS & ENTERTAINMENT

PERFORMING ARTS

When school's out on Wednesday afternoons, at weekends and during holidays, fairytales, fables and folk stories keep children entertained at the city's theatres and *café-théâtres*. The varied programme at the **Théâtre Dunois** (7 rue Louise-Weiss, 13th, 01.45.84.72.00, www.theatredunois.org) is almost entirely geared towards children. For children's theatre in an unusual setting, the **Abricadabra Péniche Antipode** (opposite 55 quai de Seine, 19th, 01.42.03.39.07, www.penicheantipode.fr) is a riverboat on the Canal de l'Ourcq.

In general, children's films are dubbed into French, but you can see VO (*version originale*) screenings of the latest Hollywood hits at most venues across town. Keep a lookout for kids' showings on Wednesdays and Saturday afternoons at the Cinémathèque Française and

ARTS & ENTERTAINMENT

ANIMAL MAGIC

Conservation is key at the handsomely revamped Parc Zoologique de Paris.

If you go down to the woods today, you're sure of a big surprise with lions, tigers, penguins, giraffes, baboons and a host of other animals once again roaming the Bois de Vincennes as the **Parc Zoologique de Paris** (www.parczoologiquedeparis.fr) reopens for business after a six-year revamp. The zoo was originally built as a temporary exhibition during the 1931 Colonial Fair, but its success led to the creation of a permanent site in 1934.

For years, the zoo's 65-metre 'Grand Rocher' (which conceals the water tower and is visible from the *périphérique*) was a legendary local landmark. But a lack of investment meant the whole place fell into disrepair in the 1980s, and concern for the animals' safety led to its closure in 2008.

Today's park, run by the Muséum National d'Histoire Naturelle (*see p246*), returns as a 'zoo of the future' with a series of 'biozones' that correspond to five global habitats: Patagonia, the Sahel (Africa), Europe, Madagascar and tropical French Guyana. The philosophy behind the project is simple. Man's enormous (and often damaging) impact on the environment during the last 50 years means that animal biodiversity is dwindling and eco-systems are being put under huge strain, and modern zoos can no longer thrive as attractions where caged creatures are treated like curiosities. Instead, they need to educate visitors and help to conserve endangered species – notably by linking up with other zoos around the world on joint breeding programmes and working to help to reintroduce certain species into the wild.

As a visitor, this means that you get to observe beautiful and endangered species in biozones that closely resemble the animals' natural habitat. And if you want to go one green step further, you can sponsor an animal (anything from an orange tomato frog to a hulking great rhinoceros) and contribute to its ongoing conservation.

IN THE KNOW GOING GREEN

Get a *diabolo menthe* in a café for a kid-friendly beverage. The alien-green drink is part mint syrup, part lemonade and all delicious. The freaky colour and minty taste is a cultural experience in itself, and it's inexpensive to boot.

L'Ecran des Enfants at the **Centre Pompidou** (*see p243*). The IMAX in La Villette's **Géode** (*see p251*) will keep kids enthralled too.

Circus

★ Cirque d'Hiver Bouglione
110 rue Amelot, 11th (01.47.00.28.81, www.cirquedhiver.com). M° Filles du Calvaire. **Shows** *Late Oct-mid Mar days vary.* **Admission** €27-€62. **Map** p409 L5.
This famous circus has been in the same family for decades. Crowds flock for its twice-yearly seasons, which include tigers, horses and very silly clowns.

Cirque Pinder
Pelouse de Reuilly, Bois de Vincennes, 12th (01.45.90.21.25, www.cirquepinder.com). M° Porte de Charenton or Porte Dorée. **Shows** *Mid Nov-mid Jan.* **Admission** prices vary.
Big cats are the stars of the show, but horses, elephants and monkeys also make Pinder the most traditional travelling circus in France.

Espace Chapiteaux
Parc de La Villette, 19th (01.40.03.75.75, www.villette.com). M° Porte de la Villette. **Shows** vary. **Admission** varies. **Map** p403 inset.
This big top hosts high-flying companies such as Cirque Plume, Centre National des Arts du Cirque and aerialists Les Arts Saut.

SWIMMING & SKATING

Aquaboulevard
4 rue Louis-Armand, 15th (01.40.60.10.00, www.aquaboulevard.com). M° Balard. **Open** 9am-11pm Mon-Thur, Sun; 9am-midnight Fri; 8am-midnight Sat; 8am-11pm Sun. **Admission** *6hrs* €22-€28; €15 reductions. **Map** p404 A10.
With year-round summer temperatures, this water park under a giant atrium is great fun for kids.

Patinoire Sonja Henie
Palais Omnisports de Paris-Bercy (01.40.02.60.67, www.bercy.fr). M° Bercy. **Open** *Sept-mid June* 3-6pm Wed; 9.30pm-12.30am Fri; 3-6pm, 9.30pm-12.30am Sat; 10am-noon, 3-6pm Sun. **Admission** €3-€5; €2.50-€4 reductions. **No credit cards. Map** p407 N9.

Bercy's Omnisports arena contains an ice rink, open on Wednesdays and weekends for skaters of all levels. Teenagers can also skate until late on Fridays and Saturdays, when disco lights colour the ice.

Piscine Butte-aux-Cailles
5 pl Paul-Verlaine, 13th (01.45.89.60.05). M° Place d'Italie. **Open** 7-8.30am, 11.30am-1.30pm, 4.30-9pm Tue; 7am-7pm Wed; 7-8.30am, 11.30am-6.30pm Thur, Fri; 7-8.30am, 10am-6.30pm Sat; 8am-6pm Sun. **Admission** €3; €1.70 reductions.
This listed complex, built in the 1920s, has one main indoor pool and two outdoor pools (open in the summer). The water is a temptingly warm 28°C, thanks to the natural sulphurous spring.

★ Piscine Josephine-Baker
Quai François-Mauriac, 13th (01.56.61.96.50). M° Quai de la Gare. **Open** 7-8.30am, 1-9pm Mon, Wed, Fri; 7-8.30am, 1-11pm Tue, Thur; 11am-8pm Sat; 10am-8pm Sun. **Admission** €3; €1.70 reductions. **Map** p407 M10.
Moored on the Seine by the Bibliothèque Nationale, the pool boasts a 25m main pool (with sliding glass roof), a paddling pool and café, and a busy schedule of exercise classes.

PARKS & THEME PARKS

Disneyland Paris/Walt Disney Studios Park
Marne-la-Vallée (www.disneylandparis.com). 32km E of Paris. RER A or TGV Marne-la-Vallée-Chessy. By car, A4 exit 14. **Open** Times vary,

Disneyland Paris.

Parc Astérix.

see website for details. **Admission** Prices vary, see website for details.

Young ones will get a real kick out of Fantasyland, with its Alice maze, Sleeping Beauty's castle and teacup rides. Walt Disney Studios focuses on special effects and the tricks of the animation trade. The Twilight Zone Tower of Terror sends daredevils plummeting down a 13-storey lift shaft and the Rock 'n' Roller Coaster in the Back Lot takes off at mega speed, before hurtling round hairpin turns and loops to the funky rhythm of Aerosmith. Themed parades and shows in the streets provide entertainment while running off to the next ride. Consider a Fastpass to avoid some of the frustrating queues.

Jardin d'Acclimatation
*Bois de Boulogne, 16th (01.40.67.90.85,
www.jardindacclimatation.fr). Mº Les Sablons.*
Open *Apr-Sept* 10am-7pm daily. *Oct-Mar* 10am-
6pm daily. **Admission** €3; €1.50 reductions;
free under-3s.
Founded in 1860, this amusement park and garden has animals, a Normandy-style farm and an aviary, plus boat rides, a funfair with mini rollercoasters, flying chairs, the Enchanted House for children aged two to four and two playgrounds. There's also a place to steer radio-controlled boats and mini golf. Many of the attractions cost €2.70 a go; others are free. A miniature train runs from Porte Maillot through the Bois de Boulogne to the park entrance, and has space for pushchairs (€2.70 return; €4.20-€5.70 with entry included).

Jardin du Luxembourg
*Main access 2 rue Auguste Compte, 6th.
Mº Odéon/RER Luxembourg.* **Open** dawn-dusk
daily. **Map** p408 H8.
The 25-hectare park is a prized family attraction. Kids come from across the city for its pony rides, ice-cream stands, puppet shows, pedal karts, sand-pits, metal swingboats and merry-go-round. The playground has an entrance fee.

★ Parc Astérix
*60128 Plailly (08.26.30.10.40, www.parcasterix.fr).
36km N of Paris. By coach from the Louvre, the*
*Eiffel Tower or RER Roissy-Charles de Gaulle 1
(check website for times). By car, A1 exit Parc
Astérix.* **Open** Times vary, see website for details.
Admission €46; €37 reductions; free under-3s.
Parking €10.
The park is split into Ancient Greece, the Roman Empire, the Land of the Vikings, the indomitable Gaulish Village and the all-new Egypt zone. Thrill-seekers can defy gravity on Goudurix, Europe's largest rollercoaster, while younger kids get wet on the Grand Splatch log flume. For a real rush of blood to the head, though, climb aboard the brand-new Oziris inverted rollercoaster. For some serious hand-shaking, Astérix, Obélix and friends wander around and a jamboree of live acts pumps up the pace.

Parc des Buttes-Chaumont
*Rue Botzaris, rue Manin, rue de Crimée, 19th.
Mº Buttes Chaumont.* **Open** *Winter* 7am-8pm
daily. *Summer* 7am-10pm daily. **Map** p403 N2.
This area, which was formerly mined for gypsum, was turned into a sumptuous park under Napoleon III. Spectacular in every way (including the views over Paris), it is a family magnet with Punch and Judy stands, pony rides, sandpits, waterfalls, picnic and games areas and drinks stands. The hilly park makes for some treacherous hikes upwards, but that just means there's fantastic tumbling potential down the grassy slopes.

★ Parc de la Villette
*Av Corentin-Cariou, 19th (01.40.03.75.75,
www.villette.com). Mº Porte de la Villette.
Av Jean-Jaurès, 19th. Mº Porte de Pantin.*
Map p403 inset.
Aside from being home to Europe's largest science museum (which also contains the brilliant Cité des Enfants, *see p161*), a music museum, an IMAX cinema, theatres, and concert and exhibition venues, the city's former abattoir district is now made up of a succession of gardens and playgrounds. Jardin des Voltiges has climbing ropes and balancing games, and the modern Jardin des Dunes et Vents has pedal windmills, waves of bouncy tubes and giant hamster wheels. The whole place makes for a won-derful family day out.

ARTS & ENTERTAINMENT

Film

ARTS & ENTERTAINMENT

During the last couple of years, French films have set tongues wagging across the globe. Michel Hazanavicius's silent, black-and-white romcom *The Artist* became the most successful French film in history, winning three Golden Globes, seven BAFTAs, six Césars and five Oscars, including best actor for Jean Dujardin. Then Olivier Nakache and Eric Toledano's *Intouchables*, a moving comedy about a quadriplegic millionaire and his petty-criminal carer, raked in $391 million worldwide. Omar Sy became the first black actor to win a César and the Weinstein Company acquired the rights for a US remake. And most recently, *La Vie d'Adèle* (Blue is the Warmest Colour), an explicit portrait of two young women falling in love, picked up the Palme d'Or and controversy galore in 2013.

There has been plenty of small-screen success, too, including critically acclaimed zombie thriller *Les Revenants* (The Returned).

MOVIEGOING IN PARIS

Happily, the rapid rise of the multiplex hasn't meant a reduction in the variety of films on offer in Paris. Multiplexes regularly show films from Eastern Europe, Asia and South America, and countless independent cinemas continue to screen a hugely eclectic assortment of cult, classic and just plain obscure films. As well as retrospectives and cut-price promotions, there are often visits from directors and stars.

Local interest is strong enough to sustain several monthly movie magazines and there's a decent selection of specialist film bookshops. Finally, French DVD labels produce some of the most expertly curated discs in the world. At **Fnac** (www.fnac.com), you're more than likely to find American and British titles otherwise unavailable in the US or UK.

INFORMATION AND TICKETS

New releases hit the screens on Wednesdays. Hollywood is well represented, of course, but Paris audiences have a balanced cinematic diet that satisfies their appetite for international films as well as shorts and documentaries. On top of this there are the 150-plus annual releases funded or part-funded with French money (the French film industry is still the world's third largest, after the US and India).

For venues, times and prices, consult one of the city's two main weekly listings magazines: *L'Officiel des Spectacles* and *Pariscope*. *Films nouveaux* are new releases, *Exclusivités* are the also-showing titles, and *Reprises* means rep. For non-francophone flicks, look out for two letters somewhere near the title: VO (*version originale*)

IN THE KNOW
SIP WITH THE STARS

Walk past the ticket office of **Studio 28** (*see p254*) and a long corridor brings you out into a magical interior courtyard that opens up every afternoon as a bar, *salon de thé* and restaurant. Part of it has been left open as a summer terrace, lined with a vast fresco of French cinema's legendary stars – Delon and Bardot, Signoret and Montand, Fernandel and Jean Gabin, Belmondo and Jean Marais.

means a screening in the original language with French subtitles; VF (*version française*) means that it has been dubbed into French.

Buy tickets in the usual way at the cinema – for new blockbusters, it pays to buy in advance. Online booking may entail a fee. Seats are often discounted by 20 to 30 per cent at Monday or Wednesday screenings, and the Mairie sponsors cut-price promotions throughout the year. If you're in town for a while, it might be a good idea to pick up a *carte illimitée*, a season ticket that allows unlimited viewing: every multiplex chain offers a version.

CINEMAS
Giant screens & multiplexes

La Géode
26 av Corentin-Cariou, 19th (01.40.05.79.99, www.lageode.fr). M° Porte de la Villette.
Admission €12; €9 reductions. **Map** p403 inset.
The IMAX cinema at the Cité des Sciences occupies a shiny dome. The vast screen lets you experience 3D plunges through natural scenery, and adventures in which figures zoom out to grab you. *Photo p252.*

★ Le Grand Rex
1 bd Poissonnière, 2nd (08.92.68.05.96, www.legrandrex.com). M° Bonne Nouvelle.
Admission €7.50-€13; €6-€11 reductions.
Les Etoiles du Rex tour €11; €9 reductions.
Map p402 J4.
With its wedding-cake exterior and the largest auditorium in Europe (2,650 seats), this listed historical monument is one of the few cinemas to upstage whatever it screens. Its blockbuster programming (usually in French) is suited to its vast screen. There are six smaller screens too.
▶ *The Etoiles du Rex tour is a 50-minute, SFX-laden taste of movie magic.*

Max Linder Panorama
24 bd Poissonnière, 9th (01.48.24.00.47, www.maxlinder.com). M° Grands Boulevards.
Admission €9.20; €7.20 reductions. **Map** p402 J4.
This state-of-the-art cinema, with THX surround sound and an 18m (60ft) screen, is named after the dapper French silent comedian who owned it between 1914 and 1925. The walls and 700 seats are all black to prevent even the tiniest twinkle of reflected light distracting the audience from what's happening on the screen. Look for all-nighters and one-off showings of rare vintage films.

★ MK2 Bibliothèque
128-162 av de France, 13th (08.92.69.84.84, www.mk2.com). M° Bibliothèque François Mitterrand or Quai de la Gare. **Admission** €10.70; €4.90-€7.90 reductions; €20.08 monthly pass. **Map** p407 M10.

IN THE KNOW REEL PARIS

The French capital makes a handsome film set and **Set in Paris: Le Movie Tour** (www.setinparis.com) gives a wonderful introduction to some of its most recent big-screen close-ups. The brilliant thing about the coach tour is that on-board video screens show you clips of the very locations as you drive by. So just as Anne Hathaway chucks her mobile phone into the fountain at Place de la Concorde in the closing scenes of *The Devil Wears Prada*, Place de la Concorde appears on your left, same angle, same shot. You can also get yourself photographed where Gil waited for Hemingway's old Peugeot in *Midnight in Paris* and the vintage car will be Photoshopped in. There's something to learn for even the most obsessive film buff on this cheerful tour that's constantly being edited just for you.

The MK2 chain's flagship offers an all-in-one night out: 14 screens, four restaurants, a bar open until 5am at weekends and two-person 'love seats'. A paragon of imaginative programming, MK2 is growing all the time; it has added ten more venues in town.

UGC Ciné Cité Bercy
2 cour St-Emilion, 12th (08.92.70.00.00, www.ugc.fr). M° Cour St-Emilion. **Admission** €10.90; €4.90-€7.70 reductions; €20.08 monthly pass. **Map** p407 P10.
This ambitious 18-screen development screens art movies as well as mainstream fodder, and hosts regular meet-the-director events. The 19-screen UGC Ciné Cité Les Halles branch (7 place de la Rotonde, Nouveau Forum des Halles, 1st, 08.92.70.00.00), serves the same mix of cinema and events.

Showcases

Auditorium du Louvre
Musée du Louvre, 99 rue de Rivoli, 1st (01.40.20.55.00, www.louvre.fr). M° Palais Royal Musée du Louvre. **Admission** prices vary. **Map** p402 H5.
The 420-seat Auditorium du Louvre was designed by IM Pei, as part of the Mitterrand-inspired renovation of the Louvre. Film screenings are often related to current exhibitions at the museum; silent movies with accompanying live music are regulars.

Centre Pompidou
Rue St-Martin, 4th (01.44.78.12.33, www.centrepompidou.fr). M° Hôtel de Ville or Rambuteau. **Admission** €6; €4 reductions. **Map** p406 K6.

ARTS & ENTERTAINMENT

The varied programme at the Centre Pompidou features themed series, experimental and artists' films, and a weekly documentary session. This is also the venue for the Cinéma du Réel festival in March (www.cinereel.org).

Le Cinéma des Cinéastes
7 av de Clichy, 17th (08.92.68.97.17, www.cinema-des-cineastes.fr). M° Place de Clichy. **Admission** €9; €7 reductions. **Map** p401 G2.
Done out to evoke the studios of old, this three-screen showcase of world cinema holds meet-the-director sessions and festivals of classic, foreign, gay and documentary films. The cinema is also big on film for kids, and is one of the hosts of the Mon Premier Festival (www.monpremierfestival.org).

★ Cinémathèque Française
51 rue de Bercy, 12th (01.71.19.33.33, www.cinematheque.fr). M° Bercy. **Admission** *Films* €6.50; €3-€5.50 reductions. *Museum* €5; €2.50-€4 reductions; free under-6s. **Map** p407 N9.
Relocated to Frank Gehry's striking, spacious cubist building, the Cinémathèque Française boasts four screens, a bookshop, a restaurant, exhibition space and the Musée du Cinéma, where it displays a fraction of its huge collection of memorabilia. The Cinémathèque hosts retrospectives, cult movies, classics, experimental cinema and Q&A sessions.

Forum des Images
2 rue du Cinéma, Forum des Halles, 1st (01.44.76.63.00, www.forumdesimages.net). M° Les Halles. **Admission** €6; €4-€5 reductions. **Map** p402 J5.
Partly a screening venue for old and little-known movies, and partly an archive for every kind of film featuring Paris. The Forum's collection numbers over 6,500 documentaries, adverts, newsreels and films, from the Lumière brothers to 21st-century reportage.

La Géode. *See p251.*

Arthouses

Accattone
20 rue Cujas, 5th (01.46.33.86.86). M° Cluny La Sorbonne/RER Luxembourg. **Admission** €7; €6 Wed, students, under-20s (except Fri nights and weekends). **No credit cards. Map** p408 J8.
This tiny Latin Quarter cinema has a clear preference for old Italian arthouse. That said, there's still plenty of room on the rolling weekly programme for the likes of Buñuel, Oshima, Roeg and Ken Russell.

Action
Action Christine *4 rue Christine, 6th (01.43.25.85.78, www.actioncinemas.com). M° Odéon or St-Michel.* **Admission** €8; €6 reductions. **No credit cards. Map** p408 J7.
Grand Action *5 rue des Ecoles, 5th (01.43.54.47.62, www.legrandaction.com). M° Cardinal Lemoine.* **Admission** €9; €6.50 reductions. **No credit cards. Map** p406 K8.
A Left Bank stalwart, the Action group is renowned for screening new prints of old movies. It's heaven for anyone who's nostalgic for Tinseltown classics and quality US independents.

★ Le Balzac
1 rue Balzac, 8th (01.45.61.10.60, www.cinema balzac.com). M° George V. **Admission** €10; €6.50-€8 reductions. **No credit cards. Map** p400 D4.
Built in 1935 and boasting a mock ocean-liner foyer, Le Balzac scores highly for design and programming. Jean-Jacques Schpoliansky, whose grandfather opened the cinema in 1935, has been the manager for the last 40 years and is often found welcoming punters in person.

Le Champo
51 rue des Ecoles, 5th (01.43.54.51.60, www.lechampo.com). M° Cluny La Sorbonne or Odéon. **Admission** €8.50; €5.50-€6.50 reductions. **No credit cards. Map** p408 J7.
The two-screen Champo has been in operation for seven decades. Novel programming includes the occasional Nuits du Champo, a trio of films beginning at midnight and ending with breakfast (€15).

★ Le Chaplin Denfert
24 pl Denfert-Rochereau, 14th (www.cinema denfert.fr). M° Denfert Rochereau/RER Denfert Rochereau. **Admission** €8.90; €6-€7.50 reductions. **No credit cards. Map** p405 H10.
This charming little cinema offers a nicely eclectic repertory selection that ranges from François Ozon and Hayao Miyazaki to shorts and animation, as well as new-release foreign films.

Le Cinéma du Panthéon
13 rue Victor-Cousin, 5th (01.40.46.01.21, www.whynotproductions.fr/pantheon). RER Luxembourg. **Admission** prices vary. **Map** p408 J8.

ESSENTIAL PARIS FILMS

You're in film-set Paris the second you get off the train.

La Haine.

HOTEL DU NORD MARCEL CARNE (1938)

The Hôtel du Nord is, thanks to Carné's film, a national monument: it, and the adjacent iron footbridge and chunk of Canal St-Martin, were re-created in the studio by Alexandre Trauner. On the bridge, Arletty gives suitor Louis Jouvet the brush-off with the immortal 'Atmosphère! Est-ce que j'ai une gueule d'atmosphère?'

LES 400 COUPS FRANCOIS TRUFFAUT (1959)

Tearaway 13-year-old kid Antoine Doisnel (Jean-Pierre Léaud in his first role) gets around large parts of Paris, helping to launch the *nouvelle vague* on the way. His troubles start when he catches his mum in an adulterous clinch on place de Clichy. Still one of the cinema's most perceptive forays into childhood.

INTOUCHABLES OLIVIER NAKACHE & ERIC TOLEDANO (2011)

François Cluzet is Philippe, a wealthy man left paralysed by an accident. Interviewing for the job of carer, he's struck by Driss (Omar Sy), a street-smart criminal who's merely applying to receive benefits. He hires Driss and moves him into his Paris mansion. Bonding ensues, amid many raised eyebrows.

SUBWAY LUC BESSON (1985)

Safecracker Christophe Lambert hides out with a bunch of eccentric social misfits in the netherworld of the Paris métro as he attempts to escape from a wealthy businessman's wife (Isabelle Adjani) with whom he has fallen in love, from her husband's thugs and from the métro police in this electrically charged 1980s punk-chic fantasy.

LA HAINE MATHIEU KASSOVITZ (1995)

Twenty-four hours in the Paris projects: an Arab boy is critically wounded in hospital, gut-shot, and a police revolver has found its way into the hands of a young Jewish skinhead, Vinz (Cassel), who vows to even the score if his pal dies. A vital, scalding piece of work.

LE FABULEUX DESTIN D'AMELIE POULAIN JEAN-PIERRE JEUNET (2001)

Jean-Pierre Jeunet's rose-tinted Parisian romance stars the wonderful Audrey Tautou as Amélie, who works in a Montmartre café (Café des Deux Moulins, 15 rue Lépic) and has a revelation that her life's work should be to bring good to others. A thoroughly charming love poem to *la vie Parisienne.*

The Cinéma du Panthéon continues to screen new, often obscure international films, and hosts meet-the-director nights and discussions.

L'Entrepôt
7-9 rue Francis-de-Pressensé, 14th (01.45.40.07.50, www.lentrepot.fr). M° Pernety or Plaisance. **Admission** €8; €4-€6.50 reductions. **No credit cards. Map** p405 F10.
This multi-disciplinary arts centre and cinema is known for its leftfield documentaries, shorts, gay repertoire and productions from developing nations. Regular debates, poetry nights and concerts complete the programme.

Le Louxor
170 bd de Magenta, 10th (01.44.63.96.96, www.cinemalouxor.fr). M° Barbès-Rochechouart. **Admission** €9; €6-€7.50 reductions. **No credit cards. Map** p402 J2.
Opened in 1921, the Egyptian art deco Louxor fell on hard times after World War II and became a drug den, 1980s club and gay disco before being left abandoned for 25 years. It reopened triumphantly as a cinema in April 2013, with a new brief to promote cultural, artistic and educational projects. Enjoy a pre-show glass of red in the new upstairs bar.

Le Mac Mahon
5 av Mac-Mahon, 17th (01.43.80.24.81, www.cinemamacmahon.com). M° Charles de Gaulle Etoile. **Admission** €7; €5 reductions. **No credit cards. Map** p400 C3.
This single-screen, 1930s-era cinema has changed little since its 1960s heyday (tickets are still of the tear-off variety), when its all-American programming fostered the label '*mac-mahonisme*' among the buffs who haunted the place. Americana still makes up the bulk of what's on the screen.

Le Nouveau Latina
20 rue du Temple, 4th (01.42.78.47.86, www.lenouveaulatina.com). M° Hôtel de Ville. **Admission** €8.50; €7 reductions. **No credit cards. Map** p406 K6.
The exciting programming at this flag-bearer for Latin cultures runs the gamut from Argentinian to Romanian films.

IN THE KNOW NEW RELEASES

The last 12 months have seen the launch of several new film venues around town, including the **Fondation Jérôme Seydoux-Pathé** (www.fondation-jeromeseydoux-pathe.com), the renovation of the grand old **Louxor** cinema (*see above*) and a new arthouse multiplex, **Ciné-Lilas** (www.etoile-cinemas.com).

★ La Pagode
57bis rue de Babylone, 7th (01.45.55.48.48, www.etoile-cinemas.com). M° St-François-Xavier. **Admission** €9; €7.50 reductions. **No credit cards. Map** p405 F7.
This glorious edifice is not, as local legend might have it, a block-by-block import, but a 19th-century replica of a pagoda. Renovated in the 1990s, this is one of the loveliest cinemas in the world.

Studio 28
10 rue Tholozé, 18th (01.46.06.36.07, www.cinemastudio28.com). M° Abbesses or Blanche. **Admission** €8.50; €7 reductions. **No credit cards. Map** p401 H1.
Studio 28 was the venue for the first screening of Buñuel's scandalous *L'Age d'Or*. It offers a decent mixture of classics and recent movies, complete with Dolby sound and a civilised bar.

Studio Galande
42 rue Galande, 5th (01.43.54.72.71, www.studiogalande.fr). M° Cluny La Sorbonne or St-Michel. **Admission** €8; €6 reductions. **No credit cards. Map** p408 J7.
Some 20 different films are screened in subtitled versions at this venerable Latin Quarter venue every week: it's mostly international arthouse fare.

Festivals & events

Festival International de Films de Femmes
Maison des Arts, pl Salvador-Allende, 94040 Créteil (01.49.80.38.98, www.filmsdefemmes.com). M° Créteil-Préfecture. **Date** Mar.
Now in its 37th year, this highly regarded festival features a selection of retrospectives and new international films by female directors.

Côté Court
Ciné 104, 104 av Jean-Lolive, 93500 Pantin (01.48.91.24.91, www.cotecourt.org). M° Eglise de Pantin. **Date** June.
Côté Court puts on a great selection of new and old short films, shown at Ciné 104 and a handful of neighbouring venues.

★ Cinéma au Clair de Lune
Various venues (01.44.76.63.00, www.forumdesimages.net). **Date** Aug.
Night-time films on giant open-air screens in squares and public gardens around town.

★ L'Etrange Festival
Forum des Images, for listing see p252 (01.44.76.63.00, www.etrangefestival.com). **Date** Sept. **Map** p404 J5.
Explicit sex, gore and weirdness in the screenings and 'happenings' at this annual feast of all things unconventional draw large crowds.

Gay & Lesbian

Paris is home to a thriving LGBT community that is visibly involved in every walk of life – and right at the top of the tree sits Bertrand Delanoë, who came out two years before running for mayor. Local gays and lesbians say that they encounter very little, if any, discrimination during their day-to-day lives, and feel integrated into mainstream society. However, the annual Marche des Fiertés (Gay Pride), held in June, is a powerful reminder of how much the gay rights movement has accomplished over the last 30 years.

GETTING OUT AND ABOUT

Beaubourg and the '**gay Marais**' are particularly gay-friendly. Most of the dedicated venues are to be found in the area bounded by rue des Archives, rue Vieille-du-Temple and rue Ste-Croix-de-la-Bretonnerie. A light lunch, coffee or cocktail at a neighbourhood café will provide ample opportunity to check out the talent, and a casual stroll through the nearby streets will introduce you to a seductive selection of shops. Fetishists, funky fashionistas, bohemians and bibliophiles will each find a boutique to suit their fancy. A good place to start is **Les Mots à la Bouche**, where you can peruse the gay and lesbian press or pick up a few of the free monthly magazines listing the hottest events.

In the evening, kick off the action at a café or a restaurant before moving on to the bars and clubs, which don't really get going until after midnight. Start by mixing it up at the **Open Café** or the nearby red-hot **Raidd Bar**. The **Queen** on the Champs-Elysées remains a clubbing institution, as does the smaller and

more intimate **Le Tango**. The oldest gay club in Paris, **Le Club 18**, is always fun. Lesbians can find a few nice bars of their own on rue du Roi de Sicile.

Information and resources

Magazines *Têtu* (www.tetu.com) and *Préf* (www. prefmag.com) report on goings-on in gay life and have text in English; *La Dixième Muse* (www.la dixiememuse.com) provides similar information for lesbians. There are also several free bi-weekly publications, distributed in gay bookshops, bars and clubs, including *Tribumove* (www.tribumove. com). And for the girls, there's *Barbi(e)turix* (www.barbieturix.com). Two excellent websites provide regularly updated listings (in English) of all things gay and lesbian in the city: www.paris-gay.com and www.gayvox.com.

Centre Gai et Lesbien

63 rue Beaubourg, 3rd (01.43.57.21.47, www.centrelgbtparis.org). M° Arts et Métiers. **Open** 3.30-8pm Mon-Fri; 1-7pm Sat. *Library* 6-8pm Mon-Wed; 3-6pm Fri; 5-7pm Sat. **Map** p402 K6.
After many years based on rue Keller, the Centre Gai et Lesbien has now moved into more central digs in the Marais. In addition to providing information on topics ranging from the sociopolitical (if you don't know what rights gays and lesbians have or don't have in France, you can find out all you need to know on the subject here) to the biomedical (the latest developments in the treatment of HIV, where to get tested for free), this multifunctional centre and library also hosts meetings for a variety of support groups and associations.

THE BEST HANGOUTS

For big wigs and ballgowns
Crazyvores. See p258.

For bears and muscle bears
Le Bears' Den. See p256.

For backroom action
Next. See p260.

Gay Pride.

Inter-LGBT

c/o Maison des Associations du 3ème, boîte 8,
5 rue Perrée, 75003 Paris (01.72.70.39.22,
www.inter-lgbt.org). **Map** p409 L5.
The Interassociative Lesbienne, Gaie, Bi & Trans
is an umbrella group of some 50 LGBT associations.
It organises the Printemps des Assoces every April
and the annual Gay Pride March in June.

SOS Homophobie

08.10.10.81.35, www.sos-homophobie.org.
Open 6-10pm Mon-Fri; 2-4pm Sat; 6-8pm Sun
(until midnight 1st Mon of mth).
Victims of and witnesses to homophobic crimes and
discrimination can report them to this confidential
service, which offers support and publishes an
annual report on homophobia.

GAY PARIS
Bars & cafés

Banana Café

13 rue de la Ferronnerie, 1st (01.42.33.35.31,
www.bananacafeparis.com). M° Châtelet.
Open 6pm-6am daily. **Map** p402 J5.
With themed soirées, drag shows and go-go boys
that could have taught Joséphine Baker a few moves,
Banana Café is a solid choice for a night on the town.
The ground-floor bar and adjacent terrace serve up
happy hour drinks (6-11pm). Afterwards, patrons
are ushered inside from the terrace and, eventually,
downstairs for some dancing and go-go boy antics.

Le Bears' Den

6 rue des Lombards, 4th (01.42.71.08.20,
www.bearsden.fr). M° Châtelet or Hôtel de Ville.
Open 4pm-2am Mon-Fri; 4pm-4am Sat, Sun.
Map p406 J6.

The Bears' Den is a friendly local for bears, muscle
bears, chubbies and their admirers. Visit the website
for details on comically named theme nights such
as 'Charcuterie'.

★ Le Café Arena

29 rue St-Denis, 1st (01.45.08.15.16). M° Châtelet.
Open 9am-6am daily. **Map** p406 J5.
This bar-restaurant has a great terrace for people-
watching and friendly staff; it's still one of the
hottest rendezvous in Les Halles.

Café Cox

15 rue des Archives, 4th (01.42.72.08.00,
www.cox.fr). M° Hôtel de Ville. **Open** 5.30pm-
2am Mon-Thur; 4.30pm-2am Fri-Sun. **No credit
cards.** **Map** p409 K6.
Beefy, hairy, shaven-headed men congregate on the
pavement in front of Café Cox for post-work drinks.
DJs spin on Thursday nights and a lengthy happy
hour on Sunday keeps the beer flowing until 2am
before the crowds head elsewhere.

Le Duplex

25 rue Michel-le-Comte, 3rd (01.42.72.80.86,
www.duplex-bar.com). M° Hôtel de Ville or
Rambuteau. **Open** 8pm-2am Mon-Thur, Sun;
8pm-4am Fri, Sat. **Map** p409 K5.

IN THE KNOW TAKE PRIDE

Don't miss out on the action in June
as a stream of outrageous floats and
flamboyant costumes parade towards
Bastille for **Gay Pride** (www.gaypride.fr);
then there's an official *fête* and various
club events.

This small bar just round the corner from the Centre Pompidou caters to a thirtysomething crowd. It's a popular meeting place for various gay associations, with friendly staff and local art on the walls.

Etamine Café
13 rue des Ecouffes, 4th (01.44.78.09.62, www.etamine-cafe.com). M° St-Paul. **Open** 7pm-midnight Tue-Sun. **Map** p409 K6.
This simple café is located very close to the lesbian bars of the Marais, and offers a contemporary and inventive twist on old classics. Excellent food, affordable prices, good atmosphere.

Le Feeling Bar
43 rue Sainte-Croix de la Bretonnerie, 4th (01.48.04.70.03). M° Hôtel de Ville. **Open** 5pm-2am daily. **Map** p409 K6.
Le Feeling is a low-key gay and lesbian hangout. It won't be to everyone's taste, but the rainbow decor, Dalida soundtrack and easy-going staff are the perfect antidote to the tumult at Spyce just over the road. The mixed clientele includes a lot of regulars, and the general atmosphere is chatty and welcoming. On the other hand, there's no wasting time – it's an enthusiastic pick-up joint for people of all tastes.

★ Open Café
17 rue des Archives, 4th (01.42.72.26.18, www.opencafe.fr). M° Hôtel de Ville or Rambuteau. **Open** 11am-2am Mon-Thur, Sun; 11am-4am Fri, Sat. **Map** p409 K6.
Cruise and be cruised in the café everybody visits at some point in the evening. Pop out on to the terrace and enjoy the people-watching potential. *Photo p258.*

★ Le Quetzal
10 rue de la Verrerie, 4th (01.48.87.99.07). M° Hôtel de Ville. **Open** 5pm-5am daily. **Map** p409 K6.

This bar is considered to be one of the 'essential stops' on the Marais circuit, as it's often filled with hot men and a few drag queens to keep things lively. You might be able to find some action in the small, dark space upstairs. *Photo p259.*

Raidd Bar
23 rue du Temple, 4th (01.42.77.04.88, www.raiddbar.com). M° Hôtel de Ville. **Open** 6pm-4am Mon-Thur; 6pm-5am Fri, Sat, Sun. **Map** p406 K6.
The Raidd is a Marais LGBT venue to be reckoned with. Famous for its bare-chested barmen straight out of a modelling agency, the major draw is surely the soap sud-covered, brief-sporting, body-building go-go dancers who flaunt their wares under the front window's built-in showers (summer only). It gets pretty wild, sometimes bordering on a riot. The red velvet rooms downstairs are cosier and more relaxed. With free entry, a warm welcome and reasonably priced drinks, this humming club is always busy, and it closes late all week. Tuesday night is nostalgia night, Wednesdays are Latino, and weekends electro, giving everyone plenty of opportunities to dress up while wearing as little as possible.

Sly
22 rue des Lombards, 4th (06.62.84.64.61, www.sly-bar.com). M° Hôtel de Ville. **Open** 5pm-3am Mon-Thur, Sun; 5pm-4am Fri, Sat. **Map** p406 J6.
A newcomer to the gay scene, Sly is a kitschy bar down the street from the Bears' Den that attracts a much younger set. The best spot is on the tiny heated terrace, but the seating inside is cosy and inviting if it's too late to snag a seat outside. Each Thursday there's a special after-work party, Single or Not, where you can wear a colour-coded bracelet identifying your relationship status. Green means 'go for it', so give it a shot.

Les Souffleurs
7 rue de la Verrerie, 4th (01.44.78.04.92, www.les-souffleurs.com). M° Hôtel de Ville or Saint-Paul. **Open** 6pm-2am daily. **Map** p409 K6.
Les Souffleurs is a hip little gay bar in the centre of the gay Marais. In the daytime, it's a quiet place to escape. But the temperature goes up quickly at night, with some out-there DJ mixes and crowds aplenty. Some nights feature concerts and shows.

Le Spyce Bar
23 rue Sainte-Croix de la Bretonnerie, 4th (no phone, www.spycebar.com). M° Hôtel de Ville. **Open** 5pm-3am Mon-Thur, Sun; 5pm-4am Fri, Sat. **Map** p409 K6.
More than an essential gay bar-club in the Marais, Le Spyce is a rallying cry. It heaves at weekends with a young, happy, sweaty, undressed, excitable crowd, ready to dance and take people home on a whim. There's an informal (read: barely there) dress code on the dancefloor, with bold guys welcome to

ARTS & ENTERTAINMENT

Open Café. See p257.

take a place on a podium and dance until 4am. Entry is free and the drinks are reasonably priced, served with a smile by topless staff.

Restaurants

Le Bar à Manger (BAM)
13 rue des Lavandières-Ste-Opportune, 1st (01.42.21.01.72). M° Les Halles. **Open** noon-3pm, 7-11pm Mon-Sat. **Map** p408 J6.
Excellent, creative cuisine in a very relaxed setting. There's a *prix fixe* menu available at lunch (€19.50).

Le Gai Moulin
10 rue St-Merri, 4th (01.48.87.06.00, www. le-gai-moulin.com). M° Hôtel de Ville. **Open** noon-midnight daily. **Map** p406 K6.
One of the oldest gay-run restaurants in Paris. The owner is famously convivial, creating a lovely, friendly atmosphere. On Tuesdays, a pianist belts out French songs, and it's not uncommon for the whole room to sing along.

Ze Restoo
41 rue des Blancs-Manteaux, 3rd (01.42.74.10.29). M° Rambuteau. **Open** 7.30pm-midnight Mon-Thur; 7.30pm-1am Fri, Sat. **Map** p409 K6.
This restaurant has become a popular place in which to eat with friends before heading out for a fun-filled evening. There's a very relaxed atmosphere.

Clubs

As well as the venues listed below, a mixed but increasingly gay crowd mingles at **Nouveau Casino** (*see p267*). Most gay clubs are very hetero-friendly.

★ Le Club 18
18 rue de Beaujolais, 1st (01.42.97.52.13, www.club18.fr). M° Palais-Royal or Pyramides. **Open** midnight-dawn Fri-Sun. **Admission** (incl 1 drink) €10. **Map** p402 H5.

The oldest gay club in Paris attracts a young and beautiful clientele. It is not very big, and the decor isn't all that great, but the music is fun and there's a very laid-back vibe. Everyone is here to dance.

Le CUD Bar
12 rue des Haudriettes, 3rd (01.42.77.44.12, www.cud-paris.com). M° Rambuteau. **Open** 11.30pm-6am Mon-Thur, Sun; 11.30pm-7am Fri, Sat. **Map** p409 K5.
Upstairs is a laid-back bar, but downstairs in the old cellar is a dancefloor that can get very crowded, especially after 2am. The crowd is a mixed bunch, and it's popular with the bears.

Les Follivores & les Crazyvores
Bataclan, 50 bd Voltaire, 11th (www.follivores.com). M° Oberkampf. **Open** times vary. **Admission** (incl 1 drink) €19. **Map** p407 M5.
Twice a month, the Bataclan concert hall transforms itself into a club to host these two parties. Crazyvores features music from the 1970s and '80s, and at Follivores the DJs spin gay classics from all eras mixed up with cutting-edge techno. These are big events with exuberant crowds; the drag queens put on their best ballgowns and biggest wigs, and the men sport their tightest tops. Great fun.

Queen
102 av des Champs-Elysées, 8th (01.53.89.08.90, www.queen.fr). M° George V. **Open** 11.30pm-6am Mon, Wed, Fri-Sun; midnight-6am Tue; 7pm-6am Thur. **Admission** €20 incl 1 drink. **Map** p400 D4.
One of the oldest and largest clubs, Queen's main gay night is Overkitsch on Sundays, but every night is a little gay. Big-name DJs often spin here to a crowd peppered with VIPs.

Scream
18 rue du Faubourg du Temple, 11th (www.scream-paris.com). M° République. **Open** midnight-7am Sat; 7am-1pm Sun. **Admission** €15. **Map** p402 L4.

If you're attractive, well-built and not afraid of getting lost, the cavernous Scream club is your ideal party. Between the covered terrace and the two underground dancefloors, there's something for everyone. If you're feeling frisky, there's a designated cruise section too. Drinks are pricey, but at least the eye candy is free – after you've paid the €15 admission, of course.

★ Le Tango (La Boîte à Frissons)

13 rue au Maire, 3rd (01.42.72.17.78, www.boite-a-frissons.fr). M° Arts et Métiers. **Open** 8pm-2am Thur; 10.30pm-5am Fri, Sat; 6-11pm Sun. **Admission** €8; free Thur. **Map** p409 K5.

Wacky crowd, Madonna songs and accordion tunes. At the Friday and Saturday Bal de la Boîte à Frissons, couples dance the foxtrot, tango, madison or *guinguette* in the early part of the evening, followed after midnight by music of every variety except techno.

Sex clubs & saunas

Le Bunker

150 rue St-Maur, 11th (01.53.36.01.16, www.bunker-cruising.com). M° Goncourt. **Open** 4pm-2am Mon-Fri; 4pm-3.30am Sat; 4pm-midnight Sun. **Admission** €8-€10. **Map** p403 M4.

This cruising club is the hottest in Paris. It features all-naked and underwear-only nights during the week, and hardcore themes at the weekend. Friday is a very popular night, as is the first Saturday of the month, when Le Bunker hosts its S&M 'Red and Black Night' – not for the faint-hearted.

Le Dépot

10 rue aux Ours, 3rd (01.44.54.96.96, www.ledepot.com). M° Etienne Marcel. **Open** 2pm-7am Mon-Thur, Sun; 2pm-8am Fri, Sat. **Admission** €15. **Map** p402 K5.

A very busy dance club upstairs with a labyrinthine maze of cubicles, glory holes and darkrooms downstairs. The Dépot's glory days are gone now, but it still draws a crowd, particularly at weekends. Pickpockets work the darkrooms, so be careful.

Full Metal

40 rue des Blancs Manteaux, 4th (www.fullmetal.fr). M° Rambuteau. **Open** 5pm-4am Mon-Thur, Sun; 5pm-6am Fri, Sat. **Admission** free. **Map** p409 K6.

The trendier of the two gay fetish clubs in the same street: don't even try to get into Full Metal unless you adhere to the night's dress code. Two backrooms host all sorts of fetish and fantasy escapades, depending on the night, and a harness is also available. Entry is free and drinks are affordable.

★ IDM

4 rue du Fbg-Montmartre, 9th (01.45.23.10.03, www.idm-sauna.com). M° Grands Boulevards. **Open** noon-1am Mon-Wed; noon-2am Thur-Sun. **Admission** €21; €15 before 9.30pm & under-35s. **Map** p402 J4.

The city's best gay sauna has three levels and plenty of cabins and corridors to prowl. The wet sauna is on two levels, and the small relaxation pool and showers are always at the perfect temperature. A few times a month, there are also performances by drag queens and other singers.

ARTS & ENTERTAINMENT

Le Quetzal. *See p257.*

Impact

*18 rue Grenata, 2nd (01.42.21.94.24, www.
impact-bar.com). M° Etienne Marcel.* **Open** 8pm-
3am Mon-Thur; 10pm-6am Fri, Sat; 3pm-3am Sun.
Admission €15 (incl 1 drink); €10 (incl 1 drink)
under-30s. **Map** p406 J5.

Two floors of antics await you at Paris's premier gay
nudist bar. Upstairs, drinking and flatscreen porn.
Downstairs, well, any variety of impacting, depending on who's there. Entrance will set you back €15
(or €10 if you're under 30), a small price to pay for
an almost guaranteed good time. If sex isn't your
thing, there's a buffet on Sunday starting at 9pm.

Next

87 rue St-Honoré, 1st (no phone). M° Les Halles.
Open noon-3am Mon-Thur; 24hrs Fri-Sun.
Admission €7 before 7pm; €10-€13 (incl 1 drink)
after 7pm; €6 (incl 1 drink) under-26s. **Map** p402 J5.
This hot sex club is located in one of the chicest parts
of the capital. It doesn't really get going until after
many clubs have closed, and at 6am on a Sunday
morning it's probably the hottest, hardest place in
town. The bar upstairs is a nice place in which to
mingle before heading down to the sexy labyrinth.

Secteur X

*49 rue des Blancs Manteaux, 4th
(www.secteurx.fr). M° Rambuteau.* **Open**
3pm-4am Mon-Thur, Sun; 3pm-6am Fri, Sat.
Admission varies. **Map** p409 K6.
Once a quaint little gay dive bar, Secteur X has transformed into one of Paris's most hardcore gay cruise
clubs. At Friday Hard Night parties, participants are
invited to dress in leather, latex or nothing at all, and
Saturday's Leather and Slave Afternoon is only for
the truly motivated. For tight budgets, there's no
cover charge and a generous happy hour until 9pm.
The two lower levels are where the fun takes place
with backrooms and corridors galore.

Sun City

*62 bd de Sébastopol, 3rd (01.42.74.31.41, www.
suncity-paris.fr). M° Etienne Marcel.* **Open** noon-
6am daily. **Admission** €19.50 Mon-Thur (€12
after 3am); €20 Fri-Sun (€15 after 3am, €12
under-26s). **Map** p402 J5.
Owned and operated by the Dépot team (*see p259*),
this Bollywood-themed venue is the largest gay
sauna in Europe, with a pool, large steam room, gym
and bar. The clientele is good-looking and knows it.

IN THE KNOW PILLOW TALK

The mixed but very gay-friendly **Hôtel Duo**
(www.duoparis.com) is a stylish place
to rest your head. What's more, it has
helpful staff at the reception – something
of a rarity in the trendy Marais.

Legay Choc.

Shops & services

Boy'z Bazaar

*5 rue Ste-Croix-de-la-Bretonnerie, 4th (www.boyz
bazaar.com). M° Hôtel de Ville or St-Paul.* **Open**
noon-8pm Mon-Sat; 1-8pm Sun. **Map** p409 K6.
Stocks some of the city's trendiest clothes for night-
clubbers, fashionistas and urban hipsters.
Other location 5 rue des Guillemites, 4th
(01.42.71.63.86).

Les Dessous d'Apollon

*15 rue du Bourg-Tibourg, 4th (01.42.71.87.37,
www.lesdessousdapollon.com). M° Hôtel de Ville
or St-Paul.* **Open** 11am-8pm Mon-Sat; 2-8pm
Sun. **Map** p409 K6.
Probably the most extensive selection of underwear
– from the functional to the downright eccentric –
that you'll ever see, plus T-shirts and accessories.

IEM

*16 rue Ste-Croix-de-la-Bretonnerie, 4th
(01.42.74.01.61, www.iem.fr). M° Hôtel de Ville.*
Open noon-8pm Mon-Thur; noon-9pm Fri, Sat;
2-8pm Sun. **Map** p403 M4.
This sex hypermarket caters for those keen on the
harder side of gay life. Videos, clothes and gadgets
can all be found, and there are leather and rubber
goods upstairs.

★ Legay Choc

*45 rue Ste-Croix-de-la-Bretonnerie, 4th
(01.48.87.56.88, www.legaychoc.fr). M° Hôtel
de Ville.* **Open** 7.30am-8pm Mon, Wed-Sun.
Map p409 K6.

Run by two brothers (one gay, one straight) whose surname just happens to be Legay, this Marais *boulangerie* and *pâtisserie* is very popular. The pastries are delightful, and the lunch-hour sandwiches are generous, so expect queues.

★ Les Mots à la Bouche

6 rue Ste-Croix-de-la-Bretonnerie, 4th (01.42.78.88.30, www.motsbouche.com). Mº Hôtel de Ville or St-Paul. **Open** 11am-11pm Mon-Sat; 1-9pm Sun. **Map** p409 K6.
An institution in the Marais, this bookshop has a large selection of gay fiction, non-fiction, magazines, and English-language books.

Nickel

48 rue des Francs-Bourgeois, 3rd (01.42.77.41.10, www.nickel.fr). Mº Hôtel de Ville or Rambuteau. **Open** 11am-7.30pm Mon, Tue, Fri, Sat; 11am-9pm Wed, Thur. **Map** p406 L6.
Body and skincare treatments, strictly for men only. A one-hour facial is €74-€82, a manicure €25 and a 50-minute massage €69-€79. Staff are adept, friendly and knowledgeable.

Plus Que Parfait

23 rue des Blancs-Manteaux, 4th (01.42.71.09.05). Mº Hôtel de Ville or St-Paul. **Open** 3-8pm Mon; 12.30-8pm Tue-Sat; 3-7pm Sun. *Clothes deposit* Mon-Fri. **Map** p409 K6.
This *dépôt vente*, where pristine second-hand designer clothing is sold on commission, is a great place for men's fashion finds.

Space Hair

10 rue Rambuteau, 3rd (01.48.87.28.51, www.space-hair.com). Mº Rambuteau. **Open** 11am-10pm Mon; 10am-10pm Tue-Sat. **Map** p409 K6.
Space Hair is divided into two salons, Cosmic and Classic, with a 1980s kitsch feel, late opening hours and cute stylists; it's best to book ahead.

LESBIAN PARIS

The girlie scene continues to flourish, especially near the corner of rue du Roi de Sicile and rue des Ecouffes in the Marais. Most of the bars welcome men accompanied by women, but a few are women only. Some girl-only parties are staged at clubs such as **Le Tango** (*see p259*); see the free monthly magazine *Barbi(e)turix* for listings.

Le 3W Kafé

8 rue des Ecouffes, 4th (01.48.87.39.26). Mº Saint-Paul. **Open** 7pm-2am Wed; 7pm-3am Thur; 7pm-5am Fri, Sat. **Map** p409 K6.
A convivial place where beautiful women go to have a drink, meet other women and listen to good music. There's a small dance space in the basement, and a number of theme nights every month. The three Ws stand for 'women with women'.

★ La Champmeslé

4 rue Chabanais, 2nd (01.42.96.85.20, www.lachampmesle.com). Mº Bourse or Pyramides. **Open** 4pm-4am Mon-Sat. **Map** p402 H4.
This veteran girlie bar remains a popular venue for lesbian locals and visitors. Beer is the drink of choice; pull up a seat and enjoy the regular cabaret nights.

Le Day Off

10 rue de l'Isly, 8th (no phone). Mº Gare St-Lazare. **Open** 11.30am-3am Mon-Fri. **Map** p401 G3.
An apt name for this weekday-only pub-restaurant – heavy drinking enjoyed by work-weary lesbians. It gets crowded in the early evening.

Dollhouse

24 rue du Roi de Sicile, 4th (01.40.27.09.21, www.dollhouse.fr). Mº St-Paul. **Open** 2-8pm Mon, Sun; 1-8pm Tue-Sat. **Map** p409 L6.
This store specialises in lingerie and gadgets for the girls. Upstairs you'll find a selection of sophisticated underwear; head downstairs for the sexcessories.

Les Jacasses

5 rue des Ecouffes, 4th (01.42.71.15.51). Mº St-Paul. **Open** 5pm-2am Wed-Sun. **Map** p409 K6.
This relaxed bar for women is located just around the corner from all the girlie bars on rue du Roi de Sicile in the Marais.

★ Le Rive Gauche

1 rue du Sabot, 6th (01.40.20.43.23, www.lerive gauche.com). Mº St-Germain-des-Prés. **Open** 11pm-5am Sat. **Admission** €15 (incl 1 drink). **No credit cards. Map** p405 G7.
This weekend women-only nightclub is one of the hottest places on the lesbian scene. The decor is '70s and the music eclectic.

Rosa Bonheur

Parc des Buttes Chaumont, 2 av de la Cascade, 19th (01.42.00.00.45, www.rosabonheur.fr). Mº Buttes Chaumont. **Open** noon-midnight Thur-Sun. **Map** p403 N2.
Bucolic delights reign at Rosa Bonheur, set in a former *guinguette*. Its name loosely translates as 'pink happiness' but refers in particular to 19th-century painter and sculptor Rosa Bonheur, famous for her depictions of animals and her role in the early feminist movement. The bar is managed by Michelle Cassaro, aka Mimi, who used to run lesbian club Pulp – and it's a popular hangout with the lesbian crowd, especially on Sunday evenings.

Le So What!

30 rue du Roi de Sicile, 4th (no phone). Mº St-Paul. **Open** 9.30pm-2am Wed-Thur; 10pm-4am Fri, Sat. **Map** p409 L6.
The So What! is primarily a girlie bar, but everyone's welcome. Recent theme nights have included live rock and drag queens.

Nightlife

Serious nighthawks may have migrated long ago to more happening cities such as London, New York and Berlin, but the French capital is fighting back with a string of great new leftfield Left Bank venues pumping out everything from gypsy jazz to electro-tropical candomblé to the Seine-side party crowds. Go early if you want to avoid the queues, but bear in mind that Parisians tend to go out clubbing late and most venues will be pretty empty if you turn up before midnight. Many of these new nightlife stars double up as gig venues too.

Paris's traditional cabarets cater to the throngs of tourists and businessmen who drop in for an eyeful of boob-bouncing, posh nosh and champers. Alternatively, if the get-your-glitz-out-for-the-boys genre isn't your cup of tea, then a Gallic giggle can still be had at old-fashioned *café-théâtres*, where songs and sketches accompany dinner.

Clubs

Ritzy places such as the **VIP Room** and **Le Baron** are still the talk of the Right Bank, but a string of new Seine-side clubs in the 13th arrondissement are now drawing hip locals south of the river for late-night fun (*see p269*). **Batofar** was the original trailblazer, but it's now been joined by the likes of **La Dame de Canton** and club venues *du jour* **Wanderlust** and **Nüba**. With everything from ping pong games to documentary screenings and free fashion workshops on offer, the emphasis on the Left Bank is more about having fun than posing.

For listings, check www.parisbouge.com, www.novaplanet.com, www.radiofg.com and www.lemonsound.com.

RIGHT BANK
Club bars

★ Andy Wahloo
69 rue des Gravilliers, 3rd (01.42.71.20.38, www.andywahloo-bar.com). M° Arts et Métiers. **Open** 7pm-2am Tue-Sat. **Admission** free. **Map** p409 K5.

Owned by the people behind Momo and Sketch in London, Andy Wahloo serves sumptuous snack food and is decorated with Moroccan artefacts and a spice rack of colours. The seating is made from upturned paint cans, and the DJs play an eclectic mix, featuring everything from hip hop to techno and stepping up the volume as the night progresses.

Café Chéri(e)
44 bd de la Villette, 19th (01.42.02.02.05). M° Belleville. **Open** noon-2am daily. **Admission** free. **Map** p403 M3.

A popular DJ bar, especially in the summer when fashionistas flock to the terrace. Live music is played from Thursdays to Saturdays after 9pm. Expect anything from electro punk to rock, funk, hip hop, rare groove, indie, dance, jazz and '80s classics.

★ Chacha Club
47 rue Berger, 1st (01.40.13.12.12, www. chachaclub.fr). M° Châtelet. **Open** 8pm-6am Tue-Sat. **Admission** varies. **Map** p402 J5.

The Chacha Club's *fumoir* is just one of the sexy attributes of this hot haunt that attracts a good-looking clientele through its doors. In the style of a private club, but with no membership requirement (only a trio of exacting 'physionomists' stand at the

ARTS & ENTERTAINMENT

door), it combines restaurant, bar and club in a suite of intimate rooms with subdued lighting and seductive, 1930s-inspired decor.

★ La Fourmi

*74 rue des Martyrs, 18th (01.42.64.70.35). M°
Pigalle.* **Open** 8.30am-2am Mon-Thur, Sun; 8am-4am Fri, Sat. **Admission** free. **Map** p402 H2.
La Fourmi was a precursor to the industrial-design, informal, music-led bars that have sprung up around Paris – and it's still very much a style leader, attracting everyone from in-the-know tourists to fashionable Parisians. Great throughout the day for coffees or a beer, it has a small seating area outside and an always busy bar with DJ decks. You can stay into the early hours at weekends, but it's also a handy pre-club rendezvous and flyer supplier.

Lizard Lounge

*18 rue du Bourg-Tibourg, 4th (01.42.72.81.34,
www.cheapblonde.com). M° Hôtel de Ville or St-Paul.* **Open** noon-2am daily. **Admission** free.
Map p409 K6.
This three-level trendy Marais hangout has a boozer upstairs serving beer in pint glasses, a mezzanine for crowd voyeurs, and a more full-on DJ bar in the booth-filled basement – often full, due to its modest proportions. Local DJs play house, hip hop and funk.

★ Panic Room

*101 rue Amelot, 11th (01.58.30.93.43,
www.panicroomparis.com). M° St-Sébastien
Froissart.* **Open** 6.30pm-2am Mon-Sat. Closed
2wks Aug. **Admission** free. **Map** p409 L5.

This newcomer has quickly carved out a niche on the rock scene, and it's not nearly as daunting as its name suggests. The excellent Goldrush collective has live acts and DJs blasting the sound system in the basement, while upstairs friendly barmen serve affordable cocktails behind a concrete counter.

Clubs

Badaboum

*2bis rue des Taillandiers, 11th (01.48.06.50.70,
www.badaboum-paris.com). M° Bastille.* **Open**
7pm-2am Wed, Sun; 7pm-7am Thur-Sat.
Admission €5-€15. **Map** p407 M7.
La Scène Bastille has been done up and relaunched by the same group behind the Panic Room, and is now the Badaboum. Inside there's a simple retro-industrial look, a sound system that makes the light-strewn ceiling shake, a restaurant and cocktail/tapas bar open to all from 7pm, and a secret room upstairs with bachelor pad allure. Nights kick off with gigs from emerging pop-rock artists, then comes clubbing with a good range of techno DJs.

Le Baron

*6 av Marceau, 8th (01.47.20.04.01, www.club
lebaron.com). M° Alma Marceau.* **Open** 11pm-6am daily. **Admission** free. **Map** p400 D5.
This small but supremely exclusive hangout for the jet set used to be an upmarket brothel, and has the decor to prove it. It only holds 150, most of whom are regulars you'll need to befriend in order to get past the door. If you do manage to get in, you'll be rubbing shoulders with celebrities and super-glossy people.

ARTS & ENTERTAINMENT

Chacha Club.

The essential guide to arts, culture and going out in Paris

timeout.com/paris

Le Cabaret Sauvage

59 bd Macdonald, 19th (01.42.09.03.09, www.cabaretsauvage.com). M° Porte de la Villette. **Open** 9pm-dawn, days vary. **Admission** €10-€33. **Map** p403 inset.
A stylish venue that's taken over by outside promoters for occasional club nights. There often used to be a world music element, but recently electronic and drum 'n' bass nights have begun to be held here, and, since the demise of Pulp, techno label Kill the DJ has started using the venue. Check the website for full details.

La Chapelle des Lombards

19 rue de Lappe, 11th (01.43.57.24.24, www. la-chapelle-des-lombards.com). M° Bastille. **Open** 11.30pm-6am Tue-Sun. **Admission** free Tue-Thur, Sun; €20 Fri, Sat (incl 1 drink and free for women before midnight Fri). **Map** p407 M7.
With Afrojazz and Latino bands and DJs providing the music, Latinos and Africans lead the dancefloor in this popular world music venue. Smart dress only.

Le Divan du Monde

75 rue des Martyrs, 18th (01.40.05.06.99, www.divandumonde.com). M° Abbesses or Pigalle. **Open** times vary. **Admission** €10-€38. **Map** p402 H2.
After a drink in the cool Fourmi opposite, pop over to the Divan for one-off parties and regular events. The upstairs specialises in VJ events, and downstairs holds dub, reggae, funk and world music nights.

Le Djoon

22 bd Vincent Auriol, 13th (01.45.70.83.49, www.djoon.com). M° Quai de la Gare. **Open** 6.30pm-1am Thur; 11.30pm-5am Fri, Sat. **Admission** free-€10. **Map** p407 M9.
Don your glad rags and get ready to party NYC style: with its loft-style lounge, large bay windows and a vast curved bar, Le Djoon wouldn't look out of place in Manhattan. Trendy thirtysomethings pile in for House, Deep House, Soul and Motown nights, spliced by a string of international DJs fresh off the plane from Detroit, Chicago, Berlin, New York and London (think Louie Vega, Theo Parrish, Deetron, Tony Humphries, Culoe de Song and DJ Spinna). Djoon's restaurant won't win any Michelin stars, but it's handy if you want to make a night of it.

★ Favela Chic

18 rue du Fbg-du-Temple, 11th (01.40.21.38.14, www.favelachic.com). M° République. **Open** 7.30pm-2am Tue-Thur; 7.30pm-4am Fri, Sat. **Admission** free Tue-Thur; €10 (incl 1 drink) Fri, Sat. **Map** p402 L4.
Past the usually steely-faced door attendants, the Brazilian-themed Favela Chic attracts an up-for-it, international crowd for some serious samba and other Latin dancing. There are decent DJs, live acts, and Brazilian food and drinks. *Photos p266.*

Le Gibus

18 rue du Fbg-du-Temple, 11th (01.47.00.78.88, www.gibus.fr). M° République or Temple. **Open** 11.30pm-6am Fri; 11.30pm-7am Sat. **Concerts** 8-11pm Fri, Sat. **Admission** €5-€20. **Map** p402 L4.
A famous 1980s punk venue, Le Gibus has gone through plenty of style changes during its life. Today, it takes in R&B, reggae, '80s pop and hip hop, plus the occasional *striptease mixte.*

Le Glaz'art

7-15 av de la Porte de la Villette, 19th (01.40.36.55.65, www.glazart.com). M° Porte de la Villette. **Open** 8.30pm-5am (sometimes 7am) on concert nights (check website). **Admission** €9.80-€20.90. **Map** p403 inset.
This converted coach station is way out to the northeast, but its strong DJ nights and live acts pull punters in from central Paris. Dub step, breakbeat, electro and drum 'n' bass nights have made the venue a magnet for breaks fans. In the summer, the outdoor area is transformed into a sandy beach with pastis, pétanque and merguez: a winning combination.

La Java

105 rue du Fbg-du-Temple, 10th (01.42.02.20.52, www.la-java.fr). M° Belleville or Goncourt. **Open** 9pm-2am Mon-Thur; midnight-dawn Fri, Sat; 6pm-2am Sun. **Admission** €5-€10. **Map** p403 M4.
Tucked inside the crumbling, disused Belleville market, La Java has been a venue for Paris night owls since the 1930s – Django Reinhardt, Edith Piaf and Jean Gabin all played here. In the decades that followed, the rebellious youth came to let their hair down to a rock soundtrack. Then, in the 1980s, the nocturnal fauna of the Parisian 'trash underground' came here to listen to punk rock. There followed a fallow period of low-quality salsa, but La Java has recently rediscovered its original vocation as an anti-establishment club, with a programme featuring garage rock, punk dub and electro-techno nights.

IN THE KNOW
FESTIVAL FEVER

Paris is home to several noteworthy rock festivals. **Solidays** (*see p35*), in mid July, features electro and dub, and leans more towards Gallic sounds than its more international rival **Rock en Seine** (*see p37*), which takes place in late August and hosted big-name bands such as Franz Ferdinand and Belle & Sebastian in 2013. The **Festival des Inrockuptibles** (*see p39*), in November, brings together a well-curated selection of indie, rock, techno and trip hop – 2013 highlights included the Foals and Suede.

ARTS & ENTERTAINMENT

Favela Chic.
See p265.

La Machine du Moulin Rouge

*90 bd de Clichy, 18th (01.53.41.88.89, www.
lamachinedumoulinrouge.com). M° Blanche.*
Open times vary. *Terrace* 7-10pm Fri-Sun.
Admission prices vary. **Map** p401 G2.

So long La Loco, enter La Machine. This three-floor
bar/club/live venue has had a substantial makeover
and is now reborn with a dash of decadence. The
main dancefloor, La Chaufferie, used to be the Moulin
Rouge's boiler room and the old pipes remain, but the
new *Alice in Wonderland*-style decor is a breath of
fresh air. If you can't take the heat, head for the new
terrace or switch to Central, a concert hall showcasing a selection of new and established acts.

MadaM

*128 rue de la Boétie, 8th (01.53.76.02.11,
www.lemadam.com). M° Franklin D. Roosevelt
or George V.* **Open** 11pm-dawn Tue-Sun.
Admission free. **Map** p401 E4.

MadaM's late-night sessions (kicking in at 4am at
weekends) are renowned for the young, moneyed
crowd they attract. The music on offer is mainly electro and house (French), with several up-to-date international tunes thrown into the mix.

★ Le Magnifique

*25 rue de Richelieu, 1st (01.42.60.70.80,
www.lemagnifique.fr). M° Palais Royal-Musée
du Louvre.* **Open** 11pm-5am daily. **Admission**
free. **Map** p401 H5.

Named after a 1970s film starring Jean-Paul
Belmondo, this snazzy cocktail bar is a real retro
treat. The decor, dominated by wood, dark leather
and animal furs, is elegant, with a hint of porno chic
that leaves you picturing Warhol and his posse partying in a corner. The place really comes to life after
midnight, when the bar turns into a club with a
soundtrack of dancefloor-fillers from the past three
decades. The fantastic cocktail menu, a selection of
sushi (€8-€30) and the separate *fumoir* add to the
overall appeal.

Mains d'Oeuvres

*1 rue Charles-Garnier, 93400 St-Ouen
(01.40.11.25.25, www.mainsdoeuvres.org). M°
Garibaldi.* **Open** 9am-midnight Mon-Fri; 11am-
midnight Sat; noon-9pm Sun. **Admission** €5-€20.

This rehearsal space and venue for new bands
(*see p274*) occasionally turns into a club venue, with
rooms devoted to different music styles.

★ New Morning

*7-9 rue des Petites-Ecuries, 10th (01.45.23.51.41,
www.newmorning.com). M° Château d'Eau.*
Open times vary. **Admission** approx €20.
Map p402 K3.

Jazz fans crowd into this hip, no-frills joint to natter,
drink and boogie to the excellent live music. Low
key it may be, but it's still worth looking out for the
occasional A-lister.

Point Ephémère.

Nouveau Casino

109 rue Oberkampf, 11th (01.43.57.57.40,
www.nouveaucasino.net). M° Parmentier.
Open times vary. **Admission** prices vary.
Map p403 M5.

Conveniently surrounded by the numerous bars of
rue Oberkampf and tucked behind the legendary
Café Charbon, Nouveau Casino is a concert venue
that also hosts some of the city's liveliest club nights.
Local collectives, international names and record
labels such as Versatile host nights here; it's worth
checking the website for one-offs and after-parties.

Le Paris Paris Club

5 av de l'Opéra, 8th (01.42.60.64.45, www.paris
parisclub.com). M° Pyramides. **Open** 11pm-6am
Tue, Thur-Sat; 10pm-6am Wed. **Concerts** 8.30pm.
Admission €5-€12. **Map** p401 H5.

Don't let the picture of Beethoven fool you: this small
club is all about electro-rock, with black-painted
walls and live acts at weekends. Gigs aren't free, but
DJ sets by the likes of MGMT and 'music label
battles' are interesting alternatives on other nights.

★ Point Ephémère

200 quai de Valmy, 10th (01.40.34.02.48,
www.pointephemere.org). M° Jaurès or Louis
Blanc. **Open** noon-2am Mon-Sat; noon-9pm Sun.
Admission varies.

This hunk of Berlin in Paris was only ever meant to
be temporary, but thankfully it's still around. An
uncompromising programming policy delivers some
of the best electronic music in town; there's also a
restaurant and bar with decks and a gallery, and terrace space by the canal in summer.

Queen

102 av des Champs-Elysées, 8th (01.53.89.08.90,
www.queen.fr). M° George V. **Open** 11.30pm-6am
Mon, Wed, Fri-Sun; midnight-6am Tue; 7pm-6am

Thur. **Admission** €20 (incl 1 drink); women free
before 1am Mon, Wed. **Map** p400 D4.

Once the city's most fêted gay club and the only venue
that could hold a torch to the Rex, with a roster of top
local DJs holding court, Queen's star faded a little in
the early noughties but is now starting to shine more
brightly again. Located along the club-laden Champs-
Elysées, this is one of the chicest addresses for clubbing in Paris, with prices to match, so bring a few
extra euros if you plan on having a drink or two
beyond the one included in the entrance fee.

► *For more on Queen's gay nights, see p258.*

★ Le Régine

49 rue de Ponthieu, 8th (01.42.66.22.78).
M° St-Philippe-du-Roule. **Open** 7pm-5am Thur;
midnight-6am Fri, Sat. **Admission** €10-€20.
Map p401 D4.

Régine was once a key figure on the Paris nightlife
scene, and the club she created is experiencing a reju-
venation. Her portrait still sits by the entrance for a
touch of '70s nostalgia, but the revamped venue has
shifted from disco to sophisticated electro, inviting
the cream of international DJs to the decks. The after-
work La French, followed by the insane Pan-Pan Cul-
Cul night (where guys get in for free if they're dressed
as girls), makes a safe bet for a wild Thursday.

★ Rex

5 bd Poissonnière, 2nd (01.42.36.10.96,
www.rexclub.com). M° Bonne Nouvelle. **Open**
11.30pm-7am Thur-Sat. **Admission** €5-€25.
Map p402 J4.

The Rex's new sound system puts over 40 different
sound configurations at the DJ's fingertips, and has
proved to be a magnet for top turntable stars. Once
associated with iconic techno pioneer Laurent
Garnier, the Rex has stayed at the top of the Paris
techno scene, and occupies an unassailable position
as the city's serious club music venue.

Showcase

Below Pont Alexandre III, 8th (01.45.61.25.43, www.showcase.fr). M° Champs-Elysées Clemenceau. **Open** 11.30pm-7am Fri, Sat. **Admission** free-€15. **Map** p401 E5.

This vast venue below Pont Alexandre III is where music-crazed insomniacs come at weekends to discover up-and-coming bands and dance until daybreak. The club has lost some of its hype over the last couple of years, but high-profile guest DJs have been setting the bar higher lately: Carl Cox, will.i.am and Calvin Harris have all made appearances.

Silencio

142 rue de Montmartre, 2nd (www.silencio-club.com). M° Bourse or Grands Boulevards. **Open** 6pm-4am Tue-Thur; 6pm-6am Fri, Sat. **Admission** varies. **Map** p402 J4.

If there's one thing Paris has been missing for years it's a decent private club – one that encourages artistic networking, before letting the public in for a night

Silencio.

of soulful partying. Cue Silencio, David Lynch's joint named after the cult venue in his 2001 movie *Mulholland Drive*. The director has designed every aspect of the decor, from the gold-leaf walls to the 1950s-style furniture. There are concerts by up-and-coming bands, film premieres, eclectic club nights and a stream of prestigious guests. If you're not up for full-blown membership (€840 plus proof of your artistic credentials), access is after midnight; but you'll have to look right to get in.

★ Le Social Club

142 rue Montmartre, 2nd (01.40.28.05.55, www.parissocialclub.com). M° Bourse or Grands Boulevards. **Open** 11pm-3am Tue, Wed; 11pm-6am Thur-Sat. **Admission** free-€15. **Map** p402 J4.

Set right in the hub of the city's club activity around Grands Boulevards, this electro venue has some of the hippest acts from the French and international scene, thanks to its owner's multidisciplinary career as a producer and founder of the record label Uncivilized World.

Toro

74 rue Jean-Jacques-Rousseau, 1st (01.44.76.00.03, www.toroparis.com). M° Les Halles. **Open** *Live performances* 9pm-midnight Thur-Sat. *Club* midnight-5am Fri, Sat. **Admission** free. **Map** p402 J5.

This no-frills tapas bar hides a small but wonderfully wacky dancefloor in the basement where DJs mix up house music with flamenco tunes.

VIP Room

188 rue de Rivoli, 1st (01.58.36.46.00, www.viproom.fr). M° Palais Royal-Musée du Louvre or Tuileries. **Open** midnight-5am Wed, Fri, Sat; 7pm-5am Thur. **Admission** free. **Map** p401 H1.

The VIP has moved from its Champs-Elysées address into the former Scala nightclub, but other than that, nothing has changed. It's still a hit with the people who also enjoy the VIP's sister venues in Cannes and Saint-Tropez during the summer, and the music is still dance-oriented. The opening of smart Italian restaurant Gioia, serving food until 5am at weekends, is a welcome addition.

Le Zéro Zéro

89 rue Amelot, 11th (01.49.23.51.00). M° Saint-Sébastien Froissart. **Open** 6pm-2am daily. **Admission** free. **Map** p409 L6.

Zéro Zéro is rammed at the weekends. The reason for all this roaring success? The music, to start with – the vinyl is expertly managed by house, minimal and hip hop/funk DJs. The style, too: a tapestry of 1970s orange flowers disappearing behind layers of graffiti. But most of all it's the staff that make it great: the enthusiastic young owners are there every evening keeping things alive.

LUCKY 13TH

The Left Bank is Paris's new clubbing capital.

Wanderlust.

The long-delayed Cité de la Mode et du Design on the quai d'Austerlitz has finally opened its doors, and its first on-site club is setting tongues wagging. **Wanderlust** (*see p270*) has joined the likes of Batofar and La Dame de Canton along the banks of the Seine, making the 13th arrondissement the new undisputed clubbing capital.

Spread across a vast space, Wanderlust includes a terrace perfect for sunset drinks, an open-air cinema, art installations and a restaurant run by TV chef Benjamin Darnaud. Running the venue is the ultra-hip Savoir Faire team (the brains behind Le Social Club, Le Baron and Silencio), so it should come as no surprise that the dress code is designer, the bouncers are unforgiving and the queues are long (come very early or late). On the plus side, though, entry is free and there are fashion-themed nights on Fridays that might include documentary screenings, catwalk shows or installations run in association with the Musée Galliera, plus free fashion workshops for children and adults. You'll also find ping pong tables, weekend yoga lessons and chill-out areas dotted with chaises longues. Music is minimal techno and house on a top-notch sound system, getting the crowd going to the point where, if you're outside, you can watch a sea of

well-dressed backsides gyrating together in the club's huge street-level bay windows.

In late 2012, the hip factor was turned up yet another notch with the opening of **Nüba** (*see p270*) on the roof. Behind the venue are Lionel Bensemoun and Jean-Marie Tassy, founders of Le Baron and Calvi on the Rocks, a popular annual electro-rock festival in Corsica. The vast rooftop terrace offers a superb panoramic view over the surrounding quays, a wooden DJ booth playing chillout world music, deckchairs, big communal tables and table football. Inside, coloured lights reveal rooms done out in copper and stone. There are gigs in the evenings, punctuated by clubby electro sets and inventive dance shows from the House of Drama collective.

ARTS & ENTERTAINMENT

Batofar.

LEFT BANK
Clubs

★ Batofar
Opposite 11 quai François-Mauriac, 13th (09.71.25.50.61, www.batofar.org). M° Quai de la Gare. **Open** *Concerts* 7-11pm Mon-Sat. *Club* 11.30pm-6am Mon-Sat; 6am-noon 1st Sun of mth. **Admission** free-€12. **Map** p407 N10.

In recent years, the Batofar lightship has gone through a rapid succession of management teams, with varying levels of success. The current managers have helped to revive the venue's tradition of playing cutting-edge music, including electro, dub step, techno and dancehall nights featuring international acts. From June to September (noon-midnight), the bar sets up a temporary beach; come and admire the sunset while sprawling in a sun lounger.

La Dame de Canton
Port de la Gare, 13th (01.53.61.08.49, www.damedecanton.com). M° Quai de la Gare. **Open** 7.30pm-2am Tue-Thur; 7.30pm-6am Fri, Sat. **Admission** free-€10. **Map** p407 N10.

The Dame de Canton, housed in a superb Chinese junk, features a concert space, a striking wooden dancefloor, a romantic restaurant in the hold and a sun-drenched bridge for *apéros*. The music is eclectic: breakbeats, electro-swing gypsy jazz, electro-tropical candomblé DJs, Thai-funk electro disco, ragga, kompa and plenty more alternative world music you've never heard of.

★ Mix Club
24 rue de l'Arrivée, 15th (01.56.80.37.37, www.mixclub.fr). M° Montparnasse Bienvenüe. **Open** 11pm-5.30am Thur; 11.45pm-6am Fri, Sat. **Admission** free-€15. **Map** p405 F8.

The Mix Club has one of the city's biggest dancefloors. Regular international visitors include Erick Morillo's Subliminal and Ministry of Sound parties, and in-house events include David Guetta's 'Fuck Me I'm Famous', 'Hipnotic' and 'One Night With Paulette', plus just about everyone else who's big in France – or anywhere in the world, for that matter.

Le Montana
28 rue St-Benoît, 6th (no phone). M° St-Germain-des-Prés. **Open** 11pm-5am daily. **Admission** free. **Map** p408 H7.

It's hard to believe that any place could out-hype Le Baron (*see p263*), and yet this exclusive St-Germain club manages it. Revamped by über-cool graphic artist André, Le Montana is a VIP magnet – Lenny Kravitz, Vanessa Bruno and Kate Moss have all hit the floor here.

Nüba
36 quai d'Austerlitz, 13th (www.nuba-paris.fr). M° Gare d'Austerlitz. **Open** 11pm-5am Wed-Sat. **Admission** free (charge for special events). **Map** p407 M9.
See p269 **Lucky 13th**.

Wanderlust
32 quai d'Austerlitz, 13th (www.wanderlust paris.com). M° Quai de la Gare. **Open** 10pm-6am Thur; 11pm-6am Fri, Sat. **Admission** prices vary. **Map** p407 M9.
See p269 **Lucky 13th**.

Cabaret, comedy & café-théâtre

The year the Eiffel Tower raised its final girders (1889), the Moulin Rouge was raising something of its own: skirts. The risqué *quadrille réaliste* (later dubbed the cancan) became such a trademark that more than 120 years later, busty babes are still slinking across the stages of Paris. These days, cabaret is an all-evening affair, traditionally served up with champagne and a meal. Male dancers and magicians complement the foxy foxtrots, the dancing is perfectly synchronised and the whole caboodle is now perfectly respectable.

RIGHT BANK

Cabaret

Crazy Horse Saloon

12 av George V, 8th (01.47.23.32.32, www.lecrazy horseparis.com). M° Alma Marceau or George V. **Shows** 8.15pm, 10.45pm Mon-Fri, Sun; 7pm, 9.30pm, 11.45pm Sat. **Admission** *Show only* €105. *Show* (incl champagne) €125. **Map** p400 D4. More risqué than the other cabarets, the Horse, whose *art du nu* was invented in 1951 by Alain Bernadin, is an ode to feminine beauty: lookalike dancers with provocative names like Daisy Blu and Zula Zazou, and identical body statistics (when standing, the women's nipples and hips are all at the same height), move around the stage, clad only in rainbow light and strategic strips of black tape. In their latest show, Désirs, the girls put on some tantalising numbers, with titles such as 'God Save Our Bare Skin' (a sexy take on the British Changing the Guard) and the sensual 'Vestel's Desire'.

Le Lido

116bis av des Champs-Elysées, 8th (01.40.76.56.10, www.lido.fr). M° Franklin D Roosevelt or George V. **Lunch** 1pm. **Matinée** 3pm Tue, Sun (dates vary). **Dinner** 7pm. **Shows** 9.30pm, 11.30pm daily. **Admission** *Lunch &*

matinée show (incl champagne) €140. *9.30pm show* €90. *11.30pm show* €80. *9.30pm show* (incl champagne) €105. *11.30pm show* (incl champagne) €145. *Dinner & show* €160-€300. *Show & backstage tour* price varies. **Map** p400 D4. This is the largest cabaret of all: high-tech touches optimise visibility, and chef Philippe Lacroix provides fabulous gourmet nosh. On stage, 60 Bluebell Girls and a set of hunky boys slink around, shaking their bodies with sequinned panache in breathtaking scenes. For a special treat, opt for the 'behind the scenes' Coulisses tour which, before the show, takes you into the heart of the action.

Moulin Rouge

82 bd de Clichy, 18th (01.53.09.82.82, www.moulin-rouge.com). M° Blanche. **Dinner** 7pm. **Shows** 9pm, 11pm daily. **Admission** *Show* (incl champagne) €109. *Dinner & show* €180-€210. *Show only* €99. **Map** p401 G2. Toulouse-Lautrec posters, glittery lamp-posts and fake trees lend tacky charm to this revue. On stage, 60 Doriss dancers cavort with faultless synchronisation. Costumes are flamboyant and the *entr'acte* acts funny. The downer is the space, with tables packed in like sardines. There are also occasional matinée performances.

Café-théâtre

Les Blancs Manteaux

15 rue des Blancs-Manteaux, 4th (01.48.87.15.84, www.blancsmanteaux.fr). M° Hôtel de Ville. **Shows** from 7pm daily (see website for details). **Admission** *Show* €20; €17 students, under-25s; *2 shows* €34 (except Sat). *Dinner & 1 show* €40. **No credit cards. Map** p409 K6.

Le Lido.

ARTS & ENTERTAINMENT

For the past 40 years, this Marais institution has been launching new talent with weekly comedy platforms. With a dinner-and-show ticket, you can dine on Thai cuisine at nearby Suan Thai.

Chez Michou
80 rue des Martyrs, 18th (01.46.06.16.04, www.michou.com). M° Pigalle. **Dinner** 8.30pm daily. **Shows** 10.30pm approx. **Admission** *Show* €32-€65. *Dinner & show* €110-€140. **Map** p402 H2.
Drag, sparkling costumes, good food and wine: Michou's show is not quite as 'blue' as his azure attire suggests. Book ahead if you want to dine.

Le Grenier
3 rue Rennequin, 17th (01.43.80.68.01, www.legrenier-dinerspectacle.com). M° Ternes. **Shows** from 7.30pm daily. **Admission** *Show* €18-€20. *Dinner & show* €27-€60. **Map** p400 D2.
If you fancy being entertained while you eat, consider a night at the Grenier, which still retains the allure of an old *café-théâtre* with an eclectic line-up of stand-up, *chansonniers* and magic acts all on the same bill.

★ Au Lapin Agile
22 rue des Saules, 18th (01.46.06.85.87, www.au-lapin-agile.com). M° Lamarck Caulaincourt. **Shows** 9pm-1am Tue-Sun. **Admission** *Show* (incl 1 drink) €24; €17 reductions. **No credit cards. Map** p402 H1.
The prices have gone up and they sell their own compilation CDs, but that's all that seems to have changed since this quaint, pink bar first opened in 1860. Tourists now outnumber the locals, but the Lapin harbours an echo of old Montmartre.

Comedy

Café de la Gare
41 rue du Temple, 4th (01.42.78.52.51, www.cdlg.org). M° Hôtel de Ville. **Shows** times vary. **Admission** €22-€24; €15 reductions. **Map** p406 K6.
Running since 1968, the most famous fringe theatre in Paris has 300 stage-hugging seats and hosts quality French stand-up and raucous comedies.

Caveau de la République
1 bd St-Martin, 3rd (01.42.78.44.45, www.caveau.fr). M° République. **Shows** 8.30pm Wed-Sat; 3.30pm Sun. Closed Aug. **Admission** €33, €39; €19.50 reductions. **Map** p402 L4.
This traditional *chanson* venue has been churning out political-satirical songs and sketches for more than a century. Nowadays, stand-up comedy is the main draw. Five artists perform each night.

Le Comedy Club
42 bd de Bonne Nouvelle, 10th (01.73.54.17.00, www.lecomedyclub.fr). M° Bonne Nouvelle. **Shows** days vary. **Admission** €8-€30. **Map** p402 J4.
Jamel Debbouze, the comic known for his one-man shows and his roles in films such as *Le Fabuleux Destin d'Amélie Poulain*, gives the comedy trade a helping hand with this theatre. Tuesdays and Wednesdays (7.30pm) are open mic nights.

★ Le Point Virgule
7 rue Ste-Croix-de-la-Bretonnerie, 4th (01.42.78.67.03, www.lepointvirgule.com). M° Hôtel de Ville. **Shows** times vary, see website for details. **Admission** €19; €15 reductions. *2 shows* €30, *3 shows* €39. *Children's show* €12; €10 children. **No credit cards. Map** p409 K6.

ARTS & ENTERTAINMENT

Au Lapin Agile.

Paradis Latin.

ARTS & ENTERTAINMENT

This small Marais theatre has become the ultimate launch pad for comedians, with shows, a *café-théâtre* school and an annual comedy festival in September. The theatre launched a new venue in Montparnasse in late 2012, the Grand Point Virgule (8bis rue de l'Arrivée, 15th, 01.42.78.67.03, www.legrandpointvirgule.com), to provide some Left Bank laughs.

LEFT BANK
Cabaret

★ **Paradis Latin**
28 rue Cardinal Lemoine, 5th (01.43.25.28.28, www.paradislatin.com). M° Cardinal Lemoine. **Dinner** 8pm. **Show** 9.30pm daily. **Admission** *Show* (incl champagne) €90. *Dinner & show* €130-€190. *Show only* €65. **Map** p406 K8.
This is the most authentic of the cabarets, not only because it's family-run (the men run the cabaret, the daughter does the costumes), but also because the clientele is mostly French, something that has a direct effect on the prices (this is the cheapest revue) and the cuisine, which tends to be high quality. Show-wise you can expect the usual fare: generous doses of glitter, live singing and cheesy *entr'acte* acts performed in a stunning belle époque room. There's also a twice-monthly matinée.

Music

Paris's music scene is bubbling with talent, and the recent emergence of some great new bands speaks volumes about the creativity of today's up-and-coming artists. The capital is overflowing with authentic concert venues,

from monster stadiums to intimate bars and jazz clubs, and venues like Nouveau Casino and L'International give precious stage space to those on the way up the musical ladder.

Chanson française is still going strong, helped by the success of Les Trois Baudets, a government-subsidised *chanson* hall in the heart of Pigalle – French law dictates that 40 per cent of music broadcast in France must be in the French language.

Jazz is having a mini revival too: after the disappearance of old flames like Le Slow Club (once one of the most famous jazz joints in Europe), Le Bilboquet and Les 7 Lézards, a handful of new joints have opened up, while flagship clubs Au Duc des Lombards, New Morning and Le Sunset/Le Sunside continue to book a range of top-notch acts from around the globe. Paris is also a European leader for world music, particularly African and Arab acts. And don't forget that every 21 June, the whole city turns into one giant music venue for the **Fête de la Musique** (*see p34*), when a party in the street is guaranteed.

INFORMATION AND RESOURCES
The weekly magazine *Les Inrockuptibles* is a valuable resource. Alternatively, try bi-monthly gig bible *Lylo*, free in bars and branches of Fnac. The **Fnac** ticket office (www.fnac.com) also displays details of up-and-coming concerts. For reduced-price tickets try www.billetreduc.com. Depending on your tastes (and your French) radio can be useful for tip-offs: Nova (101.5FM) does electro, lounge and world; TSF (89.9FM) and FIP (105.1FM) cover jazz; and Le Mouv' (92.1FM) and OuiFM (102.3FM) are for rock fans.

Box offices are usually closed in the daytime, and most venues take a break in August. Several excellent venues, like La Bellevilloise, host regular free nights – ideal if you're feeling adventurous and/or are on a budget. For concerts, it's best to turn up at the time stated on the ticket: strict noise curfews mean that start times are adhered to pretty closely.

RIGHT BANK
Rock & pop

Le Bataclan
50 bd Voltaire, 11th (01.43.14.00.30, www.le-bataclan.com). M° Oberkampf. **Open** times vary. **Map** p403 M5.
This distinctive venue, fashioned like a Chinese pagoda with a multicoloured façade, first opened in 1864 and remains admirably discerning in its booking of rock, world, jazz and hip hop acts.

Le Bus Palladium
6 rue Fontaine, 9th (01.45.26.80.35, www.lebus palladium.com). M° St-Georges, Pigalle or Blanche. **Open** *Concerts* 9pm-12.30am. *Club* 12.30-5am Thur-Sat. **Map** p401 H2.
This legendary rock venue, graced by the likes of Mick Jagger and The Beatles in its heyday, is back on the map after a 20-year spell out of the limelight with a vintage house vibe somewhere between retro rockabilly and punk psychedelia. While the new generation gets wild in the pit, former regulars are trying to catch their breath at the restaurant upstairs. Check the programme for concerts.

★ La Cigale/La Boule Noire
120 bd de Rochechouart,18th (01.49.25.89.99, www.lacigale.fr; 01.49.25.81.75, www.laboule-noire.fr). M° Anvers or Pigalle. **Open** times vary. **Map** p402 J2.
This is easily one of Paris's finest concert venues. The lovely, horseshoe-shaped theatre La Cigale is linked to more cosy venue La Boule Noire, which is good for catching cult-ish visiting indie and rock acts.

Les Disquaires
4-6 rue des Taillandiers, 11th (01.40.21.94.60, www.lesdisquaires.com). M° Bastille. **Open** 6pm-2am Tue-Sun. **Map** p407 M6.
In its newly renovated, shiny red interior, Les Disquaires' little stage directly faces the dancefloor and the decks, and exhibitions by local artists decorate the walls around the bar. The venue is a good bet for enjoying a quality gig over a cocktail or beer during happy hour, and there's plenty to choose from in the programme of jazz, funk, hip hop and soul.

Espace B
16 rue Barbanègre, 19th (01.40.37.30.29, www.espaceb.net). M° Corentin Cariou.

L'International.

Open 9am-1.30am Mon-Fri; 3pm-1.30am Sat, Sun. *Concerts* times vary. **No credit cards**. **Map** p403 inset.
On a quiet street near Parc de la Villette, Espace B is a funny little place somewhere between a neighbourhood bar, an Italian restaurant and a concert hall. The bill is varied, including synth-pop, electro-rock, hip hop, indie, shoegaze, grunge, folktronica, noise, chillwave and more. On some evenings, you can even find burlesque or avant-garde theatre.

La Flèche d'Or
102bis rue de Bagnolet, 20th (01.44.64.01.02, www.flechedor.fr). M° Alexandre Dumas. **Open** 8pm-2am Tue-Sat. *Concerts* times vary.
This much-loved indie and electro venue, which reopened a couple of years ago after a six-month shutdown, is a great place to check out the capital's live music scene, with three or four bands playing a night. It also gives monthly residencies to local groups and DJs.

★ L'International
5-7 rue Moret, 11th (01.49.29.76.45, www.linternational.fr). M° Ménilmontant. **Open** 6pm-2am daily. **Concerts** times vary. **Map** p403 N4.
This concert-bar is a breath of fresh air, with free entry and a string of on-the-up bands playing to hip indie crowds every night of the week. Once a month there's an after-party until 4am.

Mains d'Oeuvres
1 rue Charles-Garnier, 93400 St-Ouen (01.40.11.25.25, www.mainsdoeuvres.org). M° Garibaldi or Porte de Clignancourt. **Open** 9.30am-midnight Mon-Fri; 11am-midnight Sat; noon-9pm Sun. *Concerts* times vary.
A veritable hub for fringe musical and performance activity just outside Paris, the Mains d'Oeuvres is a huge former leisure centre for car factory workers that specialises in leftfield electro, rock mavericks

and multimedia artists. It frequently plays hosts to the annual Festival des Attitudes Indé (Sept-Oct) for up-and-coming bands.

La Maroquinerie

23 rue Boyer, 20th (01.40.33.35.05, www. lamaroquinerie.fr). Mº Gambetta. **Open** *Box office* (in person only) 2.30-7pm Mon-Fri. **Concerts** times vary. Closed Aug. **Map** p403 P4.
Literary discussion and rock 'n' roll coexist happily at this happening locale. It's home to the Inrocks Indie Club nights, featuring up-and-coming rock acts, but there are still plenty of traces of its world music roots on show.

★ La Mécanique Ondulatoire

8 passage Thiéré, 11th (01.43.55.69.14). Mº Bastille or Ledru Rollin. **Open** 6pm-2am Mon-Sat. **Concerts** times vary. **Map** p407 M7.
Cementing Bastille's status as the capital's prime hangout for rockers, this exciting venue is spread over three levels and alternates eclectic DJ sets with live acts in the cellar, plus there's jazz on Tuesday nights. It was forced to close in September 2012 after complaints from the neighbours, but reopened the following month.

Le Motel

8 passage Josset, 11th (01.58.30.88.52, www. lemotel.fr). Mº Ledru Rollin. **Open** 6pm-1.45am Tue-Sun. **Map** p407 M7.
This most Anglophile of Paris bars, with Stone Roses and Smiths posters adorning the walls, manages to squeeze plenty of live bands, including some of the best new local talent, on to its tiny stage. On Tuesdays, Wednesdays and alternate Sundays there's a pop quiz that attracts plenty of music-savvy regulars.

Nouveau Casino

109 rue Oberkampf, 11th (01.43.57.57.40, www.nouveaucasino.net). Mº Ménilmontant, Parmentier or St-Maur. **Open** *Concerts* times vary. **Map** p403 N5.
A bankable and loveable, albeit rather commercial, venue run by the adjacent Café Charbon, with fab gigs and club nights featuring rock, dub and garage, plus reasonable drinks prices.

Olympia

28 bd des Capucines, 9th (08.92.68.33.68, www.olympiahall.com). Mº Opéra. **Open** *Box office* noon-2pm, 6-9.30pm Mon-Fri; 5-9.30pm Sat, Sun & 2hrs before shows. By phone 10am-6pm Mon-Fri; 2-6pm Sat, Sun. *Concerts* times vary. **Map** p401 G4.
The Beatles, Frank Sinatra, Jimi Hendrix and Edith Piaf all performed at the historic Olympia. Now it's mainly home to nostalgia and *variété*, although big names do still drop by – Crystal Castles played here in 2013.

O'Sullivans by the Mill

92 bd de Clichy, 18th (01.53.09.08.49, www.osullivans-pubs.com). Mº Blanche or Place de Clichy. **Open** 3pm-5.30am Mon-Thur; 3pm-6am Fri; noon-6pm Sat, Sun. **Concerts** times vary. **Map** p401 G2.
This Irish chain bar is all about late, late nights, with grizzly weekend rock gigs that last until sunrise, DJs and open mic nights the first Wednesday of the month. Thursday nights are always wild.

Palais des Congrès

2 pl de la Porte Maillot, 17th (01.40.68.22.22, www.viparis.com). Mº Porte Maillot. **Open** times vary. **Map** p400 B2.

ARTS & ENTERTAINMENT

La Flèche d'Or.

La Bellevilloise.

ARTS & ENTERTAINMENT

The sound and the views are good wherever you sit in this state-of-the-art amphitheatre. Diana Krall and Paolo Conte have recently graced the stage.

Palais Omnisports de Paris-Bercy

8 bd de Bercy, 12th (08.92.39.04.90, www.bercy.fr). M° Bercy. **Box office** 11am-6pm Mon-Sat. **Map** p407 N9.
The traditional venue for rock and pop behemoths: Justin Bieber was a recent draw.

★ Point Ephémère

200 quai de Valmy, 10th (01.40.34.02.48, www.pointephemere.org). M° Jaurès or Louis Blanc. **Open** noon-2am Mon-Sat; noon-9pm Sun. *Concerts* times vary. **Map** p402 L2.
This converted warehouse is a classy affair, bringing together up-and-coming local rock, jazz and world gigs with a decent restaurant, dance and recording studios and exhibitions.

Le Reservoir

16 rue de la Forge-Royale, 11th (01.43.56.39.60, www.reservoirclub.com). M° Faidherbe Chaligny or Ledru-Rollin. **Open** 8pm-late Tue-Sat. **Map** p407 N7.
This classy, Anglo-inspired venue hosts regular club nights and indie gigs.

Zénith

211 av Jean-Jaurès, 19th (www.zenith-paris. com). M° Porte de Pantin. **Open** times vary. **Map** p403 inset.
State-of-the-art sound and credible bands make this the large venue of choice. Arctic Monkeys and Foals both played here in 2013.

Chanson

★ La Bellevilloise

19-21 rue Boyer, 20th (01.46.36.07.07, www. labellevilloise.com). M° Gambetta or Ménilmontant. **Open** 7pm-1am Wed, Thur; 7pm-2am Fri; 6pm-2am Sat; 11.30am-5pm Sun. **Map** p403 P4.
Is there anything that Paris's former co-operative doesn't do? There's food, drinks, DJs and live music – lashings of it, not only in the downstairs concert hall but in the Oliviers restaurant and upstairs bar too. The music selection is eclectic.

Chez Adel

10 rue de la Grange-aux-Belles, 10th (01.42.08.24.61). M° Jacques Bonsergent. **Open** noon-midnight Tue-Sun. *Concerts* 6pm Tue-Sun. **Map** p402 L3.
Patron Adel is probably the most renowned *chanson* café owner in Paris, and this fine den of kitsch attracts countless devotees with its repertoire of *chanson* and Eastern European sounds. The crowd, fuelled by rum and ginger cocktails (the house speciality), is always enthusiastic.

Le Limonaire

18 Cité Bergère, 9th (01.45.23.33.33, http://limonaire.free.fr). M° Grands Boulevards. **Open** 6pm-2am daily. *Concerts* 9pm Mon; 10pm Tue-Sat; 7pm & 9.30pm Sun. **Map** p402 J4.
Serious *chanson* takes the limelight, and performances vary from piano-led *chansonniers* to cabaret.

Sentier des Halles

50 rue d'Aboukir, 2nd (01.42.61.89.90, www.lesentierdeshalles.fr). M° Sentier. **Open** times vary. *Concerts* 8pm Mon-Fri; 8pm, 10pm Sat, Sun. Closed Aug. **Map** p402 J4.
Le Sentier has developed beyond its traditional *chanson* base to embrace a variety of modern styles plus the occasional stand-up act.

Les Trois Baudets

64 bd de Clichy, 18th (01.42.62.33.33, www.les troisbaudets.com). M° Pigalle. **Open** times vary. **Map** p401 H2.
All dolled up in black and red, with a 250-seater theatre, an enviable sound system, two bars and a restaurant, this concert hall encourages *chanson française* and other musical genres (rock, electro, folk and slam) – as long as they're in French.

★ Le Vieux Belleville

12 rue des Envierges, 20th (01.44.62.92.66, www.le-vieux-belleville.com). M° Pyrénées. **Open** 11am-3pm, 8pm-2am Thur-Sat. *Concerts* 8pm Thur-Sat. Closed mid Aug. **Map** p403 N4.
If you're looking for an authentic Belleville rendezvous, there's no better location than this old-style café with terrace, where the traditions of accordion music and croaky-voiced *chanson* endure.

ESSENTIAL PARIS ALBUMS

Sounds of the city.

AUX ARMES ET CÆTERA SERGE GAINSBOURG (1979)
Recorded in Jamaica, and featuring vocals from the I-Threes, this era-defining classic shifted more than a million copies. The title track (a variation of *La Marseillaise*) was one of the first reggae songs to hit France and so polemical that the Parisian megastar received death threats.

SUPREME NTM NTM (1998)
Essential listening from *banlieue* tough boys Nique Ta Mère (Mother Fuckers), made up of rappers Joey Starr (Didier Morville) and Kool Shen (Bruno Lopès). This controversial hip hop album influenced a generation with songs such as 'Seine Saint Denis Style' and 'Back dans les Bacs'.

HYMNE A LA MOME EDITH PIAF (2012)
Edith Piaf, who was born in Belleville, is still hailed by many as the greatest singer France has ever known. This digitally remastered box set of 45 of her most famous songs, including 'La Vie en Rose', 'L'Hymne à l'Amour' and 'Non, Je ne Regrette Rien', serves as a wonderful reminder of her raw talent.

THE NO COMPRENDO LES RITA MITSOUKO (1986)
Les Rita Mitsouko (guitarist Fred Chichin and singer Catherine Ringer) produced wacky electro pop with real musical substance and quirky text. Three tracks from the *No Comprendo* album – 'Andy', 'C'est Comme Ca' and 'Les Histoires d'a' – are still dancefloor staples today.

MY GOD IS BLUE SEBASTIEN TELLIER (2012)
Tellier's fourth album plies his trademark brand of cool, transgressive, electro-sexy pop. The bearded guru (who, bizarrely, sang for France in the 2008 Eurovision Song Contest), is the only Parisian who doles out serious electro music without taking himself too seriously.

MIDNIGHT IN PARIS VARIOUS ARTISTS (2011)
Woody Allen's *Midnight in Paris* is a love letter to a city and, like *Manhattan*, opens with an adoring montage, set to jazz, of the city by day and night. Cue this soundtrack, featuring the likes of Sidney Bechet and Josephine Baker, that added real soul to Allen's romantic ode to the capital.

ARTS & ENTERTAINMENT

ARTS & ENTERTAINMENT

World & traditional

Cité de la Musique

221 av Jean-Jaurès, 19th (01.44.84.44.84, www.cite-musique.fr). M° Porte de Pantin.
Box office noon-6pm Tue-Sat; 10am-6pm Sun.
By phone 11am-7pm Mon-Sat; 11am-6pm Sun.
Concerts times vary. **Map** p403 inset.
This excellent museum/concert complex welcomes plenty of big names, and also does a fine line in contemporary classical, avant-jazz and electronica.

Le Kibélé

12 rue de l'Echiquier, 10th (01.48.24.57.74, www.kibele.fr). M° Bonne Nouvelle. **Open** noon-2.30pm, 7pm-midnight Mon-Sat. *Concerts* 8pm & 9.30pm Mon-Sat. **Map** p402 K4.
Stashed away below a Turkish restaurant, this little basement is a landmark for new talent and small groups from far-flung places as they pass through Paris. Order a drink at the restaurant bar and head down into the cosy, softly lit vaulted room to enjoy acoustic concerts of Latin music, klezmer, jazz or *chanson française*. Early each night, actors and comedians try their luck on the little stage (check listings online).

Musée Guimet

6 pl d'Iéna, 16th (01.56.52.53.00, auditorium 01.40.73.88.18, www.guimet.fr). M° Iéna.
Open 10am-6pm Mon, Wed-Sun. *Concerts* 8.30pm some Thur, Fri & Sat. **Map** p404 C5.
Indian and Asian music by visiting troupes, as well as dance and theatre, takes pride of place in the auditorium of the Musée Guimet.

★ Théâtre de la Ville

2 pl du Châtelet, 4th (01.42.74.22.77, www.theatredelaville-paris.com). M° Châtelet.
Open *Box office* 11am-7pm Mon; 11am-8pm Tue-Sat. *By phone* 11am-7pm Mon-Sat. *Concerts* times vary. **Map** p408 J6.
Music and dance of the highest order can be found here, with jazz and music from just about anywhere you can think of (Iraq, Japan, Thailand, Brittany) amid the classical recitals.

IN THE KNOW RECORD DEAL

Born Bad (11 rue St-Sabin, 11th, www.bornbad.fr) is a don't-miss record shop with its own label that has signed excellent French rock groups such as Cheveu, Magnetix and Yussuf Jerusalem. Aside from its own bands, the shop also offers an array of cool sounds, from punk to blues and hardcore. If you want to try before you buy, ask at the counter and they'll stick it on the sound system.

Jazz & blues

Ateliers de Charonne

21 rue de Charonne, 11th (01.40.21.83.35, www.atelierch5aronne.com). M° Charonne or Ledru-Rollin. **Open** 8pm-1am daily. *Concerts* 9pm Mon-Sat; 7pm Sun. **Map** p407 M7.
This jazz club is the place in which to see the rising stars of gypsy jazz (*jazz manouche*). If you want to grab a good spot, reserve for dinner and the show.

Autour de Midi-Minuit

11 rue Lepic, 18th (01.55.79.16.48, www.autourdemidi.fr). M° Blanche. **Open** noon-2.30pm, 7pm-late Tue-Sat. *Concerts* 9.30pm Tue-Thur; 10pm Fri, Sat. **Map** p401 H2.
The Tuesday night *boeuf* (jam session) is always free, as are many other concerts – some by big names such as Laurent Epstein and Bruno Casties.

Le Baiser Salé

58 rue des Lombards, 1st (01.42.33.37.71, www.lebaisersale.com). M° Châtelet. **Open** 5pm-6am daily. *Concerts* daily (times vary). **Map** p406 J6.
The 'Salty Kiss' divides its time between passing *chanson* merchants, world artists and jazzmen of every stripe, from trad to fusion.

★ Au Duc des Lombards

42 rue des Lombards, 1st (01.42.33.22.88, www.ducdeslombards.com). M° Châtelet. **Open** 7pm-midnight Mon-Thur; 7pm-4am Fri, Sat. *Concerts* 8pm, 10pm Mon-Sat. **Map** p406 J6.
This venerable jazz spot attracts a high class of performer and a savvy crowd. Check out the '*bons plans*' section of the website for reduced-price tickets.

Jazz Club Etoile

Hôtel Méridien Etoile, 81 bd Gouvion-St-Cyr, 17th (01.40.68.30.42, www.jazzclub-paris.com). M° Porte Maillot. **Open** 7am-1am Mon, Tue, Sun; 7am-1.30am Wed-Sat. *Concerts* 9.30pm-1am Wed-Sat; 12.30-3pm Sun. **Map** p400 B2.
Created in 1975 by French jazz drummer and actor Moustache, this club continues to be a hotspot for US jazz, plus soul and funk. Connoisseurs can peruse a whisky list as long as the Mississippi.

★ New Morning

7-9 rue des Petites-Ecuries, 10th (01.45.23.51.41, www.newmorning.com). **Open** 8pm-late daily. *Concerts* times vary. **Map** p402 K3.
One of the best places in which to see the latest jazz exponents, with a policy that also embraces *chanson*, blues, world music and sophisticated pop.

Le Onze

83 rue Jean-Pierre Timbaud, 11th (01.48.06.11.97, www.onzebar.com). M° Couronnes. **Open** 10am-2am Mon-Fri; 5pm-2am Sat, Sun. *Concerts* times vary. **Map** p403 N4.

Cité de la Musique.

This little boho bar seethes with people day and night. Very hip right now, it's been done up in shabby chic – the stuffing of the big sofas is oozing out, witness to many wild parties. Daily concerts range from Balkan folk to rock'n'roll, via jazz, blues, funk or afrobeat, with people getting up to dance wherever they can find room between the tables and chairs.

Le Sunset/Le Sunside
60 rue des Lombards, 1st (01.40.26.46.60, www.sunset-sunside.com). M° Châtelet. **Open** 5pm-2am daily. *Concerts* times vary. **Map** p406 J6.
A split-personality venue, with Sunset dealing in electric groups and Sunside hosting acoustic performances. Their renown pulls in big jazz names from both sides of the Atlantic.

Théâtre du Châtelet
1 pl du Châtelet, 4th (01.40.28.28.40, www. chatelet-theatre.com). M° Châtelet. **Open** times vary. **Map** p406 J6.
This venerable theatre and classical music hall has another life as a jazz and *chanson* venue, with performances by top-notch international musicians.

LEFT BANK
Rock & pop

Batofar
Opposite 11 quai François-Mauriac, 13th (09.71.25.50.61, www.batofar.org). M° Bibliothèque François-Mitterrand or Quai de la Gare. **Open** times vary. **Map** p407 N10.
This enduringly hip party boat lays on DJs, rappers and assorted underground noise-merchants for the benefit of an up-for-it crowd. It comes into its own in the summer, when the terrace opens at 7pm.
▶ *For more on Batofar's club nights, see p270.*

Chanson

Au Magique
42 rue de Gergovie, 14th (01.45.42.26.10, www.aumagique.com). M° Pernety. **Open** 8pm-2am Wed-Sun. *Concerts* 9pm. **No credit cards**. **Map** p405 F10.
Artiste-in-residence Marc Havet serenades punters with politically incorrect *chanson* at weekends; you can also expect poetry events and exhibitions.

World & traditional

Institut du Monde Arabe (Auditorium Rafik Hariri)
1 rue des Fossés-St-Bernard, 5th (01.40.51.38.38, www.imarabe.org). M° Jussieu. **Open** 10am-6pm (8.30pm performance days) Tue-Sun. *Tickets* 10am-5pm; 90mins before show. *Concerts* usually 8.30pm Fri, Sat. **Map** p409 K7.
This huge, plush auditorium attracts some of the biggest names in the world of Arab music.

Jazz & blues

Caveau de la Huchette
5 rue de la Huchette, 5th (01.43.26.65.05, www.caveaudelahuchette.fr). M° St-Michel. **Open** 9.30pm-2.30am Mon-Thur, Sun; 9.30pm-6am Fri, Sat. *Concerts* 10pm. **Map** p408 J7.
This medieval cellar has been a mainstay for more than 60 years. Jazz shows are followed by early-hours performances in a swing, rock, soul or disco vein.

Caveau des Oubliettes
52 rue Galande, 5th (01.46.34.23.09, www. caveaudesoubliettes.fr). M° St-Michel. **Open** 5pm-2am Mon, Tue, Sun; 5pm-4am Wed-Sat. *Concerts* 10pm Wed-Sun. **Map** p408 J7.
A foot-tapping frenzy echoes in this medieval dungeon. Mondays are Pop Rock Jam nights, Tuesdays are Jazz Jam Boogaloo nights, and there are various other jam sessions during the rest of the week.

Le Petit Journal Montparnasse
113 rue du Commandant René-Mouchotte, 14th (01.43.21.56.70, www.petitjournalmontparnasse. com). M° Gaîté. **Open** 7am-2am Mon-Sat. *Concerts* 9.30pm Mon-Thur; 10pm Fri, Sat. **Map** p405 F9.
An institution for jazz amateurs, this dining/concert hall is inspired by the jazz of New Orleans and the soul of Detroit, but also gospel, blues, rock'n'roll, Latin jazz and bossa nova.

Le Swan Bar
165 bd de Montparnasse, 6th (01.44.27.05.84, www.swanbar.fr). M° Raspail or Vavin. **Open** 7pm-1am Tue-Sat. *Concerts* 7.30pm & 9.30pm Tue-Sat. **Map** p405 H9.
The Swan Bar is a modern, American-style jazz bar for traditional jazz, torch songs and jamming.

ARTS & ENTERTAINMENT

Performing Arts

The biggest news in the world of classical music is the arrival of Jean Nouvel's dramatic 2,400-seat Philharmonie in 2015. In the meantime, historic venues such as Salle Pleyel and Palais Garnier provide a stunning setting for a rich calendar of opera and classical music, and with tickets starting at just €10 accessibility isn't restricted to the *haut monde*.

Accessibility issues of a different sort come into play with Paris's theatre scene. French-speaking drama buffs can choose from some 450 productions every week, from offbeat indie shows to highbrow classics, whereas Anglophones have to make do with a handful of international companies performing in their mother tongue.

Paris is home to a thriving dance scene. There's no shortage of ballet productions at the Théâtre du Châtelet and Palais Garnier, and the Festival d'Automne features an impressive line-up.

Classical Music & Opera

The Théâtre des Champs-Elysées celebrated 100 years in the limelight with a host of big-name soloists and conductors appearing in 2013. The Opéra de Paris, meanwhile, splits its major productions between the bunker-like Bastille and the glorious Palais Garnier. The main musical provider in summer is **Paris Quartier d'Eté** (01.44.94.98.00, www.quartierdete.com), with concerts in gardens across the city. The **Festival de Saint-Denis** (01.48.13.06.07, www.festival-saint-denis.com) offers top names in a spectacular setting, while the candlelit **Chopin Piano Festival** takes place in the Jardin de Bagatelle (www.frederic-chopin.com).

INFORMATION AND TICKETS

For comprehensive listings, see *L'Officiel des Spectacles* or *Pariscope*. Monthly *Diapason* also lists classical concerts, while *Opéra* magazine provides good coverage of all things vocal. Look out too for *Cadences* and *La Terrasse*, two free monthlies distributed outside concerts. Also check the Time Out Paris website (www.timeout.fr) for comprehensive cultural listings throughout the year.

ORCHESTRAS & ENSEMBLES

★ **Les Arts Florissants**
01.43.87.98.88, www.arts-florissants.com.
William Christie's 'Arts Flo' remains France's leading Early Music group, and his conducting has become a benchmark of authentic performance. The group has not neglected passing on the secrets of Baroque ornamentation to the next generation, with the Jardin des Voix busy cultivating exciting young talent.

IN THE KNOW CLASSICAL CUTS

Many venues and orchestras offer cut-rate tickets to students under 26 an hour before curtain-up. For the Fête de la Musique (21 June) all events are free, and year-round freebies crop up at the Maison de Radio France and the Conservatoire de Paris, as well as in certain churches.

Ensemble Intercontemporain
01.44.84.44.50, www.ensembleinter.com.
German composer and conductor Matthias Pintscher has taken over from Finnish conductor Susanna Mälkki as musical director of this bastion of contemporary music founded by Pierre Boulez. The exacting standard of the 31 soloists is beyond reproach, and the ensemble has an enviable international reputation, making it one of the most popular on the Paris music scene.

Orchestre de Chambre de Paris
08.00.42.67.57,
www.orchestredechambredeparis.com.
The orchestra has struggled in recent years to find its specificity in a competitive field, but that is all set to improve after a change of name (from Ensemble Orchestral de Paris) and leadership, which has seen the wonderfully talented Thomas Zehetmair take up the baton as principal conductor.

Orchestre Colonne
01.42.33.72.89, www.orchestrecolonne.fr.
Sometimes to be found at the Salle Gaveau (*see p284*), this orchestra – led by composer Laurent Petitgirard – has intelligent programming, with every concert teaming a contemporary work with more popular repertoire. The excellent series of *concerts éveil* continues to provide bargain tickets for parents and children, making an ideal introduction to classical music.

Orchestre Lamoureux
01.58.39.30.30, www.orchestrelamoureux.com.
This reliable orchestra, which made the first recording of Ravel's *Boléro*, is now under the leadership of musical director Fayçal Karoui.

Orchestre National de France
01.56.40.15.16, www.radiofrance.fr.
Daniele Gatti is now firmly in charge of France's leading orchestra, bringing along his own brand of warm Italianate theatricality, in sharp contrast to his predecessor, veteran Kurt Masur, and his more structured Germanic approach.

★ Orchestre de Paris
01.42.56.13.13, www.orchestredeparis.com.
Many consider this orchestra to be the finest in France, and the arrival of Estonian-born Paavo Järvi as musical director a few years ago has done even more to boost its lofty reputation. Recent highlights

ARTS & ENTERTAINMENT

Computer-generated images of the **Philharmonie**, due to open in 2015.

MOULIN ROUGE ®
PARIS

125 ANS

© Jail du Moulin Rouge 2014 - Moulin Rouge - 1-1028199

0 Cédille

THE SHOW OF THE MOST FAMOUS
CABARET IN THE WORLD !
DINNER & SHOW AT 7PM FROM €185
SHOW AT 9PM & 11PM : €112

MONTMARTRE
82, BLD DE CLICHY - 75018 PARIS
TEL : 33(0)1 53 09 82 82

WWW.MOULIN-ROUGE.COM
FACEBOOK.COM/LEMOULINROUGEOFFICIE

have included a performance of Haydn's *Cello Concerto No.2* by Argentine Sol Gabetta, and Jean-Yves Thibaudet playing Saint-Saëns.

Orchestre Pasdeloup
01.42.78.10.00, www.concertspasdeloup.com.
The Pasdeloup is the oldest orchestra in Paris, and the calendar always features a great collection of concerts under the watchful eye of artistic director Patrice Fontanarosa.

Orchestre Philharmonique de Radio France
01.56.40.15.16, www.radiofrance.fr.
Myung-Whun Chung has been the musical director here for more than a decade. The standard of the orchestra is traditionally considered to lag behind that of the Orchestre National de France, but it has a dynamic programme and does plenty to try to attract younger audiences.

VENUES
Right Bank

Auditorium du Louvre
Entrance through Pyramid, Cour Napoléon, Musée du Louvre, rue de Rivoli, 1st (01.40.20.55.55, reservations 01.40.20.55.00, www.louvre.fr). M^o *Palais Royal Musée du Louvre.* **Box office** 9am-5.30pm Mon, Wed-Fri. Closed July, Aug. **Admission** €5-€32. **Map** p401 H5.
The Auditorium du Louvre packs in a full season with chamber music, lunchtime concerts and music on film. The season is divided into themed groups with artists performing a wide range of music, including a recent series of performances to coincide with the opening of the new Islamic Arts Galleries.

Châtelet – Théâtre Musical de Paris
1 pl du Châtelet, 4th (01.40.28.28.40, www.chatelet-theatre.com). M^o *Châtelet.* **Box office** (17 av Victoria) 11am-7pm Mon-Sat; 1hr before performance Sun. *By phone* 10am-7pm Mon-Sat. Closed July, Aug. **Admission** €10-€118. **Map** p408 J6.
Jean-Luc Choplin has radically changed the programming of this bastion of Paris music-making. An attempt to rediscover the theatre's popular roots has seemingly been achieved at the expense of traditional fine music subscribers. There's plenty to appeal in the diverse line-up, though, with performances by the likes of Anne Sofie von Otter and Greek songstress Nana Mouskouri.

★ Cité de la Musique
221 av Jean-Jaurès, 19th (01.44.84.44.84, www.cite-musique.fr). M^o *Porte de Pantin.* **Box office** noon-6pm Tue-Sat; 10am-6pm Sun. *By phone* 11am-7pm Mon-Sat; 11am-6pm Sun. **Admission** €8-€41. **Map** p403 inset.

Cité de la Musique.

The energetic programming here features a vast non-classical repertoire that includes world music and jazz. Concerts are frequently grouped into series with a pedagogic aim, tending to concentrate on the Baroque and the contemporary.
► *The Conservatoire de Paris (209 av Jean-Jaurès, 19th, 01.40.40.45.45) hosts world-class performers, and features many free concerts.*

IRCAM
1 pl Igor-Stravinsky, 4th (01.44.78.48.43, www.ircam.fr). M^o *Hôtel de Ville.* **Map** p406 K6.
The underground bunker next to the Centre Pompidou, set up in 1969 by avant-garde composer Pierre Boulez to create electronic microtonal music, is looking less redundant nowadays with a full programme of courses and conferences. Not many concerts take place in the building itself, but IRCAM sponsors concerts with a modernist theme across the city. See the website for details.

Maison de Radio France
116 av du Président-Kennedy, 16th (01.56.40.15.16, www.radiofrance.fr). M^o *Passy/ RER Avenue du Pdt Kennedy.* **Box office** 11am-6pm Mon-Sat. *By phone* 10am-5pm Mon-Sat. **Admission** €10-€85. **Map** p404 A7.
State-owned radio station France Musique broadcasts a broad range of classical concerts. The quality of music-making from the Orchestre National de France and the Orchestre Philharmonique de Radio France is impressive. *Photo p284.*

Opéra National de Paris, Bastille
Pl de la Bastille, 12th (08.92.89.90.90, from abroad 01.71.25.24.23, www.operadeparis.fr).

Mᵒ Bastille. **Box office** (130 rue de Lyon, 12th)
2.30-6.30pm Mon-Sat & 1hr before performance.
By phone 9am-6pm Mon-Fri; 9am-1pm Sat.
Admission €5-€180. **Map** p409 M7.
The Bastille is never going to be a beautiful building,
and the unflattering acoustics and miles of corridors
combine to create an atmosphere more akin to an
airport than an opera house. But the standard of
performance is what matters, and the Bastille has
plenty of exciting evenings under director Nicolas
Joel. The 2013 season brought to the stage great
classics such as *Falstaff*, *Siegfried* and *Carmen*.

★ Opéra National de Paris, Palais Garnier

*Pl de l'Opéra, 9th (08.92.89.90.90, from abroad
01.71.25.24.23, www.operadeparis.fr). Mᵒ
Opéra.* **Box office** 11.30am-6.30pm Mon-Sat
& 1hr before performance. *By phone* 9am-6pm
Mon-Fri; 9am-1pm Sat. **Admission** €10-€185.
Map p401 G4.
The Palais Garnier, with its extravagant decor and
ceiling by Marc Chagall, is the jewel in the crown of
Paris music-making, as well as a glistening focal
point for the Right Bank. The Opéra National often
favours the high-tech Bastille (*see above*) for new
productions, but the matchless acoustics of the
Palais Garnier are superior to the newer Bastille's,
and they were shaken by a stunning production of
Engelbert Humperdinck's *Hänsel und Gretel* in 2013.

Péniche Opéra

*Facing 46 quai de la Loire, 19th (01.53.35.07.77,
www.penicheopera.com). Mᵒ Jaurès or Laumière.*
Box office *By phone* 10.30am-6pm Mon-Fri;
2-6pm Sat. **Admission** €12-€20. **Map** p401 M1.
The Péniche Opéra is an enterprising, barge-based
company that produces chamber-scale shows and
concerts, directed by the indefatigable Mireille
Larroche. Programming ranges from Baroque rarities to contemporary creations via charming revue-
style shows.

Salle Cortot

*78 rue Cardinet, 17th (01.47.63.47.48,
www.ecolenormalecortot.com). Mᵒ Malesherbes.*

IN THE KNOW PIPE DREAMS

The regular free recitals by guest organists
at **Notre-Dame** (*see p54*) take advantage
of the building's unique acoustics and the
awesome sound of the great organ, which
was restored in 2012 for the cathedral's
850th anniversary. Programming is
eclectic, with the nave echoing to gothic
suites, carillons, fanfares, preludes and
symphonies played by visiting organists
from around the world.

Maison de Radio France. *See p283.*

No box office. **Admission** varies (phone for
details). **Map** 401 E2.
This intimate concert hall located inside the Ecole
Normale de Musique has excellent acoustics for
chamber music and master classes, which are often
free of charge.

Salle Gaveau

*45-47 rue de la Boétie, 8th (01.49.53.05.07,
www.sallegaveau.com). Mᵒ Miromesnil.* **Box
office** 10am-6pm Mon-Fri & 30mins before
performance. **Admission** €15-€75. **Map**
p401 E3.
The Salle Gaveau was built at the start of the 20th
century as a chamber music venue. Today, its ever-
growing programme includes classical concerts,
musicals, a sprinkling of comedy productions
and Les Marmots à Gaveau, aimed at kids with
performances followed by a practical workshop
called 'Osez la musique'.

Salle Pleyel

*252 rue du Fbg-St-Honoré, 8th (01.42.56.13.13,
www.sallepleyel.fr). Mᵒ Ternes.* **Box office**
noon-7pm Mon-Sat; 2hrs before show Sun.
By phone 11am-7pm Mon-Sat; 11am-2hrs
before performance. **Admission** €10-€180.
Map p400 D3.
Home to the Orchestre de Paris, the restored concert
hall looks splendid. If the improved acoustics are
only partially successful, the venue has nevertheless
regained its status as the capital's leading concert
hall for large-scale symphonic concerts, and should
keep it until the completion of the city's new concert
hall in 2015 with appearances by the likes of Sol
Gabetta and Radu Lupu.

ARTS & ENTERTAINMENT

★ Théâtre des Bouffes du Nord

37bis bd de la Chapelle, 10th (01.46.07.34.50, www.bouffesdunord.com). M° La Chapelle. **Box office** 1-6pm Mon-Sat. **Admission** €5-€24. **Map** p402 K1.

This elegant theatre boasts one of the most imaginative programmes of chamber music in the capital. Adventurous programming includes the excellent Beyond My Piano series.

Théâtre des Champs-Elysées

15 av Montaigne, 8th (01.49.52.50.50, www.theatrechampselysees.fr). M° Alma Marceau. **Box office** noon-7pm Mon-Sat; 2hrs before show Sun. *By phone* 11am-6pm Mon-Fri; 2-6pm Sat. **Admission** €5-€160. **Map** p400 D5.

This beautiful art nouveau theatre, with bas-reliefs by Bourdelle, celebrated its centenary in 2013, having hosted the scandalous première of Stravinsky's *Le Sacre du Printemps* in 1913. It remains the favourite venue for visiting foreign orchestras, and the prestigious line-up of visiting maestros has included Vladimir Jurowsky and Andris Nelsons, as well as performances by the likes of Hélène Grimaud.

Théâtre National de l'Opéra Comique

Pl Boieldieu, 2nd (01.42.44.45.40, tickets 08.25.01.01.23, www.opera-comique.com). M° Richelieu Drouot. **Box office** 11am-7pm Mon-Sat; 11am-5pm Sun. **Admission** €5-€120. **Map** p402 H4.

The Opéra Comique was founded in the early 18th century under the reign of Louis XIV and it will be celebrating its 300-year anniversary in style in 2015. Its promotion to national theatre status in 2005 has brought this jewel box of a theatre back to life under the skilful direction of Jérôme Deschamps.

Théâtre de la Ville

2 pl du Châtelet, 4th (01.42.74.22.77, www.theatre delaville-paris.com). M° Châtelet. **Box office** 11am-7pm Mon; 11am-8pm Tue-Sat. *By phone* 11am-7pm Mon-Sat. **Admission** €9-€35. **Map** p408 J6.

The programming in this concrete amphitheatre, hidden behind a classical façade, features hip chamber music outfits such as the Kronos and Takács Quartets and Early Music pioneer Fabio Biondi. World music is also well represented, with performers from as far afield as Madagascar and China.

▶ *The season here spills over to performances at Les Abbesses (31 rue des Abbesses, 18th), which shares the same phone number and box office hours, but is closed on Mondays.*

Left Bank

Musée National du Moyen Age

6 pl Paul-Painlevé, 5th (01.53.73.78.16, www.musee-moyenage.fr). M° Cluny La Sorbonne. **Admission** €13-€16. **Map** p408 J7.

The museum presents a worthy programme of medieval concerts in which troubadours reflect the museum's collection. There are also occasional 45-minute *heures musicales* in a similar style.

Musée d'Orsay

62 rue de Lille, 7th (01.40.49.47.57, www.musee-orsay.fr). M° Solférino/RER Musée d'Orsay. **Admission** €8-€35. **Map** p405 G6.

The Musée d'Orsay runs a full series of lunchtime and evening concerts. The lunchtime concerts at 12.30pm concentrate on promising young artists. Evening concerts are more prestigious, with recent performances by the likes of Dame Felicity Lott and Angelika Kirchschlager.

Palais Garnier.

ARTS & ENTERTAINMENT

FESTIVALS DANCE

What to see, when.

Faits d'Hiver (Jan-Feb, www.faitsdhiver. com) and hip hop festival **Suresnes Cités Danse** (Jan, www.theatre-suresnes.fr) start the year off with a high kick, followed by **Rencontres Chorégraphiques de Seine-St-Denis** (May-June, www.rencontres choregraphiques.com) and **Onze Bouge** (June, www.festivalonze.org). Founded in 2005, **Les Etés de la Danse** (July, www.lesetesdeladanse.com) puts the spotlight on one or two companies or choreographers, with three weeks of performances. Shows are accompanied by workshops. The ever-popular **Paris Quartier d'Eté** festival (July-Aug, www.quartierdete.com) features eclectic programmes and plenty of free outdoor performances in Paris and around the suburbs. For more than 40 years, the **Festival d'Automne** (Sept-Dec, www. festival-automne.com) has shown the way forward in the performing arts. With a focus on leading French experimental companies, the festival also invites big-name choreographers from around the world to perform.

Festival d'Automne.

Dance

The Théâtre de la Ville and Théâtre National de Chaillot attract plenty of big names, such as Anne Teresa de Keersmaeker's Rosas company and Ballets de Monte Carlo. There's no shortage of ballet productions at the Théâtre du Châtelet and Palais Garnier either, and the Festival d'Automne will again feature an impressive line-up of innovative dance. As the HQ for over 600 regional companies, the Centre National de la Danse in Pantin reaches out to its audience with well-devised performances, and smaller dance 'laboratories' such as Ménagerie de Verre and Regard du Cygne showcase new work by smaller companies.

INFORMATION AND RESOURCES

For listings, *see Pariscope* and *L'Officiel des Spectacles*. For events coverage, look out for two monthlies: *La Terrasse* (distributed free at major dance venues) and the glossy *Danser*. For shoes and equipment, **Sansha** (52 rue de Clichy, 9th, 01.45.26.01.38, www.sansha.com) has a good reputation, and **Repetto** (22 rue de la Paix, 2nd, 01.44.71.83.12, www.repetto.com) supplies the Opéra with pointes and slippers; **Menkes** (12 rue Rambuteau, 3rd, 01.40.27.91.81, www. menkes.es) sells serious flamenco gear.

MAJOR VENUES

Centre National de la Danse
1 rue Victor-Hugo, 93507 Pantin (01.41.83.27.27, box office 01.41.83.98.98, www.cnd.fr). M° Hoche/RER Pantin. **Open** *Box office* 10am-7pm Mon-Fri & performance days. **Admission** €10-€18.
This centre first opened its doors in 2004, with the express mission to bridge the divide between stage and spectator. It invites audiences to its quarterly *'Grandes leçons de danse'*, contemporary dance master classes. It also offers an expertly curated selection of performances presented in the studios, exhibitions, and a phenomenal archive of films and choreographic material.

Maison des Arts de Créteil
Pl Salvador-Allende, 94000 Créteil (01.45.13.19.19, www.maccreteil.com). M° Créteil-Préfecture. **Open** *Box office* 1-7pm Tue-Sat & show days. Closed mid July-Aug. **Admission** €23-€35.
This suburban arts centre is a vibrant hub, featuring an eclectic programme of theatre, dance, music and digital art. Don't miss the International Exit Festival of contemporary dance in the spring.

★ Palais Garnier
Pl de l'Opéra, 9th (08.92.89.90.90, from abroad 01.71.25.24.23, www.operadeparis.fr). M° Opéra.

Centre National de la Danse.

ARTS & ENTERTAINMENT

Open *Box office* 11.30am-6.30pm Mon-Sat.
Phone bookings 9am-6pm Mon-Fri; 9am-1pm Sat.
Closed 15 July-end Aug. **Admission** €10-€110
(ballet). **Map** p401 G4.

The Ballet de l'Opéra National de Paris manages to
tread successfully between classics and new productions, at the Bastille and Palais Garnier. Recent highlights have included Jirí Kylian's *Kaguyahimé* and
Pierre Lacotte's adaptation of *La Sylphide*.

Théâtre du Châtelet

*1 pl du Châtelet, 4th (01.40.28.28.40, www.
chatelet-theatre.com). M° Châtelet.* **Open** *Box
office* 11am-7pm Mon-Sat & 1hr before show
Sun. **Admission** €16.50-€80.50. **Map** p408 J6.

This classical music institution is strengthening
its reputation in other live artistic disciplines –
Benjamin Millepied's LA Dance Project are regular
visitors. The theatre also plays host to the esteemed
Etés de la Danse festival, with the San Francisco
Ballet the headline attraction for the tenth edition
in July 2014.

Théâtre National de Chaillot

*1 pl du Trocadéro, 16th (01.53.65.30.00,
www.theatre-chaillot.fr). M° Trocadéro.* **Open**
Box office 11am-7pm Mon-Sat. Closed 2wks Aug.
Admission €15-€37. **Map** p400 C5.

The Théâtre National de Chaillot's three auditoriums range from cosy and experimental to a vast
2,800-seater amphitheatre. The 2013 programme
saw the highly anticipated return of Béjart Ballet
Lausanne with *Light*.

★ Théâtre de la Ville

*2 pl du Châtelet, 4th (01.42.74.22.77, www.theatre
delaville-paris.com). M° Châtelet.* **Box office** 11am-
7pm Mon; 11am-8pm Tue-Sat. *By phone* 11am-7pm
Mon-Sat. **Admission** €20-€35. **Map** p406 J6.

This leading venue has nurtured collaborations with
international choreographers. The 2013 programme
included Anne Teresa de Keersmaeker's Rosas company performing *Drumming Live*.

▶ *Some performances take place at sister venue
Théâtre des Abbesses (31 rue des Abbesses, 18th).*

FRINGE VENUES

L'Etoile du Nord

*16 rue Georgette-Agutte, 18th (01.42.26.47.47,
www.etoiledunord-theatre.com). M° Guy Môquet.*
Open *Box office* 1hr before performance. Closed
July, Aug. **Admission** €10-€15.

This smaller venue splits its programme between
theatre and contemporary multimedia dance. The
Avis de Turbulences festival (Sept-Oct) features a
decent selection of mixed bills.

La Loge

*77 rue de Charonne, 11th (01.40.09.70.40,
www.lalogeparis.fr). M° Charonne.* **Open** *Shows*
7pm, 9pm Tue-Thur. **Admission** €5-€16.
No credit cards. Map p407 N7.

In a hidden courtyard off rue de Charonne, the 100-
seater La Loge offers performances that merge theatre, dance and music. Every summer, the Summer
of Loge festival invites eight theatre companies to
perform, followed by post-show festivities that have

IN THE KNOW RIVER DANCE

From May to September, the amphitheatres of the **Jardin Tino Rossi** (5th), a thin strip of green by the Seine, fill up with salsa, rock, tango, Irish, hip hop, traditional dance from Brittany and just about any other dance form you can think of. Informal classes are held from 7pm, then the *bal* begins, keeping everyone swaying until midnight.

previously included pyjama parties and concerts. The rest of the year, from Tuesday to Thursday, there are two shows a night.

Ménagerie de Verre
12-14 rue Léchevin, 11th (01.43.38.33.44, www.menagerie-de-verre.org). M° Parmentier. **Open** *Box office* 1hr before performance. *Phone bookings* 10am-6pm Mon-Fri. Closed July, Aug. **Admission** €13-€15. **No credit cards. Map** p403 N5.
This multidisciplinary hothouse is rooted in the avant-garde, with contemporary dance and classes given by a succession of guest teachers.

★ Le Regard du Cygne
210 rue de Belleville, 20th (01.43.58.55.93, bookings 09.71.34.23.50, www.leregarducygne. com). M° Télégraphe. **Open** *Box office* 1hr before show. Closed Aug. **Admission** free-€15. **No credit cards. Map** p403 Q3.
This pared-down studio located in the north-east of the capital is a great place to get a taste of the alternative dance scene.

▶ *The Spectacles Sauvages nights allow relative unknowns to show a ten-minute piece to the public, while the Rencontres focus on the work of a particular artist and are open to all, free of charge.*

Théâtre de la Bastille
76 rue de la Roquette, 11th (01.43.57.42.14, www.theatre-bastille.com). M° Bastille or Voltaire. **Open** *Box office* 10am-6pm Mon-Fri; 2-6pm Sat. Closed July, Aug. **Admission** €14-€26. **Map** p407 M6.
This small theatre showcases a range of innovative contemporary dance and drama pieces.

DANCE CLASSES

Centre de Danse du Marais
41 rue du Temple, 4th (01.42.77.58.19, www.parisdanse.com). M° Hôtel de Ville or Rambuteau. **Open** 9am-9pm Mon-Fri; 9am-8pm Sat; 9am-7pm Sun. **Classes** €18. **Map** p402 K5.
There's a huge choice of classes here, with big-name teachers such as belly dance star Leila Haddad and ballet's Casati-Lazzarelli team.
▶ *The five-class 'sampler' pass is a good deal at €74.*

★ Studio Harmonic
5 passage des Taillandiers, 11th (01.48.07.13.39, www.studioharmonic.fr). M° Bastille. **Open** *Office* 10am-5pm Mon-Fri. *Classes* 9.30am-10pm Mon-Fri; 9am-7.30pm Sat. Closed 3wks Aug. **Classes** €16. **Map** p407 M7.
The rising star among Paris's top dance schools. Studio Harmonic's claim to fame is the trademark Ragga Jam class – created by Laure Courtellemont – which combines ragga, dancehall, African dance and hip hop.

Le Regard du Cygne.

Theatre

The last couple of years have been tumultuous for some of Paris's most prestigious theatres, with strikes over pay and the temporary closure of the main auditorium at the Comédie Française. Fortunately, though, the Comédie has now been restored to glory, with a schedule marked by trusty old regulars such as Molière and Feydeau.

TICKETS AND INFORMATION

For weekly listings check out *L'Officiel des Spectacles* and *Pariscope* (both available from news kiosks). Tickets can be bought at the theatres, from **Fnac** (www.fnac.com) or online at www.theatreonline.com.

VENUES

Right Bank

Cartoucherie de Vincennes

Route du Champ de Manoeuvre, Bois de Vincennes, 12th. M° Château de Vincennes, then shuttle bus.
Théâtre de l'Aquarium *(01.43.74.72.74, www.theatredelaquarium.com).*
Théâtre du Chaudron *(01.43.28.97.04, www.theatreduchaudron.fr).*
Théâtre de l'Epée de Bois *(01.48.08.39.74, www.epeedebois.com).*
Théâtre du Soleil *(01.43.74.24.08, www.theatre-du-soleil.fr).*
Théâtre de la Tempête *(01.43.28.36.36, www.la-tempete.fr).*
Past the Château de Vincennes in the middle of the woods, five independent theatres offer up a first-class selection of politically committed fare. The most famous outfit is Ariane Mnouchkine's avant-garde Théâtre du Soleil, which first transformed these ex-army munitions warehouses into perfomance spaces back in 1970.

★ Comédie Française

All *www.comedie-francaise.fr.*
Salle Richelieu *2 rue Richelieu, 1st (08.25.10.16.80). M° Palais Royal Musée du Louvre.* **Box office** 11am-6pm daily. **Admission** €13-€41. *1hr before show* €6 for cheapest seats only. **Map** p401 H5.
Studio-Théâtre *Galerie du Carrousel du Louvre, 99 rue de Rivoli, 1st (01.44.58.98.58). M° Palais Royal Musée du Louvre.* **Box office** 2-5pm Wed-Sun. **Admission** €20. **Map** p401 H5.
Théâtre du Vieux Colombier *21 rue du Vieux Colombier, 6th (01.44.39.87.00). M° St-Sulpice.* **Box office** 11am-6pm Mon-Sat. **Admission** €31. **Map** p405 G7.

Théâtre des Bouffes du Nord. *See p290.*

The gilded mother of French theatres, the Comédie Française turns out season after season of classics, as well as lofty new productions. The red velvet and gold-flecked Salle Richelieu is located right by the Palais-Royal. It was closed for renovations during 2012, but reopened in early 2013. Under the same management are the Studio-Théâtre, a black box inside the Carrousel du Louvre, and the Théâtre du Vieux Colombier. The line-up generally includes plenty of Molière and Feydeau (*see p291* **Behind the Lines**).

★ Théâtre des Bouffes du Nord

37bis bd de la Chapelle, 10th (01.46.07.34.50, www.bouffesdunord.com). M° La Chapelle. **Box office** 5-8pm Mon-Fri; 2-7pm Sat. **Admission** €18-€35; €14-€28 reductions. **Map** p402 K2.
Peter Brook's former playground, the Théâtre des Bouffes du Nord treated Parisians to an adaptation of Michael Ondaatje's *The Collected Works of Billy the Kid* in 2013. *Photos p289.*
▶ *The Bouffes du Nord also has one of the best chamber music programmes in the capital.*

Théâtre du Châtelet

1 pl du Châtelet, 4th (01.40.28.28.40, www.chatelet-theatre.com). M° Châtelet. **Box office** 11am-7pm Mon-Sat; 1hr before show Sun. **Admission** €27.50-€101.50. **Map** p408 J6.
The Châtelet is fast becoming Paris's main venue for musicals hailing from Broadway and the West End – such as *My Fair Lady* – which are usually performed in the original language by visiting companies. It's the only venue in Paris to offer such quality musical theatre.

Théâtre de la Madeleine

19 rue de Surène, 8th (01.42.65.07.09, www.theatremadeleine.com). M° Madeleine. **Box office** 11am-7pm Mon-Sat. **Admission** €17-€54. **Map** p401 F4.
The theatre where Sacha Guitry composed 24 of his plays, between 1932 and 1940, continues to contribute to France's repertoire with top-notch creations by emerging and established artists.

Théâtre Marigny

Av de Marigny, 8th (08.92.22.23.33, www.theatremarigny.fr). M° Champs-Elysées Clemenceau or Franklin D. Roosevelt. **Box office** 11am-6.30pm Mon-Sat. **Admission** €25-€79. **Map** p401 E4.
Théâtre Marigny is one of the most expensive nights out for theatregoers in Paris. But then not many other theatres can boast so much: a location off the Champs-Elysées; a deluxe interior conceived by Charles Garnier (of Opéra fame); high-profile casts and an illustrious pedigree stretching back more than 150 years. The theatre is currently closed for renovations but is scheduled to reopen in late 2014.

Théâtre National de Chaillot

1 pl du Trocadéro, 16th (01.53.65.30.00, www.theatre-chaillot.fr). M° Trocadéro. **Box office** 11am-7pm Mon-Sat. **Admission** €20-€33; €15-€25 reductions. **Map** p400 B4.
Get here early, grab a cocktail and gaze in awe at the Eiffel Tower through the lobby window. Chaillot's three auditoriums range from cosy and experimental to a 2,800-seater amphitheatre. Recent highlights

Théâtre National de Chaillot.

BEHIND THE LINES
Who's who in French theatre.

From dark medieval plays to 17th-century tragicomedies and 20th-century absurdist theatre, the French have always known how to pack a punch with new acting styles and popular dramatic movements. Titles such as *Tartuffe*, *Le Cid* and *La Cantatrice Chauve* are well known; here we round up the creative talents behind them.

MOLIERE (1622-1673)
As the Sun King's official playwright and founder of the Comédie Française, Jean-Baptiste Poquelin (Molière) created powerful stories able to veer between farce and dark drama. He is associated with alexandrine, the 12-syllable-per-line metre that characterised much of 17th-century French theatre. Among Molière's best-known works are his comedies *L'Ecole des Femmes*, *Le Misanthrope*, *Tartuffe* and *Le Malade Imaginaire*.

PIERRE CORNEILLE (1606-1684)
Along with Molière and Racine, Corneille was one of France's great dramatists. Hailed as the 'founder of French tragedy', he turned out plays for over 40 years, including the world-famous *Le Cid* (based on Guillén de Castro's *Las Mocedades del Cid*) – a tale of love, loss and war.

JEAN RACINE (1639-1699)
Racine was educated by Jansenist monks, and his works are heavily influenced by Greek and Latin classics. Molière produced his second play, *La Thébaïde*, and his third, *Andromaque*, but Racine didn't enjoy the latter production and gave the text to the rival company at the Hôtel de Bourgogne. There he produced a string of successful tragedies, such as *Britannicus*, which chronicles the story of Agrippina and her son Nero, and *Phèdre*, based on Euripides' *Hippolytus*, an exploration of a woman's passion for her stepson.

Molière.

PIERRE DE MARIVAUX (1688-1763)
Marivaux's contribution to 18th-century French theatre was so great that the deft and witty bantering of his dialogues were given their own term, *marivaudage* (verbal preciousness). He wrote numerous comedies for the Comédie Française, including *La Surprise de l'Amour* and *Les Fausses Confidences*.

GEORGES FEYDEAU (1862-1921)
During his lifetime, Feydeau was frequently dismissed as a light entertainer. Now, he is considered to be one of the belle époque's greatest playwrights, and a precursor of surrealist and Dadaist theatre. His legacy of lively farces includes *La Dame de chez Maxim*, *L'Hôtel du Libre Echange* and *Hortense a dit: 'Je m'en fous!'*.

EUGENE IONESCO (1909-1994)
French-Romanian Ionesco is known for his absurdist pieces, his most famous being *La Cantatrice Chauve* (which is still played in the Théâtre de la Huchette; *see p293*). Ionesco's plays are famed for their characters being caught in hopeless situations and then forced to do repetitive or meaningless actions, with plenty of clichéd play on words and nonsense dialogue.

Jean Racine.

Théâtre de la Ville.

have included David Bobee's exciting adaptation of *Romeo and Juliet*, complete with acrobats.

Théâtre du Rond Point

2bis av Franklin D. Roosevelt, 8th (01.44.95.98.21, www.theatredurondpoint.fr). M° Champs-Elysées Clemenceau. **Box office** noon-7pm Tue-Sat; noon-4pm Sun (performance days). **Admission** €28-€36; €15 under-30s; €26 over-60s. **Map** p401 E4.
More than just a theatre, this historic venue multi-tasks as a bookshop, tearoom and restaurant. So once you've fed your mind on contemporary, avant-garde and sometimes politically slanted theatre, make a night of it and opt for dinner as well.

★ Théâtre de la Ville & Théâtre des Abbesses

01.42.74.22.77, www.theatredelaville-paris.com. **Admission** €16-€35; €9-€26 reductions. **Théâtre de la Ville** *2 pl du Châtelet, 4th. M° Châtelet.* **Box office** 11am-7pm Mon; 11am-8pm Tue-Sat. **Map** p406 J6.
Théâtre des Abbesses *31 rue des Abbesses, 18th. M° Abbesses.* **Box office** 5-8pm Tue-Sat. **Map** p402 H1.
At its two sites, the 'City Theatre' turns out the most consistently innovative programming in Paris. Instead of running a standard rep company, the house imports music, dance and theatre productions.

Left Bank

Le Lucernaire

53 rue Notre-Dame-des-Champs, 6th (01.42.22.26.50, www.lucernaire.fr). M° Notre-Dame-des-Champs or Vavin. **Box office** 11am-12.30pm, 1.30-10pm Mon-Thur; 11am-12.30pm, 1.30-11pm Fri; 1.30-11pm Sat; 1.30-10pm Sun. **Admission** €25-€30; €15-€25 reductions. **Map** p401 F4.
Three theatres, three cinemas, a restaurant and a bar make up this versatile cultural centre. Theatre-wise, Molière and other classic playwrights get a good thrashing, but so do up-and-coming authors.

★ Odéon, Théâtre de L'Europe

Pl de l'Odéon, 6th (01.44.85.40.00, bookings 01.44.85.40.40, www.theatre-odeon.fr). M° Odéon. **Box office** 11am-6pm Mon-Sat. **Admission** €12-€36; €6-€18 reductions. **Map** p408 H7.
Highlights for 2013 included Samuel Beckett's *Fin de Partie* (*Endgame*) and Molière's *Misanthrope*. The theatre also plays host to the Impatience festival.

Odéon, Théâtre de L'Europe.

Théâtre de la Huchette.

Théâtre de la Cité Internationale
*17 bd Jourdan, 14th (01.43.13.50.50, www.theatre
delacite.com). RER Cité Universitaire.* **Box office**
1hr before show. *By phone* 1-7pm Mon-Fri; 2-7pm
Sat. **Admission** €22; €7-€16 reductions.
A polished, professional theatre based on the campus
of the Cité Universitaire, the Théâtre de la Cité displays an international flair worthy of its setting. In
addition to the main theatre and dance season, the
prestigious Ecole du Théâtre National de Strasbourg
occupies the stage for a stint each summer.

Théâtre de la Huchette
*23 rue de la Huchette, 5th (01.43.26.38.99,
www.theatre-huchette.com). M° Cluny La Sorbonne
or St-Michel.* **Box office** 1.30-7pm Mon; 3.30-9pm
Tue-Sat. **Admission** €23; €16 reductions. *Double
bill ticket* €35; €25 reductions. **Map** p408 J7.
Ionesco's absurdist classic *La Cantatrice Chauve*
(The Bald Soprano) has been playing here since
1957, running on a double bill with his *La Leçon*.

Beyond the Périphérique

Culture doesn't end at the city ring road.
A combination of measures designed to bring
theatre to the masses and extortionate rental
rates for productions inside Paris has led to the
creation of several excellent out-of-town venues.
  In the north-east, **MC93 Bobigny** (1 bd
Lénine, 93000 Bobigny, 01.41.60.72.72, www.
mc93.com) is a slick institution dedicated to
promoting global cross-cultural exchange with
visiting companies from across France and
abroad – *Eugene Onegin* in Russian, perhaps.
The **Théâtre Gérard-Philipe** (59 bd Jules-
Guesde, 93200 St-Denis, 01.48.13.70.00, www.
theatregerardphilipe.com), run by Christophe

Rauck, offers consistently good fare of an
experimental nature, including the Et Moi Alors?
festival for youngsters. Just beyond La Défense's
towers, the **Théâtre Nanterre Amandiers** (7
av Pablo Picasso, 92022 Nanterre, 01.46.14.70.00,
www.nanterre-amandiers.com, shuttle bus from
RER Nanterre-Préfécture 1hr before show)
provides an eclectic mix of probing modern
theatre, as well as the great classics and
occasional opera. And the **Théâtre d'Ivry
Antoine Vitez** (1 rue Simon Dereure, 94200 Ivry,
01.43.90.11.11, www.theatre-quartiers-ivry.com)
has a theatre, dance studio and auditorium.

ALTERNATIVE THEATRE
The bastion of alternative theatre in the north
is the **Lavoir Moderne Parisien** (35 rue
Léon, 18th, 01.42.52.09.14, www.rueleon.net), a
converted washhouse where shows often tackle
themes of immigration and identity. The **Point
Ephémère** (*see p267*) and its gargantuan older
brother **Mains d'Oeuvres** (*see p266*) are
cool urban arts centres (in former warehouses)
that stage multidisciplinary performances.
Confluences (190 bd de Charonne, 20th,
01.40.24.16.46, http://confluences.jimdo.com)
is an all-in-one cultural centre equipped with
an art gallery, theatre and projection room; and
Les Laboratoires d'Aubervilliers (41 rue
Lécuyer, 93300 Aubervilliers, 01.53.56.15.90,
www.leslaboratoires.org) churns out some
wonderful, conceptualist productions.
Le Tarmac theatre (159 av Gambetta,
20th, 01.43.64.80.80, http://letarmac.fr) houses
the TILF (Théâtre International de Langue
Française), the only theatre in France dedicated
to the Francophone world.

Escapes & Excursions

Escapes & Excursions

The forests surrounding Paris were once the playground of royalty and aristocracy, and their extravagant legacy is plain to see in sumptuous châteaux such as Chantilly, Fontainebleau and Versailles. Further afield, the famous cellars of Champagne are less than an hour from the capital by train (perfect if you fancy sampling a glass or two of fizz while you're there). Even the Med is only a few hours away by TGV if you fancy combining some bouillabaisse and beach action around Marseille, 2013 Capital of Culture.

Towns & Cities

TOURS

Novelist Honoré de Balzac (1799-1850) once described his beloved birthplace as being 'more fresh, flowery and perfumed than any other town in the world', and Tours has a lot going for it today. In fact, it's a positively pleasant city, bursting with history, medieval quarters, a lively student population, colourful flower markets (Wednesday and Saturday on boulevard Béranger), and enticing bars and restaurants. Only an hour from Paris Gare Montparnasse by TGV, the city is the official gateway to the Loire Valley, and a choice place in which to refuel before overdosing on sumptuous Renaissance castles.

Sandwiched between the Loire (north) and the Cher (south) rivers, it began life as a fertile floodplain, prized by the Turones – a Celtic tribe that gave modern Tours its name. In 57 BC, Julius Caesar conquered the city, modestly changing its name to Caesarodunum (Caesar's hill). Traces of the third-century Gallo-Roman city wall and amphitheatre can still be seen in the Musée des Beaux-Arts gardens.

When Christianity arrived, St Martin, the founder of France's first monastery, became bishop of Tours. After his death in 397, his relics, laid to rest in the Basilique St-Martin, were believed to have healing powers, drawing in thousands of pilgrims en route to Santiago de Compostela in Spain, and prompting the construction of Tours' medieval quarters.

Throughout the 15th and 16th centuries, the city vied with Paris as the seat of power: Charles VII, Louis XI (who established Tours' silk industry), Charles VIII and François I all cherished Tours; Henry IV preferred Paris.

The city was bombarded by the Prussians in 1870 and suffered widespread damage during World War II, especially in the historic centre, which by the 1960s was a no-go zone of crumbling masonry. Nowadays, after 40 years of regeneration, the medieval quarter contains some of Tours' most charming streets. Pedestrianised place Plumereau, with its half-timbered façades housing cafés, galleries and boutiques, is the hub of the town. Wander down lanes such as rue Briçonnet to find concealed courtyards, more half-timbered houses and the occasional crooked tower. In place de Châteauneuf, a lone tower is the only intact segment of the original Basilique-St-Martin, sacked by the Huguenots in 1562. The neo-Byzantine **Basilique St-Martin** (www. basiliquesaintmartin.com) houses St-Martin's shrine up the road, opposite the ruined vestiges.

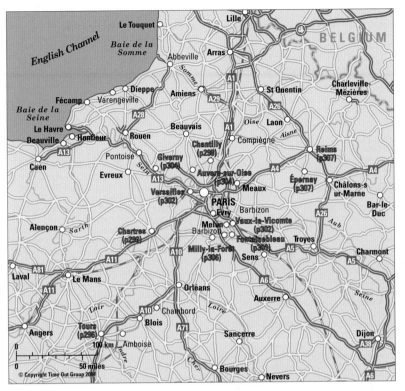

© Copyright Time Out Group 2008

The east of Tours is dominated by the **Cathédrale St-Gatien** (02.47.70.21.00, www.paroisse-cathedrale-tours.catholique.fr). Work began on this splendid building in the 13th century and ended in the 16th century, demonstrating the French Gothic style in its entirety. The stained-glass windows inside are often compared to those of Sainte-Chapelle in Paris. Next door, the archbishop's palace and **Musée des Beaux-Arts** (18 pl François-Sicard, 02.47.05.68.82, www.mba.tours.fr) has a rich collection of paintings by Degas, Rembrandt and Delacroix, plus sculptures by Rodin and Bourdelle. Check out the enormous 200-year-old cedar of Lebanon in the garden.

North of here, Tours' **Château Royal** (25 av André Malraux) looks over the Loire with dishevelled majesty. You can best take in its assorted architecture by following the river: the Tour de Guise (look out for machicolations and a pepper-pot roof) was a 13th-century fortress, and the 15th-century Logis des Gouverneurs on the quay has gable dormers and a chunk of Gallo-Roman wall at its base. Further west, the **Musée du Compagnonnage** (8 rue Nationale,

02.47.21.62.20, www.museecompagnonnage.fr) is a dinky museum, showcasing the handiwork of master craftsmen of the guilds.

For dreamy regional dishes such as *crépine de dinde* (a giant turkey meatball cooked in red wine) and *poire tappée* (poached pear), head to **Le Petit Patrimoine** (58 rue Colbert,

IN THE KNOW AMBOISE

A leisurely 20-minute drive east from Tours (*see left*), Amboise is a small town of narrow streets and quaint residences overlooking the Loire river. It is also home to two star sites: the imposing **Château Royal d'Amboise** (www.chateau-amboise. com), set on a rocky spur and one of the most historically important buildings in the region; and Leonardo da Vinci's former home, the **Clos Lucé** (www.vinci-closluce.com), an exquisitely restored manor house with landscaped gardens and a museum of da Vinci's inventions.

02.47.66.05.81). If *moules-frites* is more your thing, the **Taverne de l'Homme Tranquille** (22 rue du grand Marché, near pl Plumereau, 02.47.61.46.04) has a large selection.

For a few sneaky glasses of Touraine wine before you head back, **Au Chien Jaune** (74 rue Bernard Palissy, 02.47.05.10.17), a former brothel, is located in a handy spot by the **tourist office** (78 rue Bernard Palissy, 02.47.70.37.37, www.tours-tourisme.fr).

Cathedrals & Châteaux

CHANTILLY

From the 14th century until 1897, the town of Chantilly was the domain of the Princes of Condé, the cousins of the French kings. As well as its impressive château, Chantilly, with its hunting forests and prestigious horse-racing centres, has a rich equestrian history. The town is a half-hour train ride north of the capital (trains leave from Paris Gare du Nord).

Much of the cream-coloured **Château de Chantilly** was destroyed during the Revolution, leaving the main wing to be reconstructed in the 19th century by Henri d'Orléans, Duc d'Aumale. When the duke died in 1897, he bequeathed the entire Domaine de Chantilly – including the Grandes Ecuries, the Hippodrome and the 61sq km forest – to the Institut de France on the condition that the château be opened to the public as the Musée

Condé, and that none of the artworks would be moved or loaned to other museums. The remarkable collection includes three paintings by Raphael, and the *Très Riches Heures du Duc de Berry*, a medieval book of hours, containing the most exquisite colours imaginable. If you thought that the Middle Ages were dull, you can think again.

The main section of the château's sprawling park, designed by royal landscape architect Le Nôtre, features traditional French formal parterres and an extensive canal system, which allows visitors to see the park from electric-powered boats. Head off the beaten path to explore the English Garden, the Island of Love, the kangaroo zoo and the original hamlet that inspired Marie-Antoinette to build her own version at Versailles.

The Grandes Ecuries ('great stables') at the château were commissioned in 1719 by Prince Louis-Henri de Bourbon (who believed he would be reincarnated as a horse). Later, they became one of Napoleon's equestrian training grounds, having suffered only light damage during the Revolution. In 1982, the great horseman Yves Bienaimé restored the stables and turned them into the Musée Vivant du Cheval.

The Forêt de Chantilly is full of hiking and cycling trails. A pleasant walk of around seven kilometres circles four small lakes, the Etangs de Commelles, and passes the Château de la Reine Blanche, a mill that was converted in the 1820s into a pseudo-medieval hunting lodge. For trail details, ask at the **tourist office** (60 av Maréchal-Joffre, 03.44.67.37.37, www.chantilly-tourisme.com).

Château de Chantilly.

Château de Fontainebleau. *See p301.*

For a post-hike lunch, tuck into the *plat du jour* at **La Capitainerie** (03.44.57.15.89, www.chateaudechantilly.com), situated in the original château kitchens. For a taste of Chantilly whipped cream, stop for tea at the **Restaurant du Hameau** (03.44.57.46.21, www.chateau dechantilly.com) in the *hameau* at the château.

Château de Chantilly

Chantilly (03.44.27.31.80, www.chateaude chantilly.com). **Open** *Apr-Oct* 10am-6pm Mon, Wed-Sun (daily July, Aug). *Nov-Mar* 10.30am-6pm Mon, Wed-Sun. **Admission** *Château & park* €14; €5.50 reductions; free under-4s.

CHARTRES

Seen from a distance, the mismatched spires and dazzling silhouette of the **Cathédrale de Chartres** burst out of the Beauce cornfields and dominate the skyline of this modest town some 90km south-west of Paris (an hour by train from Gare Montparnasse). Chartres was a pilgrimage site long before the cathedral was built, ever since the Sacra Camisia (said to be the Virgin Mary's birthing garment) was donated in 876 by the king.

The cathedral is one of the finest examples of Gothic architecture in the world. The west front, or 'Royal Portal' – which was modelled in part on St-Denis – features three sculpted doorways. Inside, there's another era of sculpture, represented in the 16th-century scenes of the life of Christ that surround the choir. In particular, note the circular labyrinth of black and white stones in the floor. The cathedral is famed, above all, for its stained-glass windows depicting biblical scenes, saints and medieval trades in brilliant 'Chartres blue', punctuated by rich reds. During World War II, the windows

were removed and stored nearby for safety, only being reinstalled once the war was over. Climb the tower for a great view over the surrounding town and country. English-language tours by lecturer Malcolm Miller – one of the world's most knowledgeable and entertaining experts on the cathedral – take place from April to October (noon Mon-Sat, €10, €5 reductions). Audio guides can also be hired.

The town of Chartres is an attractive tangle of narrow, medieval streets on the banks of the river Eure. The tourist office can be found at place de la Cathédrale (02.37.18.26.26, www.chartres-tourisme.com). Two sights merit a special mention: the **Musée des Beaux-Arts** (29 cloître Notre-Dame, 02.37.90.45.80), which houses a collection of 18th-century French paintings by Watteau and others; and the memorial to **Jean Moulin**, the legendary figure of the Resistance. A wartime prefect of Chartres until he was dismissed by the Vichy government after his refusal to co-operate with the Nazis, Moulin became de Gaulle's man in France, and died under torture in Lyon in 1943. His memorial is a ten-minute walk west of the cathedral, at the corner of rue Collin d'Arleville and boulevard de la Résistance.

Hungry tourists congregate at **Café Serpente** (2 cloître Notre-Dame, 02.37.21.68.81, www.leserpente.com), in the shadow of the cathedral. But if it's full, there are plenty of easy and worthwhile options nearby. For restaurant cuisine with a riverside view, try **L'Estocade** (1 rue de la Porte Guillaume, 02.37.34.27.17, www.estocade.net). For fireside treats, **La Vieille Maison** (5 rue au Lait, 02.37.34.10.67, www.lavieillemaison.fr) has a cosy 14th-century dining room. For a local speciality, order some Chartres pâté at **Le Saint-Hilaire** (11 rue Pont St-Hilaire, 02.37.30.97.57).

TALES OF WAR

The horrors of 1914 laid bare at Meaux's new museum.

The town of Meaux played a hugely significant role in the outcome of World War I. It was here, just 40km from Paris, that French and British forces defeated the Germans at the First Battle of the Marne, forcing them to abandon their push on the capital. So near, in fact, was it to Paris that many Allied soldiers were ferried to the front by taxi. The September 1914 battle, which resulted in 500,000 casualties, saved Paris. But it unleashed the horrific trench warfare that would continue for the next three years.

Watched over by the baleful eyes of an enormous monument erected in the 1930s by the Americans, the monolithic slab of the **Musée de la Grande Guerre du Pays de Meaux** (01.60.32.14.18, www.museedelagrandeguerre.eu), half an hour by train from Paris's Gare de l'Est, is cantilevered so that it appears to hover above the ground. As you pass beneath it, you're confronted by the distant rumble of war and realise that you're standing on a map of the battleground. The weight of history hangs heavy in the air.

It was this history that so fascinated Jean-Pierre Verney when, as a child, he spent holidays with his grandparents near the Chemin des Dames World War I battle site and met an endless stream of veterans passing by on their way to revisit the killing fields. He became obsessed with the war and built up a collection of 50,000 personal objects. Now owned by the municipality of Meaux, this trove of memorabilia forms the backbone of the new museum, which opened on 11 November 2011.

The space has been designed to convey history on multiple levels. There is immersion – walking between rows of soldiers, going into a dugout, looking down on life-size trenches from the no-man's land that forms the central aisle. There is the suggestive – a montage of voices and images in a lightbox. There is the practical – a vehicle for transporting carrier pigeons, aircraft and an early tank. And then there are the side aisles containing personal objects, ranging from erotic sculptures carved from shell casings to improvised musical instruments and shaving paraphernalia. This is a social history, the shrapnel of a million lives, and it moves you all the more that men created and treasured these things in the face of death.

There are also sections tackling the origins of the war – a complex story conveyed through posters, drawings and the sudden gunshot that launched the madness – and its consequences, including recent troubles whose roots can be traced back to the Great War and its botched peace settlements. The rich cultural programme is being ramped up for 2014, the centenary year.

Cathédrale de Chartres

Pl de la Cathédrale (Cathedral 02.37.21.75.02;
Tower 02.37.21.22.07). **Open** *Cathedral* 8.30am-
7.30pm daily. *Tower* May-Aug 9.30am-12.30pm, 2-
6pm Mon-Sat; 2-6pm Sun. Sept-Apr 9.30am-noon,
2-5pm Mon-Sat; 2-5pm Sun. **Admission** *Cathedral*
free. *Tower* €7.50; €4.50 reductions; free under-18s,
under-26s (EU citizens). **No credit cards.**

FONTAINEBLEAU

Home to 14 French kings since François I, the
Château de Fontainebleau (*photo p299*) was
once a sort of aristocratic club where gentlemen
of the day came to hunt and learn the art of
chivalry. The town, which lies 60km south of
the capital (half an hour by train from Paris
Gare de Lyon), grew up around the château in
the 19th century, and is a pleasant place to visit.

The château is bite-sized in comparison to
the sprawling grandeur of Versailles. A former
hunting lodge, it is a real mix of styles. In 1528,
François I brought in Italian artists and
craftsmen to help architect Gilles le Breton to
transform the neglected lodge into the finest
Italian Mannerist palace in France. This style,
noted for its grotesqueries, contorted figures
and crazy fireplaces, is still visible in the
ballroom and Long Gallery. Henri IV added
a tennis court, Louis XIII built a double-
horseshoe entrance staircase, and Louis XIV
and XV added classical trimmings. Napoleon
and Louis-Philippe also spent a fortune on
redecoration. The château gardens include
Le Nôtre's Grand Parterre. There is also a park.

The 170sq km Forêt de Fontainebleau
features bizarre geological formations and
diverse wildlife. It's the wildest slice of nature
to be found near Paris. There are a number of
well-marked trails, such as the GR1 from Bois-
le-Roi train station, but more serious yompers
would be better off with an official map such as
the TOP25 IGN series 2417-OT, which covers
the entire forest. Trail maps are on sale at the
tourist office (4 rue Royale, 01.60.74.99.99,
www.fontainebleau-tourisme.com), which
hires out bicycles. Bikes can also be hired from
A la Petite Reine (14 rue de la Paroisse,
01.60.74.57.57, www.alapetitereine.com).

Rue Grande is lined with restaurants such
as **Au Délice Impérial** (no.1, 01.64.22.20.70)
and **Au Bureau** (no.12, 01.60.39.00.01,
www.au-bureau.fr). At no.92, picnickers
can pick up a wonderful array of cheeses at
Fromagerie Barthélémy (01.64.22.21.64).
The elegant **Hôtel Napoléon** (9 rue Grande,
01.60.39.50.50, www.hotelnapoleon-
fontainebleau.com) provides appropriately
grand meals at its restaurant.

Château de Fontainebleau

Pl du Général-de-Gaulle (01.60.71.50.70,
www.musee-chateau-fontainebleau.fr). **Open**
Château Apr-Sept 9.30am-6pm Mon, Wed-Sun.
Oct-Mar 9.30am-5pm Mon, Wed-Sun. *Park*
& gardens Mar, Apr, Oct 9am-6pm daily. May-
Sept 9am-7pm daily. Nov-Feb 9am-5pm daily.
Admission *Château* €11; €9 reductions;
free under-18s, under-26s (EU citizens).
Park & gardens free. PMP.

Château de Vaux-le-Vicomte
See p302.

VAUX-LE-VICOMTE

The lavish **Château de Vaux-le-Vicomte**
(*photo p301*), 55km south-east of Paris (half an
hour by train to Melun from Gare de Lyon then
6km taxi ride), has a valuable lesson to teach:
never, ever out-do your king. When Nicolas
Fouquet (1615-80), Louis XIV's finance minister
(and protégé of Cardinal Mazarin), decided
to build an abode fit for his position, he had
several hamlets moved away, called on three
of France's most talented men (architect Louis
Le Vau, painter Charles Lebrun and landscape
gardener André Le Nôtre), and hired star
sculptors such as Giradon, Lespagnandel and
Nicolas Poussin to chip in with the decor.

Its completion was celebrated in 1661 with a
huge party for which Molière wrote a play. All
would have gone swimmingly had it not been
for one minor detail: Fouquet invited the king.
Louis was disgusted at his minister's display of
grandeur; soon after, Fouquet was given a show
trial for the embezzlement of state funds. His
personal effects were seized by the crown and
he was sent into exile, dying 19 years later in
prison. But Fouquet's legacy did live on, as
Louis later hired Le Vau, Lebrun and Le Nôtre
to work some of their magic on Versailles.

A self-guided tour of the interior includes
Fouquet's personal suite, the servants' dining
room, the huge basement and wine cellar, and
the copper-filled kitchen. The dome, with its
unfinished ceiling – Lebrun only had time to
paint the sky and one eagle before Fouquet
was arrested – and the roof are optional extras.

On the south side, a staircase descends to the
gardens, where boxed hedges and flowerbeds
sweep into a vast expanse of lawns, grottoes,
canals, lakes and fountains. Electric cars can
be hired to help you cover the site.

Château de Vaux-le-Vicomte

*77950 Maincy (01.64.14.41.90, www.vaux-le-
vicomte.com).* **Open** *Château* Early Mar-early
Nov 10am-6pm daily. *Candlelight evenings* Early
May-early Oct 7pm-midnight Sat. **Admission**
€16; €10-€13 reductions; free under-6s. *Candlelight
evenings* €19; €17 reductions; free under-6s.

VERSAILLES

The **Château de Versailles**, 20km west of
Paris (train from Gare St-Lazare to Versailles
Rive Droite then 10min walk) is a masterpiece –
and usually packed with visitors as a result.
Allow yourself a whole day to appreciate the
sumptuous State Apartments and the Hall of
Mirrors, the highlights of any visit. The Grand
Appartement, where Louis XIV held court,
consists of six gilded salons, all opulent
examples of Baroque craftsmanship. No less
luxurious, the Queen's Apartment includes her
bedroom, where royal births took place in view
of the court. The Hall of Mirrors, where a united
Germany was proclaimed in 1871 and the
Treaty of Versailles signed in 1919, is flooded
with natural light from its 17 vast windows.
Designed to catch the last of the day's rays,
it was here that the Sun King would hold
extravagant receptions.

Château de Versailles.

IN THE KNOW HEAD SOUTH

Thanks to the TGV, you can now reach the Med city of **Marseille** from Paris in just three hours. France's second city was European Capital of Culture in 2013 and boasts steep streets, tranquil squares and bustling 19th-century thoroughfares that provide a patchwork of backdrops for souk-like markets, chic shops, and the colourful Vieux Port, where fishmongers sell their wares along the boat-lined quayside. For some breathtaking views, climb up to the Notre-Dame de la Garde basilica, or stay grounded over a plate of bouillabaisse and go shopping around the vintage boutiques on Cours Julien.

Architect Louis Le Vau first embellished the original building – a hunting lodge built during Louis XIII's reign – after Louis XIV saw Vaux-le-Vicomte, the impressive residence of his finance minister, Nicolas Fouquet. André Le Nôtre turned the boggy marshland into terraces, parterres, fountains and lush groves.

After Le Vau's death in 1670, Jules Hardouin-Mansart took over as principal architect, transforming Versailles into the château we know today. He dedicated the last 30 years of his life to adding the two main wings, the Cour des Ministres and the Chapelle Royale. In 1682, Louis moved in, accompanied by his court; thereafter, he rarely set foot in Paris. In the

1770s, Louis XV commissioned Jacques-Ange Gabriel to add the sumptuous Opéra Royal, now used for concerts by the **Centre de Musique Baroque** (01.39.20.78.10, www.cmbv.fr). The expense of building and running Versailles cost France dear. With the fall of the monarchy in 1792, most of the furniture was lost – but the château was saved by Louis-Philippe.

The gardens of Versailles are really works of art in themselves, their ponds and statues once again embellished by a fully working fountain system. On summer weekends, the spectacular jets of water are set to music, a prelude to the occasional fireworks displays of the Fêtes de Nuit. Beyond the gardens are the Grand Canal and the wooded land and sheep-filled pastures of the estate's park.

In 1687, Hardouin-Mansart built the pink marble Grand Trianon in the north of the park, away from the protocol of the court. Here Louis XIV and his children's governess and secret second wife, Madame de Maintenon, could admire the intimate gardens from the colonnaded portico. It retains the Empire decor of Napoleon, who stayed here with his second Empress, Marie-Louise.

The Petit Trianon, built for Louis XV's mistress Madame de Pompadour, is a wonderful example of neoclassicism. It later became part of the Domaine de Marie-Antoinette, an exclusive hideaway in the wooded parkland. Given to Marie-Antoinette as a wedding gift by her husband Louis XVI in 1774, the domain also includes the chapel adjoining the Petit Trianon, plus a theatre, a neoclassical 'Temple d'Amour', and Marie-Antoinette's fairy-tale farm and dairy, the Hameau de la Reine. Here, the queen escaped from the discontent of her subjects and the revolutionary fervour of Paris.

Outside the château gates are the **Potager du Roi** (the Sun King's vegetable garden, 01.39.24.62.62, www.potager-du-roi.fr), and stables that now house the **Académie du Spectacle Equestre** (01.39.02.62.75, www.acadequestre.fr), which is responsible for the elaborate shows of tightly choreographed theatrics on horseback, run by the famous horse trainer Bartabas.

In the town of Versailles, grab a Historical Places brochure free from the **tourist office** (2bis av de Paris, 01.39.24.88.88, www.versailles-tourisme.com) and explore. The Quartier St-Louis opposite the Potager was developed by Louis XV around the Cathédrale St-Louis. Just off rue d'Anjou are the Carrés St-Louis, four market squares surrounded by 18th-century boutiques. North-east of the château is the Quartier Notre-Dame, part of the 'new town' designed by the Sun King himself. Eglise Notre-Dame is where members of the royal family were baptised and married.

Around the corner is the Marché Notre-Dame, a market square dating back to 1671 and surrounded by restaurants and cafés.

Set in a building that dates back to the construction of the château, **Au Chapeau Gris** (7 rue Hoche, 01.39.50.10.81, www. auchapeaugris.com) is the oldest restaurant in Versailles, and serves up French country cuisine beneath ancient wooden beams. **Boeuf à la Mode** (4 rue au Pain, Marché Notre-Dame, 01.39.50.31.99, www.leboeuf alamode-versailles.com) is an authentic 1930s brasserie serving steak and seafood. Another long-established restaurant is the traditional **Brasserie du Théâtre** (15 rue des Réservoirs, 01.39.50.03.21, www.brasserietheatre.com).

★ Château de Versailles

78000 Versailles (01.30.83.78.00, advance tickets 08.92.68.46.94, www.chateauversailles.fr). **Open** *Apr-Oct* 9am-6.30pm Tue-Sun. *Nov-Mar* 9am-5.30pm Tue-Sun. *Garden* Apr-Oct 8am-8.30pm daily. *Park* 7am-8.30pm daily. *Garden & Park* Nov-Mar 8am-6pm daily. **Admission** €15; €13 reductions; free under-18s, under-26s (EU citizens), all 1st Sun of mth (Nov-Mar). PMP. **Grandes-Eaux Musicales** *(01.30.83.78.88).* **Open** *Apr-Oct* Sat, Sun. **Admission** €8.50; €6.50 reductions; free under-6s.

Artistic Retreats

AUVERS-SUR-OISE

This rural retreat, about an hour by train from Paris Gare du Nord, is where Vincent van Gogh spent his last weeks. His tiny attic room at the Auberge Ravoux is open to the public. Other Auvers residents included fellow artists Camille Pissarro, Paul Cézanne and Charles-François Daubigny. Today, you can explore the **Musée Daubigny** (Manoir des Colombières, rue de la Sansonne, 01.30.36.80.20, www.musee-daubigny.com) and his **studio** (61 rue Daubigny, 01.30.36.60.60, www.atelier-daubigny.com), which is still decorated with his murals. Another attraction is the **Musée de l'Absinthe** (44 rue Callé, 01.30.36.83.26, www.musee-absinthe.com), a rather modest collection of art and artefacts related to the notorious drink. Banned in France from 1915, the green concoction is once again legal. The local artistic legacy has not been overlooked by Auvers' main historical attraction, either. The 17th-century **Château d'Auvers** (rue de Léry, 01.34.48.48.48, www.chateau-auvers.fr) features a walk-through tour with an Impressionist theme. Auvers' **tourist office** is at Manoir des Colombières, rue de la Sansonne (01.30.36.10.06, www.auvers-sur-oise.com).

You can always do as Van Gogh might have done, and dine at the **Auberge Ravoux** (*see below*). Otherwise, try **L'Impressionist' Café** (Château d'Auvers, rue de Léry, 01.34.48.48.48), which does cheap lunches. The **Hostellerie du Nord** (6 rue Général-de-Gaulle, 01.30.36.70.74, www.hostelleriedunord.fr) has Joël Boilleaut running the kitchen.

Auberge Ravoux

1 pl de la Mairie, 95430 Auvers-sur-Oise (01.30.36.60.60, www.maisondevangogh.fr). **Open** *Mar-Oct* 10am-6pm Wed-Sun. **Admission** €6; €4 reductions; free under-12s.

GIVERNY

In 1883, Claude Monet moved his mistress and their eight children into a quaint pink-brick house he had rented in bucolic Giverny, less than an hour from Paris (Gare St-Lazare to Vernon, then 5km taxi or bus ride), and spent as much time cultivating a beautiful garden here as painting the water lilies in it. The leader of the Impressionist movement thrived on outdoor scenes, whether along the Seine near Argenteuil or by the Thames in London. Having once seen the tiny village of Giverny from the window of a train, he was smitten. By 1890, he had bought his dream home and soon had a pond dug, bridges built and a tableau of greenery created. As Monet's eyesight began to fail, he produced endless impressions of his man-made paradise, each trying to capture how the leaves and water reflected light. He died here in 1926.

Of the hundreds of tourists who visit here every day, not all are art-lovers; there are none of his original paintings actually on display here (though you will see the 32 Japanese woodblock prints collected by the artist). Most visitors are simply here for the lilies, and a good photo opportunity. The garden is as much a masterpiece as any of Monet's paintings, its famous water-lily pond, weeping willows and Japanese bridge still remarkably intact from the master's day; and the charming house, the **Fondation Claude Monet**, is dotted with touching mementos.

Once you're back in the village, be prepared for some difficulty finding a table at one of the scarce eating places, and long queues of impatient tourists almost everywhere you turn. Get here early, or book ahead to eat at the famous **Hôtel Baudy** museum-restaurant (81 rue Claude Monet, 02.32.21.10.03, www. restaurantbaudy.com), where Monet's American disciples (such as Willard Metcalf and Dawson-Watson) set up their easels for several decadent years, expanding the old hotel into an *art-atelier extraordinaire*, complete with ballroom, rose garden and tennis courts – Cézanne stayed here

MOVING MASTERPIECES

The capital's most visited museums make for the provinces.

Centre Pompidou Metz.

Paris's twin cultural giants, the **Louvre** and the **Centre Pompidou**, are the capital's two most visited museums, bringing in more than eight million visitors each year to gawp at the artistic treasures within. But while the galleries are stacked full of masterpieces ancient and modern, the problem has always been that their vaults are heaving with acres of unseen treasures. So the Pompidou decided to follow in the footsteps of Tate Liverpool and the Guggenheim Bilbao, and open an outpost in the eastern city of Metz (www.centre pompidou-metz.fr) in 2010 with the same *raison d'être* as the original – namely to 'present and help discover all forms of artistic expression, raise public awareness of the major works of the 20th and 21st centuries, and take part in Europe's cultural landscape'. And, presumably, to help shift some of that excess stock sitting in the basement. The experiment has been a success so far, with some 550,000 visitors checking out the Shigeru Ban-designed multidisciplinary space.

Not to be outdone, the Louvre is now playing its own regeneration game with an outpost in the gritty northern industrial town of Lens (www.louvrelens.fr). Far from the grandiose surroundings of the 1st arrondissement, the museum sprawls

across the site of an old mine works and opened in December 2012. Metz lies just 80 minutes from Paris by TGV and Lens is even closer (70 minutes), which puts it firmly in day-trip distance, as well as tapping into the Lille catchment area.

At Lens, the main display space, the 2,000sq m Galerie du Temps, displays some 300 artworks taken from every department in the Louvre. There's also a 300-seat auditorium, La Scene, which aims to bring the Louvre's collection to life through live performance.

Fondation Claude Monet.

for a month. Up the road, the **Musée des Impressionnismes Giverny** (99 rue Claude-Monet, 02.32.51.94.65, www.museedesimpressionnismesgiverny.com) houses works by the American Impressionist colony.

Fondation Claude Monet
84 rue Claude-Monet, 27620 Giverny (02.32.51.28.21, www.fondation-monet.com). **Open** 9.30am-6pm daily. Closed Nov-Mar. **Admission** *House & garden* €9.50; €4-€5 reductions; free under-7s.

MILLY-LA-FORET

As a revered poet, painter, playwright and filmmaker, Jean Cocteau has left an artistic legacy that pervades many aspects of French culture. Yet the man was always an elusive figure. But now, thanks to the hefty financial input of Pierre Bergé (partner of the late Yves Saint Laurent and a close friend of Cocteau's), his old country house in Milly-la-Forêt, less than an hour south-east of Paris (RER D to Maisse, then 7km taxi ride), is open as the **Maison de Jean Cocteau**. Cocteau moved to Milly-la-Fôret in 1947 to escape the glitz of the capital. Following his death from a heart attack at the age of 74, in 1963, his long-term partner Edouard Dhermite (who starred in Jean-Pierre Melville's 1950 film of Cocteau's 1929 novel *Les Enfants Terribles*) locked up the study, bedroom and living room, leaving more than 500 oil paintings, drawings, sculptures and photographs untouched for decades.

The three rooms have been faithfully restored, leaving one with the impression that

Cocteau left only a few minutes earlier. The living room is wonderfully flamboyant, with antique furniture and gold palm trees framing a Bérard painting of Oedipus. The bedroom, meanwhile, with its four-poster bed and a mural of a castle, boasts a fairytale quality reminiscent of Cocteau's masterful 1946 romantic fantasy film *La Belle et la Bête*. Finally the study, with its leopard-print walls and erotic memorabilia, offers the most intimate glimpse into the artist's creative process, by turns both inspiring and provocative.

The rest of the house has been converted into exhibition space with two galleries: one houses a collection of portraits of Cocteau by such artists as Picasso, Warhol and Modigliani;

the other is dedicated to temporary exhibitions. A projection room showing documentaries and Cocteau's films concludes the visit, but the adventure continues in the gardens surrounding the house, dotted with sculptures, where he used to enjoy strolling and writing.

Cocteau's body rests nearby, in the **Chapelle Saint-Blaise-des-Simples** (rue de l'Amiral de Graville, Milly-la-Forêt, 01.64.98.84.94, open 10am-12.30pm, 2-6pm Wed-Sun). The interior, like a scaled-down Sistine Chapel, is covered in murals painted by Cocteau in 1960. His epitaph, 'Je reste avec vous' (I remain with you), seems to have as much resonance today as ever.

Maison de Jean Cocteau

15 rue du Lau, 91490 Milly-la-Forêt (01.64.98.11.50, www.jeancocteau.net). **Open** *Mar-Sept* 2-7pm Wed-Sun. *Oct-early Nov* 2-6pm Wed-Sun. *Early Nov-early Jan* 2-6pm Sat, Sun. Closed mid Jan-Feb. **Admission** €7; €4.50 reductions; free under-10s.

Champagne Country
REIMS & EPERNAY

Named after the region in which it's produced, champagne – nearly all 300 million bottles a year of it – comes from the towns of Reims (nasally pronounced 'Ranse') and Epernay, some 25km apart. At less than an hour by train from Paris Gare de l'Est, both are ideal destinations for a weekend break. A tour of a champagne cellar is a big part of most visits. Most cellars give detailed explanations of how the drink is produced – from the grape varieties used to the strict name and quality controls – and guided tours finish with a sample.

Epernay developed during the 19th century as expanding champagne houses moved out from Reims to acquire more space. The best tours are at Mercier and Moët & Chandon. The tourist office is at 7 av de Champagne (03.26.53.33.00, www.ot-epernay.fr).

Some 7,000 tonnes of chalk were extracted to create the 18km (11 miles) of cellars at **Mercier**, opened in 1858. Note the 20-tonne champagne barrel at the entrance: it took 24 bulls and 18 horses to drag it from Epernay to Paris for the 1889 Exposition Universelle. The 45-minute underground tour takes place on a little train.

Moët & Chandon started life in 1743 as champagne supplier to Madame de Pompadour, mistress of Louis XV. It later supplied Napoleon and Alexander I of Russia. Since then it has kept pole position, with the largest domaine and more than 250 global outlets. In the hour-long tour, visitors are led through a section of the 28km (17 miles) of tunnels.

In Reims, most of the major champagne houses are open by appointment only: **Krug** (03.26.84.44.20, www.krug.com); **Lanson** (03.26.78.50.50, www.lanson.fr); **Louis Roederer** (by appointment *and* recommendation only, 03.26.40.42.11, www.champagne-roederer.com) and **Veuve Clicquot** (03.26.89.53.90, www.veuve-clicquot.com). **Champagne Pommery** is set in an intriguing Elizabethan building. The visit takes place some 30m (98ft) underground, in 18km (11 miles) of tunnels linking 120 Gallo-Roman chalk quarries. The tourist office is at 2 rue Guillaume-de-Machault (03.26.77.45.00, www.reims-tourisme.com).

Home of the coronation church of most French monarchs since Clovis in 496, Reims was an important city even in Roman times. Begun in 1211, the current **Cathédrale Notre-Dame** (03.26.47.55.34, www.cathedrale-reims.com) has rich Gothic decoration that includes thousands of well-preserved figures on the portals. Look out, too, for the splendid stained-glass windows in the axial chapel, designed by Chagall. The statues damaged during shelling in World War I can be seen next door in the former archbishop's palace, the **Palais de Tau** (2 pl du Cardinal-Luçon, 03.26.47.81.79).

In Reims, countless cafés and brasseries line lively place Drouet d'Erlon. In Epernay, **La Cave à Champagne** (16 rue Léon Gambetta, 03.26.55.50.70, www.la-cave-a-champagne.com) does good traditional French food, as does **Théâtre** (8 pl Pierre-Mendès-France, 03.26.58.88.19, www.epernay-restletheatre.com). Known for its champagnes, **Les Cépages** (16 rue Fauvette, 03.26.55.16.93) serves homely food.

Champagne Pommery

5 pl du Général-Gouraud, 51100 Reims (03.26.61.62.56, www.pommery.com). **Open** *Apr-Oct* 10am-6pm daily. *Nov-Mar* 10am-5pm daily. **Admission** (incl 1 glass) from €12; free under-10s.

Mercier

68 av de Champagne, 51200 Epernay (03.26.51.22.22, www.champagnemercier.fr). **Open** *Early-late Mar & mid Nov-mid Dec* 9.30-11.30am, 2-4.30pm Mon, Thur-Sun. *Late Mar-mid Nov* 9.30-11.30am, 2-4.30pm daily. **Admission** (incl 1 glass) from €13; €6 reductions; free under-10s.

Moët & Chandon

20 av de Champagne, 51200 Epernay (03.26.51.20.20, www.moet.com). **Open** *Apr-mid Nov* 9.30-11.30am, 2-4.30pm daily. *Mid Nov-Mar* 9.30-11.30am, 2-4.30pm Mon-Fri. Closed Jan. **Admission** (incl 1 glass) from €21; €10 reductions; free under-10s.

in Context

History

Heads will roll.

TEXT: NATASHA EDWARDS

The earliest settlers seem to have arrived in Paris around 120,000 years ago. One of them lost a flint spear-tip on the hill now called Montmartre, and the dangerous-looking weapon is to be seen today in the Stone Age collection at the Musée des Antiquités Nationales. There was a Stone Age weapons factory underneath present-day Châtelet, and the redevelopment of Bercy in the 1990s unearthed ten neolithic canoes, five of which are now sitting high and dry in the Musée Carnavalet.

By 250 BC, a Celtic tribe known as the Parisii had put the place firmly on the map. The Parisii were river traders, wealthy enough to mint gold coins; the Musée de la Monnaie de Paris has an extensive collection of their small change. Their most important *oppidum*, a primitive fortified town, was located on an island in the Seine, which is generally thought to have been what is today's Ile de la Cité. A superb strategic location and the capacity to generate hard cash were guaranteed to grab the attention of the Romans.

LIDO

CHAMPS-ÉLYSÉES
PARIS

THE FAMOUS CABARET OF THE CHAMPS-ÉLYSÉES:

70 artistes on stage,
600 sumptuous costumes,
23 monumental sets...

Extract of the show

Le Lido c'est Paris !

DINNER & SHOW from €160
CHAMPAGNE & SHOW from €100

116 bis avenue des Champs-Élysées 75008 Paris - Tel. : + 33 (0)1 40 76 56 10 - E-mail: reservation@lido.fr
www.lido.fr - facebook.com/lidodeparis.officiel

ROMAN PARIS

Julius Caesar arrived in southern Gaul as proconsul in 58 BC, and soon used the pretext of dealing with invading barbarians to stick his Roman nose into the affairs of northern Gaul. Caesar had a battle on his hands, but eventually the Paris region and the rest of Gaul were in Roman hands. Roman Lutetia (as Paris was known) was a prosperous town of around 8,000 inhabitants. As well as centrally heated villas and a temple to Jupiter on the main island (the remains of both are visible in the Crypte Archéologique), there were the sumptuous baths (now the Musée National du Moyen Age) and 15,000-seater Arènes de Lutèce.

CHRISTIANITY

Christianity arrived in around 250 AD in the shape of Denis of Athens, who became the first bishop of Paris. Legend has it that when he was decapitated by Valerian on Mons Martis, the mount of the martyrs (today better known as Montmartre), Denis picked up his head and walked with it to what is now St-Denis, to be buried there. The event is depicted in Henri Bellechose's *Retable de Saint-Denis*, now exhibited in the Louvre.

Gaul was still a tempting prize. Waves of barbarian invaders began crossing the Rhine from 275 onwards. They sacked more than 60 cities in Gaul, including Lutetia, where the people were massacred and the buildings on the Montagne Ste-Geneviève were pillaged and burned. The bedraggled survivors used the rubble to build a rampart around the Ile de la Cité and to fortify the forum.

It was at this time that the city was renamed Paris. Its main role was as a rear base for the Roman armies defending Gaul, and it was here in 360 that Julian was proclaimed emperor by his troops. Around 450, with the arrival of the Huns in the region, the people of Paris prepared once again to flee. They were dissuaded by the feisty Geneviève. Seeing the walls of the city defended against him, no less a pillager than Attila the Hun was forced to turn back; he was defeated soon afterwards.

CLOVIS

In 464, Paris managed to resist another siege, this time by the Francs under Childeric. However, by 486, after a further blockade

lasting ten years, Geneviève had no option but to surrender the city to Childeric's successor, Clovis, who went on to conquer most of Gaul and founded the Merovingian dynasty. He chose Paris as capital of his new kingdom, and it stayed that way until the seventh century, in spite of conflicts among his successors. Under the influence of his wife, Clotilde, Clovis converted to Christianity. He founded, and was buried in, the basilica of the Saints-Apôtres, later rededicated to Ste Geneviève when the saviour and future patron saint of Paris was interred there in 512. All that remains of the basilica today is a pillar in the grounds of the Lycée Henri IV; but there's a shrine dedicated to Ste Geneviève and some relics in the fine Gothic church of St-Etienne-du-Mont next door.

> '*Legend has it that when Denis of Athens was decapitated by Valerian on Mons Martis (Montmartre), he picked up his head and walked to what is now St-Denis, to be buried there.*'

Geneviève and Clovis had set a trend. The Ile de la Cité was still the heart of the city, but, under the Merovingians, the Left Bank was the up-and-coming area for fashion-conscious Christians, with 11 churches built here in the period (whereas there were only four on the Right Bank and one on Ile de la Cité). Not everyone was sold on the joys of city living, though. From 614 onwards, the Merovingian kings preferred the *banlieue* at Clichy, or wandered the kingdom trying to keep rebellious nobles in check. When one of the rebels, Pippin 'the Short', decided to do away with the last Merovingian in 751, Paris was starting to look passé.

Pippin's son, Charlemagne, built his capital at Aix-la-Chapelle (now Aachen in Germany), and his successors, the Carolingian dynasty,

THE FRENCH REVOLUTION

From conception to bloody execution.

In the winter of 1788-89, Louis XVI was losing grip on his country's problems. Wars had left the state almost bankrupt; harvests had failed and food prices soared. Distress and discontent reigned, and with it came demands for an end to absolute monarchy and for wider participation in government. Under pressure, Louis allowed the formation of an Assemblée Nationale, which started work on a national constitution. But behind the scenes, he began gathering troops to force it to disband; and on 12 July, he dismissed the commoner's ally, finance minister Jacques Necker. On 14 July, a crowd stormed the Bastille prison in response. Only seven prisoners were inside but the symbolic victory was huge.

The establishment of the constitution forged ahead. Tax breaks for the nobility and clergy were abolished; Church property was seized. But the price of bread remained high. In October, a mob of starving women marched to Versailles and demanded that the king come to Paris. He promised to send them grain, an offer they rejected by decapitating some of his

guards. Louis transferred to the Tuileries. In the months that followed, the Jacobins roused powerful Republican feeling. The king and his family tried to flee Paris on 20 June 1791, but were apprehended.

On 14 September, Louis accepted the constitution. But other monarchies were plotting to reinstate him. In 1792, Austrian and Prussian troops invaded France. The Republicans, correctly, suspected Louis of conspiracy, and raised an army to capture him. He and his family were incarcerated by the radical Commune de Paris, headed by Danton, Marat and Robespierre.

Then came a massacre. Republicans invaded the prisons and murdered 2,000 so-called traitors. The monarchy was abolished on 22 September; the king was executed on 21 January 1793. Headed by Robespierre, the Jacobins vowed to wage terror against all dissidents. The Great Terror of 1794 saw the guillotine slice through 1,300 necks in six weeks. Eventually there was no more stomach for killing. On 28 July 1794, Robespierre was executed and the bloodiest of revolutions was finally over.

moved from palace to palace, consuming the local produce. Paris, meanwhile, was doing nicely as a centre for Christian learning, and had grown to a population of 20,000 by the beginning of the ninth century. This was the high point in the political power of the great abbeys like St-Germain-des-Prés, where transcription of the Latin classics was helping to preserve much of Europe's Roman cultural heritage. Power in the Paris area was exercised by the counts of Paris.

PARIS FINDS ITS FEET

From 845, Paris had to fight off another threat – the Vikings. But after various sackings and seiges, the Carolingians were finally able to secure the city. The dynasty gave way to the Capetian dynasty in 987, when Hugues Capet was elected king of France. Under the Capetians, although Paris was now at the heart of the royal domains, the city did not yet dominate the kingdom. Robert 'the Pious', king from 996 to 1031, stayed more often in Paris than his father had done, restoring the royal palace on the Ile de la Cité, and Henri I (1031-60) issued more of his charters in Paris than in Orléans. In 1112, the abbey of St-Denis replaced St-Benoît-sur-Loire as principal monastery.

Paris itself still consisted of little more than Ile de la Cité and small settlements under the protection of the abbeys on each bank. On the Left Bank, royal largesse helped to rebuild the abbeys of St-Germain-des-Prés, St-Marcel and Ste-Geneviève, although it took more than 150 years for the destruction wrought there by the Vikings to be repaired. The Right Bank, where mooring was easier, prospered from river commerce, and three boroughs grew up around the abbeys of St-Germain-l'Auxerrois, St-Martin-des-Champs and St-Gervais. Bishop Sully of Paris began building the cathedral of Notre-Dame in 1163. The reign of Philippe-Auguste (1180-1223) was a turning point in the history of Paris. Before, it was a confused patchwork of royal, ecclesiastical and feudal authorities. Keen to raise revenues, Philippe favoured the growth of guilds, especially the butchers, drapers, furriers, haberdashers and merchants; so began the rise of the bourgeoisie.

Philippe also ordered the building of the first permanent market buildings at Les Halles, and a new city wall, first on the Right Bank to protect the commercial heart of Paris, and later on the Left Bank. At the western end of the wall, he built a castle, the Louvre, to defend the road from the ever-menacing Normandy, whose duke was also King of England.

A GOLDEN AGE

Paris was now the principal residence of the king and the uncontested capital of France. To accommodate the growing royal administration, the Palais de la Cité, site and symbol of power for the previous thousand years, was remodelled and enlarged. Work was begun by Louis IX (later St Louis) in the 1240s, and continued under Philippe IV ('le Bel'). This architectural complex, of which the Sainte-Chapelle and nearby Conciergerie can still be seen, was inaugurated with great pomp at Pentecost 1313.

The palace was quickly filled with functionaries, so the king spent as much of his time as he could outside Paris at the royal castles of Fontainebleau and, especially, Vincennes. The needs of the plenipotentiaries left behind to run the kingdom were met by a rapidly growing city population, piled into less chic buildings.

Paris was also reinforcing its identity as a major religious centre: as well as the local clergy and dozens of religious orders, the city was home to the masters and students of the university of the Sorbonne (established in 1253). An influx of scholars from all over Europe gave the city a cultural and intellectual cachet it was never to lose.

By 1328, Paris was home to 200,000 inhabitants, making it the most populous city in Europe. However, that year was also notable for being the last of the medieval golden age: the dynasty of Capetian kings spluttered to an inglorious halt when Charles IV died without an heir. The English quickly claimed the throne for Edward III, the son of Philippe IV's daughter. Refusing to recognise his descent through the female line, the late king's cousin, Philippe de Valois, claimed the French crown as Philippe VI. So began the Hundred Years War between France and England, which would go on for 116 years.

TROUBLES AND STRIFE

To make matters worse, the Black Death (bubonic plague) ravaged Europe from the

IN CONTEXT

1340s onwards. Citizens not finished off by the plague had to contend with food shortages, increasing taxes, riots, repression, currency devaluations and marauding mercenaries. Meanwhile, in Paris, the honeymoon period for the king and the bourgeoisie was coming to an end. Rich and populous, Paris was expected to bear the brunt of the war burden; and as defeat followed defeat (notably a disaster at Crécy in August 1346), the bourgeoisie and people of the city were increasingly exasperated by the futility of the sacrifices they were making for the hideously expensive war. To fund the conflict, King Jean II tried to introduce new tax laws – without success. When the king was captured by the English at Poitiers in 1356, his problems passed on to his 18-year-old son, Charles.

IN CONTEXT

'In 1431, Henry VI of England was crowned King of France in Notre-Dame. He didn't last. Five years later, Henry was driven back to Calais by the Valois king, Charles VII.'

The Etats Généraux, consultant body to the throne, was summoned to the royal palace on the Ile de la Cité to discuss the country's woes. The teenage king was besieged with angry demands for reform from the bourgeoisie, particularly from Etienne Marcel, then provost of the local merchants. Marcel seized control of Paris and began a bitter power struggle with the crown; in 1357, fearing widespread revolt, Charles fled to Compiègne. But as he ran, he had Paris blockaded. Marcel called on the peasants, who were raging against taxes, but they were crushed. He then called on Charles 'the Bad' of Navarre, ally to the English, but his arrival in Paris made many of Marcel's supporters

nervous. On 31 July 1358, Marcel was murdered, and the revolution was over. As a safeguard, the returning Charles built a stronghold to protect Paris: the Bastille.

By 1420, following the French defeat at Agincourt, Paris was in English hands; in 1431, Henry VI of England was crowned King of France in Notre-Dame. He didn't last. Five years later, Henry and his army were driven back to Calais by the Valois king, Charles VII. Charles owed his power to Jeanne d'Arc, who led the victorious French in the Battle of Orléans, only to be betrayed by her compatriots, who decided she was getting too big for her boots. She was captured and sold to the English, who had her burned as a witch.

By 1436, Paris was once again the capital of France. But the nation had been bled nearly dry by war and was still divided politically, with powerful regional rulers across France continuing to threaten the monarchy. Outside the French borders, the ambitions of the Austrian Habsburg dynasty represented a serious threat. In this general atmosphere of instability, disputes over trade, religion and taxation were all simmering dangerously.

RENAISSANCE AND REFORMATION

In the closing decades of the 15th century, the restored Valois monarchs sought to reassert their position. A wave of building projects was the public sign of this effort, producing such masterpieces as St-Etienne-du-Mont, St-Eustache and private homes like Hôtel de Cluny (which today houses the Musée National du Moyen Age) and the Hôtel de Sens, which now accommodates the Bibliothèque de Forney. The Renaissance in France had its peak under François I. As well as being involved in the construction of the magnificent châteaux at Fontainebleau, Blois and Chambord, François was responsible for transforming the Louvre from a fortress into a royal palace.

Despite burning heretics by the dozen, François was unable to stop the spread of Protestantism, launched in Germany by Martin Luther in 1517. Resolutely Catholic, Paris was the scene of some horrific violence against the Huguenots, as supporters of the new faith were called. By the 1560s, the situation had degenerated into open warfare. Catherine de Médicis, the scheming

Italian widow of Henri II, was the real force in court politics. It was she who connived to murder prominent Protestants gathered in Paris for the marriage of the king's sister on St Bartholomew's Day (23 August 1572). Catherine's main aim was to dispose of her powerful rival, Gaspard de Coligny, but the situation got out of hand, and as many as 3,000 people were butchered. Henri III attempted to reconcile the religious factions and eradicate the powerful families directing the conflict, but the people of Paris turned against him and he was forced to flee. His assassination in 1589 brought the Valois line to an end.

THE BOURBONS

The throne of France being up for grabs, Henri of Navarre declared himself King Henri IV, launching the Bourbon dynasty. Paris was not impressed. The city closed its gates against the Huguenot king, and the inhabitants endured a four-year siege by supporters of the new ruler. Henri managed to break the impasse by having himself converted to Catholicism (and is supposed to have said, '*Paris vaut bien une messe*' – Paris is well worth a mass).

Henri set about rebuilding his ravaged capital. He completed the Pont Neuf, the first bridge to span the whole Seine. He commissioned place Dauphine and the city's first enclosed residential square – the place Royale, now place des Vosges.

Henri also tried to reconcile his Catholic and Protestant subjects, issuing the Edict of Nantes in 1598, effectively giving each religion equal status. The Catholics hated the deal, and the Huguenots were suspicious. Henri was the subject of at least 23 attempted assassinations by fanatics of both persuasions. Finally, in 1610, a Catholic by the name of François Ravaillac fatally stabbed the king while he was in traffic on rue de la Ferronnerie.

TWO CARDINALS

Since Henri's son, Louis XIII, was only eight at the time of his father's death, his mother, Marie de Médicis, took up the reins of power. We can thank her for the Palais du Luxembourg and the 24 paintings she commissioned from Rubens, now part of the Louvre collection. Louis took up his royal duties in 1617, but Cardinal Richelieu, chief minister from 1624, was the man who ran France. Something of a schemer, he outwitted the king's mother, his wife (Anne of Austria) and a host of others. Richelieu helped to strengthen the power of the monarch, and he did much to limit the independence of the aristocracy.

The Counter-Reformation was at its height, and lavish churches such as the Baroque Val-de-Grâce were an important reassertion of Catholic supremacy. The 17th century was 'le Grand Siècle', a time of patronage of art and artists, even if censorship forced the brilliant mathematician and philosopher René Descartes into exile. The first national newspaper, *La Gazette*, hit the streets in 1631; Richelieu used it as a propaganda tool. The cardinal founded the Académie Française, which is still working, slowly, on the dictionary of the French language that he commissioned from them in 1634. Richelieu died in 1642; Louis XIII followed suit a few months later. The new king, Louis XIV, was five years old. Anne of Austria became regent, with the Italian Cardinal Mazarin, a Richelieu protégé, as chief minister. Rumour has it that Anne and Mazarin may have been married. Mazarin's townhouse is now home to the Bibliothèque Nationale de France – Richelieu.

Endless wars against Austria and Spain had depleted the royal coffers and left the nation drained by exorbitant taxation. In 1648, the royal family was chased out of Paris by a popular uprising, 'la Fronde', named after the catapults used by some of the rioters. Parisians soon tired of the anarchy that followed. When Mazarin's army retook the city in 1653, the boy-king was warmly welcomed. Mazarin died in 1661 and Louis XIV, now 24 years old, decided he would rule France without the assistance of any chief minister.

SHINE ON, SUN KING

The '*Roi Soleil*', or Sun King, was an absolute monarch. '*L'état, c'est moi*' (I am the State) was his vision of power. To prove his grandeur, the king embarked on wars against England, Holland and Austria. He also refurbished and extended the Louvre, commissioned place Vendôme and place des Victoires, constructed the Observatory and laid out the *grands boulevards* along the line

IN CONTEXT

of the old city walls. His major project was the palace at Versailles. Louis moved his court there in 1682.

Louis XIV owed much of his brilliant success to the work of Jean-Baptiste Colbert, who was nominally in charge of state finances, but eventually took control of all the important levers of the state machine. Colbert was the force behind the Sun King's redevelopment of Paris. The Hôtel des Invalides was built to accommodate the crippled survivors of Louis' wars, the Salpêtrière to shelter fallen women.

In 1702, Paris was divided into 20 quartiers (not until the Revolution was it re-mapped into arrondissements). Colbert died in 1683, and Louis' luck on the battlefield ran out. Hopelessly embroiled in the War of the Spanish Succession, the country was devastated by famine in 1692. The Sun King died in 1715, leaving no direct heir. His five-year-old great-grandson, Louis XV, was named king, with Philippe d'Orléans as regent. The court moved back to Paris. Installed in the Palais-Royal, the regent set about enjoying his few years of power, hosting lavish dinners that degenerated into orgies. The state, meanwhile, remained chronically in debt.

THE ENLIGHTENMENT

Some of the city's more sober residents were making Paris the intellectual capital of Europe. Enlightenment thinkers such as Diderot, Montesquieu, Voltaire and Rousseau were active during the reign of Louis XV. Literacy rates were increasing – 50 per cent of French men could read, 25 per cent of women – and the publishing industry was booming.

The king's mistress, Madame de Pompadour, encouraged him to finance the building of the Ecole Militaire and the laying out of place Louis XV, known to us as place de la Concorde. The church of St-Sulpice was completed in 1776. Many of the great houses in the area bounded by rue de Lille, rue de Varenne and rue de Grenelle date from the first half of the 18th century. The private homes of aristocrats and wealthy bourgeois, these would become the venues for numerous salons, the informal discussion sessions often devoted to topics raised by Enlightenment questioning.

The Enlightenment spirit of rational humanism finally took the venom out of the Catholic–Protestant power struggle, and the increase in public debate helped to change views about the nature of the state and the place and authority of the monarchy. As Jacques Necker, Louis XVI's finance minister on the eve of the Revolution, put it, popular opinion was 'an invisible power that, without treasury, guard or army, gives its laws to the city, the court and even the palaces of kings'. Thanks to the Enlightenment, and a growing burden of taxation on the poorest strata of society to prop up the wealthiest, that power would eventually overturn the status quo.

THE FRENCH REVOLUTION

The great beneficiary of the French Revolution, Napoleon Bonaparte, once remarked that lucky generals were to be preferred over good generals. The same applies to kings, and the gods of fortune certainly deserted Louis XVI in 1789, when bad weather and worse debts brought France to its knees. But few would have predicted that the next five years would see the execution of the king and most of the royal family, terror stalking the streets in the name of revolution, and the steady rise of a young Corsican soldier. For an account of the Revolution, *see p314* **The French Revolution**.

NAPOLEON

Amid the post-Revolutionary chaos, power was divided between a two-housed Assembly and a Directory of five men. The French public reacted badly to hearing of England's attempts to promote more popular rebellion; when a royalist rising in Paris needed to be put down, a young officer from Corsica was the man to do it – Napoleon Bonaparte.

Napoleon quickly became the Directory's right-hand man. When they needed someone to lead a campaign against Austria, he was the man. Victory saw France – and Napoleon – glorified. After an aborted campaign to Egypt in 1799, Napoleon returned home to put down another royalist plot, made himself the chief of the newly governing three-man Consul – and by 1804 was emperor.

After failing to squeeze out the English by setting up the Continental System to block trade across the Channel, Napoleon waged massive wars against Britain, Russia and

IN CONTEXT

RISING DAMP

It's a century since Paris's worst flooding – and it could happen again.

When the original, 19th-century Pont de l'Alma was replaced in the early 1970s by the wider, stronger version that you see today, one feature of the old bridge was retained: the Zouave statue that stands at the foot of the supporting pillar in midstream. Initially a straightforward emblem of French military success in the Crimean War, the Zouave became better known as a yardstick during the Seine's periodic floods. The fact that it was reinstated on the new bridge, alone of four statues that adorned the old one, is a measure of its stature in Paris folklore.

January 2010 was the centenary of the Zouave's dampest hour, when heavy rainfall and a badly timed thaw swelled the Seine to its highest level in recorded history, and the waters lapped around the stone soldier's neck. Hundreds of streets in central Paris were several feet deep in water, and inhabitants were obliged to get around by boat: the vast photographic record of the disaster (a boon for photographers and postcard publishers) contains scenes more reminiscent of Venice than Paris. Many residents had to get into and out of buildings via a ladder and first-storey window.

As it turns out, the Zouave's new base is higher above the average water level than previously, so if the Seine does rise to its neck, the city will be in even more trouble than it was a century ago. The deluge of 1910 was a so-called 'hundred-year flood', which means, statistically speaking, that the next one is already overdue; and since the new bridge was installed, the waters have risen as far as Zuoave's belt (in 1985). Today, flooding of the river's *berges* is a nearly annual event.

But worryingly, despite years of discussion by the city council and the government, Paris has no equivalent of London's Thames Barrier – although smaller barrages and reservoirs much further upstream have gone some way to alleviating the effects of high water runoff. So that just leaves the rather ominous 'in case of flooding' advice on the Mairie de Paris website and smart street maps shaded to show likely zones of flooded streets and electricity outage. In the meantime, the Zouave watches and waits.

Napoleon.

Austria. On his way to the disaster of Moscow, Napoleon gave France the *lycée* educational system, the Napoleonic Code of civil law, the Legion of Honour, the Banque de France, the Pont des Arts, the Arc de Triomphe, the Madeleine church (he re-established Catholicism as the state religion), La Bourse and rue de Rivoli. He was also responsible for the centralised bureaucracy that still drives the French public mad today.

As Russian troops – who had chased Napoleon's once-mighty army all the way from Moscow and Leipzig – invaded France, Paris itself came under threat. Montmartre, then named Montnapoléon, had a telegraph machine at its summit, one that had given so many of the emperor's orders and transmitted news of so many victories. The hill fell to Russian troops. Napoleon gave the order to blow up the city's main powder stores, and thus Paris itself. His officer refused. Paris accommodated carousing Russian, Prussian and English soldiers while Napoleon was sent to exile in Elba. A hundred days later, he was back, leading an army against Wellington and Blücher's troops in the mud of Waterloo. A further defeat saw the end of him. Paris

survived further foreign occupation. The diminutive Corsican died on the South Atlantic prison island of St Helena in 1821.

ANOTHER ROUND OF BOURBONS

Having sampled revolution and military dictatorship, the French were now ready to give monarchy a second chance. The Bourbons got back in business in 1815, in the person of Louis XVIII, Louis XVI's elderly brother. Several efforts were made to adapt the monarchy to the new political realities, though the new king's Charter of Liberties was not a wholly sincere expression of how he meant to rule.

When another brother of Louis XVI, Charles X, became king in 1824, he decided that enough royal energy had been wasted trying to reconcile the nation's myriad factions. It was time for a spot of old-fashioned absolutism. But the forces unleashed during the Revolution, and the social divisions that had opened as a result, were not to be ignored – and the people were happy to respond with some old-fashioned rebellion.

In the 1830 elections, the liberals won a hefty majority in the Chamber of Deputies, the legislative body. Charles's unpopular minister Prince Polignac, a returned émigré, promptly dissolved the Chamber, announced a date for new elections and curtailed the number of voters. Polishing off this collection of bad decisions was the 26 July decree abolishing the freedom of the press. The day after its issue, 5,000 print workers and journalists filled the streets and three newspapers went to press. When police tried to confiscate copies, they sparked a three-day riot, 'les Trois Glorieuses', with members of the disbanded National Guard manning the barricades. On 30 July, Charles dismissed Polignac, but it was too late. He had little choice but to abdicate, and fled to England. As French revolutions go, it was a brief affair.

Another leftover from the *ancien régime* was now winched on to the throne – Louis-Philippe, Duc d'Orléans, who had some Bourbon blood in his veins. A father of eight who never went out without his umbrella, he was eminently acceptable to the newly powerful bourgeoisie. But the poor, who had risked their lives in two attempts to change French society, were unimpressed by the new king's promise to embrace a moderate and liberal version of the Revolutionary heritage.

THE NINETEENTH CENTURY

Philosopher Walter Benjamin declared Paris 'the capital of the 19th century', and he had a point. Though it was smaller than its global rival, London, in intellectual and cultural spheres it reigned supreme. On the demographic front, its population doubled to one million between 1800 and 1850. Most of the new arrivals were rural labourers, who had come to find work on the city's expanding building sites. Meanwhile, the middle classes were doing well, thanks to the relatively late arrival of the industrial revolution in France, and the solid administrative structures inherited from Napoleon. The poor were as badly off as ever, only now there were more of them. The back-breaking hours worked in the factories would not be curbed by legislation: 'Whatever the lot of the workers is, it is not the manufacturer's responsibility to improve it,' said one trade minister. In Left Bank cafés, a new bohemian tribe of students derided the materialistic government. Workers' pamphlets and newspapers, such as *La Ruche Populaire*, gave voice to the starving, crippled poor. A wave of ill feeling was building up against Louis-Philippe.

On 23 February 1848, hundreds of Parisians – men, women and students – moved along the boulevards towards a public banquet at La Madeleine. The king's minister, François Guizot, had forbidden any direct campaigning by opposition parties in the forthcoming election, so the parties held banquets instead of meetings.

One diarist of the time noted that some of the crowd had stuffed swords and daggers underneath their shirts, but the demonstration was largely peaceful – until the troops stationed on the boulevard des Capucines opened fire, igniting a riot.

As barricades sprang up all over the city, a trembling Louis-Philippe abdicated and a liberal provisional government declared a republic. The virtual epidemic of poverty and unemployment was stemmed by creating national *ateliers*, but such 'radical' reforms made the right very nervous. A conservative government took power in May 1848, and shut down the *ateliers*. A month later, the poor were back in the streets. Some 50,000 took part in the 'June Days' protests, which were quite comprehensively crushed by General Cavaignac's troops. In total, about 1,500 Parisians died and some 5,000 were deported. As the pamphleteer Alphonse Karr said of the revolution's aftermath, '*plus ça change, plus c'est la même chose*' (the more things change, the more they stay the same). In December 1848, Louis Bonaparte – nephew of Napoleon – was elected president. By 1852, he had moved into the Tuileries palace and declared himself Emperor Napoleon III.

THE SECOND EMPIRE

The emperor appointed a lawyer as *préfet* to mastermind the reconstruction of Paris. In less than two decades, prefect Georges-Eugène Haussmann had created the most magnificent city in Europe. His goals included better access to railway stations, better water supplies, and new hospitals, barracks, theatres and *mairies*. It was a vast project, and it transformed the capital with a network of wide avenues that were more hygienic than the narrow streets they replaced.

Not everyone was happy. Haussmann's works destroyed thousands of buildings, including beautiful medieval monuments; on the whole of Ile de la Cité only Notre-Dame

IN CONTEXT

and a handful of houses survived. Entire residential areas were wiped off the map, and only the owners of the buildings were compensated; tenants were merely booted out. Writers and artists lamented the loss of the more quirky Paris they used to know, and criticised the unfriendly grandeur of the new city. But there was no going back.

At home, the rapid industrialisation of the city saw the rise of Socialism and Communism among the disgruntled working classes, and Napoleon III gave limited rights to trade unions. Abroad, though, the now constitutional monarch was a disaster. After the relatively successful Crimean War of the mid 1850s, he tried in vain to impose the Catholic Maximilian as ruler of Mexico. The Franco-Prussian war was his next misadventure. France was soon defeated. At Sedan, in September 1870, 100,000 French troops were forced to surrender to Bismarck's Prussians; Napoleon III himself was captured, never to return.

The war continued, and back in Paris a provisional government hastily took power. Elections gave conservative monarchists the majority, though the Paris vote was firmly Republican. Former prime minister Adolphe Thiers assumed executive power. Meanwhile, Prussian forces marched on Paris and laid siege to the city. Paris held out, starving, for four brave months, its citizens picking rats from the gutter for food. Léon Gambetta, a young politician, escaped in style (by hot-air balloon) but failed to raise an army in the south. In January 1871, the provisional government signed a bitter armistice that relinquished the industrial heartlands of Alsace and Lorraine and agreed to pay a five-million-franc indemnity. German troops would stay on French soil until the bill was paid.

But with occupying army camps stationed around their city, Parisians considered the treaty a dishonour and remained defiant. Thiers ordered his soldiers to enter the city and strip it of its cannons, but the insurgents cut them short. The new government scuttled off to the haven of Versailles, and on 26 March Paris elected its own municipal body, the Commune, so called in memory of the spirit of 1792. The 92 members of the Commune hailed from the left and working classes; their agenda was liberal (schools would be secularised, debts suspended) but

war-like (Germany must be defeated). Paris itself was given a little makeover: the column extolling Napoleonic glory on place Vendôme was pulled down, and statues of the great emperor were smashed all over town.

Thiers would not stand by and watch. Artillery fire picked at the Communards' sandbag barricades on the edges of Paris, and the suburbs fell by 11 April. In the sixth week of fighting, troops broke in through the Porte de St-Cloud and covered the springtime city in blood. The ill-equipped Communards faced a massacre: some 25,000 were killed in a matter of days. In revenge, around 50 hostages were taken and shot, including the Archbishop of Paris. The infamous *pétroleuses*, women wielding petrol bombs, burned off their anger, torching the Tuileries and the Hôtel de Ville. On the last day of *la semaine sanglante*, 28 May 1871, 147 Communards were trapped and shot in Père-Lachaise cemetery, against the 'Mur des Fédérés', still an icon of the Commune struggle. The dead were buried in the streets, the prisons crammed with 40,000 Communards; thousands were deported, many to penal colonies in New Caledonia.

THE THIRD REPUBLIC

Thanks mainly to the huge economic boost provided by colonial expansion in Africa and Indo-China, the horrors of the Commune were soon forgotten in the self-indulgent materialism of the turn of the century and the Third Republic. The Eiffel Tower was built as the centrepiece of the 1889 Exposition Universelle. For the next Exposition Universelle, in 1900, the Grand Palais and Petit Palais, the Pont Alexandre III and the Gare d'Orsay (now the Musée d'Orsay) were built to affirm France's position as a world power, and the first line of the métro opened. The first film screening had been held (1895), and clubs like the Moulin Rouge were buzzing. The lurid life of Montmartre – and its cheap rents – would attract the world's artistic community.

THE GREAT WAR

On 3 August 1914, Germany declared war on France. Although the Germans never made it to Paris in World War I – German troops were stopped 20 kilometres (12 miles) short of the city thanks to the French victory in the Battle of the Marne – the artillery was audible. Paris, and French society as a whole, suffered terribly, despite ultimate victory.

The nations gathered at Versailles to make the peace, and established new European states. The League of Nations was formed. Artists responded to the horrors and absurdity of the conflict with Surrealism, a movement founded in Paris by André Breton, a doctor who had treated troops in the trenches and embraced Freud's theories of the unconscious. In 1924, Surrealism had a manifesto, a year later its first exhibition. Again, artists (and photographers) flocked to Paris. Montmartre was now too expensive, and Montparnasse became the hub of artistic life. The interwar years were a whirl of activity in artistic and political circles. Paris became the avant-garde capital of the world, recorded by Hemingway, F Scott Fitzgerald and Gertrude Stein.

Meanwhile, the Depression unleashed a wave of political violence, Fascists fighting Socialists and Communists for control. At the same time, many writers were leaving Paris for Spain to cover – and, indeed, to take part in – the Civil War. Across the German border, the contentious territories of Alsace-Lorraine –

and the burden of the World War I peace agreements signed in Paris – became one of many bugbears held by the new chancellor, Adolf Hitler. As war broke out, France believed that its Maginot line would hold against the German threat. When the Nazis attacked France in May 1940, they simply bypassed the fortifications and came through the Ardennes.

WORLD WAR II

Paris was in German hands by June. The city fell without a fight. A pro-German government was set up in Vichy, headed by Marshall Pétain, and a young army officer, Charles de Gaulle, went to London to organise the Free French opposition. For Frenchmen happy to get along with the German army, the period of the Occupation presented few hardships and, indeed, some good business opportunities. Food was rationed, and tobacco and coffee went out of circulation, but the black market thrived. For people who resisted, there were the Gestapo torture chambers at avenue Foch or rue Lauriston. The Germans further discouraged uncooperative behaviour with executions: one victim, whose name now adorns a métro station, was Jacques

IN CONTEXT

The Liberation of Paris.
See p325.

ESTATES OF EMERGENCY

When rioting ripped through the suburbs.

IN CONTEXT

In November 2005, violent suburban riots in Paris sent shockwaves through the country and abroad. The run-down estates around the capital became the scene for explosive confrontations with the police, as warehouses, restaurants and thousands of cars were set ablaze. Before long, the violence spread to other French cities. The government called a state of emergency, imposing curfews and banning public meetings at the weekends. Nevertheless, it was almost three weeks before the worst of the rioting was over.

The trigger for this unprecedented outbreak of violence was the accidental death on 27 October of two North African teenagers, in the north-east Paris suburb of Clichy-sous-Bois. According to locals, Bouna Traore, 15, and Zyed Benna, 17, panicked when they saw other black youths being chased by the police, and sought shelter in an electrical substation. As they entered the site, they were electrocuted, plunging the town into a blackout. To make matters worse, the incident came just two days after then Interior Minister Nicolas

Sarkozy had made inflammatory remarks about the need to rid the *banlieue* of the '*racaille*', a highly pejorative term that can be translated as 'rabble' or 'scum'.

If this chain of events formed an explosive catalyst for the riots, the root cause went much deeper. When the economy plummeted in the 1970s, the populations of these high-rise estates found themselves struggling with factory closures and unemployment. While the wealthier moved to more desirable areas, the remaining residents – mainly North African families – were effectively left stranded in a suburban desert.

Over the three weeks of violence, nearly 3,000 arrests were made, more than 10,000 cars were set ablaze, and 300 buildings were firebombed. Initially, the government seemed to take a liberal view of its immigrant population, voting in a number of equal opportunities measures. Yet just two months later, Sarkozy's immigration bill reintroduced a hard line, laying down much stricter terms for immigrants seeking residency.

Bonsergent, a student caught fly-posting and shot because he refused to reveal the names of his friends who escaped.

The Vichy government was so eager to please the Germans, it organised anti-Semitic measures without prompting. From the spring of 1941, the French authorities deported Jews to the death camps, frequently via the internment camp at Drancy. Prime Minister Pierre Laval argued that it was a necessary concession to his Third Reich masters. In July 1942, 12,000 Jewish French citizens were rounded up in the Vélodrome d'Hiver, a sports complex on the quai de Grenelle, and then dispatched to Auschwitz.

THE LIBERATION

Paris survived the war practically unscathed, ultimately thanks to the bravery of one of its captors. On 23 August 1944, as the Allied armies of liberation approached the city, Hitler ordered his commander, Dietrich von Choltitz, to detonate the explosives that had been set all over town in anticipation of a retreat. Von Choltitz refused. On 25 August, French troops, tactfully placed at the head of the US forces, entered the city, and General de Gaulle led the parade down the Champs-Elysées. Writers and artists swept back into Paris to celebrate. Hemingway held court at the Ritz and Scribe hotels with the great journalists of the day, clinking glasses with veterans of the Spanish Civil War such as Robert Capa and George Orwell. Picasso's studio was besieged by well-wishers.

However, the Liberation was by no means the end of France's troubles. De Gaulle was the hero of the hour, but relations between the interim government he commanded and the Resistance – largely Communist – were still tricky. Orders issued to maquis leaders in the provinces were often ignored. The Communists wanted a revolution, and de Gaulle suspected them of hatching plans to seize Paris prior to August 1944. Meanwhile, de Gaulle knew that he had to commit every available French soldier to the march on Germany, or risk being sidelined by the other Allies after the war. He had to leave homeland security to the very people – the 'patriotic militias' – who were most likely to be at least sympathetic to the Communist cause; or, even more dubiously, gendarmes who had worked with the occupying power.

Recovery was slow. There were shortages of everything; indeed, many complained they had been better off under the Germans. Even in the ministries, paper was so scarce that correspondence had to be sent out on Vichy letterhead with the sender crossing out 'Etat Français' at the top and writing 'République Française' instead.

THE FOURTH REPUBLIC

On 8 May 1945, de Gaulle made a broadcast to the nation to announce Germany's surrender. Paris went wild, but the euphoria didn't last. There were strikes. And more strikes. Liberation had proved to be a restoration, not the revolution the Communists, now the most powerful political force in the land, had hoped for. The Communist Party was, in at least one respect, as pragmatic as everyone else: it did its utmost to turn parliamentary democracy to its advantage, to wit, getting as many of the top jobs as it could.

A general election was held on 21 October 1945. The Communists secured 159 seats, the Socialists got 146 and the Catholic Mouvement Républicain Populaire got 152. A fortnight later, at the Assemblée Nationale's first session, a unanimous vote was passed maintaining de Gaulle in his position as head of state – but he remained an antagonistic leader. His reluctance to take a firm grip on the disastrous economic situation alienated many intellectuals and industrialists who had once been loyal to him, and his characteristic aloofness only made the misgivings of the general populace worse. He, on the other hand, was disgusted by all the political chicanery. On 20 January 1946, de Gaulle resigned.

France, meanwhile, looked to swift industrial modernisation under an ambitious plan put forward by internationalist politician Jean Monnet. Although the economy and daily life remained grim, in 1947 brash new fashion designer Christian Dior put together a stunning collection of strikingly simple yet luxurious clothes: the New Look. Such extravagance horrified many locals, but the fashion industry boomed. Meanwhile, the divisions in Paris between its fashionable and run-down working-class areas became more pronounced. The northern and eastern edges – areas revived only in the late 20th century

IN CONTEXT

by a taste for retro, industrial decor and cheap rent – were forgotten about. Félix Gouin, the new Socialist premier, quickly nationalised the bigger banks and the coal industry. But the right wing was growing, and there was even a rise of royalist hopes. A referendum was held in May 1946 to determine the crucial tenet of the Fourth Republic's constitution: should the Assemblée Nationale have absolute or restricted power? The results were a narrow victory for people who, like de Gaulle, had insisted the Assemblée's power should be qualified. De Gaulle's prestige increased, but it was another 12 years, and a whole new constitution – the Fifth Republic – before he came back to power. He spent much of his '*passage du désert*' writing his memoirs.

THE ALGERIAN WAR AND MAY 1968
The post-war years were marked by the rapid disintegration of France's overseas interests and by her rapprochement with Germany to create what would become the European Community. When revolt broke out in Algeria in 1956, almost 500,000 troops were sent in to protect national interests. A protest by Algerians in Paris on 17 October 1961 led to the deaths of hundreds of people at the hands of the city's police force. The extent of the violence was officially concealed for decades, as was the use of torture against Algerians by French troops. Algeria became independent in 1962.

Meanwhile, the slow, painful discoveries of collaboration in World War II, often overlooked in the rush to put the country back on its feet, were also being faced. The younger generation began to question the motives of the older one. De Gaulle's Fifth Republic was felt by many to be grimly authoritarian. In the spring of 1968, students unhappy with overcrowded university conditions took to the streets of Paris at the same time as striking Renault workers. These *soixante-huitards* sprang the greatest public revolt in French living memory. Many students were crammed into universities that had been cheaply expanded to accommodate them. Political discourse grew across the campuses, turning against the government's stranglehold on the media and President de Gaulle's poor grasp of the economy. Ministers did indeed at the time have a sinister habit of leaning on the leading

newspaper editors of the day, and television was dubbed 'the government in your dining room'. Inflation was high, and the gap between the working classes and the bourgeoisie was becoming a chasm. Still, de Gaulle echoed many when he said the events of May 1968 were '*incompréhensible*'. The touchpaper was lit at overcrowded Nanterre university, on the outskirts of Paris, where students had been protesting against the war in Vietnam and the tatty state of the campus.

On 2 May, exhausted by the protests, the authorities closed the university down and threatened to expel some of the students. The next day, a sit-in was held in sympathy at the Sorbonne. Police were called to intervene, but made things worse, charging into the crowd with truncheons and tear gas. The streets were soon flooded with thousands of student demonstrators, now officially on strike. The trade unions followed, as did the *lycées*. By mid May, nine million people were on strike. On 24 May, de Gaulle intervened. His speech warned of civil war and pleaded for people's support. It didn't go down well: riots broke out, with students storming the Bourse. Five days later, as street violence peaked, de Gaulle fled briefly to Germany and Prime Minister Pompidou sent tanks to the edges of Paris. But the crisis didn't materialise. Pompidou conceded pay rises of between seven and ten per cent and increased the minimum wage; France went back to work. An election was called for 23 June, by which time the right had gathered enough momentum to gain a safe majority.

MITTERRAND
Following the presidencies of right-wingers Georges Pompidou and Valéry Giscard d'Estaing, the Socialist François Mitterrand took up the task in 1981. His *grands projets* had a big impact on Paris. Mitterrand commissioned IM Pei's Louvre pyramid, the Grande Arche de la Défense, the Opéra Bastille and the more recent Bibliothèque Nationale de France – François Mitterrand.

CHIRAC, BUSH AND IRAQ
France may still boast the world's fourth-largest economy, the nuclear deterrent and a permanent seat on the UN Security Council, but her influence on the world stage had been waning for years until President Chirac,

IN CONTEXT

flushed from re-election and aware he was on to a PR winner, stood up in 2003 to oppose the US-led invasion of Iraq. France's official disapproval of George W Bush culminated in the threat to use her Security Council veto against any resolution authorising the use of force without UN say-so. Chirac's stance brought him popularity at home and abroad. But his domestic popularity couldn't last.

Chirac's prime minister, Jean-Pierre Raffarin, and the centre-right government began attacking some of France's more prized national institutions with a programme of reforms, starting with the state pension system. This led to some of the largest nationwide protests France has seen since 1995, with striking métro staff, hospital and postal workers, teachers and rubbish collectors bringing the capital to a virtual standstill. Planned restrictions on the uniquely Gallic, exceptionally generous system of unemployment benefit for out-of-work performing-arts professionals led to a further round of protests, as well as the cancellation of France's equivalents of Edinburgh and Glyndebourne, the Avignon and Aix summer cultural festivals. Then came the official mismanagement and aloofness that characterised the two-week heatwave of August 2003, during which as many as 14,000 elderly people died. The national mood stayed gloomy through 2004, and the clouds darkened further in 2005, as Paris lost its Olympic bid.

Then, in October 2005, the accidental deaths of two North African teenagers in Clichy-sous-Bois sparked riots that spread through the *banlieue* like wildfire (*see p324* **Estates of Emergency**). Eventually Chirac declared a state of emergency that was lifted only in January 2006. Then, in March, trouble flared once again, this time provoked by an unpopular new employment bill, the CPE – which, after three months of strikes and protests, the government had to withdraw.

PRESIDENT BLING-BLING

Despite his provocations during the riots, Nicolas Sarkozy was elected president in May 2007, beating the Socialist candidate Segolène Royal. Aside from a few desultory Molotov cocktails hurled in place de la Bastille on the night of the election, the response on the Left to Sarkozy's victory was characterised more by bemusement than anger. For a few months, bemusement held sway in the population at large, especially when Sarkozy embarked on a very public whirlwind romance with *chanteuse* and ex-model Carla Bruni. But voters soon sickened of the spectacle, and of Sarkozy's parallel courtship of several tycoons; by the time 'Président Bling-Bling' married Bruni in February 2008, his popularity had plummeted to less than 35 per cent.

During the next couple of years, Sarkozy's popularity continued to decline, but 2011 brought about something of a reversal of fortune as the country geared up for the presidential elections in 2012. Pictures of himself and a pregnant Carla on the beach during the summer contrasted strongly with the coverage of his main rival on the left, Dominique Strauss-Kahn, who was fighting sexual assault charges in New York. This wholesome image, coupled with a boost from his high-profile role in the Libya crisis, saw his approval rating jump to 37 per cent by September 2011.

HOLLANDE TO THE FORE

With the scandal engulfing Strauss-Kahn, François Hollande came to the fore as the leading Socialist candidate, defeating rival Martine Aubry in a run-off for the party candidacy in October 2011 with 56 per cent of the vote. The first round of the presidential election took place on 22 April 2012. Hollande came in first place and faced Sarkozy in the second round run-off on 6 May 2012, when he was duly elected 24th President of the French Republic and the first Socialist president in almost two decades. But Hollande's post-election elation was short-lived and a flagging economy, sliding opinion polls and close media scrutiny of his love life – his current partner is Valérie Trierweiler, but his former partner was Ségolène Royal, the mother of his four children and herself a former Socialist party presidential candidate – mean Hollande's honeymoon period is most definitely over.

In a November 2013 poll, his approval rating had hit a new low with just 15% of those polled backing him. Sarkozy, meanwhile, is waiting quietly in the wings, and rumour has it that he may yet challenge for the presidency again in 2017.

IN CONTEXT

Architecture

A city of monumental ambitions.

TEXT: NATASHA EDWARDS

Paris's rulers have always understood the key role of architecture in the exercise of power. Long before François Mitterrand made his presidential mark on the capital in the 1980s with his *grands projets* – including the Opéra Bastille, Grande Arche de la Défense, Louvre Pyramid and Ministry of Finance – Colbert had glorified Louis XIV with the place Vendôme, place des Victoires and a series of triumphal arches. Yet the city is also one of Europe's most densely inhabited and lived-in capitals. For all its apparent uniformity, caused in large part by the prevalence of golden stone, Paris has never ceased to evolve and experiment, with aristocratic mansions, Baroque churches and Haussmannian apartments existing happily alongside concrete avant-garde houses, industrial premises, the cast iron of the Eiffel Tower, the high-tech Centre Pompidou, and Rudy Ricciotti and Mario Bellini's dramatic new Islamic Arts department set beneath the Louvre's Cour Visconti.

IN CONTEXT

ROMANESQUE TO GOTHIC

Medieval Paris congregated on the Ile de la Cité and the Latin Quarter. Although the clusters of medieval housing around Notre-Dame were razed by Haussmann in the 19th century, much of the medieval street plan remains. A few churches still survive as examples of simple Romanesque architecture, including the tower of **St-Germain-des-Prés** (see p192) and **St-Julien-le-Pauvre** (see p174).

The Gothic trademarks of pointed arches, ogival vaulting and flying buttresses had their start at the **Basilique St-Denis** (see p236), begun in the 12th century and completed in the 13th by master mason Pierre de Montreuil. **Notre-Dame** (see p51) continued the style with its sculpted façade, rich, delicate rose windows and fine, tendon-like buttresses. Montreuil's **Sainte-Chapelle** (see p54), built 1246-48, represents the peak of Gothic design, reducing stonework to a minimum between the expanses of stained glass. The Flamboyant Gothic style that followed unleashed an orgy of decoration. **Eglise St-Séverin** (see p175), with its twisting spiral column, is particularly original. Civil architecture can be seen in the impressive vaulted halls of the **Conciergerie** (see p51). The **Tour Jean Sans Peur** (see p84) is a rare fragment of an early 15th-century mansion. The city's two finest medieval mansions are the Hôtel de Cluny (now the **Musée National du Moyen-Age;** see p175) and the **Hôtel de Sens**.

RENAISSANCE

Italianate town planning, with its ordered avenues and neat squares and public spaces, came late to Paris. It was instigated by François I, who installed Leonardo da Vinci at Amboise, brought over Primaticcio and Rosso to work on his palace at **Fontainebleau** (see p301), and began transforming the **Louvre** (see p64) with the Cour Carrée. The **Eglise St-Etienne du Mont** (see p181) and the massive **Eglise St-Eustache** (see p84) display a transitional style, adding the classical motifs of the Renaissance over an essentially Gothic structure. Aristocratic quarters were established in St-Germain-des-Prés and the developing Marais; the latter has the **Hôtel Carnavalet** (see p131) and the **Hôtel de Lamoignon** (24 rue Pavée, 4th), the finest examples of Renaissance mansions in Paris.

THE ANCIEN REGIME

Henri IV took control of Paris in 1594 after a long siege. He found a city knee-deep in bodies and rubble, and promptly organised public building projects. Half-timbering was banned for façades, to be replaced by brick and stone, and bridges over the Seine were cleared of houses and shops. **Place Dauphine** (1st) and **place des Vosges** (see p131) reflected Henri's taste for classicism; the latter is irresistibly elegant, with symmetrical design, red-brick vaulted galleries and steeply pitched roofs, reflecting the influence of northern Renaissance style as well as Italy.

The nouveaux riches flocked to build mansions in the Marais and on the Ile St-Louis. Those in the Marais follow a symmetrical U-shaped plan, with the main residence at the rear of an elegant *cour d'honneur,* look through the entrance archways of the **Hôtel de Sully** (see p127) or the **Hôtel Salé** (see p127), where façades are richly decorated, in contrast with the face they present to the street.

The **Palais du Luxembourg** (see p199), built in the 1620s by Salomon de Brosse in Italianate style for Marie de Médicis, combines classic French château design with the more dramatic rustication of the Pitti Palace in Marie's native Florence. The 17th century was a high point in French power, and the monarchy desired buildings that reflected its grandeur. Great architects emerged under court patronage: de Brosse, François Mansart, Libéral Bruand and André le Nôtre, who redesigned the Tuileries gardens, created the park and fountains at Versailles and planned the Champs-Elysées. The **Eglise du Val-de-Grâce** (see p181),

Château de Fontainebleau.

Gare du Nord.

designed by Mansart and finished by Jacques Lemercier, is a grand Baroque statement designed to promote the Catholic Counter-Reformation, with its painted dome and barley sugar columns. Hospitals got the royal treatment: Libéral Bruand created the grand classical façades and polygonal chapel at the **Salpêtrière** (13th) and **Les Invalides** (*see p223*), with its grandiose galleried courtyard and domed double church. But even at **Versailles** (*see p302*), ultimate architectural symbol of royal absolutism in the scale and glittery reflections of the Hall of Mirrors, Baroque never reached the decorative excesses of Italy or Austria.

Under Colbert, Louis XIV's chief minister, the creation of stage sets to magnify the Sun King's power proceeded apace. The Louvre grew as Claude Perrault created the sweeping west wing, triumphal arches at **Porte St-Denis** and **Porte St-Martin** (*see p82*) commemorated military victories, while Hardouin-Mansart's circular **place des Victoires** (*see p75*) and **place Vendôme** (*see p66*), an elegant octagon, were designed to show off equestrian statues of the king.

ROCOCO AND NEOCLASSICISM

In the early 18th century, the Faubourg St-Germain overtook the Marais as the city's most fashionable quarter, as the nobility built smart mansions with tall windows and elegant wrought ironwork, such as the **Hôtel Matignon**, today home of the French prime minister. However, the finest example of frivolous rococo decoration is the **Hôtel de Soubise** (60 rue des Francs-Bourgeois, 3rd), with panelling, plasterwork and paintings by celebrated decorators of the day, including Boucher, Restout and van Loo. In furniture-makers' **Faubourg St-Antoine**, a different sort of accommodation grew up, with workshops around courtyards and lodgings up above.

Under Louis XV, several sumptuous buildings were commissioned, among them La Monnaie (now **Musée de la Monnaie de Paris**; *see p192*), the **Panthéon** (*see p182*), the **Ecole de Droit** (place du Panthéon, 5th) and many new theatres. Soufflot's Panthéon, like Jacques-Ange Gabriel's neoclassical **place de la Concorde** (*see p66*), was inspired by ancient Rome, as were the toll gates put up in 1785 by Nicolas Ledoux, famed for his almost minimalist geometrical style (still visible at Nation, Denfert-Rochereau and Parc Monceau) for the Mur des Fermiers Généraux.

THE 19TH CENTURY

The street fighting of the Revolution left Paris in a dilapidated state. Napoleon redressed this situation with a suitably grandiose vision to make Paris the most beautiful city in the world. He confiscated land from the aristocracy and the Church, and ordered a massive building spree. As well as five new bridges and 56 ornamental fountains, he built the **Eglise de la Madeleine** (*see p79*), a mock Greek temple in honour of the Grande Armée, plus a rash of statues and arches, most notably the **Arc de Triomphe** (*see p91*) and the **Arc du Carrousel** (*see p59*).

In 1853, Bonaparte's nephew Louis Napoleon appointed Baron Haussmann as the *préfet* of Paris, with a brief to remake the city. A fearsome administrator rather than an architect, Haussmann faced problems of

IM Pei's Louvre Pyramid.

Institut du Monde Arabe.

IN CONTEXT

sanitation, sewage and traffic-clogged streets. He set about bringing order, cutting broad, long boulevards through the urban fabric. An estimated 27,000 houses were razed in the process. The Haussmannian apartment block has endured, setting an adaptable format that endured well into the 20th century, its utilitarian lines set off by mansarded roofs and rows of wrought-iron balconies. Haussmann also introduced English-style public parks, such as the **Buttes-Chaumont** (*see p168*), along with prisons, hospitals, train stations and sewers. Amid the upheaval, one building epitomised the grand style of the Second Empire: Charles Garnier's sumptuous **Palais Garnier** (1862-75; *see p284*).

Haussmann could also be an innovator, persuading Baltard to build new market pavilions at Les Halles in lacy iron rather than stone. Iron frames had already been used by Henri Labrouste in his lovely reading room at the Bibliothèque Ste-Geneviève (1844-50; 10 place du Panthéon, 5th), and they became increasingly common: stations such as Hittorff's **Gare du Nord** (1861-65; *see p161*) and Laloux's Gare d'Orsay (now **Musée d'Orsay**; *see p225*) are simply shells around an iron frame, producing spacious, light-filled interiors. The most daring iron construction of them all was, of course, the **Eiffel Tower** (*see p231*). When it was built in 1889, it was the tallest structure in the world. Stylistically, eclecticism ruled, from the neo-Renaissance **Hôtel de Ville** (*see p126*) to neo-Byzantine **Sacré-Coeur** (*see p116*).

EARLY 20TH CENTURY

An outburst of extravagance for the 1900 Exposition Universelle marked the beginning of the 20th century, notably the **Grand Palais** (*see p94*), with its massive glass and steel nave, and the **Petit Palais**, awash in sculptures, mosaics, marble and wrought iron. The **Train Bleu** brasserie in the Gare de Lyon (*see p157*) is an ornate example of the heavy, florid Beaux Arts style of this period. Art nouveau at its most fluid and flamboyant can be seen in Hector Guimard's instantly recognisable métro stations and his 1901 **Castel Béranger** (*see p108*).

All this was a long way from the roughly contemporary work of Henri Sauvage, who created a large social housing project in rue des Amiraux (18th), tiled artists' studio flats in **rue La Fontaine** (16th), and the 1920s extension of **La Samaritaine** (19 rue de la Monnaie, 1st). Funded by philanthropists, social housing began to appear in the city.

THE MODERN MOVEMENT

After World War I, two people stand out by virtue of their innovation and influence: Auguste Perret, architect of the **Théâtre des Champs-Elysées** (*see p285*), and Le Corbusier. A third architect, Robert Mallet-Stevens, is unrivalled for his elegance, best seen in his villas on rue Mallet-Stevens. Paris is one of the best cities in the world for Modern Movement houses and studios (many situated in the 16th and Montparnasse), but also in a more diluted form for town halls and schools built in the socially minded 1930s.

Perret stayed largely within a classical aesthetic, but was a pioneer in the use of reinforced concrete. Le Corbusier tried out his ideas in private houses, such as the Villa La Roche in the 16th (now **Fondation le Corbusier**). His **Pavillon Suisse** at the **Cité Universitaire** (*see p216*) and **Armée du Salut** hostel (12 rue Cantagrel, 13th) can be seen as a mid point between these villas and his Villes Radieuses mass housing schemes, which became so influential after 1945.

Meanwhile, the new love of chrome, steel and glass found its way into art deco cafés such as **La Coupole** (*see p214*). As in the 19th century, world fairs provided an excuse for grandiose state architecture, with a return to monumental classicism in the **Palais de la Porte Dorée**, built for the 1931 Exposition

Coloniale, and the **Palais de Chaillot** (*see p95*) and **Palais de Tokyo** (*see p96*), built for the 1937 Exposition Internationale.

POST-WAR PARIS

The aerodynamic aesthetic of the post-war era yielded the 1958 **UNESCO building** (*see p231*) by Bernard Zehrfuss, Pier Luigi Nervi and Marcel Breuer, and the beginnings of **La Défense** (*see p236*) with the same architects' **CNIT** building, then the largest concrete span in the world. In the 1960s and '70s, tower blocks sprouted in the suburbs and new towns to replace the *bidonvilles* (shanty towns) that had served as immigrant housing. Inside the city redevelopment was limited, but new regulations allowed taller buildings; in 1960, the 23-storey **33 rue Croulebarbe** marked Paris's first high-rise residential block.

President Georges Pompidou embraced modernity, too, disastrously in the case of the expressways along the Seine, and more benignly in the form of the **Centre Pompidou** (*see p124*), opened in 1977. But after the construction of the **Tour Montparnasse** (*see p212*), Pompidou's successor, Valéry Giscard d'Estaing, prevented the Paris horizon from rising any higher.

THE 1980S AND '90S

President François Mitterrand's *grands projets* dominated the 1980s and '90s, with Jean Nouvel's **Institut du Monde Arabe** (*see p184*), IM Pei's **Louvre Pyramid** (*see p64*) and Johan Otto Von Sprecklesen's **Grande Arche de la Défense** (*see p236*), as well as Carlos Ott's **Opéra Bastille** (*see p283*), Dominique Perrault's **Bibliothèque Nationale** (*see p188*) and Chemetov & Huidobro's **Bercy** finance ministry. The buzzword was 'transparency', from Pei's pyramid to Nouvel's **Fondation Cartier** (*see p209*).

THE 21ST CENTURY

Jacques Chirac managed to squeeze one last project into his reign with the completion of Nouvel's **Musée du Quai Branly** (*see p231*) in 2006, a highly colourful baroque structure. Younger architects are making their mark too: Manuelle Gautrand's **Citroën** showcase on the Champs-Elysées plays on the firm's logo in a fine example of architecture as branding, and she was also behind the revamp of the **Gaîté Lyrique** (*see p128*).

Other areas have also come up for a makeover: the much-maligned 1970s **Forum des Halles** (*see p87*) complex is currently being revamped with a new glass canopy and landscaped gardens, while plans to pedestrianise a 2.5km stretch along the banks of the Seine between the Musée d'Orsay and the Pont de l'Alma were finally approved in 2012, with a riverside park, pedestrian promenades, floating gardens, restaurants and more. But the biggest project of all will soon start to take shape at La Défense with the construction of Hermitage Plaza, a pair of skyscrapers courtesy of Norman Foster, topping London's Shard by a few metres.

Meanwhile, the city also continues to benefit from exciting new cultural buildings. After the appearance of **104** (*see p161*) in the former municipal undertakers in 2008, Frank Gehry's cloudlike glass Fondation Louis Vuitton in the Bois de Boulogne (due to open 2014), Renzo Piano's egg-like Fondation Pathé (due to open 2014) on avenue des Gobelins, and Jean Nouvel's new Philharmonic concert hall at La Villette (due to open 2015) are all well under way. And one long-awaited cultural creation that has finally come to fruition is the opening of the new Islamic Arts department in the **Cour Visconti** (*see p64*) at the Louvre. Led by Rudy Ricciotti and Mario Bellini, the project is the museum's greatest architectural work since the Grand Louvre.

The Louvre's Islamic Arts department.

IN CONTEXT

Essential Information

Hotels

A fter a slew of new hotel openings in the last couple of years, the big news during 2013 was all about closures, with two of the city's most famous hotels shutting their doors for major renovations. The Ritz (www.ritzparis.com) and the Crillon (www.crillon.com) will be shut for business until 2014 and 2015 respectively, as they freshen themselves up to try to contend with the influx of Asian super-luxury from the likes of Shangri-La, Raffles, Mandarin Oriental and, from early 2014, Peninsula Paris. In the meantime, these new arrivals have taken service and design to a new level, although rack rates can be eye-watering. For something a little less luxe, the city's burgeoning boutique hotel selection means you can still afford good design, as long as you can make do without the uniformed doormen.

STAYING IN PARIS

Paris's poshest hotels continue to offer the ultimate luxury experience: at the **Bristol**, the **George V** and the **Plaza Athénée** uniformed flunkeys whisk you through the revolving doors to an otherworldly domain of tinkling china, thick carpets and concierges for whom your wish is their desire, for a generous tip. And the last few years have brought even more competition to the luxury sector with the completion of a new **Shangri-La** in the 16th, the complete makeover of the **Royal Monceau** on avenue Hoche by Philippe Starck, plus the arrival of the **W Paris-Opéra** and **Mandarin Oriental** – one can only wonder why it took

quite so long for Mandarin Oriental to set up in a city seemingly made for its brand of high-end, low-key chic.

If palaces are beyond your pocket, then opt for one of Paris's increasingly luxurious boutique hotels. You can be soothed by fine linen, marble baths and a dreamy pool and hammam at **Le Metropolitan**, walk through silk taffeta curtains to your own terrace at **Le Petit Paris**, fall into a deep sleep at the pure white technological marvel that is the **Hôtel Gabriel**, gaze across the Marais rooftops from the cool new **Jules et Jim**, and fraternise at the trendy cava bar of the Spanish-owned **Banke**. For those who like a bit more glitz, the sparkly **Opéra Diamond** and unabashedly sexy **Sublim Eiffel** use fibre optics to create your own starry galaxy. All of these hotels have made the smooth move of abandoning petty pay-per-hour Wi-Fi in favour of providing it free, and Nespresso machines and iPod docks are making an appearance in bedrooms too.

Further down the scale, there is now a wide choice of moderately priced and even budget design hotels, especially in the trendy east and north-east of the city, such as the Starck-designed **Mama Shelter**, **Standard Design Hotel**, **20 Prieuré** and **Hôtel Crayon**. And shoestring travellers should consider **St Christopher's Inn** on the Canal d'Ourcq,

THE BEST SUITES

For romantic assignations
Sublim Eiffel. *See p363.*

For a view from your pillow
Le Metropolitan. *See p349.*

For Montmartre magic
Hôtel Particulier Montmartre. *See p350.*

whose façade is lit up like an art installation at night (or, more centrally, at their new outpost opposite the Gare du Nord).

Hotels are graded according to an official star rating system designed to sort the deluxe from the dumps – but we haven't followed it in this guide, as the ratings merely reflect room size and amenities such as lifts or bars, rather than other important factors such as decor, staff or atmosphere. Instead, we've divided the hotels by area, then listed them in four categories, according to the standard prices (not including seasonal offers or discounts) for one night in a double room with en suite shower/bath. For **Deluxe** hotels, you can expect to pay more than €350; for properties in the **Expensive** bracket, €250-€350; for **Moderate** properties, allow €150-€250; while **Budget** rooms go for less than €150. For **gay hotels**, *see p260*.

Note that all hotels in France charge a room tax (*taxe de séjour*) of around €1 per person per night, although this is sometimes included in the rate. Children under 12 often stay for free when sharing a room with parents (check when booking), and small pets usually cost between €10 and €20 extra per night.

THE ISLANDS

Expensive

★ Hôtel du Jeu de Paume
54 rue St-Louis-en-l'Ile, 4th (01.43.26.14.18, www.jeudepaumehotel.com). M° Pont Marie. **Map** p409 K7.
With a discreet courtyard entrance, 17th-century beams, a private garden and a unique timbered

breakfast room that was once a real tennis court built under Louis XIII, this is a charming and romantic hotel. These days, it is filled with an attractive array of modern and classical art, and has a coveted billiards table. A dramatic glass lift and catwalks lead to the guestrooms as well as two self-catering apartments, which are simple and tasteful, the walls hung with Pierre Frey fabric.

Moderate

Hôtel des Deux-Iles
59 rue St-Louis-en-l'Ile, 4th (01.43.26.13.35, www.deuxiles-paris-hotel.com). M° Pont Marie. **Map** p409 K7.
This peaceful 17th-century townhouse offers 17 rooms kitted out in toned-down stripes, *toile de Jouy* fabrics and neo-colonial style furniture. Its star features are a tiny courtyard off the lobby and a vaulted stone breakfast area. All the bedrooms and bathrooms were freshened up a few years ago (fortunately saving the lovely tiles on the bathroom walls).
▶ *The equally pleasant Hôtel le Lutèce (65 rue St-Louis-en-l'Ile, 01.43.26.23.52, www.paris-hotel-lutece.com) is run by the same team.*

Budget

Hospitel Hôtel Dieu
1 pl du Parvis-Notre-Dame, 4th (01.44.32.01.00, www.hotel-hospitel.com). M° Cité or Saint-Michel. **Map** p408 J7.
If the thought of sleeping in a working hospital doesn't put you off (half the rooms here are used by families of the Hôtel Dieu hospital's in-patients and staff), you can stay in one of 14 recently renovated, spotless rooms with colourful contemporary decor,

Hôtel du Jeu de Paume.

ESSENTIAL INFORMATION

right in the middle of Ile de la Cité. A medical smell is present but not strong, bathrooms are quite large, and you couldn't ask for a better sightseeing base.

Hôtel Henri IV
25 pl Dauphine, 1st (01.43.54.44.53, www.henri 4hotel.fr). M° Pont Neuf. **Map** p408 J6.
On tree-lined, triangular place Dauphine, surrounded by some of Paris's most expensive real estate on Ile de la Cité and a stone's throw from Notre-Dame, the Henri IV remains Paris's best-value budget hotel. You therefore need to book well ahead. Rooms are simple and unadorned, but clean, and the three paupers' penthouses with balconies and rooftop views go first. Eleven of the 15 rooms have en suite bathrooms; the others offer very, very cheap rates.

THE LOUVRE & PALAIS-ROYAL

Deluxe

Hôtel Costes
239 rue St-Honoré, 1st (01.42.44.50.00, www.hotelcostes.com). M° Concorde or Tuileries. **Map** p401 G5.
Attitude definitely counts in this temple of notoriety – a place so trendy its website contains an online boutique of its own *ultra-branché* products, and where innumerable A-listers still gravitate to the low-lit bar after all these years. The Costes boasts one of the best pools in Paris, a sybaritic, Eastern-inspired affair with an underwater music system. Rooms are a modern take on Napoleon III, designed by Jacques Garcia.

Hôtel Westminster.

Hôtel Sofitel le Faubourg
15 rue Boissy-d'Anglas, 8th (01.44.94.14.14, www.sofitel.com). M° Concorde or Madeleine. **Map** p401 F4.
This hotel is close to all the major couture boutiques, which is no surprise, as it used to house the *Marie Claire* offices. The rooms have Louis XVI armchairs, large balconies, walk-in wardrobes and Roger & Gallet goodies in the bathrooms; for shopping widowers, there's a small gym and a hammam. It's quiet too: the street has been closed to traffic since 2001 because the American embassy is on the corner.
Other locations Sofitel Arc de Triomphe, 14 rue Beaujon, 8th (01.53.89.50.50); Hôtel Scribe, 1 rue Scribe, 9th (01.44.71.24.24).

★ Le Meurice
228 rue de Rivoli, 1st (01.44.58.10.10, www.lemeurice.com). M° Tuileries. **Map** p401 G5.
With its extravagant Louis XVI decor, mosaic-tiled floors and modish restyling by Philippe Starck, Le Meurice is looking grander than ever. All 160 rooms are done up in distinct historical styles; the Belle Etoile suite on the seventh floor provides panoramic views of Paris from its terrace. You can relax in the Winter Garden to the strains of regular jazz performances; for more intensive intervention, head over to the lavish spa with treatments by Valmont.
▶ *Don't miss dinner at the hotel's three Michelin-starred restaurant, but come with plenty of euros – the degustation menu is €280; see also p67.*

Le Westin
3 rue de Castiglione, 1st (01.44.77.11.11, www. thewestinparis.com). M° Tuileries. **Map** p401 G5.
In the heart of shopping HQ, the Westin mixes belle époque features with pale limestone walls, beautiful vintage-style furniture (inspired by the 1930s and '40s), a neoclassical fountain and a patio. Its sleek modern bedrooms, decked out with top-end gadgets and the award-winning Heavenly Bed, sport balcony views over the Tuileries gardens. The bathrooms are sumptuous, and some have their own balconies. There's an excellent restaurant, Le First, with a sleek, boudoir-like interior by Jacques Garcia.

Moderate

★ Hôtel Brighton
218 rue de Rivoli, 1st (01.47.03.61.61, www.esprit-de-france.com). M° Tuileries. **Map** p401 G5.
With several rooms overlooking the Tuileries gardens, the Brighton is great value, so book well ahead for a room with a view. Recently restored, it has a classical atmosphere, from the high ceilings in the rooms to the faux-marble and mosaic downstairs.

Hotel du Lion d'Or
5 rue de la Sourdière, 1st (01.42.60.79.04, www.hotel-louvre-paris.com). M° Tuileries. **Map** p401 G5.

ESSENTIAL INFORMATION

Mandarin Oriental. *See p341.*

The fashion pack adores this 18th-century hotel (the staircase is listed), located in prime shopping territory. Done out with ethnic rugs, a smattering of animal prints, bright art and antique furniture, the 26 comfy bedrooms feel like they belong more in an eccentric family home than a central Paris hotel.

Le Relais du Louvre
19 rue des Prêtres St-Germain-l'Auxerrois, 1st (01.40.41.96.42, www.relaisdulouvre.com). M° Pont Neuf or Louvre-Rivoli. **Map** p402 H6.
The cellar of this characterful hotel, with its antiques and wooden beams, was once used by revolutionaries to print anti-royalist literature. It also inspired Puccini's Café Momus in *La Bohème*. The rooms are decorated in floral fabrics, and the front ones look out on to St-Germain-l'Auxerrois church. There's also a top-floor apartment for up to five people.

OPERA TO LES HALLES
Deluxe

Hotel W Paris-Opéra
4 rue Meyerbeer, 9th (01.77.48.94.94, www.wparis opera.fr). M° Opéra/RER Auber. **Map** p401 H4.
The Starwood hotel group's latest venture took two and a half years to finish, but it was worth the wait, with 91 rooms that ooze NYC style from every nook and cranny. For an all-out treat, the 'Extreme Wow' suite will set you back a whopping €2,300 (don't worry, standard doubles start at €390), but you'll get 88sq m of smart modern design all to yourself, and the feeling that you've walked on to the set of a James Bond movie.

Hôtel Westminster
13 rue de la Paix, 2nd (01.42.61.57.46, www. warwickwestminsteropera.com). M° Opéra/ RER Auber. **Map** p401 G4.
This luxury hotel near place Vendôme has more than a touch of British warmth about it, no doubt owing to the influence of its favourite 19th-century guest, the Duke of Westminster (after whom the hotel was named). The hotel fitness centre has a top-floor location, with a tiled steam room and views over the city, and the cosy bar features deep leather chairs, a fireplace and live jazz at weekends.

★ InterContinental Paris Le Grand
2 rue Scribe, 9th (01.40.07.32.32, www.intercontinental.com/paris). M° Opéra. **Map** p401 G4.
This 1862 hotel is the chain's European flagship – but, given its size, perhaps 'mother ship' would be more appropriate: this landmark establishment occupies the entire block (three wings, almost 500 rooms) next to the opera house; some 80 of the honey-coloured rooms overlook the Palais Garnier. The space under the vast *verrière* is one of the best oases in town, and the hotel's restaurant and coffeehouse, the Café de la

Simple, brightly coloured rooms and fully furnished studios (with kitchenettes) that can sleep up to five make the Golden Lion a popular choice for families and groups of friends.

Hôtel Mansart
5 rue des Capucines, 1st (01.42.61.50.28, www.esprit-de-france.com). M° Madeleine or Opéra. **Map** p401 G4.
This spacious hotel has real style, with a light, roomy lobby decorated with murals inspired by formal gardens. The 57 bedrooms feature pleasant fabrics, antiques and paintings; five of the rooms have an excellent view of place Vendôme.

Hôtel des Tuileries
10 rue St-Hyacinthe, 1st (01.42.61.04.17, www.hotel-des-tuileries.com). M° Tuileries. **Map** p401 G5.

LE MARCEAU BASTILLE ★★★★

Hôtel-Gallery
13 rue Jules César
75012 Paris
Tél: 00.33(0)1 43 43 11 65
Fax: 00.33(0)1 43 41 67 70
infos@hotelmarceaubastille.com
Géneral Manager: Christophe Diallo

Le Marceau Bastille – Hotel gallery is a charming and contemporary 4 stars hotel, located nearly a few steps away from the Bastille square, as well as the "Gare de Lyon" train station and the historic Marais neighbourhood. The hotel interiors denote a characteristically contemporary style.

Le Marceau Bastille Hotel offers 55 rooms of two kinds: First, the "urban" option guarantees a cozy and resolutely avant-garde type atmosphere swathed in vibrant color, still seeped in elegance. The "ecological" option provides calm and sunny rooms set off by bright yet soft tones, natural materials, organic forms and sleek lines. The furnishings are contemporary and combine delicacy with modern technology. The living room and the restaurant walls are dedicated to the Art with the permanent collections of contemporary artists.

Hotel Facilities

General

Bar, 24-Hour Front Desk, Newspapers, Non-Smoking Rooms, Rooms/Facilities for Disabled Guests, Elevator, free Safety Deposit Box, Heating, Design Hotel, Luggage Storage, Air-conditioning, Fitness room.

Services

Massage Room Service, Laundry, Dry Cleaning, Breakfast in the Room, Fax/Photocopying.

Free! All children under 2 years stay free of charge for cots.

Free! Wi-Fi is available in the entire hotel and is free of charge.

Free! Pets are allowed on request. No extra charges.

Extra beds are available on request only. Any type of extra bed or baby cot is upon request and needs to be confirmed by the hotel. Public parking is possible at a location nearby with preferential rates for clients of the hotel.

Hotel Policies

Check-in 13:00 & Check-out 12:00

Accepted credit cards

American Express, Visa, Euro/MasterCard, Carte Bleue, Diners Club, JCB

Area Information

Architect, Historic and Art Area.

Place de la Bastille - L'Opéra Bastille - L'Hôtel Sully - L'Hôtel Carnavalet - L'Institut du Monde Arabe et la Mosquée de Paris - Le Pavillon de l'Arsenal. Le Quartier du Marais - La Place des Vosges - Cour Saint - Emilion

Stroll and Walk Area

La Promenade Plantée - Le Port de Plaisance de Paris Arsenal - Le Jardin des Plantes and Muséum National d'Histoire Naturelle - L'Ile Saint Louis

Paix, is overseen by the hotel's head chef, Christophe Raoux. For a relaxing daytime break, head to the I-Spa by Algotherm for one of its seawater treatments.

Mandarin Oriental
251 rue St-Honoré, 1st (01.70.98.78.88, www.mandarinoriental.com). M° Tuileries.
Map p401 G4.

Set in a 1930s building on rue St-Honoré, the Mandarin Oriental has a wonderfully indulgent location – and the interior doesn't disappoint either, with 138 luxurious rooms, fusion restaurants, a vast interior garden, and smart spa with pool and seven spa suites with private hammams. Decor-wise, think art deco meets oriental boudoir with chic, kitschy touches throughout. In the lobby, fake diamonds decorate the curtain holders and the imposing grey walls are encrusted with stripes of jewels. The boudoir theme continues into the bedrooms, where steely grey, gold or white walls are contrasted with plum-pink cushions and trimmings. Back on the ground floor, the main draw is the choice of eateries, all managed by top chef Thierry Marx. Marx's gastronomic offering is the Sur Mesure restaurant, an all-white affair where the chef creates Asian-influenced delights. Next door sits Bar 8, replete with a theatrical marble bar, walls inlaid with raindrop Lalique crystals, and snazzy cocktails. It's a top spot for a sophisticated slurp, especially in summer when tables spill out into the gardens. *Photos p339.*

Expensive

★ Hôtel Chavanel
22 rue Tronchet, 8th (01.47.42.26.14, www.hotel chavanel.com). M° Madeleine. **Map** p401 G3. *See p342* **Sweet Dreams**.

Hôtel Concorde Opéra Paris
108 rue St-Lazare, 8th (01.40.08.44.44, www. concorde-hotels.com). M° St-Lazare. **Map** p401 G3.
Guests here are cocooned in soundproofed luxury. The 19th-century Eiffel-inspired lobby with jewel-encrusted pink granite columns is a historic landmark: the high ceilings, walls and sculptures look much as they have for over a century. Rooms are spacious, with double entrance doors and exclusive Annick Goutal toiletries; the belle époque brasserie, Café Terminus, and sexy Golden Black Bar were designed by Sonia Rykiel. Guests have access to a nearby fitness centre.

Paris Marriott Opera Ambassador Hotel
16 bd Haussmann, 9th (01.44.83.40.40, www.marriott.com). M° Chaussée d'Antin or Richelieu Drouot. **Map** p401 H4.
If you're looking for some vintage style but can't face another gilded Louis XIV interior, check into this historic, Haussmann-era hotel, which sets traditional furniture against contemporary decor in each of the 294 bedrooms. The low-lit Lindbergh Bar is named

Hôtel Amour.

after the pilot, who dropped in for a celebratory drink and cigar after his solo transatlantic flight in 1927. The hotel is perfect for the *grands magasins.*

Moderate

Hôtel Amour
8 rue Navarin, 9th (01.48.78.31.80, www.hotel amourparis.fr). M° St-Georges. **Map** p402 H2.
Opened back in 2006, this boutique hotel is a real hit with the in crowd. Each of the 20 rooms is unique, decorated on the theme of love or eroticism by a coterie of contemporary artists and designers, such as Marc Newson, M&M, Stak, Pierre Le Tan and Sophie Calle. Seven of the rooms contain artists' installations, and two others have their own private bar and a large terrace on which to hold your own party. The late-night brasserie has a coveted outdoor garden, and the crowd is young and beautiful and loves to entertain.

ESSENTIAL INFORMATION

SWEET DREAMS

Exquisite detail abounds at the Hôtel Chavanel.

The **Chavanel** (*see p341*) is a thoroughly dreamy place to lay your head. It cocoons you in a fantasy world, a modern-day Narnia peopled by the curious, alluring furniture and lighting that give the place its character. Birch tree trunks lined up against mirrors in the foyer create the illusion of a sylvan glade, with Moby Dick whale-like ceiling lamps by Matteo Ugolini suspended above a Louise Campbell Prince chair and Confluences couch by Ligne Roset. The name-dropping could go on, but suffice to say that everything here is an original and you feel it – in the quality of the fabrics, the smoothness of the wood, the finesse of the design. Even the window blinds feature French lace from Sophie Hallette, who supplied the material for Kate Middleton's wedding dress.

Twenty-five rooms of differing sizes and shapes are arranged across five floors, with two suites in the eaves, including one with a circular bed. The exquisite bathrooms feature tiles by Porcelanosa that resemble crushed silk, and all rooms – even the smallest – come with robes and slippers. Despite all these indulgent luxuries, Wi-Fi is free and the minibar reasonable. Breakfast is all-organic, including smoked salmon, and an astonishing array of cereals and breads.

Located just a few steps away from place de la Madeleine and the Palais Garnier opera house, the Chavanel is superbly positioned for high-end shopping and highbrow culture, and the surrounding backstreets are home to time-warp restaurants and cocktail bars completely off the hipster radar, and all the more delightful for it.

Hôtel Arvor Saint Georges

8 rue Laferrière, 9th (01.48.78.60.92, www.arvor-hotel-paris.com). M° St-Georges. **Map** p402 H2.

Don't be put off by the slightly austere façade; the owner intended it this way to contrast with the homely atmosphere that reigns inside. Although you're right in the middle of the city, the hotel has the feel of a quiet country house. The decor is delicate and uncluttered, and most of the 30 spacious rooms, including six suites, overlook the rooftops (no.503 has the best view of the Eiffel Tower). The small terrace is the ideal spot to take a break from the Paris buzz.

Hôtel Britannique

20 av Victoria, 1st (01.42.33.74.59, www.hotel-britannique.fr). M° Châtelet/RER Châtelet les Halles. **Map** p408 J6.

Smiling staff in stripy waistcoats welcome you to this adorable hotel, where guest areas and rooms are cocooned in thick drapes, luscious carpets and a mishmash of British colonial-style furniture that make you feel like you've stepped into an English country cottage. Enjoy deeply delicious pastries in the warm, rustic breakfast room, or book a top-floor *chambre* and eat them on your plant-filled balcony – a rare oasis of greenery for such a central and reasonably priced hotel.

★ Hôtel Crayon

25 rue du Bouloi, 1st (01.42.36.54.19, www.hotelcrayon.com). M° Les Halles. **Map** p402 H5.

Brilliantly situated near the Louvre in a neighbourhood full of great restaurants, Hôtel Crayon offers colour therapy with rooms painted top to toe in a choice of 16 hues. Each also features a life-size hand-drawn nude pencilled on the wall in a Matisse style, a white bathroom with colour accents where vintage furniture has been adapted to support contemporary sinks, silky smooth cotton bedlinen and random vintage holiday snaps collected from flea markets and mounted in frames. You can order a selection of meals via room service, and a copious breakfast is served in the vaulted breakfast room. The ground floor also has an honesty bar decked out with 1950s furniture and a selection of newspapers and magazines. For the same price as a run-of-the-mill three-star, this boutique hotel offers a wonderful experience in a great location. *Photo p345.*

Hôtel Langlois

63 rue St-Lazare, 9th (01.48.74.78.24, www.hotel-langlois.com). M° Trinité. **Map** p401 H3.

Built as a bank in 1870, this belle époque building became the Hôtel des Croisés in 1896. In 2001, after featuring in the Jonathan Demme film *Charade*, it changed its name to Hôtel Langlois in honour of the founder of the Cinémathèque Française. Its 27 spacious, air-conditioned bedrooms are decorated in art nouveau style; the larger ones have delightful hidden bathrooms.

Hotel O

19 rue Hérold, 1st (01.42.36.04.02, www.hotel-o-paris.com). M° Palais Royal-Musée du Louvre or Les Halles. **Map** p402 J5.

The new Hotel O is a sleek, 29-room venture that adds some welcome hip to the arrondissement accommodation options. Rooms (styled by cool young design company Ora-Ito, hence the 'O' in the hotel's name) are small but exquisitely done out, with retro-futuristic features that make you feel like you're on board a 1970s spaceship, with clean lines, gracious curves and blocks of pink, grey, purple and dark turquoise.

Budget

Hôtel Chopin

10 bd Montmartre (46 passage Jouffroy), 9th (01.47.70.58.10, www.hotel-chopin.com). M° Grands Boulevards. **Map** p402 J4.

Handsomely set in a historic, glass-roofed arcade next door to the Grévin museum, the Chopin's original 1846 façade adds to its old-fashioned appeal. The 36 rooms are quiet and functional, done out in an assortment of salmons, greens, yellows and blues.

Hôtel du Cygne

3 rue du Cygne, 1st (01.42.60.14.16, www.hotelducygne.fr). M° Etienne Marcel/RER Châtelet Les Halles. **Map** p402 J5.

This traditional hotel located in a handsome 17th-century building has 20 compact, cosy and simple rooms embellished with touches such as antiques and home-made furnishings. It's on a pedestrianised street in the bustling Les Halles district, so light sleepers might prefer to book one of the rooms overlooking the courtyard.

Résidence Hôtel des Trois Poussins

15 rue Clauzel, 9th (01.53.32.81.81, www.les3poussins.com). M° St-Georges. **Map** p402 H2.

Set just off the beaten track in a pleasant *quartier*, and within walking distance (uphill) of Montmartre, the Résidence Hôtel des Trois Poussins offers hotel accommodation in the traditional manner, and also offers some rare self-catering studios for people who'd rather cook than eat out. Now completely redone, the decor is pleasantly traditional, with a preference for yellow.

IN THE KNOW NO VACANCIES

Hotels are often booked solid and cost more during the major trade fairs (January, May, September), and it's also hard to find a good room during Fashion Weeks. At quieter times, hotels can often offer special deals at short notice; phone ahead or check their websites.

LA VILLA MAILLOT
& SPA

★★★★

PARIS

FOR BUSINESS OR LEISURE,
THE PERFECT PLACE TO STAY.

Full renovation in 2013,
Chic & cosy, contemporary & warm atmosphere,
42 rooms & Suites, 'V' Lounge bar, 'M' Spa.
Valet parking . Daily turndown service . Discreet & personalized service
Free Wifi . Ipad, Playstation, Wii available on request . Ipod, Iphone station

www.lavillamaillot.fr

La Villa Maillot & Spa . 143 avenue de Malakoff 75116 Paris, France
reservation@lavillamaillot.fr . www.facebook.com/lavillamaillot . #lavillamaillot

CHAMPS-ELYSEES & WESTERN PARIS

Deluxe

Buddha Bar Hotel

4 rue d'Anjou, 8th (01.83.96.88.88, www.buddha barhotelparis.com). M° Concorde or Madeleine. **Map** p401 F4.

Opened in June 2013, this latest instalment in the Buddha Bar empire is a wonderful mix of French style and neo-Asian extravagance set in a handsome 18th-century *hôtel particulier*. The Le Vraymonde restaurant is headed by acclaimed Senegalese chef Rougui Dia.

★ Four Seasons George V

31 av George V, 8th (01.49.52.70.00, www. fourseasons.com/paris). M° Alma Marceau or George V. **Map** p400 D4.

There's no denying that the George V is serious about luxury: chandeliers, marble and tapestries; glorious flower arrangements; divine bathrooms; and ludicrously comfortable beds in some of the largest rooms in all of Paris. The Versailles-inspired spa includes whirlpools, saunas and a menu of treatments for an unabashedly metrosexual clientele; non-guests can now reserve appointments. If you can afford it, it's worth every euro.

Hôtel le A

4 rue d'Artois, 8th (01.42.56.99.99, www. paris-hotel-a.com). M° Franklin D. Roosevelt or St-Philippe-du-Roule. **Map** p401 E4.

The black-and-white decor of this designer boutique hotel provides a fine backdrop for the models, artists and media types hanging out in the lounge bar area; the only splashes of colour come from graffiti-like artworks by conceptual artist Fabrice Hybert. The 26 rooms all have granite bathrooms, and the starched white furniture slip covers, changed after each guest, make the smallish spaces seem larger than they are. The dimmer switches are a nice touch – as are the lift lights changing colour at each floor.

Hôtel le Bristol

112 rue du Fbg-St-Honoré, 8th (01.53.43.43.00, www.hotel-bristol.com). M° Champs-Elysées Clémenceau. **Map** p401 E4.

Set on the exclusive rue du Faubourg St-Honoré, near luxury boutiques such as Christian Lacroix, Azzaro, Salvatore Ferragamo, Givenchy and Dolce & Gabbana, the Bristol is a luxurious 'palace' hotel with a loyal following of fashionistas and millionaires drawn by the location, impeccable service, larger than average rooms, sixth-floor pool and sundeck, and a three Michelin-starred restaurant, Epicure, with Eric Fréchon at the helm.

Hôtel Daniel

8 rue Frédéric-Bastiat, 8th (01.42.56.17.00, www.hoteldanielparis.com). M° Franklin D. Roosevelt or St-Philippe-du-Roule. **Map** p401 E4.

A romantic hideaway close to the monoliths of the Champs-Elysées, this Relais & Châteaux property is decorated in chinoiserie and a palette of rich colours, with 26 rooms cosily appointed in *toile de Jouy* and an intricately hand-painted restaurant that feels like a courtyard. The gastronomic restaurant is a good deal for this neighbourhood; the bar menu is served at all hours.

Hôtel Fouquet's Barrière

46 av George V, 8th (01.40.69.60.00, www.fouquets-barriere.com). M° George V. **Map** p400 D4.

Hôtel Crayon. *See p343.*

ESSENTIAL INFORMATION

Hôtel le Bristol. *See p345.*

This grandiose five-star hotel is built around the famous *fin-de-siècle* brasserie Le Fouquet's. Five buildings form the hotel complex, housing 81 rooms (including 33 suites), upmarket restaurant Le Diane, the U Spa, an indoor pool and a rooftop terrace for hire. Jacques Garcia, of Hôtel Costes and Westin fame, was responsible for the interior design, which retains the Empire style of the exterior while incorporating luxurious touches inside – flatscreen TVs and mist-free mirrors as standard in the marble bathrooms. And, of course, it's unbeatable in terms of location: right at the junction of avenue George V and the Champs-Elysées.

Hôtel Plaza Athénée
25 av Montaigne, 8th (01.53.67.66.65, www. plaza-athenee-paris.com). M° Alma Marceau. **Map** p400 D5.
This palace is ideally placed for power shopping at Chanel, Louis Vuitton, Dior and other avenue Montaigne boutiques. Material girls and boys will enjoy the high-tech room amenities, such as remote-controlled air con, internet and video-game access on the TV via infrared keyboard, and mini hi-fi.
▶ *The Plaza Athénée closed in October 2013 for renovations and is due to reopen in May 2014.*

Hôtel de Sers
41 av Pierre-1er-de-Serbie, 8th (01.53.23.75.75, www.hoteldesers.com). M° Alma Marceau or George V. **Map** p400 D4.
Behind its stately 19th-century façade, the Hôtel de Sers calls itself a baby palace, displaying an ambitious mix of minimalist contemporary furnishings, with a few pop art touches. Original architectural details, such as the grand staircase and reception, complete the picture. The large top-floor apartment affords dreamy views over Paris's rooftops.

★ Hôtel de la Trémoille
14 rue de la Trémoille, 8th (01.56.52.14.00, www.hotel-tremoille.com). M° Alma-Marceau. **Map** p400 D4.
The recent opening of a new restaurant-bar-lounge and improved spa and fitness facilities have made the Trémoille a serious competitor to the other palaces nearby. The 93 rooms are decorated to evoke no fewer than 31 different 'atmospheres', and the bathrooms are filled with Molton Brown products. A unique feature is the 'hatch', which enables room service to deliver your meal without disturbing you.

Hôtel de Vigny
9-11 rue Balzac, 8th (01.42.99.80.80, www.hotel devigny.com). M° George V. **Map** p400 D3.
This hotel has the feel of a private, plush townhouse. Although it's just off the Champs-Elysées, the Vigny pulls in a discerning, low-key clientele. Its 37 bedrooms and suites are decorated in tasteful stripes or florals, with marble bathrooms. Enjoy dinner in the art deco Baretto restaurant.

Les Jardins de la Villa. *See p349.*

★ Jays Paris
6 rue Copernic, 16th (01.47.04.16.16, www. jays-paris.com). M° Kléber or Victor Hugo. **Map** p400 C4.

Jays is a luxurious *boutique-apart* hotel that trades on a clever blend of antique furniture, modern design and high-tech equipment. The marble staircase, lit entirely by natural light filtered through the glass atrium overhead, gives an instant feeling of grandeur, and leads to five suites, each with a fully equipped kitchenette. A cosy salon is available to welcome in-house guests and their visitors.

Opéra Diamond
4 rue de la Pépinière, 8th (01.44.70.02.00, www. bestwestern.com). M° St-Lazare. **Map** p401 F3.

This sparkling Best Western Premier hotel lives up to its name with a night-sky decor made up of black granite resin punctuated with crystals and LEDs. The 30 rooms are equally splendid, with Swarovski crystal touches to the furniture, black bathrooms and satin curtains that close to become a huge photomontage of a female nude crossed with architectural imagery. The Executive rooms on the fifth floor have iPod stations, Nespresso machines, and speakers in the bathrooms. A grassy courtyard with a fountain adds to the appeal. Unashamedly bling, but rather magical when night falls. Check the website as rates are often heavily discounted.

Pershing Hall
49 rue Pierre-Charron, 8th (01.58.36.58.00, www. pershinghall.com). M° George V. **Map** p400 D4.

The refreshing mix of 19th-century grandeur and contemporary comfort makes Pershing Hall feel quite large, but this luxury establishment is really a cleverly disguised boutique hotel with just 26 rooms. Fashionable locals frequent the stylish bar and restaurant terrace. Designed by Andrée Putman, the neat bedrooms emphasise natural materials, with stained grey oak floors and fine mosaic-tiled bathrooms with geometric styling and copious towels. There's also a small spa and gym.

Renaissance Paris Arc de Triomphe
39 av de Wagram, 17th (01.55.37.55.37, www.marriott.com). M° Ternes. **Map** p400 C3.

You can't miss it. This six-storey undulating glass façade on avenue de Wagram is like no other part of the neighbourhood. All rooms are stylishly done out in pale greys, charcoals and dark wood, with Eames-style furniture. Nice high-tech touches include an iPod dock on the bedside radio and a large flatscreen TV with Wi-Fi keyboard. Bathrooms are a glory of polished metal, tasteful tiles and gleaming glass. The Makassar restaurant serves delicate and delicious Franco-Asian fusion food.

Royal Monceau
37 Avenue Hoche, 8th (01.42.99.88.00, www.leroyalmonceau.com). M° Charles de Gaulle Etoile. **Map** p400 D3.

This Starck-designed incarnation of the legendary old grande dame opened to the public (or at least those who could afford it) in October 2010, offering everything from cosy studio rooms to the 190sq m Royal Monceau suite. In 2013, it was granted 'palace status', joining an elite group. With no fewer than three restaurants (two of which have recently been awarded a Michelin star each), desserts from star pastry chef Pierre Hermé and an indoor pool and spa, the Royal Monceau is firmly back in the big league.

Le Sezz
6 av Frémiet, 16th (01.56.75.26.26, www.hotel sezz.com). M° Passy. **Map** p404 B6.

ATELIER **103**
RIVE GAUCHE

A stylish aparthotel
in the heart of Paris

Tel: +33 (0)1 53 63 25 50
welcome@atelier103.fr

Saint Germain-des-Prés

www.atelier103.fr

105 rue de Vaugirard
F - 75006 Paris

Tel: +33(0)153632550
welcome@aviatichotel.com

depuis 1856
★ ★ ★
AVIATIC
H O T E L
Saint Germain-des-Prés

BEST PRICE
GUARANTEE

www.aviatichotel.com

Le Sezz opened its doors in 2005 with 27 deluxe rooms and suites – the work of acclaimed French furniture designer Christophe Pillet. The understated decor represents a refreshingly modern take on luxury, with black parquet flooring, rough-hewn stone walls and bathrooms partitioned off with sweeping glass façades. The bar and public areas are equally chic.

Shangri-La Paris
10 av d'Iéna, 16th (01.53.67.19.98, www. shangri-la.com). Mº Iéna. **Map** p404 C5.
Pierre-Yves Rochon's design at the Shangri-La is an ode to French imperialism, with lavish colonial-style paintings, knick-knacks and light fittings, artfully mixed with century-old marble floors, stained-glass windows and thick velveteen fabrics. Half of the 81 rooms and suites look out on to Eiffel's filigree tower, and the top-floor Suite Panoramique provides what could easily be Paris's best panorama over the Left Bank. Shangri-La may be a Chinese company, but it has gone out of its way to ensure that the building's 'French' architectural heritage remains intact: the mansion, built in 1896, drips in Napoleonic carvings and gilding; and there's a Louis XIV-style salon, the splendour of which rivals Versailles. The 15-metre indoor pool is stunning too, bathed in natural light. Dining-wise, expect the best of France and Asia, including Shang Palace.

Expensive

Hôtel Keppler
10 rue Keppler, 16th (01.47.20.65.05, www. keppler.fr). Mº George V or Charles de Gaulle Etoile. **Map** p400 C4.
This newly renovated boutique hotel is a family-run treasure, decorated with striped wallpaper, funky mirrors, animal prints and various knick-knacks. None of the 39 rooms is huge, but all are cleverly thought through, so that lack of space is never an issue and the whole experience is pleasantly cosy. The top-floor suites have their own (large) balcony – perfect for an alfresco breakfast – and views over Paris's rooftops towards the Eiffel Tower.

Hôtel Pergolèse
3 rue Pergolèse, 16th (01.53.64.04.04, www.pergolese.com). Mº Argentine. **Map** p400 B3.
The Pergolèse was one of the first designer boutique hotels in town, but still looks contemporary a decade or so after being kitted out by Rena Dumas-Hermès with art deco-style furniture by Philippe Starck and rugs by Hilton McConnico. Rooms feature pale wood details and cool, white-tiled bathrooms, and there's also a large, two-bedroom family apartment.

★ Hôtel Regent's Garden
6 rue Pierre-Demours, 17th (01.45.74.07.30, www.hotel-regents-paris.com). Mº Charles de Gaulle Etoile or Ternes. **Map** p400 C2.

This elegant hotel – built for Napoleon III's physician – features Second Empire high ceilings and plush upholstery, and a lounge overlooking a lovely walled patio. There are 39 large bedrooms, some with gilt mirrors and fireplaces. It's an oasis of calm just ten minutes from the Champs-Elysées, and was the first hotel in Paris to receive an Ecolabel, for its recycling and energy- and water-saving efforts.

Hôtel Square
3 rue de Boulainvilliers, 16th (01.44.14.91.90, www.hotelsquare.com). Mº Passy/RER Avenue du Pdt Kennedy. **Map** p404 A7.
This courageously modern hotel has a dramatic yet welcoming interior, and attentive service that comes from having to look after only 22 rooms. They're decorated in amber, brick or slate colours, with exotic woods, quality fabrics and bathrooms seemingly cut from one huge chunk of Carrara marble. View the exhibitions in the atrium gallery or mingle with the media types at the Zebra Square restaurant/bar.

Les Jardins de la Villa
5 rue Bélidor, 17th (01.53.81.01.10, www.jardins delavilla.com). Mº Porte Maillot. **Map** p400 B2.
Behind a sober frontage, this 33-room boutique hotel is an unexpectedly playful affair, with a couture theme and a penchant for fuchsia pink. It's dotted with surreal touches – not least the high heel-shaped couch in reception. Beautifully appointed rooms pair modern luxuries (Nespresso machines, free Wi-Fi, sleek flatscreen TVs) with old-fashioned attention to detail (proper soundproofing and thick, light-blocking curtains). The location is off the tourist trail, though close to the métro. *Photo p347.*

★ Le Metropolitan
10 pl de Mexico, 16th (01.56.90.40.04, www. radissonblu.com). Mº Trocadéro. **Map** p400 B5.
This 40-room offering from Radisson Blu is supremely sleek. The discreet entrance is only a few metres wide, but once inside the triangular structure opens out into surprising volumes, with a monumental art deco-style fireplace, and cream leather and black granite reminiscent of New York in the 1930s. The first floor contains a swank insiders' cocktail bar, but the biggest surprise of all is the breathtaking view of the Eiffel Tower from the front façade, best enjoyed through the huge oval window while lying on the four-poster bed of the sixth-floor suite. All rooms exude *luxe, calme et volonté* with solid oak floors, linen curtains and baths or showers carved from black or cream marble. Below ground is a sublime pool and hammam reserved for guests.

Moderate

Hôtel Elysées Ceramic
34 av de Wagram, 8th (01.42.27.20.30, www.elysees-ceramic.com). Mº Charles de Gaulle Etoile. **Map** p400 D3.

ESSENTIAL INFORMATION

Hôtel Particulier Montmartre

Situated between the Arc de Triomphe and place des Ternes, this comfortable hotel has one of Paris's finest art nouveau ceramic façades, dating from 1904; inside, the theme continues with a ceramic cornice around the reception. All 57 rooms have been renovated in sophisticated chocolate or pewter tones with modern, art nouveau-inspired wallpaper and light fixtures. Outside is a terrace garden perfect for taking afternoon tea or evening cocktails.

MONTMARTRE & PIGALLE

Deluxe

★ Hôtel Particulier Montmartre

23 av Junot, 18th (01.53.41.81.40, www.hotel-particulier-montmartre.com). M° Lamarck Caulaincourt. **Map** p401 H1.

Visitors lucky (and wealthy) enough to manage to book a suite at the Hôtel Particulier Montmartre will find themselves in one of the city's hidden gems. Nestled in a quiet passage off rue Lepic, in the heart of Montmartre and opposite a mysterious rock known as the Rocher de la Sorcière (witch's rock), this sumptuous Directoire-style house is dedicated to art, with each of the five luxurious suites personalised by an avant-garde artist. The private garden conceived by Louis Bénech (famous for the Tuileries renovation) adds the finishing touch.

Expensive

Hôtel Banke

20 rue La Fayette, 9th (01.55.33.22.22, www.derbyhotels.com). M° Le Peletier. **Map** p401 H3.

The Banke may well have the most eye-popping lobby in the city, a huge two-storey space done in outrageous belle époque style, all crimson, black pillars and gold leaf beneath a whopping glass roof. After such opulence, the rooms are perhaps something of a let-down; but they are stylish and comfortably equipped. The mezzanine bar partakes of the lobby's luxe, and the Josefin restaurant serves nouvelle Med cuisine. There's also a gym and hammam for a post-sightseeing wind-down.

Kube Hotel

1-5 passage Ruelle, 18th (01.42.05.20.00, www.kubehotel.com). M° La Chapelle. **Map** p402 K1.

The younger sister of the Murano Urban Resort (*see p351*), Kube is an edgier and more affordable hotel. Like the Murano, it sits behind an unremarkable façade in an unlikely neighbourhood – in this case, the ethnically diverse Goutte d'Or. The Ice Kube bar by Grey Goose serves up vodka glasses that, like the bar itself, are carved from ice; drinkers pay €38 to down four vodka cocktails in 30 minutes. Also on the menu, 'aperifood' and 'snackubes' by culinary designer Nicolas Guillard. The Arty Brunch (€34) on Sundays introduces a different artist each month, with DJs and a buffet. To top off the futuristic style, access to the 41 rooms is by fingerprint technology.

Moderate

Hôtel des Arts

5 rue Tholozé, 18th (01.46.06.30.52, www.arts-hotel-paris.com). M° Abbesses or Blanche. **Map** p401 H1.

This Montmartre gem is pleasantly decorated with oriental rugs, wooden bookcases and Provençal-style furniture. The rooms here are simple but inviting, some affording pleasant views of the hidden roof gardens and windmills of the Butte. Art by local artists is displayed in the basement breakfast room.

Hôtel Royal Fromentin

11 rue Fromentin, 9th (01.48.74.85.93, www.
hotelroyalfromentin.com). M° Blanche or Pigalle.
Map p401 H2.
Wood panelling, art deco windows and a vintage
glass lift echo the hotel's origins as a 1930s cabaret
hall; its theatrical feel attracted Blondie and Nirvana.
It's just down the road from the Moulin Rouge, and
many of its 47 rooms overlook Sacré-Coeur. Rooms
have been renovated in French style, with bright fabrics and an old-fashioned feel.

Terrass Hotel

12-14 rue Joseph-de-Maistre, 18th (01.46.06.72.85,
www.terrass-hotel.com). M° Place de Clichy.
Map p401 H1.
There's nothing spectacular about this classic hotel,
but for people willing to pay top euro for the best
views in town, it fits the bill. Ask for room 704 and
you can lie in the bath and look at the Eiffel Tower.
In decent weather, head up for brunch on the sev-
enth-floor terrace, open from June to September.

Timhotel Montmartre

11 rue Ravignan, 18th (01.42.55.74.79, www.
timhotel.fr). M° Abbesses or Pigalle. **Map** p401 H1.
The location adjacent to picturesque place Emile-
Goudeau makes this one of the most popular hotels
in the Timhotel chain. It has 59 rooms, comfortable
without being plush; try to bag one on the fourth or
fifth floor for stunning views.

Budget

Hôtel Eldorado

18 rue des Dames, 17th (01.45.22.35.21, www.
eldoradohotel.fr). M° Place de Clichy. **Map** p401 G1.
This eccentric hotel is decorated with flea market
finds. The Eldorado's winning features include a
wine bar, one of the best garden patios in town and
a loyal fashionista following. The cheapest rooms
have shared bathrooms and toilets.

Hôtel Ermitage

24 rue Lamarck, 18th (01.42.64.79.22,
www.ermitagesacrecoeur.fr). M° Lamarck
Caulaincourt. **No credit cards**. **Map** p402 J1.
This 12-room townhouse hotel stands on the calm,
non-touristy north side of Montmartre, only five
minutes from Sacré-Coeur. The bedrooms are large
and endearingly overdecorated, with bold floral
wallpaper; those higher up have fine views.

BEAUBOURG & THE MARAIS

Deluxe

★ Murano Urban Resort

13 bd du Temple, 3rd (01.42.71.20.00, www.
muranoresort.com). M° Filles du Calvaire or
Oberkampf. **Map** p409 L5.

Kube Hotel.

Hôtel du Petit Moulin.

Behind this unremarkable façade is a super cool and supremely luxurious hotel, popular with the fashion set for its lounge-style design, excellent restaurant and high-tech flourishes – including coloured light co-ordinators that enable you to change the mood of your room at the touch of a button. The handsome bar has a mind-boggling 140 varieties of vodka to sample, which can bring the op art fabrics in the lift to life and make the fingerprint access to the hotel's 43 rooms and nine suites (two of which feature private pools) a late-night godsend.

Expensive

Hôtel Bourg Tibourg

19 rue du Bourg-Tibourg, 4th (01.42.78.47.39, www.hotelbourgtibourg.com). M° Hôtel de Ville. **Map** p409 K6.

The Bourg Tibourg has the same owners as Hôtel Costes (*see p338*) and the same interior decorator – but don't expect this jewellery box of a boutique hotel to be a miniature replica. Aside from its enviable location in the heart of the Marais and its fashion-pack fans, here it's all about Jacques Garcia's neo-Gothic-cum-Byzantine decor – impressive and imaginative. Scented candles, mosaic-tiled bathrooms and luxurious fabrics in rich colours create the perfect escape. There's no restaurant or lounge – posing is done in the neighbourhood bars.

Moderate

★ Hôtel de la Bretonnerie

22 rue Ste-Croix-de-la-Bretonnerie, 4th (01.48.87.77.63, www.bretonnerie.com). M° Hôtel de Ville. **Map** p409 K6.

With wrought ironwork, exposed stone and wooden beams, the labyrinth of corridors in this 17th-century *hôtel particulier* is full of atmosphere. Tapestries, rich

colours and the occasional four-poster bed give the 29 rooms individuality. Location is convenient too.

Hôtel Duo

11 rue du Temple, 4th (01.42.72.72.22, www.duo paris.com). M° Hôtel de Ville. **Map** p406 K6.

An unbeatable location, designer decor, a gym with sauna and a convivial cocktail bar make this a popular choice for laptop-wielding young professionals. Its Jean-Philippe Nuel decor is so striking that passers-by sometimes enquire about the price of the outsize lampshades and mustard-coloured armchairs in the huge lounge lobby, which also has a bamboo courtyard garden. Based on a palette of brown with contrasting turquoise, mustard, lime green, pink or blue, each room is different and you can request a balcony, beams, wallpaper, a bath, separate loo, and road or courtyard preference.

Hôtel Jules & Jim

11 rue des Gravilliers, 4th (01.44.54.13.13, www.hoteljulesetjim.com). M° Arts et Métiers. **Map** p409 K5.

Located in the heart of the Marais, this modern hotel is surrounded by two paved courtyards and has lovely rooftop views. Guest rooms are comfortable, with all mod cons (iPod dock, flatscreen TV), while a continental buffet breakfast is served in the chic dining area. Guests can enjoy cocktails at the bar or on the terrace.

★ Hôtel du Petit Moulin

29-31 rue de Poitou, 3rd (01.42.74.10.10, www.hoteldupetitmoulin.com). M° St-Sébastien Froissart. **Map** p409 L5.

Within striking distance of the hip shops around rue Charlot, this turn-of-the-century façade masks what was once the oldest *boulangerie* in Paris, lovingly restored as a boutique hotel by Nadia Murano and

BED AND BOARD

Book in at the wonderful Auberge Flora.

There's nothing better after an exceptional meal than being able to slip between crisp white sheets without even having to leave the building. Flora Mikula, the hugely talented chef behind Les Olivades and Les Saveurs de Flora, left the smart 8th for the more boho 11th to pursue her dream of creating an urban inn – the **Auberge Flora** (*see p354*).

'It's a restaurant with rooms rather than a hotel with a restaurant,' she says, but as much care has gone into the decor and comfort of the rooms as goes into her Mediterranean cuisine. From the laughter behind the kitchen hatch to the unique decorative touches – Bernardaud china on the restaurant walls, watering cans lining the stairs – everything is imbued with Flora's ebullient personality. The fabulously affordable *bistronomie*-style menu features a course of French tapas served on a three-tier cake stand and rich main courses that manage to be both satisfying and refined. And with Flora herself in charge in the kitchen, it feels almost like you're being invited into the chef's home.

Upstairs, the 21 bedrooms are spread across three floors and themed around *bohème* (brocade throws, fringed

lampshades, vivid colours), *potager* (aubergine-coloured walls, vast pumpkin pictures as headboards), and *nature* (stone sinks, mirrors framed with tiny rounds of wood). All the rooms have iPod docks and flatscreen TVs, and the top two categories offer bathrobes too.

As you would expect, breakfast is a treat, and it's made all the more enjoyable by the steady stream of locals popping in for coffee and pastries at the bar. Unsnobbish, warm and welcoming, feminine and joyful, Auberge Flora is a unique place to stay with a real heart.

Denis Nourry. The couple recruited no lesser figure than Christian Lacroix for the decor, and the result is a riot of colour, trompe l'oeil effects and a savvy mix of old and new. Each of its 17 exquisitely appointed rooms is unique, and the walls in rooms 202, 204 and 205 feature drawings and scribbles taken from Lacroix's sketchbook.

Hôtel St-Louis Marais

1 rue Charles V, 4th (01.48.87.87.04, www.saint louismarais.com). M° Bastille or Sully Morland. **Map** p409 L7.
Built as part of a 17th-century Célestin convent, this peaceful hotel had its bathrooms redone and Wi-Fi access installed a few years ago. Rooms are compact and cosy, with wooden beams, tiled floors and simple, traditional decor.
Other location Hôtel St-Louis Bastille, 114 bd Richard Lenoir, 11th (01.43.38.29.29).

Les Jardins du Marais

74 rue Amelot, 11th (01.40.21.20.00, www.les jardinsdumarais.com). M° Bastille. **Map** p409 L5.
The centrepiece of this ultra-swish hotel is a vast courtyard, filled with tables, potted plants and lampposts that wouldn't look out of place in Narnia. Inside, it's smart and modern; the lobby looks tastefully trendy in its steely black and white marble, with purple furnishings and Philippe Starck chairs.

Budget

Grand Hôtel Jeanne d'Arc

3 rue de Jarente, 4th (01.48.87.62.11, www. hoteljeannedarc.com). M° Chemin Vert or St-Paul. **Map** p409 L6.
The Jeanne d'Arc's strong point is its great location on a quiet road close to pretty place du Marché-Ste-Catherine. A recent refurbishment has made the reception area striking, with a huge mirror adding the illusion of space. The bedrooms are colourful and comfortable.

Hôtel Paris France

72 rue de Turbigo, 3rd (01.42.78.00.04, www. paris-france-hotel.com). M° Temple. **Map** p402 L5.
A great central location, sweet lift, spruce staff and clean, pleasant rooms are on offer here. The attic has views of Montmartre and (if you lean out far enough) the Eiffel Tower.

BASTILLE & EASTERN PARIS

Deluxe

Hôtel Marceau Bastille

13 rue Jules César, 12th (01.43.43.11.65, www.hotelmarceaubastille.com). M° Bastille. **Map** p409 M7.
This slick boutique hotel has 55 rooms divided into three different styles: urban, *écolo* (eco-friendly) or

privilège, some with a balcony. The bar-lounge, overlooking a pleasant, bamboo-planted patio, is surrounded by a gallery that exhibits works by contemporary artists.

Moderate

Auberge Flora

44 bd Richard Lenoir, 11th (01.47.00.52.77, www.aubergeflora.fr). M° Richard Lenoir. **Map** p407 M6.
See p353 **Bed and Board**.

Hi Matic

71 rue de Charonne, 11th (01.43.67.56.56, www.hi-matic.net). M° Charonne. **Map** p407 N7.
The decor at the eco-friendly Hi Matic hotel near Bastille is positively multicoloured: every inch of wall space is either blue, lime, purple or yellow. The rooms are titchy but multi-task, so you can whip out your duvet at night and roll it back up in the day. Breakfast is organic, and a masseur will come to your room if you fancy a well-being massage (€85).

Le Pavillon Bastille

65 rue de Lyon, 12th (01.43.43.65.65, www. pavillonbastille.com). M° Bastille. **Map** p407 M7.
The best thing about this hotel is its location between the Bastille opera and the Gare de Lyon. The 25 rooms may be small, but you're a stone's throw from the Viaduc des Arts (*see p157*).

Standard Design Hotel

29 rue des Taillandiers, 11th (01.48.05.30.97, www.standard-design-hotel-paris.com). M° Ledru Rollin. **Map** p407 M6.
The Standard Design's black and white interior, with the occasional splash of colour, is a winner with visitors looking for a break from the sometimes rather heavy atmosphere of more traditional hotels. The rooms have all mod cons, the breakfast room awakens the senses with bold stripes, and you can roll into bed after a night out in Bastille's cool bars and restaurants.

Budget

★ Mama Shelter

109 rue de Bagnolet, 20th (01.43.48.48.48, www.mamashelter.com). M° Alexandre Dumas, Maraîchers or Porte de Bagnolet.
Philippe Starck's latest design commission is set a stone's throw east of Père Lachaise, and its decor appeals to the young-at-heart with Batman and Incredible Hulk light fittings, dark walls, polished wood and splashes of bright fabrics. Every room comes equipped with an iMac computer, TV, free internet access and a CD and DVD player; and when hunger strikes, there's a brasserie with a romantic terrace. If you're sure of your dates, book online and take advantage of the saver's rate.

ESSENTIAL INFORMATION

Mama Shelter.

★ Le Quartier Bercy Square
*33 bd de Reuilly, 12th (01.44.87.09.09,
www.lequartierhotelbs.com). M° Daumesnil
or Dugommier.* **Map** p407 P9.
You'd never think that lime green and brown stripes
would match bold silver and white replica 19th-century
wallpaper, but it does at the boutique Quartier
Bercy Square in the trendy 12th arrondissement.
Rooms are small but inviting, often using coloured
light to create atmosphere.

NORTH-EAST PARIS
Moderate

Le 20 Prieuré Hôtel
*20 rue du Grand Prieuré, 11th (01.47.00.74.14,
www.hotel20prieure.com). M° République.*
Map p402 M5.
In a road where budget sleeps are fast metamorphosing
into hip hotels, this young, funky place benefits
from particularly welcoming staff. Each bedroom
features an enormous blow-up of a Paris landmark
covering the entire wall behind the bed, giving you
the illusion that you are sleeping halfway up the
Eiffel Tower, or on Bir-Hakeim bridge as the métro
speeds by (great for *Last Tango in Paris* fans).
Bathrooms are mundane in comparison, but things
brighten up again in the breakfast room, with pop
art portraits and a reworked 1970s look.

Hôtel Gabriel
*25 rue du Grand Prieuré, 11th (01.47.00.13.38,
www.gabrielparismarais.com). M° République.*
Map p402 M5.
Paris's first 'detox hotel' is a shrine to quality kip.
The air-conditioned, pure white rooms are not short
on techno wizardry: there's an iPod station, free Wi-Fi,
and the *sine qua non* of sleep aids, the NightCove
device. This white box is easily programmed to emit
sounds and light that stimulate melatonin: choose
between sleep, nap or wake-up programmes. If you're
still feeling run-down, grab a detox massage courtesy
of Franco-Japanese masseuse Mitchiko and her
colleagues. A partner gym, jogging routes and green
taxis complete the healthy vibe. *Photo p357.*

Hôtel Le Général
*5-7 rue Rampon, 11th (01.47.00.41.57, www.
legeneralhotel.com). M° République.* **Map** p402 L5.
A fashionable find near the nightlife action, Le
Général was one of Paris's first boutique bargains
when it opened a decade ago. It is still notable for its
moderate rates and sleek, neutral-toned interior.

Budget

Hôtel Beaumarchais
*3 rue Oberkampf, 11th (01.53.36.86.86,
www.hotelbeaumarchais.com). M° Filles du
Calvaire or Oberkampf.* **Map** p409 L5.

Dear Mary,

I followed your advice and checked the ParisAddress website to look for an apartment. This place we booked is just amazing, it has everything we were expecting and even more !

> Instant availability
> Instant booking
> Easy process
> Prices all included, no hidden fees !
> Personal greeting
> Assistance 7/7

WWW.PARISADDRESS.COM

You wish to live like a true Parisian ?
Saint-Germain-Des-Prés, the Latin Quarter, St Louis Island, the Marais, Eiffel Tower and so many other great areas for you to discover !
To make your next trip in Paris an unique and unforgettable experience, rent an apartment and discover Paris from 'within'.
ParisAddress invites you to discover picturesque and fully furnished apartments !

www.parisaddress.com - booking@parisaddress.com - +33 1 43 20 91 57   Parisaddress

This contemporary hotel is located in the heart of the Oberkampf area. Its 31 rooms are brightly decorated with colourful walls, bathroom mosaics and wavy headboards; breakfast is served on the tiny garden patio or in your room.

Hôtel Garden Saint-Martin
35 rue Yves Toudic, 10th (01.42.40.17.72, www.hotel-gardensaintmartin-paris.com). M° Jacques Bonsergent. **Map** p402 L4.
The shops, cafés and bars along the Canal St-Martin draw visitors to this hotel, where creature comforts are guaranteed at an excellent rate. No prizes will be won for the ordinary decor, but there is a very pleasant patio garden, and the staff are helpful.

THE LATIN QUARTER & THE 13TH
Expensive

Hôtel Résidence Henri IV
50 rue des Bernardins, 5th (01.44.41.31.81, www.residencehenri4.com). M° Cardinal Lemoine. **Map** p406 K7.
This belle-époque-style hotel has a mere eight rooms and five apartments, so guests are assured of the staff's full attention. Peacefully situated next to leafy square Paul-Langevin, it's just a few minutes' walk away from Notre-Dame. The four-person apartments come with a handy mini-kitchen featuring a hob, fridge and microwave.

★ Le Petit Paris
214 rue St-Jacques, 5th (01.53.10.29.29, www.hotelpetitparis.com). M° Maubert Mutualité/RER Luxembourg. **Map** p408 J8.
This Latin Quarter venture is a dynamic exercise in taste and colour. The 20 rooms, designed by Sybille de Margerie, are arranged by era, running from the puce and purple of the medieval rooms to the wildly decadent orange, yellow and pink of the swinging '60s rooms, replete with specially commissioned sensual photographs of Paris monuments. Luxury abounds with finest silks, velvets and taffetas. Some of the rooms have small terraces, and those with baths have a TV you can watch while soaking. An honesty bar in the lounge and ultra-modern jukebox encourage conviviality.

Moderate

★ Five Hôtel
3 rue Flatters, 5th (01.43.31.74.21, www.thefivehotel.com). M° Les Gobelins or Port Royal. **Map** p406 J9.
The rooms in this stunning boutique hotel may be small, but they're all exquisitely designed. Fibre optics built into the walls create the illusion of sleeping under a starry sky, and you can choose from four different fragrances to subtly perfume your room (the

Hôtel Gabriel. *See p355.*

hotel is entirely non-smoking). Guests staying in the suite have access to a private garden with a jacuzzi.

Hôtel la Demeure
51 bd St-Marcel, 13th (01.43.37.81.25, www.hotel-paris-lademeure.com). M° Les Gobelins. **Map** p406 K9.
This comfortable, modern hotel has 43 air-conditioned rooms, plus suites with sliding doors to separate sleeping and living space. The wraparound balconies of the corner rooms offer lovely views of the city, and bathrooms feature either luxurious tubs or shower heads with elaborate massage possibilities.

Select Hôtel
1 pl de la Sorbonne, 5th (01.46.34.14.80, www.selecthotel.fr). M° Cluny La Sorbonne. **Map** p408 J8.
Located at the foot of the Sorbonne, this 68-room hotel delivers pure, understated chic with its clever blend of modern art deco features, traditional stone walls and wooden beams. The winter garden and airy common areas have recently been redone in a sleek, contemporary style.

Budget

Familia Hôtel
11 rue des Ecoles, 5th (01.43.54.55.27, www.hotel-paris-familia.com). M° Cardinal Lemoine or Jussieu. **Map** p406 K8.

Hôtel de l'Abbaye Saint-Germain.

This old-fashioned Latin Quarter hotel has balconies hung with tumbling plants and walls draped with replica French tapestries. Owner Eric Gaucheron extends a warm welcome, and the 30 rooms have personalised touches such as sepia murals, cherry-wood furniture and stone walls. The Gaucherons also own the Hôtel Minerve next door.

★ Hôtel les Degrés de Notre-Dame

10 rue des Grands-Degrés, 5th (01.55.42.88.88, www.lesdegreshotel.com). M° Maubert-Mutualité or St-Michel. **Map** p406 J7.
On a tiny street across the river from Notre-Dame, this vintage hotel is an absolute gem. Its ten rooms are full of character, with original paintings, antique furniture and exposed beams (nos.47 and 51 have views of the cathedral). It has an adorable restaurant and, a few streets away, two studio apartments that the owner rents out to preferred customers only.

Hôtel Résidence Gobelins

9 rue des Gobelins, 13th (01.47.07.26.90, www.hotelgobelins.com). M° Les Gobelins. **Map** p406 K10.
A tiny lift leads to colourful rooms, all equipped with satellite TV and telephone. The breakfast room overlooks a private garden, and there's free internet use available at the reception.

★ Hôtel de la Sorbonne

6 rue Victor-Cousin, 5th (01.43.54.58.08, www.hotelsorbonne.com). M° Cluny La Sorbonne/RER Luxembourg. **Map** p408 J8.

It's out with the old at this charming, freshly renovated hotel, with bold, designer wallpapers, floral prints, lush fabrics and quotes from French literature woven into the carpets. Rooms are all equipped with iMac computers.

ST-GERMAIN-DES-PRES & ODEON
Expensive

Artus Hotel

34 rue de Buci, 6th (01.43.29.07.20, www.artus hotel.com). M° Mabillon. **Map** p408 H7.
The recently renovated Artus Hotel is the ideal spot for a classic taste of Paris – you couldn't be any closer to the heart of the Left Bank action if you tried. Inside, the look is chic boutique, with 27 individually designed rooms and suites, ranging from cosy to capacious. Staff are eager to help and full of local tips. The cocktail bar, Playtime, is handy for an *apéro* before stepping out into St-Germain.

★ L'Hôtel

13 rue des Beaux-Arts, 6th (01.44.41.99.00, www.l-hotel.com). M° Mabillon or St-Germain-des-Prés. **Map** p408 H6.
Guests at the sumptuously decorated L'Hôtel these days are more likely to be models and film stars than the starving writers who frequented the place during Oscar Wilde's last days (the playwright died here in November 1900). Under Jacques Garcia's careful restoration, each room has its own special theme: Mistinguett's *chambre* retains its art deco mirror bed, while Oscar's tribute room is appropriately clad in green peacock murals. Don't miss out on dinner in the fabulously decadent restaurant or on the hotel's glorious underground swimming pool, which you can reserve by the hour for private relaxation.

Hôtel de l'Abbaye Saint-Germain

10 rue Cassette, 6th (01.45.44.38.11, www.hotel abbayeparis.com). M° Rennes or St-Sulpice. **Map** p405 G7.
A monumental entrance opens the way through a courtyard into this tranquil hotel, originally part of a convent. Wood panelling, well-stuffed sofas and an open fireplace in the drawing room make for a relaxed atmosphere, but, best of all, there's a surprisingly large garden. The 43 rooms and duplex apartments (some with terrace) are tasteful and luxurious.

Hôtel Lutetia

45 bd Raspail, 6th (01.49.54.46.46, www.lutetia-paris.com). M° Sèvres Babylone. **Map** p405 G7.
This historic Left Bank hotel is a masterpiece of art nouveau and early art deco architecture that dates from 1910. It has a plush jazz bar and lively brasserie. Its 230 spacious rooms, revamped in purple, gold and pearl grey, maintain a 1930s feel. Big-name guests in years gone by have included Picasso,

ESSENTIAL INFORMATION

LUXURY LOUNGING

Take your pick from Paris's palaces.

For years, it seemed that the only criteria required for hotel palace status were a grand historic building, a gastronomic restaurant (preferably with Michelin stars and a well-known chef attached), plenty of suites and enough staff to fulfil the whims of every client.

So imagine the uproar when, in 2010, the French government tightened the rules and demoted the Ritz, Crillon and George V – three of the city's most famous establishments – to humble five-stars. The George V, which was undergoing refurbishment at the time, quickly regained its palace status. But the Ritz closed for full-scale renovations in 2012, followed shortly after by the Crillon. Then, at the end of 2013, the Plaza Athénée decided to undergo a preventative revamp and build an extension. Add to all this the opening of two new palace hotels in 2010 (the Shangri-La and Royal Monceau Raffles Paris), and another one in 2011 (the Mandarin Oriental), and you'd be forgiven for thinking that the city's luxury hotel scene was in a state of ferocious flux.

But fortunately the dust is settling: in 2014, the Plaza Athénée and the Ritz will reopen (the Crillon is planned for 2015); and the spanking new Majestic (a Peninsula hotel) will swing wide the doors of a vast mansion on avenue Kléber in the 16th, offering 200 rooms, all-day dining, a posh Chinese restaurant, cigar lounge, rooftop bar, huge spa and indoor pool. The end of 2014 should also see the opening of the new Hôtel du Cheval Blanc, set in the iconic La Samaritaine building in Châtelet. Run by LVMH, it will incorporate 80 luxury suites and rooms, a Givenchy spa and a boutique selling the group's high-end wares (think Vuitton, Dior and Eres).

According to the Paris tourist office, other palaces could soon be joining the ranks too. The Hôtel Lutetia, which was bought by Israeli group Alrov in 2010, would become the Left Bank's first palace hotel if it made the grade; and rumour has it that the art nouveau HSBC building at 103 avenue des Champs-Elysées – a former hotel where spy Mata Hari was arrested in 1917 – could be next in line for a luxury makeover.

The iconic Samaritaine building is being transformed in 2014.

ESSENTIAL INFORMATION

Hôtel Aviatic. *See p362.*

Josephine Baker and de Gaulle. It was also the Abwehr (German military intelligence) HQ during the Nazi occupation.

▶ *The Hôtel Lutetia is scheduled to close in April 2014 for a three-year overhaul (see p359).*

★ Relais Saint-Germain

9 carrefour de l'Odéon, 6th (01.44.27.07.97, www.hotel-paris-relais-saint-germain.com). M° Odéon. **Map** p408 H7.

The rustic, wood-beamed ceilings remain intact at the Relais Saint-Germain, a 17th-century hotel bought and renovated by much-acclaimed chef Yves Camdeborde (originator of the *bistronomique* dining trend) and his wife Claudine. Each of the 22 rooms has a different take on eclectic Provençal charm, and the marble bathrooms are positively huge by Paris standards.

▶ *Hotel guests get an added bonus – first dibs on a sought-after seat in Le Comptoir restaurant next door; see p200.*

La Villa

29 rue Jacob, 6th (01.43.26.60.00, www.villa-saintgermain.com). M° St-Germain-des-Prés. **Map** p408 H6.

The charismatic La Villa features cool faux crocodile skin on the bedheads and crinkly taffeta over the taupe-coloured walls. Wonderfully, your room number is projected on to the floor outside your door; very useful for any drunken homecomings.

Villa d'Estrées

17 rue Gît-le-Coeur, 6th (01.55.42.71.11, www.villadestrees.com). M° St-Michel. **Map** p408 J7.

Jewel colours, sumptuous fabrics, stripes and patterns are the hallmarks of this polished boutique hotel; there's nothing at all minimalist about Villa d'Estrées, which was designed by Jacques Garcia. Each of the ten rooms and suites is individually decorated, all with a nod to Empire style and a crisp, slightly masculine feel.

Moderate

Le Clos Médicis

56 rue Monsieur-le-Prince, 6th (01.43.29.10.80, www.closmedicis.com). M° Odéon/RER Luxembourg. **Map** p408 H8.

More like a stylish, private townhouse than a hotel, Le Clos Médicis is located by the Luxembourg gardens. Decor is refreshingly modern, with rooms done out with taffeta curtains and chenille bedcovers, and antique floor tiles in the bathrooms. The cosy lounge has a working fireplace.

Grand Hôtel de l'Univers

6 rue Grégoire-de-Tours, 6th (01.43.29.37.00, www.hotel-paris-univers.com). M° Odéon. **Map** p408 H7.

Making the most of its 15th-century origins, this hotel features exposed wooden beams, high ceilings, antique furnishings and toile-covered walls. Manuel Canovas fabrics lend a posh touch, but there are also useful services such as a laptop for hire.

Hôtel du Globe

15 rue des Quatre-Vents, 6th (01.43.26.35.50, www.hotel-du-globe.fr). M° Odéon. **Map** p408 H7.

The Hôtel du Globe has managed to retain much of its 17th-century character – and very pleasant it is too. Gothic wrought-iron doors open into the florid corridors, and an unexplained suit of armour supervises guests from the tiny salon. The rooms with baths are somewhat larger than those with showers, and if you're an early booker you might even get the room with the four-poster bed (ask when reserving).

Hôtel des Saints-Pères

65 rue des Sts-Pères, 6th (01.45.44.50.00, www.espritfrance.com). M° St-Germain-des-Prés. **Map** p405 G7.

Built in 1658 by one of Louis XIV's architects, this hotel has an enviable location near St-Germain-des-Prés' designer boutiques. It boasts a charming garden and a sophisticated, if small, bar. The most coveted room is no.100, with its fine 17th-century ceiling by painters from the Versailles School; it also has an open bathroom, so you can gaze at scenes from the myth of Leda and the Swan while you scrub.

Hôtel Villa Madame

44 rue Madame, 6th (01.45.48.02.81, www.hotelvillamadameparis.com). M° St-Sulpice. **Map** p408 G7.

This revamped hotel (formerly the Regents) located in a quiet street is a lovely surprise, its courtyard garden used for breakfast in the summer months. Honey- and chocolate-coloured woods mix with warm-toned velvets to make the rooms (all with plasma screens) feel cosy and inviting; some even have small balconies with loungers.

Le Placide

6 rue St-Placide, 6th (01.42.84.34.60, www.leplacidehotel.com). M° Sèvres-Babylone, St-Placide or Vanneau. **Map** p405 G7.

With only ten rooms, the Placide is just about as bijou as it gets. White, chrome and neutral tones reign throughout (as does bark- or bamboo-inspired wallpaper), broken only by the occasional funky cushion and throw. Rooms are spacious: all have large bathrooms as well as their own sitting area. The stylish ground-floor duplex has been designed for disabled guests.

Budget

Hôtel de Nesle

7 rue de Nesle, 6th (01.43.54.62.41, www.hoteldenesleparis.com). M° Odéon. **Map** p408 H6.

Only nine of the 20 rooms are en suite, but all are decorated with colourful murals, and many overlook a charming garden courtyard.

MONTPARNASSE

Expensive

★ Hôtel Aviatic

105 rue de Vaugirard, 6th (01.53.63.25.50, www.aviatic.fr). M° Duroc, Montparnasse Bienvenüe or St-Placide. **Map** p405 F8.

This historic hotel has masses of character, from the Empire-style lounge and garden atrium to the bistro-style breakfast room and polished marble floor in the lobby. New decoration throughout, in beautiful steely greys, warm reds, elegant, striped velvets and *toile de Jouy* fabrics, lends an impressive touch of glamour, and the service is consistently with a smile.

Moderate

Hôtel des Académies et des Arts

15 rue de la Grande Chaumière, 6th (01.43.26.66.44, www.hotel-des-academies. com). M° Notre-Dame des Champs, Raspail or Vavin. **Map** p405 G8.

This small boutique hotel scores highly on style. There are cosy salons, fireplaces and an extensive collection of art books. The 20 immaculate rooms are individually designed around four *ambiances* (Paris Rive Gauche, Comédienne, Man Ray or Rulhmann), and offer wonderful views across the rooftops or down on to the spectacular Jérôme Mesnager mural in the courtyard.

Hôtel Delambre

35 rue Delambre, 14th (01.43.20.66.31, www.delambre-paris-hotel.com). M° Edgar Quinet or Vavin. **Map** p405 G9.

Occupying a narrow slot in a small street between Montparnasse and St-Germain, this hotel was home to Surrealist André Breton in the 1920s. Today it's modern and friendly, with cast-iron details in the 13 rooms and newly installed air-conditioning. The mini suite in the attic, comprising two separate rooms, is particularly pleasant and sleeps up to four.

Budget

Hôtel Istria Saint-Germain

29 rue Campagne-Première, 14th (01.43.20.91.82, www.hotel-istria-paris.com). M° Raspail. **Map** p405 G9.

Behind this unassuming façade is the place where the artistic royalty of Montparnasse's heyday – the likes of Man Ray, Marcel Duchamp and Louis Aragon – once lived. The Istria Saint-Germain has been modernised since then, but it still has plenty of charm, with 26 bright, simply furnished rooms.

▶ *Film fans take note: the artists' studios next door featured in Godard's A Bout de Souffle.*

Solarhôtel

22 rue Boulard, 14th (01.43.21.08.20, www.solarhotel.fr). M° Denfert Rochereau. **Map** p405 G10.

This hotel has managed to strike a great balance between price and sustainability. The simple en suite bedrooms are all equipped with low-energy lamps, and corridors are fitted with sensor-operated lights. Clients and staff are encouraged to recycle, with sep-

St Christopher's Inn. *See p364.*

ESSENTIAL INFORMATION

arate bins for plastics, paper, glass and batteries, and biodegradable waste from the organic breakfast gets turned into compost in a barrel in the garden.

THE 7TH & WESTERN PARIS

Deluxe

★ Le Bellechasse

8 rue de Bellechasse, 7th (01.45.50.22.31, www.lebellechasse.com). M° Assemblée Nationale or Solférino/RER Musée d'Orsay. **Map** p405 F6.
A former *hôtel particulier*, the Bellechasse fell into the hands of Christian Lacroix, already responsible for the makeover of the Hôtel du Petit Moulin (*see p352*). It reopened in July 2007, duly transformed into a trendy boutique hotel. It offers 34 splendid – though rather small – rooms.

Expensive

Hôtel La Bourdonnais

111-113 av de La Bourdonnais, 7th (01.47.05.45.42, www.hotellabourdonnais.com). M° Ecole Militaire. **Map** p405 F6.
The Bourdonnais feels more like a traditional French bourgeois townhouse than a hotel, with 56 bedrooms decorated in rich colours, antiques and Persian rugs. The lobby opens on to a winter garden. The hotel is due to reopen in March 2014 after renovations.

Hôtel Duc de Saint-Simon

14 rue de St-Simon, 7th (01.44.39.20.20, www.hotelducdesaintsimon.com). M° Rue du Bac. **Map** p405 G6.

A lovely courtyard leads the way into this popular hotel situated on the edge of St-Germain-des-Prés. Of the 34 romantic bedrooms, four have terraces over a closed-off, leafy garden. It's perfect for lovers, though if you can do without a four-poster bed there are more spacious rooms than the Honeymoon Suite.

★ Le Montalembert

3 rue Montalembert, 7th (01.45.49.68.68, www.hotel-montalembert.fr). M° Rue du Bac. **Map** p405 G6.
Grace Leo-Andrieu's impeccable boutique hotel is a benchmark of quality. It has everything that *mode* maniacs (who flock here for Fashion Week) could want: bathrooms stuffed with Molton Brown toiletries, a set of digital scales and plenty of mirrors with which to keep an eye on their figure. Clattery stairwell lifts are a nice nod to old-fashioned ways in a hotel that is otherwise *tout moderne*.

Moderate

Hôtel Lenox

9 rue de l'Université, 7th (01.42.96.10.95, www.lenoxsaintgermain.com). M° St-Germain-des-Prés. **Map** p405 G6.
This is a venerable literary and artistic haunt. The art deco-style Lenox Club Bar, open to the public, features comfortable leather club chairs and jazz instruments on the walls. Bedrooms, reached by an astonishing glass lift, have more traditional decor and city views.

Sublim Eiffel

94 bd Garibaldi, 15th (01.40.65.95.95, www.sublimeiffel.com). M° Sèvres-Lecourbe. **Map** p405 E8.
Some Barry White on your iPod is essential for this luuurve hotel not far from the Eiffel Tower. Carpets printed with paving stones and manhole covers lead to the rooms, where everything has been put in place for steamy nights. It's all to do with the lighting effects, which include a starry Eiffel Tower or street-scene lights above the bed and sparkling LEDs in the showers, filtered by coloured glass doors. Lovers should head for the suite, with its jacuzzi, huge shower, bathrobes and DVDs, and book the Romance package (rose petals on the bed and champagne). All guests get the use of the mini-gym and hammam, and there is a massage room too. The bar adds a bit of jazz to an area in need of some action.

Budget

Hôtel Eiffel Rive Gauche

6 rue du Gros-Caillou, 7th (01.45.51.51.51, www.hotel-eiffel.com). M° Ecole Militaire. **Map** p404 D6.
The Provençal decor and warm welcome make this a pleasant retreat. For the quintessential Paris view at a bargain price, ask to stay on one of the upper floors: you can see the Eiffel Tower from nine of the

29 rooms. All of them feature Empire-style headboards and modern bathrooms. Outside, there's a tiny, tiled courtyard.

YOUTH ACCOMMODATION

Auberge Internationale des Jeunes

10 rue Trousseau, 11th (01.47.00.62.00, www.aijparis.com). M° Ledru-Rollin. **Map** p407 N7.
Cleanliness is a high priority at this large, 120-bed hostel close to Bastille. Rooms accommodate between two and four people, and the larger ones have their own shower and toilet. With the lowest hostel rates in central Paris, the place does tend to fill up fast during the summer months, but advance reservations can be made. Although the hostel is open all hours without any late-night curfew, the rooms are closed for cleaning (11am-3pm). Under-35s only.

Auberge Jules-Ferry

8 bd Jules-Ferry, 11th (01.43.57.55.60, www. hihostels.com). M° République. **Map** p402 M4.
This friendly IYHF hostel has 100 beds in rooms for two to six. There's no curfew, though rooms are closed between 10am and 2pm.

BVJ Paris/Quartier Latin

44 rue des Bernardins, 5th (01.43.29.34.80, www.bvjhotel.com). M° Maubert Mutualité. **No credit cards.** Map p406 J7.
The BVJ hostel has 121 beds with homely tartan quilts in clean but bare modern dorms (accommodating up to ten), and rooms with showers. There's also a TV lounge and a work room.
Other location BVJ Paris/Louvre, 20 rue Jean-Jacques-Rousseau, 1st (01.53.00.90.90).

★ MIJE

6 rue de Fourcy, 4th (01.42.74.23.45, www.mije. com). M° St-Paul. **No credit cards.** Map p409 L6.
MIJE runs three 17th-century Marais residences – one is a former convent – that provide the most attractive hostel sleeps in Paris. Its plain, clean rooms have snow-white sheets and sleep up to eight people; all have a shower and basin. The Fourcy address has its own restaurant (evenings only).
Other locations (same phone) 12 rue des Barres, 4th; 11 rue du Fauconnier, 4th.

St Christopher's Inn

159 rue de Crimée, 19th (01.40.34.34.40, www. st-christophers.co.uk/paris-hostels). M° Crimée, Jaurès, Laumière or Stanlingrad. **Map** p403 N1.
If you don't mind bunking up with others, you could try this branch of the youth hostel chain on the Canal de l'Ourcq. The decor in the bedrooms has a sailor's cabin feel, with round mirrors, bubble-pattern wallpaper and 1950s-inspired cabin furniture. The hostel really comes into its own in its bar Belushi's, where the backpack brigade are joined by Parisians bent on taking advantage of the canal setting. *Photos p362.*

▶ *The company has just opened a second, more central hostel right opposite Gare du Nord (same website as above).*

BED & BREAKFAST

Alcove & Agapes

(01.44.85.06.05, www.bed-and-breakfast-in-paris.com).
This B&B booking service offers over 100 *chambres d'hôtes* (€80-€320 for a double, including breakfast; three-, four- and five-bed rooms available too) with hosts who range from artists to grannies. Extras can include anything from dinner to cooking classes.

Good Morning Paris

43 rue Lacépède, 5th (01.47.07.28.29, www.goodmorningparis.fr).
This company has 100 rooms in the city. Prices range from €84 to €129 for doubles, and €116 for an apartment that sleeps two to four people. There's a minimum stay of two nights.

APART-HOTELS & FLAT RENTAL

A deposit is usually payable on arrival. Small ads for private short-term lets run in fortnightly anglophone mag *FUSAC* (www.fusac.fr); or check out www.frenchconnections.co.uk, which has a selection of furnished apartments for four or more people, and www.apartmentservice.com.

Citadines Apart'hotel

01.41.05.79.05, www.citadines.com.
The 16 modern Citadines complexes across Paris tend to attract a mainly business clientele. Room sizes vary from slightly cramped studios to quite spacious two-bedroom apartments.

Paris Address

01.43.20.91.57, www.parisaddress.com.
Paris Address has over 280 apartments for rent in the heart of Paris and offers a friendly reception service – a great alternative to staying in a hotel.

Paris Appartements Services

20 rue Bachaumont, 2nd (01.40.28.01.28, www.paris-apts.com). M° Sentier. **Open** 9am-6pm Mon-Fri. *Key pick-up* 24hrs.
This organisation specialises in short-term rentals, offering furnished studios and one-bedroom flats in the first to fourth arrondissements.

Swell Apartments

11 rue Duhesme, 18th (+44 (0)7725 056 421, www.swell-apartments.co.uk). M° Lamarck Caulincourt. **Map** p401 H1.
Don't be put off by the tatty entrance; this flat on the north side of Montmartre (sleeping two) is lovely inside. The bedroom, with blue and white walls, has a crystal chandelier and marble fireplace.

ESSENTIAL INFORMATION

Getting Around

ARRIVING & LEAVING

By air

Roissy-Charles-de-Gaulle airport
39.50, www.adp.fr.
Most international flights use
Roissy-Charles-de-Gaulle airport,
which is situated 30km (19 miles)
north-east of Paris. Its three main
terminals are some way apart, so
check which one you need for your
return flight. The terminals are
linked by the free CDGVAL
driverless train.

The **RER B** (RATP helpline,
36.58, www.transilien.com) is the
quickest way to central Paris (about
30mins to Gare du Nord; 35mins
to RER Châtelet-Les Halles; €9.25
single). RER trains run every
10-15mins, 4.56am-11.56pm daily
from the airport to Paris.

Air France buses
(08.92.35.08.20, www.cars-
airfrance.com; €15 single, €24
return, €7.50 under-11s, free under-
2s) leave every 20-30mins, 6am-
11pm daily, from terminals, and
stop at porte Maillot and place
Charles-de-Gaulle (35-50min trip).
Air France buses also run to Gare
Montparnasse and Gare de Lyon
(€16.50 single, €27 return, €8
under-11s, free under-2s) every
30mins (45-60min trip), 6am-10pm
daily; there's a shuttle bus between
Roissy and Orly (€19 single,
€9.50 under-11s, free under-2s)
every 30mins, 5.55am-10.30pm
daily from Roissy; 6.30am-10.30pm
Mon-Fri, 7am-10.30pm Sat, Sun
from Orly.

The **RATP RoissyBus** (32.46,
www.ratp.fr; €10) runs every
15-20mins, 5.45am-11pm daily,
between the airport and the corner
of rue Scribe/rue Auber (at least
45mins); buy tickets on the bus.
Paris Airports Service is a door-
to-door minibus service between
airports and hotels, 24/7. The more
passengers on board, the less each
one pays. Roissy prices go from
€27 for one person to €100 for
eight people, 6am-8pm (minimum
€43, 4-6am, 8-10pm); book on
01.55.98.10.80, www.parisairport
service.com. A **taxi** to central
Paris takes 30-60mins depending
on traffic conditions. Expect to
pay approx €40-€50, plus €1 per
item of luggage.

Orly airport
39.50, www.adp.fr.
Domestic and international flights
use Orly, 18km (11 miles) south of
the city. It has two terminals: Orly-
Sud (mainly international) and
Orly-Ouest (mainly domestic).

Air France buses
(08.92.35.08.20, www.cars-
airfrance.com; €11.50 single, €18.50
return, €5.50 under-11s, free under-
2s) leave both terminals every 20-
30mins, 6am-11.30pm daily, and
stop at Invalides and Montparnasse
(30-45mins). The **RATP Orlybus**
(32.46, www.ratp.fr; €7) runs
between the airport and Denfert-
Rochereau every 15mins, 5.35am-
11.40pm daily (30min trip); buy
tickets on the bus. The high-speed
Orlyval (www.orlyval.fr) shuttle
train runs every 4-7mins (6am-
11pm daily) to RER B station
Antony (€11.30 to Châtelet-les-
Halles); getting into central Paris
takes about 35mins.

You could also catch the
Paris par le train bus (€6.45,
www.parisparletrain.fr) to Pont
de Rungis, where you can take
the RER C into central Paris. Buses
run every 20mins, 4.34am-11.24pm
daily from Orly-Sud; 35min trip.
Orly prices for the **Paris Airports
Service** door-to-door facility
(*see left*) are the same as for Roissy-
Charles-de-Gaulle. A **taxi** into town
takes 20-40mins and costs €16-€26,
plus €1 per piece of luggage.

Paris Beauvais airport
08.92.68.20.66,
www.aeroportbeauvais.com.
Beauvais, 70km (44 miles) from
Paris, is served by budget airlines
such as Ryanair (08.92.78.02.10,
www.ryanair.com). Buses (€16)
leave for Porte Maillot 15-30mins
after each arrival; buses the other
way leave 3hrs 15mins before each
departure. Get tickets from arrivals
lounge or buy them on the bus.

Major airlines

Aer Lingus
08.21.23.02.67,
www.aerlingus.com.
Air France
36.54, www.airfrance.fr.
American Airlines
08.26.46.09.50,
www.americanairlines.fr.

British Airways
08.25.82.54.00,
www.britishairways.fr.
Continental
01.71.23.03.35,
www.continental.com.
Easyjet
08.20.42.03.15, www.easyjet.com.
KLM & NorthWest
08.92.70.26.08, www.klm.com.
United
08.10.72.72.72, www.united.fr.

By car

Options for crossing the
Channel with a car include:
Eurotunnel (08.10.63.03.04,
www.eurotunnel.com); **Brittany
Ferries** (08.25.82.88.28,
www.brittanyferries.com);
P&O Ferries (08.20.90.00.61,
www.poferries.com); and **My
Ferry Link** (08.11.65.47.65,
www.myferrylink.com).

Shared journeys

Allô-Stop
01.53.20.42.42, www.allostop.net.
Call several days ahead to be put
in touch with drivers. There's a fee
(€5 under 250km, 155 miles; €8
over 250km), plus a contribution
towards the petrol expenses, paid
to the driver (from €5 under 100km,
62 miles, up to €95 for over
2,000km, 1,243 miles).

By coach

International coach services arrive
at the Gare Routière Internationale
Paris-Gallieni at Porte de Bagnolet,
20th. For reservations (in English),
call **Eurolines** on 08.92.89.90.91
(€0.34 per min) or 01.41.86.24.21
from abroad, or visit www.
eurolines.fr. Fares start from as
little as £19 for a single ticket
from London to Paris.

By rail

From London, **Eurostar**
services (UK: 0044.8432.186186,
www.eurostar.com) to Paris depart
from the dedicated terminal at
St Pancras International. Thanks
to the new high-speed track, the
journey from London to Paris now
takes 2hrs 15mins direct, slightly
longer for trains stopping at

Ashford and Lille. Eurostar services from the new terminal at Ebbsfleet International, near junction 2 of the M25, take 2hrs 5mins direct. Fares start at £69/€88 for a London-Paris return ticket. Passengers must check in at least 30mins before departure time. Trains arrive at Gare du Nord (www.sncf.fr), with easy access to public transport and taxi ranks.

Cycles can be taken as hand luggage if they are dismantled and carried in a bike bag. You can also check them in at the EuroDespatch depot at St Pancras (Esprit Parcel Service, 0844 822 5822) or the Geoparts depot at Gare du Nord (01.55.31.58.33). Check-in should be done at least 24 hours ahead; a Eurostar ticket must be shown. The service costs £25/€29.

MAPS

Free maps of the métro, bus and RER systems are available at airports and métro stations. Other brochures from métro stations are *Paris Visite – Le Guide*, with details of transport tickets and a small map, and *Plan de Paris*, a fold-out one showing *Noctambus* night bus lines. A Paris street map (*Plan de Paris*) can be bought from newsagents. The blue *Paris Pratique* is clear and compact.

PUBLIC TRANSPORT

Almost all of the Paris public transport system is run by the **RATP** (Régie Autonome des Transports Parisiens; 32.46, www.ratp.fr): the bus, métro (underground) and suburban tram routes, as well as lines A and B of the RER (Réseau Express Régional) suburban express railway, which connects with the métro within the city centre. National rail operator **SNCF** (36.35, www.sncf.com) runs RER lines C, D and E, and serves the Paris suburbs (*Banlieue*), as well as French regions and international destinations (*Grandes Lignes*).

Fares & tickets

Paris and suburbs are divided into six travel zones; zones 1 and 2 cover the centre. RATP tickets and passes are valid on the métro, bus and RER. Tickets and *carnets* can be bought at métro stations, tourist offices and *tabacs* (tobacconists); single tickets can also be bought on buses. Hold

on to your ticket in case of spot checks; you'll also need it to exit RER stations.
● A single ticket *T+* costs €1.70, but it's more economical to buy a *carnet* of ten for €13.30.
● A one-day *Mobilis* pass costs from €6.60 for zones 1 and 2 to €15.65 for zones 1-5.
● A one-day *Paris Visite* pass for zones 1-3 is €10.55; a five-day pass is €33.70, with discounts on some attractions.
● One-week or one-month passes (passport photo needed) offer unlimited travel in the relevant zones; if bought in zones 1 or 2, each is delivered as a Navigo swipe card. A *forfait mensuel* (monthly pass valid from the first day of the month) for zones 1 and 2 costs €65.10; a weekly *forfait hebdomadaire* (weekly pass valid Mon-Sun inclusive) for zones 1 and 2 costs €19.80 and is better value than *Paris Visite* passes.

Métro & RER

The Paris **métro** is the fastest and cheapest way of getting around the city. Trains run 5.30am-12.40am Mon-Thur, 5.30am-1.30am Fri-Sun. Individual lines are numbered, with each direction named after the last stop. Follow the orange *Correspondance* to change lines. Be prepared for the fact that some interchanges, such as Châtelet-Les-Halles, Montparnasse-Bienvenüe and République, involve long walks. The exit (*Sortie*) is indicated in blue. The driverless line 14 runs from Gare St-Lazare to Olympiades. Pickpockets and bag-snatchers are rife on the network – pay special attention as the doors are closing.

The five **RER** lines (A, B, C, D and E) run 5.30am-1am daily through Paris and into the suburbs. Within Paris, the RER is useful for faster journeys – Châtelet-Les-Halles to Gare du Nord is one stop on the RER, and six on the métro. Métro tickets are valid for RER journeys within zones 1 and 2.

Buses

Buses run 6.30am-8.30pm, with some routes continuing until 12.30am, Mon-Sat; limited services operate on selected lines on Sunday and public holidays. You can use a métro ticket, a ticket bought from the driver (€2) or a travel pass to travel on the bus. Tickets should be punched in the machine next to the driver; passes should be

shown to the driver. When you want to get off, press the red request button.

Night buses
After the métro and normal buses stop running, the only public transport – apart from taxis – are the 47 **Noctilien** lines, running between place du Châtelet and the suburbs (hourly 12.30am-5.30am Mon-Thur; half-hourly 1am-5.35am Fri, Sat); look out for the Noctilien logo on bus stops or the N in front of the route number. A ticket costs €1.70 (€2 from the driver); travel passes are valid.

River transport

Batobus
(08.25.05.01.01, www.batobus.com). River buses stop every 20-25mins at: Eiffel Tower, Musée d'Orsay, St-Germain-des-Prés (quai Malaquais), Notre-Dame, Jardin des Plantes, Hôtel de Ville, Louvre, Champs-Elysées (Pont Alexandre III). They run Sept-Mar 10am-7pm; Apr-Aug 10am-9.30pm. A one-day pass is €15 (€7, €9 reductions); two-day pass €18 (€9, €12 reductions); annual pass €60 (€38 reductions). Tickets can be bought at Batobus stops, online at www.batobus.com, RATP ticket offices and the Office de Tourisme (*see p378*).

Trams

Three modern tram lines (www.ratp.fr) operate in the suburbs. They connect with the métro and RER; fares are the same as for buses. The network is set to grow to seven lines and nearly 100km of track by 2016, making it the third largest in Europe in terms of passenger numbers.

RAIL TRAVEL

Suburban destinations are served by the RER. Other locations farther from the city are served by the SNCF railway; the TGV high-speed train has slashed journey times and is being extended to all the main regions. There are few long-distance bus services. Tickets can be bought at any SNCF station (not just the one from which you'll travel), SNCF shops and travel agents. If you reserve online or by phone, you can pay and pick up your tickets from the station or have them sent to your home. SNCF automatic machines (*billeterie automatique*) only work with French credit/debit cards. Regular trains have full-rate White (peak) and cheaper Blue (off-peak) periods. You can save on TGV fares by buying special cards. The *Carte 12/25* gives under-26s a 25-50 per cent reduction; even without it, under-26s are entitled to 25 per cent off. Buy tickets in advance to secure the cheaper fare. Before you board any train, stamp your ticket in the orange *composteur* machines located on the platforms, or you might have to pay a hefty fine. *See also p374* **Lost Property**.

SNCF reservations & tickets

National reservations & information 36.35 (€0.34 per min), www.sncf.com. **Open** 7am-10pm daily.

Mainline stations

Gare d'Austerlitz
Central and south-west France and Spain.
Gare de l'Est
Alsace, Champagne and southern Germany.
Gare de Lyon
Burgundy, the Alps, Provence and Italy.
Gare Montparnasse
West France, Brittany, Bordeaux, the south-west.
Gare du Nord
Eurostar, Channel ports, north-east France, Belgium and the Netherlands.
Gare St-Lazare
Normandy.

TAXIS

Paris taxi drivers are not known for their flawless knowledge of the Paris street map; if you have a preferred route, say so. Taxis can also be hard to find, especially at rush hour or early in the morning. Your best bet is to find a taxi rank (*station de taxis*, marked with a blue sign) on major roads, crossroads and at stations. A white light on a taxi's roof indicates the car is free; an orange light means the cab is busy. Rates (low to high) are based on zone and time of day: **A** (10am-5pm Mon-Sat central Paris); **B** (5pm-10am Mon-Sat, 7am-midnight Sun central Paris; 7am-7pm Mon-Sat inner suburbs and airports); **C** (midnight-7am Sun central Paris; 7pm-7am Mon-Sat, all day Sun inner suburbs and airports; all times outer suburbs).

Most journeys in central Paris cost €7-€15; there's a minimum charge of €6.20, plus €1 for more than one piece of luggage over 5kg or bulky objects, and a surcharge from mainline stations. Most drivers will not take more than three people, but they should take a couple and two children. There is a charge of €3 for a fourth adult passenger.

Don't feel obliged to tip, although rounding up to the nearest euro is polite. Taxis are not allowed to refuse rides if they deem them too short and can only refuse to take you in a certain direction during their last half-hour of service (both rules are often ignored). If you want a receipt, ask for *un reçu* or *la note*. Complaints should be made to the **Bureau des Taxis et des Transports Publics**, 36 rue des Morillons, 75732 Paris Cedex 15 (01.55.76.20.05). *See also p374* **Lost Property**.

Phone cabs

These firms take phone bookings 24/7; you also pay for the time it takes your taxi to reach you. If you wish to pay by credit card, mention this when you order.

Alpha
01.45.85.85.85, www.alphataxis.fr.
G7
36.07, www.taxis-g7.fr.
Taxis Bleus
36.09, www.taxis-bleus.com.

DRIVING

If you bring your car to France, you must bring its registration and insurance documents.

As you come into Paris, you will meet the Périphérique, the giant ring road that carries traffic into, out of and around the city. Intersections, leading on to other main roads, are called *portes* (gates). Driving on the Périphérique is not as hair-raising as it might look, though it's often congested. Some hotels have parking spaces that can be paid for by the hour, day or by types of season tickets.

In peak holiday periods, the organisation Bison Futé hands out brochures at motorway *péages* (toll gates), suggesting less crowded routes. French roads are categorised as *Autoroutes* (motorways, with an 'A' in front of the number), *Routes Nationales* (national 'N' roads), *Routes Départementales* (local, 'D' roads) and rural *Routes Communales* ('C' roads). *Autoroutes* are toll roads;

some sections, including most of the area around Paris, are free.

Infotrafic *08.92.70.77.66 (€0.34 per minute), www.infotrafic.fr.*
Bison Futé
08.00.10.02.00, www.bison-fute.equipement.gouv.fr.

Breakdown services

Beaking down in France can be an expensive business, so it's advisable to take out additional breakdown insurance cover before you travel, for example with a company such as the **AA** (www.theaa.com) or **Green Flag** (www.greenflag.com). **Dan Dépann Auto** (08.00.25.10.00, www.dandepann.fr) operates a 24-hour breakdown service in the Paris area.

Driving tips

● At junctions where no signposts indicate right of way, the car coming from the right has priority. Many roundabouts now give priority to those on the roundabout. If this is not indicated (by road markings or a sign with the message *Vous n'avez pas la priorité*), priority is for those coming from the right.
● Drivers and all passengers must wear seat belts.
● Under-tens are not allowed to travel in the front of a car, except in baby seats facing backwards.
● You should not stop on an open road; you must pull off to the side.
● When drivers are flashing their lights at you, this often means they will not slow down and are warning you to keep out of the way.

Parking

If you park illegally, you risk getting your car clamped or towed away. It's forbidden to park in zones marked for deliveries (*livraisons*) or taxis. Parking meters have now been replaced by *horodateurs*, pay-and-display machines, which take a special card (*carte de stationnement* at €15 or €40, available from *tabacs*). Many also now accept payment by credit/debit cards. Parking is often free at weekends, after 7pm and in August.

Car hire

To hire a car, you must be 25 or over and have held a licence for at least a year. Some agencies accept drivers aged 21-24, but a supplement of €20-€25 per day

ESSENTIAL INFORMATION

is usual. Take your licence and passport with you. Bargain firms may have an extremely high charge for damage: make sure you read the small print.

Hire companies

Ada
www.ada.fr.
Avis
08.21.23.07.60, www.avis.fr.
Budget
08.25.00.35.64, www.budget.fr.
EasyCar
www.easycar.com.
Europcar
08.25.35.83.58,
www.europcar.fr.
Hertz
01.55.31.93.21, www.hertz.fr.
Rent-a-Car
08.91.70.02.00,
www.rentacar.fr.

Chauffeur-driven cars

Chauffeur Services Paris
(01.80.40.00.86, www.csparis. com). **Open** 24hrs daily. **Prices** from €105 airport transfer; €240 for 4 hours.

CYCLING

In 2007, the mayor launched a municipal bike hire scheme, **Vélib** (www.velib.paris.fr), which has become a model for similar projects around the world. There are now more than 20,000 bicycles available 24 hours a day, at nearly 1,800 'stations' across the city. Just swipe your travel card to release the bikes from their stands. The *mairie* actively promotes cycling in the city and the Vélib scheme is complemented by the 400km (250 miles) of bike lanes snaking their way around Paris.

The Itinéraires Paris-Piétons-Vélos-Rollers – scenic strips of the city that are closed to cars on Sundays and holidays – continue to multiply; www.paris.fr can provide an up-to-date list of routes and a downloadable map of cycle lanes. A free *Paris à Vélo* map can be picked up at any mairie or from bike shops. Cycle lanes (*pistes cyclables*) run mostly N–S and E–W. N–S routes include rue de Rennes, av d'Italie, bd Sébastopol and av Marceau. E–W routes take in the rue de Rivoli, bd St-Germain, bd St-Jacques and av Daumesnil. You could be fined if you don't use them. Cyclists are also entitled to use certain bus lanes (especially the new ones, set off by a strip of kerb

stones); look out for traffic signs with a bike symbol. Don't let the locals' blasé attitude to helmets and lights convince you it's not worth using them.

Cycles & scooters for hire

Bike insurance may not cover theft; check when you book.

Freescoot
63 quai de la Tournelle, 5th (01.44.07.06.72, www.freescoot.fr). Mº Maubert Mutualité or St-Michel. **Open** 9am-1pm, 2-7pm daily; closed Sun Oct-mid May. Hires out bicycles (from €15 per day) and scooters (from €45 per day).
Left Bank Scooters
(06.82.70.13.82, www.leftbankscooters.com). This company hires out vintage-style Vespas (from €70 per day), with delivery and collection from your apartment or hotel. Various tours also available.

WALKING

Walking is easily the best way to explore Paris; just remember to remain vigilant at all times. Brits should be aware that traffic will be coming from the 'wrong' direction and that zebra crossings mean very little. By law, drivers are only obliged to stop at a red traffic light – even then, many will take a calculated risk.

TOURS

Bus tours

The following companies offer hop-on, hop-off bus tours of the city with commentary available in a variety of languages.

Les Cars Rouges
01.53.95.39.53, www.carsrouges. com. **Tickets** €31; €15 4-11s. Tours leave every 7-15mins and the round trip takes 2hrs 15mins. You can hop on and off along the way and tickets are valid for two consecutive days.
Paris City Vision
01.44.55.61.00, www.pariscity vision.com. **Tickets** €31; €16 4-11s. Choose beetween four different Open Tour routes around Paris.

Bike tours

Fat Tire Bike Tours
01.56.58.10.54, http://fattire biketours.com/paris. **Tickets** €30; €28 reductions.

Bike tours of the city, with the main tour starting at the south leg of the Eiffel Tower. Tours run daily at 11am, with a 3pm tour added in summer. Check online for details.

Boat tours

Cruising along the River Seine is a delightful way to see Paris. The companies below all run a variety of tours on the river. Most boats depart from the quays in the 7th and 8th, and proceed to go on a circuit around the islands. Check online for full tour details and times: many companies operate more than one type of tour, though the basic tour usually runs every 20-60mins in summer. Rates are for one day only, though other tickets may be available.

Bateaux-Mouches
Pont de l'Alma, 8th (01.42.25.96.10, www.bateaux-mouches.fr). Mº Alma-Marceau. **Tickets** €12.50; €5.50 reductions; free under-4s.
Bateaux Parisiens
Port de la Bourdonnais, 7th (www.bateauxparisiens.com). RER Champ de Mars. **Tickets** €13; €5 reductions; free under-3s.
Batobus Tour Eiffel
Various stops (08.25.05.01.01, www.batobus.com). **Tickets** €15; €7 reductions.
Vedettes de Paris
Port de Suffren, 7th (01.44.18.19.50, www. vedettesdeparis.com). Mº Bir-Hakeim. **Tickets** €13; €5 reductions; free under-4s.
Vedettes du Pont-Neuf
Sq du Vert-Galant, 1st (01.46.33.98.38, www.vedettes dupontneuf.com). Mº Pont-Neuf. **Tickets** €13; €7 under-12s; free under-4s.

Walking tours

Paris Walking Tours
01.48.09.21.40, www.paris-walks.com. **Tickets** €12; €8-€10 reductions.
Led by long-term resident expats, these daily two-hour walking tours (times vary by season) explore various city locales.
Visites Spectacles
01.48.59.92.97, www.visites-spectacles.com. **Tickets** €25; €15-€21 reductions; free under-4s. Combining historical tours with interactive theatre performances, Visites Spectacles' themed treats range from the Spirit of Montmartre to Eiffel Tower Romance.

Resources A-Z

TRAVEL ADVICE

For up-to-date information on travel to a specific country – including the latest on safety and security, health issues, local laws and customs – contact your home country government's department of foreign affairs. Most have websites with useful advice for would-be travellers.

AUSTRALIA
www.smartraveller.gov.au

CANADA
www.voyage.gc.ca

NEW ZEALAND
www.safetravel.govt.nz

REPUBLIC OF IRELAND
foreignaffairs.gov.ie

UK
www.fco.gov.uk/travel

USA
www.state.gov/travel

ADDRESSES

Paris arrondissements are indicated by the last two digits of the postal code: 75002 denotes the second, 75015 the 15th, and so on. The 16th arrondissement is divided into two sectors, 75016 and 75116. Some business addresses have a more detailed postcode, followed by a Cedex number, which indicates the arrondissement; *bis* or *ter* is the equivalent of 'b' or 'c' after a building number.

AGE RESTRICTIONS

For heterosexuals and homosexuals, the age of consent is 15. You must be 18 years old to drive, and to consume alcohol in a public place. You must be 16 years old to buy cigarettes.

ATTITUDE & ETIQUETTE

Parisians take manners seriously and are generally more courteous than their reputation may have led you to believe. If someone brushes you accidentally when passing, they will more often than not say *'pardon'*; you can do likewise, or say *'c'est pas grave'* (don't worry). In shops it is normal to greet the assistant with a *'bonjour madame'* or *'bonjour monsieur'* when you enter, and say *'au revoir'* when you leave. The business of *'tu'* and *'vous'* can be tricky for English speakers. Strangers, people significantly older than you and professional contacts should be addressed with the respectful *'vous'*; friends, relatives, children and pets as *'tu'*. When among themselves, young people will often launch straight in with *'tu'*.

BUSINESS

The best first stop for initiating business is the CCIP (Chambre de Commerce et d'Industrie de Paris; *see p370*). Banks can refer you to lawyers, accountants and tax consultants.

Conventions & conferences

CNIT *2 pl de la Défense, BP 321, 92053 Paris La Défense (01.40.68.22.22, www.viparis.com). M°/RER Grande Arche de La Défense.* Mainly computer fairs.
Palais des Congrès *2 pl de la Porte-Maillot, 17th (01.40.68.22.22, www.viparis.com). M° Porte-Maillot.*
Parc des Expositions de Paris-Nord Villepinte *Zac Paris Nord 2, 93420 Villepinte (01.40.68.22.22, www.viparis.com). RER Parc des Expositions.*
Trade fair centre near Roissy.
Paris-Expo *1 pl de la Porte de Versailles, 15th (01.40.68.22.22, www.viparis.com). M° Porte de Versailles.*
The city's biggest expo centre.

Courier services

ATV *08.11.65.56.05, www.coursiers.com.* **Open** 24hrs daily.
Bike or van messengers 24/7. Rates rise after 8pm and at weekends.
Chronopost *08.25.80.18.01, www.chronopost.fr.* **Open** 9am-8pm Mon-Fri; 9am-1pm Sat (in post offices).
This overnight delivery offshoot of the state-run post office is the most widely used service for parcels.
UPS *08.21.23.38.77, www.ups.com.* **Open** 8am-7pm Mon-Fri; 8am-1pm Sat.
International courier services.

Secretarial services

ADECCO Experts *57-59 bd Malesherbes, 8th (01.77.69.12.12, www.adecco.fr). M° St-Augustin.* **Open** 8.30am-12.30pm, 2-6.30pm Mon-Fri.
Employment agency specialising in bilingual secretaries and staff. **Other locations** throughout the city.

Translators & interpreters

Documents such as birth certificates, loan applications and so on must be translated by certified legal translators, listed at the CCIP (*see p370*) or embassies. For business translations there are dozens of reliable independents.

Association des Anciens Elèves de l'Esit *01.44.05.41.46, www.aaeesit.com.* **Phone enquiries** 8am-8pm Mon-Fri; 8am-6pm Sat. **Booking** (via email only) at mdttraducteurs@aaeesit.com.
A translation and interpreting co-operative whose 900 members are graduates of the Ecole Supérieure d'Interprètes et de Traducteurs.
International Corporate Communication *3 rue des Batignolles, 17th (01.43.87.29.29, www.iccparis.com). M° Place de Clichy.* **Open** 9am-1pm, 2-6pm Mon-Fri.
Translators of financial and corporate documents, plus simultaneous translation.

Useful organisations

American Chamber of Commerce *77 rue de Miromesnil, 8th (01.56.43.45.67, www.amcham france.org). M° Miromesnil.*
Closed to the public, calls only.

British Embassy Commercial Library *35 rue du Fbg-St-Honoré, 8th (01.44.51.31.00, www.ukin france.fco.gov.uk). M° Concorde.* **Open** by appointment.
Stocks trade directories, and assists British companies that wish to develop or set up in France.
CCIP (Chambre de Commerce et d'Industrie de Paris) *27 av de Friedland, 8th (08.20.01.21.12, www.ccip.fr). M° Charles de Gaulle Etoile.* **Open** 8.30am-6.30pm Mon-Fri.
A variety of services for people doing business in France, and very useful for small businesses. Pick up the free booklet *Discovering the Chamber of Commerce* from its head office. There's also a legal advice line (08.92.70.51.00, 9am-4.30pm Mon-Thur, 9am-1pm Fri).
Other locations: Bourse du Commerce, 2 rue de Viarmes, 1st (has a free library and bookshop); 2 rue Adolphe-Jullien, 1st (support for businesses wishing to export goods and services to France).
US Commercial Service *Postal address: US Embassy, 2 av Gabriel, 8th. Visit: US Commercial Service, NEO Building, 14 bd Haussmann, 9th (01.43.12.71.28, www.buyusa. gov/france). M° Richelieu Drouot.* **Open** by appointment 9am-6pm Mon-Fri.
Helps American companies looking to trade in France.

CONSUMER

In the event of a serious problem, try one of the following:

Direction Départementale de la Concurrence, de la Consommation et de la Répression des Fraudes *8 rue Froissart, 3rd (01.40.27.16.00). M° St-Sébastien Froissart.* **Open** 9am-noon, 2-5pm Mon-Fri.
Come here to file a consumer complaint concerning problems with Paris-based businesses.
Institut National de la Consommation *80 rue Lecourbe, 15th (01.45.66.20.20, www.conso. net). M° Sèvres Lecourbe.* **Open** by phone 9am-12.30pm Mon-Fri; recorded information at other times.
Deals with questions on housing, consumer, regulatory and administrative issues.

CUSTOMS

Custom declarations are not usually necessary if you arrive from another EU country and are carrying legal

goods for personal use. The amounts given below are a guide only: if you come close to the maximums in several categories, you may still have to explain your personal habits to customs.

● 1,000 cigarettes, 400 small cigars, 200 cigars or 1kg loose tobacco.
● 10 litres of spirits (more than 22% alcohol), 90 litres of wine (of which 60 litres sparkling wine) or 110 litres of beer.

Coming from a non-EU country, you can bring:
● 200 cigarettes, 100 small cigars, 50 cigars or 250g tobacco.
● 1 litre of spirits (more than 22% alcohol; 2 litres if less than 22% alcohol), 4 litres of wine or 16 litres of beer.
● 50g (1.76oz) of perfume.

Tax refunds

Non-EU residents can claim a refund or *détaxe* (around 12 per cent) on VAT if they spend over €175 in any one day in one shop and if they live outside the EU for more than six months in the year. At the shop concerned ask for a *bordereau de vente à l'exportation*, and when you leave France have it stamped by customs. Then send the stamped form back to the shop. *Détaxe* does not cover food, drink, antiques, services or works of art.

Customs Information Centre *(08.11.20.44.44).*

DISABLED

It's always wise to check up on a site's accessibility and provision for disabled access before you visit. There is information (in French) available on the **Secrétaire d'Etat aux Personnes Handicapées** website: www.handicap.gouv.fr, telephone 08.20.03.33.33.

Association des Paralysés de France *13 pl de Rungis, 13th (01.53.80.92.97, www.apf.asso.fr). M° Place d'Italie.* **Open** 9am-12.30pm, 1.30-5.30pm Mon-Thur; 9am-12.30pm, 1.30-5pm Fri.
Publishes *Guide 98 Musées, Cinémas* (€3.81) listing accessible museums and cinemas, and also has a guide to restaurants and sights.
Fédération APAJH (Association pour Adultes et Jeunes Handicapés) *29th Floor, Tour Montparnasse, 33 av du Maine, 15th (01.44.10.23.40, www.apajh. org). M° Montparnasse Bienvenüe.*

Advice for disabled people living in France.
Maison Départementale des Personnes Handicapées de Paris *69 rue de la Victoire, 9th (08.05.80.09.09, www.mdph.fr).* **Open** 9am-4pm Mon, Tue, Thur, Fri; 9am-5pm Wed.
Advice available in French to disabled persons living in or visiting Paris. The Office de Tourisme website (www.parisinfo.com) also provides plenty of useful information for disabled visitors.

Getting around

The métro and buses are not wheelchair-accessible, with the exception of métro line 14 (Méteor), stations Barbès-Rochechouard (line 2) and Esplanade de la Défense (line 1), and bus lines 20, 21, 22, 24, 26, 27, 28, 29, 30, 31, 32, 38, 39, 42, 43, 46, 47, 48, 52, 53, 54, 56, 57, 58, 60, 61, 62, 63, 64, 65, 66, 67, 68, 69, 70, 72, 73, 74, 75, 76, 80, 81, 82, 83, 84, 85, 86, 87, 88, 89, 91, 92, 93, 94, 95, 96 and PC (Petite Ceinture) 1, 2 and 3. Forward seats on buses are intended for people with poor mobility. RER lines A, B, C, D and some SNCF trains are wheelchair-accessible in parts. For a full list of wheelchair-accessible stations: 08.10.64.64.64, www.infomobi.com. All Paris taxis are obliged by law to take passengers in wheelchairs.

DRUGS

French police have the power to stop and search anyone. It's wise to keep prescription drugs in their original containers and, if possible, to carry copies of the original prescriptions. If you're caught in possession of illegal drugs, you can expect a prison sentence and/or a fine.
See also p371 **Health**.

ELECTRICITY

Electricity in France runs on 220V. Visitors with British 240V appliances can change the plug or use an adaptor (*adaptateur*). For US 110V appliances, you'll need to use a transformer (*transformateur*), available at BHV, Fnac and Darty.

EMBASSIES & CONSULATES

For a full list of embassies and consulates, see the *Pages Jaunes* (www.pagesjaunes.fr) under 'Ambassades et Consulats'. Consular services (passports, etc) are for citizens of that country only.

Australian Embassy *4 rue Jean-Rey, 15th (01.40.59.33.00, www.france.embassy.gov.au). Mº Bir-Hakeim.* **Open** *Consular services* 9am-noon, 2-4pm Mon-Fri.
British Embassy *35 rue du Fbg-St-Honoré, 8th (01.44.51.31.00, www.ukinfrance.fco.gov.uk). Mº Concorde. Consular services: 18bis rue d'Anjou, 8th. Mº Concorde.* **Open** 9.30am-12.30pm Mon-Fri.
British citizens wanting consular services (new passports, etc) should ignore the long queue stretching along rue d'Anjou for the visa department, and instead walk straight in at no.18bis.
Canadian Embassy *35 av Montaigne, 8th (01.44.43.29.00, www.amb-canada.fr). Mº Franklin D. Roosevelt.* **Open** 9am-noon, 2-5pm Mon-Fri. *Consular services:* 01.44.43.29.02. **Open** 9am-noon Mon-Fri. *Visas: 37 av Montaigne, 8th (01.44.43.29.16).* **Open** 8.30-10.30am Mon-Fri.
Irish Embassy *12 av Foch, 16th. Consulate 4 rue Rude, 16th (01.44.17.67.00, www.embassyofireland.fr). Mº Charles de Gaulle Etoile.* **Open** *Consular/visas* 9.30am-noon Mon-Fri; by phone 9.30am-1pm, 2.30-5.30pm Mon-Fri.
New Zealand Embassy *7ter rue Léonard-de-Vinci, 16th (01.45.01.43.43, www.nz embassy.com/france). Mº Victor Hugo.* **Open** 9am-1pm Mon-Fri.
South African Embassy *59 quai d'Orsay, 7th (01.53.59.23.23, www.afriquesud.net). Mº Invalides.* **Open** 8.30am-5.15pm Mon-Fri. *Consulate & visas: 01.47.53.99.70.* **Open** 9am-noon Mon-Fri.
US Embassy *2 av Gabriel, 8th (01.43.12.22.22, http://france. usembassy.gov). Mº Concorde. Consulate & visas: 4 av Gabriel, 8th (08.10.26.46.26). Mº Concorde.* **Open** *Consular services* 9am-12.30pm, 1-3pm Mon-Fri. *Visas* 08.92.23.84.72 or check website for non-immigration visas.

EMERGENCIES

Most of the following services operate 24 hours a day. In a medical emergency, such as a road accident, phone the Sapeurs-Pompiers, who have trained paramedics. *See also* **Health: Accident & Emergency; Doctors; Helplines;** and **Police.**

Ambulance (SAMU) 15
Police 17
Fire (Sapeurs-Pompiers) 18

Emergency (from a mobile phone) 112
Centre anti-poison 01.40.05.48.48

GAY & LESBIAN

For information on HIV and AIDS, *see below* **Health**. *See also pp255-261* **Gay & Lesbian**.

HEALTH

Nationals of non-EU countries should take out insurance before leaving home. EU nationals staying in France can use the French Social Security system, which refunds up to 70 per cent of medical expenses. UK residents travelling in Europe require a European National Health Insurance Card (EHIC). This allows them to benefit from free or reduced-cost medical care while travelling in a country belonging to the European Economic Area (EEA) or Switzerland. The EHIC is free of charge. For further information, refer to www.dh.gov.uk/travellers.

If you're staying for longer than three months, or working in France but still making National Insurance contributions in Britain, you will need form E128 filled in by your employer and stamped by the NI contributions office in order to get a French medical number. Consultations and prescriptions have to be paid for in full on the spot, and are reimbursed on receipt of a completed *fiche*. If you undergo treatment, the doctor will give you a prescription and a *feuille de soins* (bill of treatment). Stick the small stickers from the medication boxes on to the *feuille de soins*. Send this, together with the prescription and details of your EHIC card, to the local **Caisse Primaire d'Assurance Maladie** for a refund. For those resident in France, more and more doctors now accept the **Carte Vitale**, which lets them produce a digital *feuille de soins* and allows you to pay only the non-reimbursable part of the bill. Information on health insurance can be found at www.ameli.fr, where you can also track refunds online. See also the Ministry of Health's website at www.sante.gouv.fr.

Accident & emergency

Hospitals specialise in one type of emergency or illness – refer to the Assistance Publique's website (www.aphp.fr). In a medical emergency, call the Sapeurs-Pompiers or SAMU (*see left* **Emergencies**). The following

(arranged in order of district) have 24-hour accident and emergency services:

ADULTS
Hôpital Hôtel-Dieu *1 pl du Parvis Notre-Dame, 4th (01.42.34.82.34).*
Hôpital St-Louis *1 av Claude-Vellefaux, 10th (01.42.49.49.49).*
Hôpital St-Antoine *184 rue du Fbg-St-Antoine, 12th (01.49.28.20.00).*
Hôpital de la Pitié-Salpêtrière *47-83 bd de l'Hôpital, 13th (01.42.16.00.00).*
Hôpital Cochin *27 rue du Fbg-St-Jacques, 14th (01.58.41.41.41).*
Hôpital Européen Georges Pompidou *20 rue Leblanc, 15th (01.56.09.20.00).*
Hôpital Bichat-Claude Bernard *46 rue Henri-Huchard, 18th (01.40.25.80.80).*
Hôpital Tenon *4 rue de la Chine, 20th (01.56.01.70.00).*

CHILDREN
Hôpital Armand Trousseau *26 av du Dr Arnold-Netter, 12th (01.44.73.74.75).*
Hôpital St-Vincent de Paul *74-82 av Denfert-Rochereau, 14th (01.58.41.41.41).*
Hôpital Necker *149 rue de Sèvres, 15th (01.44.49.40.00).*
Hôpital Robert Debré *48 bd Sérurier, 19th (01.40.03.20.00).*

PRIVATE HOSPITALS
American Hospital in Paris *63 bd Victor-Hugo, 92200 Neuilly (01.46.41.25.25, www.american-hospital.org). Mº Porte Maillot, then bus 82.* **Open** 24hrs daily. English-speaking hospital. French Social Security refunds only a small percentage of the total treatment costs.
Hertford British Hospital (Hôpital Franco-Britannique) *3 rue Barbès, 92300 Levallois-Perret (01.46.39.22.22, www. british-hospital.org). Mº Anatole-France.* **Open** 24hrs daily. Most staff here speak English.

Contraception & abortion

To get the pill (*la pilule*) or coil (*stérilet*), you need a prescription, available on appointment from the two places listed below, from a *médecin généraliste* (GP) or from a gynaecologist. The morning-after pill (*la pilule du lendemain*) can be had from pharmacies without prescription but is not reimbursed. Condoms (*préservatifs*) and spermicides are sold in pharmacies and supermarkets, and there are condom machines in most métro stations, club lavatories and on some street corners.

Centre de Planification et d'Education Familiales
27 rue Curnonsky, 17th (01.48.88.07.28). M° Porte de Champerret. **Open** 9am-5pm Mon-Fri.
Free consultations on family planning and abortion.

MFPF (Mouvement Français pour le Planning Familial)
10 rue Vivienne, 2nd (01.42.60.93.20, www.planning-familial.org). M° Bourse. **Open** 2-7pm Mon; 11am-1pm Tue; 1.30-4.30pm Wed; noon-3pm Thur.
Phone for an appointment for prescriptions and contraception advice. For abortion advice, turn up at the centre at one of the designated time slots.

Dentists

Dentists are found in the *Pages Jaunes* under *Dentistes*. For emergencies, contact:

Hôpital de la Pitié-Salpêtrière
(*see p371*) also offers 24hr emergency dental care.

SOS Dentaire
87 bd Port-Royal, 13th (01.43.37.51.00). M° Les Gobelins/RER Port-Royal. **Open** *by phone* for appointment after 6pm.
A telephone service for emergency dental care.

Doctors

You'll find a list of GPs in the *Pages Jaunes* under *Médecins: Médecine générale*. For a social security refund, choose a doctor or dentist who is *conventionné* (state registered). Consultations cost €22 or more, of which part can be reimbursed.

Centre Médical Europe
44 rue d'Amsterdam, 9th (01.42.81.93.33, www.centre-medical-europe.com). M° St-Lazare. **Open** *With appointment* 8am-7pm Mon-Fri; 8am-6pm Sat.
Practitioners in all fields; modest consultation fees.

SOS Médecins
36.24, www.sosmedecins.com. House calls cost approx €35 before 7pm; from €50 after and on holidays; prices are higher if you don't have French social security.

Urgences Médicales de Paris
01.53.94.94.94, www.ump.fr. Doctors make house calls for approx €35 during the day (€60 if you don't have French social security); €50/€80 until midnight; €65/€90 after midnight. Some speak English.

Opticians

Branches of **Alain Afflelou** (www.alainafflelou.com) and **Lissac** (www.lissac.fr) stock hundreds of frames and can make up prescription glasses within the hour. For an eye test, you'll need to go to an *ophtalmologiste* – ask the optician for a list. Contact lenses can be bought over the counter if you have your prescription details with you.

Hôpital des Quinze-Vingts
28 rue de Charenton, 12th (01.40.02.15.20). Specialist eye hospital offers on-the-spot consultations for eye problems.

SOS Optique
01.48.07.22.00, www.sosoptique.com.
Offers a 24-hour repair service for glasses.

Pharmacies

French *pharmacies* sport a green neon cross. A rota of *pharmacies de garde* operate at night and on Sundays; see below for a list of these night pharmacies. If closed, a pharmacy will have a sign indicating the nearest one open. Staff can provide basic medical services such as bandaging wounds (for a small fee) and will indicate the nearest doctor on duty. *Parapharmacies* sell almost everything pharmacies do but cannot dispense prescription medication. Toiletries and sanitary products are often less expensive in supermarkets.

Grande Pharmacie de la Nation
13 pl de la Nation, 11th (01.43.73.24.03). M° Nation. **Open** 8am-midnight daily.

Matignon
1 av Matignon, 8th (01.43.59.86.55). M° Franklin D. Roosevelt. **Open** 8.30am-2am daily.

Pharmacie des Champs-Elysées
84 av des Champs-Elysées, 8th (01.45.62.02.41). M° George V. **Open** until 2am daily.

Pharmacie Européene de la Place de Clichy
6 pl de Clichy, 9th (01.48.74.65.18). M° Place de Clichy. **Open** 24hrs daily.

Pharmacie des Halles
10 bd de Sébastopol, 4th (01.42.72.03.23). M° Châtelet. **Open** 9am-midnight Mon-Sat; 9am-10pm Sun.

Pharmacie d'Italie
61 av d'Italie, 13th (01.44.24.19.72). M° Tolbiac. **Open** 8am-midnight daily.

Pharma Presto
01.61.04.04.04, www.pharma-presto.com. **Open** for emergencies 24hrs daily. Delivery (€45 8am-6pm; €55 6pm-8am & during weekends) of medication.

STDs, HIV & AIDS

Cabinet Médico-Social Municipal Figuier
2 rue Figuier, 4th (01.49.96.62.70). M° Pont-Marie. **Open** *HIV test walk-in* 1.30-6.30pm Tue, Thur, Fri. *With appointment* 9am-12.15pm, 1.30-6.30pm Mon; 1.30-6.30pm Wed; 9am-1.15pm Thur; 9.15am-noon Sat. *STD tests walk-in* 9am-noon Mon-Fri.
Free, anonymous tests (*dépistages*) for HIV, hepatitis B and C and syphilis (wait one week for results). Good counselling service, too.

Le Kiosque Infos Sida-Toxicomanie
48 rue François Miron, 4th (01.44.78.00.00, www.lekiosque.org). M° St-Paul. **Open** *Walk-in* 11am-7pm Mon; 10am-7pm Tue-Fri; noon-6pm Sat.
Youth association offering information and counselling on AIDS, sexuality and drugs, and fast AIDS tests for gay men. Also works with Checkpoint (36 rue Geoffroy l'Asnier, 4th, 01.44.78.24.44).

SIDA Info Service
08.00.84.08.00, www.sida-info-service.org. **Open** 24hrs daily.
Confidential AIDS information in French.

HELPLINES

Alcoholics Anonymous in English
01.46.34.59.65, www.aaparis.org. A 24hr recorded message gives details of AA meetings at the American Cathedral or American Church (*see p375*).

Allô Service Public
39.39, www.service-public.fr. **Open** 8am-8pm Mon-Fri; 8.30am-6pm Sat.
A source of information and contacts for all aspects of tax, work and administration matters. They even claim to be able to help out if you have problems with neighbours. The catch: operators speak only French. Foreigners can call Info Migrants on 01.53.26.52.82.

Counseling Center
01.47.23.61.13, www.american cathedral.org. Walk-in clinic 11am-1pm 1st & 3rd Thur of mth. English-language counselling, based at the American Cathedral.

Drogues Info Service
08.00.23.13.13, Ecoute Alcool 08.11.91.30.30, Ecoute Cannabis 08.11.91.20.20, Tabac Info Service 39.89, www.drogues.gouv.fr. Phone service, in French, for help with drug, alcohol and tobacco problems.

Narcotics Anonymous
01.43.72.12.72, www.narcotiquesanonymes.org.

ESSENTIAL INFORMATION

The helpline is open daily 8-10pm.
Meetings in English are held
every week.
SOS Dépression *01.40.47.95.95,*
http://sos.depression.free.fr.
Open 24hrs daily.
People listen and/or give advice to
those suffering from depression.
SOS Dépression can send round a
counsellor or psychiatrist in case
of a crisis.
SOS Help *01.46.21.46.46,*
www.soshelpline.org. **Open**
3-11pm daily.
English-language helpline.

ID

French law requires that some
form of identification be carried at
all times. You should be prepared
to produce your passport or **EHIC**
card (*see p371*).

INSURANCE

See p371 Health.

INTERNET

ISPs

Free *10.44, www.free.fr.*
Open 24hrs daily.
SFR *10.23, www.sfr.fr.*
Open 8am-10pm daily.
Orange *39.00, www.orange.fr.*
Open 24hrs daily.
Bouygues *10.34,*
www.bouyguestelecom.fr.
Open 8am-8pm Mon-Sat.

Internet access

An increasing number of public
spaces now offer Wi-Fi hotspots.

Milk *31 bd de Sébastopol, 1st*
(01.42.33.68.17, www.milklub.com).
M° Châtelet/RER Châtelet Les Halles.
Open 24hrs daily.
The biggest internet café in Paris.
Other locations 28 rue du
Septembre, 2nd (01.40.06.00.70);
5 rue d'Odessa, 14th (01.43.20.10.37).

LANGUAGE

See p379 Vocabulary; for a
glossary of food terms, *see p380*
Eating out.

LEFT LUGGAGE

Gare du Nord

There are self-locking luggage
lockers (6.15am-11.15pm daily)
situated on Level -1 under the main
station concourse.

Roissy-Charles-de-Gaulle airport

Bagages du Monde
(01.34.38.58.90,
www.bagagesdumonde.com).
Terminal 1 *Niveau Départ, Porte*
14 (01.34.38.58.82). Open 9am-
1.35pm, 3.30-7pm daily. **Between**
Terminal 2C & 2E *Gare TGV*
Niveau 4 (01.34.38.58.90). Open
6am-9.30pm daily.
Company with counters in Roissy-
Charles-de-Gaulle and an office
in Paris (102 rue de Chemin-Vert,
11th, 01.43.57.30.90, open 9am-
noon, 2-5.30pm Mon-Fri). Can ship
baggage worldwide or store it.

LEGAL HELP

Mairies can answer some legal
enquiries; ask for times of their
free *consultations juridiques.*
See also p370 Embassies.

**Direction Départementale
de la Concurrence, de la
Consommation et de la
Répression des Fraudes** *8 rue*
Froissart, 3rd (01.40.27.16.00).
M° St-Sébastien Froissart. **Open**
9am-noon, 2-5pm Mon-Fri.
Part of the Ministry of Finance;
deals with consumer complaints.
**Palais de Justice Galerie de
Harlay** *Escalier S, 4 bd du Palais,*
4th (01.44.32.52.52). M° Cité.
Open 9.30am-noon Mon-Fri.
Free legal consultation. Make sure
you arrive early and obtain a ticket
for the queue.
SOS Avocats *08.25.39.33.00.*
Open 7-11.30pm Mon-Fri.
Free legal advice by phone.

LIBRARIES

Every arrondissement has a free
public library. To get a library card,
you need to provide ID and evidence
of a fixed address in Paris.

American Library *10 rue du*
Général-Camou, 7th (01.53.59.12.60,
www.americanlibraryinparis.org).
M° Ecole-Militaire/RER Pont de
l'Alma. **Open** 10am-7pm Tue-Sat;
1-7pm Sun (shorter hours in Aug).
Admission day pass €14; €10
reductions; annual €110.
A useful resource: this is the largest
English-language lending library
on the continent. It receives 400
periodicals, as well as popular
magazines and newspapers.
**Bibliothèque Historique de
la Ville de Paris** *Hôtel Lamoignon,*
24 rue Pavée, 4th (01.44.59.29.40).
M° St-Paul. **Open** 10am-6pm Mon-

Sat. **Admission** free (bring
passport photo and ID).
A decent range of books and
documents on Paris history.
**Bibliothèque Marguerite
Durand** *79 rue Nationale, 13th*
(01.53.82.76.77). M° Tolbiac. **Open**
2-6pm Tue-Sat. **Admission** free.
This library holds some 40,000
books and 120 periodicals on
women's history. The feminism
collection includes letters of Colette
and Louise Michel.
**Bibliothèque Nationale de
France François Mitterrand**
quai François-Mauriac, 13th
(01.53.79.59.59, www.bnf.fr). M°
Bibliothèque. **Open** 2-7pm Mon;
9am-7pm Tue-Sat; 1-7pm Sun.
Closed 2wks Sept & bank holidays.
Admission day pass €3.50; annual
€38; €20 reductions.
Books, papers and periodicals, plus
titles in English. An audio-visual
room lets you browse photo, film
and sound archives.
**Bibliothèque Publique
d'Information (BPI)** *Centre*
Pompidou, 4th (01.44.78.12.33,
www.bpi.fr). M° Hôtel de Ville/
RER Châtelet Les Halles. **Open**
noon-10pm Mon, Wed-Fri; 11am-
10pm Sat, Sun. Closed 1 May.
Admission free.
Now arranged across three levels,
the Centre Pompidou's vast library
has a huge global press section,
reference books and language-
learning facilities.
BIFI (Bibliothèque du Film) *51*
rue de Bercy, 12th (01.71.19.32.32,
www.bifi.fr). M° Bercy. **Open** 10am-
7pm Mon, Wed-Fri; 1-6.30pm Sat.
Closed 2wks Aug. **Admission**
€3.50 day pass; €34 annual;
€15 reductions.
Housed in the same building as the
Cinémathèque Française, this world-
class researchers' and film buffs'
library offers books, magazines, film
stills and posters, as well as films
on video and DVD.
Documentation Française
29-31 quai Voltaire, 7th (01.40.15.
71.10, www.ladocumentation
francaise.fr). M° Rue du Bac.
Open 10am-6pm Mon-Fri. Closed
Aug & 1st wk Sept.
The official government archive
and central reference library has
information on French politics and
economy since 1945.

LOCKSMITHS

There are many round-the-clock
repair services handling locks, plumb-
ing and, sometimes, car repairs. Most
of them charge a minimum €18-€20
call-out (*déplacement*) and €30 per

hour, plus parts. Charges are higher on Sunday and at night.

Allô Serrurerie *01.40.29.44.68, www.alloserrurerie.com.*
SOS Dépannage *08.20.22.23.33, www.okservice.fr.*
SOS Dépannage is double the price of most services, but claims to be twice as reliable.

LOST PROPERTY

Bureau des Objets Trouvés
36 rue des Morillons, 15th (08.21.00.25.25, www.prefecture depolice.interieur.gouv.fr). M° Convention. **Open** 8.30am-5pm Mon-Thur; 8.30am-4.30pm Fri.
Visit in person to fill in a form specifying details of the loss. This may have been the first lost property office in the world, but it is far from the most efficient. Huge delays in processing claims mean that if your trip to Paris is short, you may need to nominate a proxy to collect found objects after you leave, although small items can be posted. If your passport was among the items lost, you'll need to go to your consulate to get a single-entry temporary passport in order to leave the country.

SNCF lost property
Some mainline SNCF stations have their own lost property offices. *See also p367.*

MONEY

The amount of currency visitors may carry is not limited. However, sums worth over €10,000 must be declared to customs when entering or leaving the country.

The euro

Non-French debit and credit cards can be used to withdraw and pay in euros, and currency withdrawn in France can be used subsequently all over the euro zone. Daylight robbery occurs, however, if you try to deposit a euro cheque from any country other than France in a French bank: they currently charge around €15 for this service, and the European parliament has backed down on its original decision that cross-border payments should be in line with domestic ones across the euro zone. This is good news for the British, though: if you transfer money from the UK to France in euros, you will pay the same charges as if Britain were within the euro zone (but it pays to watch the exchange rate carefully).

ATMs

Withdrawals in euros can be made from bank and post office automatic cash machines. The specific cards accepted are marked on each machine, and most can give instructions in English. Credit card companies charge a fee for cash advances, but rates are often better than at banks.

Banks

French banks usually open 9am-5pm Mon-Fri (some close during lunchtime); some banks also open on Sat. All are closed on public holidays, and from noon on the previous day. Note that not all banks have foreign exchange counters. The commission rates vary between banks; the state-owned Banque de France usually offers good rates. Most banks accept travellers' cheques, but may be reluctant to accept personal cheques even with the Eurocheque guarantee card, which is not widely used in France.

Bank accounts

To open an account (*ouvrir un compte*), French banks require proof of identity, address and your income (if any). You'll probably be required to show your passport, an electricity, gas or phone bill in your name and a payslip/letter from your employer. Students need a student card and may need a letter from their parents. Of the major national banks (BNP, Crédit Lyonnais, Société Générale, Banque Populaire, Crédit Agricole), Société Générale tends to be the most foreigner-friendly. Most banks don't hand out a Carte Bleue/Visa card until several weeks after you've opened an account. A chequebook (*chéquier*) is usually issued in about a week. Payments made with a Carte Bleue are debited directly from your current account, but you can arrange for purchases to be debited at the end of every month. French banks are tough on overdrafts, so try to anticipate any cash crisis in advance and work out a deal for an authorised overdraft (*découvert autorisé*) or you risk being blacklisted as '*interdit bancaire*' – forbidden from having a current account – for anything up to ten years. Depositing foreign currency cheques can be slow, so try to use wire transfer or a bank draft in euros to receive funds from abroad.

Bureaux de change

If you happen to be arriving in Paris early in the morning or late at night, you will be able to change money at the **Travelex** bureaux de change in Roissy terminals 1 (7.30am-8pm Mon-Sat, 7am-2.30pm Sun), 2A (7am-5pm & 6am-10.30pm), 2C (7.30am-7pm & 6am-10.30pm), 2D (6.30am-10.30pm), 2F (6am-10.30pm & 6.30am-10.30pm), and 3 (6.30am-10.30pm), and at Orly Sud. Travelex also has bureaux de change at the following stations:

Gare Montparnasse
01.42.79.03.88. **Open** 9am-7pm Mon-Sat; 10am-5pm Sun.
Gare du Nord *01.40.82.96.59.* **Open** 6.45am-10.30pm Mon-Sat; 6.45am-9.30pm Sun.
Gare St-Lazare *01.42.93.74.58.* **Open** 8am-7pm Mon-Sat; 10.30am-5pm Sun.

Credit cards

Major international credit cards are widely used in France; Visa (more commonly known in France as *Carte Bleue*) is the most readily accepted. French-issued credit cards have a security microchip (*puce*) in each card. The card is slotted into a reader, and the holder keys in a PIN to authorise the transaction. In case of credit card loss or theft, call one of the following 24hr services with English-speaking staff on hand to help:

American Express
01.44.77.72.00.
Diners Club *08.20.82.01.43.*
MasterCard *08.00.90.13.87.*
Visa *08.92.70.57.05.*

Foreign affairs

American Express *11 rue Scribe, 9th (01.47.77.70.00, www.americanexpress.com). M° Opéra.* **Open** 9am-6.30pm Mon-Sat.
Travel agency, bureau de change, *poste restante* (you can leave messages for other card holders), card replacement, travellers' cheque refund service, money transfers and cash machine for AmEx cardholders.
Barclays *6 rond-point des Champs-Elysées, 8th (01.44.95.13.80, www.barclays.fr). M° Franklin D. Roosevelt.* **Open** 9.15am-4.30pm Mon-Fri.
Barclays' international Expat Service handles direct debits, international transfer of funds, and so on.

Citibank *1-5 rue Paul Cézanne, 8th (01.70.75.50.00, www.citibank.fr).* M° *St-Philippe-du-Roule.* **Open** 10am-5.30pm Mon-Fri.
Bank clients get good rates for international money transfers, preferential exchange rates and commission-free travellers' cheques.
Travelex *52 av des Champs-Elysées, 8th (01.42.89.80.33, www.travelex.com/fr).* M° *Franklin D. Roosevelt.* **Open** 9am-10.30pm Mon-Sat; 10am-9pm Sun.
Travelex issues travellers' cheques and insurance and also deals with bank transfers.
Western Union Money Transfer *www.westernunion.com.* Many post offices in the city (*see right*) provide Western Union services. Transfers from abroad should arrive within 15 minutes; charges paid by sender.

Tax

French VAT (*taxe sur la valeur ajoutée* or TVA) is arranged in three bands: 2.1 per cent for items of medication and newspapers; 5.5 per cent for food, books, CDs and DVDs; and 19.6 per cent for all other types of goods and services (the TVA for restaurants has been reduced from 19.6 per cent to 5.5 per cent).

NATURAL HAZARDS

Paris has no natural hazards as such, though in recent years the town hall has produced evacuation plans to cover flooding.

OPENING HOURS

Standard opening hours for shops are 9 or 10am to 7 or 8pm Monday to Saturday. Some shops are closed on Monday. Shops and businesses often close at lunchtime, usually 12.30-2pm; many shops close in August. Sunday opening is found in the Marais, on the Champs-Elysées, at Bercy Village and in the Carrousel du Louvre. Most areas have a local grocer that stays open into the night and will often open on Sundays and public holidays too.

24hr florist Elyfleur *82 av de Wagram, 17th (01.84.88.43.59, www.elyfleurs.com).* M° *Wagram.*
24hr garage Shell *6 bd Raspail, 7th (01.45.48.43.12).* M° *Rue du Bac.*
This garage has an extensive array of everyday supermarket products on sale from the Casino chain. No alcohol is sold 10pm-8am.

24hr newsagents include: *33 av des Champs-Elysées, 8th,* M° *Franklin D. Roosevelt. 2 bd Montmartre, 9th,* M° *Grands Boulevards.*
Late-night tabacs Le Brazza *86 bd du Montparnasse, 14th (01.43.35.42.65).* M° *Montparnasse-Bienvenüe.* **Open** 7am-12.30am daily. **La Favorite** *3 bd St-Michel, 5th (no phone).* M° *St-Michel.* **Open** 8am-2am daily.

POLICE

The French equivalent of 999 or 911 is **17 (112** from a mobile), but don't expect a speedy response. That said, the Préfecture de Police has no fewer than 94 outposts in the city. If you're assaulted or robbed, report the incident as soon as possible. You'll need to make a statement (*procès verbal*) at the *point d'accueil* closest to the site of the crime. To find the nearest, call the Préfecture Centrale (01.53.71.53.71) or go to www.prefecturedepolice.interieur. gouv.fr. Stolen goods are unlikely to be recovered, but you'll need a police statement for insurance. *See also p371* **Emergencies**.

POSTAL SERVICES

Post offices (*bureaux de poste*) are open 8am-8pm Mon-Fri; 9am-1pm Sat, apart from the 24-hour post office listed below. Details of all branches are included in the phone book: under 'Administration des PTT' in the *Pages Jaunes*; under 'Poste' in the *Pages Blanches*. Most post offices contain automatic machines (in French and English) that weigh your letter, print out a stamp and give change, saving you from wasting time in an enormous queue. You can also usually buy stamps and sometimes envelopes at a tobacconist (*tabac*). For more information refer to www.laposte.fr.

Main Post Office *52 rue du Louvre, 75001 Paris, 1st (36.31).* M° *Les Halles or Louvre Rivoli.* **Open** 7.30am-6am Mon-Sat; 24hrs daily for poste restante, telephones, stamps, faxes, photocopying and a modest amount of banking operations. This is the best place to arrange to have your mail sent to if you haven't got a fixed address in Paris. Mail should be addressed to you in block capitals, followed by Poste Restante, then the post office's address. There will be a charge of approximately €0.50 for each letter received.

RECYCLING & RUBBISH

The city has a system of colour-coded domestic recycling bins. A yellow-lidded bin can take paper, cardboard cartons, tins and small electrical items; a white-lidded bin takes glass. All other rubbish goes in the green-lidded bins, except for used batteries (shops that sell batteries should accept them), medication (take it back to a pharmacy), toxic products (call 01.43.61.57.36 to have them picked up) or car batteries (take them to an official tip or return to garages exhibiting the '*Relais Verts Auto*' sign). Green, hive-shaped bottle banks can be found on many street corners. More information is available at www.environnement.paris.fr.

RELIGION

Churches and religious centres are listed in the *Pages Jaunes* under 'Eglises' and 'Cultes'. Paris has several English-speaking churches.

American Cathedral *23 av George V, 8th (01.53.23.84.00, www.americancathedral.org).* M° *George V.*
American Church in Paris *65 quai d'Orsay, 7th (01.40.62.05.00, www.acparis. org).* M° *Invalides.*
Emmanuel International Church of Paris *56 rue des Bons Raisins, Rueil-Malmaison (01.47.51.29.63, www.eicparis. org).* RER Reuil-Malmaison, then bus 244.
Kehilat Gesher *10 rue de Pologne, 78100 St-Germain-en-Laye (01.39.21.97.19, www.kehilatgesher.org).* RER St-Germain-en-Laye.
The Liberal English-speaking Jewish community has services in Paris and the western suburbs.
La Mosquée de Paris *2bis pl du Puits de l'Ermite, 5th (01.45.35.97.33, www.mosquee-de-paris.org).* M° *Place Monge.*
St George's Anglican Church *7 rue Auguste-Vacquerie, 16th (01.47.20.22.51, www.stgeorges paris.com).* M° *Charles de Gaulle Etoile.*
St Joseph's Roman Catholic Church *50 av Hoche, 8th (01.42.27.28.56, www.stjoeparis. org).* M° *Charles de Gaulle Etoile.*
St Michael's Church of England *5 rue d'Aguesseau, 8th (01.47.42.70.88, www.saint michaelsparis.org).* M° *Madeleine.*

ESSENTIAL INFORMATION

RENTING A FLAT

Rental apartments are generally cheapest in northern, eastern and south-eastern Paris. You can expect to pay approximately €20 per square metre per month (which works out as, for example, €700 per month for a modest 35sq m apartment). Studios and one bedroom flats fetch the highest prices proportionally; the provision of lifts and cellars will also boost the rent.

Flat-hunting Given the scarcity of housing stock in Paris, it's a landlord's world; you'll need to search actively, or even frenetically, in order to find an apartment. The internet is a decent place to start: www.explorimmo.fr lists rental ads from *Le Figaro* and specialist real estate magazines; you can place a classified ad or check lettings on www.avendrealouer.fr. Thursday morning's *De Particulier à Particulier* (www.pap.fr) is a must for those who want to rent directly from the owner, but be warned– most flats go within hours. Fortnightly *Se Loger* (www.seloger.com) is also worth getting, though most of its ads are placed by agencies.

Landlords keen to let to foreigners advertise in the English-language *FUSAC* (www.fusac.fr); rents tend to be higher than in the French press. There are also assorted free ad brochures that can be picked up from agencies. Private landlords often set a visiting time; prepare to meet hordes of other flat-seekers and have your documents and cheque book to hand.

There's also the option of flat-sharing – one that's been growing in popularity in recent years. To look for housemates, pick up a copy of *FUSAC* or browse the 3,000-odd weekly announcements found at www.colocation.fr, which also organises monthly soirée Le Jeudi de la Colocation, a chance to meet potential flatmates in the flesh.

Rental laws The minimum lease (*bail de location*) on an unfurnished flat is three years (though the tenant can give notice and leave before this period is up); furnished flats are generally let on one-year leases. During this period the landlord can raise the rent only by the official construction inflation index. At the end of the lease, the rent can be adjusted, but tenants can object before a rent board. Tenants can be evicted for non-payment, or if the landlord wishes to sell the

property or use it as his own residence. It is illegal to throw people out in winter.

Landlords will probably insist you present a dossier with pay slips (*fiches de paie/bulletins de salaire*) showing income equivalent to three to four times the monthly rent, and for foreigners in particular, provide a financial guarantor (someone who will sign a document promising to pay the rent if you abscond). When taking out a lease, payments usually include the first month's rent, a deposit (*caution*) of the equivalent of two months' rent, and an agency fee, if applicable.

It's customary to have an inspection of the premises (*état des lieux*) at the start and end of the rental, the cost of which (around €150) is shared by landlord and tenant. Landlords may try to rent their flats *non-declaré* – without a written lease – and get rent in cash. This can make it difficult for tenants to establish their rights – which is one reason why landlords do it.

Centre d'information et de défense des locataires *9 rue Severo, 14th. M° Pernety.* **Open** *by appointment* 10am-12.30pm, 2.30-3.30pm Mon-Thur. Helps sort out problems with landlords, rent hikes, etc.

SAFETY & SECURITY

Beware of pickpockets, especially around the city's crowded tourist hotspots and métro stations. *See also p366* **Métro & RER** and *p375* **Police**.

SHIPPING SERVICES

Hedley's Humpers *6 bd de la Libération, 93284 St-Denis (01.48.13.01.02, www.hedleys humpers.com). M° Carrefour Pleyel.* **Open** 9am-1pm, 2-6pm Mon-Fri. Closed 2wks Aug. Specialist in transport of furniture and antiques. **In UK:** 3 St Leonards Road, London NW10 6SX (020 8965 8733). **In USA:** 271 Scholes Street, Brooklyn, New York NY 11101 (1-718 433 4005).

SMOKING

Although smoking seems to be an essential part of French life (and death), the French state and public health groups have recently waged war against the cigarette on several fronts. Smoking is now banned in all enclosed public spaces, including bars, cafés, clubs, restaurants, hotel

foyers and shops, as well as on public transport. Many bars, cafés and clubs offer smoking gardens or terraces. There are also increasingly strident anti-smoking campaigns in France. Prices have soared.

For information about stopping smoking, contact the Tabac Info Service (39.89, www.tabac-info-service.fr). If you're a dedicated smoker, you'll soon learn that most *tabacs* close at 8pm (for a few that don't, *see p375* **Opening hours**). Some bars sell cigarettes behind the counter, generally only to customers who have a drink.

STUDY

Language

Most of the large multinational language schools, such as **Berlitz** (01.40.74.00.17, www.berlitz.com), have at least one branch in Paris.

Alliance Française *101 bd Raspail, 6th (01.42.84.90.00, www.alliancefr.org). M° St-Placide.* The Alliance Française is a non-profit French-language school. Beginner and specialist courses start every month.
Institut Catholique de Paris *21 rue d'Assas, 6th (01.44.39.52.68, www.icp.fr/ilcf). M° St-Sulpice.* Courses in French culture and language. You must hold a *baccalauréat*-level qualification and be 18 or over (but you don't have to be Catholic).
La Sorbonne – Cours de Langue et Civilisation *47 rue des Ecoles, 5th (01.44.10.77.00, www.ccfs-sorbonne.fr). M° Cluny-La Sorbonne/RER Luxembourg.* Classes for foreigners ride on the name of this eminent institution. Teaching is grammar-based.
University of London Institute in Paris *9-11 rue Constantine, 7th (01.44.11.73.83, www.ulip.lon.ac.uk). M° Invalides.* Linked to the University of London, this 4,000-student institute offers English courses for Parisians, and French courses at university level.

Specialised

Many of the prestigious Ecoles Nationales Supérieures (including film schools La FEMIS and ENS Louis Lumière) offer summer courses in addition to their full-time degree courses – ask for *formation continue*.

Adult education courses *www.paris.fr or your local mairie.*

A huge range of inexpensive adult education classes is run by the city of Paris, including French as a foreign language, computer skills and applied arts.

American University of Paris
6 rue du Colonel Combes, 7th (01.40.62.07.20, www.aup.edu). M° Ecole-Militaire/RER Pont de l'Alma.
International college awarding four-year American liberal arts degrees (BA/BSc).

Cordon Bleu *8 rue Léon-Delhomme, 15th (01.53.68.22.50, www.cordon bleu.edu). M° Vaugirard.*
Courses range from three-hour sessions on classical and regional cuisine to a nine-month diploma for those starting a culinary career.

Ecole du Louvre *Palais du Louvre, porte Jaujard, place du Carrousel, 1st (01.55.35.18.00, www.ecoledulouvre.fr). M° Palais Royal Musée du Louvre.*
Art history and archaeology courses. Foreign students not wanting to take a degree can attend lectures.

INSEAD *bd de Constance, 77305 Fontainebleau (01.60.72.40.00, www.insead.edu).*
Highly regarded international business school offering a ten-month MBA course in English as well as PhDs in a range of business subjects.

Parsons School of Design *14 rue Letellier, 15th (01.45.77.39.66, www.parsons-paris.com). M° La Motte-Picquet-Grenelle.*
Subsidiary of the New York art college offering BFA programmes in fine art, photography, fashion, marketing and interior design.

Ritz-Escoffier Ecole de Gastronomie Française *38 rue Cambon, 1st (01.43.16.30.50, www.ritzparis.com). M° Madeleine.*
Everything from afternoon demonstrations in the Ritz kitchens to diplomas. Courses in French with English translation.

TELEPHONES

Mobile phones

A subscription (*abonnement*) will normally get you a free phone if you sign up for at least one year. Two hours' calling time a month costs about €35 per month. International calls are normally charged extra – a lot extra.

Remember that using your UK mobile phone in France can cost considerably more than at home, especially if you use data roaming.

The three companies that rule the mobile phone market in France are:

Bouygues Télécom *10.64, www.bouyguestelecom.fr.*
France Télécom/Orange *39.70, www.orange.fr.*
SFR *10.23, www.sfr.fr.*

Dialling & codes

All French phone numbers have ten digits. Paris and Ile-de-France numbers begin with 01; the rest of France is divided into four zones (02-05). Mobile phone numbers start with 06. 08 indicates a special rate; numbers beginning with 08 can only be reached from inside France. If you are calling France from abroad, leave off the 0 at the start of the ten-digit number. The country code is 33. To call abroad from France dial 00, then the country code, then the number.

Operator services

Operator assistance, French directory enquiries
(*renseignements*) *12*. To make a reverse-charge call within France, ask to make a call *en PCV*.
Airparif *01.44.59.47.64, www.airparif.asso.fr.*
Information about pollution levels and air quality in Paris and Ile-de-France: invaluable for asthmatics.
International directory enquiries *32.12*, then country code. €3 per call.
International news (France Inter recorded message, in French), *08.92.68.10.33* (€0.34 per min).
Telegram *all languages, international 08.00.33.44.11; within France 36.55.*
Telephone engineer *10.13.*
Time *36.99.*
Traffic news *08.26.02.20.22.*
Weather *08.99.70.12.34* (€1.39 then €0.34 per min) for enquiries on weather in France and abroad, in French or English; you can also dial *08.92.68.02.75* (€0.34 per min) for a recorded weather announcement for Paris and the region.

Public phones

Most public phones in Paris, almost all of which are maintained by France Télécom, use *télécartes* (phonecards), which are sold at post offices, *tabacs*, airports and train and métro stations. For cheap international calls, you can also buy a *télécarte à puce* (card with a microchip) or a *télécarte pré-payée*, which features a numerical code you dial before making a call; these can be used on domestic phones too. Travelex's International Telephone

Card can be used in more than 80 countries (available from **Travelex** agencies, *see p375*). Cafés have coin phones, while post offices usually have card phones. In a phone box, the display screen will read '*Décrochez*'. Pick up the phone. When '*Introduisez votre carte*' appears, put your card into the slot; the screen should read '*Patientez SVP*'. '*Numérotez*' is your signal to dial. '*Crédit épuisé*' means you have no more units left. Hang up ('*Raccrochez*') – and don't forget your card. Some public phones take credit cards. If you're using a credit card, insert the card, enter your PIN number and '*Patientez SVP*' will appear.

Telephone directories

Telephone books can be found in all post offices and most cafés. The *Pages Blanches* (White Pages) list people and businesses alphabetically; the *Pages Jaunes* (Yellow Pages) list businesses and services by category order. Online versions can be found at www.pagesjaunes.fr.

Telephone charges

All local calls in Paris and Ile-de-France (to numbers beginning with 01) cost €0.11 for three minutes, standard rate and €0.04/min thereafter. This applies only to calls to other landlines. Calls beyond a 100km radius (*province*) are charged at €0.11 for the first 39 seconds, then €0.24 per minute.

International destinations are divided into 16 zones. Reduced-rate periods for calls within France and Europe are 7pm-8am during the week and all day Saturday and Sunday. Reduced-rate periods for the US and Canada are 7pm to 1pm Monday to Friday and all day Saturday and Sunday.

Cheap providers

Getting wise to the market demand, the smaller telephone providers are becoming increasingly popular, as rates from France Télécom are not exactly at bargain-basement levels. The following can offer alternative rates – although you will still need to rent your telephone line from France Télécom:

AT&T Direct (local access) *08.00.99.00.11.*
Free *10.44, www.free.fr.*
With the Freebox (Free's modem for ADSL connection), €29.99 per month

ESSENTIAL INFORMATION

ESSENTIAL INFORMATION

gets you ten hours of free calls to landlines (additional calls cost €0.01 per minute), €0.19 per minute to mobiles and €0.03 per minute for most international calls.
IC Télécom *08.05.13.26.26, www.ictelecom.fr.*
Onetel *08.92.13.50.50, www.onetel.fr.*

Special-rate numbers

0800 Numéro Vert
Freephone.
0810 Numéro Azur
€0.11 under three minutes, then €0.04/min.
0820 Numéro Indigo
€0.118/min.
0825 Numéro Indigo II
€0.15/min.
0836.64/0890.64/0890.70
€0.112/min.
0890.71 €0.15/min.
0891.67/0891.70 €0.225/min.
0836/0892 €0.337/min. This line is for the likes of ticket agencies, cinema and transport information.
10.14 France Télécom information; free (except from mobile phones).

TIME

France is one hour ahead of Greenwich Mean Time (GMT). France uses the 24hr system (for example, 18h means 6pm).

TIPPING

A service charge of ten to 15 per cent is legally included in your bill at all restaurants, cafés and bars. However, it is polite either to round up the final amount for drinks, or to leave a cash tip of €1-€2 or more for a meal, depending on the restaurant and, of course, the quality of the service.

TOILETS

The city's automatic street toilets are not really as terrifying as they first appear. Each loo is completely washed down and disinfected after use.

If a space age-style lavatory experience doesn't appeal, you can nip into the toilets of a café; although theoretically reserved for customers' use, a polite request should win sympathy with the waiter – and you may find you have to put a €0.20 coin into a slot in the door-handle mechanism, customer or not. Fast-food chain toilets often have a code on their toilet doors that is made known to paying customers only.

TOURIST INFORMATION

Office de Tourisme et des Congrès de Paris *25 rue des Pyramides, 1st (08.92.68.30.00 recorded information available in English & French, www.paris info.com). Mº Pyramides.* **Open** *Summer* 9am-7pm daily. *Winter* 10am-7pm daily.
Information on Paris and the suburbs, shop, bureau de change, hotel reservations, phonecards, museum cards, travel passes and tickets. Multilingual staff.
Other locations: *Gare de Lyon* 20 bd Diderot, 12th. Mº Gare de Lyon. **Open** 8am-6pm Mon-Sat. *Gare du Nord* 18 rue de Dunkerque, 10th. Mº Gare du Nord. **Open** 8am-6pm daily. *Anvers* 72 bd Rochechouart, 18th. Mº Anvers. **Open** 10am-6pm daily. *Porte de Versailles* 1 pl de la Porte de Versailles, 15th. **Open** 11am-7pm during trade fairs.

VISAS & IMMIGRATION

EU nationals don't need a visa to enter France, nor do US, Canadian, Australian, New Zealand or South African citizens for stays of up to three months. Nationals of other countries should enquire at the nearest French embassy or consulate before leaving home. If they are travelling to France from one of the countries in the Schengen agreement (most of the EU, but not Britain or Ireland), the visa from that country should be sufficient.

EU citizens may stay in France for as long as their passport is valid. Non-EU citizens who wish to stay for longer than three months must apply to the French embassy or consulate in their own country for a long-term visa. For more information, contact:

CIRA (Centre Interministeriel de Renseignements Administratifs) *39.39, www.service-public.fr.* **Open** 8am-7pm Mon-Fri; 8am-noon Sat. CIRA gives advice on most French administrative procedures via its local-rate phone line.
Préfecture de Police de Paris Service Etrangers *7-9 bd du Palais, 4th (01.53.73.53.73, www.prefecturedepolice.interieur. gouv.fr). Mº Cité.* **Open** 9am-4pm Mon-Fri.
This office can provide information on residency, along with work permits for foreigners.

WEIGHTS & MEASURES

France uses only the metric system; remember that all speed limits are in kilometres per hour. One kilometre is equivalent to 0.62 miles (1 mile = 1.6km). Petrol, like other liquids, is measured in litres (one UK gallon = 4.54 litres; 1 US gallon = 3.79 litres).

WHAT TO TAKE

Binoculars for studying high-altitude details of monuments, a pocket knife with corkscrew (for improvised picnics) and – vital for getting around the city on foot – comfortable shoes.

WHEN TO GO

In July and August, during the long school holidays, there are often great deals to be had on hotels and a good range of free events laid on by the city (such as Paris-Plages), but many family-run restaurants and shops close as the locals go off *en vacances*. Avoid October, with its fashion weeks and trade shows.

WOMEN

Although Paris is not an especially threatening city for women, the precautions you would take in any major metropolis apply here: be careful at night in certain areas, including Pigalle, the rue St-Denis, Stalingrad, La Chapelle, Château Rouge, Gare de l'Est, Gare du Nord, the Bois de Boulogne and Bois de Vincennes. If you receive unwanted attention, a politely scathing *N'insistez pas!* (Don't push it!) will make your feelings abundantly clear. If things get too heavy, go into the nearest shop or café.

CIDFF (Centre d'Information sur les Droits des Femmes et des Familles) *17 rue Jean Poulmarch, 10th (01.83.64.72.01, www.info femmes.com). Mº Porte de Pantin.* **Open** 10am-12.30pm, 1.30-5.30pm Mon-Thur; 10am-12.30pm Fri.
The CIDFF offers plenty of health, legal and professional advice for women.
Violence Conjugale: Femmes Info Service *39.19.* **Open** 10am-7pm Mon-Fri.
A hotline for the victims of domestic violence, directing them to medical aid, shelters and other services.
Viols Femmes Informations *08.00.05.95.95.* **Open** 10am-7pm Mon-Fri. Freephone service.
Help and advice available, in French, to rape victims.

Vocabulary

In French, the second person singular (you) has two forms. Phrases here are given in the more polite *vous* form. The *tu* form is used with family, friends, children and pets; you should be careful not to use it with people you do not know sufficiently well. Courtesies such as *monsieur*, *madame* and *mademoiselle* are used more than their English equivalents.

For food terms, *see p380*.

GENERAL

Good morning/afternoon, hello bonjour; **good evening** bonsoir; **goodbye** au revoir; **OK** d'accord; **yes** oui; **no** non; **how are you?** comment allez vous?/vous allez bien?; **how's it going?** comment ça va?/ça va? (familiar)

Sir/Mr monsieur (M.); **madam/Mrs** madame (Mme); **miss** mademoiselle (Mlle); **please** s'il vous plaît; **thank you** merci; **sorry** pardon; **excuse me** excusez-moi; **I am going to pay** je vais payer

Do you speak English? parlez-vous anglais?; **I don't speak French** je ne parle pas français; **I don't understand** je ne comprends pas; **speak more slowly, please** parlez plus lentement, s'il vous plaît

It is c'est; **it isn't** ce n'est pas; **good** bon/bonne; **bad** mauvais/mauvaise; **small** petit/petite; **big** grand/grande; **beautiful** beau/belle; **well** bien; **badly** mal; **a bit** un peu; **a lot** beaucoup; **very** très

With avec; **without** sans; **and** et; **or** ou; **because** parce que; **who?** qui?; **when?** quand?; **what?** quoi?; **which?** quel?; **where?** où?; **why?** pourquoi?; **how?** comment?; **at what time/when?** à quelle heure?

Forbidden interdit/défendu; **out of order** hors service (HS)/en panne; **daily** tous les jours (tlj)

ON THE PHONE

Hello allô; **who's calling?** c'est de la part de qui?/qui est à l'appareil?; **this is… speaking** c'est… à l'appareil; **I'd like to speak to…**

j'aurais voulu parler à…; **hold the line** ne quittez pas; **please call back later** rappelez plus tard s'il vous plaît; **you must have the wrong number** vous avez dû composer un mauvais numéro

GETTING AROUND

Where is the (nearest) métro? où est le métro (le plus proche)?; **when is the next train for…?** c'est quand le prochain train pour… ?; **ticket** un billet; **station** la gare; **platform** le quai; **entrance** entrée; **exit** sortie; **left** gauche; **right** droite; **straight on** tout droit; **far** loin; **near** pas loin/près d'ici

SIGHTSEEING

Museum un musée; **church** une église; **exhibition** une exposition; **ticket** (*museum*) un billet; (*theatre, concert*) une place; **open** ouvert; **closed** fermé; **free** gratuit; **reduced price** un tarif réduit

ACCOMMODATION

Do you have a room (for this evening/for two people)? avez-vous une chambre (pour ce soir/pour deux personnes)?; **full** complet; **room** une chambre; **bed** un lit; **double bed** un grand lit; **(a room with) twin beds** (une chambre à) deux lits; **with bath(room)/shower** avec (salle de) bain/douche; **breakfast** le petit déjeuner; **included** compris

EATING OUT

I'd like to book a table (for three/at 8pm) je voudrais réserver une table (pour trois personnes/à vingt heures); **lunch** le déjeuner; **dinner** le dîner; **coffee** (espresso) un café; **tea** un thé; **wine** le vin; **beer** une bière; **mineral water** eau minérale; **tap water** une carafe d'eau; **the bill, please** l'addition, s'il vous plaît

SHOPPING

Cheap pas cher; **expensive** cher; **how much?/how many?** combien?; **have you got change?** avez-vous de la monnaie?; **I'll take**

it je le prends; **I would like…** je voudrais…; **may I try this on?** est-ce que je pourrais essayer cet article?; **do you have a smaller/larger size?** auriez-vous la taille en-dessous/au dessus?; **I'm a size 38** je fais du 38

STAYING ALIVE

Be cool restez calme; **I don't want any trouble** je ne veux pas d'ennuis; **I only do safe sex** je ne pratique que le safe sex

NUMBERS

0 zéro; 1 un, une; 2 deux; 3 trois; 4 quatre; 5 cinq; 6 six; 7 sept; 8 huit; 9 neuf; 10 dix; 11 onze; 12 douze; 13 treize; 14 quatorze; 15 quinze; 16 seize; 17 dix-sept; 18 dix-huit; 19 dix-neuf; 20 vingt; 21 vingt-et-un; 22 vingt-deux

30 trente; 40 quarante; 50 cinquante; 60 soixante; 70 soixante-dix; 80 quatre-vingts; 90 quatre-vingt-dix; 100 cent

1,000 mille; 10,000 dix mille; 1,000,000 un million

DAYS, MONTHS & SEASONS

Monday lundi
Tuesday mardi
Wednesday mercredi
Thursday jeudi
Friday vendredi
Saturday samedi
Sunday dimanche

January janvier
February février
March mars
April avril
May mai
June juin
July juillet
August août
September septembre
October octobre
November novembre
December décembre

Spring le printemps
Summer l'été
Autumn l'automne
Winter l'hiver

ESSENTIAL INFORMATION

EATING OUT

Except for the very simplest restaurants, it's wise to book ahead. This can usually be done on the same day as your intended visit, although really top-notch establishments require bookings weeks or months in advance and confirmation the day before. Many venues close for their annual break in August, and some also close at Christmas. All bills include a service charge, but an additional tip of a few euros (for the whole table) is polite unless you're unhappy with the service.

Meals (repas)

petit déjeuner breakfast. **déjeuner** lunch. **dîner** dinner. **souper** late dinner, supper.

Preparation (la préparation)

en croûte in a pastry case. **farci** stuffed. **au four** baked. **flambé** flamed in alcohol. **forestière** with mushrooms. **fricassé** fried and simmered in stock, usually with creamy sauce. **fumé** smoked. **garni** garnished. **glacé** frozen or iced. **gratiné** topped with breadcrumbs or cheese and grilled. **à la grècque** vegetables served cold in the cooking liquid with oil and lemon juice. **grillé** grilled. **haché** minced. **julienne** (vegetables) cut into matchsticks. **lamelle** very thin slice. **mariné** marinated. **pané** breaded. **en papillote** cooked in a packet. **parmentier** with potato. **pressé** squeezed. **râpé** grated. **salé** salted.

Cooking type (la cuisson)

cru raw. **bleu** practically raw. **saignant** rare. **rosé** (of lamb, duck, liver, kidneys) pink. **à point** medium rare. **bien cuit** well done.

Basics (essentiels)

ballotine stuffed, rolled-up piece of meat or fish. **crème fraîche** thick, slightly soured cream. **épices** spices. **feuilleté** 'leaves' of (puff) pastry. **fromage** cheese. **fruits de mer** shellfish. **galette** round flat cake of flaky pastry, potato pancake or buckwheat savoury crêpe. **gelée** aspic. **gibier** game. **gras** fat. **légume** vegetable. **maison** of the house. **marmite** small cooking pot. **miel** honey. **noisette** hazelnut; small, round portion of meat. **noix** walnut. **noix de coco** coconut. **nouilles** noodles. **oeuf** egg; – **en cocotte** baked egg; – **en meurette** egg poached in red wine; – **à la neige** see *île flottante*. **parfait** sweet or savoury mousse-like mixture. **paupiette** slice of meat or fish, stuffed and rolled. **timbale** dome-shaped mould, or food cooked in one. **tisane** herbal tea. **tourte** covered pie or tart, usually savoury.

Meat (viande)

agneau lamb. **aloyau** beef loin. **andouillette** sausage made from pig's offal. **bavette** beef flank steak. **biche** venison. **bifteck** steak. **boudin noir/blanc** black (blood)/white pudding. **boeuf** beef; – **bourguignon** beef cooked Burgundy style, with red wine,

onions and mushrooms; – **gros sel** boiled beef with vegetables. **carbonnade** beef stew with onions and stout or beer. **carré d'agneau** rack of lamb. **cassoulet** stew of white haricot beans, sausage and preserved duck. **cervelle** brains. **châteaubriand** thick fillet steak. **chevreuil** young roe deer. **civet** game stew. **cochon de lait** suckling pig. **contre-filet** sirloin steak. **côte** chop; – **de boeuf** beef rib. **croque-madame** sandwich of toasted cheese and ham topped with an egg. **croque-monsieur** sandwich of toasted cheese and ham. **cuisses de grenouille** frogs' legs. **daube** meat braised in red wine. **entrecôte** beef rib steak. **escargot** snail. **estouffade** meat that's been marinated, fried and braised. **faux-filet** sirloin steak. **filet mignon** tenderloin. **foie** liver; – **de veau** calf's liver. **gigot d'agneau** leg of lamb. **hachis parmentier** shepherd's pie. **jambon** ham; – **cru** cured raw ham. **jarret** ham shin or knuckle. **langue** tongue. **lapin** rabbit. **lard** bacon. **lardon** small cube of bacon. **lièvre** hare. **marcassin** wild boar. **merguez** spicy lamb/beef sausage. **mignon** small meat fillet. **moelle** bone marrow; **os à la** – marrowbone. **navarin** lamb and vegetable stew. **onglet** cut of beef, similar to *bavette*. **pavé** thick steak. **petit salé** salt pork. **pied** foot (trotter). **porc** pork. **porcelet** suckling pig. **pot-au-feu** boiled beef with vegetables. **queue de boeuf** oxtail. **ragoût** meat stew. **rillettes** potted pork or tuna.

ris de veau veal sweetbreads.
rognons kidneys. **rôti** roast.
sang blood. **sanglier** wild boar.
saucisse sausage. **saucisson
sec** small dried sausage. **selle**
(*d'agneau*) saddle (of lamb). **souris
d'agneau** lamb knuckle. **tagine**
slow-cooked North African stew.
tartare raw minced steak (also tuna
or salmon). **tournedos** small slices
of beef fillet, sautéed or grilled.
travers de porc pork spare ribs.
veau veal.

Poultry (volaille)

aiguillettes (*de canard*) thin slices
(of duck breast). **blanc** breast. **caille**
quail. **canard** duck; **confit de –**
preserved duck. **coquelet** baby
rooster. **dinde** turkey. **faisan**
pheasant. **foie gras** fattened goose
or duck liver. **gésiers** gizzards.
magret duck breast. **oie** goose.
perdrix partridge. **poulet** chicken.
suprême (*de poulet*) fillets (of
chicken) in a cream sauce.

Fish & seafood (poissons & fruits de mer)

anguille eel. **bar** sea bass. **belon**
smooth, flat oyster. **bisque** shellfish
soup. **bouillabaisse** Mediterranean
fish soup. **brochet** pike. **bulot**
whelk. **cabillaud** fresh cod.
carrelet plaice. **colin** hake.
coquille shell. **coquilles St-
Jacques** scallops. **crevettes**
prawns (UK), shrimp (US). **crustacé**
shellfish. **daurade** sea bream.
eglefin haddock. **escabèche**
sautéed and marinated fish, served
cold. **espadon** swordfish. **fines
de claire** crinkle-shelled oysters.
flétan halibut. **hareng** herring.
homard lobster. **huître** oyster.
langoustine Dublin Bay prawns,
scampi. **limande** lemon sole.

lotte monkfish. **maquereau**
mackerel. **merlan** whiting. **merlu**
hake. **meunière** fish floured and
sautéed in butter. **moules** mussels;
– à la marinière cooked with
white wine and shallots. **morue**
dried, salted cod; **brandade de –**
cod puréed with potato. **oursin**
sea urchin. **palourde** type of
clam. **poulpe** octopus. **raie** skate.
rascasse scorpion fish. **rouget**
red mullet. **St-Pierre** John Dory.
sandre pike-perch. **saumon**
salmon. **seiche** squid. **truite** trout.

Vegetables (légumes)

aligot mashed potatoes with melted
cheese and garlic. **asperge**
asparagus. **céleri** celery. **céleri
rave** celeriac. **cèpe** cep mushroom.
champignon mushroom; **– de Paris**
button mushroom. **chanterelle**
small, trumpet-like mushroom.
choucroute sauerkraut; **– garnie**
with cured ham and sausages.
ciboulette chive. **citronelle**
lemongrass. **coco** large white bean.
cresson watercress. **échalote**
shallot. **endive** chicory (UK), Belgian
endive (US). **épinards** spinach.
frisée curly endive. **frites** chips
(UK), fries (US). **gingembre** ginger.
girolle small, trumpet-like
mushroom. **gratin dauphinois**
sliced potatoes baked with milk,
cheese and garlic. **haricot** bean;
– vert green bean. **mâche** lamb's
lettuce. **morille** morel mushroom.
navet turnip. **oignon** onion. **oseille**
sorrel. **persil** parsley. **pignon** pine
nut. **poivre** pepper. **poivron** red or
green (bell) pepper. **pomme de terre**
potato. **pommes lyonnaises**

potatoes fried with onions. **riz** rice.
truffes truffles.

Fruit (fruits)

ananas pineapple. **cassis** black-
currants. **citron** lemon; **– vert** lime.
fraise strawberry. **framboise**
raspberry. **groseille** redcurrant; **– à
maquereau** gooseberry. **myrtille**
blueberry. **pamplemousse**
grapefruit. **pomme** apple.
prune plum. **pruneau** prune.
quetsche damson.

Desserts & cheese (desserts & fromage)

bavarois moulded cream dessert.
beignet fritter or doughnut. **chèvre**
goat; goat's cheese. **clafoutis** baked
batter filled with fruit. **crème
brûlée** creamy custard dessert
with caramel glaze. **crème
chantilly** sweetened whipped
cream. **fromage blanc** smooth
cream cheese. **glace** ice-cream.
île flottante whipped egg white
floating in vanilla custard. **réglisse**
liquorice. **tarte aux pommes** apple
tart. **tarte tatin** warm, caramelised
apple tart cooked upside down.

Soups & sauces (soupes & sauces)

aïoli garlic mayonnaise. **anchoïade**
spicy anchovy and olive paste. **béarnaise** sauce of butter and egg
yolk. **blanquette** 'white' stew made
with eggs and cream. **potage** soup.
velouté stock-based white sauce;
creamy soup. **vichyssoise** cold leek
and potato soup.

Further Reference

BOOKS

Non-fiction

Robert Baldick *The Siege of Paris* A gripping account of the Paris Commune of 1871.
Antony Beevor & Artemis Cooper *Paris after the Liberation* Rationing, freedom, Existentialism.
NT Binh *Paris au cinéma* Attractively illustrated hardback round-up of Paris sights on film.
Henri Cartier-Bresson *A propos de Paris* Classic black-and-white shots by a giant among snappers.
Vincent Cronin *Napoleon* A fine biography of the emperor.
Léon-Paul Fargue *Le Piéton de Paris* The city anatomised, just before World War II.
Jean-Marie Gourio *Brèves de comptoir* An anthology of wisdom and weirdness overheard at café counters. A French classic.
Alastair Horne *The Fall of Paris* Detailed chronicle of the Siege and Commune 1870-71.
J-K Huysmans *Croquis Parisiens* The world that Toulouse-Lautrec painted.
Ian Littlewood *Paris: Architecture, History, Art* Paris's history and its treasures.
Henri Michel *Paris Allemand*; *Paris Résistant* Detailed, two-volume account of life in Paris during the Occupation.
Noel Riley Fitch *Literary Cafés of Paris* Who drank what, where.
Virginia Rounding *Les Grandes Horizontales* Entertaining lives of four 19th-century courtesans.
Simon Schama *Citizens* Epic, readable account of the Revolution.
Thibaut Vandorselaer *Paris BD* A lovely series of walking trails around the city, illustrated entirely with 'BD' (cartoon) panels.

Fiction & poetry

Honoré de Balzac *Illusions perdues*; *La Peau de chagrin*; *Le Père Goriot*; *Splendeurs et misères des courtisanes* Much of the 'Comédie Humaine' cycle of novels is set in Paris.
Charles Baudelaire *Le Spleen de Paris* Prose poems, Paris settings.
Louis-Ferdinand Céline *Mort à crédit* Vivid, splenetic account of an impoverished Paris childhood.

Victor Hugo *Notre Dame de Paris* Romantic vision of medieval Paris. Quasimodo! Esmeralda! The bells!
W Somerset Maugham *Christmas Holiday* Young, middle-class Brit spends Christmas with a prostitute in Paris.
Gérard de Nerval *Les Nuits d'octobre* Late-night Les Halles and environs, mid 19th century.
Georges Perec *La Vie, mode d'emploi* Cheek-by-jowl life in a Haussmannian apartment building.
Raymond Queneau *Zazie dans le Métro* Paris in the 1950s: bright and very *nouvelle vague*.
Nicolas Restif de la Bretonne *Les Nuits de Paris* The sexual underworld of Louis XV's Paris.
Georges Simenon *Rue Pigalle*; *Maigret et les braves gens*, etc. Many of the famous Maigret books are set in Paris.
Emile Zola *L'Assommoir*; *Nana*; *Le Ventre de Paris* Accounts of the underside of the Second Empire from the master Realist.

The ex-pat angle

Janet Flanner *Paris Journal* Three volumes of reports on post-war Paris arts and politics, written for the *New Yorker*.
Henry Miller *Tropic of Cancer* Love and low life: lusty and funny.
George Orwell *Down and Out in Paris and London* Work in a Paris restaurant, hunger in a Paris hovel, suffering in a Paris hospital.

FILM

Luc Besson *Subway* Christophe Lambert goes underground.
Marcel Carné *Hôtel du Nord* Arletty stars in this poetic slice of life by the Canal St-Martin.
René Clair *Paris qui dort* Clair's surrealist silent comedy is one of the best Paris films ever made.
Louis Feuillade *Fantômas* Supervillain Fantômas repeatedly outwits Paris law enforcers in Feuillade's masterful silent serials.
Jean-Luc Godard *A Bout de Souffle* Belmondo, Seberg, Godard, the Champs-Elysées, the attitude, the famous ending. Essential.
Michel Hazanavicius *The Artist* Silent black-and-white blockbuster that won five Oscars, including best actor for Jean Dujardin.

Abdellatif Kechiche *La Vie d'Adèle* An explicit portrait of two young women falling in love, picked up the Palme d'Or and controversy galore in 2013.
Edouard Molinaro *Un Témoin dans la ville* Lino Ventura on the run in 1950s Paris. Superb *noir*.
François Truffaut *Les 400 Coups* The first of the Antoine Doinel cycle.
Agnès Varda *Cléo de 5 à 7* The *nouvelle vague* heroine spends an anxious afternoon in the city.

MUSIC

Miles Davis *Ascenseur pour l'échafaud* The soundtrack to Louis Malle's film is superb after-dark jazz.
Baptiste Trotignon *Song Song Song* Jazz-chanson from this supremely talented pianist.
Fréhel *1930-1939* The immortal Fréhel sings of love, drugs and debauchery in true *chanson réaliste* style.
Naive New Beaters *Wallace* Great pop from a hot Paris band.
Sebastien Tellier *My God is Blue* Transgressive electro pop.
Serge Gainsbourg *Le Poinçonneur des Lilas* Classic early Gainsbourg.

WEBSITES

www.parisinfo.com Official site of the Office de Tourisme.
www.ratp.fr Everything you'll need to know about using the buses, métro, RER and trams.
www.timeout.fr Your critical guide to arts, culture and going out in Paris (English and French).
www.velib.paris.fr All you need to know about using Velib'.

IPHONE APPS

Time Out (free) The ultimate guide to the capital's culture at your fingertips.
Patrimap (free) Pinpoints nearby monuments along with potted descriptions, and also features a series of itineraries.
RATP (free) Access a wide range of Paris transport maps.
Vélib' (free) Tells you where bikes are available around the city.
Louvre (free) All you need to know before you visit the Louvre.

Index

INDEX

INDEX

Bags packed, milk cancelled, house raised on stilts.

You've packed the suntan lotion, the snorkel set, the stay-pressed shirts. Just one more thing left to do – your bit for climate change. In some of the world's poorest countries, changing weather patterns are destroying lives.

You can help people to deal with the extreme effects of climate change. Raising houses in flood-prone regions is just one life-saving solution.

Climate change costs lives.
Give £5 and let's sort it *Here & Now*

www.oxfam.org.uk/climate-change

Oxfam is a registered charity in England and Wales (No.202918) and Scotland (SCO039042). Oxfam GB is a member of Oxfam International.

Be Humankind (X) Oxfam

Advertisers' Index

Please refer to the relevant pages for contact details.

ADVERTISERS' INDEX

Maps

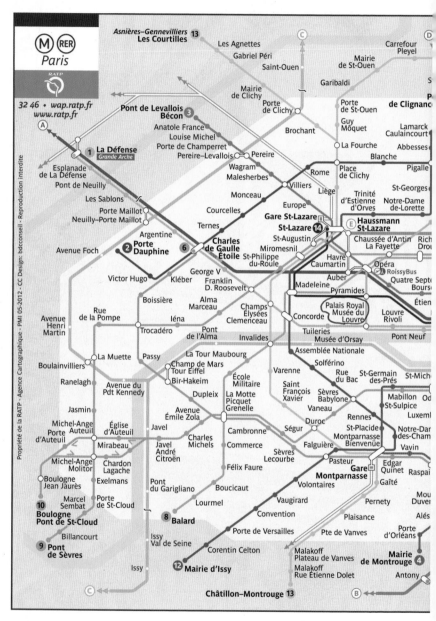

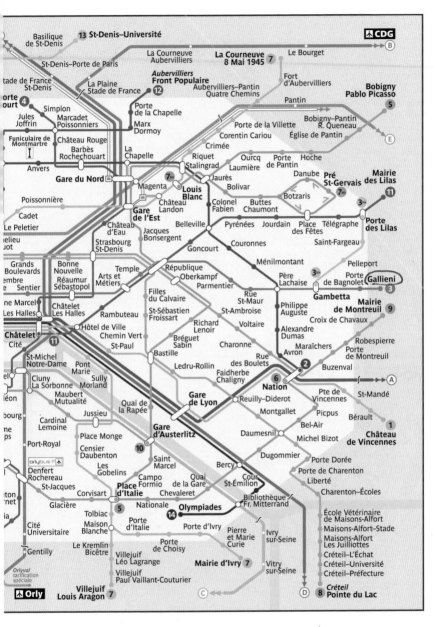

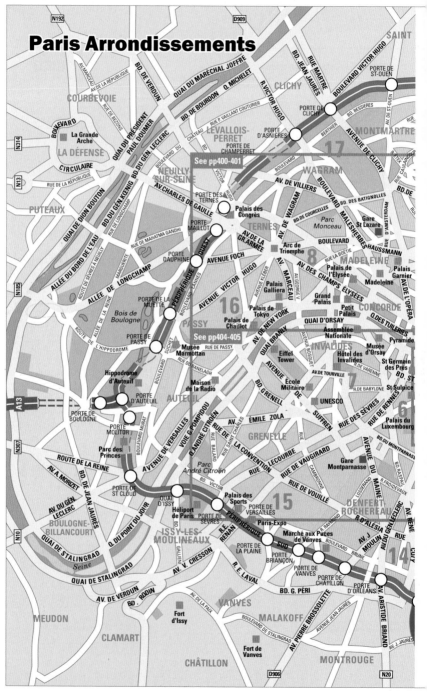

Paris Arrondissements

MAPS

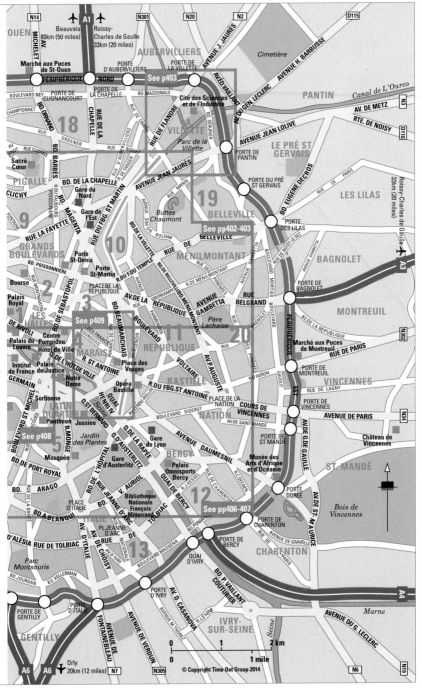

© Copyright Time Out Group 2014

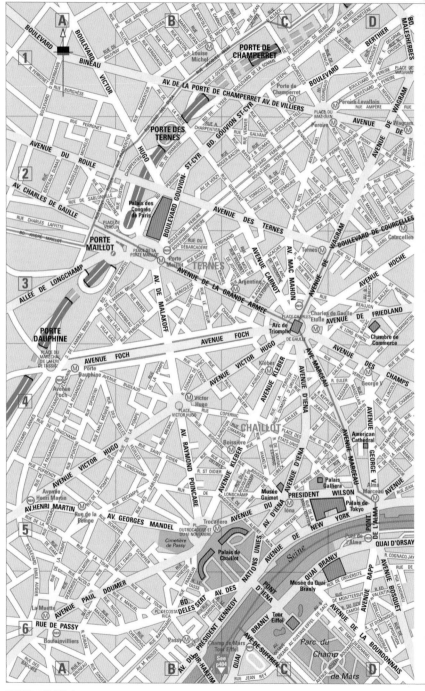

MAPS

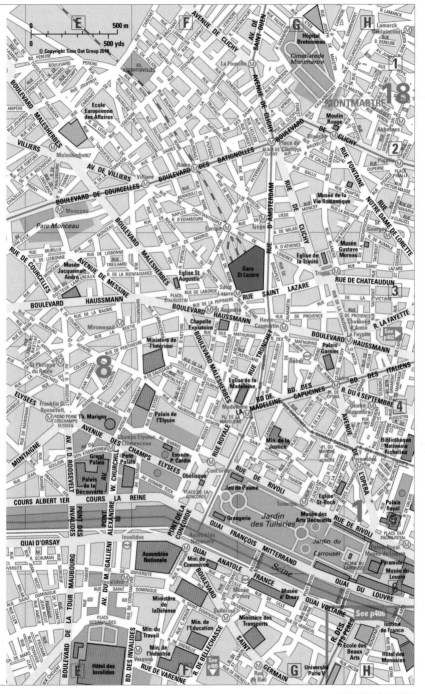

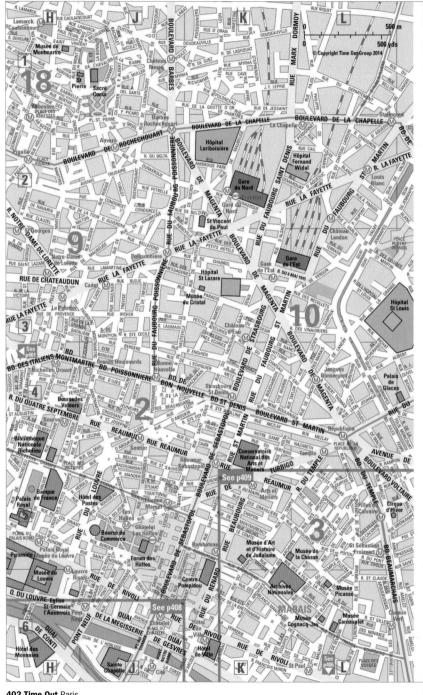

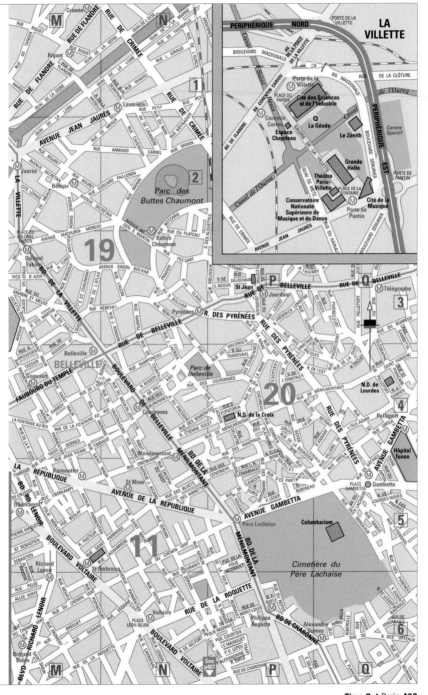

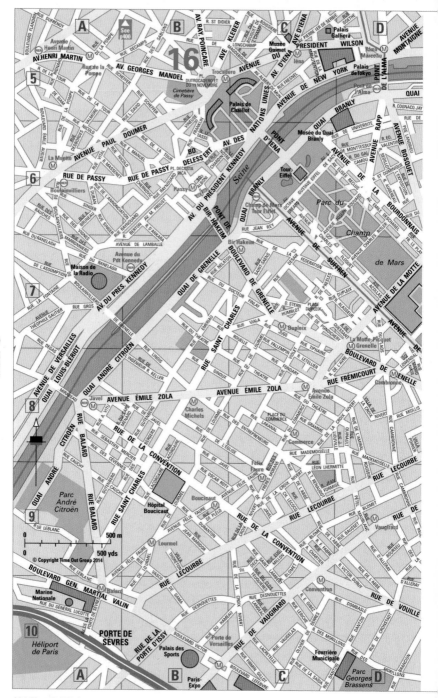

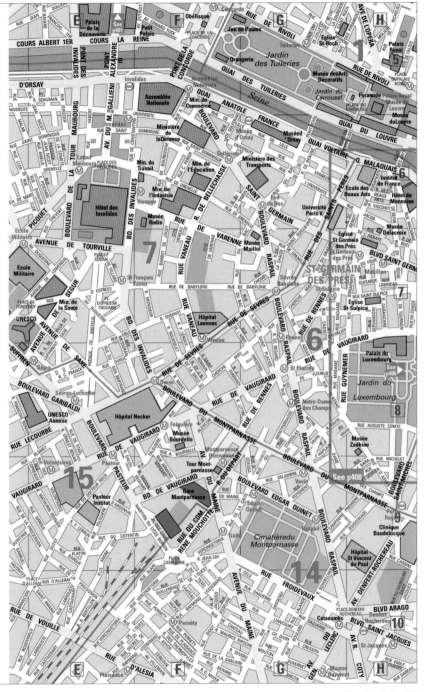

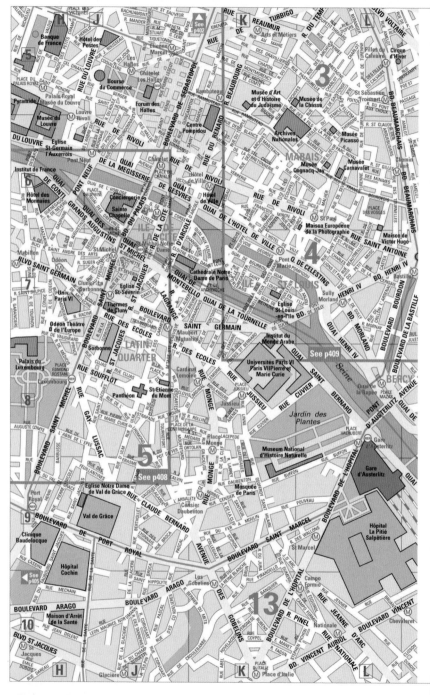

MAPS

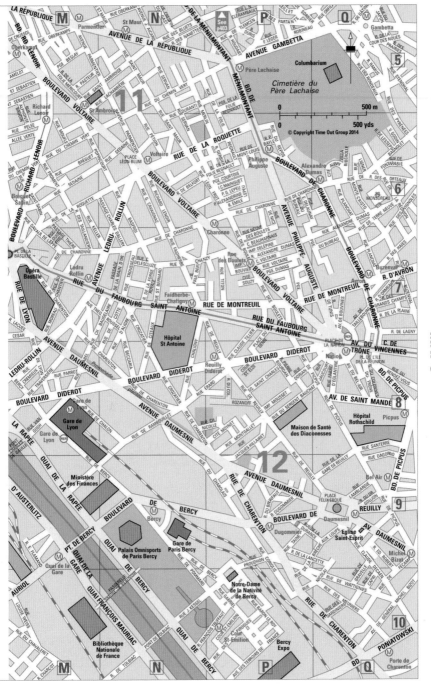

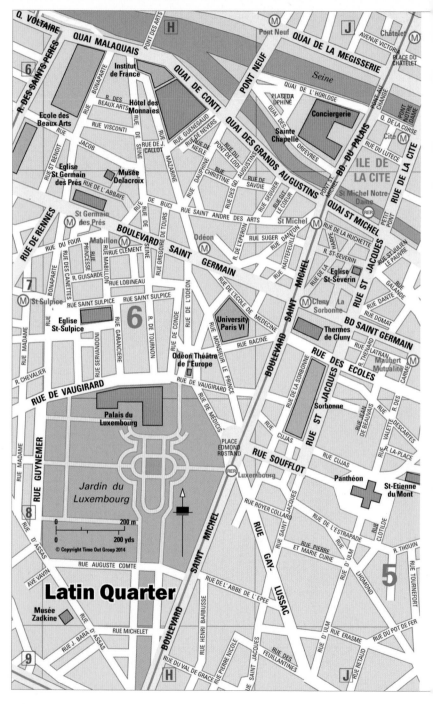

Latin Quarter

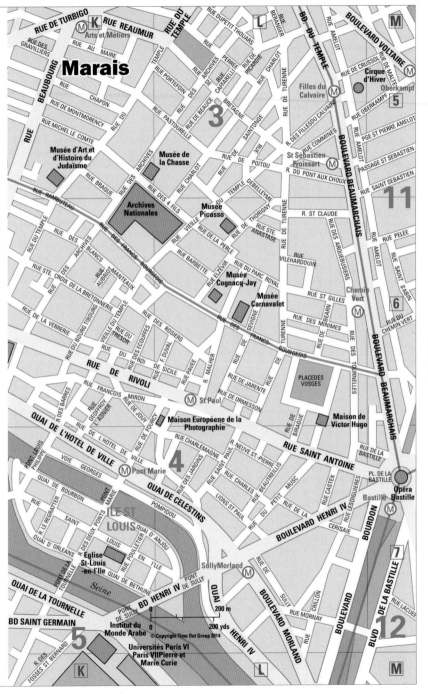

Marais

Street Index

STREET INDEX

STREET INDEX